Society and Individual in Renaissance Florence

Sandro Botticelli, Portrait of a Man with a Medal of Cosimo the Elder. Uffizi, Florence, Italy. Copyright Scala/Art Resource, N.Y.

Society and Individual in Renaissance Florence

EDITED BY WILLIAM J. CONNELL

University of California Press

BERKELEY   LOS ANGELES   LONDON

Chapter 11 was previously published as "San Lorenzo in Florence: Liturgical Perspectives," in *La Toscane et les Toscans autour de la Renaissance: Cadres de vie, société, croyances. Mélanges offerts à Charles-M. de La Roncière* (Aix-en-Provence: Université de Provence, 1999 [2000]), pp. 283–99.

University of California Press
Berkeley and Los Angeles, California

University of California Press, Ltd.
London, England

Library of Congress Cataloging-in-Publication Data

Society and individual in Renaissance Florence / edited by William J. Connell.
    p.   cm.
    Includes bibliographical references and index.
    ISBN 0-520-23254-2 (alk. paper)
    1. Florence (Italy)—Civilization.   2. Renaissance—Italy—Florence.   I. Connell, William J.
DG735.6 .S73   2002
945'.51—dc21

                        2001006436

Manufactured in the United States of America
11 10 09 08 07 06 05 04 03 02
10 9 8 7 6 5 4 3 2 1

The paper used in this publication meets the minimum requirements of ANSI/NISO Z39.48–1992 (R 1997) *(Permanence of Paper)*. ♾

To Gene Brucker,
friend and teacher

Contents

Acknowledgments

The editor would like especially to thank Stanley Chojnacki, F. W. Kent, and Sharon Strocchia, who served as an editorial committee for this volume, and who gave friendly assistance and advice throughout its creation. Randolph Starn was unstinting with his time and offered many helpful suggestions. The editor is also grateful to William Bouwsma, Robert Brentano, and Marion Brucker for their encouragement; to Gina Paolercio, for assistance in preparing the typescript; and to James Clark, of the University of California Press, for his support of the project.

Abbreviations of Archival Sources

ASF	Florence, Archivio di Stato
AD	Acquisti e doni
CP	Consulte e pratiche
CPGNR	Capitani di parte guelfa. Numeri rossi
CRSGF	Corporazioni religiose soppresse dal Governo francese
CRSPL	Corporazioni religiose soppresse da Pietro Leopoldo
CS	Carte strozziane
Dipl.	Diplomatico
LC	Signoria. Carteggi. Legazioni e commissarie
MAP	Archivio Mediceo avanti il Principato
MC	Monte comune
Misc. rep.	Miscellanea repubblicana
Miss. I canc.	Signoria. Carteggi. Missive. Prima Cancelleria
NA	Notarile antecosimiano
OGBR	Otto di guardia e balia. Periodo repubblicano
PP	Provvisioni. Protocolli
PR	Provvisioni. Registri
RAP	Riformagioni. Atti pubblici
SC Delib. ord.	Signoria. Collegi. Deliberazioni fatte in forza di ordinaria autorità
SC Delib. spec.	Signoria. Collegi. Deliberazioni fatte in forza di speciale autorità
ASM	Milan, Archivio di Stato
Pot. est.	Potenze estere
ASV	Vatican City, Archivio Segreto Vaticano
RA	Registra Avenionensia
RV	Registra Vaticana
ASVe	Venice, Archivio di Stato
CI	Cancelleria inferiore

GP	Giudici di petizion
SG	Sentenze a giustizia
Test.	Testamenti
BAM	Milan, Biblioteca Ambrosiana
BAV	Vatican City, Biblioteca Apostolica Vaticana
Vat. lat.	Fondo Vaticano latino
BLF	Florence, Biblioteca Medicea Laurenziana
Ashb.	Manoscritti Ashburnham
ASL	Archivio di San Lorenzo
Conv. soppr.	Conventi soppressi
BNF	Florence, Biblioteca Nazionale Centrale
F.P.	Fondo principale
Magl.	Fondo Magliabechiano
Pal.	Fondo Palatino
Strozz.	Fondo Strozziano
BRF	Florence, Biblioteca Riccardiana
Ricc.	Fondo Riccardiano
BSS, AC	Borgo San Sepolcro, Archivio comunale
Paris, BN	Paris, Bibliothèque Nationale
Ms. Ital.	Manuscrits Italiens

Introduction
William J. Connell

Among scholars, but also in the general learned public, there has been a slow but dramatic change in the way we understand Renaissance Florence. It used to be said that Florence was one of a very few special historical places that gave birth to the modern understanding of the individual. The individual of the Renaissance was described most famously by the Swiss historian Jacob Burckhardt in his *Civilization of the Renaissance in Italy* (1860) with words that are as well remembered as they are often now challenged: "In the Middle Ages . . . [m]an was conscious of himself only as a member of a race, people, party, family or corporation—only through some general category. In Italy this veil first melted into air; an objective treatment and consideration of the state and of all things of this world became possible. The subjective side at the same time asserted itself with corresponding emphasis; man became a spiritual individual and recognized himself as such."[1] Although one of the novel aspects of Burckhardt's account was his emphasis on princely and despotic states in the process he called the "development of the individual" (*Entwicklung des Individuums*), he reserved special consideration for the republican city of Florence. In a faction-prone republic such as Florence, the formation of men as individuals was encouraged, he wrote, since "the more frequently the governing party was changed, the more the individual was led to make the utmost of the exercise and enjoyment of power." Defeat in political struggle, more-

1. J. Burckhardt, *The Civilization of the Renaissance in Italy*, trans. S. G. C. Middlemore, intro. P. Burke, annot. P. Murray (London, 1990), p. 98; Burckhardt, *Die Kultur der Renaissance in Italien: Ein Versuch*, ed. W. Goetz, 10th ed. (Stuttgart, 1976), p. 123.

1

over, imposed on certain individuals an "involuntary leisure" that led them to cultivate areas of taste and endeavor that lay outside the political realm. Lengthy periods of absence from one's native city (*patria*), whether the result of banishment or of voluntary emigration (usually for reasons of commerce), encouraged among Florentines a "cosmopolitanism" that was itself a sign of the self-sufficiency of the man of the Renaissance. In Dante Alighieri (who peopled Hell with his fellow Florentines), Burckhardt found an early example of the *uomo universale*, "the all-sided man."[2] Predictably, Dante was treated as a forerunner to those two other "all-sided" Florentines, Leon Battista Alberti and Leonardo da Vinci. Burckhardt was especially struck by the achievements of the Florentine biographers and history writers who, he claimed (in a way that seems exaggerated in our present age of confession), explored ways of revealing the inner selves of their subjects. Thus Filippo Villani's *On the Famous Citizens of Florence*, Burckhardt said, included "the inward and outward physiognomy in the same sketch."[3] But this "individualism" was not confined to writers and artists. "The statesmen and popular leaders, especially in Florentine history," Burckhardt wrote, "acquired so marked a personal character that we can scarcely find, even exceptionally, a parallel to them in contemporary history."[4]

To say that the "modern individual" was discovered during a given period and in a given place sounds like a very strong claim, but perhaps it is worth remembering that the idea did find some support in quite specific Renaissance changes in the way individuals were described and portrayed, and that most of them either involved Florentines or took place in Florence. Thus humanist philology, with its project of critical and comparative study of a wide range of evidence, destabilized the way such writers as Petrarch and Leonardo Bruni portrayed persons from the past and gave them new confidence in bringing out what they thought was essential to their character.[5] A similar confidence in literary description may also be seen in the

---

2. Burckhardt, *The Civilization*, pp. 100–101; Burckhardt, *Die Kultur*, pp. 126–28.

3. Burckhardt, *The Civilization*, p. 215; Burckhardt, *Die Kultur*, p. 307. For the text, see now F. Villani, *De origine civitatis Florentie et de eiusdem famosis civibus*, ed. G. Tanturli (Padua, 1997).

4. Burckhardt, *The Civilization*, p. 100; Burckhardt, *Die Kultur*, p. 126.

5. See the crisis registered in Petrarch, *Ad familiares*, XXIX, 3, in Francesco Petrarca, *Prose*, ed. G. Martellotti et al. (Milan and Naples, 1955), pp. 1023–25; and compare Leonardo Bruni's new approach to biography in his lives of Dante, Petrarch, and Cicero. See also G. Ianziti, "A Life in Politics: Leonardo Bruni's *Cicero*," *Journal of the History of Ideas* 61 (2000): 39–58. For the likening of the philological method to modern psychology, see C. Ginzburg, "Clues: Roots of an Eviden-

way Florentines and other Italians wrote about their contemporaries.[6] There was a radical change, too, in the way individuals were represented in the visual arts at Florence. Freestanding, larger-than-life-size statues of human beings were sculpted for the first time since antiquity.[7] The use of linear perspective resulted in representations of human beings that conformed with measurements of the space around them.[8] And there also developed at Florence a tradition of domestic portraiture, both painted and sculpted, that treated not only saints and statesmen but also merchants and their families.[9] These were and remain impressive historical changes, and there is nothing surprising in the fact that one hundred years after Burckhardt such scholars as Hans Baron and Erwin Panofsky were still attempting general syntheses that saw these developments as aspects of a new attitude toward the individual that developed in Renaissance Florence. In the words of Panofsky (as quoted by Ernst Gombrich), "Something must have happened."[10]

From early on in the historiography, however, there has also been considerable resistance to the notion of Florentine individualism. There were socialist critics like Karl Schalk, who in 1901 argued that class allegiance rather than individual choice was determinative in Florentine history, and

---

tial Paradigm," in Ginzburg, *Clues, Myths, and the Historical Method* (Baltimore, 1989), pp. 96–125.

6. H. Gmelin, *Personendarstellungen bei den florentinischen Geschichtsschreibern der Renaissance* (Leipzig, 1927); M. Phillips, "The Disenchanted Witness: Participation and Alienation in Florentine Historiography," *Journal of the History of Ideas* 44 (1983): 191–206, repr. in *Renaissance Essays*, 2 vols., ed. P. O. Kristeller, P. P. Wiener, and W. J. Connell (Rochester, N.Y., 1993), 2:251–66. On Renaissance biography, see T. F. Mayer and D. R. Woolf, eds., *The Rhetorics of Life-Writing in Early Modern Europe: Forms of Biography from Cassandra Fedele to Louis XIV* (Ann Arbor, Mich., 1995).

7. M. Bergstein, *The Sculpture of Nanni di Banco* (Princeton, N.J., 2000).

8. J. White, *The Birth and Rebirth of Pictorial Space* (London, 1957); S. Y. Edgerton Jr., *The Renaissance Rediscovery of Linear Perspective* (New York, 1975).

9. A. Warburg, "The Art of Portraiture and the Florentine Bourgeoisie. Domenico Ghirlandaio in Santa Trinita: The Portraits of Lorenzo de' Medici and His Household," in Warburg, *The Renewal of Pagan Antiquity*, trans. D. Britt (Los Angeles, 1999), pp. 185–221; R. Hatfield, "Five Early Renaissance Portraits," *Art Bulletin* 47 (1965): 315–34.

10. H. Baron, *The Crisis of the Early Italian Renaissance: Civic Humanism and Republican Liberty in an Age of Classicism and Tyranny*, rev. 1 vol. ed. (Princeton, N.J., 1966), pp. 201–5; E. Panofsky, *Renaissance and Renascences in Western Art* (New York, 1972), pp. 1–41. Gombrich is quoted by D. R. Kelley, "Something Happened: Panofsky and Cultural History," in *Meaning in the Visual Arts: Views from the Outside*, ed. I. Lavin (Princeton, N.J., 1995), p. 113.

Schalk has had numerous followers in more recent years.[11] From a somewhat different perspective, in the 1930s Hans Baron argued that Renaissance Florence was distinguished by a new civic ethic that was contrary to the private, often apolitical individualism expounded by Burckhardt. Baron did not discard individualism—it was still an important part of his interpretation of Florentine history—but he thought the individual achieved affirmation through participation in the political process at Florence, not through selfish withdrawal.[12] A less sympathetic critique, aimed not just at Burckhardt's individualism but at the writing of his kind of cultural history, was developed by Paul Kristeller, who in an influential essay of the 1940s argued for the need to study the disciplines of philosophy and rhetoric along their separate historical trajectories.[13] The internal history of the discipline of rhetoric, he suggested, was more likely to explain changes in the humanist movement than were external events or changes in other scholarly fields. E. H. Gombrich made a similar argument concerning the visual arts, suggesting that they tended to be more influenced by craft-specific technological developments and by the intramural competition and emulation of their practitioners than by the cross-fertilization among fields supposed by Burckhardt, Baron, and Panofsky.[14]

11. K. Schalk, "Sociale Momente in der Verfassungsgeschichte der florentinischen Republik," *Mittheilungen des Instituts für Oesterreichische Geschichtsforschung*, Ergänzungsband 6 (Innsbruck, 1901), p. 319: "Nach Dantes Ausspruch müsste man die Florentiner für wankelmüthige Menschen halten, indem die Individuen selbst ihre Anschauungen in kurzen Zeiträumen änderten. Aber die Verfassungsgeschichte zeigt, dass der Wechsel der wichtigsten Einrichtungen nicht auf die Wandelbarkeit der Individuen, sondern auf den Wechsel der politischen Macht der wirtschaftlichen Classen zurückzuführen ist." Compare the measured response to Schalk's intellectual descendants in the chapter by F. W. Kent in this volume.

12. H. Baron, "Das Erwachsen des historischen Denkens im Humanismus des Quattrocento," *Historische Zeitschrift* 147 (1932); and Baron, "La Rinascita dell'etica statale romana nell'umanesimo fiorentino del quattrocento," *Civiltà moderna* 7 (1935); both now in Baron, *In Search of Florentine Civic Humanism: Essays on the Transition from Medieval to Modern Thought*, 2 vols. (Princeton, N.J., 1988), 1:24–42, 134–57. See also Baron, "The Limits of the Notion of 'Renaissance Individualism': Burckhardt after a Century," ibid., 2:155–81.

13. P. O. Kristeller, "Humanism and Scholasticism in the Italian Renaissance," *Byzantion* 17 (1944–45): 346–74, now in Kristeller, *Studies in Renaissance Thought and Letters*, 4 vols. (Rome, 1955–96), 1:553–83. See also his essay "Changing Views of the Intellectual History of the Renaissance since Jacob Burckhardt," in ibid., 2:3–23; and J. E. Seigel, "'Civic Humanism' or Ciceronian Rhetoric? The Culture of Petrarch and Bruni," *Past and Present* 34 (1966): 3–48.

14. E. H. Gombrich, "The Renaissance Conception of Artistic Progress and Its Consequences," in Gombrich, *Gombrich on the Renaissance*, vol. 1, *Norm and Form*, 4th ed. (London, 1996), pp. 1–10. Cf. also Gombrich, "From the Revival of Letters

The most sustained attack on the thesis of Florentine and, by extension, Renaissance individualism has been by three generations of social historians, most of them English-speaking, who since the 1960s have published remarkable studies of Florentine society based on the systematic use of archival sources. Thanks to the unusual wealth of material surviving in Florence, these scholars have demonstrated in extraordinarily well-documented books and essays that Renaissance Florentines tended to think of themselves not as self-sufficient individuals but as weak and fragile beings whose identities (as both observers and observed) resulted from their place in intersecting networks of institutions and social groups. There was little that fifteenth-century Florentines feared more than the solitary life of the individual so praised by Burckhardt.[15]

For historians in the late twentieth and early twenty-first centuries, Florence during the Renaissance belonged to a more distant, less recognizable premodern world of extended families, artisan guilds, and tightly knit neighborhoods.[16] In the 1960s one prominent economic historian argued that the highly refined and impersonal division of labor in the Florentine wool industry demonstrated its modernity and efficiency; but the most recent treatment instead emphasizes the personal ties that pervaded the workplace.[17] Where one historian once argued that Florentine aristocrats were among the first Europeans to live in nuclear families, others have demonstrated the survival of the values of the extended family.[18] A political way

to the Reform of the Arts: Niccolò Niccoli and Filippo Brunelleschi," in *The Essential Gombrich*, ed. R. Woodfield (London, 1996), pp. 411–35: "But perhaps it is no mere paradox to assert that this movement had its origin not so much in the discovery of man as in the rediscovery of diphthongs" (p. 435). On Gombrich's "nominalism" as opposed to Panofsky's "Platonism," see Kelley, "Something Happened."

15. For descriptions of this fear, and the psychological dependency it engendered, see R. C. Trexler, *Public Life in Renaissance Florence* (New York, 1980), pp. 131–86; and R. F. E. Weissman, *Ritual Brotherhood in Renaissance Florence* (New York, 1982), chap. 1. On the meaning of being connected to others in Florentine society, see F. W. Kent, "Essay," in F. W. Kent and G. Corti, *Bartolomeo Cederni and His Friends: Letters to an Obscure Florentine* (Florence, 1991), pp. 3–47.

16. A. Molho, "The Italian Renaissance, Made in the USA," in *Imagined Histories: American Historians Interpret the Past*, ed. A. Molho and G. S. Wood (Princeton, N.J., 1998), pp. 263–94; R. F. E. Weissman, "Dal dialogo al monologo: La storia tra i fiorentini," *Cheiron* 8, no. 16 (1991): 95–111.

17. Cf., for example, R. de Roover, "Labor Conditions in Florence around 1400: Theory, Policy and Reality," in *Florentine Studies: Politics and Society in Renaissance Florence*, ed. N. Rubinstein (London, 1968), pp. 277–313; and F. Franceschi, *Oltre il "Tumulto": I lavoratori fiorentini dell'Arte della Lana fra Tre e Quattrocento* (Florence, 1993).

18. R. Goldthwaite, *Private Wealth in Renaissance Florence: A Study of Four Families* (Princeton, N.J., 1968): "The modern conception of a family as a private

of life that was once described by Baron as "democratic" and committed to "modern values" has been shown to have been riddled with patronage ties of a traditional sort.[19]

That this new understanding of Florentine society has gone well beyond the intramural revisionism of historians and found more general acceptance in the learned community is indicated by two influential accounts of the rise of modern individualism. Alasdair MacIntyre's 1981 book, *After Virtue,* which argued that the scope of moral philosophy was strikingly reduced with the development of modern individualism, cited Gene Brucker's magnum opus, *The Civic World of Renaissance Florence* (1977), as offering a careful description of a premodern society guided by corporate rather than individualistic values.[20] Charles Taylor's *Sources of the Self* (1989), a rich account of the development of modern understandings of the individual, barely treated the Renaissance at all, instead attributing to the Enlightenment many of the features Burckhardt had assigned to fifteenth- and sixteenth-century Italy.[21] In the minds of most historians, the thesis of a particular Florentine "individualism" has by now been discarded as a serious theory. Like an ancient flying machine in a provincial air museum, it dangles by wires in simulated flight and is visited only by the occasional graduate student who marvels that anyone could have thought such an invention might ever leave the ground.

Still, if "individualists" in the modern sense were rare in Renaissance

---

association of a man, his wife, and their children, held together by the bonds of affection, has one of its first manifestations here and certainly it was a distinctive feature of Florentine society at the time" (p. 263). Cf. F. W. Kent, *Household and Lineage in Renaissance Florence: The Family Life of the Capponi, Ginori and Rucellai* (Princeton, N.J., 1978); and my comment in "*Libri di famiglia* and the Family History of Florentine Patricians," *Italian Culture* 8 (1990): 277–92. See also the collection *Art, Memory, and Family in Renaissance Florence,* ed. G. Ciappelli and P. L. Rubin (Cambridge, England, 2000).

19. Cf. Baron, *The Crisis of the Early Italian Renaissance,* with the political realities described by G. Brucker, *The Civic World of Early Renaissance Florence* (Princeton, N.J., 1977); D. Kent, *The Rise of the Medici: Faction in Florence, 1426–1434* (Oxford, 1978); and N. Rubinstein, *The Government of Florence under the Medici (1434–1494),* 2d ed. (Oxford, 1997). On patronage networks and their impact on politics, see also J. Padgett, "Robust Action and the Rise of the Medici, 1400–1434," *American Journal of Sociology* 98 (1993): 1259–319; W. J. Connell, *La città dei crucci: Fazioni e clientele in uno stato repubblicano del '400* (Florence, 2000), pp. 151–77, 195–200.

20. A. MacIntyre, *After Virtue: A Study in Moral Theory,* 2d ed. (Notre Dame, Ind., 1984), p. 237. (The first edition was published in 1981.)

21. C. Taylor, *Sources of the Self: The Making of the Modern Identity* (Cambridge, Mass., 1989).

Florence, it remains true that the unusually rich sources for Florentine history—a city whose archives have been spared the catastrophes of warfare and major fires, but not floods[22]—allow the historian to "meet" and even get to know rather well an extraordinary number of individuals who once lived there. Florentine historians of the later twentieth century (and now the early twenty-first) have given themselves over wholeheartedly to the task of studying the social practices and institutions that constrained these men and women of the city on the Arno. Contributors to this volume were asked to address ways in which Renaissance Florentines expressed or shaped their identity in interaction with their society.[23]

Chapters one through six address the exceptionally resilient and homogeneous Florentine merchant elite that functioned as the true protagonist of much of Florentine history.[24] They explore relations of this class with other classes, its marriages, its domestic space, its testamentary and legitimation practices, and its politics. In a powerful contribution to ongoing debates about the nature of the Florentine social hierarchy, F. W. Kent shows that patronage, charity, and friendship overlapped with class antagonisms in fifteenth-century Florence. John Najemy's new interpretation of Leon Battista Alberti's dialogue, *Della famiglia*, contradicts recent readings of the work as a patriarchal text and argues that the author instead reveals the "shaky foundations" of patriarchal ideology. Julius Kirshner discusses the costly transactions that took place in the course of Renaissance marriages. Expensive gifts from Florentine grooms to their wives, he says, were not (as others have argued) compensation for the hefty dowries their wives brought them but were "investments in auspiciousness and honor," since

22. On working conditions for historians in Florence prior to 1987, when the Florentine State Archive was transferred to a new building, see A. Molho, "The Closing of the Florentine Archive," *Journal of Modern History* 60 (1988): 290–99.

23. This is the agenda of S. Greenblatt, *Renaissance Self-Fashioning: From More to Shakespeare* (Chicago, 1980). See also M. de Grazia, M. Quilligan, and P. Stallybrass, eds., *Subject and Object in Renaissance Culture* (Cambridge, England, 1996); J. Martin, "Inventing Sincerity, Refashioning Prudence: The Discovery of the Individual in Renaissance Europe," *American Historical Review* 102 (1997): 1309–42; J. S. Amelang, *The Flight of Icarus: Artisan Autobiography in Early Modern Europe* (Stanford, Calif., 1998). A. Grafton, *Leon Battista Alberti: Master Builder of the Italian Renaissance* (New York, 2000), brings this approach to bear on Burckhardt's preferred example of the *uomo universale*.

24. The durability of the Florentine elite has been emphasized by J. N. Stephens, *The Fall of the Florentine Republic, 1512–1530* (Oxford, 1983); R. B. Litchfield, *Emergence of a Bureaucracy: The Florentine Patricians, 1530–1790* (Princeton, N.J., 1986), pp. 362–82; and A. Molho, *Marriage Alliance in Late Medieval Florence* (Cambridge, Mass., 1994), pp. 1–11.

they remained the property of the groom and were later sold or transferred to others. Dale Kent attempts to reconstruct the "ways of seeing the world" of fifteenth-century Florentines. Through a study of accounts of oral performances and a reading of the "memory house" of an accountant, she shows the remarkable extent to which the "high" culture of the Renaissance permeated everyday life. Michele del Giogante's "house of memory" appears in the form of a typical household inventory written down in his *zibaldone*, a personal book of literary passages. Michele lists the places in his house and the images he associated with them, offering clues to how he saw his world and thoughts as being organized. Thomas Kuehn shows how the law and personal identity interacted in Florence in the delightfully complicated case of a legitimated bastard who was also a murderer who, with top-notch legal assistance, successfully laid claim to his dead father's estate. According to Kuehn, the jurists involved consciously adapted their legal reasoning to suit the empirical interests of the case. Although a person's identity as a bastard was established by law, the law proved remarkably flexible in conforming with unusual circumstances. Margery Ganz's essay on a conflict between families within the Medici party illustrates a crucial turning point in the history of the Medici regime. Before 1466, the Medici were first among equals in a party that sought the advantage of all its leading families. After 1466, Ganz writes, "the Medici were to be the sole patrons in the political arena; everyone else was to be a client."

Chapters 7 through 11 address Florentine religion. In a sweeping treatment of Florentine relations with the church, ranging from the city's war with the papacy, known as the War of the Eight Saints, down to the mid–fifteenth century and beyond, David Peterson demonstrates that the future course of Florentine republican ideology was profoundly shaped by the memory of the fourteenth-century commune's contest with the papacy, when Florence seriously shed its identity as a Guelf city. Sharon Strocchia offers a perceptive look at a world that historians have insufficiently appreciated—the world of cloistered nuns. Her study of the renaming of nuns when they entered convents reveals a change that occurred in the later fifteenth century. Before 1450, girls entering convents tended to keep their secular names; by 1500, it was customary for girls to take on new names. Strocchia shows that the names chosen helped to fashion a collective identity for the convent, establishing ties to particular saints and angels, identifying spiritual exemplars for the nuns, and offering a way of keeping alive the names of fondly remembered nuns who had died. Donald Weinstein's study of an often-ignored confessor's manual written by Girolamo Savonarola reveals the friar at work in a role quite different from that of fiery preacher. The manual, which advises priests on questions of pastoral care, reveals a "kinder, gentler" Savonarola, Weinstein argues. The manual does not belong to a late-fifteenth-century trend toward greater surveillance and social control, nor does it suggest a shift toward self-discipline of the kind other historians have seen in this period. His other concerns notwithstanding, Savonarola's views on pastoral care were rather moderate, and they probably help to explain why so many people were attracted to him as a spiritual adviser. Lauro Martines studies anticlerical verse in the fifteenth century, which he shows to have been written principally by Florentines. Why was this so? The answer would seem to lie, at least in part, in the account of rivalry with the church presented by Peterson. William Bowsky's chapter on liturgy at the Florentine Church of San Lorenzo presents itself as a lesson in the difficulty of reconstructing the spiritual life of a past community. He shows how nearly impossible it is to really know anything about what was said and done, let alone believed, by the clerics of San Lorenzo. Spirituality, Bowsky implies, is something for historians to talk about at their peril.

Chapters 12 through 16 treat persons who in one way or another occupied positions "outside" of Florentine society. These chapters treat criminals, the inhabitants of a subject town, Florentines who were exiled, Florentine merchants residing in Venice, and the Florentine pope who endured the Sack of Rome. John Brackett's study of the sixteenth-century *Cronaca* of Giuliano de' Ricci and of the criminal records of the Eight (Otto di guardia) shows that Florence in the later Renaissance, unlike the Quattrocento in F. W. Kent's reading, was radically divided between an upper-class elite and the numerous poor, who lived in segregated areas and were subject to new methods of social control. James Banker's chapter on the men of the town of Borgo San Sepolcro tackles directly the question of self-fashioning by carefully describing the universe of available roles and options through which an ordinary citizen of the town might establish an identity for himself. Alison Brown argues in her essay on exile that this punishment did not, as some have suggested, lose its sting in the fifteenth century. The Medici, she says, adopted a new approach that targeted not just specific opponents but also the identity and power of entire families. Paula Clarke's study of Florentine expatriates in Venice shows that wealthier individuals tended to maintain their identity as Florentines, while those of lower class tended to assimilate to Venetian society more rapidly. Paul Flemer's treatment of Clement VII and the Sack of Rome attempts to understand the Florentine pope's inner psychological turmoil as he lived through a horrible political trauma. Flemer suggests that the events in Rome caused

Clement to relive the tragic assassination of his father, Giuliano de' Medici, during the Pazzi Conspiracy of 1478, and he shows how Clement made specific use of an example from ancient Roman history in his efforts to recover politically from the ordeal.

In both its format and variety of subjects, this volume might well be compared with a collection published in 1968 that consisted of fifteen essays by leading English-speaking historians of Florence (with the exception of one French contributor) edited by Nicolai Rubinstein.[25] In particular, differences in the subject matter of the essays offer a good indication of changes in the direction of Florentine scholarship during the past thirty-three years. Most obviously, perhaps, religion has assumed a much greater importance in the writing of Florentine history, since not one of the essays in the Rubinstein collection treated the subject directly. Similarly, women, marriage, family life, and the household were not included in the earlier collection, although these have become central topics in Florentine studies today, thanks especially to the pioneering work of Christiane Klapisch-Zuber, first published in the 1970s.[26] Economic history, which was well represented in the earlier collection, is still an active area of research in Florence, but in recent years economic and social historians have tended to shy away from addressing the same questions.[27] Social patronage has become a very important topic in the years since the publication of the Rubinstein collection;[28] as has the ritual life of Florentines, thanks above all to Richard Trexler's masterpiece, *Public Life in Renaissance Florence.*[29] An area of continuing interest since the 1960s, represented here by Banker's contribu-

25. N. Rubinstein, ed., *Florentine Studies: Politics and Society in Renaissance Florence* (London, 1968). See also the excellent review by R. Starn in *Bibliothèque d'Humanisme et Renaissance* 32 (1970): 677–84.

26. See her essays collected in C. Klapisch-Zuber, *Women, Family, and Ritual in Renaissance Italy*, trans. L G. Cochrane (Chicago, 1985); Klapisch-Zuber, *La maison et le nom: Stratégies et rituels dans l'Italie de la Renaissance* (Paris, 1990).

27. S. K. Cohn Jr., e.g., in his recent *Creating the Florentine State: Peasants and Rebellion, 1348–1434* (Cambridge, England, 1999); and R. A. Goldthwaite, in his *Wealth and the Demand for Art in Italy, 1300–1600* (Baltimore, 1993), are two economic historians of Florence who have consistently attempted to address questions of importance to social and cultural historians.

28. See D. V. Kent and F. W. Kent, *Neighbours and Neighbourhood in Renaissance Florence: The District of the Red Lion in the Fifteenth Century* (Locust Valley, N.Y., 1982); R. F. E. Weissman, *Ritual Brotherhood in Renaissance Florence* (New York, 1982); the essays in a special number of the journal *Ricerche storiche* 15, no. 1 (1985); F. W. Kent and P. Simons, eds., *Patronage, Art, and Society in Renaissance Italy* (Canberra, 1987); and N. A. Eckstein, *The District of the Green Dragon: Neighbourhood Life and Social Change in Renaissance Florence* (Florence, 1995).

29. R. C. Trexler, *Public Life in Renaissance Florence*, 2d ed. (Ithaca, N.Y., 1991).

tion, has been the territorial expansion of Florence in the fourteenth and fifteenth centuries, and the relations between the capital city and subject jurisdictions.[30]

This volume is dedicated to an admired scholar who throughout his long and distinguished career as a teacher and writer of early modern European history has always shown an extraordinary appreciation for the place of individuals in what he calls their "social world."[31] In his authoritative writings on Renaissance Florence, Gene Brucker has emphasized the social bonds of kinship, patronage, neighborhood, and religious devotion as factors in the construction of Florentine identities. In so doing, he has been responsible more than any other single scholar for changing our common conception of the first city of the Renaissance. Today, when we think of Florence and the Renaissance, we think first of a world dominated by powerful families, merchant guilds, and a corporatist ethos—of the world Gene Brucker has described in a series of penetrating studies. Although many historians (including all the contributors to this volume) have participated in the project of charting the structures, institutions, and relationships by which Florentines of the fourteenth, fifteenth, and sixteenth centuries defined themselves, no one has done more than Brucker over the past forty years to synthesize these findings, to situate them against the political and institutional background of Renaissance Italy, and to open new fields for exploration.

That there were institutional structures, social relations, and belief systems that both bound Florentines together and limited their scope of action as individuals has been a constant theme in Brucker's work. In one of his earliest essays, "The Structure of Patrician Society in Renaissance Florence," he argued that far from beginning an age of unfettered individualism, the Renaissance saw the rise of a new relationship of patron and client, a bond so strong and so prevalent, he suggested it functioned as a new kind of feudalism.[32] In other essays and books, Brucker has argued that the older corporate ties that characterized the guild society of the medieval commune were replaced in the late fourteenth century by the regime of a political elite that ruled through a carefully managed consensus concerning the major issues facing the republic and the composition of the ruling

30. For recent essays on these issues, see W. J. Connell and A. Zorzi, eds., *Florentine Tuscany: Structures and Practices of Power* (Cambridge, England, 2000).

31. G. Brucker, ed., *The Social World of Renaissance Florence: A Documentary Study*, reprint ed. (Toronto, 1998).

32. G. Brucker, "The Structure of Patrician Society in Renaissance Florence," *Colloquium* 1 (1964): 2–11.

class.[33] Kinship, marriage, poverty, the guilds, popular superstition, the administration of justice, the university, religious life, and ecclesiastical politics have been among the aspects of Florentine society Brucker has discussed in notable ways—always with a careful eye to the documentary evidence. His reading of Renaissance Florence as a society in which lives were largely lived in interaction with these institutions and their particular features has today almost entirely supplanted the romantic Burckhardtian notion of Florence.[34]

In Brucker's more recent work, including *Giovanni and Lusanna* and "Florentine Voices from the *Catasto*," he has made a particular effort to go beyond the description of the structures and normative terms by which people lived, to explore what can be learned about the attitudes and experiences of individuals in Renaissance Florence.[35] A turn from the idealized Florentine "Individual" to the study of many Florentine individuals as they relate to their society seems wholly appropriate. The essays contained in this volume are dedicated to a historian without whose patient work and friendly encouragement our own efforts should have fallen far short of the mark.

33. See especially G. Brucker, *The Civic World of Early Renaissance Florence* (Princeton, N.J., 1977). The argument has been refined further by J. M. Najemy, *Corporatism and Consensus in Florentine Electoral Politics, 1280–1400* (Chapel Hill, N.C., 1982); and R. Fubini, "Dalla rappresentanza sociale alla rappresentanza politica: Alcune osservazioni sull'evoluzione politico-costituzionale di Firenze nel Rinascimento," *Rivista storica italiana* 102 (1990): 279–301.

34. G. Brucker, *Renaissance Florence*, 2d ed. (Berkeley and Los Angeles, 1983), remains his classic statement.

35. G. Brucker, *Giovanni and Lusanna: Love and Marriage in Renaissance Florence* (Berkeley and Los Angeles, 1986); Brucker, "Florentine Voices from the *Catasto*, 1427–1480" (1993), repr. in Brucker, *Renaissance Florence: Society, Culture, and Religion* (Goldbach, Germany, 1994), pp. 133–54.

1 "Be Rather Loved Than Feared"

Class Relations in Quattrocento Florence

F. W. Kent

I

One night in October 1486, Maria Villani was murdered as she slept, her infant son beside her, in her villa near Carmignano. Florence's police magistracy, the Eight of Ward (Otto di guardia), found Maria's black slave, Lucia, guilty of the crime, charging that it had been long premeditated with three accomplices: Marsilia, the daughter of a local peasant; the manservant of her husband Alberto, Giovanni da Cascia; and a second man with a humble surname. According to the sentence, Lucia, having failed to poison Maria, had crept into her mistress's bedroom dressed in the manservant's clothes and, after a violent struggle during which the eighteen-year-old attacker bit off the dying woman's finger, succeeded in strangling her. The punishments handed out on 31 December for "so important and so cautionary an affair," as the Eight put it,[1] were as terrible as the deed and prompted Bartolomeo Dei to send a detailed description in a letter to his uncle, Benedetto. The latter was relieved that their friend, Alberto Villani, a direct descendant of the city's celebrated chroniclers, Giovanni and Matteo Villani, was subsequently cleared of suspicion and released from custody.[2]

Gene Brucker, who has written with such distinction on the Villani's

I am, as ever, grateful to Gino Corti for research help and more than usually obliged to Carolyn James for her advice and assistance. I much appreciated Ian Robertson's shrewd comments and Alison Brown's helpful suggestions. Research for this essay has been funded by Monash University and the Australian Research Grants Council. Villa I Tatti and its director, Walter Kaiser, generously provided ideal conditions in which to write it.

1. ASF, OGBR, 75, fols. 61r–62v, 29 December 1486: "questo caso di tanta importantia e di tanto exemplo." See fols. 137v, 138v, 140r for other references to the "caso della moglie d'Alberto Villani." As in this case, quotations translated in the text will be given in the original in the notes only when the document is unpublished.

2. See below, note 186, for Dei's letter. Benedetto's comments are in ASF, CRSGF, 78, 318, fol. 268, 15 January 1486/87.

Florence, was the first in the postwar generation to bring to our attention sobering stories such as this; to ask detailed questions about class relations and social structures suggested by a sensitive reading of a wide range of private and public sources touching all sections of Florentine society.[3] Having opened up so much of Florence to our gaze, so to speak, thereby enabling us to see within it the dramatic inequalities of wealth, status, and authority revealed in the story of Maria's murder and the tortured death of her slave, Brucker insisted, in the tradition of Nicola Ottokar, that social relationships other than those of class—bonds of kinship, neighborhood, and friendship—were also important to the Florentines, certainly to the patrician class but also to others. He argued that, from the late fourteenth century onward, there developed ties of dependence between men of the same, and different, social groups: bonds of friendship, *amicizie,* as contemporaries called them, or patron-client relationships in the more utilitarian language of modern historians.[4] Most scholars, including those, such as Alessandro Stella, who continue to emphasize the centrality of class conflict in Florentine life,[5] now accept that ties of friendship and dependence acted as a social "lubricant," in Anthony Molho's phrase, within the ranks of a large political class.[6] But, as Christiane Klapisch-Zuber has written of Stella's recent study of the Ciompi Revolt, if Florence were as torn by class conflict, born of yawning economic and social divisions, as he argues, then how could ties of clientage and friendship have bridged this abyss and created the "vertical solidarities" that some historians, the present writer included, have suggested existed in the Quattrocento?[7] How, to put the question another way, might such historians account for the violent events of late 1486 with which this chapter began?

Anyone familiar with the evidence, and the historical literature, can acknowledge the force of the argument that Florence remained into the Quat-

3. See particularly G. Brucker, ed., *The Society of Renaissance Florence: A Documentary Study* (1971; Toronto, 1998); with the documents published in the original Latin and Italian in Brucker, *Firenze nel Rinascimento* (Florence, 1980), pp. 233–399.

4. Among his numerous studies, see G. Brucker, "The Structure of Patrician Society in Renaissance Florence," *Colloquium* 1 (1964): 2–11; Brucker, *Renaissance Florence,* 2d ed. (Berkeley and Los Angeles, 1983), chap. 3, pp. 89–127.

5. A. Stella, *La révolte des Ciompi* (Paris, 1993), esp. pp. 268–70.

6. A. Molho, "Patronage and the State in Early Modern Italy," in *Klientelsysteme im Europa der frühen Neuzeit,* ed. A. Mączak (Munich, 1988), pp. 233–42, quotation on p. 242.

7. In the preface to Stella, *La révolte,* p. 15. Cf. F. W. Kent and P. Simons, "Renaissance Patronage," in *Patronage, Art and Society in Renaissance Italy,* ed. F. W. Kent and P. Simons (Oxford, 1987), pp. 1–21, esp. 8–11.

trocento what, according to Stella, it had been during the turbulent later fourteenth century: *"deux Florence,"* or, in Klapisch-Zuber's gloss, *"une ville double, deux villes plutôt."* [8] The huge disparities in wealth to which Stella points continued to apply, a tiny minority of the population controlling most of Tuscany's resources. [9] The textile workers, the descendants of the Ciompi, stayed topographically isolated, and marginalized from civic life, in largely plebeian areas of the city. As Samuel Cohn and Molho have suggested, working-class protest and violence continued; there was more of it, indeed, than they have described. [10] On such occasions, the Eight stepped in with their armed retainers (a network of spies and a well-paid executioner waiting in the wings). There was no lack of vigorous state action in response to this popular protest during the Quattrocento, for patrician memory of the Ciompi Revolt was long, the violence of those months exaggerated in hindsight. Thousands of "wool beaters, called *ciompi*," had invaded the church of Santa Maria degli Angeli, it was remembered, whereupon "women and whores came in, everyone plundering." [11] Many citizens remained wary, not to say fearful, of the popular classes and their "country cousins," building in the post-Ciompi years a new style of urban palace, with imposing, "bossy," rustication on the ground floor where previously there had been arched areas open to the street. [12]

The "very poor and wretched people," [13] thus shut out, themselves lived in tiny cottages and were described by some upper-class observers as if they almost belonged to another race or came from another planet. "Do not look up at the heights" of the great city buildings, a poet warned a visitor, "watch that you don't move / Like a man who is from the country." [14] The Servite church was to other noble buildings "what the fine gentleman is to

8. Stella, *La révolte,* pp. 15, 263.

9. A theme influentially elaborated in D. Herlihy and C. Klapisch-Zuber, *Les Toscans et leurs familles: Une étude du catasto florentin de 1427* (Paris, 1978).

10. S. K. Cohn, *The Laboring Classes in Renaissance Florence* (New York, 1980); Cohn, *Women in the Streets* (Baltimore, 1996); A. Molho, "Cosimo de' Medici: 'Pater Patriae' or 'Padrino'?" *Stanford Italian Review* 1 (1979): 5–33. For other major working-class protests, see below, pp. 24–28.

11. *Leggende di alcuni santi e beati venerati in S. Maria degli Angeli di Firenze* (1864; repr., Bologna, 1968), pt. 2, pp. 125–27. See N. Rubinstein, "Il regime politico dopo il tumulto dei Ciompi," in *Il Tumulto dei Ciompi: Un momento di storia fiorentina ed europea* (Florence, 1981), pp. 105–24, esp. 123–24.

12. F. W. Kent, "Palaces, Politics and Society in Fifteenth-Century Florence," *I Tatti Studies* 2 (1987): 41–70, esp. 54–57.

13. Cited in ibid., p. 57.

14. Brunetto Latini, *Il Tesoretto (The Little Treasure),* ed. and trans. J. B. Holloway (New York, 1981), pp. 90–91.

the wretched peasant," wrote Feo Belcari.[15] Such country folk were "evil villeins with no regard for anyone," Francesco di Nerone reminded Giovanni de' Medici, who had recommended a peasant to him: "I know you cherish the least skerrick of a citizen's honor rather than that of a villein."[16] As for the urban mob—the *vulgo* or *popolazzo*—it spread false rumors ("jailbirds' gossip," in a guildsman's phrase),[17] for "the truth is rarely seen where the mob foregathers."[18] For this, and countless other reasons, ordinary people, like women, were unfit to participate in politics, let alone to govern. "Pity the city that falls into the hands of the *popolo*," Vespasiano da Bisticci observed.[19] Niccolò Niccoli is supposed to have said that the Latin of Dante's letters was so poor that "I would exclude [him] from the company of literate men and leave him to the woolworkers."[20] Any specialist can multiply beyond necessity such examples of citizen disdain and cite a few pithy, proletarian responses.

Movement across this literal and rhetorical divide was powerfully and prayerfully discouraged. The city's influential archbishop in midcentury insisted that Florentines subdue their restless spirits and stay within their allotted social places, a message other mendicant preachers reiterated, to some effect.[21] Invited by Bolognese emissaries to lead that city's Bentivolesco regime, the illegitimate Sante Bentivoglio, a young woolworker in a Florentine shop, was "astonished," one citizen reported, and spent "all of Thursday believing he was being made a fool of, and still he went on stretching the wool."[22] Sante's subsequent elevation to authority in Bologna be-

---

15. Cited in N. Newbigin, ed., *Nuovo corpus di sacre rappresentazioni fiorentine del Quattrocento* (Bologna, 1983), p. xxiii n. 21.

16. ASF, MAP, VII, 186, 10 September 1459: "costoro son mali villani e non churono persona . . . ; so ami più ongni picolo honore di uno cittadino che di uno villano." See, in general, M. S. Mazzi and S. Raveggi, *Gli uomini e le cose nelle campagne fiorentine del Quattrocento* (Florence, 1983).

17. Cited by F. W. Kent and G. Corti, *Bartolommeo Cederni and His Friends* (Florence, 1991), p. 45.

18. Francesco Datini, quoted by D. V. Kent and F. W. Kent, *Neighbours and Neighbourhood in Renaissance Florence* (Locust Valley, N.Y., 1982), p. 59.

19. G. M. Cagni, *Vespasiano da Bisticci e il suo epistolario* (Rome, 1969), p. 175.

20. Quoted by E. H. Gombrich, "From the Revival of Letters to the Reform of the Arts: Niccolò Niccoli and Filippo Brunelleschi," in *Essays in the History of Art Presented to Rudolf Wittkower*, ed. D. Fraser, H. Hibbard, and M. J. Lewine (London, 1967), pp. 71–82, quotation on p. 72.

21. P. F. Howard, *Beyond the Written Word: Preaching and Theology in the Florence of Archbishop Antoninus, 1427–1459* (Florence, 1995), chap. 8; B. Paton, *Preaching Friars and the Civic Ethos: Siena, 1380–1480* (London 1992), pp. 320–22.

22. ASF, MAP, VIII, 156, 26 March 1446, Bartolomeo Sassetti to Giovanni de' Medici: "e lui maravigliandosi stette tutto dì giovedì che se ne facie[v]a beffe, e at-

came one of the century's most extraordinary tales of social mobility, re-counted over and over as if, in Pope Pius II's words, "he had changed his character and spirit with his garments."[23] "Listen Sante," Cosimo de' Me-dici was supposed to have said to him, "if you are Ercole [Bentivoglio's] son, your nature will draw you to Bologna and great affairs. If you are Agnolo da Cascese's son, you will remain pettily engaged in your workshop."[24] Such a story lends credence to Molho's contention that "intense class con-sciousness and . . . class conflict" were the Florentine Quattrocento's prin-cipal characteristics.[25]

II

And yet to read the Florentine sources in all their infinite variety and rich-ness is also to find much evidence that complicates, at times contradicts, such a conclusion. The "double-city," or two-city, model itself, to a large extent constructed from statistical data, is not invulnerable to attack from scholars who have immersed themselves in the luxuriant if entangled qual-itative evidence, against which the validity of any abstract construction must, in my view, finally be tested. Such evidence throws up numerous de-tails and tendencies, exceptions and contradictions, which combine to blur and even at times dissolve the outlines of the model; begin to shake, if not destroy, the foundations and scaffolding of its twin construction, the two-tiered society.

One thinks of Franco Franceschi's meticulous demonstration of the nu-merous gradations of skill and status existing within the woolen industry itself,[26] of the abundant evidence that Florentine society at large was simi-larly many-layered and hardly immobile. The very insistence of Quattro-cento moralists that people remain dutifully in their ordained social place, that they adhere to the sumptuary laws that sought to make distinctions of rank clearly visible, revealed, as has been observed of an earlier period,[27]

---

tendeva pure a tirare g[i]ù la lana a bottegha." Carolyn James and I will publish this letter shortly.

23. *The Commentaries of Pius II*, trans. F. A. Gragg and L. C. Gabel, Smith Col-lege Studies in History, 25 (Northampton, Mass., 1939–40), pp. 175–76.

24. Neri Capponi, *Commentarj di cose sequite in Italia dal 1419 al 1456*, in *Re-rum italicarum scriptores*, 18, ed. L. A. Muratori (Milan, 1731), col. 1209.

25. Molho, "Cosimo," p. 9.

26. F. Franceschi, *Oltre il "Tumulto": I lavoratori fiorentini dell'Arte della Lana fra Tre e Quattrocento* (Florence, 1993), esp. pt. 2, pp. 81–231.

27. A. Murray, *Reason and Society in the Middle Ages*, (Oxford, 1986), esp. pp. 96–98; for sumptuary laws, see Paton, *Preaching Friars*, pp. 320–22.

the energies many Florentines were putting into doing exactly the opposite. Individuals and families, even small social groups, sought to move up
from one tier of Florentine society to another. Families of skilled artisans
and artists—the Gaddi, Rosselli, Canacci, Pucci, della Robbia, and many
others—knew a marked social mobility, as Richard Goldthwaite and Margaret Haines have emphasized; Niccolò da Uzzano endowed scholarships to
encourage poor provincial students.[28] Manno Temperani, a close friend of
the painter of marriage chests Apollonio di Giovanni and a man whose own
social background may have predisposed him to be more understanding of
such aspirations than were most patricians, went so far as to praise his city's
"popular" government because "more than others it opens the way for talented men."[29] Such political and social mobility, so marked a feature of Florentine public life, Piero Guicciardini deplored in 1484 while acknowledg-
ing its almost irresistible force: "And thus continuously new men make the
grade, and in order to give them a place in the governing class it is necessary to eliminate from it long-established citizens," by which means "good
government is destroyed."[30] This porous political class was itself subject to
infiltration from below. Ten years later, Piero Capponi felt compelled to
propose the exclusion from the newly created Great Council of men with
spurious claims to membership of established families and of those whom
he called "country cousins (consorti contadini)."[31] For peasants, too, could
be rich and da bene (respectable)[32] and might entertain political ambitions;
patricians might be very poor indeed, reduced to living like peasants, as the
saying went.

Kinship ties might extend themselves vertically, as well as horizontally,
throughout the city and beyond its walls, blurring distinctions of class. The
Rinieri, rich bankers, were clearly nonplussed to discover that a certain
"Mariotto di ——— woodworker, claims to be our paternal kinsman

28. ASF, NA, 9042, fol. 170v, 27 December 1430; R. A. Goldthwaite, *The Building of Renaissance Florence* (Baltimore, 1980), pp. 272–86; M. Haines, "Artisan
Family Strategies: Proposals for Research on the Families of Florentine Artists," in
Art, Memory and Family in Renaissance Florence, ed. G. Ciappelli and P. Rubin
(New York, 1999), pp. 163–75.
29. Cited by D. V. Kent and F. W. Kent, "Two Vignettes of Florentine Society in
the Fifteenth Century," *Rinascimento* 23 (1983): 237–60, quotation on p. 249.
30. Cited by N. Rubinstein, *The Government of Florence under the Medici
(1434 to 1494)*, 2d ed. (Oxford, 1997), pp. 246–47. See also A. Molho, *Marriage Alliance in Late Medieval Florence* (Cambridge, Mass., 1994), pp. 198–201.
31. Published by S. Bertelli, "Constitutional Reforms in Renaissance Florence,"
Journal of Medieval and Renaissance Studies 3 (1973): 165.
32. See below, p. 35.

[*chonsortto*]."[33] More willing to acknowledge his cross-class family was the eminent knight Temperani, four times Standard Bearer of Justice, whose intricate paternal network included his lower guild cousins and city neighbors, the Carradori, and at least two families of obscure peasants from Petriolo.[34] These latter men were remembered in several of Messer Manno's wills. One such rural cousin, Francesco del Nero, worked and was cared for by both the Carradori and the Temperani, reminding one of Beatrice Webb's discovery that her upper-middle-class family's beloved servant, "Dada," was "a blood relation . . . from her mother's connections among the Lancashire weavers."[35] Only further research will establish if such apparently unlikely connections between citizen and peasant were at all common. Possibly they were. It is well established that poorer households were small, but beyond their nuclear families some members of the working class, and especially the peasantry, may have had kinship networks more extensive than the reticent census data can reveal. Such wider family bonds would have provided support for the members of a small household and, as in Temperani's case, may have forged links with Florentines of higher social standing. Here and there one finds intriguing references to the intricacy of humble kin groups: to a baker bequeathing dowries among his "parentela, mascholini e feminine,"[36] or to one Lorenzo del Passera, whose peasant "parentela" was so extensive that the institution administering his dowry bequest decided to draw up a proper genealogy.[37] Perhaps when a full study of the social structure of Renaissance Florence comes to be written (when some brave scholar analyzes in detail the contemporary language of social hierarchy), the city may be seen more closely to resemble, mutatis mutandis, feudal society as recently described by Susan Reynolds—"the layers of society were more like those of a trifle than a cake: its layers were blurred, and the sherry of accepted values soaked through . . . ; a very rich and deep trifle with a lot of layers"[38]—than the two-tiered, or double, city of Leonardo da Vinci's architectural imagination. There the "gentlemen" inhab-

33. Bernardo Rinieri's *Ricordanze*, cited in Kent and Kent, "Two Vignettes," p. 249.

34. Ibid., pp. 237–52.

35. *The Diary of Beatrice Webb*, ed. N. Mackenzie and J. Mackenzie (London, 1986), 1:7.

36. ASF, AD, 41, *Libro memoriale* of the Company of S. Frediano, fol. 9r.

37. AD, 42, fol. 36r–v. See, too, the suggestive remarks of D. Herlihy, *Medieval Households* (Cambridge, Mass., 1985), chap. 6., pp. 131–56.

38. S. Reynolds, *Fiefs and Vassals* (Oxford, 1996), p. 40. See, too, G. A. Brucker, "Florentine Voices from the *Catasto*, 1427–1480" (1993); repr. in Brucker, *Renaissance Florence: Society, Culture, and Religion* (Goldbach, Germany, 1994), pp. 133–

ited the higher level of the *urbs* while lower down the rest of the population labored away on their behalf among the stables and latrines.[39]

Recent historians of Florence have suggested several ways in which the layers of this Tuscan *zuppa inglese* came to be blurred, how it was that working people might be found walking and talking on the upper levels of the city Leonardo had preserved for gentlefolk. Where the statistical evidence suggests clear and profound social divisions, a wide variety of documents reveals Florentines mixing together in what was, after all, a small and concentrated series of urban spaces inhabited by some forty thousand people. Ronald Weissman pointed out years ago that most lay confraternities drew their membership from the city at large and from a range of social groups. As subsequent studies have confirmed, great patricians and humble artisans became Christian brothers together when singing Mary's praises in the *laudesi* companies or when a confraternal captain ritually humbled himself by washing the feet of his companions at Easter.[40] If certain flagellant confraternities were more socially exclusive, there were also neighborhood companies, such as those of the district of the Green Dragon (Drago verde) studied by Nicholas Eckstein, whose predominantly artisan memberships made it their special mission to comfort the destitute, "poveri nostri," of their own area, where by the mid-Quattrocento many of the Ciompi's descendants forgathered.[41]

It is notable that recent studies of social and work relationships in Renaissance Florence, however different their historiographical points of view, have converged in regarding the city's "neighborhoods," variously defined, to be sure, as the places where most Florentines learned to interact with one another. In Stella's view, the class consciousness of the original Ciompi was forged from overlapping neighborhood and occupational loyalties; it was such local bonds that later sustained their defeated successors, according to Cohn.[42] For Franceschi, the Quattrocento woolworkers more creatively

54. I am sensible of the fact that this essay hardly begins the close study of Florentine social terminology that is needed, and that "class" is as treacherous a word now as it ever was: see P. J. Corfield, ed., *Language, History and Class* (Oxford, 1991).

39. On this text, published by G. Fumagalli, *Leonardo, omo sanza lettere* (Florence, 1952), pp. 313–14, see E. Garin, "La città in Leonardo," in *Leonardo da Vinci: Letture Vinciani I–XII (1960–1972)*, ed. P. Galluzzo (Florence, 1974), pp. 311–25.

40. R. F. E. Weissman, *Ritual Brotherhood in Renaissance Florence* (New York, 1982), esp. pp. 58–105; and, among many other studies, B. Wilson, *Music and Merchants: The Laudesi Companies of Republican Florence* (Oxford, 1992).

41. N. A. Eckstein, *The District of the Green Dragon: Neighbourhood Life and Social Change in Renaissance Florence* (Florence, 1995), esp. pp. 132–38.

42. Stella, *La révolte*; Cohn, *Laboring Classes*.

used their parish bases to better their conditions and work out more flexible relations with their employers.[43] Other historians have argued that more or less cordial cross-class ties might exist within the city's sixteen *gonfaloni* (administrative districts) and its some sixty-two parishes. However patrician the administrations of the districts were, quite humble citizens (even a handful known only by nicknames) participated formally in local business and were active in community life.[44] John Henderson has found that Christian charity often began very near to home, in one's parish or neighborhood, and was first extended to poor people whom one knew or had reliable information about.[45] Real empathy for a destitute neighbor can be found in the Florentine sources, alongside generic denunciations of the vile and lowborn: "Incline your thoughts rather towards the men whose bed has been taken from under them, who suffer from the cold or have to give up buying wine, and, in the name of God's charity, weep for them rather than for yourself," Lapo Mazzei admonished the wealthy Francesco Datini, who had complained of his tax burden.[46]

Literary sources in particular reveal the verbal interplay, the sociability, and wrangling between the classes, which occurred as people mixed informally in the streets and piazzas. Humble men might also penetrate their masters' grand houses, where they witnessed notarial documents (a reminder that the notaries themselves, repositories of civic information many of whom had very socially mixed clienteles, were catalysts of sociability).[47] Men of all social ranks gambled in the public and family loggias of the city, repairing afterward to the taverns where the Piovano Arlotto found good fellowship, and others found trouble! It is in the anonymous stories about the priest Arlotto, whose social world—between city and country, rich and poor—was extensive indeed, that we can perhaps best eavesdrop on the conversations between Florentines.[48] Such talk went on in the countryside and in the city: in the barbershops frequented by all manner of men, in the

---

43. Franceschi, *Oltre il "Tumulto,"* pp. 312–15.

44. Kent and Kent, *Neighbours and Neighbourhood;* F. W. Kent, "Ties of Neighbourhood and Patronage in Quattrocento Florence," in *Patronage, Art and Society,* pp. 79–98; Eckstein, *District of the Green Dragon,* esp. chaps. 5–6.

45. J. Henderson, *Piety and Charity in Late Medieval Florence* (Oxford, 1994), esp. pp. 421–25. See, too, P. Spilner, "*Ut civitas amplietur:* Studies in Florentine Urban Development, 1282–1400" (Ph.D. diss., Columbia University, 1987), chap. 4, esp. pp. 330–447.

46. Quoted in Kent and Kent, *Neighbours and Neighbourhood,* p. 60.

47. Examples abound in the notarial archives of the ASF.

48. G. Folena, ed., *Motti e Facezie del Piovano Arlotto* (Milan and Naples, 1953); F. W. Kent and A. Lillie, "The Piovano Arlotto: New Documents," in *Flor-*

botteghe of master craftsmen where patricians flocked to see some new creation, and, above all, *in piazza.*[49] While watching his palace being built in early December 1465, Giovanni Boni was physically assaulted by his Marsuppini brother-in-law, upon which "Matteo di Tano, the woodworker, called me across the piazza to him," Boni recorded, apparently not put out by what one might have thought to be an impertinence, "saying to me: 'It seems to me Gregorio's very vexed with you. Would you have had words with him previously?'"[50] On occasion, an upper-class observer could write admiringly of a workingman's taking center stage. Some ten thousand people, including the diarist Giuliano Bartoli, watched the weaver of gold cloth called "Il Baccino" celebrate the Peace of Lodi in the Piazza della Signoria; the artisan "had a small bagpipe which he made to talk rather than played, precisely as if it were a person."[51]

The frequent sexual alliances formed between Florentines of unequal social standing presupposed physical and emotional contexts in which the classes could intermingle with some ease (sexual and class exploitation at times, no doubt, going hand in hand). Domestic intimacy between masters and servants or slaves provided only one such sexual opportunity, for a patrician Giovanni della Casa might meet his Lusanna, daughter of the artisan Benedetto di Girolamo, in the streets of their parish of San Lorenzo.[52] Men and youths often made homosexual love across lines of class, as Michael Rocke has shown, and chose neighbors for partners. There was no inevitable tendency for the well-off to take the active, "virile," role in these affairs. Such enduring affection and dependency could spring from these

ence and Italy: Renaissance Studies in Honour of Nicolai Rubinstein, ed. P. Denley and C. Elam (London, 1988), pp. 347–67.

49. On meeting places and talk, see F. W. Kent, "'Un paradiso habitato da diavoli': Ties of Loyalty and Patronage in the Society of Medicean Florence," in *Le radici cristiane di Firenze*, ed. A. Benvenuti, F. Cardini, and E. Giannarelli (Florence, 1994), pp. 183–210, esp. 202–4. F. W. Kent, "Lorenzo di Credi, His Patron Iacopo Bongianni and Savonarola," *Burlington Magazine* 125 (1983): 539–41, quotation on p. 540 n. 4, notes examples of visits to workshops. For sociability in wool shops, see Franceschi, *Oltre il "Tumulto,"* p. 318.

50. The provenance of this *ricordo* by Boni is uncertain. It exists in a late copy in BNF, Manoscritti Passerini, 186 (insert 38, "Boni"), unfoliated: "Matteo di Tano legnaiolo mi chiamò quivi su la piazza a sè, e dissemi queste parole: 'E mi pare che Gregorio [Marsuppini] t'abbi fatto un cattivo viso; havesti tu havuto dipoi altre parole con lui?'"

51. *Ricordanze* of Bartoli, ed. I. del Badia, *Miscellanea fiorentina di erudizione e storia* 1 (1886): 127.

52. G. A. Brucker, *Giovanni and Lusanna: Love and Marriage in Renaissance Florence* (Berkeley, 1986).

"forbidden friendships" that some contemporaries suspected that they became the bases of political factions.[53] Citizens and patricians, in life and in
love more involved with artisans and the disenfranchised than one might
have expected, might also choose to be buried in the, as it were, purifying
presence of the poor. Bartolomeo Panciatichi was to be escorted to his burial
by twelve paupers; five hundred attended the funeral of Niccolò Alberti.[54]

III

The close, and at times harmonious, exposure of members of one class to
another in this small and rather fluid hierarchical society could hardly in
itself, however, have defused all violent social resentment and smothered
all conflict. Such contact must at times have exacerbated the tensions that
surface so frequently in the evidence. To know is not necessarily to love
your enemy. The Ciompi, I am persuaded, though they could hardly have
been in 1378 prematurely "modern" revolutionaries possessed of a class
ideology, did have a rational political program that, with its demand for the
inclusion of workingmen's organizations in communal politics, was revolu-
tionary in late Trecento terms and was perceived to be so by all sides in the
conflict.[55] After the defeat of the Ciompi, the social and political conditions
of, and motives for, continuing, serious conflict remained—all unrest in the
woolen industry did not end with the Ciompi's downfall—and were quite
as compelling as those social circumstances and tendencies that might at
times have acted to ease those tensions. "Many ignorant men and Ciompi
are demanding the earth," one citizen complained in May 1412.[56]

As Alison Brown has emphasized, discussion of political issues and civic
events among the popular classes continued into the Quattrocento, as difficult as it may be now to recapture more than its general sense. If citizens
usually dismissed such talk as ill-informed gossip, one anonymous contemporary was more sympathetic to the desire of ordinary men "denied knowledge of the secret affairs dealt with by rulers of states and great princes" to
discuss "the news that's going around" in an attempt to penetrate the fog

53. M. Rocke, *Forbidden Friendships: Homosexuality and Male Culture in Renaissance Florence* (New York, 1996), esp. pp. 134–46, and chap. 5, pp. 148–91.
54. L. Polizzotto, "'Dell'arte del ben morire': The Piagnone Way of Death
1494–1545," *I Tatti Studies* 3 (1989): 27–87 (42); Henderson, *Piety and Charity*,
p. 161; S. T. Strocchia, *Death and Ritual in Renaissance Florence* (Baltimore, 1992),
pp. 64, 76–77.
55. Stella, *La révolte*, esp. pp. 64–65.
56. Cited by G. A. Brucker, *The Civic World of Early Renaissance Florence*
(Princeton, N.J., 1977), p. 336. See Franceschi, *Oltre il "Tumulto,"* pp. 320–25, for
the wool industry.

that, Francesco Guicciardini later said, hovered between the palace of government and the piazza.[57] In the Arlotto stories, and some other *novelle*, humble people are as often made to talk sharply and shrewdly as they are presented as foolish, so preserving for us some sense of the flow of discussion and speculation among the lower classes. Citizen critics were perhaps supercilious about such "gossip" precisely because it gave the power of ridicule to people outside the political process. "The wretched man finds himself the talk of the mob and the butt of people's jokes, deprived of honor and of life," Cristoforo Landino wrote of the well-connected herald Filarete, who had been caught making love to a girl within the sacrosanct space of the Priors' palace.[58] The retailers of lying "gossip" who frequented the city's benches had no respect for "rank or gentlemen," a critic observed.[59]

The *popolo minuto* (little people, or lower class) did not confine its commentary on civic events to ridiculing its betters. Some of the people took action in the collective interest at times of disease and famine by demanding a regular supply of affordable grain. It is too easy to dismiss bread riots, especially by women (many of whom worked in the textile industries) as nonpolitical, or to construe government reaction as merely the subduing of the mob in the name of order. As Brucker pointed out years ago, post-Ciompi governments remained sensitive to the political need to ensure the grain supply, aware that the very stability of a regime might be at risk if popular unrest became uncontrollable.[60] Lorenzo de' Medici was quick personally to subsidize the price of grain at moments of crisis in the 1470s.[61] It was perhaps not a coincidence that after the expulsion of the Medici and

57. Folena, *Motti e Facezie*, p. 146. For Guicciardini, and also on this theme, see A. Brown, "Lorenzo and Public Opinion in Florence," in *Lorenzo il Magnifico e il suo mondo*, ed. G. C. Garfagnini (Florence, 1994), pp. 61–85, esp. 65–66; and A. Molho and F. Sznura, eds., *"Alle bocche della piazza": Diario di anonimo fiorentino (1382–1401)* (Florence, 1986), esp. pp. xxxv–xlviii. More generally, see *La circulation des nouvelles au moyen âge* (Rome, 1994).

58. Published by A. della Torre, *Storia dell'Accademia Platonica di Firenze* (Florence, 1902), pp. 402–3.

59. "Canzona delle Pancaccie," in *Trionfi e canti carnascialeschi toscani del Rinascimento*, 2 vols., ed. R. Bruscagli (Rome, 1986), 1:185–88.

60. G. A. Brucker, "The Florentine *Popolo Minuto* and Its Political Role, 1340–1450" (1972); repr. in Brucker, *Renaissance Florence: Society, Culture and Religion*, pp. 81–109, esp. 97–99. See, too, Henderson, *Piety and Charity*, pp. 274–77; and S. Tognetti, "Problemi di vettovagliamento cittadino e misure di politica annonaria a Firenze nel XV secolo (1430–1500)," *Archivio storico italiano* 157 (1999): 419–52. For women in the workforce, see Franceschi, *Oltre il "Tumulto,"* pp. 116–17, 174.

61. Brown, "Lorenzo and Public Opinion," p. 77.

during the worst famine the city had known in decades, some fifteen poor women went toward the Priors' palace in April 1497, shouting "bread, bread" and quickly recruiting some three thousand companions, some of whom began to cry "palle, palle (Medici, Medici)." Shops were closed, and in the subsequent scuffle with the Eight's men, one woman attacked a retainer who had injured her daughter, as if to imitate the vigorous assault by an aged woman on a grotesque old man very unusually portrayed in a contemporary Florentine drawing. Peace was only restored by the distribution of grain throughout the city.[62] These humble women, many of whom would have come in from the country where "Christians were eating grass like beasts, many dying of hunger," as a diarist said,[63] had taken a political action, had in effect called for a change of regime in the volatile atmosphere of Savonarolan Florence if their needs were not met. During that terrible spring, citizens feared that "Florence was about to be turned upside down," as Giovanni Borromei reported of a tumult in the Cathedral during which a servant of the Eight was torn to pieces.[64] A change of regime "suits rather the poor, the dishonest and the desperadoes," Otto Niccolini had earlier observed at a tense moment for the Medici in 1458.[65]

These patrician comments take for granted a plebeian interest not only in those economic concerns that most pressed upon the poor—grain shortages, taxation, and changes to the currency[66]—but also in political events. As difficult as it is to determine the political conceptions and allegiances

---

62. C. Carnesecchi, "Un tumulto di donne," *Miscellanea fiorentina di erudizione e storia* 2 (1895): 45–47. For a grain riot in February during which the crowd shouted "palle, palle," see G. Pampaloni, "La crisi annonaria fiorentina degli anni 1496–1497 e le importazioni di grano dalla Romagna," *Atti e memorie della Deputazione di storia patria per le provincie di Romagna*, n.s., 15–16 (1963–65): 277–309, quotation on p. 290; and G. Praticò, "Spigolature savonaroliane nell'Archivio di Mantova," *Archivio storico italiano* 60 (1952): 223. See, too, Henderson, *Piety and Charity*, pp. 401–6. Upon the Medici victory in 1530, "per tutta la città non s'attende se non a dire 'palle,' 'palle' et 'pane,'" according to a correspondent of Lucrezia Salviati: ASF, CS, ser. 1, 335, fol. 82r, 24 August 1530, a reference I owe to Natalie Tomas. For the anonymous drawing, see G. Dillon in *Il disegno fiorentino del tempo di Lorenzo il Magnifico*, ed. A. Petrioli Tofani (Milan, 1992), pp. 120–23, fig. 5.2.

63. ASF, Carte Bagni, 65, insert 15, *ricordanze* of Tomaso Ginori, fol. 189: "i cristiani mangiavano l'erbe come le bestie et assai numero morivono di fame." This important diary, known to nineteenth-century scholars, has been recently relocated by Richard Goldthwaite, whom I thank for the reference. Alison Brown kindly shared her notes on it.

64. Letter of 4 May 1497, published in P. Villari, *La storia di Girolamo Savonarola e de' suoi tempi*, new ed., 2 vols. (Florence, 1926), 2.

65. Cited by Rubinstein, *Government*, p. 112.

66. See Brown, "Lorenzo and Public Opinion," esp. pp. 77–80.

of members of the popular classes, more such research could be done. The registers of the Eight tantalizingly record many crimes by, or involving, obscure Florentines that one might well decide were "political" rather than "criminal" if only the charge had been recorded; as when, to take only one example, some thirty or forty men led by an official of the Calimala guild attacked the Servite church in 1481. The group included some friars, men "from the city, others from the countryside," a patrician, a guildservant, and some woodworkers.[67] Men of humble origin were at times exiled by the Eight, a few of them, without doubt, for political acts or opinions.[68] Prison outbreaks, often violently suppressed, occurred with some frequency and might at times have had a political context.[69]

There was a consistent critique of the Eight's arbitrary administration of criminal justice explicit in the repeated acts of popular hostility directed against that magistracy, including concerted attempts to free prisoners. In one such incident in May 1456, which significantly occurred at a time of grain shortage, Bartoli reported that "it appeared to the populace [populo] that a great wrong was being done" to two foreigners about to be executed. Though its anger grew during the condemned men's procession through the city, "the mob [populazo] restrained itself," finally "rising as one man" in the Piazza del Grano and seizing the prisoners "with a great scream as if they had won all the world's treasures," after which they were given sanctuary in the church of Santa Croce and the Priors' palace itself.[70] A second account of this mass intervention, which resulted in the pardoning of the prisoners, emphasizes the crucial role played in their release by two citizens, persuaded by the popular belief that the punishment was unjust.[71] On

67. ASF, OGBR, 58, fol. 28r: "parte della città e parte del nostro contado." See, too, fols. 21v, 22r–23r, 24r–v.

68. See below, p. 29, and the sentences in ASF, OGBR, 224, passim. In general, see S. Cohn, "The Character of Protest in Mid-Quattrocento," in Il Tumulto dei Ciompi, pp. 199–220, esp. 199–200.

69. See, e.g., ASF, OGBR, 221, fol. 63r; Alessandra Strozzi, Lettere di una gentildonna fiorentina del secolo XV ai figliuoli esuli, ed. C. Guasti (Florence, 1877), pp. 487–88, 604–5.

70. Bartoli, Ricordanze, ed. del Badia, p. 127. For the grain shortage, D. Buoninsegni, Storia della città di Firenze dall'anno 1410 al 1460 (Florence, 1637), p. 117.

71. Pietro Pietribuoni, priorista, in BNF, Conventi soppressi, C.4.895, fol. 171r: "duo nostri cittadini commossi a passione intendendo quello si diceva per la terra, del torto fatto era a chostoro, subito se n'andorono alla Signoria per innarrare il detto caso. Et in questo 'stante così il popolo era grande lor dirieto. Et i detti duo cittadini, non potendo parlare sì tosto alla Signoria, mandorono un famiglio a que' battuti ch'eran colla detta giustitia, che andassino adagio." Molho, "Cosimo," p. 14 n. 20, drew attention to this account. See, too, Eckstein, District of the Green Dragon, pp. 15–16.

another occasion the patrician Giovanni di Francesco Cavalcanti was punished in 1486 for having broadcast criticism of the Eight.[72] In the same decade the police magistracy was forced to repeat decrees against interference with the due execution of justice.[73]

Some citizens might not only agree with members of the *popolo* on such issues but also act together with them in the factional politics of the city. There are important, if necessarily vague, contemporary references to such popular political participation in most of the major partisan crises, as when a thousand leading citizens "and many others of lower social standing from the city and beyond" combined in 1466 to defend the Medici palace from assault when the regime split.[74] "Some servants and men of base condition" were implicated in a minor anti-Medicean plot by several patricians in the next year.[75] Eleven years later, the Pazzi conspirators had hoped to start a popular uprising by overthrowing the Medici, although in the bloody event, as the government emphasized in a letter to Donato Acciaiuoli, the citizens and the people (*popolo*) acted in concert to resist, "the wrath of the people" proving itself awesome.[76] The same strategy was adopted by several patricians who planned to kill Lorenzo in the early summer of 1481. The conspirators, shouting "Long live the people," were to carry a flag bearing the arms of the *popolo* through the working-class districts of the city.[77] The Medici were finally expelled in 1494 when "there rose up a goodly part of the Florentine populace together with many great citizens," the artisan Piero Masi reported.[78] To buy plebeian support with food during the famine of 1497 was one strategy of the pro-Medicean conspirators executed by the republic in that year.[79]

72. ASF, OGBR, 75, fols. 27v–28r.

73. Ibid., 74, fol. 41v; 221, fols. 40r, 42r, 90r, 173r. See G. Antonelli, "La magistratura degli Otto di Guardia a Firenze," *Archivio storico italiano* 112 (1954): 3–39; and Rubinstein, *Government*, p. 229.

74. G. Zippel, *Ricordi e sonetti inediti di Jacopo Cocchi Donati* (Nozze Fabris-Zambelli) (Trent, 1894), p. 16.

75. Ten of War to Otto Niccolini, 20 February 1467, in G. Niccolini, "Lettere di Piero di Cosimo de' Medici a Otto Niccolini," *Archivio storico italiano*, ser. 5, 20 (1897): 33–59, quotation on p. 49 n. 1.

76. ASF, Signori, Carteggio, Missive, Minutari, 11, fols. 26v–27r, without date: "l'ira del populo."

77. Lorenzo de' Medici, *Lettere*, vol. 5 (1480–81), ed. M. Mallett (Florence, 1989), pp. 226–27 n. 12.

78. ASF, Manoscritti, 88, fol. 142r: "si levò el popolo di Firenze buona partte, e chosì molti citadini grandi dela cità. . . ."

79. L. Martines, *Lawyers and Statecraft in Renaissance Florence* (Princeton, N.J., 1968), p. 442.

It would appear that the popular classes of town and country were a more active force, some of their members more politically conscious, than has been argued; that contemporaries regarded them as a volatile factor in the political equation, despite their exclusion from formal politics. Not only might the politically disenfranchised be courted by, and attach themselves to, the city's "parties"; they also retained some sense of possessing collective interests that might manifest itself in group action. Patricians feared them, especially peasants and mountainmen, for their sheer numerousness and (no doubt exaggerated) reputation for violence. A good deal of official correspondence is devoted to the blood feuds and livestock raids, the boundary disputes and insults to citizen honor, perpetrated by *contadini*, especially in the ill-defined frontier areas to the north and northeast on which Florence kept an anxious eye for unexplained troop movements. Even in the more tranquil country nearer to town, most patrician villas were still fortified houses whose owners were well aware of the rural potential for turbulence.[80] In the city, fear of that violence was more palpable. It became proverbial after the Ciompi Revolt to say, with Giovanni Cavalcanti, that "who controls the piazza always wins the city."[81] When Niccolò Soderini planned in 1466 to gather an armed crowd to assault the Medici palace, he only restrained himself from doing so, according to one contemporary, because of "the fear that, once the lower class [*populo minuto*] was armed and had defeated Piero de' Medici and plundered his house and property, it might be stirred to such rage that, having savored the sweetness of the prey, it might desire to turn against others of the well-to-do, hoping by this means to leave its poverty and wretchedness behind and to become rich; and, perhaps, as its confidence increased, once more to become involved in politics and to take over the regime as it had done in 1378."[82] The dramatic events of the Ciompi years were long remembered precisely because the descendants of those who had participated in the revolt remained a numerous and active force to be reckoned with.

Yet despite this fact, and the indubitable inequalities and injustices of late medieval Florentine existence, the Quattrocento was remarkable — scholars of all ideological persuasions agree — for the absence of Ciompi-

80. A. Lillie, "The Humanist Villa Revisited," in *Language and Images of Renaissance Italy*, ed. A. Brown (Oxford, 1995), pp. 193–215; Cohn, *Women*, passim.

81. For the quotation from Cavalcanti, and in general, see N. Rubinstein, *The Palazzo Vecchio, 1298–1532* (Oxford, 1995), pp. 89–92; and P. Pissavino, "Piazza e potere," in *Vigevano e i territori circostanti alla fine del Medioevo*, ed. G. Chittolini (Abbiategrosso, 1997), pp. 324–32.

82. Marco Parenti, *Cronica*, cited in F. W. Kent, "Palaces," p. 57.

like revolt. There was a positive easing of social tension, or so some would say. The standard explanation of this phenomenon has been that the state repressed a demoralized proletariat in the interests of the victorious patrician class. Stern action against popular unrest continued, to be sure. Molho cites Francesco Giovanni's comment, made in 1458 after the quelling of an attempt to free a condemned prisoner, that "we disabused the people [*popolo*] of their bad habits."[83] Unlike Giovanni, Lorenzo de' Medici was not even a member of the Eight when he intervened thirty-one years later during a riotous protest in front of the Priors' palace against the execution of a man guilty of killing a servant of that hated police magistracy. Despite pleas for mercy from several ambassadors and from his Medici cousins, to which he had apparently responded sympathetically, Lorenzo secretly directed that the prisoner be executed on the spot and that four of his would-be rescuers in the crowd be tortured and exiled.

Repression, indeed, and yet this act, which the Ferrarese ambassador seems to have found as chilling as it was unconstitutional,[84] hardly represented Lorenzo's normal policy toward the popular classes of the city and countryside, for all that it does reveal an underlying determination to keep control of the populace by almost any means, his patrician fear of plebeian violence. Lorenzo's preferred method was to cultivate the support of the *popolo*, as Richard Trexler eloquently suggested years ago,[85] and for the sake of the present argument one needs to rehearse how he did so. A mere three months after his violent intervention in the riot, Lorenzo loaned "the King of Camaldoli two bowls with the Medici arms, two goblets with the arms of the Medici and Rucellai and 12 clean cups," presumably for a feast.[86] This elected monarch of one of the city's numerous working-class *potenze*, or festive brigades, which imposed on the city a topography of their own, "reigned" over an area south of the river given over to textile workers and known for its unruliness. Lorenzo had earlier concerned himself with the

---

83. Molho, "Cosimo," p. 14 and passim, for this argument; and Cohn, "Character of Protest." Alternatively, see Brucker, "Florentine *Popolo Minuto*," pp. 81–109; and Franceschi, *Oltre il "Tumulto,"* pp. vii, 305, 334, and passim.

84. Reported by Aldobrandino Guidoni to Ercole d'Este on 19 January 1489, this incident has been most recently discussed by Brown, "Lorenzo and Public Opinion," pp. 76–77.

85. R. C. Trexler, *Public Life in Renaissance Florence* (New York, 1980), esp. pp. 399–418. See, too, M. M. Bullard, *Lorenzo il Magnifico: Image and Anxiety, Politics and Finance* (Florence, 1994), pp. 34–39.

86. Noted in Trexler, *Public Life,* p. 413. See M. del Piazzo, ed., *Protocolli del Carteggio di Lorenzo il Magnifico per gli anni 1473–74, 1477–92* (Florence, 1956), p. 448.

Camaldoli district. From around 1470 onward, when with some of his clos-
est associates he joined Sant'Agnese, the popular religious confraternity
that dispensed local corporate charity, Lorenzo had assumed control of the
ritual distribution of bread to the plebeian needy at Easter and Christmas.
He may have done so because he feared the rising influence there of the
Soderini family, closely identified with its native *gonfalone* of the Green
Dragon and its artisan religious companies.[87] Nearer to home, behind the
Medici palace, Lorenzo had a close association with another *potenza*, that
of the Millstone King, some thirty young members of which had apparently rushed to his armed defense during the Pazzi Conspiracy.[88] Lorenzo
also cultivated a reputation as a "father of charity" and, like his ancestors
before him, was an active dispenser of alms. His mother, Lucrezia Tornabuoni, became a specialist in such holy causes. According to one contemporary, she was a patron more concerned than Lorenzo himself with the
humble, the destitute, and the afflicted, a veritable "pious madonna of the
poor."[89] Cosimo had earlier displayed a similar sensitivity to plebeian opinion. The Milanese ambassador reported that he had been very self-effacing
during debates in January 1458 concerning the introduction of a new catasto "because on the one hand he doesn't want to offend the rich, while on
the other he doesn't wish to lose the grace of the little people."[90]

The Medici were building on an existent tradition that, if it predated the
Ciompi Revolt, certainly became stronger afterward, and that encouraged
citizens to seek the benevolence of the populace in preference to simply re-
pressing it. Contemporaries praised politicians who could be, as Giovanni
Rucellai wrote of an ancestor, "very much in the good graces of the merchants, the middling sort and the people"[91] — a man such as the virtuous
and genial Franco Sacchetti, of whom it was said that "it's quite something,
in a republic, to be acceptable to everyone."[92] For reasons of commercial

87. Eckstein, *District of the Green Dragon*, pp. 205–17. On *potenze*, see Trexler,
Public Life, pp. 399–418; Henderson, *Piety and Charity*, pp. 434–38.

88. Kent and Kent, "Two Vignettes," pp. 252–60.

89. For this quotation and theme, see F. W. Kent, "Sainted Mother, Magnificent
Son: Lucrezia Tornabuoni and Lorenzo de' Medici," *Italian History and Culture* 3
(1997): 3–34, quotation on p. 21.

90. Cited in Rubinstein, *Government*, p. 100 n. 4. Rocke, *Forbidden Friendships*, speculates that Cosimo's regime reduced penalties against sodomy "partly . . .
to attract the support" of lower-class members (p. 65).

91. Published by G. Marcotti, *Un mercante fiorentino e la sua famiglia nel secolo XV* (Florence, 1881), p. 55.

92. Vespasiano da Bisticci, *Le vite*, 2 vols., ed. A. Greco (Florence, 1970–76),
2:214.

prudence, great textile manufacturers such as the Alberti might be, in one worker's opinion, "always good merchants and fine men, and they have always given excellent wages and sustenance to poor men."[93] But it was surely for larger, political, considerations that Piero Alberti, according to his humanist kinsman, Leon Battista, sought "to be seen and heard to be gracious and genial even to the plebeians and the lowest of the low," a policy continued by the Alberti family's Medici friends. It is telling that in 1441, Leon Battista himself and Piero de' Medici combined to suggest that a poetic contest be held to decide "who best can describe 'Amicitia' in the Tuscan tongue."[94] As a matter of "practical prudence," Cavalcanti wrote early in the century, "always . . . keep your eye on the man most esteemed by the plebeians among the populace [*nel vulgo del popolo*]" and "don't oppose the people's will. Love the people and honor the nobility." It was harder for a plebeian than a great citizen to attract "true friendship," Cavalcanti recognized. "Indeed it is a saying of the vulgar [*plebe*]: 'I denounce friendship, I send it to the devil.' A powerful man is either loved or feared."[95]

Unlike Machiavelli's future prince, many Florentines sought during the Quattrocento to be "rather loved than feared"[96]—as Rucellai enjoined his sons to be when discussing their relations with domestics—by a populace distrustful of such overtures of friendship. The Quattrocento witnessed the emergence among the governing class of a series of charitable practices and patronal attitudes that amounted almost to a policy, haphazardly conceived and falteringly implemented to be sure, the intention of which was to encourage peaceful coexistence between itself and the *popolo minuto*. The changed economic circumstances of, and internal developments within, the woolen industry discussed by Franceschi provided a favorable context for the emergence of such attitudes, as did the larger improvement in working conditions and the economy insisted upon by Goldthwaite.[97] Patrician gov-

93. Brucker, *Firenze nel Rinascimento*, p. 122.

94. Leon Battista Alberti, *Opere volgari*, 3 vols., ed. C. Grayson (Bari, 1960–73), 1:278–79. On popular support for the Alberti, see Brucker, *Civic World*, pp. 337–39. I am grateful to a seminar at Wesleyan University that pointed out to me the importance of this well-known literary event for my theme: *De vera amicitia: I testi del primo Certame coronario*, ed. L. Bertolini (Modena, 1993), p. 516.

95. Giovanni Cavalcanti, *The "Trattato Politico-Morale" of Giovanni Cavalcanti*, ed. M. T. Grendler (Geneva, 1973), pp. 132, 155.

96. Published by A. Perosa in *Giovanni Rucellai ed il suo Zibaldone*, 2 vols. (London, 1960–81), 1:13, a passage not taken from Rucellai's authority. Niccolò Machiavelli, *Il Principe e Discorsi*, ed. S. Bertelli (Milan, 1960), chap. 17.

97. Franceschi, *Oltre il "Tumulto,"* passim; Franceschi, "Florence and Silk in the Fifteenth Century," *Italian History and Culture* 1 (1995): 3–22; Goldthwaite, *Building*, chap. 6, pp. 287–350.

ernments seized the moment. There was "increased intervention by the republic in the administration of charity and a considerable expansion of the city's poor relief facilities," Henderson has argued,[98] as well as a growing willingness by the authorities of church and state to allow the creation of craft confraternities, which had been repressed as seditious in the previous century.[99] Some fourteen of these were formed, under tight supervision. Humanist rhetoricians from Leonardo Bruni onward developed and shaped older republican traditions into the unifying ideology Hans Baron called "civic humanism," a cluster of ideas by no means incompatible with increasing Medicean exercise of power. The *Summa* of Saint Antoninus, widely diffused in the second half of the century, insisted that the rights and humanity of working people be respected, that there existed a sort of civic contract, indistinguishable from Christian love, which obliged people of different social status to cooperate with each other.[100] In the confraternities men were taught humbly and ritually to forget social differences. "And so, each of us ought to wash the feet of the others, even the feet of our servants," Alamanno Rinuccini believed.[101] The festive activities of the *potenze*, whose membership overlapped with that of the craft confraternities, signaled the continued (Trexler would say reborn)[102] vitality of a plebeian culture more or less benignly observed and encouraged by patricians, some of whom, including Lorenzo de' Medici, were not loathe to participate in it by writing bawdy carnival songs.

98. Henderson, *Piety and Charity*, p. 349; and G. Pinto, ed., *La società del bisogno* (Florence, 1989).

99. Henderson, *Piety and Charity*, pp. 426–30; Trexler, *Public Life*, pp. 394–418; and Weissman, *Ritual Brotherhood*, pp. 63–66. Successive governments sought to provide a secure grain supply in a period of growing population and uncertain employment: Tognetti, "Problemi," passim.

100. Howard, *Beyond the Written Word*, chap. 8, on Antoninus. C. Stinger has recently surveyed Florentine humanism in *Renaissance Humanism: Foundations, Forms, and Legacy*, 3 vols., ed. A. Rabil (Philadelphia, 1988), 1:175–208. A. Brown reexamines Baron's legacy in *The Medici in Florence: The Exercise and Language of Power* (Florence, 1992), pp. 327–37. See also the essays of Q. Skinner and J. M. Najemy in *Language and Images*, ed. Brown, chaps. 3 and 10, respectively; and now M. Jurdjevic, "Civic Humanism and the Rise of the Medici," *Renaissance Quarterly* 52 (1999): 994–1020.

101. Cited by Weissman, *Ritual Brotherhood*, p. 101; see also pp. 99–105.

102. Trexler, *Public Life*, p. 401; Kent and Kent, "Two Vignettes," pp. 252–60. David Rosenthal of Monash University is completing a doctoral thesis on *potenze* under the Grand Duchy. See now his "The Genealogy of Empires: Ritual Politics and State Building in Early Modern Florence," *I Tatti Studies* 8 (1999): 197–234. Cecilia Hewlett of Monash University is pursuing similar themes in her Ph.D. thesis on several rural Tuscan communities during the Renaissance period.

Such ideas as those of Saint Antoninus had of course been preached before, and communal charity offered to the poor was hardly a Quattrocento invention and by no means banished poverty. It is, however, hard to escape the impression, which only further research can test, that various ideas, policies, and social impulses began to cohere in the course of the Quattrocento, and that we are dealing with a more or less conscious patrician and civic response to the turbulent events of the Ciompi Revolt, shaped by an enduring perception that the plebeian orders continued to be a force to be reckoned with. If the descendants of the Ciompi were so cowed and lacking in bargaining power, so irrelevant to patrician lives, as some historians have argued, then how to explain that many Florentines, and the Medici regime itself, strove to placate them? How to explain that, as well as extending a benevolent and charitable hand to the humble in general, many patricians succeeded in establishing with individuals and families of the *popolo minuto* and peasantry those ties of interdependence, both functional and affectionate, which contemporaries called *amicizia?*

IV

As unlikely as some scholars have found it that this could have occurred, others have detected the existence of such bonds of clientage between men and women of very different social status in the fifteenth century. David Herlihy and Christiane Klapisch once suggested, indeed, that "the skewed distribution of wealth [within towns] favored the development of patronage systems and of factions and parties based upon them."[103] Charity and patronage dispensed by rich people and institutions "became almost indistinguishable," Henderson has suggested.[104] Molho observed that class relations may have been easier in the country than the city and, while hardly converted from skepticism on the subject, has now handsomely acknowledged that the republic's dowry fund "attracted the deposits of a number of middling, even poor families," both from city and country, a fair proportion of the investments coming from third persons motivated by "patron-

---

103. D. Herlihy and C. Klapisch-Zuber, *Tuscans and Their Families* (New Haven, Conn., 1985), p. 107. See, too, D. Herlihy, "The Distribution of Wealth in a Renaissance Community: Florence, 1427," in *Towns in Societies*, ed. P. Abrams and E. A. Wrigley (Cambridge, England, 1978), pp. 131–57, esp. 154. For Venice, see D. Romano, *Patricians and Popolani: The Social Foundations of the Venetian Renaissance State* (Baltimore, 1987), esp. chap. 6.

104. Henderson, *Piety and Charity*, p. 424.

age or charity."[105] Franceschi finds it "difficile non definire di tipo cliente-lare" the bonds of dependence and even affection his sensitive analysis reveals in the records of the Wool Guild (Arte della Lana) in which men of different social rank are described as "friends."[106]

It is in the voluminous letter collections of the Florentines, and in other family documents, that one finds perhaps the firmest and most extensive evidence of the extent to which citizens labored on behalf of obscure individuals, that one reads the language of friendship and clientage invoked not only with reference to equals but also to men and women from despised social groups. Letters in support of such humble people date from every decade of the century and come from Florentines as modest as Bartolomeo Cederni and as grand as Lorenzo de' Medici, from women as well as men. I cannot survey all this evidence here, nor have I read it so systematically as to be able to offer a quantitative analysis, even were I qualified to do so. Yet now to draw attention to and to sample these letters, to begin to seek some understanding of the human actions, relationships, and feelings to which, however allusively, they refer, is not to indulge in what has been dismissed as "un tipo di biografismo belletristico"[107] but rather to pursue with appropriate evidence a subject of capital importance.

Among the numerous Quattrocento letters that recommend the affairs of the humble, only a minority of them are wholly devoted to some obscure petitioner. Such a letter was the detailed and committed defense of Piero da Santo Sano written by Bartolomeo Sassetti to Giovanni de' Medici to explain why the latter should instruct Piero's master not to prosecute him for leaving his farm fallow, a petition the local priest also actively supported: "because of the war, and the serious famine, he (Piero) had no alternative."[108] Sassetti was perhaps unusual in being apparently disinterestedly moved by compassion. Most letters in support of peasants concerned people whom the writers knew, even if indirectly, or to whom they felt some responsibility. So Bernardo Cresci commended to another citizen, Bastiano Giovannegli, "the worker of my brother Bernardo's sister-in-law," and

105. Molho, *Marriage Alliance*, pp. 91, 104, 109; Molho, "Cosimo," pp. 12–13.

106. Franceschi, *Oltre il "Tumulto,"* p. 311 n. 24. Goldthwaite, *Building*, p. 314, emphasizes that the building industry had "a marketplace where . . . personal relations were not yet left out of the cash nexus."

107. A. Molho, "Il padronato a Firenze nella storiografia anglofona," *Ricerche storiche* 15 (1985): 5–16, quotation on p. 14.

108. ASF, MAP, V, 464, 16 August 1442: "per rispetto della ghuerra e della fame grande non potè fare altro."

Piero Tornaquinci described Meo di Guerriere as "very much my friend and a respectable peasant."[109]

Clarice Orsini made explicit her motives for strongly supporting "Lorenzo di Bartolo, my worker here at Bagno," in a court case: "[H]elp him in such a way that, given that he's a peasant and has no one on his side, his rights are not encroached upon. Handle this as if it were our affair."[110] More concerned with his own *bella figura* was a certain Don Benedetto, who requested a friend to defend "one of our workers" in the podestà's court because in fact the guilty party was Lazzaro Fiorini's peasant "and since we try to be neighborly, I take it badly that we are being treated in this way."[111] Any Quattrocento letter collection contains such passages concerning the peasantry, who were helped not only in legal disputes but also in finding "a corner to live in" or a new wife.[112] In need of protection and guidance as they often were, peasant petitioners were not, however, passive recipients of patrician patronage. Some letters make it clear that the humble client had taken the initiative by approaching someone who could, as it were, switch on a current of recommendations that might flow to very powerful patrons indeed. Lorenzo Rucellai wrote to his influential kinsman, Palla, recommending some friends "as requested by my workers."[113]

Common soldiers, too, themselves often country men or mountainmen, actively sought patrician patronage. In a careful letter to Forese Sacchetti, Captain of Cortona, written "to serve" Pieraccino da San Cascino, a guard there, Palla Strozzi also mentions Rinaldo Gianfigliazzi's interest in the soldier's case.[114] Decades later, Guglielmo Capponi commended Biagio di Giovanni to Francesco Valori as "our very intimate friend . . . just the man to stand guard over some strategic place."[115] Governments and citizens, in their turn, recruited these almost anonymous *fanti* and *provvigionati* as re-

109. ASF, CRSGF, 78, 322, fol. 115r, 14 November 1522: "lavoratore della suocera di Bernardo mio fratello"; CS, ser. 3, 150, fol. 108, 1 June 1445: "molto mio amicho ed è uno chontadino da bene."

110. BNF, Fondo Ginori Conti, 29, 38 bis, fol. 23, 3 May 1487: "aiutatelo e fate in modo che le sua ragioni, per essere contadino et per non havere chi sia per lui, non gli habbino a essere ocupate. Fatene come di cosa nostra."

111. BLF, Ashb., 1839, fol. 21r, 13 March 1470/71: "facciendo noi buona vicinanza, mi pare male ci sia fatto a nnoi a questo modo."

112. ASF, NA, 11403, unfoliated letter of Giuliano Lanfredini, 12 June 1476: "uno cantuccio di casa"; MAP, VII, 164, Mariotto Lippi, 9 February, without year.

113. ASF, CRSGF, 78, 322, fol. 102r, 8 October 152[o?]: "chome preghata da mia lavoratori."

114. Ibid., 78, 325, fol. 425.

115. ASF, CS, ser. 1, 336, fol. 140r, 9 July 1495: "amico nostro familiarissimo . . . molto acto a guardare qualche . . . dubbioso luogo."

tainers or bodyguards and, as we have seen, sought to attract armed partisans in times of civic crisis. Letters by or concerning such retainers are common in the correspondence of the Medici, who throughout the century secured the more or less personal allegiance of tough countrymen, such as the three who wrote the following in an uncertain hand to Cosimo when he was Standard Bearer of Justice in early 1435: "We've heard some things down here; if by any chance you need men, we are three brothers, and the bearer of the present letter is our nephew [living in Florence] and him aside, we can get together 12 or 15 loyal companions should we wish, and this nephew of ours can get hold of 6 or 8, all ready to sacrifice themselves."[116] "A huge multitude of wild and fierce peasants," led by Papi de' Medici, had defended the Priors' palace against the Albizzi upon Cosimo's return from exile in September of the year before.[117] Lorenzo recruited Medici partisans among the *contadini* during the challenge to his family's authority in 1465–66, when the Medici also received pledges of armed support from clients in provincial towns such as Arezzo, where—an impressive body of recent research has shown—they successfully cultivated ties with the local elites, who in turn had their own followings. By means of such bonds, which Machiavelli later sought to sever when organizing the Florentine militia, the Medici secured not only local influence but also potential support in Florence itself.[118] A Medici document of Lorenzo's period, describing some sixty "friends of Donato di Gusto di Bertino dal Chastro living at Bruscoli," may refer to such a network of rural partisans.[119] After his brother's murder in

116. ASF, MAP, V, 639, Antonio, Biagio, and Piero, 8 January 1434/35: "nnoi abiamo sentito alchuna chosa chosstag[i]ù se per chagone veruna voi avesse bisongno di fanti, noi siamo tre fratelgli e lla portatore. . . . è nnosstro nipote; e oltra a di quessto, qua[n]do noi vorremo dodici o quindici chonpangni fedeli noi gli aremo, e quessto nosstro nipote n'arà anch' legli [sic] sei o otto, tutti quanti d'a[n]dare alla croce."

117. Cited by D. Kent, *The Rise of the Medici* (Oxford, 1978), pp. 337–38.

118. I have in mind research by R. Black, W. J. Connell, S. Milner, P. Salvadori, and others, the most recent fruits of which appear in W. J. Connell and A. Zorzi, eds., *Florentine Tuscany: Structures and Practices of Power* (Cambridge, 2000). On Lorenzo, see F. W. Kent, "The Young Lorenzo, 1449–1469," in *Lorenzo the Magnificent, Culture and Politics*, ed. M. Mallett and N. Mann (London, 1996), pp. 1–22, esp. 14; and M. Phillips, *The Memoir of Marco Parenti* (Princeton, N.J., 1987), p. 191. For peasant support of the Medici marshaled by their Bardi relatives, see now O. Gori, "La crisi del regime mediceo del 1466 in alcune lettere inedite di Piero dei Medici," in *Studi in onore di Arnaldo d'Addario*, 4 vols., ed. L. Borgia et al. (Lecce, 1995), 3:809–25; and Gori, "Per un contributo al carteggio di Lorenzo il Magnifico: Lettere inedite ai Bardi di Vernio," *Archivio storico italiano* 154 (1996): 253–78. See, too, Niccolò Machiavelli, *Arte della guerra*, ed. S. Bertelli (Milan, 1961), pp. 95–100.

119. ASF, MAP, LXXXVIII, 397, without date.

1478, Lorenzo had a bodyguard largely made up of men with provincial surnames, although one of these *staffieri* was from his own city parish.[120] The tradition continued. An early-sixteenth-century chronicler describes one "Ramazzotto da Scaricalasino, once the lowliest peasant but because of his friendship with the Medici house, made a guard at Bologna by Pope Leo and given preferment, and so become rich and made captain."[121]

My impression, and that of a number of other scholars, is that there are fewer recommendations of the urban laboring classes to be found in letters, which has been taken to indicate a patrician predilection for recruiting country rather than city clients.[122] The subject invites further scrutiny. One might observe, meanwhile, that the comparative scarcity of references to the urban poor may be explained in part by the fact that such petitions as they made were likely to have been presented *a bocca* (face-to-face), by either themselves or their spokesmen, so making unnecessary the letters that inform us about rural petitioners, who found it harder to be on the spot in Florence where most patronal business was done. Prisoners, one category of urban petitioners well represented in contemporary letter collections (especially that of the Medici), were, for obvious reasons, forced to write letters rather than approach personally their prospective liberators. And it goes without saying that among these incarcerated petitioners there were many poor and humble people, such as the brassworker Lorenzo, nicknamed "Ipichia povero," imprisoned by the Wool Guild for debt, who requested Lorenzo de' Medici's charity because Piero di Cosimo "loved me . . . ; indeed together we learned arithmetic, together."[123] The letters of religious, whose own movements might be constrained, provide a steady stream of recommendations on behalf of the needy and powerless. Concerned that "a creature of ours, as poor as he can be, named Master Iacopo the weaver," was being victimized by the Wool Guild, which had deprived the artisan of his loom and his work, the abbess of Le Murate asked Lorenzo de' Medici to pursue the matter in 1475.[124] She addressed other such requests to Lorenzo, "my sweetest son, so merciful a father to the poor."[125]

---

120. ASF, OGBR, 67, fol. 5r; Catasto, 1017, pt. 1, fol. 112v.

121. Giuliano Ughi, "Cronica," *Archivio storico italiano*, ser. 1, app. VII (1849): 147.

122. Molho, "Cosimo," esp. pp. 12–13.

123. ASF, MAP, XXIII, 552, 6 October 1473: "Piero vostro . . . mi voleva bene i[n]però stemo i[n]sieme al'abaco a [im]parare i[n]sieme."

124. Ibid., XXXII, 586, 23 December 1475: "una nostra creatura, poveretto quanto può."

125. Ibid., XXV, 316, 20 May 1474: "Dilectissimo figliuolo et padre clementissimo de' poveri." See F. W. Kent, "Lorenzo de' Medici, Madonna Scolastica Ron-

The many building sites that dotted the city as the Quattrocento went on, giving scores of artisans and laborers work, "a very great help to poor men" as Vespasiano said of the Medici projects, could also become sites of patronage. In April 1497 Antonio Strozzi recommended on behalf of "a poor woman, friend of my mother's house," that her stonecutter son be employed in building the great Strozzi palace "especially as this stonecutter is a good worker, at other times employed at this site." [126] Filippo Strozzi had earlier acted as godfather to the son of Cronaca, "master of my stonecutters," and numerous building workers attended his funeral, though it is true that Strozzi's son called them "a vile crowd." [127]

In the nature of things, one can rarely discover what became of a petition on behalf of an obscure client such as this stonecutter. What is certain, however, above all from his *Protocolli*, is that Lorenzo de' Medici wrote frequently indeed on behalf of humble people, some of whom he knew ("our family butcher"),[128] while others were recommended to him by third parties: "for a porter friend of the Santa Croce friars," "for a poor slave woman," or "for an uncle of Girolamo the tailor." [129] He was not atypical in so doing. Groups of citizens might combine to marshal such support, as when Andrea di Ser Tino suggested to Giovanni de' Medici that he help a lower guildsman whom the patricians Manno Temperani and Martino dello Scarfa "loved more dearly than Christ himself." [130] Very occasionally, we witness in detail this mobilization of patrician forces and glimpse the complicated bonds between citizens and noncitizens that called it into being. On 25 February 1451, Pandolfo Pandolfini wrote to the vicar of Poppi, Francesco Caccini, asking urgently that he punish "as lightly as possible" the brother of the bearer Giovannino da Spugnano, who was implicated in some scandal concerning the salt tax, on the grounds that the accused was also "brother

---

dinelli e la politica di mecenatismo architettonico nel convento delle Murate a Firenze (1471–72)," in *Arte, committenza ed economia a Roma e nelle corti del Rinascimento 1420–1530*, ed. A. Esch and C. L. Frommel (Turin, 1995), pp. 353–82.

126. ASF, CS, ser. 1, 180, 17 April 1497, fol. 90r: "una povera donna, amica di chasa di mia madre . . . ; maxime che dicto scharpellino è buon maestro e altre volte ha lavorato ad esta muraglia." For Vespasiano's comment, see F. W. Kent, "Palaces," p. 56. For the Strozzi palace labor force, see Goldthwaite, *Building*, pp. 167–68, 297–301.

127. Strocchia, *Death and Ritual*, pp. 194–96. See Strozzi's *ricordanze* (ASF, CS, ser. 5, 41, fol. 178) for the references to Cronaca, also an intimate of Filippo's son: I. del Badia, *Tre lettere di Simone del Pollaiuolo detto il Cronaca* (Nozze Andreini-Biagini) (Florence 1869).

128. Medici, *Lettere*, vol. 6 (1481–82), ed. M. Mallett (Florence 1990), p. 264.

129. Del Piazzo, ed., *Protocolli*, pp. 83, 99, 132, and passim.

130. ASF, MAP, V, 521, 21 May 1444: "che gli vogliono meglio che a Cristo."

of Pulito, messenger of the *Mercanzia*, who is one of our creatures."[131] By the same bearer, Caccini received a second letter, from Bernardo de' Medici, which repeated the request on different grounds: Giovannino "and his family are as close to us as could be," which made him "your and our possession," "because all of our friends are yours, and especially the men of that territory [Poppi]." "You are a sensible man," Bernardo concluded, "and don't need to be taught how one rescues a friend who's gone astray. You don't fall into the rector's hands if you've not erred, but he who errs needs compassion."[132]

The three da Spugnano brothers had evidently formed "friendships" with several Florentine patricians, themselves *amici*, who were willing to cooperate to exert (undue) influence on their behalf. To read not only the correspondence but also the testaments and family papers of citizens is to be persuaded that many, perhaps most, prominent Florentines must have had some such cross-class friendships. Whatever view individuals might have had of the *popolo minuto* or peasantry en masse, they numbered among their acquaintances associates or even intimates from those classes, humble people whom, in most cases, they employed or had other close contact with, or near whom they lived in town or country. The language of brotherhood and friendship, standard in letters of commendation exchanged between citizens, might be extended to include such dependents, and if many recommendations of the humble were, of course, perfunctory and one-off (as were many concerning a writer's peers!), some just as clearly expressed enduring relationships.

In a few, well-documented, cases we can be precise and nuanced about these more durable bonds. In his will of 1465, the childless Castello Quaratesi remembered not only his wife and three (probably not very affluent) Quaratesi kin but also his German servant and, less generously, his other domestics and slaves. The daughters of his laborer, Piero da Casavecchia, were to receive dowries from his estate, and he released all his workers

131. ASF, AD, 140, insert 8, pt. 1, fol. 88: "che la punizione ... sia più leggiere si può perchè il sopradetto è fratello del Pulito, donzello della Merchatantia, il quale è una nostra chreatura."

132. Ibid., fol. 89, 26 February 1450/51: "Et perchè detto Giovanino e sua famigla sono tanto nostri quanto essere potesino ed essendo nostri non può essere non sieno anche di voi, perchè tutti e nostri amici son vostri e massimamente gl' uomini di chotesto paese ... ; e prieghovi che la vi sia rachomandato sichome nostra e vostra cosa. Voi siete prudent' uomo, e a voi non bisogna insegnare in che modo si salva uno amicho che erri; chi nonn erra non capita a mano di Rettore, ma chi erra à bisogno di misirichordia. ...." The brothers presumably came from Sprugnano, near Pratovecchio.

from their debts to him. Four other dowries were to be distributed to needy girls.[133] This last, typical, bequest was also made by one of Castello's contemporaries, Giovanni Rucellai, who wanted to dower peasant girls from the district where his estate was. There, at Quaracchi, he had leased land for several generations to the same peasant families, whose conversation supplied his diary with details about past harvests and weather. These men later agreed to maintain Giovanni's beloved country garden at their own expense. "Be liberal and courteous to domestic servants," Rucellai had counseled his sons, and he was as good as his word. Of Marco da Vicchio, his manservant who was his proxy in a vital land purchase, Giovanni wrote to Piero de' Medici, "I love him and very much wish to do him this favor." Rucellai also backed Domenico da Signa for a post, perhaps because earlier the servant had nursed his son, Bernardo, back to health: "He's always been very dear to me," Bernardo Rucellai himself wrote, "but during my illness he's behaved towards me as I believe very few other men would have done." It was to such household servants that Giovanni had given twelve pairs of stockings bearing his device upon Bernardo's marriage into the Medici, "numerous servants and friends of the house" receiving a further seventy pairs. His peasant dependents sent gifts on this occasion, including "a magnificent olive tree in a cart," to which Rucellai responded with "four vealers, to feed the peasants."[134]

Greater landholders such as the Medici, men more preoccupied with politics than Giovanni Rucellai, were nevertheless kept closely informed about their estates. When a peasant family, in her view, deserved help, Lucrezia Tornabuoni was warm in her recommendations to Lorenzo.[135] He should make Matteo di Viviano, "our farm worker," a loan of six florins, an estate manager advised Giovanni de' Medici in 1441, because "they're good people" with a large family and "are settling down very well to running your place."[136] Away from Florence on public business in the spring of 1438, Cosimo was informed of such details as that the farmer at Careggi with whom he had discussed "straightening the vines . . . leaving a path in the middle, says that the suckers are too abundant," and that "Biagio, the cellarer, is sick with a pain in his side and has ended up in hospital, and for now

133. ASF, NA, 1740, fols. 23r–28v, 27 April 1465.
134. All quotations are in F. W. Kent, "The Making of a Renaissance Patron of the Arts," in *Giovanni Rucellai ed il suo Zibaldone*, 2:72–75.
135. Lucrezia Tornabuoni, *Lettere*, ed. P. Salvadori (Florence, 1993), p. 77.
136. ASF, MAP, V, 428, Bartolomeo di Francesco, 24 September 1441: "nostro lavoratore alla tera . . . ; sono buone persone e anchora mi pare s'adattino molto bene e ghovernare il vostro luogho e lla famiglia è pure grande. . . ."

he can't see to selling the wine."[137] The first passage, irresistibly recalling as it does Vespasiano's statement that even Cosimo did not disdain to prune his own vines,[138] may suggest far too rosy and cozy a view of peasant-master relations. What does seem to emerge from such letters is that great lords might talk to and in a sense know their peasant employees, with whom they might forge bonds, which wills and bequests then remembered.

So Alessandra Strozzi mentions in her letters the old peasant Agnolo da Quaracchi, "who handles all our business" and whose debts she partly canceled in 1453 "because he's poor." Having sent him to Rome at her expense, she hoped that the aged Agnolo would be willing to travel on to Naples to see her sons, who were to "show him a good time."[139] "To please them," Bernardo Machiavelli had sheltered his farmworkers' sister in Florence "with my wife and my daughters" during an outbreak of war. When Bernardo's son later chatted with woodcutters and caroused at a common inn while writing *The Prince*, he was hardly discovering a novel social world.[140] Men speak explicitly of having rural friends, and in documents other than letters of recommendation where the word can be merely formulaic. A country artisan was "my good friend, tried and tested time and time again," wrote the aristocratic Francesco Castellani.[141] Cured of his illness by Antonio Benivieni, a certain countryman "retained and cherished assiduously to this day . . . the friendship thus contracted with me," wrote the famous physician.[142] Countrymen visited Giovanni Petrucci as he lay dying, for, as his brother explained, he had ties with "many peasants . . . because he was very well known in the countryside on account of holding several rural posts in which he had been of service to many."[143]

137. Ibid., V, 645, Matteo di Ser Giovanni, 11 March 1437/38: "et raderizando quelle viti come voi ragionaste con lui, rimanendo uno viottolo in mezo, dice che questi magliuoli vi sono troppi . . ."; "Biagio, chanovaio, è amalato di fiancho; èssi ridotto a Santa Maria Nuova et per ora non può attendere a vendere i vini."

138. Vespasiano da Bisticci, *Le vite*, 2:194–95.

139. Strozzi, *Lettere*, pp. 48, 50, 102; Alessandra Strozzi, *Ricordanze*, ASF, CS, ser. 5, 15, fol. lxxxi r.

140. Bernardo Machiavelli, *Libro di ricordi*, ed. C. Olschki (Florence, 1954), pp. 75–76 (and see 28, 85); Niccolò Machiavelli, *Lettere*, ed. F. Gaeta (Milan, 1961), pp. 301–6.

141. Francesco Castellani, *Ricordanze*, vol. 2, *Quaternuccio e Giornale B (1459–1485)*, ed. G. Ciappelli (Florence, 1995), p. 137 (and index under Bartolomeo di Piero da Cioffoli).

142. Antonio Benivieni, *De abditis nonnullis ac mirandis morborum et sanationum causis*, trans. C. Singer (Springfield, Ill., 1954), pp. 48–49.

143. Cited by E. G. Rosenthal, "Lineage Bonds in Fifteenth Century Florence: The Giovanni, Parenti and Petrucci" (Ph.D. diss., University of London, 1988), p. 158.

Men and women less influential or less aristocratic than a Strozzi, a Medici, or a Quaratesi had their friends and clients among the humble. The linen manufacturer Andrea di Berto in midcentury bequeathed the newly founded carders' confraternity of Sant'Andrea, his tenants, a permanent meeting place, and obliged his heirs annually "to feed, or rather have to dine, twelve of God's poor, as I have done." Less anonymous charity he extended as dowries to the daughters of a named laborer.[144] An obscure and hardly affluent citizen such as Bartolomeo Cederni, himself the familiar of much more powerful Florentines, included among his own dependent friends a rural goldsmith who described Cederni as "my living brother," a cowherd named Lioncino, and the Florentine doublet maker, Betto di Miniato. Cederni's slave, Caterina da Slavonia, he remembered in his will with almost lavish care; a contemporary document calls her "Caterina de' Cederni."[145]

The charity to the humble, often expressive of friendship and obligation, offered by such men and women may have been exceptional in its comprehensiveness or generosity; or perhaps their activities are just better documented. Whatever the case, more scattered documents reveal other citizens to have had similar concerns. In will after will one finds, for example, the provision of dowries for poor girls, a charitable act increasingly popular from the thirteenth century onward and given fresh impetus by Savonarola. Citizens frequently contracted to find dowries for servant girls in their employ. Burdened with providing for their own daughters' or sisters' respectable marriages, Florentines evidently could understand a poor family's more desperate attempts to marry off its girls and were willing to help save them from a possible life of dishonor "amore Dei et pro remedio anime sue," as the formula went.[146] Bartolomeo Lenzi was only atypical in the generosity of his bequest: fifteen gold florins for each of eight girls.[147] In many cases, testators expressed the wish that the dowries be distributed to girls from a particular rural district, usually where their estates lay. In the eventual distribution, what Alfonso della Casa explicitly requested

144. ASF, NA, 81, insert 18 (1394–1458), no folio, 23 May 1457: "a dare mangiare overo desinare ogni anno a dodici poveri di Dio, come ò fatto io." For the Sant'Andrea company, see Henderson, *Piety and Charity*, pp. 426–28.

145. Kent and Corti, *Bartolommeo Cederni*, pp. 40–41.

146. Will of Tomaso Spinelli, ASF, NA, 16842, fol. 70r. See Polizzotto, "'Dell'arte,'" pp. 53–54; Herlihy, *Medieval Households*, pp. 99–100; Molho, *Marriage Alliance*; J. Kirshner, *Pursuing Honor While Avoiding Sin* (Milan, 1978), pp. 13–14; C. Klapisch-Zuber, *Women, Family and Ritual in Renaissance Italy* (Chicago, 1985), chap. 8, pp. 165–77.

147. ASF, NA, 21063, insert 4, fols. 96r–100v, 29 September 1467.

must often have happened. His ten dowries were to go to girls from two rural parishes, "and if there should be among the above number some who are my [responsibility, daughters of] a laborer or tenant, they should be preferred."[148] In a few cases, indeed, the testator names the daughters of a particular laborer. There are also occasionally "personalized" endowments to urban families whose precise relationship to the donor one cannot know.[149] One's impression is that dowries or other alms were usually distributed in the light of local or specialized knowledge, often that of an ecclesiastic. The pious Feo Belcari himself nominated the "poor persons" to whom his gift of a hundred florins to the Badia Fiorentina was to go. After his death, the widow Veronica, mother of a shoemaker, was to make the decisions.[150]

Alessandra Strozzi and Castello Quaratesi were in no sense alone in releasing rural laborers from the debts so many incurred. "I desire that all my workers, past or present, who contracted debts with me be free of them for love of God," Carlo Serristori was unexceptional in writing in 1485.[151] An urban dependent of the Castellani, such as Niccolò di Piero, might also have his debt discharged "because the said Niccolò is poor and has been good and faithful to our house,"[152] but it was apparently a far more usual practice to provide free lodging in the city, a very charitable act according to a moralist. The tax records are full of such arrangements, undertaken "for the love of God," the Medici wrote, offered "as alms" according to the del Cicca brothers.[153] Very likely, the parties knew each other. Lodging was provided for "a creature of ours," in an example cited by Isabel Chabot, who has observed that among women there existed "networks of private charity . . . based on personal ties of friendship or neighborhood solidarities."[154] Such groups of caring friends and neighbors were clearly at work

---

148. NA, 13757, fol. 5v, 6 April 1492: "e se vi fusse alchuna dale sopradette che fussino nel mio per lavoratore o pigonale vadino innanzi al altre."

149. E.g., ASF, Catasto, 26, fol. 1103r; ibid., 1005, pt. 1, fol. 291v; CRSGF, 95, 220, fol. 6r; NA, 19628, fols. 15r–20r, 13 June 1417.

150. ASF, CRSGF, 78, 261, fols. 125r, 137v.

151. ASF, NA, 10198, fol. 396v, 15 August 1485: "voglio che tutti i mia lavoratori che sono o sono stati se mi fussino debitori voglio siano lasciati loro per l'amore di Dio."

152. ASF, CRSGF, 90, 132, no folios, 20 May 1452: "perchè detto Niccolò è povera persona e stato buono e fedele da chasa."

153. D. Kent, *Rise of the Medici*, p. 78 n. 43; ASF, Catasto, 805, fol. 1009r. See Henderson, *Piety and Charity*, p. 270.

154. I. Chabot, "Widowhood and Poverty in Late Medieval Florence," *Continuity and Change* 3 (1988): 291–311, quotations on pp. 304, 311 n. 69.

in the lives of the aged ex-baker who admitted in 1480 that "I live with difficulty and if it were not for the good people who support me, I should die of hunger,"[155] and of the much younger *lavorante* who stayed at home living "on the charity of gentlemen."[156] These were people even poorer than poor, as that state was defined succinctly by contemporaries: "poor girls, namely those whose fathers own no immovable goods"; "poor men, who live from day to day."[157]

The solicitude, even love, shown toward particularly faithful domestic servants was not confined to the house of Giovanni Rucellai. If much female service was of an "episodic and temporary nature," in part because for the first part of the Quattrocento the labor market was not unfavorable to employees,[158] it was perhaps for this very reason that a long-lived attachment might be valued by both parties. Piero da Pistoia, "ten years in our house,"[159] was warmly recommended by Gino Ginori to Lorenzo de' Medici for one of those minor government posts, as messenger or attendant, so sought after by manservants who had proved themselves in domestic service. Numerous wills and tax reports refer to careful arrangements made for long-serving family retainers. "Considering his good service, . . . and because he has served him since he was a boy," Carlo Pandolfini gave Francesco d'Antonio the right to live in his house and some subsistence.[160] Decades after his father's will of 1428, Carlo Carradori still honored it by supporting in his house one Caterina, "who is ancient indeed, over eighty years old, unwell, and can hardly get about or do a thing; and she has to be looked after because half in her dotage."[161] One senses a certain exasperation here, perhaps even the resentment that surely emerges in Domenico Simoni's remark that "he got nothing out of" the eighty-year-old slave he let live in a "small, low, cottage" behind his own house.[162] Heirs might be tempted to shortchange superannuated servants, as testators realized. His

155. ASF, Catasto, 1017, pt. 1, fol. 2r: "a faticha posso vivere, et se non fussino le buone persone che mi sovenghono mi morrei di fame."

156. Catasto, 992, fol. 35r: "sto alle mercé degl' uomini da bene."

157. ASF, NA, 13757, fol. 5v: "povere, cioè che 'l padre non abia beni immobili"; MAP, XX, 688, Stefano, *miniatore*, to Lorenzo de' Medici, no date: "huomini poveri e che vivono dì per dì."

158. Klapisch-Zuber, *Women*, p. 176.

159. ASF, MAP, XXXIII, 719, 30 August 1476: "è stato in chasa nostra X anni."

160. ASF, AD, 268, insert 3, no folios, 20 November 1470: "considerando il ben servito . . . et perchè lo ha servito da fanciullo."

161. ASF, Catasto, 919, pt. 1, fol. 180v: "la quale è vechissima d'età d'anni ottanta o più, e inferma, e non può quasi più andare nè fare nulla; e bisogna ce la fare ghovernare ch' è meza rimbambita."

162. Catasto, 80, pt. 1, fol. 156v: "e niente se ne chava."

freed slave should be given good, "not powdery," grain each year and wine that had "not turned to vinegar," Lorenzo Vettori stipulated, observing that since the woman had "well and faithfully served me for many years past," he wanted to show gratitude, "so that in her old age she can support herself and not have to go begging."[163] A few domestics, like Cederni's slave, permanently entered the family, as it were, and took part in its cult of remembrance. The patrician painter Alesso Baldovinetti followed his wife's instructions in taking special care of Mea, a crippled servant "not likely to find a husband since she is not sound in body," to whom he gave permission to be buried in his own tomb. In a reversal of the normal order of things, the Circassian ex-servant of Temperani bequeathed property to the knight's family on condition that masses be said for her in his chapel.[164] Ties of godparenthood, which contemporaries took very seriously, frequently crossed class lines, as Klapisch-Zuber has pointed out, creating a kind of spiritual kinship between people of very different social status.[165]

Wet nurses, at the pinnacle of domestic servitude, were better paid even than manservants and might enjoy special access to their employers.[166] A soldier trying to gain the Medici ear wrote to the *balia* of Lorenzo's son, "Monna Piera di Casentino . . . a casa Lorenzo de' Medici," but his timing was poor; she was replaced some days later.[167] Luckier were the "peasants, . . . close relations of my wet nurse," whom Maddalena de' Medici recommended to her brother.[168] Unlike the Medici children, most babies were wet-nursed away from home. Nevertheless, some citizens remembered wet nurses long after their usefulness was over, Alessandra Strozzi among

163. ASF, NA, 1740, fol. 327v, 23 August 1479: "m' à servito bene e fedelmente più e più anni passati per non essere ingrato e che lla in sua vecchiezza si possa substentare e non abbia andare mendicando." Agnolo Vettori made a similar bequest in ibid., fol. 53v, 17 May 1470.

164. R. W. Kennedy, *Alesso Baldovinetti* (New Haven, Conn., 1938), pp. 196, 251–52; Kent and Kent, "Two Vignettes," p. 247.

165. C. Klapisch-Zuber, "Compérage et clientélisme à Florence (1360–1520)" (1985), repr. in Klapisch-Zuber, *La maison et le nom: Stratégies et rituels dans l'Italie de la Renaissance* (Paris, 1990), pp. 123–33.

166. C. Klapisch-Zuber, *La famiglia e le donne nel Rinascimento a Firenze* (Rome and Bari, 1988), chap. 9, p. 275. See, too, P. Gavitt, "*Perche non avea chi la ghovernasse:* Cultural values, family resources and abandonment in the Florence of Lorenzo de' Medici, 1467–85," in *Poor Women and Children in the European Past,* ed. J. Henderson and R. Wall (London, 1994), pp. 65–93.

167. ASF, MAP, LXXXV, 65, 3 August 1472; Tornabuoni, *Lettere,* pp. 72–73; Medici, *Lettere,* vol. 1 (1460–1474), ed. R. Fubini (Florence, 1977), p. 392.

168. Matteo Franco, *Lettere,* ed. G. Frosini (Florence, 1990), p. 152, 23 August 1492.

them; Giovanni Minerbetti supported an old nurse and filled out her tax form.[169] Some wet nurses went on to act as nannies, establishing long-lived ties of affection. Such a person was the ex-slave Agnese, "who raised Bartolomea my wife," as Lorenzo Pitti noted of her death in his house. Agnese, buried at Pitti's expense, had, however, left a cottage and "some household goods of little worth" to her ex-ward.[170] In recommending "a certain Mona Agniola," Pandolfo Pandolfini pointed out that she "brought up Costanza my wife, and [is] a good and needy person."[171] For much of her life one Caterina di Brunetto was close to Bernardo Rinieri. Upon his marriage in 1459, the banker employed Caterina, once his wet nurse, as a domestic servant and later actively protected her financial interests. Caterina died in Rinieri's house in 1471.[172]

Such enduring ties of loyalty and affection between patricians and their familiars would have existed in only a small minority of cases. They were nurtured, however, in a working and civic context rather more amenable to social intercourse between individuals and families from different milieux than proponents of the double-city model of Florentine society would allow. Even the Eight frequently intervened on behalf of humble people (ordering a bed to be restored to a provincial widow on one occasion) and exerted more personal patronage. It was surely not coincidental that the particular magistracy of the Eight that absolved Pierfilippo Pandolfini's laborer from a charge in June 1492 included that patrician's son, Alessandro.[173] And insofar as this intercourse allowed "the sherry of accepted values" to seep through the layers of Florentine society, that gentle process might even defy social gravity by persuading a few gentlemen to emulate artisans. Did the patrician Alesso Baldovinetti make the highly unusual decision to become a painter, what contemporaries, notwithstanding Alberti's efforts, still regarded as a manual worker, not only because he was illegitimate but also because he had mixed familiarly as a boy with the *dipintori* who rented

169. Rosenthal, "Lineage Bonds," p. 119; ASF, Catasto, 43, fols. 1107r–1108v. For other examples, see ASF, NA, 10638, fol. 133r, 12 August 1428; ASF, CS, ser. 5, 1747, fol. 39v.

170. Florence, Archivio contemporaneo G. P. Vieusseux, Fondo Ginori Conti (Fondo Rinuccini), 105, account book of Lorenzo Pitti, fol. 208v: "che alevò la Bartolomea mia donna . . . ; chosì le lasciò alcuna maserizie di pocho conto."

171. ASF, AD, 148, insert 8, pt. 1, fol. 92, 19 April 1450: "una mona Angniolo [sic] . . . alevò la Costanza mia donna e buona persona e bisognosa."

172. ASF, CRSGF, 95, 212, Rinieri's *ricordanze*, fols. cliiii, 162, 165.

173. ASF, OGBR, 74, fol. 21v; 91, fol. 106v.

workshops below the houses of his Baldovinetti kinsmen?[174] Perhaps so. Wet-nursed among the stonemasons of Settignano, Michelangelo told Vasari that "I . . . sucked in with my nurse's milk the chisels and hammer with which I make my figures."[175]

v

Almost all Quattrocento artists, however, even the majority of architects, were artisans by social origin and professional training, which serves to remind us that the Renaissance in the visual arts was the creation of a collaboration between craftsmen and their patrons, most of whom were patrician citizens or institutions. Perhaps the finest, most enduring achievement of the processes of social and political negotiation and collaboration, of cultural osmosis, which I have only begun to describe here, was the Florentine Renaissance itself, which could hardly have been the product of an utterly polarized city. This social and cultural osmosis begs for further investigation, for a fuller explication of why a Michelangelo Buonarotti became a sculptor and why his namesake, the humble trumpeter Michelangelo di Cristofano da Volterra, who loved "to read and hear all about those grand deeds of old, to gain a fuller understanding and to flee boredom," begged parents to have their children taught to read: "because, truly, in this world a person who can't read is, in effect, like a lifeless marble statue."[176]

Just as the Medici themselves, and their later admirers, claimed that they had brought into being that cultural Renaissance, Florence's principal family took credit for the easing of social tensions in the later Quattrocento, for the creation, indeed, of a golden age of harmony. "How rightly you circle your temples with oak leaves, you who protect not only the citizen but the people," Poliziano was prompted to write of Lorenzo.[177] As in so many other respects, however, Lorenzo and his immediate ancestors in

174. See ASF, Catasto, 74, fols. 38r, 162v. Kennedy, *Alesso Baldovinetti*, does not mention this in discussing his early career (pp. 3, 20–21, 25, 199–200.)

175. Cited by K. Weil-Garris Brandt, "'The Nurse of Settignano': Michelangelo's Beginnings as a Sculptor," in *The Genius of the Sculptor in Michelangelo's Work*, ed. P. C. Marani (Montreal, 1992), pp. 21–43, quotation on p. 23. See, too, W. E. Wallace, *Michelangelo at San Lorenzo* (New York, 1994), p. 2 and passim; and P. Barolsky, *The Faun in the Garden* (University Park, Pa., 1994), pp. 17–18. Cf. G. Duby, "The Diffusion of Cultural Patterns in Feudal Society," in Duby, *The Chivalrous Society* (Berkeley and Los Angeles, 1977), pp. 171–77.

176. L. Pescetti, "Michelangnolo di Cristofano, 'Canterino,' volterrano," *Rassegna volterrana* 24–26 (1958): 8.

177. I. D. McFarlane, *Renaissance Latin Poetry* (New York, 1980), pp. 20–21.

fact were doing more systematically and extensively what other Florentines and their governments had already done, and continued to do, in
offering benevolence and "friendship" to the Ciompi's descendants. (It is
true that, as Lorenzo increasingly became "maestro della bottega," able to
put at the disposal of clients the patronal resources provided by his other
friendships inside and outside of Florence, he almost certainly became a
more effective friend of humble petitioners than any previous Florentine
had been.)[178] Piero Capponi, struggling in the summer of 1495 to decide
how the post-Medicean city might survive in difficult circumstances, acknowledged having learned the lesson that the Florentine elite could govern only with the cooperation and tacit consent of the popular classes: "I
am persuaded that Florence can only be ruled by twenty-five or thirty aristocrats who, putting aside all sectarian passion, ambition and avarice, undertake to look after and not let go to ruin that wretched city: with the people's
agreement [consenso del popolo], implicitly given rather than by law."[179]
Nor was this Florentine and Medicean realization, though powerfully
shaped by the city's particular history, unique, since other contemporary
regimes, such as those of the Estensi in Ferrara and the Sforza in Milan,
also "devoted considerable energy towards cultivating, at least outwardly,
an amicable working relationship with the popolo."[180]

There is no cause to romanticize the "amicable working relationship"
established between many Florentines of different classes during the Quattrocento. Long-lived affection and mutual dependence could develop between individuals and families from different social strata, and yet the language of class disdain, not to say hatred, retained a certain vigor, fed by the
suspicion and fear apparent on all sides. Individuals from one class might,
as we say, identify with individuals from another, while holding in fear or
contempt the social group as a whole to which their "friend" belonged. It
was indubitably the citizens' wary sense of the potential power of the numerous laboring classes—as soldiers and partisans, even as derisive critics—that dictated their "policy" of appeasement and friendship. Humble
people, formally cut off from civic institutions controlled by patricians

178. F. W. Kent, "Patron-Client Networks in Renaissance Florence and the
Emergence of Lorenzo as 'Maestro della Bottega,'" in Lorenzo de' Medici: New Perspectives, ed. B. Toscani (New York, 1993), pp. 279–313.

179. Letter to F. Valori, 28 July 1495, ed. G. Aiazzi, Archivio storico italiano 4,
pt. 2 (1853): 59.

180. R. G. Brown, "The Politics of Magnificence in Ferrara 1450–1505" (Ph.D.
diss., University of Edinburgh, 1982), chap. 1, pt. 1, p. 6; E. S. Welch, Art and Authority in Renaissance Milan (New Haven, Conn., 1995).

whom they, in their turn, had some cause to fear, came to realize their bargaining power in the post-Ciompi era and entered into relationships of friendly clientage that gave them access to dowries for their daughters, protection in court, employment, and other valued prizes.

It is anachronistic (perhaps patronizing) to describe as "quelques petits avantages personnels" these benefits humbler Florentines wrung from citizen patronage,[181] to regard these descendants of the Ciompi as merely passive recipients of charity. Their relations with patrons were reciprocal if, inevitably, unequal, each side having something to offer and, just as important, to withhold. From this perspective, the laboring classes participated in Quattrocento Florentine history with more dignity, and more successfully, than we have been taught. John Najemy has recently argued that Quattrocento patricians and their elite regimes were as much influenced by, as they influenced, the popular guild community, that there was a "dialogue between classes," a "process by which the elite learned from the *popolo* to speak the language of popular sovereignty, representation and consent as the surest foundation of its own leadership role."[182] Such a "dialogue," more muted, expressed more often in actions than words, was also taking place between the laboring classes of town and country and the citizens as a whole, each group shaping the other's behavior as the negotiating went on. It was the humble who, in effect, taught their masters that it was preferable to be "loved than feared," the citizens who persuaded the noncitizens not "to send friendship to the devil."

Violence, or the threat of violence, called into being this dialogue and remained the last resort when it broke down. Lorenzo de' Medici, the friend of the poor, could act arbitrarily against the *popolo* in 1489; Giovanni Rucellai, having counseled loving-kindness to servants, added that sometimes they had to be beaten.[183] The people, in their turn, might riot to obtain bread or a prisoner's release. If indeed they were guilty of Maria Villani's death, the slave Lucia and her companions had, for reasons that are unclear, decided to commit murder. No more complete or tragic a breakdown of relations between domestics and their mistress could be imagined, compel-

181. Stella, *La révolte*, p. 269.

182. J. M. Najemy, "The Dialogue of Power in Florentine Politics," in *City States in Classical Antiquity and Medieval Italy*, ed. A. Molho and K. Raaflaub (Ann Arbor, Mich., 1991), pp. 270–88, quotation on p. 284. On the reciprocal nature of patronage relationships, see Bullard, *Lorenzo*, chap. 4, pp. 109–30; and T. E. Cooper, "*Mecenatismo* or *Clientelismo*? The Character of Renaissance Patronage," in *The Search for a Patron in the Middle Ages and Renaissance*, ed. D. S. Wilkins and R. L. Wilkins (New York, 1996), pp. 19–32.

183. Ed. Perosa in *Giovanni Rucellai*, 1:13.

ling us to acknowledge how fragile bonds between the classes might be; and how delicately short-lived was to be whatever social equilibrium Quattrocento Florentines had achieved. Machiavelli, the child of a far more turbulent period in Florentine and Italian history, was soon to grasp this and came to the conclusion that the conflicted nature of the city's society and politics made it imperative for a leader to be more feared than loved.

Official horror at Lucia's crime certainly sprang from a fundamental fear of "the domestic enemy," [184] but it also expressed shock, I would submit, that the bonds of trust and friendship desirable and attainable in such a domestic relationship, as Quattrocento experience had revealed, had been so brutally severed. And even in this story, there are still hints, however unpleasant, of collaboration and complicity between classes. Lucia and the servant, Marsilia, were said by the Eight to have committed their crime because they hated Maria for disgraceful, lustful motives. No further explanation is given, but the initial arrest of the murdered woman's husband strongly suggests that there existed an early official suspicion that he was the lover of one or another of his domestics and possibly implicated in the crime. Why, one might also speculate, did the slave girl approach her mistress's bed dressed as the manservant? [185] Furthermore, the popular classes from which they came apparently consented without protest to the execution of Lucia and Marsilia and the punishment of their friends. In his description, Dei mentions no plebeian tumult during the grim event, no attempt by the people to free the condemned. It was, tragically for these particular prisoners, as if the Florentines as a whole, rich and poor, patrician and plebeian alike, agreed for once with the despised Eight.[186]

184. I. Origo, "The Domestic Enemy: The Eastern Slaves in Tuscany in the Fourteenth and Fifteenth Centuries," *Speculum* 30 (1955): 321–66. On "household revolt" in the Quattrocento, see Cohn, "Character of Protest," pp. 210–21.

185. Ibid.; ASF, OGBR, 75, fol. 61r: "acce[n]se odio, malivolentia et malo animo ob quasdam turpes causas amoris et libidinis contra ed adversus dominam Mariam...." So far, I have found nothing more concerning the crime. Maria di Lorenzo Lamberteschi married Alberto Villani in 1471: P. Litta, *Celebri famiglie italiane*, vol. 8 (Milan, 1819), table II. For Alberto as galley captain, see M. E. Mallett, *The Florentine Galleys in the Fifteenth Century* (Oxford, 1967), p. 98.

186. ASF, CRSGF, 78, 316, fol. 151r, 31 December 1486: "solo come questa mattina pel caso occorso della dona d' Alberto Villani stata strangolata ... è ito in sul charro per la terra, e dipoi alla giustizia a essere apicchate, quella sciava che fè l'omicidio d' età d' anni 18 o circha, et un' altra contadina che era conscia del fatto; e in loro compagnia andarono 2 giovani in sul detto carro a quali avea a esser mozi gli orecchi, de' quali uno era stato favorevole al male commisso e l'altro alcuni furti avea facti non molto gravi. D' Alberto, el quale si dice non havere colpa, non s' è facto nulla; stimasi lo licenzieranno, che così abbi a essere in suo servigio...."

2 Giannozzo and His Elders
Alberti's Critique of Renaissance Patriarchy
John M. Najemy

Giannozzo Alberti has recently become a notorious figure. In life, he was a moderately important merchant and an otherwise undistinguished member of a great Florentine family, who, like the rest of the Alberti men of his time, spent many years in exile. He does not seem to have been particularly influential or prominent either among the Alberti or, in the years before and after the exile, within the Florentine ruling class. Giannozzo is of course much better known as the character who dominates the third book of the dialogues on family life written by his famous cousin, Leon Battista. This is the Giannozzo who has become notorious, largely because of the pages in which he explains how he instructed his young wife to be "an excellent mother of the household"; to be faithful, obedient, and submissive to him; to refrain from even giving the appearance of flirting or calling attention to herself in public; to shun the use of cosmetics; and to be an efficient manager of the household, with access to and supervision over everything in it—except for Giannozzo's books and the family papers bequeathed to him by his ancestors.[1] There is little use hiding the fact that today, by contrast with even a couple of decades ago, these pages make for embarrassing reading and some awkward classroom experiences. Giannozzo Alberti is now regularly invoked as the chief spokesman for what many literary and so-

My sincere thanks to William Connell and Julia Hairston for their perceptive and critical readings of an earlier draft. I also thank the Department of History of Stanford University, the New College Medieval and Renaissance Conference of the University of South Florida, Sarasota, and the European History Colloquium at the University of Buffalo for the opportunity to read and/or discuss this essay and for the useful criticisms I received on these occasions.

1. Leon Battista Alberti, *I libri della famiglia*, ed. R. Romano and A. Tenenti (Turin, 1972). Giannozzo's account of his instruction to his wife is on pp. 264–95; for the prohibition against her seeing his papers in his private study, see pp. 267–68. This edition will be cited below as *Della famiglia*.

cial historians of Renaissance Italy see as that society's deeply patriarchal and misogynist ideology and practices, and his reputation has suffered as a consequence. Even as recently as the late 1960s, Alberti's translator, Renée Watkins, who has certainly not been indifferent to feminism, could refer to the "charm" of Giannozzo's "healthy countenance and . . . temperate ways" and describe him as "reliable, . . . honest, benevolent [and] generous with relatives, friends, sometimes even with strangers." About the "instruction" of his wife, Watkins commented, somewhat neutrally, that Giannozzo's lessons both borrow heavily from Xenophon's treatise on household management and also give us "vivid glimpses of the Florentine home."[2]

But to many readers Giannozzo now seems decidedly less charming and benevolent. Two examples will suffice. In *Renaissance Feminism*, Constance Jordan summarizes Giannozzo's training of his wife as a combination of techniques designed to keep her ignorant of his affairs, to isolate her from "persons in general" and even from "the society of women," and above all to contain the danger represented by her speech and her sexuality through constant "humiliation" and "dehumanization." According to Jordan, Giannozzo's wife "is made to feel wholly incapable of correct judgment." "Scolded" and "chastened," she "is forgiven," says Jordan in the angriest moment of a strong paragraph, "when she behaves like a dog."[3] In a similar vein, Carla Freccero also refers to Giannozzo's "strategy" of "sa-

---

2. *The Family in Renaissance Florence*, trans. R. N. Watkins (Columbia, S.C., 1969), pp. 12–13. In chapters 7–10 of Xenophon's *Oeconomicus*, Socrates tells Critobulus about the conversation he had with Ischomachus in which the latter described how he "trained" or "educated" his wife in the principles of household management. In addition to the basic framework in which an older husband imparts such knowledge to a much younger wife who has come directly from her parents' household to her husband's, Alberti borrowed two major themes from Ischomachus's lessons: first, the wife's responsibility for the internal management of the household, in particular for maintaining the order in which all possessions must have their assigned place, and in which the servants respect and obey her; and second, the warnings against the use of cosmetics. But there are important differences as well. Giannozzo's account of the instruction of his wife is much longer than the corresponding portion of the *Oeconomicus*, and neither the emphasis in *Della famiglia* on the wife's potential infidelity or flirtatiousness as a threat to Giannozzo's honor nor the strategy of compelling her obedience by humiliating her has any parallel in Xenophon. In general, whereas Giannozzo treats his wife like a child, Ischomachus considers his to be (at least more of) an equal partner. I have consulted the *Oeconomicus* in the Loeb edition: *Xenophon: Memorabilia and Oeconomicus*, ed. and trans. E. C. Marchant (New York, 1923), pp. 362–525; chapters 7–10 are on pp. 413–53. For commentary, see L. Strauss, *Xenophon's Socratic Discourse: An Interpretation of the Oeconomicus* (with a translation by C. Lord) (Ithaca, N.Y., 1970).

3. C. Jordan, *Renaissance Feminism: Literary Texts and Political Models* (Ithaca, N.Y., 1990), pp. 51–53.

distic humiliation" in dissuading his wife from the use of cosmetics.[4] Different times produce different readings, and my purpose is certainly not to defend Giannozzo. It is not, in any case, with the harsh assessments of Giannozzo's lessons to his wife that one might wish to take issue. The recent feminist readings of this section of Alberti's book are trenchant and provocative. It is rather about the interpretations of Alberti himself built from such readings that questions might be raised. The general tendency has been to assume, first, that Giannozzo's attitudes reflect and represent those of Florentine or Italian society in the Renaissance, which I think is partly true, and second, that Alberti himself was speaking through Giannozzo and thus embracing and promoting these attitudes, which I think is not the case. Both Giannozzo and Alberti are now routinely summoned to represent this misogynist patriarchy. Two questionable steps are involved here: the first is the conflation of Giannozzo with his author—a conflation evident, for example, when Jordan, referring to Giannozzo's infamous training of his wife, asks how Alberti imagines "that such brutal methods will be successful"; the second is the conflation of Alberti's text with what is presumed to be the dominant ideology of Renaissance patriarchy—the assumption that the *Libri della famiglia* are a treatise whose purpose is to represent, promote, and justify a view of society based on the strict control of women and the presumption of their intellectual and moral inferiority. Such modes of reading are by no means limited to feminist criticism, with its special interest in Giannozzo. Social and intellectual historians with very different agendas frequently lift passages from the text and claim to find in them either a description of actual social practices and/or Alberti's prescription for the same.

In drawing attention to the obvious fact that Alberti's book is a series of dialogues, not a treatise, and that it is essential to look carefully at how the text constructs its characters, I am not simply suggesting that a more literary reading will reveal the complexity of the interaction among the speakers and thus the difficulty of seeing in the text the promotion of any particular ideology.[5] That is part of what I will argue. But it is not my intention

4. C. Freccero, "Economy, Woman, and Renaissance Discourse," in *Refiguring Woman: Perspectives on Gender and the Italian Renaissance*, ed. M. Migiel and J. Schiesari (Ithaca, N.Y., 1991), p. 206. For an overview of Alberti's misogyny, see R. Contarino, *Leon Battista Alberti moralista* (Caltanissetta and Rome, 1991), pp. 95–154.

5. On the character of the dialogues in *Della famiglia*, see D. Marsh, *The Quattrocento Dialogue: Classical Tradition and Humanist Innovation* (Cambridge, Mass., 1980), pp. 78–99. Marsh calls attention to the ways in which an "initial di-

to isolate the reading of the text from social history. Alberti does indeed reproduce the patriarchal ideology of Florentine patrician society in these dialogues, not, I think, to promote it but to dramatize its shaky foundations and self-defeating contradictions. In short, I propose that *Della famiglia* can be read as a parody of Renaissance patriarchy and, more specifically, as a critique of the oppressiveness of the power that fathers exercised over their sons, and of the resulting fears and resentments that led these sons to anxious attempts later in life to control every aspect of their lives, including their wives.

It is sometimes assumed—too easily, I think—that Renaissance patriarchy was a deep structure beyond the possibility of critical reflection or challenge from within this society and thus a system of attitudes and practices so powerful as to preclude even the full awareness of its power. As Thomas Kuehn has noted, historians often take rather too much for granted "the organic structural solidarity of the family and the central position of the father-son relationship within it." Typically assuming the cohesiveness and internal harmony of the family, they see the "familial ideology embedded in [Renaissance Italian] culture . . . as a reflection of the nature of the family and of the historical patterns of family activity."[6] To be sure, there is no reason to doubt the prevalence of the patriarchal structures and marriage and inheritance strategies of the agnatic lineages that were the typical form of family organization in the Florentine upper class. The patrilineal system sought to accumulate and preserve in the hands of male descendants two precious commodities, property and honor, that had to be protected from a variety of dangers. Among these dangers were women, or at least the marriage customs that governed their passage from one family to another. Daughters and sisters needed dowries in order to be married, and, because dowries were increasing steadily, this alone could be a threat to family patrimonies.[7] The families into which women married expected

---

versity of viewpoints" (p. 83) among the speakers gives way, at the end of each book, to some form of consensus. P. Marolda, in his *Crisi e conflitto in Leon Battista Alberti* (Rome, 1988), pp. 9–57, emphasizes even more strongly the coexistence of contrasting and at times mutually irreconcilable positions in the dialogues. By contrast, much of the scholarship on *Della famiglia* either ignores the dialogical dimension of the work or seeks to assert the fundamental unity of Alberti's thought despite what is taken to be the rhetorical practice of presenting it through different voices.

6. T. Kuehn, *Law, Family, and Women: Toward a Legal Anthropology of Renaissance Italy* (Chicago, 1991), p. 131.

7. On Florentine marriage customs and dowries, see A. Molho, *Marriage Alliance in Late Medieval Florence* (Cambridge, Mass., 1994); and L. Fabbri, *Alleanza*

them to bring dowries and then produce the male children on whom the survival of a patriline depended. But if a woman became widowed and wished to remarry, she had the right to reclaim her dowry, in which case she both abandoned her children in the household of her deceased husband and deprived them of what could have been a part of their inheritance. From the point of view of her natal family, the decision not to remarry, and thus to remain with her children, meant the loss of the dowry and of the possibility of a new marriage alliance. In the absence of prospects for marriage, girls were sent off to convents, because a woman's independence, whether before or after marriage, was considered a potential threat to the honor of her male relatives. These practices marginalized women within their own families. As Christiane Klapisch-Zuber has argued, women often seemed little more than "passing guests" in the families into which they married and never fully belonged to either their natal or their marital families.[8] The family, or *casa*, was the patriline, the transgenerational community of males in which, according to F. W. Kent, "the father-son relationship was a pivotal one."[9] The patriarchal ideology of the family centered on the identification of the family with the patriline, on the unquestioned authority of fathers, the obedience of sons, and the exclusion of women. As Marsilio Ficino put it, the father was a "second God," the son a "mirror and image" of the father, and "the house . . . nothing other than the union of the father with his sons in one residence"[10]—a masculine trinity of the father, the son, and the holy house.[11]

matrimoniale e patriziato nella Firenze del '400: Studio sulla famiglia Strozzi (Florence, 1991).

8. On the dilemmas faced by women in upper-class lineages, see Klapisch-Zuber's fundamental essays in her *Women, Family, and Ritual in Renaissance Italy*, trans. L. G. Cochrane (Chicago, 1985); for women as "passing guests," see pp. 117–20. On widows, remarriage, and Florentine inheritance law, see I. Chabot, "La loi du lignage: Notes sur le système successoral florentin (XIVe/XVe–XVIIe siècles)," *Clio: Histoire, femmes et sociétés* 7 (1998): 51–72; and also by Chabot, "Seconde nozze e identità materna nella Firenze del tardo medioevo," in *Tempi e spazi di vita femminile tra medioevo ed età moderna*, ed. S. Seidel Menchi, A. J. Schutte, and T. Kuehn (Bologna, 1999), pp. 493–523.

9. F. W. Kent, *Household and Lineage in Renaissance Florence: The Family Life of the Capponi, Ginori, and Rucellai* (Princeton, N.J., 1977), p. 45 and passim.

10. Kent's translation (ibid., p. 47) of passages from Ficino's 1455 "Epistola ad fratres vulgaris," ed. in P. O. Kristeller, *Supplementum ficinianum*, 2 vols. (Florence, 1937), 2:109–23. The *casa*, says Ficino, "non è altro che congiunctione del padre con figliuoli in un domicilio" (p. 122).

11. Two good, but rather different, introductions to prevailing notions of paternal power and the relationship between fathers and sons are offered by Kent, *Household and Lineage*, and by T. Kuehn, *Emancipation in Late Medieval Florence* (New

But much of this patriarchal system, in Florence at least, was a fairly recent development that neither went back into the mists of time nor emerged from the deep currents of "Mediterranean culture." [12] And the exaggerated notions of paternal power that became attached to the agnatic lineage were, I believe, a still later development of fourteenth-century and early-fifteenth-century politics and political thought, which had the effect of intensifying the rhetoric of patriarchy in precisely the generation of Leon Battista Alberti's youth. Those developments were, in essence, the process by which Florentine politics moved away from the social and class conflicts of the thirteenth and fourteenth centuries and came under the firm control of the upper class of elite families. The central feature of this more conservative and hierarchical republicanism was the emergence of an inner elite —an oligarchy—of leaders from prominent families who, whether from positions of formal leadership or with influence exerted behind the scenes, presented themselves as the collective fathers of the civic family. [13]

The hegemony of the elite needed and generated a new republican ideology to enhance its legitimacy. The ruling families had little use for the older popular republican notions of the active consent and representation of the republic's constituent social or institutional parts. The legitimation of elite hegemony was the work of civic humanism, which drew from Roman moral philosophy and an idealization of Roman *pietas*—duty to family, elders, and the state—the elements for the construction of a language of politics, grounded in the metaphor of the family, that promoted the natural leadership of an elite of elders identified with the "best" families. It also offered consolation to those excluded from the inner circles of power through a moral discourse of dutiful passivity that ennobled their acquiescence. The language of political paternalism was applied both to the "descent" of the Florentines from their Roman fathers and to the relationship between the Florentine ruling class and its citizen-children. [14] In the mid–fifteenth

---

Brunswick, N.J., 1982), pp. 55–71. Kuehn's approach stresses the structural nature of the tensions and conflicts that characterized relations between fathers and sons, a theme he has further explored in "Honor and Conflict in a Fifteenth-Century Florentine Family," in Kuehn, *Law, Family, and Women*, pp. 129–42.

12. Carol Lansing has shown that the agnatic lineage was still taking shape as late as the thirteenth century; Lansing, *The Florentine Magnates: Lineage and Faction in a Medieval Commune* (Princeton, N.J., 1991).

13. On this fundamental transformation of Florentine politics, see, above all, G. Brucker, *The Civic World of Early Renaissance Florence* (Princeton, N.J., 1977).

14. In Leonardo Bruni's *Laudatio Florentinae Urbis*, an extended discussion of the father-son relationship between Romans and Florentines includes the assertion of Florentine dominion over the world by hereditary right as a "paternarum rerum

century this language was routinely applied to the Medici, most famously with the decision to honor Cosimo de' Medici as *pater patriae*.[15] With the family as the dominant metaphor in this system of thought, republics and families began to be spoken of as species within the same genus, governed by the same laws of natural hierarchy and benevolent but absolute power. If the republic was a family writ large, then the family had to serve as a model of the kinds of power relations that were meant to structure civic life. The new civic ideology thus engendered heightened expectations of control by fathers over sons and by husbands over wives—a concept of family governance that was by no means new but that received greater intensity and urgency precisely because it was now seen as the foundation of authority in the civic world.[16] My hypothesis is that Leon Battista Alberti saw the connections among these political changes, the spread of civic humanism within the ruling class, and the claims of an ever more assertive patriarchy, and that he appropriated the figure of his distant cousin Giannozzo to illustrate the connection and to reveal the darker side of this convergence of ideas.

---

possessio." The text is in H. Baron, *From Petrarch to Leonardo Bruni* (Chicago, 1968), pp. 232–63, quotation on p. 244. Bruni also compares the governance of the city to the solicitous management of the household by a paterfamilias; see note 37. See also the more extended treatment of the relationship of civic humanism to Florentine political developments that I offer in my "Civic Humanism and Florentine Politics," in *Renaissance Civic Humanism*, ed. J. Hankins (Cambridge, England, 2000), pp. 75–104; and my *Corporatism and Consensus in Florentine Electoral Politics, 1280–1400* (Chapel Hill, N.C., 1982), pp. 301–17.

15. See A. Brown, "The Humanist Portrait of Cosimo de' Medici, Pater Patriae," *Journal of the Warburg and Courtauld Institutes* 24 (1961): 186–221; repr. in Brown, *The Medici in Florence: The Exercise and Language of Power* (Florence, 1992), pp. 3–52. On Donato Acciaiuoli's role in promoting the Medici as fathers to the Florentines, see M. A. Ganz, "Donato Acciaiuoli and the Medici: A Strategy for Survival in '400 Florence," *Rinascimento* 22 (1982): 33–73. His father, Neri, died when Donato was an infant, and Acciaiuoli later wrote that because of his father's early death "nullam iocunditatem, nullum adiumentum ad honores, nullum stimulum ad virtutes percipere unquam potui"; ibid., p. 38 n. 3. Ganz theorizes that Acciaiuoli's heavy sense of the loss and deprivation he suffered because of his father's death increased the appeal of the Medici as surrogate fathers.

16. An important example of this early-fifteenth-century trend—and another text that Alberti no doubt had in mind as he wrote *Della famiglia*—is the *De re uxoria* of the Venetian humanist Francesco Barbaro, who, like Alberti, studied with Gasparino Barzizza in Padua. Barbaro's treatise, written in 1415–16, was dedicated and addressed to Lorenzo di Giovanni de' Medici (Cosimo's brother) on the occasion of his marriage to Ginevra Cavalcanti. The text is edited by A. Gnesotto in *Atti e memorie della R. Accademia di Scienze, Lettere ed Arti in Padova*, n.s., 32 (1915–16): 7–100. An English translation by B. G. Kohl of the preface and book 2 is in *The Earthly Republic: Italian Humanists on Government and Society*, ed. B. G. Kohl and R. G. Witt (Philadelphia, 1978), pp. 179–228.

So, back to Giannozzo. The real—or historical—Giannozzo was born in 1357, the great-grandson of Lapo, the brother of Leon Battista's great-great-grandfather Alberto di Jacopo. Although they apparently knew each other, they were distant cousins separated in age by almost two generations. Giannozzo belonged to the generation of Alberti sent into exile as adults; in fact, he had already married his wife, Niccolosa Pazzi, in 1386 or 1387.[17] In the years of exile, Giannozzo periodically reminded the governors of Florence that he was not a political man and had had no part in the conspiracies in which the Alberti were accused of participating. In 1413, he and his brothers petitioned the Signoria from Venice and asked to be exempted from the law, passed the year before, that prohibited Florentines from having any business dealings with the Alberti within two hundred miles of Florence. They pleaded that they resided in Venice "as merchants," attending only to their business and having nothing to do with politics.[18] A year later Giannozzo and his brother Antonio asked that their daughters be exempted from the punitive tax imposed in 1412 on anyone marrying an Alberti. Once again, they based their appeal on the claim that they were merchants and had "never done anything against the government of the city of Florence."[19] And in 1418 Giannozzo and three of his brothers successfully petitioned for exemption from the law that required exiled Alberti to stay at least two hundred miles away from the city.[20]

In 1424, when Giannozzo was sixty-seven, he petitioned the Florentine government to be allowed to return to the city.[21] He pleaded that in exile

17. For Alberti marriages and genealogy, see S. K. Foster [Baxendale], "The Ties That Bind: Kinship Association and Marriage in the Alberti Family, 1378–1428," 2 vols. (Ph.D. diss., Cornell University, 1985). See 2:737–43 for the genealogical tables and 2:757 for Giannozzo's marriage.

18. ASF, PR, 102, fols. 17v–18 (28 April 1413): "Quod ipsi iam diu steterunt et stant in civitate Venetiarum ut mercatores et ibidem fecerunt et faciunt mercantias et ad aliud non intendunt nec unquam de statu civitatis Florentie se impediverunt nec contra presentem statum ipsius civitatis aliquid ullo tempore fecerunt nec attentaverunt dicto vel facto quoquomodo ut notorium est et clarum."

19. ASF, PR, 103, fols. 17v–18 (27 April 1414): "numquam contra regimen civitatis Florentie aliquid tentaverunt." For the context of these petitions and the circumstances of exile faced by the Alberti, see S. Foster Baxendale, "Exile in Practice: The Alberti Family In and Out of Florence 1401–1428," *Renaissance Quarterly* 44 (1991): 720–56; petitions discussed on pp. 738–39.

20. Foster Baxendale, "Exile in Practice," p. 739; ASF, PR, 107, fols. 284v–285v (9 February 1417/18).

21. An earlier attempt in 1421—the same year Alberti selected as the fictional moment of *Della famiglia*—had failed; see Molho, *Marriage Alliance in Late Medieval Florence*, p. 28 n. 6.

"he had always patiently obeyed the order of banishment" and had considered this and all other decrees of the government to be "most just and enacted for a most excellent purpose, even though . . . he had never done, or said, or even thought of doing anything harmful to the government of Florence or to the *patria*." For this reason, and "because of the innate humanity of the Florentine people," he hoped to gain the government's favor and sympathy. Referring to himself in the third person as was common in official petitions, he wrote: "Having arrived at old age, he ardently desires, because of the sweetness of the fatherland, to see it and his relatives and friends again before he dies, and to provide for marriages in Florence for his many daughters and nieces who are now of marriageable age."[22] The Signoria and the legislative councils met his request with a two-year exemption from the general ban against the Alberti. It was not until 1428—four years later—that the general ban was lifted.[23]

Giannozzo's petitions echo the cultural and political pieties of civic humanism: declarations of complete loyalty to the *patria* even though its laws had imposed unmerited suffering on him;[24] the acknowledgment that the lure of the fatherland's "sweetness" was undiminished after so many years of exile; faith in the *humanitas* of the Florentine people; and eagerness to embrace again relatives and friends. In petitions in which he was begging the goodwill of the regime, Giannozzo naturally said what he thought the governors of Florence wanted to hear, and that certainly included the plan to marry his daughters and nieces to Florentines, which was in effect a

22. ASF, PR, 113, fols. 294v–295v (19 February 1423/24), quotation on fol. 295: "Et quod ipse Giannozus . . . semper ut debebat patienter ordinamento paruit et reputavit et reputat quecumque ordinamenta dicti populi et communis fuisse et esse iustissima et ob perfectum finem firmata, quamquam numquam reperiri posset ipsum quicquid florentino regimini molestum aut patrie nocuum nedum operasse vel dixisse sed nec cogitasse. Et ob id et etiam ob innatam humanitatem populi florentini semper speravit et in presenti ferventius gratiam et misericordiam a vestra benigna dominatione et toto florentino dominio indubie reportare. Et quod ipse ad senium deductus summe percuperet ob patrie dulcedinem ante mortem illam et consanguineos et amicos revidere, et filias suas quamplures neptesque virorum potentes ibidem maritare." See also Baxendale, "Exile in Practice," p. 750.

23. ASF, PR, 119, fols. 229–230v, 245v–247, and 257. Other laws readmitting individual members of the family apparently not covered by the 1428 law were passed from August 1429 to February 1430; see ASF, PR, 120, fols. 311v, 451–452, 453v–454v, 464v–465v, 468–468v, 470v–471, 484, 485–485v, 487–487v.

24. Such loyalty in the face of official injustice is precisely what Leonardo Bruni, writing a decade later in his *Life of Dante*, says Dante lacked; text in H. Baron, *Leonardo Bruni Aretino: Humanistisch-philosophische Schriften* (Leipzig, 1928), pp. 51–63.

declaration of his intention to merge his own interests and resources—in the form of dowries[25]—with those of the larger civic family. The strategy worked. Giannozzo reestablished himself as a trustworthy citizen apparently not identified with either of the factions. Even though the exile had come to an end under the oligarchical regime led by the Albizzi, the *balìa* that brought the Medici to power in 1434 restored the Alberti to *popolano* status and full officeholding rights. Several members of the family, including Giannozzo, were approved in the first Medici electoral scrutiny, and he and his sons and brother soon began holding important offices: Giannozzo himself as a member of the advisory college of the Sixteen Gonfalonieri di compagnia in 1435, and his brother Antonio as a member of the priorate in 1439.[26] Although it seems to have been limited to Giannozzo's branch of the family, this was a remarkable political recovery, probably due in no small part to Giannozzo's willingness to embrace the civic ethic of virtuous but politically unambitious citizenship.

But the Giannozzo we meet in book 3 of *Della famiglia*, which was drafted in the early 1430s and revised in subsequent years, is much less sure of the compatibility of his own interests with those of the family, and of his and the family's interests with those of the republic. The better known part of the skepticism expressed by Alberti's Giannozzo is his angry denunciation and rejection of politics: the harsh insistence that political life is all "pretence, vanity, and lies, . . . madness, . . . pride, and tyranny," a "perversion of moral life" in which one is constantly beset by favor seekers and "encircled by vice-ridden men."[27] The historical Giannozzo may or may

25. In fact, according to Baxendale, in their 1427 Catasto declaration Giannozzo and Antonio "listed Monte credits in the names of their various daughters and grand-daughters. It is likely that these credits were destined as future dowries although not specifically designated as such"; "Exile in Practice," p. 749 n. 118.

26. Giannozzo's son Tommaso was drawn for the priorate in 1439 but was barred from assuming the office, presumably because his uncle Antonio had been drawn for the same office. The information on Alberti office-holding here and in the text comes from an unpublished essay of Luca Boschetto, "La *Famiglia* e la famiglia: Ricerche su Leon Battista Alberti e gli Alberti di Firenze negli anni trenta del Quattrocento." My thanks to Dr. Boschetto for permission to cite his important paper. See now also Boschetto's *Leon Battista Alberti e Firenze: Biografia, storia, letteratura* (Florence, 2000), pp. 34–35.

27. *Della famiglia*, pp. 218–22. The English translations are generally borrowed from Watkins (cited above in note 2, and hereafter as Watkins), where Giannozzo's denunciation of politics is on pp. 174–77. I have also consulted the translation by G. A. Guarino in *The Albertis of Florence: Leon Battista Alberti's Della Famiglia* (Lewisburg, Pa., 1971). In some cases I have provided my own translation of particular words or phrases.

not have shared these views, but, if he did, he would never have expressed them so openly in the years in which he was asking the Florentine government for all those exemptions and privileges. After Giannozzo regained his modest place in the political sun, the sentiments about politics spoken by the character bearing his name could only have embarrassed him. Whatever Leon Battista's motive may have been in attributing such antipolitical cynicism to "Giannozzo," the diatribe against politics loudly announces that among *Della famiglia's* purposes is a critical examination of the assumptions behind the optimistic civic humanist notions of active citizenship.

Alberti's Giannozzo seems equally, though more quietly, skeptical about his connection to the rest of the family and in particular to the Alberti elders. The very first thing he says about himself at the beginning of book 3 is a recollection of the quarrels he had as a young man many decades earlier with the family elders over his wish to join the jousting and other public games that were a major part of the entertainment of the city's elite families. He recalls that

> there always used to be sharp disagreements [*contenzione*] between my elders and myself because I wanted, above all things, to go along with the others into the midst of it all and prove my worth. The men from our house always came home with high praises and honor. I enjoyed their triumph myself, it is true, yet I also grieved because I was not among those whose noble exertions won the honors. . . . I used to watch them, joyful, spirited, full of strength as they performed feats of arms. . . . You can imagine how I delighted in the great acclaim thus enjoyed, and justly, by our men. Imagine, on the other hand, . . . how a youth with a lively and manly spirit [*l'animo desto e virile*] such as I then possessed would suffer at being prevented from taking his own place among his kinsmen as he longed to do, and making everyone praise and admire him.

"This," he adds, "happened to me." Giannozzo's memory of those disagreements then turns surprisingly ugly: "I hated everyone who kept me away from the joust, and every word my elders spoke seemed a stone smiting my ears. . . . I could not listen to what they said when they all warned me that jousting was dangerous, useless, expensive. . . . And I—silent, sullen."

Giannozzo makes it clear, of course, that he would never have disobeyed his elders. But he tried everything to persuade them: "You would laugh if I told you how many devices [*astuzie*] I hit on to gain their permission, for I still would not have done this, or anything else, without the permission of my elders. I would get kinsmen, friends, and friends of friends to intercede with them for me. . . . Nothing helped." Then Giannozzo makes a startling admission:

Thus there were times when I did not love them as I usually did. I well knew that they did all this because I was all too dear to them, and because they, in their love, feared lest some disaster befall either my person or my honor, as often happens to a strong and courageous boy. But they still seemed hateful [*odiosi*] to me when they opposed me and stood firm against my manly will [*mia virile voglia*]. I was angrier still whenever I thought they acted as they did from motives of economy, for they were, as you know, excellent and careful managers, as I, myself, have since learned to become. In those days I was young, I spent and gave away my money.[28]

This recollection of youthful anger and even hatred toward unnamed elders—Giannozzo never tells us whether they included his own father, whom he mentions only once, briefly and in passing[29]—is quickly set aside as the dialogue moves on to the topic of thrift and good management. But a few pages later the elders make another awkward appearance. When his interlocutor and cousin, the humanist Lionardo, asks Giannozzo whether he invented these "remarkable and holy precepts" concerning thrift by himself or whether he learned them from others, Giannozzo first ignores the question, then approaches it indirectly by attempting to remember the year in which he was present at meetings of the family elders in the home of Messer Niccolaio, the cousin of Leon Battista's grandfather Benedetto. Recalling some of the participants in those meetings, Giannozzo reconstructs a portion of the family genealogy. Lionardo then asks whether the ancestors to whom Giannozzo assigns the honorific *messer*, a title normally indicating knighthood, were "all really knights" or were "so called only by virtue of age and position." "They were indeed knights," responds Giannozzo, "and very eminent ones, almost all knighted for some particular merit. . . . Often do I think to myself that from the earliest times to the present there has never been anyone born in our house of Alberti who was not father or son or uncle or grandson of some knighted person of our blood."[30] Giannozzo, of course, was *not* a knight, and one senses that at this moment he must have been remembering with some sourness his own exclusion by the elders from the jousting and chivalric games that constituted the festive dimension of knightly culture. He registers his embarrassment by quickly urging Lionardo to "pass over this matter of genealogy"—

28. *Della famiglia*, pp. 193–95; Watkins, pp. 157–58.
29. *Della famiglia*, p. 209: "e fu questo Lapo avolo di messer Iacobo cavaliere, il quale messer Iacobo fu fratello di messer Tomaso nostro padre"; Watkins, p. 168.
30. *Della famiglia*, pp. 208–9; Watkins, p. 168.

which he himself had introduced—because "it is irrelevant to both the subject of thrift . . . and to the question you raised as to my having developed my own precepts or learned them from others." So he again recalls the family meetings at which he and the other young men used to crowd around and listen to the elders as they talked about important matters affecting the honor and well-being of the family. Pointedly addressing his humanist cousin, Giannozzo remembers that the elders "constantly read these books of yours [the works of classical antiquity] and were always in the government palace giving their counsel to the *patria*." [31] Whether or not the mid-fourteenth-century Alberti were as devoted to ancient literature as Giannozzo claims, this image of his elders combines both the protohumanist reverence for the books of antiquity and the ethic of political duty central to civic humanism. It underscores the mutual reinforcement of patriarchal authority within the family and the ideal of civic participation supported by humanistic studies.

But book learning and politics are of course precisely the two things that Giannozzo tells us over and over he has no use for. In repeatedly reminding us that he does not "know letters"—in other words, that he is unfamiliar with those Latin books that he claims his elders read—and that he wants no part of politics, Alberti's Giannozzo distances himself from the traditions of the family elders: so much so that, just after saying that he used to listen to them "in order to show them reverence," he admits that the person who made the greatest impression on him at those meetings was not any of the family elders but "a certain old priest," a "man of many excellent thoughts" who "said many things that [the elders] admitted they had never heard before." It was to this priest that Giannozzo gave his "rapt and fixed attention" and whose "weighty thoughts" he has never forgotten.[32] And he never does say that he actually learned lessons about thrift or anything else from the elders.

Alberti thus gives us a Giannozzo estranged and alienated from the family elders and their traditions, which makes it especially ironic that so much current scholarship assumes Giannozzo to be the voice of his family's and society's patriarchal values. But to realize the depth of Giannozzo's "silent, sullen" repudiation of the patrilineal bond at the center of this patriarchal world, in particular the crucial relationship between young men and their

31. *Della famiglia*, p. 210: ". . . sempre stavano o leggendo questi vostri libri, sempre o in palagio a consigliare la patria"; Watkins, p. 169.
32. *Della famiglia*, pp. 211–12; Watkins, pp. 169–70.

elders, we need to turn back to the long and solemn speech of Leon Battista's father, Lorenzo, at the beginning of book 1.[33] Lorenzo's mortal illness is the occasion for the fictional (and perhaps also actual) reunion of the Alberti in Padua in 1421, and he has just enough energy to deliver a long oration on the duties and burdens of fathers, on the collective responsibilities of all the family's elders toward its young men, and on the duty of the latter unquestioningly to obey. In the middle of this speech Lorenzo invokes the memory—and claims to represent the exact words—of his own father, Benedetto, who is quoted for a full three pages, after which Lorenzo continues in his own voice. This speech-within-a-speech re-creates—and in some sense brings back to life—the long-dead grandfather, even as the father is himself dying: a joining of two voices and two generations, and, behind them of course, countless generations of patrilineal tradition within a lineage that never dies. Alberti quite deliberately evokes here the structure and myth of the Florentine upper-class agnatic lineage, conceived of as a descent group in the male line only, in which, as F. W. Kent puts it, a strong sense of the continuity of identity between fathers and sons led to the belief that sons "in a real sense replaced [their] father[s]," "almost as if the ancestor were reincarnated."[34] Lorenzo brings his father back to life, just before joining him in the afterlife, for the purpose of forming his own sons in the image of their father and grandfather and thus ensuring the survival of the lineage into future generations.

Lorenzo restates what he assumes to be the "ancient" truths of this family tradition. But this vision of family unity and paternal authority is in fact grounded in language that again echoes the fairly recent pieties of civic humanism: in the image of fathers who make themselves loved rather than feared, and obeyed because of their constant devotion to the good of those under their care; in the metaphor of the family ship, on which the father must be the "experienced expert navigator [*pratico ed essercitatissimo navichiero*]" who knows how to steer through tempestuous weather and dangers of every sort;[35] in the extension of these responsibilities to all the family's elders, who must "be ever alert and busy for the well-being and honor of the whole family"; in the duty of the young to show reverence to the elders; and in the telling analogy, adduced by Benedetto, of "those good ancient Lacedaemonians"—the Spartans—whose "most useful system of moral discipline [*disciplina de' costumi*]" made "their land glorious and

33. *Della famiglia*, pp. 18–33; Watkins, pp. 35–45.
34. Kent, *Household and Lineage*, pp. 46–47.
35. *Della famiglia*, p. 21; Watkins, p. 37.

honored." [36] This is language that could have come from the archpriest himself of Florentine civic humanism, Leonardo Bruni, who had become chancellor, and thus chief spokesman of the republic's moral virtues, in 1427, just a few years before Alberti wrote the first three dialogues of *Della famiglia*. Benedetto's sentence about the moral discipline of the Spartans echoes a passage in Bruni's *Panegyric to the City of Florence* in which, after outlining the specific merits of the institutions of Florentine government, he remarks that "under these magistracies this city has been governed with such diligence and excellence that one could not find better discipline [*disciplina*] even in a household ruled by a solicitous *paterfamilias*." [37] Civic humanism and the patriarchal ideology of Lorenzo and Benedetto share the assumption that the overriding duty of the elders is to take charge of the moral discipline of the young men who would one day replace them but who will also allow them to live forever. Both family and republic have thus become theaters, or schools, of virtue, and among the many virtues that, according to Lorenzo, the house of Alberti possessed in abundance—prudence, intelligence, constancy of spirit, and so on—we also find "manliness [*virilità*]." [38]

Curiously, despite all this praise of family unity, Lorenzo assumes that the young men will inevitably oppose and evade the civic and moral discipline of the elders. He worries about the "dubious ways" and hidden vices of the young, "depraved and corrupted by their own native inclinations, [and] sometimes inspired to evil and wholly ruined by the bad conversation and customs around them." [39] As he acknowledges the recalcitrance and defiance of the young, Lorenzo (speaking as his father, Benedetto) begins to describe the authority of fathers over their sons in more openly authoritarian and repressive terms. Chief among the duties of fathers, he says, is "to watch over and guard the family from all sides, ... to examine all the practices of every member ... and to correct and improve every bad habit. ... [Fathers] must never allow [their sons] to try something irresponsible and wild, either for revenge or to satisfy some youthful and frivolous idea" (presumably including ideas about jousting).[40] Something still more troubling emerges when Lorenzo quotes Benedetto's dictum that "the son's vir-

---

36. *Della famiglia*, pp. 23–24; Watkins, p. 39.

37. Text in Baron, *From Petrarch*, p. 262: "ita diligens et preclara est huius urbis gubernatio ut nulla unquam domus sub frugi patre familias maiori disciplina fuerit instituta." Translation, modified, from Kohl and Witt, *The Earthly Republic*, p. 173.

38. *Della famiglia*, p. 30; Watkins, p. 43.

39. *Della famiglia*, p. 19; Watkins, p. 36.

40. *Della famiglia*, pp. 20–21; Watkins, pp. 36–37.

tue lies in the watchfulness of the father,"[41] which is reinforced by Lorenzo's belief that to their fathers the young "owe all too much," because "your father, with his sweat and care and hard work has led you to be the man you are in your age, your fortune, and your condition."[42] Such notions not only exclude any role for mothers in the formation of the young; they also deny the sons any moral autonomy, and thus any merit for whatever virtue they acquire. At certain points this defense of paternal authority begins to sound like a legitimation of the republic's ruling oligarchy. Benedetto asserts that a family's elders "should be common fathers to all the young,"[43] and, borrowing the old metaphor of the body in order to assert the naturalness of hierarchy and subordination, he declares that the elders must be "mind and soul to the whole body of the family [*come mente e anima di tutto il corpo della famiglia*]." Praising the Lacedaemonians for their "most useful system of moral discipline," and claiming that the same system will make families strong, he observes that "there was but a single will among them all [*una sola volontà fra tutti commune*], and that directed to making the country virtuous and disciplined. . . . The old offered their counsel, their memories, and their good example, while the young gave their obedience and imitation."[44] Obedience to and imitation of the single collective will of the elders are narrow grounds for the emergence of an autonomous subject.

Lorenzo's long opening speech presupposes and embodies the compatibility of these venerable family traditions with the wisdom of antiquity that was the object of humanism.[45] The example of the Spartans directly

41. *Della famiglia*, p. 21: ". . . nella sollecitudine del padre sta la virtù del figliuolo"; Watkins, p. 38.

42. *Della famiglia*, p. 26; Watkins, p. 40.

43. As Guarino notes (*The Albertis of Florence*, p. 330), the likely source of this idea is Plutarch's *Lycurgus*, 17.1: "The elderly men also kept close watch of them . . . with the idea that they were all in a sense the fathers and tutors and governors of all the boys. In this way, at every fitting time and in every place, the boy who went wrong had someone to admonish and chastise him." But Alberti must also have remembered (especially given that Plutarch's *Lives* were becoming a very popular text in the fifteenth century, as evidenced by the many translations) that this chapter of *Lycurgus* begins with a matter-of-fact statement about the practice of homosexuality in the education of the boys: "When the boys reached this age, they were favoured with the society of lovers from among the reputable young men"; translation by B. Perrin from the Loeb edition of *Plutarch's Lives*, 11 vols. (Cambridge, Mass, 1982), 1:259. This is an early indication that Alberti need not be read at the same high level of solemnity assumed by his patriarchal characters.

44. *Della famiglia*, pp. 23–24; Watkins, p. 39.

45. Marsh believes that "much of the inspiration" for Lorenzo's long speech came from Cicero's *De senectute;* see *The Quattrocento Dialogue*, p. 85. In the pas-

summons ancient history in support of what are alleged to be old Alberti traditions.[46] Lorenzo thus echoes the prologue to *Della famiglia*, written in a very civic humanist voice, which explicitly links family traditions and humanist learning as the twin sources of the wisdom that can enable families to survive the onslaught of fortune.[47] But after Lorenzo's speech, without ever saying so, *Della famiglia* splits apart these twin pillars of family tradition and humanist learning and never reunites them. Giannozzo defends his peculiar vision of paternal authority exclusively from experience, mostly in fact his own, supplemented by occasional references to the wise sayings and habits of this or that family member, but with no reference to ancient history or moral philosophy, which he has never studied. The civic and humanist defense of patriarchy is entrusted to the character of Lionardo, who lacks any direct experience of what he is defending. He is young (twenty-nine), unmarried, childless, and a scholar who has spent his life reading the ancients, on the basis of whose authority he vigorously promotes the rights and duties of fathers in book 1. In fact, his interlocutor, Adovardo, pointedly calls attention to the fact that Lionardo argues from theory and books alone when he comments that Lionardo's opinions will

---

sages to which Marsh points (paragraphs 17–20), one does indeed find a defense of the vigor, wisdom, and authority of older men, as well as the same comparison of the wise elder to a ship's pilot (the "gubernator") invoked by the voice of Benedetto. But in the Ciceronian text these themes are not specifically related to the authority of fathers or the structure of agnatic lineages.

46. But, as I have already suggested, Lorenzo's praise of the Lacedaemonians (through the voice of Benedetto) must be—in Alberti's intention, but not Lorenzo's—ironic, and even a joke, given the prevalence of homosexuality in the education of boys. And there is much more that should alert us to the likelihood that Alberti was poking fun at the civic humanist use of ancient sources to buttress the patriarchal family values of fifteenth-century Florentines. In both Plutarch's *Lycurgus* (15.6–10) and the short description of the "Government of Lacedaemon" (1.6–10), which was traditionally attributed to Xenophon and from which Plutarch drew much of the material for his biography, it is claimed that Lycurgus explicitly permitted married persons of either sex to have children with anyone else they fancied. As Plutarch puts it, "Lycurgus did not regard sons as the peculiar property of their fathers, but rather as the common property of the state." Lacedaemonian customs, in these accounts at least, make a mockery of paternal identity and lineage purity. Lorenzo, of course, is evidently unaware of this. For Alberti's complex use of classical sources, in ways that sometimes subvert the arguments of his speakers, see A. Grafton, *Commerce with the Classics: Ancient Books and Renaissance Readers* (Ann Arbor, 1997), pp. 53–92.

47. *Della famiglia*, p. 12: "E credo io, poiché voi arete meco riveduto e' ditti e le autorità di que' buoni antiqui, e notati gli ottimi costumi de' nostri passati Alberti, sarete in questa medesima sentenza, e giudicarete in voi stessi come la virtú cosí stare ogni vostra fortuna"; Watkins, p. 31.

please him more when he hears them supported by experience as well.[48] Alberti's selection of the book-trained but otherwise inexperienced Lionardo as the chief spokesman for the power of fathers and the escalating claims of patriarchy is no accident: the choice of Lionardo underscores just how much of this vision of the family came from the theoretical postulates of political humanism and its tendency to appropriate a hierarchical and quasi-authoritarian notion of the patriline as a model for republican government by an oligarchy of self-styled patrician families.

In the light of Lionardo's defense of the absolute power of fathers over sons, it is particularly significant that he is also the one who introduces misogyny into the rationale for strict paternal control. Lorenzo (and Benedetto) had largely ignored women in their mythmaking about the family. Much can be read into that silence, but Lionardo makes its implied hostility against women explicit by asserting that among the duties of fathers is that of protecting their sons' masculinity, or manliness—their *virilità*—against specifically feminine dangers. Lionardo urges fathers to make sure that their sons develop a "manly spirit," and he advises against keeping little boys, "as some mothers do, always in a room or in a lap," or letting them sit in "feminine leisure [*ozio femminile*]" or "skulk among the girls [*covando tra le femmine*]." Nor should young boys be allowed to live in solitude, which is a breeding ground for "corrupt desires" and sensuality. "From the first day of life," they should "be accustomed to life among men," where "they can be made virile" and kept "segregated from all feminine activities and habits [*storli da tutti i costumi e maniere femminile*]." Here, too, the ancients are summoned in support: the warnings against solitude come from Plato and Cato (an odd combination), and the Lacedaemonians (again through Plutarch)[49] provide the model of manly avoidance of the feminine: they "used to make their boys go out at night among the tombs in the dark, to accustom them to fearlessness and teach them not to believe the inventions and fables of old women [*le maschere e favole delle vecchie*]."[50]

Adovardo, the family elder who calls attention to Lionardo's lack of experience in these matters, frequently warns him about putting too much pressure on both fathers and sons: "Beware lest you give us fathers too much to do. . . . What father, my dear Lionardo, could manage to supervise so many activities? What son could ever be induced to learn all the things

48. *Della famiglia*, p. 97; Watkins, p. 90.

49. Plutarch, *Lycurgus*, 27.1. For the identification of the source, see Guarino, *The Albertis of Florence*, p. 331.

50. *Della famiglia*, pp. 57–58; Watkins, pp. 62–63.

you have indicated to us?"[51] To Lionardo's high sense of paternal power, Adovardo consistently opposes greater caution about the difficulties fathers face in trying to shape sons. But Lionardo comes back each time with escalating claims for the ever more obviously political powers that he would give to fathers: he speaks of their *signoria* over their sons[52]—the word means "lordship" and was used by the Florentines to refer to the highest office of their government—and, although he argues that a *signoria* maintained by love is more stable than an *imperio* sustained by force, he nonetheless urges fathers to consider a bad son an "enemy" and to be "less sorry to have one of your children in prison or in chains than to have an enemy free in your house or a public disgrace outside."[53] Alberti was suggesting, I think, that the concept of fatherhood was being overburdened with expectations that came from two directions—from the patrilineal ideology in which sons were expected to become, replace, and reproduce their fathers in endless succession; and from civic humanism's conflation of paternal authority with the authoritarian paternalism of the ruling elite. Lionardo is the voice of this overextension of the notion of fatherhood beyond its natural psychological limits. It is Lionardo who tells fathers that their children are "their own works"—he explicitly compares a father's love for his children to the love that painters, writers, and poets feel for their works ("l'opere sue"). Even Adovardo, usually skeptical of Lionardo's theories but willing at least to recognize the power of the irrational in such matters, adds that "there is by nature something in a father—I don't know exactly what—a kind of greater need . . . to take delight in seeing [his children] express his very image and likeness."[54] This is indeed precisely the biblical language— "la imagine e similitudine sua"—and it anticipates Ficino's notion that the son is a "mirror and image" of the father, and the father a "second God" whose commands sons should obey with reverence and fear.[55]

Far from promoting such exaggerated notions of paternal power, Alberti's text underscores the impossible nature of their reach. And if Lionardo, not

---

51. *Della famiglia,* pp. 88–89; Watkins, p. 84.

52. *Della famiglia,* p. 94: "E ricordisi ciascuno padre e maggiore che lo imperio retto per forza sempre fu manco stabile che quella signoria quale sia mantenuta per amore"; Watkins, p. 88.

53. *Della famiglia,* p. 95; Watkins, p. 89.

54. *Della famiglia,* pp. 36–37; Watkins, p. 47.

55. In the "Epistola ad fratres vulgaris," Ficino will also compare children to the "opere" of writers and artists: "el figliuolo è opera del padre, et non è cosa che l'uomo ami più che l'opera sua. Et per questo Iddio ama tanto l'umana natura, et gli auctori e loro libri, e dipintori le figure da loro facte"; Kristeller, *Supplementum ficinianum,* 2:113.

Giannozzo, is the defender of such views, how should we read Giannozzo? Although often misunderstood as a spokesman for the family patriarchy, is he not in fact (perhaps without fully realizing it) the book's most powerful indictment of the patriarchal and civic pieties outlined by Lorenzo and Benedetto in book 1 and promoted thereafter by Lionardo?[56] Not only does Giannozzo reject politics, humanist education, and the fundamental civic assumption of the essential goodness of community, government, and the active life; he also quietly turns his back on the larger Alberti family. When Lionardo asks him what he means by "family" ("Che chiamate voi famiglia?"), Giannozzo gives a narrow definition—"children, wife, and other members of the household, servants and staff"[57]—that contrasts in the starkest possible way with Lorenzo's, Benedetto's, and Lionardo's vision of the moral unity of all those carrying the Alberti name, that grand masculine assemblage of the imagination in which women have no place and the elders are collective fathers to all the young men. If Lionardo is, as it were, all theory and ideology and book learning about fathers, families, and civic duty, Giannozzo stands for what this convergence of high-minded ideas in fact produced: a private and fearful man who has processed old anger against his elders into quiet alienation from his whole family and mistrust of everything and everyone around him, including his father, who, as we saw, is mentioned only incidentally, his sons, whom he never mentions, and of course his wife. Subdued and domesticated by the moral discipline of the elders, Giannozzo has never overcome the resentment he feels toward them for the suffocation of his autonomy. But, deprived of the opportunity to settle old psychic scores with long-dead elders, it is instead with his wife that Giannozzo attempts to recuperate the manliness he lost in the early battles with the elders. And he does so, whether he is aware of it or not, by combining conventions from the already established genre of advice on domestic management that ran from Xenophon to Francesco Barbaro with the same language of gendered power relations that Lionardo uses in book 1 of *Della famiglia* concerning the education of young men. In one

56. Thus I would not fully agree with the contention of David Marsh that "the figure of the merchant Giannozzo . . . combines typically Florentine attitudes with the author's own moral strictures"; *The Quattrocento Dialogue*, p. 97. Some of Giannozzo's ideas are typically Florentine; others are at odds with Florentine tradition. And while Giannozzo no doubt says some things with which Alberti agreed, I believe that Alberti used the figure of Giannozzo to point to the contradictions that permeated Florentine ideas and assumptions about the lineage, especially once civic humanism exaggerated and politicized the notion of paternal authority.

57. *Della famiglia*, p. 226: "E' figliuoli, la moglie, e gli altri domestici, famigli, servi"; Watkins, p. 180.

passage of the account of his long instruction to his wife, Giannozzo reveals how much the deeply ingrained need to train and control his wife emerges from the same gendered stereotypes that characterize Lionardo's civic humanist advice about the proper training of boys:

> All wives are thus obedient to the extent that their husbands know how to be husbands. But some [husbands] I see quite unwisely suppose that they can win obedience and respect from a wife to whom they openly and abjectly subject themselves and show by word and gesture that their spirit is all too deeply lascivious and effeminate, whereby they make their wives no less immodest than rebellious. I have never wanted, with either words or gestures, even in the slightest way to submit to my wife in anything. It would not have seemed possible to make myself obeyed by one to whom I had confessed myself a slave. Always, therefore, I showed myself virile and a man.[58]

The submission to his wife that Giannozzo simultaneously fears and refuses in this passage takes on the quality of a displaced memory of the submission and humiliation he suffered at the hands of his elders, and if he could no longer prove himself a man in their eyes, he would at least do so with his own wife.

This passage can perhaps also shed some light on the psychological— one is tempted to say pathological—complexities of the bizarre analogy that Giannozzo offers a few pages earlier between the good father and the industrious spider that builds its web and sits at the center, alert, watchful, and ready both to protect its little world and to capture unsuspecting prey.[59] As a way of talking about the responsibilities of fathers, it is a curious image indeed, since the spider is of course imprisoned in its own creation, and also because, as Alberti knew from Pliny (whose *Natural History* is cited or alluded to several times in books 3 and 4),[60] it was commonly thought

---

58. *Della famiglia*, pp. 277–78: "E cosí tutte le moglie sono a' mariti obediente quanto questi sanno essere mariti. Ma veggo alcuni poco prudenti che stimano potere farsi ubidire e riverire dalle moglie alle quali essi manifesto e miseri servono, dimonstrano con loro parole e gesti l'animo suo troppo lascivo ed effeminato, onde rendono la moglie non meno disonesta che contumace. A me mai piacque in luogo alcuno né con parole né con gesto in quale minima parte si fusse sottomettermi alla donna mia; né sarebbe paruto a me potermi fare ubidire da quella a chi io avessi confessato me essere servo. Adunque sempre mi li monstrai virile e uomo. . . ." I have somewhat modified the translation by Watkins, p. 217.

59. *Della famiglia*, p. 263; Watkins, p. 206.

60. Guarino, *The Albertis of Florence*, pp. 337–41. For an analysis of passages from the *Theogenius* that demonstrate Alberti's familiarity with Pliny's *Natural History*, see Contarino, *Leon Battista Alberti moralista*, pp. 159–63.

that the female makes the web and that, among certain kinds of spiders at least, the offspring devour the mother, and sometimes the father too, in the first moments of their life.[61] Had Giannozzo spent a little more time reading those books of the ancients that he treated with such bemused indifference,[62] he might have remembered that the spider was a figure denoting punishment for the crime of overstepping proper bounds. In Ovid's *Metamorphoses* (6.1–145) Arachne is changed into a spider for the twin presumptions of having denied that she learned the art of weaving from Minerva (Giannozzo, as we know, was similarly reluctant to acknowledge that he learned the art of thrift from his elders) and of having challenged the goddess to a contest of skill in that art. In letting Giannozzo offer as a model for the diligent father, of all creatures, the spider,[63] which, as one commentator on the story from Ovid has written, "is a compulsive weaver whose work is always liable to sudden destruction,"[64] Alberti was pointing to the

61. Pliny the Elder, *Natural History*, 11.28: "Feminam putant esse quae texat, marem qui venetur; ita paria fieri merita coniugio." The passage about the young devouring their parents follows in 11.29.

62. In another of his dialogues Alberti has one of the speakers say about Giannozzo that all he lacked to be counted among the greatest citizens of the republic was a knowledge of letters. In the *Profugiorum ab erumna libri*, ed. G. Ponte (Genoa, 1988), pp. 6–7, Alberti has Nicola di Vieri de' Medici report the character Battista's opinion that only two men—Giannozzo Alberti and Agnolo Pandolfini—"seem to him to be adornments of our fatherland, fathers of the senate, and true governors of the republic. . . . If only Giannozzo had much knowledge of literature, I would wonder what two men could be found anywhere else so complete in their merits or so similar in their worth? [Se a Giannozzo fusse molta cognizione di lettere, direi: qual due uomini altrove si troverebbono o sì compiuti d'ogni pregio, o sì simili in ogni laude?]" (my translation). According to Martin L. McLaughlin, however, Giannozzo's "unsophisticated" style of speech "continues the Albertian polemic against sophistry and literary philosophizing"; McLaughlin, *Literary Imitation in the Italian Renaissance* (Oxford, 1995), p. 160.

63. It is by no means easy to discern what the figure of the spider meant to Alberti. Perhaps influenced by the Aesopic fable of the gnat and the elephant, Alberti devoted one of his own fables, *Aranea*, in the *Intercenales*, to the story of a high-minded and eloquent spider who rebukes an elephant for trying to attack a man. But when the spider's arguments fail, it jumps into the elephant's ear and administers a deadly sting. See Leon Battista Alberti, *Dinner Pieces*, trans. David Marsh (Binghamton, N.Y., 1987), pp. 186–89. Marsh observes (p. 258) that the "theme of a small animal overcoming a large beast," common to *Aranea* and to several Aesopic fables, "is traditional." On Alberti and Aesop, see A. Borghini, "Un'altra probabile fonte del 'Momo' di L. B. Alberti: Esopo," *Rivista di letteratura italiana* 5 (1987): 455–56. On Alberti and animals, see Contarino, *Leon Battista Alberti moralista*, pp. 157–93.

64. E. W. Leach, "Ekphrasis and the Theme of Artistic Failure in Ovid's *Metamorphoses*," *Ramus* 3 (1974): 102–42, quotation on p. 118. For more comment on the story of Arachne and Minerva and its echoes in the Renaissance, see L. Barkan,

confusion, danger, and anxiety surrounding Giannozzo's aspirations to notions of natural hierarchy between the sexes.

The question of paternal power continued to fascinate and trouble Alberti in later works, and by way of conclusion I would like briefly to call attention to two places where he revisits the subject. Among the *Intercenales*, or *Dinner Pieces*, is a crazy little story called *Uxoria*, set, probably not accidentally, among the ancient Lacedaemonians.[65] Here, too, a dying father calls together his sons and, evoking the memory of his own father whom he has sought to emulate, urges his sons in turn to live exactly the same kind of life. In order to stimulate their desire for and willingness to compete in virtue, he says he will leave the insignia he has received from his fellow citizens in recognition of his merits to the one of his three sons who will display the greatest virtue. The father dies, and the sons convene the wisest and noblest of the family elders as judges to decide who shall be awarded the father's insignia.

Two of the sons make speeches before the elders on the subject of marriage, each claiming to have adopted the wisest and most virtuous policy in dealing with their very difficult wives. The oldest son, Mizio (mildness), recounts in misogynist detail his wife's quarrelsome, obstinate, and promiscuously unfaithful behavior and his own decision, after much soul-searching, simply to ignore it all and to pretend not even to notice her escapades. His virtue consists in keeping her happy, thus containing the scandal and preserving his equanimity. The second son, Acrino (harshness), has an equally intolerable wife and shares with his brother the conviction that "every woman is wanton, inconstant, troublesome, proud, querulous, shameless, and stubborn."[66] But his preferred approach has been to lock her up and keep her under watchful supervision, to make sure that she would never have even the opportunity to harm him. The third and youngest son, Trissofo (thrice-wise), heaps scorn on both his brothers and presents his own decision—absolute refusal to marry—as the only prudent course of action. Trissofo is especially harsh on Acrino, the second brother whose handling

---

The Gods Made Flesh: Metamorphosis and the Pursuit of Paganism (New Haven, Conn., 1986), pp. 1–5 and passim.

65. *Uxoria* exists in both a Latin and a Tuscan version, both published in Leon Battista Alberti, *Opere volgari*, 3 vols., ed. C. Grayson (Bari, 1960–73), 2:302–43; English translation in Marsh, *Dinner Pieces*, pp. 134–48.

66. *Opere volgari*, 2:328–31; Marsh, *Dinner Pieces*, p. 143.

of his wife comes closest to the methods advocated by Giannozzo in *Della famiglia*. To render and reinforce this severe judgment, Trissofo invokes the voice of their dead father, imagining the terms in which, if he were to come back to life, he would denounce the elders if Acrino were awarded the insignia: "Do you award them," says the father, "to a man whose suspicions and foolish meddling have completely destroyed his domestic peace and quiet, and who has basely enslaved himself and his household?" And, now addressing Acrino, the father says: "If your diligence thwarted your wife's sins, and if your duty as a husband lay in surveillance, restraint, and repression [*S'ella per te non peccò, se tu con custodirla e contenerla facesti el debito tuo / Sin tua diligentia non peccavit mulier, si observando coercendo continendo functus mariti officio extitisti*], why do you boast that you merit these tokens?"[67] The elders retire to deliberate, and the insignia are deposited with the priests of Cybele. Why Cybele? She was the Phrygian goddess, mother of the gods, known to the Romans as Great Mother (Magna Mater), whose priests were eunuchs.[68] Alberti very likely knew the description of Cybele in Lucretius's *De rerum natura*, whose full text had just been rediscovered by Poggio. Lucretius explains the meaning of the eunuch priests as follows: "They give her eunuchs, as wishing to indicate that those who have violated the majesty of the Mother, and have been found ungrateful to their parents, should be thought unworthy to bring living offspring into the regions of light."[69] The patriarchy in *Uxoria* has failed and is unmanned: the insignia are not handed on to any of the sons (we never do learn the decision of the elders) and are instead entrusted to the emasculated devotees of the Great Mother. In this story (located among those same ancient Lacedaemonians that Benedetto, Lorenzo, and Lionardo had so admired in *Della famiglia*), misogyny emerges in, and perhaps from, a competition among brothers instigated by their father in the effort to preserve and transmit masculine and civic virtue through three generations of a patriline. Mocking fathers, elders, and sons alike, the story ridicules any notion of patrilineal transmission of either masculine virtue or virtuous masculinity. The sons seek to display a virtue grounded in the hatred of

67. *Opere volgari*, 2:338–41; Marsh, *Dinner Pieces*, pp. 146–47.
68. On Cybele, also known as Rhea in the Cretan version of her cult, see O. Seyffert, *Dictionary of Classical Antiquities*, ed. H. Nettleship and J. E. Sandys (Cleveland, 1956), pp. 542–43.
69. Lucretius, *De rerum natura* 2.614–17: "gallos attribuunt, quia, numen qui violarint / matris et ingrati genitoribus inventi sint, / significare volunt indignos esse putandos, / vivam progeniem qui in oras luminis edant." Text and translation from the Loeb Lucretius, trans. W. H. D. Rouse (New York, 1924), pp. 128–29.

women and are forced to surrender the symbols of masculinity and paternal inheritance to the mutilated worshipers of a cult of maternal power and authority.

Did Alberti have any sense of an alternative to the patriarchal ideology he critiques in *Della famiglia* and *Uxoria?* That he was at least thinking in this direction emerges from *De iciarchia,* a somewhat more ponderous dialogue that he wrote around 1470,[70] in which the character Battista outlines the kind of guidance and supervision that successful families need from their leaders. But the odd thing is that Battista speaks for pages and pages about the qualities and virtues required in those who have responsibility for families without once using the word *padre.* Even when one of his interlocutors mentions "fathers" in a question, Battista avoids the term and prefers "elders" (*maggiori* and *vecchi*).[71] When he himself finally asks, "What shall we call this one [we have been describing]?" he suggests *iciarco*—a term invented by Alberti himself and adapted from the Greek words for household (*oikia*) and ruler, or leader (*archon*).[72] Battista defines *iciarco* as the "chief man and first leader of his family [*supremo omo e primario principe della famiglia sua*]."[73] Why did Alberti need and invent a new word here? For one thing, it gave him a way of talking about elders and their duties toward the young that avoided or elided biological paternity and all the assumptions of patrilineal reproduction of fathers in their sons. In fact, Alberti uses *iciarco* to subject the concept of father to a critique built on the distinction between mere biological paternity and true fatherhood. Battista says that if someone pointed to a child of his and said, "'This

70. *Opere volgari,* 2:185–286. On this less well known dialogue, which like *Della famiglia* combines political and family themes, see G. Ponte, *Leon Battista Alberti, umanista e scrittore* (Genoa, 1981), pp. 115–20; H. Baron, "Leon Battista Alberti as an Heir and Critic of Florentine Civic Humanism," in Baron, *In Search of Florentine Civic Humanism: Essays on the Transition from Medieval to Modern Thought,* 2 vols. (Princeton, N.J., 1988), 1:281–85; and especially L. Boschetto, "Note sul 'De iciarchia' di Leon Battista Alberti," *Rinascimento* 31 (1991): 183– 217. Boschetto reads the dialogue as a protest against the excessive power assumed by the Medici in the aftermath of the failed attempt in 1465–66 by leading *ottimati* to restore the collective hegemony of the oligarchy—an interpretation that is broadly compatible with what I see as *De iciarchia*'s polemic against all forms of excessive paternal authority.

71. *Opere volgari,* 2:270. (The translations from *De iciarchia* are mine.)

72. According to the *Grande dizionario della lingua italiana,* vol. 7, ed. S. Battaglia (Turin, 1972), p. 198, "Tanto iciarchia quanto iciarco sono voci introdotte da L. B. Alberti nel suo trattato in volgare *De iciarchia.*" Baron also recognized it as "a newly coined Italian term"; *In Search of Florentine Civic Humanism,* 1:281.

73. *Opere volgari,* 2:273.

is my boy,' I will say: 'Right. But you made him similar to other two-footed animals; I made him similar, on account of his virtue, to an earthly god.'" Battista rhetorically asks his young listeners to whom they think such a child would be more beholden, to his "babbo"—his daddy—or "to me, his true and best father."[74] The search for truer and better fathers always points an accusing finger at actual fathers, and it should be noted that, in all three works considered here, Alberti removes, or displaces, the biological father: *Della famiglia* and *Uxoria* both begin at the deathbed of the father, and in *De iciarchia* the *iciarco* competes with mere "daddies" for their sons' affections.

The *iciarco's* duties include the predictable one of preventing discord and contention within the family. Alberti clearly has generational conflict in mind here. According to Battista, differences between the desires of the young and those of their elders are natural, and just as similarity of customs, inclinations, and desires makes for reciprocal benevolence, so dissimilarity in such matters prohibits and rejects that perfect unity required for genuine love. Faced with this dilemma, the Lorenzos, Benedettos, and Lionardos of *Della famiglia* unanimously responded that the whole purpose of paternal authority and moral discipline is to make stubborn young men abandon the inclinations that divide them from their fathers and thus to mold and shape them in the paternal "image and likeness." But the Battista of *De iciarchia* will have none of this. He recommends what he calls "skillful adaptability [*adattezza competente*]" on the part of "the elders, who should join the young often in lighthearted familiarity, especially at dinners," since the "pleasure of irreverent conversation does so much to win favor and intimacy." It will be sufficient, he thinks, if the young show just enough modesty as is required by the good manners and reverence of the elders, and if the elders in turn "set aside that severe *gravitas* of theirs [*quella severa gravità loro*] and present themselves as good-natured, relaxed, and affable, in order to show that they are willing to be like the young without frivolity [*che degnino aguagliarsi alla gioventù senza levità*]." Battista makes it clear that it is the elders who should do most of the adjusting: "It will be much less difficult for us, who are already mature in years, to resume the joyful and festive mood that we had in the flower of our youth, especially when the grace of the good customs of these young men invites us to take pleasure and amuse ourselves, than it would be for the young to put aside their youthful joy and cheerfulness and to feign in

74. Ibid., p. 274.

themselves the harshness and sadness of old age."[75] So Battista recommends that conversations between young and old should focus on the pleasures of the young: on horsemanship and dogs and birds of prey and fishing and swimming, and similar things, which will make the young men more inclined to share their thoughts and ask advice from the elders. The *iciarco* must become expert at investigating and recognizing the particular circumstances, needs, and thoughts of each person committed to his care. When a biological father knows how to do all this, says Battista, then he will be loved as a true father. Battista's *iciarchia* is the antithesis of that program of moral discipline whose purpose was to make of the son the "mirror and image" of the father. He underscores this difference by warning the would-be *iciarco* that "the purpose of this undertaking should not be for you to want always to be obeyed in your commands merely to give yourself satisfaction."[76]

This was no doubt a utopian, perhaps whimsical, countervision to the patriarchal practices and notions that prevailed in Alberti's time. But the very fact that he could parody the pieties of family ideology and envision any alternative to its dominant assumptions suggests that there were cracks in the patriarchy, cracks that would get wider in the next generation.[77] We need only think of Machiavelli's ridicule of Florentine fathers in *Mandragola*, where Messer Nicia's obsession with paternity leads him to accept a plan for his own cuckolding and for the production of an heir who, unbeknownst to him, will not be his child, or in *Clizia*, where Nicomaco, an elderly father mad with senile lust, competes with his own son for the opportunity to bed the young woman who came to them as a foster child when abandoned by her own father. But of course Machiavelli was writing when the political fathers of Italy—the sons and grandsons of Alberti's generation—had already been exposed as abject failures.

To suggest that Alberti linked misogyny to the oppressive rule of fathers over their sons does not make him a feminist. But his search for a less authoritarian notion of fatherhood, no doubt born at some level from his own experience,[78] was also the product of what he observed and did not like

75. Ibid., pp. 275–76.

76. Ibid., p. 283.

77. For an intriguing hypothesis about what might be called the crisis of patriarchal authority in fifteenth-century Florence, see R. Trexler, "Ritual in Florence: Adolescence and Salvation in the Renaissance," first published in *The Pursuit of Holiness in Late Medieval and Renaissance Religion*, ed. C. Trinkaus and H. Oberman (Leiden, 1974), pp. 200–264; and now in Trexler, *Dependence in Context in Renaissance Florence* (Binghamton, N.Y., 1994), pp. 259–325.

78. His illegitimate birth may have played a role in this. As Thomas Kuehn has observed in commenting on the passages on adoption in book 2 of *Della famiglia*, Al-

3 *Li Emergenti Bisogni Matrimoniali* in Renaissance Florence

Julius Kirshner

Li emergenti bisogni matrimoniali[1]—namely, the urgent necessity at the outset of marriage to adorn brides with extravagant clothing and jewelry, to decorate the nuptial chamber, and to arrange wedding festivities—entailed sizable expenditures of capital on the part of new husbands and their kin in Renaissance Florence. In a legal opinion written in 1400, the Florentine jurist Filippo Corsini observed that "even before sexual intercourse, it is necessary for the husband to shoulder the expenses for his wife's clothing and other accessories, as well as other expenses related to the wedding."[2] In another opinion, Paolo di Castro, who taught and practiced law in early-fifteenth-century Florence, emphasized that in both Florence and Bologna the outfitting of the bride and expenses for the wedding consumed the whole dowry even before the couple had exchanged marriage vows and rings.[3]

This chapter was substantially completed in Florence in the spring of 1996, while I was in residence as a visiting professor at Villa I Tatti, the Harvard University Center for Italian Renaissance Studies. I am especially grateful to its director, Walter Kaiser, for his convivial support. A version of this chapter was presented at the the Eleventh Biennial New College Conference on Medieval-Renaissance Studies, Sarasota, Florida, and at the International Medieval Congress, University of Leeds. An earlier version has appeared in *"Visibilità" delle donne tra Medioevo ed Età moderna: Carte private e pubbliche apparenze, lusso e prescrizioni,* Università degli studi di Perugia, *Annali della Facoltà di Lettere e Filosofia,* 2. *Studi Storico-Antropologici,* 34–35 (= n.s. 20–21) (1996/97–1997/98): 59–83.

1. The pungent expression *li emergenti bisogni matrimoniali* was used by Piero di Marco Parenti in his *ricordanze* (ASF, CS, ser. 2, 17bis, fol. 127v).

2. I have edited Corsini's *consilium* in J. Kirshner, "*Maritus lucretur dotem uxoris sue premortue* in Late Medieval Florence," *Zeitschrift der Savigny-Stiftung für Rechtsgeschichte (Kanonistische Abteilung)* 77 (1991): 138: "... quia etiam ante carnalem copulam opportet maritum subire expensas propter vestes et alia ornamenta uxoris et alia preparatoria nuptiarum."

3. *Consilia* (Venice, 1580), fol. 76va, cons. 154: "Et per experientiam videmus tam Florentiae quam Bononiae, ubi non pervenitur ad verba de presenti et annuli dationem, nisi ea die qua ducitur vel praecedenti, et tamen omnia praeparamenta

By law, husbands retained ownership of all the nuptial gifts they personally transmitted to their wives, with the exception of ordinary apparel for
everyday wear.[4] In the estimation of contemporaries, however, the financial demands that marriage imposed on new husbands made them forlorn
figures who would derive marginal, if any, benefits from the dowries they
were promised. Planning for the marriage of her sons, Alessandra Macinghi Strozzi despaired that "the world is in a sorry state, and never has so
much expense been loaded on the backs of women as now. No dowry is so
big that when the girl goes out she doesn't have the whole of it on her back,
between silks and jewels."[5] With righteous indignation, San Bernardino of
Siena reproved wives with small dowries who demanded from their husbands a precious woolen cloth (rosado) in return.[6] He also reproved brides

---

sunt facta et expensae vestium et iocalium, ut tota dos sit consumpta." Paolo di Castro's opinion concerned the rights of a husband to the dowry of his predeceased
wife. Dealing with the identical issue, the Florentine jurist Rosello de' Roselli noted
that "maritus facit magnas expensas in nuptiis pro indumentis et aliis honeribus
matrimonii, que valde transcedunt fructus dotis, et tunc communiter matrimonium
carnali copula consumatur." Roselli's consilium is edited in Kirshner, "Maritus,"
p. 145.

4. Upon the husband's predecease, ownership of precious nuptial items passed
to his heirs, not to his wife. But the husband's heirs, acording to the jurists, could
not reclaim precious vestments and jewelry that a testator-husband had specifically
bequeathed to his wife. See T. M. Izbicki, "Ista questio est antiqua: Two Consilia on
Widows Rights," Bulletin of Medieval Canon Law 8 (1978): 47–50; Bartolo to Dig.
24. 3. 66. 1, In hiis, § Servis uxoris (Venice, 1570–71), fols. 30v–31r; and his Consilia (Venice, 1570–71), fol. 14va, cons. 50: "Veritas est quod vestes festive et pre-
tiose non sunt uxoris, nec eidem a viro donate videntur, et sic non potest morte con-
firmari rerum datio, cum ei tradere videntur ad usum tantum, ut tamen magis sint
apud virum quam quesita uxoris." This regulation conformed to the legal presumption, derived from Roman law (Dig. 24. 1. 51), that whatever a wife received, she
received from her husband, unless she could prove otherwise. On this legal issue,
see also M. T. Guerra Medici, L'aria di città: Donne e diritti nel comune medievale
(Naples, 1996), pp. 39ff.; and J. F. Bestor, "The Groom's Prestations for the Ductio
in Late Medieval Italy: A Study in the Disciplining Power of Liberalitas," Rivista
internazionale di diritto comune 8 (1997): 129–77. Bestor's study enlarges our understanding of the jurisprudential context in which the nuptial items the bridegroom
sent to his bride came to be treated as gratuitous loans of things that the borrower
(the wife) or her heirs were required by law to return to the lender (the husband)
or his heirs.

5. Lettere di una gentildonna fiorentina, ed. C. Guasti (Florence, 1877), pp. 548–
49; trans. in E. Cochrane and J. Kirshner, eds., The Renaissance (Chicago, 1986),
p. 116.

6. San Bernardino, Prediche volgari sul Campo di Siena, 1427, 2 vols., ed. C. Del
Corno (Milan, 1989), 2:1075, sermon 37. See also T. M. Izbicki, "Pyre of Vanities:
Mendicant Preaching on the Vanity of Women and Its Lay Audience," in De ore
Domini: Preacher and the World in the Middle Ages, ed. T. L. Almos, E. A. Green,

with large dowries (*le grandi dote*) who sought parity by cravenly demanding from their husbands expensive clothing, adornments, and jewels.[7] And he directed his biblical fury at wives who kept the whole dowry in a chest yet forced their husbands to resort to credit on unfavorable terms in order to afford things beyond their meager resources.[8] Giovanni della Casa, in his misogynistic screed, *An uxor sit ducenda*, protested that taking a wife reduces a man to poverty, "for he must support, clothe, and adorn her at tremendous expense [*ali, vestiri ornarique maximo sine impendio*]."[9] Machiavelli cast as his central character in *Belfagor* a husband ruined by his new wife's extravagant demands, among which were "dressing her in the newest fashions and keeping her in the latest novelties which our city habitually changes."[10] Renaissance audiences responded with familiarity to the figure of the nagging wife in Plautus's *Aulularia*, who expected a quid pro quo for her dowry: "I brought you a dowry far bigger than the money you had; so it is fair that I should be given purple clothes, gold jewelry, slave girls, mules, grooms, footmen, pages, and a carriage."[11]

It would be easy, but fruitless, to multiply contemporary denunciations making women's inherent greed and Venus envy directly responsible for the ills of their husbands and society, a well-known topos of the European misogynist imagination.[12] These denunciations raise questions whose an-

---

and B. M. Kienzle (Kalamazoo, Mich., 1989), pp. 211–34; M. G. Nico Ottaviani, "*De vanitate mulierum*: Donne, lusso, moderazione e stile di vita nel tardo medioevo," in "*Visibilità*" *delle donne*, pp. 45–53. For an overview of San Bernardino's views on marriage, see R. Rusconi, "S. Bernardino da Siena, la donna e la 'roba,'" in *Mistiche e devote nell' Italia tardomedievale*, ed. D. Bornstein and R. Rusconi (Naples, 1992), pp. 171–86; for the English translation, see "St. Bernardino of Siena, the Wife and Possessions," in *Women and Religion in Medieval and Renaissance Italy*, trans. M. J. Schneider (Chicago, 1996), pp. 182–96.

7. *Prediche volgari sul Campo di Siena*, 2:1017–19, sermon 35.

8. *Le prediche volgari: Predicazione del 1425 in Siena*, ed. C. Cannorozzi (Florence, 1957), 2:92, sermon 28; trans. in Cochrane and Kirshner, *The Renaissance*, pp. 119–28.

9. I cite the edition in *Prose di Giovanni della Casa*, ed. A. Di Benedetto (Turin, 1970), pp. 126–27.

10. Niccolò Machiavelli, *Belfagor*, in his *Opere*, ed. M. Bonfantini (Milan and Naples, 1954), pp. 1035–44, quotation on p. 1038; trans. in *The Portable Machiavelli*, ed. P. Bondanella and M. Musa (New York, 1979), p. 423.

11. *Aulularia*, 499–501, ed. and trans. P. Nixon, vol. 1 of *Plautus* (London, 1928), p. 499.

12. The deep-seated belief that the vanity of women discouraged men from marriage, resulting in the inability of Italians to increase their numbers in the years after 1348, was recycled in the twentieth century by G. Gentile, "Le leggi suntuarie nel comune di Pisa nei secoli XIII e XIV," in Gentile, *La vita e il pensiero* (Florence, 1972), 4:210; and M. Pierro, "Le leggi suntuarie e il problema demografico nel me-

swers are critical to any assessment of the role played by dowries in Florentine society. First and foremost, what sociocultural logic made dressing nubile women and young brides a duty that fathers and husbands could not fail to perform? Second, should we take at face value assertions that uxorious husbands spent sums equivalent to the entire dowry or the dowry itself on the wedding and the dressing of vain and mercenary wives? Put another way, was the promise of a dowry simply a promise to compensate husbands for expenses already incurred at the time of marriage and for indulging their wives in the latest fashions during marriage? Third, what legal remedies and financial arrangements were available to husbands who received only partial payment of the promised dowry or nothing at all? Finally, did husbands violate the usury prohibition by demanding and accepting compensation or interest payments on dowries promised but not paid?

(IN)VESTMENTS IN AUSPICIOUSNESS

An indispensable requisite for the sumptuous weddings and indulgent craze for luxuries, scholars agree, was the conspicuous affluence of the Renaissance city-states, especially Florence.[13] Affluence, in turn, triggered competitive displays of wealth for the purpose of signaling family rank,[14] an enduring social dynamic brilliantly analyzed by Veblen, Simmel, and Bourdieu.[15] As dress was employed as a primary visual means by medieval

---

dioevo," in *Politica sociale: La legislazione sociale del regime fascista e la più avanzata del mondo* 1 (1930): 13–23.

13. D. Herlihy, "Family and Property in Renaissance Florence," in *The Medieval City*, ed. H. A. Miskimin, D. Herlihy, and A. L. Udovitch (New Haven, Conn., 1977), pp. 3–24; R. A. Goldthwaite, *Wealth and Demand for Art in Italy, 1300–1600* (Baltimore, 1993), pp. 13–71—but see L. Martines's critical review of Goldthwaite's book: "The Renaissance and the Birth of a Consumer Society," *Renaissance Quarterly* 51(1998): 197–203.

14. See R. Levi Pisetsky, *Il costume e la moda nella società italiana* (Turin, 1978), pp. 17–30; G. A. Brucker, *Renaissance Florence* (New York, 1969), pp. 123ff.; S. Mosher Stuard, "Gravitas and Consumption," in *Conflicted Identities and Multiple Masculinities: Men in the Medieval West*, ed. J. Murray (New York, 1999), pp. 215–42, who relates the extravagant dress of Florentine and Venetian merchants to their untold wealth and desire to comport themselves as European nobility. For an exceptionally informed and panoramic study of medieval clothing, see M. G. Muzzarelli, *Guardaroba medievale: Vesti e società dal XIII al XVI secolo* (Bologna, 1999).

15. T. Veblen, *A Theory of the Leisure Class* [1899] (New Brunswick, N.J., 1992), esp. pp. 126–27; G. Simmel, "Fashion [1904]," in Simmel, *On Individuality and Social Forms* (Chicago, 1971), pp. 294–323; P. Bourdieu, *Distinction: A Social Critique of the Judgment of Taste* (Cambridge, Mass., 1979). In the economy of symbolic violence, according to Bourdieu, women contribute to their own domination

and Renaissance elites to manifest rank and magnificence publicly, socio-cultural logic dictated that Florentine fathers and husbands, independently of their personal wishes, invest considerable sums in adorning their daughters and wives. Sociocultural logic also dictated that a wife existed as an appendage of her husband and his family, whose image of prestige and power was reflected in her dress. In the idiom of the period, they were pursuing honor, a heartfelt quest made strikingly tangible by the wife's clothing and ornaments and dramatized by nuptial festivities. As the jurist Angelo degli Ubaldi of Perugia explained, the husband conveys precious clothing and accessories to his wife, "so that she may appear in public proudly and honorably." [16]

In his treatise *Wifely Duties*, dedicated to Lorenzo di Giovanni de' Medici, Francesco Barbaro urged wives to dress with moderation but advised that "if they are of noble birth, they should not wear mean and despicable clothes if their wealth permits otherwise." [17] What alarmed Barbaro and like-minded contemporaries was the ostentatious display (*pompa*) of wealth by aristocratic elites, which wasted patrimonies, and the unrestrained use of expensive clothing and adornments by upwardly mobile commoners seeking to rise beyond their inferior status. Spurred by these fears, lay and ecclesiastical authorities in Florence and elsewhere had attempted repeatedly, but in vain, to legislate modesty and regulate social competition by curbing nuptial pomp and vestimentary excess. [18] Despite recurring bouts of invasive

---

by reflexively performing the roles assigned to them by a male-dominated society. See his *La domination masculine* (Paris, 1998).

16. "Vestimenta vero pretiosa et alia ornamenta, que uxori traduntur, ut magis con[ten]ta et magis honorifice incedat, illa sunt viri." This view was shared by virtually all the jurists who treated the issue of nuptial vestments and ornaments. Angelo's *consilium* is found in BAV, Vat. lat. 8069, fol. 189rv. Since the *consilium* was imperfectly edited by Izbicki (note 4 above), Osvaldo Cavallar of Nanzan University in Nagoya and I have prepared a new edition. A translation of Angelo's *consilium* will appear in our forthcoming volume, *Medieval Italian Jurisprudence: A Selection of Texts in Translation*.

17. Francesco Barbaro, *De re uxoria*, ed. A. Gnesotto, *Atti e memorie della R. Accademia di Scienze, lettere ed arti di Padova*, n.s., 32 (1915): 65; trans. in *The Earthly Republic: Italian Humanists on Government and Society*, ed. B. G. Kohl and R. G. Witt (Philadelphia, 1978), p. 206. See also P. Allerston, "Wedding Finery in Sixteenth-Cenury Venice," in *Marriage in Italy, 1300–1500*, ed. T. Dean and K. J. P. Lowe (Cambridge, England, 1998), pp. 25–40; S. Chojnacki, "From Trousseau to Groomgift," in his *Women and Men in Renaissance Venice* (Baltimore, 2000), pp. 76–94.

18. On Florentine sumptuary laws from the fourteenth into the sixteenth century, see R. E. Rainey, "Sumptuary Legislation in Renaissance Florence," 2 vols. (Ph.D. diss., Columbia University, 1985)—an exhausting as well as exhaustive

moralism, sumptuary laws were ultimately doomed to failure because social competition, an insatiable appetite for luxuries, and ostentatious display had taken deep root in the psyche of fourteenth- and fifteenth-century
Florentines. By the late fourteenth century, the statutory penalties imposed
on conspicuous status wearers for violating sumptuary laws were mitigated
and transformed into excise taxes or fees. By paying fees, fathers and husbands were able to purchase immunities from sumptuary regulations, enabling their daughters and wives to dress as social necessity demanded.[19]

An alternative thesis, rejecting this totalizing conception of social competition and the sociopsychological conception of conspicuous consumption,
was advanced in 1982 by Christiane Klapisch-Zuber to explain the behavior of the bridegroom and his family.[20] Applying the insights of the ethnol-

study. For analytical discussions, see D. O. Hughes, "Sumptuary Law and Social
Relations in Renaissance Italy," in *Disputes and Settlements: Law and Human Relations in the West*, ed. J. Bossy (Cambridge, England, 1983), pp. 69–100; J. A.
Brundage, "Sumptuary Laws and Prostitution in Late Medieval Italy," *Journal of
Medieval History* 13 (1987): 343–56; M. G. Muzzarelli, "La disciplina delle apparenze: Vesti e ornamenti nella legislazione suntuaria bolognese fra XIII e XV secolo," in *Disciplina dell'anima, disciplina del corpo e disciplina della società tra medioevo ed età moderna*, ed P. Prodi (Bologna, 1994), pp. 757–84; Muzzarelli, *Gli
inganni delle apparenze: Disciplina di veste ed ornamenti alla fine del medioevo*
(Turin, 1996); L. Berti, "I capitoli *De vestibus mulierum* del 1460, ovvero 'status'
personale e distinzioni sociali nell'Arezzo di metà Quattrocento," in *Studi in onore
di Arnaldo d'Addario*, 5 vols., ed. Luigi Borgia et al. (Lecce, 1995), vol. 4, pt. 1,
pp. 1171–214; M. A. Ceppari Ridolfi and P. Turrini, *Il mulino delle vanità: Lusso
e cerimonie nella Siena medievale* (Siena, 1996); M. G. Nico Ottaviani, "De glie
ariede e fregiature: Alcune considerazioni sulla legislazione suntuaria tra Tre e
Quattrocento," in *Studi sull'Umbria medievale e umanistica*, ed. M. Donnini and
E. Menestò (Spoleto, 1999), pp. 1–32.

19. C. Kovesi Killerby, "Practical Problems in the Enforcement of Italian Sumptuary Law, 1200–1500," in *Crime, Society and the Law in Renaissance Italy*, ed.
T. Dean and K. J. P. Lowe (Cambridge, England, 1994), pp. 99–120; R. Rainey,
"Dressing Down the Dressed-Up: Reproving Feminine Attire in Renaissance Florence," in *Renaissance Society and Culture: Essays in Honor of Eugene F. Rice, Jr.*,
ed. J. Monfasani and R. G. Musto (New York, 1991), pp. 217–37. O. Cavallar and
J. Kirshner, "*Licentia navigandi . . . prosperis ventibus aflantibus*: L'esenzione dei
doctores e dello loro mogli da norme suntuari," in *A Ennio Cortese*, 3 vols. (Rome,
2001), 1:204–27. Lax and sporadic enforcement punctuated by bouts of moral rigorism was also the experience beyond the Alps; see N. Bulst, "Kleidung als sozialer
Konfliktstoff: Probleme kleidergesetzlicher Normierung im sozialen Gefüge,"
Saeculum 44 (1993): 32–46.

20. C. Klapisch-Zuber, "Le complexe de Griselda," *Mélanges de l'Ecole Fran-
çaise de Rome* 94 (1982): 7–43. For the English and Italian translations, see Klapisch-
Zuber, *Women, Family and Ritual in Renaissance Italy*, trans. L. G. Cochrane
(Chicago, 1985), pp. 213–46; and Klapisch-Zuber, *La famiglia e le donne nel Rinascimento a Firenze* (Bari, 1988), pp. 151–91. Klapisch-Zuber discusses her method-

ogist Marcel Mauss into the relationship between gifts and social cohesion in archaic societies, she holds that gifts exchanged between families at the time of marriage were not weapons in the battle for social prestige but, on the contrary, part of a system of compulsory reciprocities that secured peace among neighbors and maintained the stability of the social structure. With the demise of the Germanic *Morgengabe* and the reduction of the Roman *donatio propter nuptias*, or counterdowry, into a token gift by the opening of the thirteenth century,[21] "the reciprocal and almost equal exchange" that existed for over half a millennium between the families of the bridegroom and bride had disappeared. However, the gifts given to the bride by the bridegroom and his family served to perpetuate the function that *Morgengabe* once fulfilled:

> Even more important than the material worth of these gifts, in fact, was the need that people engaged in the process of alliance felt—on all levels of society—to make such offerings. They took great pains to reestablish an equilibrium perturbed by the official modalities of the dowry system when an alliance was made and a new couple set up housekeeping. The obligation honored by the husband to "dress" his wife thus *acted* as a countergift. It reestablished equality between the partners, an equality that had been destroyed by the initial gift [the dowry] and by the superiority that it momentarily conferred to the giver over the receiver.[22]

Beyond reciprocity, matrimonial gifts, like linens and rings, had symbolic attributes that gave meaning to the passage of the bride from her own

---

ological approach in "Écriture de famille, écriture de l'histoire," the introduction to her *La Maison et le nom: Stratégies et rituels dans l'Italie de la Renaissance* (Paris, 1990), pp. 5–15. Her study of nuptial prestations is also critically discussed by Bestor (note 4 above). See also Bestor, "Marriage Transactions in Renaissance Italy and Mauss's *Essay on the Gift," Past and Present* 164 (1999): 6–46.

21. The *Morgengabe* was a substantial gift (equalvalent to one-third of the dowry in Salic law, one-fourth in Lombard law) given to the bride on the morning after the consummation of marriage. In late Roman law, the *donatio propter nuptias* comprised the gifts given by the husband's family to the wife before or during the marriage. In general, the *donatio propter nuptias* had to be equal to the dowry (Cod. 5. 14. 9–10). See L. Anné, *Les rites des fiançailles et la donation pour cause de mariage sous le bas-empire* (Louvain, 1941), pp. 318ff. On the decline of the *donatio propter nuptias* in medieval Italy, see M. Bellomo, *Ricerche sui rapporti patrimoniali tra coniugi: Contributo alla storia della famiglia medievale* (Milan, 1961), pp. 27–60, 223–44; on the decline of the *Morgengabe*, see B. M. Kreutz, "The Twilight of the *Morgengabe*," in *Portraits of Medieval and Renaissance Living: Essays in Honor of David Herlihy*, ed. S. K. Cohn and S. A. Epstein (Ann Arbor, Mich., 1996), pp. 131–47.

22. Klapisch-Zuber, "The Griselda Complex: Dowry and Marriage Gifts in the *Quattrocento*," p. 224 (English translation).

household into her husband's.[23] The bridegroom's adornment of his bride-to-be, in particular, with articles of clothing and jewels bearing his family's coat of arms, signaled that this woman was spoken for and that her initiation into married life had begun. Similarly, the gifts he gave to her on the morning after the consummation of the marriage signaled the husband's claim to sexual rights over his wife. Other gifts provided by the husband's relatives marked the acceptance of the bride into the husband's kin group and brought into relief new ties of *parentado*. A year or two after the right of passage of marriage was completed, it was expected that almost all nuptial gifts would be returned to their donors, which, for Klapisch-Zuber, shows that their primary role was to give symbolic meaning to ritual action. Since the husband remained the owner of all nuptial gifts that he personally gave his wife, with the exception of ordinary apparel for everyday wear, he had the right to dispose of them as he wished. Husbands in need of cash could sell them or lend them for a premium to other new husbands in need of nuptial gifts. Far from causing the diversion of productive capital into wasteful nuptial gifts, according to Klapisch-Zuber, Florentine wives were pitiable creatures, relegated to the role of passive agents of social solidarity and equilibrium, and ultimately sacrificed on the altar of patrilineal interests. Like Boccaccio's Griselda, they were victims of a ritual process stripping them of their clothing and adornments. Her image of men dressing and undressing women becomes a searing metaphor of the emotional bondage and dismemberment of women fated to live in a heterosexist, patriarchal society. And far from facing financial ruin caused by the obligation to dress their wives, husbands not only recouped their initial investment but could also turn a profit as nuptial gifts shuttled back and forth between the sphere of ritualized generosity and self-interest and the sphere of commodities.

Klapisch-Zuber's illuminating and evocative analysis grounded in empirical evidence and ethnographic theory marked a watershed in our understanding of the role played by nuptial gifts in Florentine society and deservedly became the starting point for all subsequent studies of nuptial expenditures in Renaissance Italy. Nonetheless, I remain unpersuaded by the view that Florentine husbands and their families, responding to a deep-seated cultural predisposition, were compelled to spend large sums on nuptial gifts and festivities for the *almost exclusive* purpose of counterbalancing incoming dowries, thereby engendering social solidarity. This view, predi-

23. On the symbolism of rings, see the critical discussion of Anné, *Les rites des fiançailles*, pp. 11–62.

cated on the assumption that rituals of exchange in medieval and early modern societies function to promote social equilibrium, slights the prevalence of social competition in Florentine society. It also ignores an outstanding feature of nuptial gifts, crucial to any explanation of why husbands and their families felt obliged to give them: that gifts of gemstones, pearl-studded garlands, richly decorated silver belts or girdles, clothing, and marriage chests were primarily regarded as investments in auspiciousness.

The magical powers attributed to nuptial gifts were believed to ward off evil spirits, to mediate the emotional and sexual relationship of the betrothed couple, and to create circumstances favorable to the successful consummation of their marriages.[24] Medieval and Renaissance lapidaries informed their readers that rubies dispersed poison in the air and guaranteed love and good fortune. Their fiery color, the humanist and Roman noble Marco Antonio Altieri explained, signified the body, repository of the heart, which was burning with the flame of love. The bridegroom who gave his bride rubies (*balasci*) had symbolically given her his heart. His soul was tenderly conveyed by gifts of sky blue sapphires.[25] Besides the medicinal value of emeralds to repel poison, pestilence, dysentery, evil dreams, madness, and witchcraft, it was also believed that they preserved the chastity of the wearer and assisted women at childbirth. Gifts of diamonds and pearls showered on Florentine brides were considered antidotes to assorted ills. Such gifts were not restricted to members of patrician and wealthy

24. For Florence, see P. Castelli, "Le virtù delle gemme: Il loro significato simbolico e astrologico nella cultura umanistica e nelle credenze popolari del Quattrocento," in *L'oreficeria nella Firenze del Quattrocento* (Florence, 1977), pp. 307–64; R. Kieckhefer, "Erotic Magic in Medieval Europe," in *Sex in the Middle Ages* ed. J. E. Salisbury (New York, 1991), pp. 30–55. On the medical value of pearls, see R. A. Donkin, *Beyond Price: Pearls and Pearl-Fishing: Origins to the Age of Discoveries* (Philadelphia, 1998). On the medicinal qualities of coral, see D. Alexandre-Bidon, "La dent et le corail ou la parure prophylactique de l'enfance à la fin du Moyen Age," in *Razo* (Cahiers du Centre d'Études Médiévales de Nice) 7 (1987): 5–35. For an example of the apotropaic use of coral in Florence, see J. M. Musacchio, *The Art and Ritual of Childbirth in Renaissance Italy* (New Haven, Conn., and London, 1999), p. 132.

25. Marco Antonio Altieri, *Li nuptiali*, ed. E. Narducci (Rome, 1873), p. 53. *Balasci*, or balas-rubies of rose red or orange, are found near Samarkand in modern Uzbekistan and were treated as precious gemstones in late medieval and Renaissance Italy. *Grande dizionario della lingua italiana*, vol. 1, ed. S. Battaglia (Turin, 1961), p. 950, s.v. *balascio*. There are myriad references to *balasci* in Florentine *ricordanze*. For example, Ugolino di Niccolò Martelli, *Ricordanze dal 1433 al 1483*, ed. F. Pezzarossa (Rome, 1989), p. 104; Francesco di Matteo Castellani, *Ricordanze A (1436–1459)*, ed. G. Ciappelli (Florence, 1992), 1:132, 165.

families,[26] but were also given by shopkeepers and weavers,[27] and even *contadini*.[28]

Among the talismanic gifts traditionally given by the bridegroom, none carried more meaning than the erotically charged nuptial belt (*cingulum*, *zona*) or girdle molding the bride's breasts.[29] A fine example of a nuptial belt is depicted in an early-fourteenth-century miniature illustrating the title, *De donationibus inter virum et uxorem* in Justinian's *Digest* (24. 1). Here the pledge and the counterpledge to marry (*sponsalia*) are sealed by

26. *Ricordanze* of Niccolò del Buono di Bese Busini (ASF, CS, ser. 4, 564, fol. 2r): "1 ghirlanda di perle a fruscholi"; *ricordanze* of Giovanni Buongirolami (CS, ser. 2, 23, fols. 129r–130r); Alessandra Machinghi Strozzi, *Lettere*, pp. 17–20 (pearls given by Marco Parenti to his future wife, Caterina Strozzi); *Giovanni Rucellai ed il suô zibaldone*, pt. 1, *Il zibaldone quaresimale*, ed. A. Perosa (London, 1960), p. 29; G. Biagi, *Due corredi nuziali fiorentini, 1320–1493, da un libro di ricordanze dei Minerbetti* (Florence, 1899), p. 13.

27. Luca Landucci, *Diario fiorentino*, ed. I. Del Badia (Florence, 1888), pp. 6–8. In her *L'arte della seta a Firenze nei secoli XIV e XV*, ed. S. Tognetti (Florence, 2000), the late Florence Edler de Roover provides information on the rings, belts, gems, silk fabrics, and accessories weavers purchased for their wives. C. Carnesecchi has published a marvelous document (1452) regarding a professional garland maker who made expensive garlands decorated with pearls for Florentine brides, but acquired the pearls by stealing them from wives who already possessed such garlands. Some of these pearls he gave to his lover, some as payment to a prostitute. See "Niccolò delle Grillande," *Rivista d'arte* 4 (1906): 56–61.

28. M. S. Mazzi and S. Raveggi, *Gli uomini e le cose nelle campagne fiorentine del Quattrocento* (Florence, 1983), pp. 107–9; G. Piccini, "Le donne nella mezzadria toscana delle origini: Materiali per la definizione del ruolo femminile nelle campagne," *Ricerche storiche* 15 (1985): 172–73.

29. In general, see I. Fingerlin, *Gürtel des hohen und späten Mittelalters* (Berlin, 1971); Pisetsky, *Il costume*, pp. 148–51; V. Viale, "Cinture nuziali del XV secolo," *Bolletino della Società Piemontese di Archeologia e di Belle Arti*, n.s., 1 (1947): 44–60. In Andreas Capellanus's *De amore* (II, 21, ed. and trans. P. G. Walsh), a *cingulum* is included among the legitimate gifts a lover may accept from her partner (thanks to Paolo Cherchi for this reference). For references to marriage girdles and belts in Florence, see H. Hoshino, "Francesco di Iacopo Del Bene cittadino fiorentino del Trecento," *Annuario dell' Istituto Giapponese di Cultura* 4 (1966–67): 35; *Il libro di ricordanze dei Corsini (1362–1457)*, ed. A. Petrucci (Rome, 1965), p. 66; Strozzi, *Lettere*, p. 20; *Ricordi storici di Filippo di Cino Rinuccini dal 1282 al 1460*, ed. G. Aiazzi (Florence, 1840), p. 251, where Cino Rinuccini in 1461 commissioned Antonio del Pollaiuolo to make a *cintola d'ariento* for his sister-in-law. For another commission, see J. Beck, "Desiderio da Settignano (and Antonio del Pollaiuolo): Problems," *Mitteilungen des Kunsthistorischen Institutes in Florenz* 28 (1984): 213, doc. 3. Luca Landucci, *Diario fiorentino*, p. 6, presented his bride with "una fetta per la cintola e arienti e doratura." The damask weaver Giovanni di Luca gave his wife a girdle (*cinto*) made of crimson damask with a fringe of gold metallic, cited in Edler de Roover's *L'arte della seta*, p. 81. For the sumptuary legislation regulating the wearing of belts by men as well as women, see Rainey, "Sumptuary Legislation in Renaissance Florence."

the fiancé who gives his fiancée a belt with a purse and in exchange receives a ring (figure 3.1). Sanctified heteroeroticism is symbolized on a Quattrocento nuptial belt depicting a maiden embracing a youth and a girl holding a carnation, the symbol of marriage.[30] Known as the girdle of Venus (*cesto*), the nuptial belt was believed to endow the bride with the graces of beauty and love. It was also a symbol of the bride's virginity, which she preserved for her husband and which remained intact until the consummation of marriage. Boccaccio informed readers of his *Genealogy of the Gods* that "some have asserted the girdle which binds the bride affirms the marriage's legitimacy."[31] Marco Antonio Altieri related that among his contemporaries brides were formally girded in memory of the *cesto* given by Vulcan to Venus. Without the performance of this ritual, it was generally held that the marriage was neither legitimate nor true, but impure (*incesto*).[32] A valid marriage was linked to the couple's ability to perform sexual intercourse,[33] which began, Sextus Pompeius Festus maintained, when the husband unfastened the bride's girdle in bed. Indeed, "the beginning of marriage

30. A. M. Hind, *Nielli, Chiefly Italian of the XV Century* (London, 1936), p. 34 nn. 87–88.

31. *Genealogie deorum gentilium libri*, ed. V. Pontano (Bari, 1951), 1:142, chap. 22: "Dicunt insuper huic cingulum esse quod ceston nominant, quo cinctam eam asserunt legitimis intervenire nuptiis." On Boccaccio's treatment of dress, see E. Weaver, "Dietro il vestito: la semiotica del vestire nel 'Decameron,'" in *La novella italiana* (Rome-Salerno, 1989), pp. 701–10; on dress as a class marker in the visual representation of Boccaccio's women, see B. Buettner, *Boccaccio's "Des cleres et nobles femmes": Systems of Signification in an Illuminated Manuscript* (Seattle, 1996), pp. 6off.

32. *Li nuptiali*, p. 52: "Ma appresso anche de molti la Arraglia medesmamente se exequisce col cegnere la sposa, in memoria de cesto cioè vinculo se dunassi per Vulgano alla sua Venere; del qual senne hebbe sì meravigliosa opinione, che quando vese defecti presentarlo, se tenga essere incesto, et non legitimo et vero matrimonio." By virtue of giving his bride a nuptial belt before the exchange of marriage vows, the bridegroom had legally pledged to fulfill the promise he made to marry her. See D. Bizzarri, "Per la storia dei riti nuziali in Italia," in her *Studi di storia del diritto italiano*, ed. F. Patetta and M. Chiaudano (Turin, 1937), pp. 619, 628. Relevant here is a matrimonial case brought before the Curia Patriarcale of Udine. The relatives of a certain Lucretia found her together with her lover, Leonardo. They threatened to injure Leonardo on the spot if he did not marry Lucretia. He refused, claiming that he could not marry because he had neither a ring with him nor a marriage girdle to give Lucretia. This excuse became the basis for his contention that he had no intention to marry: "Ego non attuli mecum neque anulum neque cingulum quia non erat facturus nuptias et accepturus uxorem . . ."; cited by P. Rasi, "La conclusione del matrimonio prima del Concilio di Trento," *Rivista di storia del diritto italiano* 16 (1943): 255.

33. J. A. Brundage, *Law, Sex, and Christian Society in Medieval Europe* (Chicago, 1987), pp. 504ff.

Figure 3.1.   Miniature: "De donationibus inter virum et uxorem." Tübingen, Universitätsbibliothek, Ms. 293, fol. 315r. Courtesy of the Universitätsbibliothek.

occurs with the unfastening of the girdle, by which brides were bound."[34] Dressing and undressing the wife was thus a necessary prelude to legitimate sexual intercourse and procreation.

In the conventional medieval psychophysiology of love, the eyes were the opening through which the image of the beloved entered the heart, the

34. Festus was the epitomizer of the *De significatu verborum* of Verrius Flaccus. His epitome was in turn epitomized in the eighth century by Paul the Deacon: *Sexti Pompei Festi De verborum significatu quae supersunt cum Pauli epitome*, ed. W. M. Lindsay (Leipzig, 1913), p. 63: "*Cingillo* nova nupta praecingebatur, quod vir in lecto solvebat . . . ; *Cinxiae Iunonis* nomen sanctum habebatur in nuptiis, quod initio coniugii solutio erat cinguli, quo nova nupta erat cincta." On the custom of the Spartan husband removing his bride's ceremonial belt before consummating marriage, see Lapo da Castiglionchio the Younger's (d. 1438) Latin translation of Plutarch's *Lycurgus* (15): *Vitae illustrium virorum Lapo florentino interprete* (Venice, 1491): "ac sponsae cingulum solvens, eam sublatam in lectum transferebat." For the ancient Greek customs of young maidens dedicating their belts to Athena

seat of the sensitive soul and the appetites. Andreas Capellanus famously defined love "as an inborn suffering which results from the sight of, and uncontrolled thinking about, the beauty of the other sex."[35] A wife dressed to attract her husband's gaze would naturally give him pleasure and excite his sexual desire, leading him to bed her. From a Freudian perspective, the husband's visually derived libidinal pleasure was predictable. "Visual impressions," Freud posited, "remain the most frequent pathway along which libidinal excitation is aroused."[36] Small wonder, then, that a husband was moved to transform his wife into an erotic object, just as her parents had done in order to attract potential husbands. Even San Bernardino, the apostle of conspicuous parsimony and uncompromising preaching, grudgingly admitted that it was acceptable for wives to deck themselves out in fineries within the confines of the *casa* to please their husbands, but only if they behaved discreetly and decently and without lascivious intention.[37]

The large majority of married couples, Bernardino believed, were actually incapable of exercising the self-restraint necessary to limit themselves to the three legitimate ends of sexual intercourse: procreation, rendering the marital debt, and avoidance of fornication. He assumed that the eroticized wife would inflame her husband to love her too ardently and therefore sinfully, and worse, that she would attract lovers outside matrimony.[38]

Apatouria and the loosing of the bride's belt prepatory to sexual intercourse, see P. Schmitt, "Athéna Apatouria et la ceinture: Les aspects féminins des Apatouries à Athens," *Annales Économies Sociétés Civilisations* 32 (1977): 1059–73.

35. *De amore* (I, 1, ed. and trans. P. G. Walsh); for the fourteenth-century Tuscan translations, see Andrea Capellano, *Trattato d'amore*, ed. S. Battaglia (Rome, 1947). See also R. H. Cline, "Heart and Eyes," *Romance Philology* 25 (1972): 263–97; L. K. Donaldson-Evans, *Love's Fatal Glance: A Study of Eye Imagery in the Poets of the École lyonnaise*, University of Mississippi Romance Monographs, vol. 39 (Oxford, Miss., 1980), pp. 9–49; I. P. Couliano, *Eros and Magic in the Renaissance*, trans. M. Cook (Chicago, 1987).

36. S. Freud, *On Sexuality*, Pelican Freud Library, ed. A. Richards (Harmondsworth, 1977) 7:69.

37. *Prediche volgari sul Campo di Siena*, 2:1092, sermon 37: ". . . sì bene ch' io voglio che tu stia ornata e dilicata, ma con discrezione ogni cosa, e con modo onesto." The Franciscan moralist Angelo Carletti da Chivasso agreed with Bernardino: *Summa angelica* (Venice, 1569), fol. 258, s.v. *ornatus:* "Nam vir ornat se vel mulier ut non appareat in contemptu honestis personis, vel ut placeat vir uxori sue et uxor viro et huiusmodi ex tali intentione licitus quilibet ornatus. . . ."

38. Bernardino's chilling condemnation of passionate marital love derived from mainstream canon law and moral theology. On the sins of the "too ardent lover of his own wife," see E. Sastre Santos, "Sobre el aforismo: 'Adulter est in suam uxorem amator ardentior,' allegado en el Decreto: C. 32 q.4 c.5," *Apollinaris* 57 (1984): 587–626; R. Weigand, "Liebe und Ehe bei den Dekrestisten des 12. Jahrhunderts," in Weigand, *Liebe und Ehe im Mittelalter* (Goldbach, Germany, 1993), pp. 59–76;

No meretrix was as meretricious as the eroticized bride. He recounted the arrival of a bride at the house of her husband, adorned with a garland of silver acorns, her fingers laden with rings, glittering with gold, her face painted. She was greeted with joy and after three days of feasting, "it seems that her husband has fallen madly and fiendishly in love with her [*impazzato e indiavolato di lei*]."[39] As for wives who tell confessors that they dress sumptuously and paint their faces "to please our husbands," Bernardino replied, "you're blatantly lying. And the confessors are fooled by you if they believe it, and they are fooled by their generosity to you."[40] Leon Battista Alberti also pointed his accusatory finger at women who "take great pains to please the public eye. . . . When a woman is looked at, she thinks that you desire her beauty, and she regards your gaze as a sort of tribute."[41] Alberti, to apply the words of Maria Wyke, "operates as a hyperbolically normative male who has the power to dismantle the mask that constitutes the deceitful sex."[42]

Other moralists, however, openly approved the behavior of a wife who adorned herself in sexually alluring, formfitting dress to capture her husband's wandering libidinous eye, even if it caused other men to sin by desiring her body.[43] Here transgressive sexualized voyeurism was considered

P. J. Payer, *The Bridling of Desire: Views of Sex in the Later Middle Ages* (Toronto, 1993), pp. 118–31; J. Gordley, "*Ardor quaerens intellectum*: Sex within Marriage According to the Canon Lawyers and Theologians of the 12th and 13th Centuries," *Zeitschrift der Savigny-Stiftung für Rechtsgeschichte (kanonistische Abteilung)* 114 (1997): 305–32. For Bernardino's views on the spiritual reasons permitting wives to refuse sex with their husbands, see D. Elliot, "Bernardino of Siena versus the Marriage Debt," in *Desire and Discipline: Sex and Sexuality in the Premodern West*, ed. J. Murray and K. Eisenbichler (Toronto, 1996), pp. 168–200.

39. *Prediche volgari sul Campo di Siena*, 2:1241, sermon 42.

40. *Le prediche volgari*, 2:86, sermon, 28; trans. in Cochrane and Kirshner, *The Renaissance*, pp. 119–28.

41. Leon Battista Alberti, *Dinner Pieces: A Translation of the Intercenales*, trans. D. Marsh (Binghamton, N.Y., 1987), p. 141. Alberti anticipated John Berger's famous formulation that "men look at women. Women watch themselves being looked at" (*Ways of Seeing* [London, 1972], p. 46). Alberti's stance on women is discussed by C. Freccero, "Economy, Woman, and Renaissance Discourse," in *Refiguring Woman: Perspectives on Gender and the Italian Renaissance*, ed. M. Migiel and J. Schiesari (Ithaca, N.Y., 1991), pp. 192–208.

42. "Woman in the Mirror: The Rhetoric of Adornment in the Roman World," in *Women in Ancient Societies*, ed. L. J. Archer, S. Fischler, and M. Wyke (New York, 1994), pp. 134–51, quotation on p. 147.

43. Bartolomeo Fumi, *Summa* (Venice, 1554), fol. 364v, s.v. *ornatus*: "Si non habet malam intentionem, neque propter hoc ornat se vel hoc facit, ut proprio marito placeat, vel propter alium respectum, qui non est peccatum mortale, non mortaliter agit, etiam multi peccent eam personam appetendo, et ipsa sciat se appeti, hoc

morally acceptable because it was principally intended to incite the husband to perform the "duties of the flesh," not as a provocation to lust.[44] The Dominican moral theologian Antoninus of Florence, named archbishop of his native city in 1446, advised that if a wife dresses to please her husband, lest he abandon her for other women, or because he directs her to wear seductive dress, she does not commit a sin.[45] Contemporaneously, Antonio Roselli of Arezzo, who taught canon and civil law at the University of Florence and the University of Padua, enlisted the *Digest*, the *Decretum* of Gratian, Aristotle, Augustine, Thomas Aquinas, and above all the biblical models of the virtuously adorned Judith and Esther to support his contention that adornment in dress is not evil of its own nature but only in its abuse. Against the validity of an episcopal ordinance imposing limitations on women's dress and adornment, he argued that the civil law "permits men to provide potions and ointments to their wives, so that they may appear more beautiful." It permits them to send their wives gold and silver orna-

---

enim scandulum tantum passivum in ea secundum Caietanum (Thomas de Vio) ibi in Summa."

44. N. Denholm-Young and H. Kantorowicz, "*De ornatu mulierum:* A Consilium of Antonius de Rosellis with an Introduction on Fifteenth-Century Sumptuary Legislation," *La Bibliofilia* 35 (1933): 25 n. 3; 37–38 nn. 25–26; repr. in Kantorowicz's *Rechtshistorische Schriften* (Karlsruhe, 1970), pp. 341–76. The *consilium* was written in 1447 at Padua in response to an episcopal decree, the author and place of which have not been determined. Roselli's views were shared by Giovanni Petrucci da Montesperello—namely, "quod uxor teneatur obedire marito, non obstante statuto episcopali in talibus ornamentis." It is possible that Petrucci may have addressed his opinion to the same episcopal ordinance; see his *Consilia* (Venice, 1590), vol. 1, fols. 219–21, cons. 104. Earlier, Baldo degli Ubaldi had defended the behavior of married women, who, at the insistence of their husbands, wore dresses with low-cut necklines revealing their breasts in violation of an episcopal ordinance. Although Baldo affirmed that women could be excommunicated for wearing seductive dresses to church or on holy days, he rejected the bishop's claim to interfere with sartorial behavior sanctioned by lay customs. For the text, see P. J. Lally, "Baldus de Ubaldis on the *Liber sextus* and *De regulis iuris*: Text and Commmentary," 2 vols. (Ph.D. diss., University of Chicago, 1992), 2:304–5.

45. *Summa theologica* (Verona, 1740), pt. 2, tit. 4, cap. 5 (*De praesumptione, in quo agitur de ornamentu mulierum inordinato, utrum sit mortalis*), col. 596: "Demum si intendit praecise placere viro, ne huiusmodi omittendo, reddatur ei odiosa, et sic inclinetur ad aliarum concupiscentiam, vel quia imperatur sibi hoc a viro, peccatum siquidem nullus erit." On this and related texts, see also Izbicki, "Pyres of Vanities." For Archbishop Antonino's strictures on the painting of naked women, see C. Gilbert, "The Archbishop on the Painters of Florence, 1450," *Art Bulletin* 41 (1959): 75–87. The argument that women deserved qualified exemption from sumptuary regulations to attract hubands and please them was a standard defense: see C. Kovesi Killerby, "*Heralds of a Well-Instructed Mind:* Nicolosa Sanuti's Defence of Women and Their Clothes," *Renaissance Studies* 13 (1999): 257–58.

ments, gems and stones and toiletries, especially when such gifts and practices are sanctioned by regional custom. For Roselli, "in these matters no one can rule the wills of wives except their husbands, to whom God wished females to be subordinate."[46] Consequently, there is nothing cupidinous or sinful about married women who, at the command of their own husbands, adorn themselves with expensive garments and ornaments with the intention of pleasing them and stimulating their desire for sexual intercourse (*proprios maritos ad coitum provocent*).

Images of the wife's acquiescence to her husband's authority over her body and her will were customarily inscribed on the pair of marriage chests (*forzieri*) packed with the gifts the bridegroom sent his bride before the wedding ceremony. Marriage chests illustrated the classical virtues that the bridegroom wished to associate with his family: generosity, magnanimity, and prudence, as well as the selflessness and sacrifices expected of his bride. Among the most popular images depicted were the figures of the submissive Griselda dressed and undressed by her lord and husband; humble Esther, who appeared before King Xerxes dressed in her finest robes; and the queen of Sheba rewarded with royal bounty for journeying far to hear the wisdom of Solomon.[47]

The power of *forzieri* and *forzerini* (jewel boxes), as well as the gifts they contained, to convey moral and spiritual allegories was seized by the Florentine Dominican friar Giovanni Dominici. Like his contemporary Bernardino of Siena, Dominici was a master of performative rhetoric, leavening his devotional writings with the imagery of lived experience to es-

---

46. *De ornatu mulierum*, p. 363, n. 4: "Set voluntates mulierum in istis non habent regulare nisi maritum, quibus deus voluit feminas subesse."

47. Although modern writers use the term *cassoni* to refer to Florentine wedding chests, they were customarily called *forzieri* in the fourteenth and fifteenth centuries. By custom the bridegroom gave the bride two *forzieri*. See E. Callman, *Apollonio di Giovanni* (Oxford, 1974), esp. pp. 40ff.; P. F. Watson, *The Garden of Love in Tuscan Art of the Early Renaissance* (Philadelphia, 1979); C. L. Baskins, "La Festa di Susanna: Virtue on Trial in Renaissance Sacred Drama and Painted Wedding Chests," *Art History* 14 (1991): 329–45; Baskins, *Cassone Painting, Humanism and Gender in Early Modern Italy* (Cambridge, England, 1998); C. Klapisch-Zuber, "Les Noces Feintes—sur quelques lectures de deux thèmes iconographiques dans les *cassoni* florentins," *I Tatti Studies* 6 (1995): 11–30; B. Witthoft, "Riti nuziali e loro iconografia," in *Storia del matrimonio*, ed. M. De Giorgio and C. Klapisch-Zuber (Bari, 1996), pp. 119–48. J. M. Musacchio suggests that the image of the Rape of the Sabine Women was meant to encourage a new bride to produce children for the sake of her husband's lineage. See "The Rape of the Sabine Women on Quattrocento Marriage Panels," in *Marriage in Italy, 1300–1500*, pp. 66–84. See also Musacchio, *The Art and Ritual of Childbirth in Renaissance Italy*, pp. 132–34.

tablish a rapport with his largely lay female audience.[48] In Italy of the late Middle Ages and the Renaissance, the practice of arranged marriages coupled with the taboo against courtship precluded the romantic, passionate attachments and the drama of the flesh that have become and remain a precondition of modern Western marriages. For Florentine girls the prospective husband was necessarily a stranger, and for many an overbearing imaginary figure.

In a rapturous passage indebted to the story in the *Golden Legend* of the Roman virgin martyr Agnes, Dominici conflated the phantasm of the new, yet unseen, bridegroom with that of a loving Jesus Christ, who sends his chaste bride a *forzerino* overflowing with "glowing seraphim, shining cherubim and resplendent thrones, domains like sapphires, green and virtuous emeralds, strong diamonds of power, red rubies of princedoms, the finest beryl of archangels, white pearls, big and round of the blessed angels. Of these companions you make together with Saint Agnes crowns, decorations, buckles, rings, and the richest belts."[49] These precious gifts signaled the bridegroom's fidelity and served to reward the chastity of his betrothed and to guarantee her future fidelity by garbing her in invincible virtue. For Dominici, marital love and fidelity were activated by the imagination of the seeing self. Sumptuous nuptial gifts would arouse in the mind of the young bride a phantasm of the bridegroom as the beloved: "Now as a bride receiving the rich *forzerino* from that husband whom she never saw, she feels much beloved when she is so richly rewarded, and she creates a noble image of him who so nobly sends, and not seeing, she loves and desires to see

---

48. D. Bornstein, "Le donne di Giovanni Dominici: Un caso nella recezione e trasmissione dei messagi religiosi," *Studi medievali* 36 (1995): 355–61.

49. *Il libro d'amore di carità del fiorentino B. Giovanni Dominici*, ed. A. Ceruti (Bologna, 1889), p. 432 (thanks to Lydia G. Cochrane and Osvaldo Cavallar for assistance with Dominici's text). Agnes's martyrdom was set in motion when she rejected the offer of marriage and gifts of jewels from the son of a Roman prefect who had fallen madly in love with the winsome twelve-year-old girl *at first sight*. For remaining faithful to her true lover and spouse, Christ, Agnes was richly rewarded. Jacobus de Voragine, *The Golden Legend*, trans. W. G. Ryan (Princeton, N.J., 1993), 1:102: "'He [Christ] has placed a wedding ring on my right hand,' she [Agnes] said, 'and a necklace of precious stones around my neck, gowned me with a robe woven with gold and jewels, placed a mark on my forehead to keep me from taking any lover but himself, and his blood has tinted my cheeks. Already his chaste embraces hold me close, he has united his body to mine, and has shown me incomparable treasures, and promised to give them to me if I remain true to him.'" For the ideological context in which Agnes was transformed from *virago* into *virgo*, see V. Burrus, "Reading Agnes: The Rhetoric of Gender in Ambrose and Prudentius," *Journal of Early Christian Studies* 3 (1995): 25–46.

his figure. Much more does that love entering in you inflame you for God Almighty . . . and in the bed of heavenly repose, naked by these gifts, make you your abode."[50] Here Dominici adeptly transformed the phantasm of the prospective husband into an intimate gift-giving lover pledging everlasting fidelity to his betrothed.

Undeniably, the desire for honor impelled Florentine husbands and their families to spend lavishly on nuptial gifts, while the desire for alliances initiated a sequence of exchanges between the families of the bridegroom and bride. Yet the forces of social competition counterbalanced by the forces of social equilibrium provide an incomplete context for understanding the role of nuptial gifts in inaugurating and fostering the interpersonal bonds between bride and bridegroom. Nuptial gifts announced the figure of the unknown husband before marriage, kindled marital love, intimacy, and fidelity, protected the new bride from maladies, assisted childbirth, and represented the authority of the husband over his deferential wife. The distinctive attributes and meanings of what was actually given by Florentine bridegrooms to their brides constitute the basis of my contention that nuptial gifts were principally an investment in auspiciousness.

NUPTIAL EXPENSES

Lacking a detailed study of nuptial expenses, it is not possible to answer definitively what proportion of the dowry was spent on gifts at the beginning of marriage. However, a reliable survey of *ricordanze* indicates that on average from the mid–fourteenth century through the early sixteenth century, Florentine husbands and their families spent on nuptial gifts and wedding festivities an amount representing from one-third to two-thirds of the promised dowry.[51] My own research, admittedly fragmentary, supports this finding. In 1356 Francesco di Iacopo Del Bene spent 647 florins on his wedding, dressing his bride, Dora di Domenico Guidalotti, and furnishing their bridal chamber. In return, he received a dowry of 950 florins paid in five installments between May 1356 and May 1357.[52] A century later it cost

---

50. *Il libro d'amore*, p. 433: "Or come sposa ricevente il ricco forzerino da quel marito, lo quale mai non vidde, si sente molto amata, quando è così altamente presentata, si fa concetto nobil sia chi nobilmente manda, non vedendo ama e desidera l' aspetto. Molto più tu del sommo Dio t' infiamma, lasciando lo 'ntelletto per questo specchio scuro fuori della divina essenzia, l' amor dentro entrando, dove nel letto del divin riposo, da' doni nominati ignuda, faccia tua residenzia."

51. Klapisch-Zuber, "The Griselda Complex."

52. ASF, Carte Del Bene, 48, filza 50. See also Hoshino, "Francesco di Iacopo Del Bene," pp. 35–36, who gives a partial transcription of the text listing del Bene's wedding expenditures.

Bartolomeo di Filippo Valori more than 1,200 florins when he married Caterina di Piero Pazzi, who brought him a dowry of 2,000 florins.[53] Tribaldo de' Rossi limited his expenditures to 324 florins, representing 26 percent of his wife's 1,250-florin dowry.[54] Rarely did nuptial expenses exceed the promised dowry. The lavish expenditures that sealed the marriage of Bernardo di Giovanni Rucellai to Nannina di Piero de' Medici and exceeded her dowry stand as a remarkable exception to the norm.[55] If we can say that nuptial expenses were inflated by the rhetorical virtuosity of their detractors, they nevertheless constituted a substantial drain on the husband's assets, especially from the mid–fifteenth century on when the city's Dowry Fund (Monte delle doti) failed to pay husbands promised dowries as they came due.[56] For instance, new husbands like Tribaldo de' Rossi had to borrow money from their in-laws to cover nuptial expenses, while others, like Marco Parenti, arranged for advanced payment of their dowries.[57] Bartolomeo Valori's annoyance is noticeable when he recorded that his wife's Monte dowry had not yet come due and that he had received from his in-laws only 300 florins in cash, though he had forked out more than 1,200 florins for his bride's clothing and jewelry.[58] All these husbands were anxious to receive the dowries promised them to compensate, in part, for their nuptial expenses. In recognition of their plight, the government in 1433 allowed husbands to deduct nuptial expenses from their dowries, which were treated as taxable assets.[59]

HUSBANDS IN NEED

In his *Della famiglia*, Leon Battista Alberti cautioned new husbands that their pockets as well as their peace of mind would be better served by a dowry that was "modest, certain, and payable immediately [*presente*] than

53. *Ricordanze* of Bartolomeo di Filippo Valori in BNF, Panciatichiano, 134, fol. 5r.

54. BNF, II.II.357 (formerly Magl., XXVI, 25), fols. 2r–6v. In 1510 Primerano di Piero Primerani spent 478 lire, 19 soldi, and 4 denari to outfit his wife, Fiametta di Soldo Cegia. His expenditure represented a mere 17 percent of the 700-florin dowry he was promised. See *Ricordanze* of Primerano di Piero Primerani, ASF, Corporazioni religiose soppresse (S. Ambrogio), n. 348, fol. 7r.

55. *Giovanni Rucellai ed il suo zibaldone*, ed. Perosa, pp. 28–34.

56. On the *Monte delle doti*, see A. Molho, *Marriage Alliance in Late Medieval Florence* (Cambridge, Mass., 1994).

57. For Tribaldo, see note 97 below; for Parenti, see Strozzi, *Lettere*, pp. 3–9.

58. *Ricordanze* of Bartolomeo di Filippo Valori, fol. 5r.

59. E. Conti, *L'imposta diretta a Firenze nel Quattrocento (1427–1494)* (Rome, 1984), pp. 171–72.

large, doubtful, and payable over a period of time [*a tempo*]."[60] This prudent admonition fell on deaf ears. The steady increase in the size of dowries in the fourteenth and early fifteenth centuries, in Florence and far beyond the city's walls, made it ever more difficult for dowries to be paid fully before a husband inducted his wife into his house. The Perugian jurist Pier Filippo della Corgna was on target when observed that "in many places it is the custom that almost always the husband acknowledges receiving the dowry, and yet on the same day, in the same place, and with the same witnesses (notwithstanding the acknowledgment), he is promised the same amount for the said dowry."[61] In Florence and elsewhere it was not unusual for husbands to agree to payment of their dowries "sub spe future numerationis" and in installments that might drag on for years.[62] But what remedies were available to a husband who was reluctant, or who refused outright, to wait and demanded his dowry immediately? A husband was entitled to sue his delinquent in-laws, but that was not a socially viable option.[63] As Alberti observed, litigation was counterproductive on account of the expenses incurred and enmities aroused. The alternative was for a new husband to suffer in silence, which would likely happen once he began living with his bride:

60. *I libri della Famiglia*, ed. R. Romano and A. Tenenti (Turin, 1969), p. 135; trans. in Cochrane and Kirshner, *The Renaissance*, p. 87. See also Giovanni di Pagolo Morelli's admonition in his *Ricordi*, ed. V. Branca (Florence, 1956), p. 211: "Della dote non volere per ingordigia del danaio afforgarti, però che di dota mai si fece bene niuno; e se l'hai a rendere, ti disfanno. Sia contento a questo: avere quello ti si richiede secondo te e secondo la donna togli."

61. *Consilia D. Petri Philippi Cornei*, 4 vols. (Venice, 1572), 1:60ra, cons. 62; Angelo degli Ubaldi, *Consilia* (Lyon, 1551), fol. 74r, cons. 145: "Gener a socero confessus fuit se habuisse dotem et non obstante dicta confessione dictus socer promisit dicto genero mille nomine dotis."

62. When Vieri di Francesco del Bene married Salvaggia di Giovanni Aldobrandini in 1405, he received 400 florins of the 700-florin dowry promised him. He was paid another 100 florins in 1406, while the remainder was paid in installments over the next five years; ASF, NA, 13528 (16 May 1428). Numerous references to overdue dowries can be found in the *catasto*. See, for instance, ASF, Catasto of 1427, 61, fol. 606v (Cardinale di Neri); fol. 608r (Ciaro di Pagolo, notaio); fol. 859r (Guglielmo di Piero Adimari); ibid., 34, fol. 14v (Niccolò del Buono Busini); fol. 364r (Baldassare di Cione della Testa da Panzano); Catasto of 1433, 33, fol. 34r (Giovanni di Antonio di Gini); fol. 290v (Ser Nuto di Feo Nuti); fol. 300v (Nigri di Lippo da Montelungo); Catasto of 1480, 992, fol. 162r (Bernardo di Marco); fol. 337v (Francesco di Domenico).

63. For a rare exception, see the lawsuit brought by Ser Giuliano di Giovanni Lanfredini against his father-in-law, Filippo de' Ricci, for the remainder of his overdue dowry; ASF, Podestà, 4823, unfoliated (29 November 1447).

For the bride now lives in your house, and during the first year it seems impermissible to do other than strengthen the new bonds of kinship [*parentado*] through frequent visits and convivialities. Perhaps you will feel it impolite to bring up the question of payment during festivities, for new husbands generally try not to interfere with the still tender bonds of kinship. . . . And if you try to act with more force, the in-laws will start lamenting their infinite needs, their bad fortune, the hardships of the times. . . . Moreover, no matter how harsh you may be toward them, you will not be able to resist the sweet and prayerful requests made by your wife in your own house and bedchamber on behalf of her father and brothers. Accordingly, you are bound in the end to suffer financial damage and enmity. . . . That is why the dowry should be certain, payable immediately, and not too great.[64]

Husbands were authorized by law to support their wives only in proportion to the amount of dowry they received.[65] They could also refuse to support and live with spouses for whom a dowry was promised but not fully paid. Paolo di Castro opined that "when a husband is promised a dowry, if it is not paid to him fully, he is not obligated to support the expenses of marriage [*onera matrimonii*]; on the contrary, he can drive his wife away and send her back to her father's house."[66] The Florentine jurist Alessandro Strozzi concurred: "A husband who is promised a dowry by his brother-in-law that is not paid can send his wife back to her brother's house and even

64. *I libri della famiglia*, pp. 135–36; partial translation in Cochrane and Kirshner, *The Renaissance*, p. 87. It is conceivable that in addition to voicing conventional wisdom, Alberti was expressing the fears of Xenophon (*Oeconomicus* 13) and Aristotle (*Nicomachean Ethics* 1161A3), who believed that a wealthy wife would threaten the husband's superiority.

65. For the canonists: Hostiensis to X. 4. 20. 7, *Per vestras* (Venice, 1581), fol. 47r; Antonio da Budrio to X. 4. 20. 7 (Venice, 1575), fol. 62r; Panormitanus to X. 4. 20. 7 (Lyon, 1521), fol. 50r. For the civilian position: Bartolomeo Saliceto to Cod. 5. 12. 20, *Pro oneribus* (Lyon, 1515), fol. 18r; Angelo degli Ubaldi to Dig. 24. 3. 42. 2, *In insulam*, § *Usuras* (Lyon, 1548), fol. 12v; Lodovico Pontano to Dig. 24. 3. 5, *De divisione* (Venice, 1580), fol. 14r, n. 16; Francesco Accolti to Dig. 44. 2. 4, *Rei iudicatae exceptio* (Venice, 1589), fol. 31v, n. 7; and Alessandro Tartagni to Dig. 24. 3. 42. 2 (Venice, 1595), fol. 58v, nn. 1–2. However, the canonists insisted, while the majority of civilian jurists concurred, that since husband and wife were partners in spiritual life and two in one flesh, a husband was thereby obliged to provide her basic support (*alimenta:* food, clothing, and shelter), even if she was dowerless. Even without his wife's dowry, a husband is said to benefit (*utitur*) from her body and service. See G. Savino Pene Vidari, *Ricerche sul diritto agli alimenti* (Turin, 1972), pp. 449ff.

66. Paolo di Castro to Dig. 24. 3. 42. 2 (Lyon, 1553), fol. 32v, n. 2: ". . . quia quando maritus promittitur dos, si sibi non solvitur integraliter, non tenetur onera matrimonii subire, imo potest uxorem repellere et ad domum patris remittere."

deny her basic necessities." [67] But Alberti did not counsel new husbands to avail themselves of this drastic, shame-producing remedy, which was seldom employed by husbands belonging to the highest levels of Florentine society.

The plight of the lay canon lawyer Francesco di ser Benedetto Marchi offers a telling example of the countless Florentine husbands who resided with their wives, even though he had not received full payment of the 650-florin dowry promised him. In his catasto declaration of 1427, Marchi reported that he was in financial hell. His father-in-law, Filippo di Tommaso Guidetti, owed him 500 florins for the remainder of his promised dowry, which, he declared, would be recoverable only after long delay and with great difficulty. [68] Marchi's financial woes were aggravated by a string of debts, among which were 84 florins he owed his brother-in-law, Berto di Milano Salvini, for his own sister's dowry and 25 florins owed to the commune for the tax on the full dowry of 650 florins publicly acknowledged in a confessio dotis. Debts arising from nuptial expenses forced him to borrow money at usury from a Pratese Jew, with whom he left in pawn two belts that he had given to his wife. [69] For debts incurred on behalf of his father-in-law, he was also compelled to place in pawn his wife's apparel with a used-clothes dealer. Worse, Marchi's law practice had come to a halt. Miserable and humiliated, he had not left his home (where he lived with his wife, Diana, and their three-month old son, Marco), except on holidays, for more than ten months, and accordingly asked the catasto officials to take

67. Alessandro Strozzi, Repertorium, in ASF, CS, ser. 3, 41, vol. 18, fol. 177r: "Vir propter dotem promissam a fratre et non solutam potest uxorem remittere ad domum fratris et denegare alimenta ei necessaria."

68. ASF, Catasto of 1427, 61, fol. 727r: "Filippo di Tommaso Guidetti mio suocero mi resta a dare per resto di dota fiorini cinquecento o circa, cioè f. 500. Non ne posso ritrarre danaro, benchè pure gli credo ritrarre, ma chon lunghezza e faticha."

69. Ibid.: "Il giudeo da Prato dee avere di chapitale lire 24 piccoli e l'usura mesi otto o circa; àe in pegno due cintole della donna mia." Interestingly, Niccoletto Tartagni of Imola (apparently the grandfather of the celebrated jurist Alessandro Tartagni) also deposited with a Jewish pawnbroker precious vestments that he had given his wife on the occasion of their marriage. These vestments were subsequently sold. After Nicoletto's death a dispute arose over his widow's claim to be compensated by her husband's heirs for loss of the nuptial gifts she once possessed; see Angelo degli Ubaldi, Consilia, fol. 189r–v, cons. 339, who denied the widow's claim on the grounds that ownership of the vestments was transmitted by the husband to his heirs. Klapisch-Zuber, "The Griselda Complex," p. 244, cites Tivoli's sumptuary law (1308), which gave as a primary justification for limiting nuptial expenses the new husband's financial straits that compelled him to borrow at usury from the city's Jews and as security place in pawn the very vestments he had sent his bride.

into consideration his financial troubles when assessing his tax.[70] A self-serving appeal, to be sure. Nonetheless, although Marchi had received only 150 florins of a promised 650-florin dowry, the remainder of which he had faint hope of collecting,[71] he, like the overwhelming majority of partially endowed husbands of his station, was residing with and maintaining his wife.[72]

On the other hand, there is the oft-cited case of *contractus interruptus* occasioning *matrimonium interruptum* in which Paolo Niccolini waited three years (1430–33) before he introduced his bride, Cosa di Bernardo Guasconi, into his household. "During this period," Paolo recorded sourly, "I received the dowry in many installments and at many times. On the day I took her [to my house] some of it was still owing to me. I was not satisfied with so many small sums, and this was the reason why I waited so long to take her, because I wished to have the dowry first, to avoid quarrels."[73] Paolo Niccolini's behavior, however, was not representative of his station but was more typical of less well-to-do husbands in Florence and in the *contado* and *distretto*.[74] The weaver Antonio di Bastiano, for example, was not willing to live with his wife, Agnoletta d'Andrea, until he received the entire dowry. In her catasto declaration of 1480, Nanna, Agnoletta's widowed mother, described her daughter as "married but

---

70. ASF, Catasto of 1427, 61, fol. 727r: "E per dette chagioni, e anche per detti miei debiti per non avere avuta la dota, non sono uscito di chasa se non i dì feriati già sono mesi dieci e più, e no' ò potuto exercitare l'arte mia, benchè pocho si faccia. Et pertanto vi priegho consideriate lo stato mio per modo io vi sia rachamandato." Cited also by Gene Brucker, "Florentine Voices from the *Catasto*," *I Tatti Studies* 5 (1993): 23.

71. According to Marchi's tax declaration of 1433, Filippo Guidetti still owed his son-in-law 500 florins for the dowry; ASF, Catasto of 1433, 482, fol. 515rv.

72. Not surprisingly, whether or not fathers received a promised dowry, they were bound to support their children and, as a practical matter, their wives, too. Niccolò Adimari was living with his wife, Maria, the daughter of the jurist Francesco di Iacopo da Empoli, even though he had received only 275 florins of his 800-florin dowry (Catasto of 1427, 81, fol. 96r).

73. Quoted from G. Niccolini da Camugliano, *The Chronicles of a Florentine Family* (London, 1933), p. 114. In another example, Remigio di Lanfredino Lanfredini expressed fears that his sister Lippa might be returned to her family, even after she had been inducted into her husband's household, because her dowry had not been fully paid. See T. Kuehn, "Honor and Conflict in a Fifteenth-Century Florentine Family," *Ricerche toriche* 10 (1980): 307.

74. Fifteenth-century *catasti* are the main source of evidence for husbands who refused to cohabit with their wives because they had not yet received their dowries; see D. Herlihy and C. Klapisch-Zuber, *Les Toscans et leurs familles: Une étude du catasto florentin de 1427* (Paris, 1978), p. 592; Mazzi and Raveggi, *Gli uomini e le cose*, p. 109; H. Gregory, "Daughters, Dowries and Family in 15th Century Florence," *Rinascimento* 27 (1987): 221.

not gone to her husband [*maritata et non ita a marito*]," with a Monte dowry worth ninety florins but not payable until 1481. Meanwhile, Nanna gave her son-in-law temporary possession of a small house as partial payment of his dowry and as an inducement to begin living with his bride. If after six years Antonio had not yet begun to live with his wife, the house would revert to Nanna. It would belong to Antonio, with no strings attached, only when he installed Agnoletta in his household.[75] For brides whose impoverishment prevented them from living with their husbands, assistance from religious foundations and benevolent relatives was necessary.[76]

Many husbands were unable to collect the entire Monte dowry immediately because they had entered marriage before the initial, or subsequent, deposits made on behalf of their wives were payable. The evidence I have been able to unearth suggests that, contrary to Alberti's dire forecasts, a husband eager to collect a Monte dowry, either before or after the date of maturity, did not have to suffer in silence. He could demand that his in-laws consign to him, for his own use, property that would be returned on receipt of the Monte dowry. Temporary consignments of property represented a favored expedient. In her catasto return of 1480, the widowed mother of Frescobalda di Piero of San Miniato al Tedesco explained that she had married her daughter to Giorgio di Simone of Prato. Since Frescobalda's Monte dowry of 230 florins was not due for at least another three years, she consigned 230 florins of her own goods, which her son-in-law promised to return when he received the Monte dowry.[77] If the husband's demands were resisted by his in-laws, he might have his claim settled by arbitration. When Giovencho de' Medici married Francesca di Giovanni di

75. ASF, Catasto of 1480 (Campione del Monte), 40, fol. 217r; MC, 3735, fol. 10r; MC, 3742, fol. 137r.

76. J. Henderson, *Piety and Charity in Late Medieval Florence* (Oxford, 1994), pp. 316–21. However, Henderson mistakenly states (p. 317) that as a rule a husband would consummate his marriage only after he received the dowry due him. On dotal assistance, see also I. Chabot and M. Fornasari, *L'economia della carità: Le doti del Monte di Pietà di Bologna (secoli XVI–XX)* (Bologna, 1997); M. Fubini Leuzzi, "*Condurre a onore": Famiglia, matrimonio e assistenza a Firenze in Età moderna* (Florence, 1999); D. Balestracci, "Il testamento di Giacomo Galganetti mercante lucchese: Una fonte per lo studio della povertà nella Lucca di metà Trecento," in *La Toscane et les Toscans autour de la Renaissance: Cadres de vie, société, croyances. Mélanges offerts à Charles-M. de La Roncière* (Aix-en-Provence, 1999), pp. 161–69.

77. ASF, Catasto of 1480 (Campione del Monte), 39, fol. 308rv (Francesca di ser Piero di Michele). The first installment of Frescobalda's dowry was paid in 1484 (MC, 3742, fol. 256r).

Niccolò Manelli in 1462, he was promised a Monte dowry of 1,500 florins, with 413 collectible in November 1463 and another 591 in February 1464. He had already received 496 florins at the beginning of marriage. According to the terms of an arbitrated settlement of August 1463, Francesca and her husband were given use of a farm in Antella until her entire dowry was finally paid.[78]

Typically, any fruits appropriated by the husband from these arrangements would not count as payment of the dowry. At the time the dowry was fully paid, could the husband's in-laws, therefore, demand restoration of such fruits by claiming that they were usurious, an illegitimate addition to the dowry? No, the canonists and civilians replied. Fruits from property pledged to the husband, according to the decretal *Salubriter*, should not suffer the stigma of usury, since it often happens the fruits of the dowry itself were insufficient to meet the expenses of marriage. They should be sanctioned as a legitimate supplement to the dowry.[79] Commenting on *Salubriter*, the canonists added that such fruits served as a licit interim substitute for dotal fruits and as an incentive to the husband to begin living with his bride.[80] The canonists' position was endorsed both by Antoninus of Florence and by San Bernardino in a Lenten sermon treating the morality of *interesse* (licit compensation).[81] Civilian jurists, too, affirmed the husband's claim to receive *interesse* for suffering damages because of nonpayment of the dowry.[82]

---

78. MC, 3734, fols. 201r, 208r. The first payment was made on 5 December 1463, the second on 15 March 1464.

79. X. 5. 19. 6, *Salubriter*—a fragment of a letter of Pope Innocent III incorporated by Raymond of Penafort into the *Decretals* of Pope Gregory IX.

80. See T. P. McLaughlin, "The Teaching of the Canonists on Usury (XII, XIII, & XIV Centuries)," *Mediaeval Studies* 1 (1939): 131–34; J. T. Noonan, *The Scholastic Analysis of Usury* (Cambridge, Mass., 1957), pp. 103–4; A. Blomeyer, "Aus der Consilienpraxis zum kanonischen Zinsverbot," *Zeitschrift der Savigny-Stiftung für Rechtsgeschichte (Kanonistische Abteilung)* 66 (1980): 327–30.

81. Antonino, *Summa theologica*, pt. 2, tit. 1, cap.7 (De avaritia), n. 27, cols. 106–7; San Bernardino, *Quadregesimale de evanglio aeterno*, sermon 42, art. 1, cap. 2, *Opera omnia*, 5 vols. (Quaracchi, 1956), 4:352–54. Their views were shared by the Franciscan moralist Angelo Carletti, *Summa angelica*, s.v. *usura*, n. 25, fol. 350r–v; and by Battista Trovamala de Salis, *Summa casuum conscientiae*, s.v. *usura*, n. 21 (Venice, 1499), fol. 259.

82. For the civilians, see Bartolo to Cod. 5. 12. 31. 5, *Cum quidam*, § *Praeterea sancimus*, fols. 476va-477ra; to Dig. 24. 3. 42. 2 *In insulam*, § *Usuras*, ibid., fol. 27b; Baldo to Dig. 24. 3. 42. 2 (Lyon, 1498), unfoliated; Raffaele Raimondi to Dig. 24. 3. 42. 2 (Lyon, 1554), fol. 18va; Lodovico Pontano to Dig. 24. 3. 42. 2, fol. 77rb; Paolo di Castro to Dig. 24. 3. 42. 2, fol. 32va; Giovanni da Imola to Dig. 24. 3. 42. 2, fol. 20vb; Alessandro Tartagni to Dig. 24. 3. 42. 2, fol. 58vb.

Some husbands had no option but to accept interest instead of the dowry itself. Based on data from the catasto of 1427, Pampaloni has shown that the going rate on overdue dowries in nearby Prato was 10 percent. That corresponded to the going rate of 9 to 10 percent that husbands expected to receive on overdue dowries in fifteenth-century Florence and its environs. Carlo di Scolaio Salterelli reported in his catasto declaration of 1480 that he owed his son-in-law 150 florins for the remainder of the dowry he had promised. Without sufficient resources and incapacitated by age, Salterelli could only pay his son-in-law 13.5 florins in three installments—that is, an annual rate of 9 percent.[83] Earlier, Bernardo di Nofri Mellini had acknowledged in his catasto declaration of 1427 that he and his brothers owed 230 florins on the dowry promised his brother-in-law, Romolo di Lorenzo, a secondhand-clothes dealer. They were paying Romolo "fiorini 10 per 100" and anticipated paying him in full from the proceeds of the future sale of a farm that served as collateral for their dotal obligation.[84]

For the influential canonist Giovanni d' Andrea (d. 1348) and his immediate followers, such cash payments to husbands, despite the in-laws' failure to fulfill their contractual obligations, were strictly speaking in violation of the usury prohibition.[85] But by the fifteenth century the leading canonists and moral theologians had joined with civilian jurists in allowing "dowerless" husbands to accept cash, so long as they applied it to the expenses of marriage. They explicitly sanctioned cash payments to husbands reputed to be merchants, reasoning that delayed payment of the dowry would force them to shoulder the expenses of marriage with cash earmarked for their commercial undertakings. The arguments sanctioning cash payments were made by jurists and moralists who recognized that accommodations were necessary in a commercial society in which cash was the primary medium of funding dowries, but who were equally adamant in upholding the usury prohibition. Indeed, they gave notice that the fruits from property consigned to husbands could neither exceed the expenses of marriage nor derive from

83. ASF, Catasto of 1480 (Campione del Monte), 34, fol. 117v: "Io Carlo Salteregli non fo nulla; sono vecchio d'età d'anni 65 e o debito con mio genero Tommaso di Bernardo di mona Biagia, fiorini 150 di resto di dota . . . e a mio genero pagho 9 per cento l'anno in 3 paghe; sono fiorini 13½ di sugiello." Based on data from the *catasto* of 1427, Pampaloni has calculated that the going rate on overdue dowries in Prato was 10 percent; G. Pampaloni, "Prato nella Repubblica fiorentina," in *Storia di Prato, secolo XIV–XVI*, 3 vols. (Prato, 1980), 2:44.

84. ASF, Catasto of 1427, 34, fol. 395r.

85. For what follows, see MacLaughlin's study and the texts cited in notes 81 and 82.

fraudulent arrangements, where the son-in-law willingly and intentionally forwent payment of the dowry with the purpose of collecting interest.

So far I have been dealing with husbands who sought compensation on overdue dowries. There were instances, as legal opinions (*consilia*) dating from the fourteenth and fifteenth centuries testify, where a husband was entitled, but failed, to demand *interesse* on a dowry that was promised but never paid. One question legal consultors tried to answer was whether a husband, after the death of the person who had promised the dowry, could sue that person's heirs for compensation. Another was whether, after a husband's death, his own heirs could sue those responsible for paying the dowry. In general, *consilia* lent support to these claims, though the circumstances of the cases varied.

One opinion, written in the mid–fifteenth century by Galeotto de Gualdis, an official of the Mercanzia in Florence, dealt with a suit brought by a certain Battista di Iacopo.[86] On the decease of his father, Battista claimed compensation on a dowry that was promised, but not paid, to Iacopo by his mother (Lucrezia), her brother, and her own mother. Galeotto followed the principle set forth by Battista's lawyer in an earlier opinion (which I have not been able to locate): that a husband who bears the expenses of marriage can demand usury from the promissor of a dowry who delays payment. But referring to Papinian's opinion in Dig. 24, 1, 54, *Vir usuras*, Galeotto raised the issue of whether Iacopo, by failing to demand compensation during marriage and by giving his wife clothing and other items for her use, had thereby acquitted her from the obligation to compensate him for his marital expenses. Basing his own opinion on *Vir usuras*, Galeotto determined that Iacopo had so released his wife. In consequence, Battista could not act against his mother but only against his grandmother and uncle. Regrettably, we remain ignorant of whether Battista ultimately succeeded in his quest.

Another opinion was written in 1517 by Antonio Strozzi, the most active lawyer in Florence at the turn of the fifteenth century and at the beginning of the sixteenth. These are the facts of the case. Giovanni promised to deliver to Nicola, his son-in-law, within a certain time one-half of a farm as payment of a 250-florin dowry. Nicola then inducted his wife into his household (*duxit uxorem*) yet never received the property. Instead he received many small payments of cash totaling 170 florins. At the time of Giovanni's death—twenty-six years after he had promised to consign the property—he owed 80 florins to his son-in-law, described as "creditor pro

---

86. ASF, CS, ser. 3, 41, n. 10, fols. 250r–251v, and for what follows.

dote sibi promissa."[87] Now it is asked whether Nicola can legitimately demand compensation. Citing the decretal *Salubriter*, Strozzi contended that since Nicola bore the burdens of marriage and thus fulfilled his part of the dotal contract, while his father-in-law dishonored the contract, he was unquestionably entitled to compensation. There remained the question of whether Nicola had in effect forfeited his claim, because he waited so long to exercise it. Referring to other *consilia* on this issue, Strozzi argued that for reasons of equity, one must not presume that Nicola had released his father-in-law from paying compensation. As for the amount of compensation, Strozzi reckoned that it should be commensurate with the estimated value of the fruits that would have been produced by the property over the course of the twenty-six years. Nicola was also entitled to receive income (*redditus*) for the outstanding portion of the dowry due him. The responsibility for satisfying Nicola's claim rested squarely on the shoulders of his father-in-law's heirs: "For such a debt should be paid by the heirs in equal shares, because it is their duty to pay the creditors of the inherited estate."[88]

More fortunate husbands like the jurist Francesco Guicciardini received an advance on the remainder of their Monte dowries, serving to alleviate the *onera matrimonii* and cement the ties between the spouses' families.[89] When the Monte dowry finally became collectible, it was not the husband but his father-in-law or brothers-in-law who would receive the payment as

87. ASF, CS, ser. 3, 41, n. 5, fols. 332v–333r: "Consideratis his que in facto presuponuntur. Iohannes promisit consignare infra certum tempus Nichole eius genero quedam bona immobilia, scilicet dimidiam unius poderis pro florenis 250 in quibus restabat creditor pro dote sibi promissa. Quod Nichola duxit uxorem et Iohannes nunquam consignavit dictum predium, mortuus est dictus Iohannes et lapsi sunt anni XXVI vel circa a die quo erat consignanda dicto Nichole dicta bona. Interim tamen dictus Nichola recepit in pecunia numerata in pluribus vicibus de summa predicta florenorum 250, florenis 170, adeo quod hodie restat creditor in florenis 80 tantum."

88. Ibid., "Unde puto dictum generum posse petere interesse quod passus fuit propter non solutam integram dotem tempore statuto, quod interesse debet attendi et commensuari secundum fructum illorum bonorum que promiserit sibi consignare hoc modo, estimando quantum valebat dimidia illius predii. Item quantum fructabat dicta dimidia, quia si socer servasset promissa, gener debebat habere dicta bona pro quantitate extimata et habuisset fructus illorum bonorum quibus caruit propter non servata promissa, et plus tales redditus dari debet tantum pro centenario dicto genero, eius in quo remanet creditor. Et tale debitum solvi per heredes equali portione, quia est honus hereditarium solvere creditoribus iuxta l. 1, C. si cer. pe. (Cod. 4. 2. 1), et l. Pro hereditariis, C. de heredit. act. (Cod. 4. 16. 2)."

89. Francesco Guicciardini, *Ricordi, diari, memorie*, ed. M. Spinella (Rome, 1981), p. 86; ASF, MC, 3746, fol. 123r (the account of Guicciardini's wife, Maria Salviati).

recompense for the advance. The transfer of the Monte dowry was typically effected through assignment of the husband's claims (*cessio iuris*)—that is, by appointing his in-laws as his legal agents for the purpose of collecting the Monte dowry.[90] Numerous examples of such assignments, employed by those with relatively small as well as large dowries, could be presented, but two should suffice. Luca da Panzano, acting with power of attorney from his son-in-law, Iacopo di Ducino Mancini, received 627 florins from the Dowry Fund in January 1452. He had advanced Mancini the Monte portion of his daughter's dowry in February 1447.[91] Simone di Domenico, who had already received a dowry at the time he married Caterina di Tedice Villani, appointed both his father-in-law and brother-in law as his legal agents in order to collect his wife's Monte dowry of 61 florins.[92]

Regardless of who actually received payment from the Dowry Fund, the husband remained obligated to make formal acknowledgment of its receipt. Rather inadvertently, this regulation gave rise to legal complications. In November 1459 Niccolò di messer Carlo Federighi married Tita di Stefano Segni and acknowledged full payment of a dowry totaling 2,000 florins from his father-in-law. The 2,000 florins had been paid in lieu of Tita's Monte dowry. Two deposits in the Dowry Fund, each worth 1,000 florins, had been made on her behalf. One had matured in November 1459, but payment was delayed. Another was to mature several years later.[93] After Stefano died, his sons in July 1460 entered into an agreement concerning the disposition of Tita's Monte dowry. A preface to the agreement underscores the mutual understandings that made prepayment of the Monte dowry both desirable and feasible:

In truth it has been customary that the dowry be handed over especially so that the expenses of marriage can be more easily supported, which are

---

90. On the assignment of Monte credits and Monte dowries, see J. Kirshner, "Encumbering Private Claims to Public Debt in Renaissance Florence," in *The Growth of the Bank as Institution and the Development of Money-Business Law,* ed. V. Piergiovanni (Berlin, 1993), pp. 19–75.

91. See Luca da Panzano's *ricordanze* in ASF, CS, ser. 2, n. 9, fol. 126v; MC, 3734, fol. 11r. For additional examples, see ibid., fol. 34r (account of Angelica di Antonio di Piero); MC, 3727, fol. 77r (Caterina di Morello Morelli); MC, 3738, fol. 160r (Oretta di Caterina di Buonafidanza Gherardini); MC, 3739, fol. 12v (Agnola di Luigi di Tommaso da Panzano); MC, 3743, fol. 60r (Ginevra di Giorgio Aldobrandini); MC, 3744, fol. 155r (Lucrezia di Giovanni Migliorelli).

92. Ibid., fol. 1r.

93. Owing to gaps in the record of the registers of the Dowry Fund, I have information only for Tita's original account opened in 1444 and scheduled to mature fifteen years later (MC, 3734, fol. 18r).

great first and foremost in the city of Florence. For that reason Stefano handed over and paid the dowry in cash to Niccolò, not having waited for the day on which the dowry credits in the Monte fell due. Not, however, with the intention that afterward, when the Monte credits fell due, he would give yet another dowry or that he would assign the said credits to augment the dowry, but rather with the intention that the amount given in cash would be assigned in place and would stand in place of Tita's Monte dowry for the greater advantage of Niccolò, and with the intention of recovering from the Monte credits the amount in cash he had handed over and paid to Niccolò.[94]

In the presence of witnesses, Niccolò and Tita first confirmed the arrangement with Stefano and then consigned to Tita's brothers the 1,000 florins in her original dowry account that was now collectible. Niccolò was still required to present the Dowry Fund's officials with a *confessio dotis* before they would disburse the 1,000 florins—an act that obligated him for restitution of that amount, even though it had been consigned as repayment for the advance. Accordingly, on their acceptance of the 1,000 florins, his brother-in-laws agreed not to hold Niccolò liable for restitution.

Starting in 1475, the Dowry Fund paid husbands only 20 percent of their dowries in cash and the remainder in Monte credits.[95] Even these payouts were delayed as long as three years. With the launching of the Seven Percent Fund in the autumn of 1478, partial and delayed payments had become permanently institutionalized.[96] These events decreased confidence in the ability of new husbands to repay from their Monte dowries the advances they had received from their in-laws. In 1494 Tribaldo d'Amerigo de' Rossi admitted that he was unable to repay at 8 percent 610 florins he

---

94. ASF, NA, 10183, fols. 46r–49v (19 July 1460), fols. 46v–47r: "Verum quia dos dari consuevit maxime ut onera matrimonii, que presertim in civitate Florentie magna sunt, facilius supportari possint. Idcirco dictus Stefanus ut supra dedit et solvit de contanti dicto Niccholao dictam dotem non expectato die dicti crediti dotis super dicto monte descripte. Non tamen animo et intentione ut postmodum eveniente dicto tempore dicti crediti montis aliam etiam dotem daret et seu in augumentum dotis cederet dictum creditum, sed animo et intentione ut dicta quantitas data de contanti cederet in locum et esset loco dicte dotis super monte predicto descripte predicta Tita pro maiori utilitate dicti Niccholai, et animo et intentione rehabendi ex dicto credito montis illud quod di contanti dederat et solverat dicto Niccholaio . . ."; and for what follows.

95. Molho, *Marriage Alliance*, pp. 66ff.

96. J. Kirshner and J. Klerman, "The Seven Percent Fund of Renaissance Florence," in *Banchi pubblici, banchi privati e monti di pietà nell' Europa preindustriale: Amministrazione, techniche operative e ruoli economici*, 2 vols. (Genoa, 1991), 1:67–98.

borrowed from his father-in-law in 1481, since the "evil times" that had descended on the city prevented him from collecting the remainder of his Monte dowry.[97] In 1501 Niccolò d'Andrea degli Agli was promised a dowry of 1,600 florins, 960 of which was due from the Dowry Fund the following year, upon his marriage to Caterina di Piero Parenti. Piero agreed to advance Niccolò 250 florins when he consummated his marriage. Niccolò, in turn, agreed to repay this amount when he himself was paid by the Dowry Fund. Yet, in the event that Niccolò failed to receive payment from the fund, he would nonetheless remain obligated to repay his father-in-law from his own pocket.[98]

The Florentine husbands depicted in this chapter are intended to be contrasted with the stereotype of the overbearing *capi di famiglia* evoked by historians of medieval and Renaissance Italy. Far from being fortune hunters devouring their wives' dowries, a considerable number of Florentine husbands were lucky to receive full payment of the dowries to which they were legally entitled. Husbands like Francesco Marchi were hapless creatures, who would have been much better off by following Alberti's advice to seek a modest dowry that was payable rather than a large one that was unpayable. But where the economy of auspiciousness and honor override bare calculations of cash, and where the size of a dowry one family promises another reflects each family's worth in the eyes of society, large dowries are taken for granted. It was the desire to keep intact their honor as well as the bonds of *parentado*, I suggest, that moved husbands to seek remedies other than litigation to collect the dowries promised them. Private settlements regularly involved payment of compensation in lieu of the dowry and financial arrangements that appeared to be in violation of the usury prohibition. Yet, from the mid–fourteenth century on, the interest paid to husbands on overdue dowries was sanctioned by virtually all jurists and moral theologians in recognition of *li emergenti bisogni matrimoniali*.

97. BNF, II.II.357 (formerly Magl., XXVI.25), fol. 8r: ". . . non avendo el modo a dargli perchè la dota non si poteva ritrarre per li temporali chativi."
98. ASF, CS, ser. 2, n. 17 bis, fol. 10v.

4 Michele del Giogante's House of Memory

Dale Kent

In his *Renaissance Florence*, Gene Brucker described Florentine identity as forged from an amalgam of four distinct elements; Christian, feudal, mercantile, and communal; in the fifteenth century, the classical tradition fused with these to create the city's distinctive Renaissance culture.[1] The truth of his observations can be demonstrated in many contexts: this chapter is concerned with how the merchant's penchant for making records, lists, and inventories provided the framework within which the literature of the classical and feudal worlds, which shaped Christian and civic ideals, was preserved and ordered in the construction of a house of memory.

The merchant-adventurer Benedetto Dei is the best known of Florentine list makers. Dei, who described himself as "a good writer, and good on the abacus, and a good accountant," wrote several books filled with lists of things he counted and named—friends, enemies, places he had been, things he had, and things he lacked, the landmarks of Florence (churches, piazzas, palaces, artists' workshops), and the songs, poems, and stories he liked best and had memorized. His *Cronica* documents the interaction of oral performance and the written word in creating the memory of Florentine popular culture. It is obvious from the structure and rhythm of Dei's prose, and from the repetition of key phrases—"somma delle somme" (to sum up), "correvano gli anni" (time went by)—that his accounts were written from memory and spoken aloud in order to be memorized by others, even had he not larded them with the frequent address "leggitori e uditori miei" (my readers and listeners).[2]

1. G. Brucker, *Renaissance Florence*, 2d ed. (Berkeley and Los Angeles, 1983), p. 101, and chap. 6 (pp. 213–55).

2. Benedetto Dei, *La cronica dall'anno 1400 all'anno 1500*, ed. R. Barducci (Florence, 1985); for these and other phrases that serve as memory markers, see, e.g., pp. 59, 79, 81, 85, 91, 127. Cf. Ser Alesso Pelli, Cosimo de' Medici's household factotum, on the oral transmission of news; "et cantòssi et suonasi siamo fuori di quello impaccio"; ASF, MAP, V, 376, 5 January 1440/41. See also Dei's list in G. Corti, "Una

Dei was merely an extreme example of the compulsive record-keeping citizen, shaped by the practice of large-scale international trade and banking on which Florentine prosperity depended. Presumably to serve the needs of business, Florence had developed an educational system that created what appears to be the highest rate of literacy of any European society in the fifteenth century—over 30 percent of the population. Vernacular schools were attended by a large range of tradesmen, including the sons of butchers, bakers, shoemakers, and tailors. The revised tax laws of 1427 required that every citizen with any taxable property at all, down to the chicken feathers from which one man, nicknamed "Pennuccia," made pens and pillows, or the tiniest plots of land owned by almost everyone above the level of *miserabile,* or pauper, declare his assets in a detailed written report. The majority of these, including the returns of wool carders and cooks barely able to grasp the principle of separating words with spaces, were written, or at the very least signed, by the thousands of literate inhabitants of Florence. The city's unusually deep-rooted educational system also created the fullest surviving body of record for any premodern society. From it we can reconstruct not only the economic, political, and quotidian experience of the Florentine people but also their rich civic culture.[3]

---

lista di personaggi del tempo di Lorenzo il Magnifico, caratterizzati da un motto o da una riflessione morale," *Rinascimento* 3 (1952): 154–57; L. Frati, "Cantari e sonetti ricordati nella *Cronaca* di B. Dei," *Giornale storico della letteratura italiana* 4 (1884): 162–202; M. Phillips, "Benedetto Dei's Book of Lists" (paper presented at a conference to honor Michel de Certeau, University of San Diego, 1988). Dei, born in 1417, was related to several key literary and political figures. His brother Miliano married Papera, daughter of Feo Belcari, and his brother Bernardo's wife was Bartolomea di Goro di Stagio Dati. In Dei's list of letters received "in quarant'anni di tempo" were communications from Cosimo, Piero, Lorenzo, and Antonio de' Medici.

3. See P. Grendler, "Schooling in Western Europe," *Renaissance Quarterly* 43 (1990): 775–87; Grendler, *Schooling in Renaissance Italy: Literacy and Learning 1300–1600* (Baltimore, 1989), esp. pp. 71–74. The fundamental study of the catasto is D. Herlihy and C. Klapisch-Zuber, *Les Toscans et leurs familles: Une étude du catasto florentin de 1427* (Paris, 1978); the authors used the *campioni* copied by tax officials from the original returns, or *portate.* For evidence from the catasto of the wide diffusion of literacy among workers, see particularly E. Conti, *L'imposta diretta a Firenze nel Quattrocento, 1427–1494* (Rome, 1984); Brucker, "The Florentine *Popolo Minuto* and Its Political Role, 1340–1450," and Brucker, "Florentine Voices from the Catasto, 1427–1480," both repr. in Brucker, *Renaissance Florence: Society, Culture and Religion* (Goldbach, Germany, 1994), pp. 81–109, 133–54; see also Brucker, *The Society of Renaissance Florence: A Documentary Study,* repr. ed. (Toronto, 1998). In "Voices from the Catasto," Brucker observes that "most Florentine lower guildsmen were able to read, write and keep accounts, skills that distinguished them from the majority of salaried workers. Their tax returns are a rich source for studying the levels of literacy and numeracy in this society" (pp. 139–

The need to create memory—of personal, domestic, political, and economic milestones—sprang from the desire to lay down foundations; for successful business ventures, for the growth and prosperity of family and city, and for individual and social salvation, by learning from past exempla of moral and Christian virtue.[4] All these goals and values were ultimately related, as we may see from the expansion of the business account book to include personal and familial gains and losses (births, marriages, and deaths), family participation in city government, and the civic balance sheet of conquests, crises, and celebrations. In the resulting *ricordi* a man could pass on to his sons and heirs the wisdom he had taken pains to acquire, as valuable a part of their patrimony as the wealth he had worked to accumulate. *Ricordi* and cognate forms of the vast Florentine literature of private record—account books, *prioriste*, family genealogies and memoirs, chronicles, and literary compilations—shaded into one another and eventually into a new conception of the writing of history, exemplified in the works of Machiavelli and Guicciardini.[5]

---

40). He also cites examples of the many citizens who boasted at the bottom of their declarations, "I have drafted this return with my own hand." The signature of a cook, "Io Piero di Fruosino o rechato la sopra detta iscrita," ASF, Catasto, 28, fol. 344r, is reproduced in "Voices" as it appears in his *portata:* the words all run together. F. W. Kent and Dale Kent, who used the *portate* extensively in their studies (F. W. Kent, *Household and Lineage in Renaissance Florence: The Family Life of the Capponi, Ginori and Rucellai* [Princeton, N.J., 1977]; D. Kent, *The Rise of the Medici: Faction in Florence, 1426–1434* [Oxford, 1978]; and D. V. Kent and F. W. Kent, *Neighbours and Neighbourhood in Renaissance Florence* [Locust Valley, N.Y., 1982]), found that most heads of households wrote their own returns; those who did not almost always added their own signatures. On Pennuccia, see Kent and Kent, *Neighbours and Neighbourhood*, p. 114. For discussion and reproductions of citizens' original returns, see also L. De Angelis et al., eds., *La civiltà fiorentina del Quattrocento* (Florence, 1993), pp. 229–45.

4. On collective spiritual goals, see D. Weinstein, "The Myth of Florence," in *Florentine Studies: Politics and Society in Renaissance Florence*, ed. N. Rubinstein (London, 1968), pp. 15–44.

5. On the relation between private record and public history, see F. Gilbert, *Machiavelli and Guicciardini: Politics and History in Sixteenth-Century Florence* (Princeton, N.J., 1965); N. Rubinstein,"The *Storie fiorentine* and the *Memorie di famiglia* by Francesco Guicciardini," *Rinascimento* 4 (1953): 171–225; R. Starn, "Francesco Guicciardini and His Brothers," in *Renaissance Studies in Honor of Hans Baron*, ed. A. Molho and J. A. Tedeschi (De Kalb, Ill., 1971), pp. 412–16; L. Green, *Chronicle into History: An Essay on the Interpretation of History in Florentine Fourteenth-Century Chronicles* (Cambridge, England, 1977); M. Phillips, *Guicciardini: The Historian's Craft* (Toronto, 1977); Phillips, *The Memoir of Marco Parenti* (Princeton, N.J., 1987). For an imaginative use of assorted private records and a comment on their variety, see J. S. Grubb, *Provincial Families of the Renaissance: Private and Public Life in the Veneto* (Baltimore, 1996), esp. pp. xi–xii.

Among the least explored documents of this genre surviving in Florentine libraries and archives are the thousands of personal literary compilations, *quaderni* or *zibaldoni*, in which citizens from international merchants to saddlewrights, wool trimmers, cobblers, and soapmakers transcribed the oral performances and texts that were the foundation on which a constantly evolving Florentine popular culture was built.[6] Inscriptions written on the flyleaves of these *zibaldoni*, as they passed from one generation to another, testify to the fulfillment of hopes that they would bring knowledge, profit, and delight to the author "and to his descendants" or "his friends."[7] The first entry on the flyleaf of one, consisting largely of a vulgarization of the fourth *Decade* of Livy, reads: "This book belongs to me, Simone d'Alessandro di Iacopo Arrighi, and I wrote it in my own hand in the year 1451 and 1452." It passed eventually to "Simone Girolamo di Giovambatista di Simone di Bartolomeo, who is the heir of the aforesaid Simone di Alessandro di Iacopo Arrighi, who wrote this history in his own hand in the year 1451; and today as I write this, we are in the year of our Lord 1584; and the said Simone di Girolamo was born in the year 1583, on the 15th day of June, at 19½ hours or thereabouts, a Wednesday. God grant him the grace to be nourished, grow and live in fear of Him and of the most glorious ever Virgin mother Mary."[8]

Commenting on Boethius's *Consolation*, the first text that he transcribed in his collection, Francesco di Albizzo di Luca di Ser Albizzo at the same time described the purpose of compilations of such literature. "[This] book dealing with the misery of life . . . gives comfort to those who feel themselves weighed down by the tribulations of the world, and gives advice to those who have taken the wrong path, to humble themselves and take a new direction . . . and it gives comfort and strength to the virtuous, to improve themselves through the hope of knowing how to conduct themselves." Francesco's *zibaldone* also included the cleric Feo Belcari's verses of spiritual advice to his many correspondents, and his much-performed *Sacra rappresentazione* of *Abraham and Isaac*, which turns on paternal love and

---

6. On these see primarily F. Flamini, *La lirica toscana del Rinascimento anteriore ai tempi del Magnifico* (Pisa, 1891); S. Morpurgo, *I manoscritti della R. Biblioteca Riccardiana di Firenze: Manoscritti italiani 1* (Rome, 1893); A. Lanza, *Lirici toscani del Quattrocento*, 2 vols. (Rome, 1973–75); G. Tanturli, "Rapporti del Brunelleschi con gli ambienti letterari fiorentini," in *Filippo Brunelleschi: La sua opera e il suo tempo*, 2 vols. (Florence, 1980), 1 : 125–44.

7. Lodovico d'Antonio, BNF, II.II.81, flyleaf. Another compilator noted that "Questo libro si è d'Alessandro Cerretani e suorum amicorum"; BLF, Plut. 90, inf. 35, fol. 1, flyleaf.

8. BRF, Ricc., 1556.

filial obedience and God's expectations of man. The anthologist's commentary on this work addressed his own son: "I will begin in the name of God, for every good and perfect gift proceeds from the father of light. My paternal charity takes such love and delight in your filial subjection to me as I can scarcely convey to you . . . wishing that in time I may inform you, my son, as to the customs you should follow and of the love . . . of God . . . and teach you the nature of the virtuous life."[9]

Texts were selected for their relevance to personal problems, practical and moral, reflecting above all the Quattrocento preoccupation with religious instruction and observance, preserved in lists of offices and the forms of their celebration, treatises on the nature and function of the mass, prayers, meditations, confessions, and *laude*, addressed particularly to the Virgin, selections from Scripture, especially the Psalms, the didactic writings of the church fathers and modern religious leaders, and the exemplary lives of the saints. The creation and conservation of civic traditions was fostered by early accounts of Florence's Roman foundation, stories emphasizing the central role of merchants in her culture, poems in praise of the city, descriptions of her festivals and celebrations, and transcriptions of speeches by civic officials addressed to distinguished visitors like the pope and the emperor, and to the *condottieri*, military captains and princes hired to preserve the city's much-prized liberty from foreign aggression.[10]

Michele del Giogante was an accountant who compiled some of the most interesting anthologies, several of which contained a memory treatise.[11]

9. BLF, Ashb., 539, fols. 1r, 80r; on Belcari's *Abram e Isaac* and its dedication to Giovanni de' Medici in a verse hoping that his "glory and honor and fame" would equal those of his father Cosimo, see N. Newbigin, "Il testo e il contesto dell'Abramo e Isaac di Feo Belcari," *Studi e problemi di critica testuale* 13 (1981): 13–37.

10. For an extensive account of the nature, form, and content of these compilations, see D. Kent, *Cosimo de' Medici and the Florentine Renaissance: The Patron's Oeuvre* (New Haven, Conn., and London, 2000), chap. 6.

11. A group of three volumes, BRF, Ricc., 2729, 2734, 2735, compiled by Michele del Giogante, Giovanni Pigli, Giovan Matteo di Meglio, and Sandro Lotteringhi, are written in alternating hands and include comments and notations addressed by one to another. Ricc. 2734 contains the memory treatise transcribed below. See F. Tocco, "Un trattatello Mnemonico di Michele del Giogante," *Giornale storico della letteratura italiana* 32 (1898): 327–28, and O. Bacci, "Di Michele del Giogante e del codice riccardiano 2734," *Giornale storico della letteratura italiana* 32 (1898): 328–54. Other of his *zibaldoni* include BNF, II.II.39, inscribed on the flyleaf: "Questo libro è di me Michele di Nofri del Giogante ragioniere da Firenze scritto *il forte* di mia mano nel 1453 et 1454"; Pal., 215; and Strozz., XXV.9.650 (formerly Magl. XXV.650), which also includes a memory treatise. Magl., XXV.676, is his book for Piero de' Medici. Magl., XXI.87, and BRF, Ricc., 1591 and 2805, contain similar selections, including *Geta e Birria*. On this work, see also note 74 below. These books

Born in 1387 and dying in 1463, he was a precise contemporary of Cosimo de' Medici and a key figure on the scene of popular culture in Cosimo's lifetime.[12] He kept account of popular culture by transcribing works he heard performed. The established venue for popular performers was the piazza outside the church of San Martino al Vescovo. In the shadow of the Badia and close by Orsanmichele, a traditional site of popular devotion, charity, and ritual, it stood at the center of one of the city's main wool manufacturing districts. A variety of sources, from letters to tax reports, refer from at least the 1420s to those "che canta in panca a San Martino"—who sing on the benches at San Martino.[13] The most popular days for performances were Sundays and feast days, which amounted to almost a hundred holidays in each working year; however, transcriptions of recitals also show that often they continued for several days in succession. Performers described their audience at San Martino as including distinguished patricians as well as plebeians—artisans and laborers.[14]

These popular entertainers were praised particularly for their extraordinary feats of memory, their special skill being to extemporize new works based on a core of familiar themes. This necessitated the memorization and frequent rehearsal of a broad range of learning. Singers' repertoires consisted of a mixture of their own works and those of their friends and con-

---

have all been attributed to Michele; more are likely to be identified. Individual hands are hard to distinguish, and signatures hidden in the body of a book are easily missed. Many *quadernucci* are composites, with quires in different hands and from different periods bound together at a date unknown, some with multiple numeration and others with none; there is much room for confusion and error.

12. Cosimo was born in 1389 and died in 1464. Michele lived at the Canto alla Macina, just behind the Medici houses on the corner of the present Via de' Ginori and Via Guelfa; see ASF, Catasto, 676, fols. 85r–87v; he was buried in San Marco. For his biography, the details of his relations with the Medici, and his role in popular culture, see Flamini, *La lirica,* pp. 238ff.; and D. Kent, *Cosimo de' Medici,* pt. 2.

13. On San Martino, see Flamini, *La lirica;* B. Becherini, "Un canta in panca fiorentino, Antonio di Guido," *Rivista musicale italiana* 5 (1948): 241–47; Becherini, "Poesia e musica in Italia ai primi del XV secolo," in *Les Colloques de Wégimont II, 1955* (Paris, 1959), pp. 239–59. Performances of popular literature in public *piazze* were apparently common in northern Italian cities in an earlier age; by the fifteenth century they persisted mainly in Florence; see BLF, Plut. 90, inf. 47, fols. 119v–120r: "Veduto già di molti piazze / per diverse città ma di vicini / vorà cantare lasciando l'altre razza. / Bella mi pare quella de' perugini. . . ."

14. R. Renier, ed., *Strambotti e sonetti dell'Altissimo* (Turin, 1886), pp. xxv–xxvi. On feast days, see Iacopo da Voragine, *The Golden Legend,* 2 vols., trans. W. G. Ryan (Princeton, N.J., 1993); also R. de Roover, *The Rise and Decline of the Medici Bank* (Cambridge, Mass., 1963), who notes, pp. 184–86, that the holidays prescribed by guild statutes left only 275 workdays each year.

temporaries, and of traditional selections conserved in various *zibaldoni*, including manuals written specifically by and for popular singers. The best-known of these were the *zibaldone* attributed to Antonio Pucci and the *Cantare dei Cantari*, whose anonymous author, writing sometime between 1380 and 1420, collected the works he had found to be most popular with audiences. The songs and recitations that moved the audience at San Martino "to tears or admiration" included everything from popular sayings and moral exempla; observations about such subjects of perennial popular appeal as the disposition of women, the education of children, and the character of priests, doctors, and notaries; sacred songs of penance or instruction; songs of love fulfilled, or more often unrequited; medieval romance or historical narrative epics based on the deeds of ancient heroes, or the origins and history of Florence; to the Bible and the works of Latin poets and prose writers, translated and transposed into vernacular rhyme.[15]

Singers accompanied themselves on the viola or *chitarra*, with simple melodies such as Gregorian chants, or *melopee* like those favored at Florentine festivals and sacred dramas.[16] The most talented improvisers were artisans—shoemakers or barbers like Antonio *calzaiuolo*, Burchiello, and Antonio da Bacchereto, "who was a barber and now sings on the benches"[17] —and professionals like the heralds of the Signoria, or like Antonio di Guido and Niccolò Cieco (who devised Michele del Giogante's memory treatise), full-time singers who also entertained at the table of the Priors in the palace of the Signoria, or in the homes of wealthy citizens such as the Medici.[18] When Cosimo gave a dinner at the Medici villa of Careggi in 1459

15. Flamini, *La lirica*, pp. 155–57; P. Rajna, "Cantare dei cantari," *Zeitschrift für romanische Philologie* 2 (1868): 220–54, 419–37; A. Graf, "Il Zibaldone attribuito ad Antonio Pucci," *Giornale storico della letteratura italiana* 1:294ff. There are two known codices of the Pucci *zibaldone*: BNF, Magl., XXIII.135; and BRF, Ricc., 1922.

16. Flamini, *La lirica*; Becherini, "Un canta in panca," "Poesia e musica"; F. D'Accone, "Alcune note sulle Compagnie fiorentine dei Laudesi durante il Quattrocento," *Rivista italiana di musicologia* 10 (1975): 86–114, esp. 109–14. On music and performance, see also C. Barr, "Music and Spectacle in Confraternity Drama of Fifteenth-Century Florence," in *Christianity and the Renaissance: Image and Religious Imagination in the Quattrocento*, ed. T. Verdon and J. Henderson (Syracuse, N.Y., 1990); B. Wilson, *Music and Merchants: The "Laudesi" Companies of Republican Florence* (Oxford, 1992).

17. BLF, Conv. soppr., 109 (SS. Annunziata), fol. 49r.

18. On the Florentine entertainment establishment, see Flamini, *La lirica*; Becherini, "Una canta in panca"; and Lanza, *Lirici toscani*. On the heralds, see *The "Libro Cerimoniale" of the Florentine Republic, by Francesco Filarete and Angelo Manfidi*, ed. R. Trexler (Geneva, 1978); S. Branciforte, "'Ars poetica rei publicae':

to honor the young Galeazzo Maria Sforza, son of the duke of Milan, the popular poet Antonio di Guido was chosen to provide the entertainment. In a letter to his father, Galeazzo Maria described the impression the singer had made on him. "We heard a maestro Antonio sing, accompanying himself on the chitarra; I think if Your Excellency does not know him, you must at least have heard him spoken of." Ranking Antonio, the son of an unnamed artisan, with the greatest of classical and Christian poets, he continued: "I don't know if Lucan or Dante ever did anything more beautiful, combining so many ancient stories, the names of innumerable ancient Romans, fables, poets, and the names of all the Muses. . . . I was greatly impressed by him." The apothecary Luca Landucci's equally enthusiastic praise of Antonio as "a singer of improvisations who has surpassed all others in that art" indicates the social breadth of the poet's appeal.[19]

Michele del Giogante, poet, anthologist, and accountant, was a close associate of the Medici, Florence's leading citizens, and a major conduit linking them with the world of popular culture. Michele wrote to Cosimo's son Piero in 1454, beginning his letter with a *quartina* written in red ink, "A pious man, according to Augustine / has one foot on the ground, and the other in heaven. / Therefore, my dear Signor, with the warm zeal / of love please sample my letter." This was a recommendation to Piero's charity of "a young Florentine of ours, aged about sixteen or seventeen," and at that time in the service of a captain of the Venetian army. "And this boy, whom I already put to singing improvisations on the bench at San Martino, of fine intellect and imagination [*buono ingiengno e fantasia*], naturally gifted in this art, . . . you already heard sing in Lionardo Bartolini's house, at a splendid dinner he gave for you, where I brought him, and he sang a few stanzas; you must remember it. . . . I think you were also acquainted with his work when he brought with him a very pleasing little book I made for him, and he had sung a good part of the material written in it at San Martino, including a little work Maestro Niccolò Cieco performed as a motet at San Martino, which made hundreds of people there weep in sympathy."[20]

The famous singer known as "L'Altissimo" alluded in his songs to the

The Herald of the Florentine Signoria" (Ph.D. diss., University of California, Los Angeles, 1990).

19. For Sforza's letter, B. Buser, *Die Beziehungen der Mediceer zu Frankreich während der Jahre 1434–1494 in ihrem Zusammenhang mit den allgemeinen Verhältnissen Italiens* (Leipzig, 1879), pp. 347–48. See also Luca Landucci, *Diario fiorentino dal 1450 al 1516*, ed. I. del Badia (Florence, 1883), p. 3.

20. ASF, MAP, XVII, 108, 24 May 1454.

financial support he received from his audience: some of this shaded seamlessly into charity and patronage. At least one singer of *laude* at San Martino received charity from the Buonomini of San Martino, a charitable confraternity attached to the church, founded by Cosimo de' Medici and his friends with the support of Pope Eugenius and Archbishop Antoninus.[21] The Medici also contributed personally to the support of singers with the encouragement of their friends Feo Belcari and Michele del Giogante. Michele himself was a recipient of their charity. In 1450 he wrote to "that most famous man, Coximo [*sic*] de' Medici," thanking him for the dowry he gave through the agency of Antonio Martelli to his son Piero for his marriage to Antonio's daughter Felice; Cosimo had also arranged the *parentado*.[22]

One of Michele's many services to the Medici was his compilation of a celebratory anthology for Cosimo's elder son, Piero, when Francesco Sforza became duke of Milan. Cosimo and his family were friends, allies, and admirers of the *condottiere*, who was also a great hero of the Florentine *popolo*. A decade before Sforza's son praised the performance of Antonio di Guido at Careggi, the crowd at San Martino had acclaimed the news of his own acquisition of Milan, and several poems were recited there in his honor. This was almost certainly the occasion for the poem in praise of Sforza attributed to Cosimo himself.[23] On 6 March 1450, Sforza sent an envoy with trumpet and olive branch in hand to announce his victory to the Signoria of Florence. His letter appears in several *zibaldoni* besides the volume for the Medici, which Michele described as the book "I made, that is, more wrote than made, at the behest of my more than superior Piero di Cosimo de' Medici." He prefaced it with a dedicatory poem: "O famed

21. In canto 67 of his poetic cycle on the kings of France, L'Altissimo acknowledged the "uditor degni, uditor singular' / Che purch'io canti in versi questa historia / Mi sovvenite coi vostri denari . . . ," Renier, *Strambotti e sonetti*, p. xvii. On Medici charity at San Martino, see D. Kent, "The 'Buonomini di San Martino': Charity for 'the glory of God, the honour of the city, and the commemoration of myself,'" in *Cosimo "il Vecchio" de' Medici, 1389–1464*, ed. F. Ames-Lewis (Oxford, 1992), pp. 49–67. The main Quattrocento books of this confraternity are in BNF, Tordi, 1–3; see esp. 3, fols. 13r, 27v. For praise of Cosimo's charity by popular poets and his own perception of its role in his salvation, see D. Kent, *Cosimo de' Medici*, pp. 117–21 and chap. 9.

22. ASF, MAP, XII, 201.

23. See D. Kent, *Cosimo de' Medici*, p. 20 (on Cosimo's poem), pp. 52–54 (on popular *condottieri*), and pp. 268–81 (on Cosimo's admiration for military heroes). The poems by Belcari, Antonio di Meglio, and Cosimo are published by Lanza, *Lirici toscani*. See BNF, Pal., 215, fol. 35v, for Niccolò Cieco's poem "fatto in commendazione del Magnifico Conte Francescho Sforza nostro capitano, il qual fece in firenze in chasa Michele di Nofri del Giogante in dì 22 di Novenbre 1435."

Piero mine, son of Cosimo, / this little book of mine I call yours, / because 'il Forte' [his own nickname] made it with your advice, / dreaming, as you know, of serving you in some small way, / with certain additions which you will see that I found over time, and we know where; / from that source from which these things / always spring, and known to all the crowd." Putting the best of popular culture at his patron's disposal, Michele used this compilation to instruct him in matters of morals and duty. He thought Sforza's letter so important to every Florentine "that he should have it engraved on his heart forever," as indeed it was by its preservation in Michele's *zibaldoni*, a house of memory he built to accommodate Florentine popular culture.[24]

Transcribing performances and texts was only the first step. The knowledge conserved in compilations had then to be activated in memory. Among the wealth of information Benedetto Dei conserved were lists of things he had memorized. The record in his *Cronica* of 1473 of the first lines of "Cantari e Sonetti," those he had committed to memory, helps to define the corpus of popular literature in Cosimo's lifetime. It included, like many *zibaldoni*, a poem about the great snowfall of 1408, when citizens made snowmen in the shape of Hercules and of Florence's symbolic lion, the Marzocco. Other popular items memorized and transcribed by Dei were Cosimo's poem in praise of Sforza; the *Sfera* of Goro Dati, describing the wonders of the three regions of the Renaissance world; Lo Za's *Buca di Monte Ferrato*, exposing the associations of Florentine homosexuals; the cobbler Giovanni's poem on the consecration of the cathedral after the completion of Brunelleschi's cupola; one of the architect's own poems; Boccaccio's *Ninfale*; the *Credo* attributed to Dante; Burchiello's verse denouncing the recall of the Medici in 1434; and a poem celebrating the exploits of the English *condottiere* Sir John Hawkwood, whom the commune had memorialized in Uccello's fresco for the Duomo in 1436. Dei committed to memory altogether ten *novelle* and 139 histories and poems, showing just how much information a well-ordered mind could house.[25]

Zanobi di Pagholo d'Agnolo Perini noted in his *quadernuccio*, alongside the verse describing the snowfall, "In the name of God and his mother Saint Mary and of all the holy court of Paradise amen, amen. Here I record the memory of how on the 17th of January 1407[8], on the day of Saint

24. BNF, Magl., XXV, 676; for Sforza's letter, fols. 7–10. On the apparently original cover is inscribed "Senper felix," an obvious play on the Medici motto "Semper." The manuscript is liberally adorned with hands pointing to passages Michele considered of particular significance "to you, my Piero."

25. For the complete list see Frati, "Cantari e Sonetti."

Anthony, the great snow which continued all that month began to fall . . . for I would not consider myself to have even the smallest knowledge if I created no records for the sake of memory of that which I saw in my Florence."[26] As Machiavelli told his friend Vettori, describing how he communed with ancient writers in his study at night, "where I am not ashamed to speak with them and to ask them the reason for their actions, and they in their kindness answer me," he later noted down what he had learned, "because Dante says it does not produce knowledge when we hear but do not remember."[27]

The relation in Renaissance minds between hearing, writing, reading, memorizing, and knowing explains the inclusion in many compilations of a treatise on memory. These took various forms, some with striking individual variations, such as the one built by Ser Piero di Ser Bonaccorso around the image of Santa Quaresima.[28] But all basically derived from the prescriptions of classical writers. Among the most personal variants, and the most popular, were those promulgated by Michele del Giogante.[29] The one I will examine was devised by the blind poet and popular entertainer Niccolò Cieco, who performed his improvisations frequently at San Martino and was praised by his fellow poets as "the lodging-house of memories."[30] A native of the Marches, Niccolò Cieco came to Florence in 1432 and moved into Michele's house in 1435. Michele was an indefatigable recorder of Niccolò's performances, and indeed in one of his *zibaldoni* he included a sonnet of apology to his friend, which refers to a falling-out on this account: "Three stanzas that Michele di Nofri del Giogante wrote for Maestro Niccolò Cieco of Florence on December 30, 1435. Michele, wish-

26. BNF, Magl., VII, 375, fol. 61r. Perini's chapbook included Aesop's *Fables* and a water-colored table for calculating the dates of church festivals.

27. Niccolò Machiavelli to Francesco Vettori, 10 December 1513, in *The Letters of Machiavelli*, ed. and trans. A. Gilbert (Chicago, 1961), pp. 139–44. See also E. R. Curtius, *European Literature and the Latin Middle Ages* (New York, 1953), p. 526, on Dante and "the book."

28. Ricc., 1122, dated 1422; cf. his Ricc., 1402, which also contained a memory treatise. See also BNF, Pal., 54, fols. 1–5v, copyist not identified, the treatise attributed to Cicero; and BLF, Plut. 90, inf. 47, fol. 106v.

29. E.g., Ricc., 1159, fol. 12r, "Cicerone della memoria artificiale," attributed originally to Aristotle's *Ethics;* the book is in Michele's hand and belonged to Michele Grazzi. It also contained a vulgarization of the *Rosarium odor vite*, a compendium of wise sayings of the ancients, organized under categories for memorization.

30. "Albergo delle memorie." Cf. the description of Mariotto Davanzati by Feo Belcari, as "L'immenso ingegno e l'etterna memoria," in Lanza, *Lirici toscani*, 2:217.

ing to take down in writing the stanzas [Niccolò] sang at San Martino in a correct manner, and with the aid of others, and having explained this to Niccolò, who replied that he was happy about this, Niccolò later became upset, and refused to sing any more. For this reason they didn't speak to one another for three days, after which Michele decided to make peace with him by sending him these three stanzas."[31]

Introducing Niccolò's memory treatise, Michele wrote:

> Here I Michele di Nofri di Michele di Maso del Giogante, accountant, will show the principle of learning the art of memory, which was explained to me by Maestro Niccholò Ciecho of Florence in December 1435 when he came here, beginning by allotting places in my house according to the way he told me to, saying that the first five spaces should be called the first category, and then another five the second, and another five the third, . . . and so on. . . . And for each place I assigned a symbol on top of it which related to what was named underneath, and so I began with the first place outside the front door, on the bench, and then for the second, the entrance, and for the third, the chest beside the entrance, and for the fourth the window, and for the fifth the corner of the wall, and this was the first group, and then the sixth was the woodwork, and the seventh the door of the cellar, . . . and so on, as I shall show.[32]

This treatise is a Florentine artisan domestication of the schema outlined in Cicero's *De oratore*, Quintilian's *Institutio oratoria*, and the letter *Ad Herennium*, attributed erroneously to Cicero. These classical texts were well known in Florence in the early Renaissance, and there were copies in Cosimo's library, for example, by 1418.[33] The two basic models for memory treatises were the wax tablet, embodying the notion of "engraving" information on the memory, and the "storage room," which could be expanded into a house of memory. The author of *Ad Herennium* recommended that to train oneself in the art of memory, one should choose a well-lit, spacious house, with a variety of rooms through which the mind can run freely.

---

31. BNF, Pal., 215; published in Lanza, *Lirici toscani*, 2:671.

32. Ricc., 2734, fol. 28r.

33. See A. C. De La Mare, "Cosimo and His Books," in *Cosimo "il Vecchio*," pp. 115–56; also Grendler, *Literacy and Learning;* and C. Bec, *Les Livres des Florentins (1413–1609)* (Florence, 1984). As W. J. Connell pointed out, *Archivio storico italiano* 147 (1989): 369–70 n. 4, the inventory generally known as that of 1418 was begun and probably largely completed in 1417. The original date of June 1417 on the initial folio was crossed out and replaced by that of March 1418, representing presumably the completion at that date of revisions and additions to the inventory.

"Begin by fixing the plan in your imagination; then order the ideas, words, or images that you wish to remember, placing the first thing in the vestibule, the second in the *atrium*, then move around the *impluvium*, into side rooms, and even onto statues or paintings. Once you have put everything in its place, whenever you wish to recall something, start again at the entrance and move through the house, where you will find all the images linked one to another as in a chain or a chorus." Once inside his house of memory, a man could start anywhere and move either backward or forward from that point, for it was the spatial order of the storage that allowed for retrieval.[34] The advice to the student of memory to form his own images is followed faithfully in Michele del Giogante's scheme based on his own house; by contrast, Frances Yates noted in most postclassical treatises "the regular arrangement of the places in . . . memory rooms (not chosen for their unlikeness to one another and irregularity, as advised in the classical rules)."[35]

It is interesting that Florentine artisan-poets, in the city that gave such impetus to the revival of classical architecture, as well as literature, chose to base their schema on the building model in preference to the metaphor of the book. The latter might have seemed the natural choice of men so steeped in the culture of the word, especially the allegorical images of the Scriptures, which were represented in so much devotional art along with open books displaying decipherable scriptural texts.[36] However, figures and symbols associated with the arts of painting and sculpture do appear in Michele's house of memory, and not simply as signs for the objects to be found there. In his treatise *On Painting*, written in 1435, the year that Michele transcribed his treatise, Alberti expounded "a view of painting as an art of

34. See Cicero, *De oratore*, Loeb Classical Library, 2.86.351–54; Quintilian, *Institutio oratoria*, ibid., II.2.17–22; *Ad Herennium*, ibid., 3, 16–24. Also F. Yates, *The Art of Memory* (Chicago, 1966); M. Carruthers, *The Books of Memory: A Study of Memory in Medieval Culture* (Cambridge, England, 1990), esp. 33–37; B. Bergmann, "The Roman House as Memory Theater," *Art Bulletin* 76 (1994): 225–55, esp. 225.

35. Yates, *Art of Memory*, p. 109.

36. See, e.g., Angelico's paintings, including those for Cosimo at San Marco, in which there are decipherable books in several frescoes, and in the altarpiece. Petrarch's remarks in his *Secretum*, which took the form of a dialogue with Saint Augustine on the model of Augustine's own *sortes Biblicales* in the garden, recounted in *Confessions*, VIII, are an example of "regarding books as personal sources whose function is to provide memorial cues to oneself, divine influences being able to prophesy through the images of letters on the page just as they are during sleep through the images written in the memory"; Carruthers, *Books of Memory*, p. 163.

memory";[37] Michele's scheme illuminates the relation between images and memory in the popular mind.

The second part of the treatise deals with the eight "figures" of memory, moving from the known to the unknown, with the aid of imagination.[38] The "actual figure" is for "men, women and other things that you have seen and known and dealt with . . . what you can see and touch," to be associated with places, "or their symbols or devices." The "imaginative figure" is for people or objects "which you have not seen or known or had experience of, except for what you have heard or found in writing. . . . You will have heard it said that Hercules was a just and powerful man, and you want to keep his name in your mind, but never having seen or known him . . . you must have faith in your imagining of what he is . . . this is necessary to all the other figures, and none . . . can work without it, because imagination is always open to all forms of language or means of communication [*ydioma*]." The "significative figure" takes the first letter of a name and links it to one beginning with the same letter, "which you cannot forget; if you want to remember Sant' Ambrogio and you are called Antonio, use your own name; . . . in this chain and group you can retain the other." The "figure of pronunciation" is similarly simple; faced with a word without associations, like "a name in a language you don't understand, divide it into syllables which have meaning in your own language."

The "figure of the skill," involves a principle upon which many Florentine lists or descriptions of people were based; "for a man, think of his craft or profession . . . for a thing, in what profession it is used." The "figure of fame" accords with both classical and Florentine social values, being the recall of the object by its fame or reputation, good or evil. The "figure of the will" depends, like the choice of texts to be preserved in *zibaldoni* and memorized, upon an imaginative conception of the relevance of something to oneself: "Think of this man or woman or thing, of what you would like to do with it . . . or what you would like to see happen to it, whether good or ill . . . like a beautiful palace . . . saying to yourself, if it were mine, I would like to have it all decorated with images and stories in mosaics of gold; if you hate it, you should say, let it be set on fire today rather than tomorrow,

37. For both the Latin and Italian versions, see Leon Battista Alberti, *Opere volgari*, 3 vols., ed. Cecil Grayson (Bari, 1960–73); also M. Pardo, "Memory, Imagination, Figuration: Leonardo da Vinci and the Painter's Mind," in *Images of Memory: On Remembering and Representation*, ed. S. Küchler and W. Melion (Washington D.C., 1991), esp. pp. 47–48.

38. Ricc., 2734, fols. 30r–32r.

so that I may see it reduced to ashes down to the foundations, together with him who had it built." The eighth, the "effective figure," required attaching to a man or object the opposite of the truth, "like imagining that you would like to see a good man hanged." Michele assured his readers that "these eight figures of artificial memory constitute every method and manner of being able to remember every name of a man or a woman or other animal or other memorable thing . . . numbers, events, prose, allegories in sermons, the speeches of ambassadors, readings, each and every thing."

Both Quintilian and the author of *Ad Herennium* discussed at length the importance of symbolism and historical allegory, and Cicero equated this with "translation" or "the connection of many metaphors, so that one thing may be said and another understood."[39] As Kristeller observed of the contents of literary anthologies, in these metaphorical language became a philosophical medium.[40] That is the principle underlying preachers' analyses of images of the Passion of Christ, which specifically relate metaphor and memory to visual images and their viewing. Confraternal devotion and constant listening to sermons, carefully constructed to be memorized, accustomed Florentines to the habit of mind recommended in a Venetian text, *The Garden of Prayer:*

> The better to impress the story of the Passion on your mind, and to memorize each action of it more easily, it is helpful and necessary to fix the places and people in your mind: a city, for example, which will be the city of Jerusalem—taking for this purpose a city that is well known to you. In this city find the principal places in which all the episodes of the Passion would have taken place—for instance, a palace with the supper-room where Christ had the Last Supper with the disciples, and the house of Anne and that of Caiaphas, . . . etc. And then too you must shape in your mind some people, people well-known to you, to represent for you the people involved in the Passion—the person of Jesus Himself, of the Virgin, Saint Peter, Saint John the Evangelist.[41]

39. On this, see D. C. Allen, *Mysteriously Meant: The Recovery of Pagan Symbolism and Allegorical Interpretation in the Renaissance* (Baltimore, 1970), pp. viii–ix.

40. P. O. Kristeller, "Marsilio Ficino as a Man of Letters and the Glosses Attributed to Him in the Caetani Codex of Dante," *Renaissance Quarterly* 36 (1983): 1–34. On sermons, see R. F. E. Weissman, *Ritual Brotherhood in Renaissance Florence* (New York, 1982), pp. 63, 83–85; also I. Origo, *The World of San Bernardino* (London, 1964), pp. 39–40.

41. M. Baxandall, *Painting and Experience in Fifteenth-Century Italy*, 2d ed. (Oxford, 1988), p. 46.

Michele's treatise offers a formal method for this imaginative exercise, which works in reverse in the extensive use of visual images and metaphors in popular devotional poetry.[42] As the author of *Ad Herennium* observed, "The artificial memory includes backgrounds and images. . . . we first go over a given verse twice or three times to ourselves, and then represent the words by means of images. In this way art will supplement nature."[43]

Popular culture and Michele del Giogante's personal identity are equally enshrined in his memory treatise, built upon the foundation of his own house. The contents of his home and his mind are inventoried in the following list from his treatise, of one hundred places in his house and the associations they evoked for him:[44]

1. The bench outside, and I call it "The first Seat, the first place," and upon it a king. (He is put on top of these places as a coat of arms.)[45]

2. The door to the street . . . the sword.

3. The large chest [*cassa*] beside the door . . . the keys of the door.

---

42. A translation of metaphorical language characterized alternatively as "ut rhetorica pictura" or "ut pictura poesis"; for the popular application of these precepts, see Kent, *Cosimo de' Medici*, pp. 104–6.

43. On memory treatises, see Kent, *Cosimo de' Medici*, pp. 91–93. For a brilliantly articulated example of the imaginative use of images along the lines suggested in these passages, eliding play, dream, and rite, see C. Klapisch-Zuber, "Holy Dolls: Play and Piety in Florence in the Quattrocento," in Klapisch-Zuber, *Women, Family, and Ritual in Renaissance Italy*, trans. L. G. Cochrane (Chicago, 1985), pp. 310–29.

44. Ricc., 2374, fols. 28r–29v, new numeration. Omitted are the repetitions of the number of each object, except at the beginning of each new category. My translation for the benefit of the general reader is offered with some trepidation. Many obscure terms are arcane, colloquial, or architectural; I am grateful to Gino Corti and to Brenda Preyer for their advice on meaning and translation. Specialists will no doubt wish to consult the original document, bringing their own expertise to bear on its translation, but for their benefit, terms referring to architecture and furniture are translated once, and then left in Italian. Some usages seem to express the poet's taste for intentional ambiguity and multivalent wordplay. Since there is no such thing as a "most likely" translation where there is no context, the author being engaged in fanciful and wholly personal association of words and images, alternative English equivalents are offered in some cases. Occasionally the Trecento and Quattrocento usage of problematic words is documented, especially if the texts cited appear in Michele's *zibaldoni* or the compilations of his close friends. An asterisk (*) signifies an archaic usage. References are to B. Reynolds, *Cambridge Italian Dictionary*, vol. 1 (Cambridge, England, 1981); and N. Tommaseo, *Dizionario della lingua italiana*, 20 vols. (Milan, 1983).

45. The passage in parentheses was inserted above this line, signaled by a pointing hand (*manina*).

4. The closed-off window above the *cassa* . . . hanging from it the arms for defense.

5. The corner by the window, fifth place and first category . . . the banner hanging there.

6. The woodwork along the floor of that wall . . . a body shield.

7. The door of the cellar . . . a lantern upon it.

8. The console [*mensola*] as you go in to the cellar underground . . . a cockerel upon it.

9. A funnel for filling casks [*pevera*] next to that *mensola*, nearer the entrance of the cellar . . . a Barbary ape/old busybody [*bretuccia*] upon it.[46]

10. The stair of the cellar, tenth place and second category, the fairy upon it.

11. The bucket of olives on the landing of the stair . . . a mouse upon it.

12. The basket of kitchen utensils hanging on the wall in the cellar . . . a charcoal burner upon it.

13. Casks of vinegar on the right-hand side of the cellar . . . a Jew upon them.

14. The supply of oil in that hollowed-out place facing the street . . . the bat upon it.

15. The dark corner next to the cellar on the right-hand side, fifteenth place and third category, the idle man [*lo nighittoso*] upon it.[47]

16. White wine from the piazza in small casks from four adjacent barrels . . . the pig upon it.

17. Distilled *vermiglio* wine in the other casks alongside . . . the bell upon it.

18. The ewer on the protective wall [*ritegno*] around the stairs at the door of the cellar . . . a rope/halter [*capresto*] upon it.

19. The water dipper beside the door of the cellar, or rather the taster . . . flames of fire upon it.

20. The arch of the granary at ground level where today one gains access to it, twentieth place and fourth category, the flail/strap/belt [*correggaio*][48] upon it.

21. The lion of the staircase on the ground floor, twenty-first sign . . . the weasel upon it.

---

46. Tommaseo: a Barbary ape; * pej. a ridiculous old woman or witch, a gossip, cf. *la cenerina, la spinetta;* sources, *Volgarizzamento della Biblia;* Sacchetti, *Novelle.*

47. Tommaseo: * Che fugge la fatica, lento, pigro: sources, *Trattato dei Sette peccati mortali;* Brunetto Latini, *Tesoretto;* Petrarch, *Canzoni;* Sacchetti, *Rime.*

48. Since many of Michele's signs have moral significance, and many Florentines belonged to a flagellant confraternity, flail seems very likely.

22. The staircase up from the ground floor to the main room [*sala*] . . . the wheel of fortune upon it.

23. The door at the half-landing of the stair below the *sala* . . . Hope dressed in green upon it.

24. The bread box [*cassa*] up in the *sala* next to the stair . . . a missal upon it.

25. The shelf [*schianceria*] of the *sala* coming from the stairs, twenty-fifth place and fifth category, the cat upon it.

26. The landing [*lassito*] outside the *sala*, that is, the banister [*paratio*] of the stair going upward . . . vainglory upon it.

27. The pinewood stair going from the *sala* up to the kitchen . . . King Herod upon it.

28. The door in the guardrail [*guardia*] halfway up the stairs from the *sala* to the kitchen . . . Geta upon it.

29. The store-cupboard [*armaro*] of the treasure, that is, the cupboard in the kitchen up above . . . the snake upon it.

30. The wood supply, that is, the *armaro* underneath it, up in the kitchen, thirtieth place and sixth category, the donkey upon it.

31. The dustpan, that is, the place near the dustpan . . . the white rabbit upon it.

32. The bread supply, that is, the shelf above in the kitchen . . . a bunch of leaves on it.

33. The servant's room up above, upon it . . . two sieves, one fine and one coarse.

34. The servant's bed in that room above . . . upon it the spider/spider's web.

35. The outside terrace/balcony, that is, above on the other side of that room, thirty-fifth place and seventh category, two peacocks upon it.

36. The wall of the birdseed, going back into the room on the right-hand side . . . a dovecote upon it.

37. The black corner of that room on the right-hand side, coming out of the *razze* and this is because there are *bracie* there . . . the salamander upon it.[49]

38. The surface of the window of that room, in fact with a spy-hole . . . a bow upon it.

---

49. There are numerous possible translations of these terms; I leave the reader to imagine or envisage the image for himself, in accordance with Michele's advice, above, pp. 123–24.

39. The flour supply on the shelf on the right-hand side of the bread...
Abundance in the figure of a woman.

40. The big fireplace of the kitchen as you go along the wall where the stair is, fortieth place and eighth category, an oiled skin upon it.

41. The small window [*finistretta*] above the canopy/roof [*tetto*] down in the kitchen by the big fireplace ... the window box upon it.

42. The wood column between two windows in the kitchen that look over the street ... a pair of snares [*tranpoli*].

43. The corner of the guttering [*doccioni*] up in the kitchen next to the flasks by the bread ... a cloud upon it.

44. The double column, that is, the wall of the fireplace of the kitchen... the duck on it.

45. The reinforced wall [*la faccia del cerchio*] beside the wall of the fireplace that goes up from the *sala* into the kitchen, forty-fifth place and ninth category, the saw upon it.

46. The shield of the authority of the keys on the stair in the kitchen... Paradise on it.

47. The new room up above the kitchen ... the broom upon it.

48. The first corner on the right of that new room above ... a grappling hook upon it.

49. The white column in the middle of the wall of that room on the right side ... a pigeon upon it.

50. The pantry [*guardaspensa*] of that new room up above the kitchen, fiftieth place, tenth category, Avicenna the doctor there.

51. The wall of the flask, that is, coming out of the *guardaspensa* on the right-hand side in that new room, there is a flask hung on the wall (this was put in that place to serve as a crest/device)[50] ... on it the sleeping man.[51]

52. The column of the maiden/serving woman [*donzella*], that is, on the column on that wall there was a Dacian woman painted on a sheet of paper ... the parrot upon it.

53. The *anticameretta* of that new room called the dark one, because the window over the courtyard is closed off ... the witch inside it.

54. The corner of the keyhole [*toppa*], that is, the first corner on the right-hand side of that *cameretta* to which is attached a large lock of worked gold [*a oro aguto*] ... on it the clock.

---

50. The passage in parentheses was inserted above the line.

51. Tommaseo: Augustine, in his *City of God*, describes the ecstatic visions "delli dormenti"; Michele's reference to his crest may be a joke about drinking.

55. The big window of the *cameretta* over the courtyard, fifty-fifth [place] and eleventh category, the goose upon it.

56. The entrance to my room from the main *sala*, that is, after coming down again into the *sala* as you go up into my room . . . a French carpet hanging there.

57. My big bed as you go into that room . . . Adam and Eve upon it.

58. The first chest [*cassone*] behind the bolster of the bed . . . upon it an inscription [*breve*] which says "Keep your hands to yourself."[52]

59. The chessboard above the *cassone* between two things hung there . . . a Saracen and a Corsican upon it.

60. The *guardaspensa* of that *camera*, sixtieth place and twelfth category . . . an orange upon it.

61. The small new cupboard [*armaretto*] outside the door of the *guardaspe[n]sa* . . . a bronze mortar with a pestle.

62. The cot [*letuccio*] in my room . . . a trumpet/whore upon it.

63. The backboard of the *lettuccio* . . . upon it Cato as an old man wearing a small hat.

64. The *cassone* for linens in the *cameretta* above the study . . . a thief with a bundle on his back.

65. The corner of the sword in the *cameretta* above the study, sixty-fifth place and third category, a painting of Hector upon it.

66. The window opening of the woodpile, that is, the one that looks over the courtyard there . . . Serena upon it.

67. The corner of the boots, that is, after you pass the window . . . a messenger upon it.

68. The place of the nets, that is, hung on the wall on the left . . . the fisherman upon it.

69. The place of the arms, that is, in a storage area [*armaro*] for armguards [*braciali*] and other arms . . . the frog upon it.

70. The place of Our Lady, when you come down again into my room, seventieth place and fourteenth category, upon it David with an open book.

71. The little window of the alcove [*chiostro*] when you come out of my room beside the study outside it . . . the crow upon it.[53]

---

52. A *breve* is also a small pouch for devotional objects, worn around the neck, such as Michele might have done when attending confraternal meetings, or it may simply refer to an inscription, perhaps on a cartouche, attached either to the *cassone* or possibly to such a pouch.

53. The crow's mainly negative symbolism derives from the Bible and was popularized by Brunetto Latini's *Tesoro*, Iacopo Passavanti's *Specchio di vera Penitenza*,

72. The door of the laurel, that is, the door of the study . . . a garland of laurel.

73. The study with the scholar . . . half a loaf for firm faith [*mezzo pane per fede sobrio*].[54]

74. The cupboard [*armaro*] of knowledge, with many drawers . . . Averroës the philosopher, who wrote the great commentary.

75. The *cassone* for provisions in the study, seventy-fifth place, fifteenth [category], the sheep upon it.

76. The corner of the arrow in the study by the *cassone* and the window . . . the fox upon it.

77. The *finestruzza* of that study . . . upon it the cruel tiger who is malevolent.

78. In the corner of the ironware beside the window, the face of Vulcan.

79. The place of the fallen [*guati*] as you go into the study on the wall on the right . . . (these are the arms of the places for arms)[55] upon it the nettle.

80. The plaster table in that place on that wall nearest the door of the study, eightieth place and sixteenth category, the chair of the master [*la cattedra del maestro*].

81. The well of the Samaritan woman, that is our well . . . Jesus upon it.

82. The greasy door in the kitchen to the covered porch [*verone*] . . . a pig run through with a skewer.[56]

83. The piazza of the saucepans, that is, the flat place where there is a large tray on the right-hand side as you go into the kitchen . . . the tree of the sausages.

84. The corner of the vinegar, that is, the corner on the right-hand side

---

Sacchetti's *Novelle* and letters, and Tuscan proverbs, referring to someone who is not coming or will not return. Cf. Boccaccio's *Corbaccio*.

54. Obviously a proverb; see Tommaseo for a sample of those involving bread.

55. The passage in parentheses was inserted above the line. It thus contributes to the significance of one of the more obscure sets of association, of which the first term (*guati*) may include a concrete reference to structural damage to the house but in Quattrocento usage almost always refers to those fallen in battle (see Tommaseo); the nettle is something that, however painfully, must be grasped. This pairing should perhaps be related to the other associations Michele's study evoked in his mind, esp. nos. 71, 72, 73, and 77, which might add up to a wry suggestion of some difficulties in his confrontations with literature and learning.

56. Giovanni dalle Celle's letter to Guido del Palagio, which Michele transcribed in several *zibaldoni*, referring to the pig fattened only for slaughter, "as the world fattens its lovers," might add moral resonance to the obvious association of roast pigs with kitchen grease.

as you go into the kitchen, beside the stair to go down, where there is a barrel of vinegar . . . a beehive.[57]

85.   The place of the onion, that is, a small bar above that street [*una stanghetta sopr' al detta *borghora*][58] . . . a yoke [*giogho*].

86.   The customary walled-up window [*la costumata quella finestra murata*] which is the only window that remains of the house of Ser Baldese, known as "the well-mannered" [*lo costumato*, a play on words] . . . a pair of dice.

87.   The soup-plate place, that is, the tray for the dishes next to it . . . a rabbit in a trance.

88.   The shelf [*schianceria*] by the tray . . . the dog [blank] with the eyes.[59]

89.   The door of the *camera* above the kitchen . . . a wheel of archangels (below, canceled, "crown . . .").[60]

90.   The black column, that is, a small column on the wall next to the door of that *camera* . . . a papal miter.

91.   The cage for hunting on that wall, beside the window that was there . . . the goat.

92.   The closed-off window of the kitchen . . . wise Merlin.

93.   The fireplace of the kitchen . . . a river to receive it.

94.   The glass supply, that is, a hole for the glass next to the fireplace . . . a furnace.

95.   The water dipper in the kitchen . . . la Cichogna.

96.   The place of the branch as you come out of the kitchen onto the porch [*verone*] on the right-hand side . . . a scabrous man [*tignoso*].

97.   The mirror, that is, because there was a mirror right beside the wall on the right of the terrace, as you go out of the kitchen, opposite the well . . . la Marta.[61]

98.   The large table laid out on the terrace . . . the bride prepared for her wedding.

---

57.   Nos. 82–85, 96, and 40–41 may imply an outside staircase.

58.   Tommaseo: in Villani, as in Borgo Pinti, street.

59.   The dog is generally associated with faithfulness and watchfulness. Michele left a space apparently to insert the name of a particular dog; he may have had in mind Cerberus, the three-headed dog that guarded the entry to Hades, brought back by Hercules, associated also with Virgil's *Aeneid*, and Christ's descent into Limbo, described in the *Golden Legend*, and Dante's *Inferno*, cantos 3 and 4.

60.   The wheel or crown of angels, an image derived from Revelations, is often represented in later Renaissance painting.

61.   Martha and Mary were the sisters of Lazarus, whom Christ raised from the dead: John 11–12. They symbolized the active and the contemplative life.

99.   The column on the wall . . . Blind Samson.

100.   The falconer's lure [*logoro*], that is, a lure which hung from the wall next to the column, going toward the door of our room . . . a falcon.

Seen from the most pedestrian point of view, Michele's treatise resembles the inventories of houses and possessions that many Florentines made regularly in accordance with mercantile practice.[62] However, even inventories could inspire flights of fancy not as foreign as some scholars seem to imagine to commerce, and to "gouty old bankers," as they like to represent Cosimo de' Medici.[63] De Robertis artfully observes that nonsense verses in which others desperately seek some deeper meaning are more likely wordplays on the random nature of the inventory, representing simply the pure fantasy of which the popular poets sang.[64] "I write," said Burchiello, ". . . because my head is full of fantasy."[65] Even Machiavelli, he of the hardest-nosed image of them all, remarked that "each man governs himself according to his fantasy."[66] Solid objects as well as ideas could be woven into this airy fabric; in Michele's mental game of ambivalent and ambiguous wordplay, concrete and abstract are maintained in continuous but uncertain balance.

Many of Michele's signs obviously sprang from the elaboration of personal fantasy, impossible to recapture or reconstruct. Some of the objects and their symbols are clearly drawn from a memory bank of elements from familiar Christian, classical, or popular traditions, with a few exotic images thrown in. The missal and the pope's miter were associated with the church and its ceremonies. A witch naturally dwelt in a dark place. The orange and

62. R. Goldthwaite, "The Florentine Palace as Domestic Architecture," *American Historical Review* 77 (1972): 977–1012, first suggested how much the furnishings of palaces might reveal about the values of their owners. See also J. K. Lydecker, "The Domestic Setting of the Arts in Renaissance Florence" (Ph.D. diss., Johns Hopkins University, 1987); M. Spallanzani, ed., *Inventari Medicei 1417–1465* (Florence, 1996).

63. See particularly A. Field, *The Origins of the Platonic Academy of Florence* (Princeton, N.J., 1988), chap. 1, pp. 3–9; J. Hankins, "Cosimo de' Medici and the Platonic Academy," *Journal of the Warburg and Courtauld Institutes* 53 (1990): 144–62.

64. "L'esperienza poetica del Quattrocento: Una proposta per Burchiello," *Rinascimento*, ser. 2, 8 (1968): 110–20.

65. ". . . perchè il mio capo è pien' di fantasia"; A. Lanza, *Polemiche e Berte Letterarie nella Firenze del primo Rinascimento* (Rome, 1989), p. 377. This pleasing notion was adopted by other poets, such as Bernardo Biffoli; see Lanza, *Lirici toscani*, 1:298.

66. Machiavelli noted this in the margin of a letter discussed by P. Bondanella and M. Musa, eds., *The Portable Machiavelli* (New York, 1979), p. 62.

the falcon were devices adopted by the Medici: Michele wrote a whole sonnet for them about oranges.[67] Symbols in more general use in Florence included the wheel of fortune and the laurel wreath. The Saracino and the Corsiano on the chessboard may refer to the forms of the chessmen, but their use as signs was likely inspired by a fascination with the exotic worlds of northern Africa and the East, described in popular anthology items like Dati's *Sfera*[68] and the letters of Prester John, king of Ethiopia, which Michele transcribed in several collections.[69] The numerous animals he names, particularly the salamander, could be elements of heraldry but more likely relate to medieval bestiaries, which provided moral exempla, and most likely of all to the *Fables* of Aesop, which appear, accompanied sometimes by illustrations, in many popular compilations.[70] Wise Merlin belongs to the cycle of Arthurian tales probably told, along with the epic deeds of the Trojan War and of Charlemagne's battles, at San Martino.[71] Hector and the aged Cato are classical exempla, respectively, of military and domestic virtue and of Stoic integrity, while Blind Samson and King Herod, representing the betrayal of strength and trust, are exempla from the Bible. Lists of such exempla are included in most *quaderni*, along with proverbs and the closely related genre of *facetiae*, moral tales supposedly referring to real people and events.[72] The warning on the object behind Michele's bed, "Keep your hands to yourself," and the presumably admonitory reminder of vainglory in the banister of the stair are in a similar vein.

67. Ricc., 2729, 50. On Medici arms, S. McKillop, "L'ampliamento dello stemma mediceo e il suo contesto politico," *Archivio storico italiano* 150 (1992): 641–73.

68. This text appears in BNF, Magl., II.II.81, fol. 47v; ibid., II.IX.137, fols. 11r–21r; Pal., 215; BRF, Ricc., 1091, 1163, 1185, 2729; BLF, Conv. soppr., 109, fol. 51r; Plut. 90, sup. 103.

69. BNF, II.II.39; BRF, Ricc., 2729. They were also included in compilations by other authors: BNF, II.I.102; II.I.195; Strozz., II.II.102; BRF, Ricc., 1279; Ricc., 1475, and mentioned in a letter of Ser Alesso Pelli to Giovanni de' Medici, ASF, MAP, V, 418, 22 August 1441. On both of these texts, see D. Kent, *Cosimo de' Medici*, pp. 90–91, 313.

70. The owner of Ricc. 1591 noted that "chostò lire tre e mezo la dipintura a 'ndre del verrochino," referring to illustrations of selections from Aesop and *Geta e Birria*. The same texts are similarly illustrated in BRF, Ricc., 2805; and BNF, Magl., XXI.87; for further comment, see Tanturli, "Ambienti letterari fiorentini"; Kent, *Cosimo de' Medici*, p. 76.

71. Kent, *Cosimo de' Medici*, pp. 52, 278.

72. On *facetiae* in general, and for particular comment on Herod's image in proverbial wisdom, see A. Brown, "Cosimo de' Medici's Wit and Wisdom," in *Cosimo "il Vecchio,"* pp. 95–113. Poggio Bracciolini ridiculed a member of the audience at San Martino for his absorption in the singer's tale of Hector's death; Bracciolini, *Facezie*, ed. M. Ciccuto (Milan, 1993), no. 83, p. 203.

Michele's household well evoked by obvious association Jesus' meeting at Jacob's well with the Samaritan woman, the water of life, and the prophecy of the coming of Christ, so appropriately its symbol was Jesus.[73] Averroës and Avicenna were Arab scholars integrated into the late medieval compendium of learning by Aquinas and Dante, and represented in Michele's memory by their writings. Geta (and Birria) was the name of a risqué popular poem satirizing scholars of the classics, which derived from a Plautus comedy via a Goliardic version by Gilles of Blois. Much copied and quoted in the Quattrocento, it was this work that diverted Machiavelli as he lay under the olive trees on lazy afternoons.[74] "The shield of the authority of the keys on the stairs in the kitchen" Michele naturally connected with the keys of the kingdom of heaven, and so paradise was its symbol; he might have meant either the place of the blessed or the third volume of the Divine Comedy, since so many of his signs were books. The sign of the door to the study was the laurel wreath bestowed on poets and victors of contests, like the Certame Coronario organized by Alberti and sponsored by Piero de' Medici, in which Michele took part.[75] David holding the open book of his Psalms was an image of great resonance for members of devotional confraternities, which incorporated the Psalms into their services, and all patriotic Florentines saw the young and valiant David as the symbol of their city opposing the aggression of great powers, identified with Goliath.[76]

The image of Hector seems to have been an actual picture, like the Dacian woman painted on a sheet of paper attached to a column. Michele may also have owned a painting or bust of Cato which he envisaged on the backboard of the daybed. "Abbondanza in the figure of a woman" was probably a replica of Donatello's statue, which stood on an antique column in the Mercato Vecchio, symbolizing charity, and was associated with the communal provision of grain for the poor; not surprisingly, it was linked in Michele's mind with his household grain store.[77] The other theological virtues

73. John 4:5–30.
74. On the place of this work in fifteenth-century popular culture, see Kent, Cosimo de' Medici, pp. 73, 82; and Machiavelli's letter to Vettori, 1512, cit. supra. On Machiavelli's debt to Geta and Birria, see J. M. Najemy, Between Friends: Discourses of Power and Desire in the Machiavelli-Vettori Letters of 1513–1515 (Princeton, N.J., 1993), pp. 221–30.
75. On this, see Kent, Cosimo de' Medici, p. 28 and passim.
76. Ibid., esp. pp. 52, 282.
77. See esp. D. Wilkins, "Donatello's Lost Dovizia for the Mercato Vecchio: Wealth and Charity as Florentine Civic Virtues," Art Bulletin 45 (1983): 401–23; S. Blake Wilk McHam, "Donatello's Dovizia as an Image of Florentine Political Propaganda," Artibus et Historiae 14 (1986): 9–28.

appear in his house of memory in the form of a proverb, "half a loaf for firm faith," being the sign of the scholar in his study, and the figure of Hope, dressed in green. Michele's association of Adam and Eve with his own large bed and of the table laid out on the balcony with a bride prepared for her wedding are particularly memorable. Ultimately, given that the point of constructing a personal house of memory was to fill it with exceptional images, things striking or even disfigured, or associations drawn from childhood, considered to be what we remember best, the significance of Michele's choices must remain conjectural.[78]

Perhaps the most substantial interest of this document lies in its very rare description of the layout and contents of a modest fifteenth-century house, not the palace of a wealthy patrician but the relatively humble home of a notary. As such, it is interesting that it contains a number of decorative pieces like *pennoni,* and various pictures and statues, including the lion at the foot of the stairs. This may have been an image of Florence's symbolic Marzocco, like the one carved by Donatello, which occupied the same position on the staircase of the papal residence at Santa Maria Novella. Michele owned a few luxury items, among them a French carpet, a clock, and a mirror, removed but still remembered. However, the house was generally sparsely furnished, as was the norm in this period, apart from the exceptional case of the Medici palace. There were several tables, including one of *gesso,* and a number of *armadi* and *cassoni,* but only a few beds and chairs.[79]

Like many ordinary houses reconstructed from inventories and surviving structures, the plan of Michele's home seems to have been irregular, built on three or four levels, with storage and other spaces between floors connected by flights of stairs. One of these went down to a cellar where wine, vinegar, water, oil, grain, and olives were kept. The main staircase in the entrance hall led up to the main living room, the *sala;* above it was the kitchen with a fireplace. Above the kitchen was a servant's room and a new *camera* with *anticamera,* and a terrace open to the street. Above the *sala* was Mi-

---

78. See *Ad Herennium,* III. xvi–xxiv. Since what one sees in texts depends on what one brings to them, others may well discern in this one associations that have escaped me.

79. On furniture in domestic inventories, see Lydecker, "Domestic Setting," pp. 46–47, which Richard Goldthwaite describes (Goldthwaite, "The Empire of Things," in *Patronage, Art and Society in Renaissance Italy,* ed. F. W. Kent and P. Simons [Oxford, 1987], pp. 153–75) as established practice only toward the end of the century. Cf. Marco Parenti's list of household goods, Phillips, *Memoir,* pt. 1, pp. 23–96. On ordinary Florentines' patronage of art, see S. K. Cohn Jr., *The Cult of Remembrance and the Black Death: Six Cities in Central Italy* (Baltimore, 1992); Kent, *Cosimo de' Medici,* pp. 110–15.

chele's room. One storage space containing arms was reached by a stair, and may have been an attic. The windows overlooked either the street or a court-yard with a well, and the house of Ser Baldese, nicknamed "il costumato." [80]

This memory treatise, which Michele del Giogante based on Niccolò Cieco's scheme, has many implications for our understanding of Florentine Renaissance culture, especially popular culture, and particularly for the or-dinary man's conception of art and architecture and the cultural equipment he brought to its viewing. What Michele's memory scheme tells us, apart from what was in his own house, is that the minds of Renaissance men were a mass of associations, things that "stood for" other things. This is some-thing we need to understand about Florentine ways of looking at the world, and its representation in works of art. Artists themselves, as Francis Has-kell observes, create memory with the "self-conscious citation of one work of art by another." [81] That was particularly true of Renaissance artists, who built up a framework of customarily connected classical and Christian im-ages that helped viewers to interpret new ones and tended to make the prac-tice of viewing an exercise in the rehearsal of learning. [82] The Muses, the goddesses of creative inspiration in poetry, music, and history, were after all the daughters of Jupiter and Mnemosyne, literally born out of memory that forged the links between past and present, words and images, and the various distinct but ingeniously integrated elements of Florentine culture.

80. For some architectural reconstructions, see H. Saalman and P. Mattox, "The First Medici Palace," *Journal of the Society of Architectural Historians* 44 (1985): 329–45; and B. Preyer's studies, particularly "The 'chasa overo palagio' of Alberto di Zanobi," *Art Bulletin* 45 (1983): 613–60.

81. *History and Its Images: Art and the Interpretation of the Past* (London, 1993), p. ix.

82. R. Starn, in a lecture for the Renaissance Society of America, New York, 1988, an early version of his "Seeing Culture in 'A Room for a Renaissance Prince,'" in *The New Cultural History*, ed. L. Hunt (Berkeley and Los Angeles, 1989).

5 Inheritance and Identity in Early Renaissance Florence

The Estate of Paliano di Falco

Thomas Kuehn

HONOR AND LITIGATION

In his novel about a Sardinian village in the early twentieth century, Salvatore Satta, himself a jurist, depicted a society wracked with ubiquitous, never-ending lawsuits. "It was not a question of winning or losing it, and indeed it was vital to do neither, for otherwise the lawsuit would be over and done with. A lawsuit was part of the personality, if not the only visible sign of it, to such an extent that there was often no real animosity between the litigants, because they both needed each other."[1] Satta's Sardinian villagers used the impersonal and abstract nature of codified law and state-run courts for their own purposes. In a culture of honor, forms of antagonism and assertions of ownership were necessary and frequently expressed.[2] To have enemies, especially prominent and important ones, was a sign of one's weight in the community. Law furnished means of self-definition, personhood, and social identity. This was no less true in the Italian cities of the Renaissance.[3] It is the intent of this chapter to examine identity forged in the crucible of law from the evidence provided by a single Florentine family from the early fifteenth century.

1. Salvatore Satta, *The Day of Judgment*, trans. P. Creagh (New York, 1987), p. 291.

2. Cf. J. G. Peristiany, ed., *Honour and Shame: The Values of Mediterranean Society* (Chicago, 1966); J. Davis, *People of the Mediterranean: An Essay in Comparative Social Anthropology* (London, 1977), esp. pp. 89–101; J. K. Campbell, *Honour, Family and Patronage* (Oxford, 1964); P. Bourdieu, *Outline of a Theory of Practice*, trans. R. Nice (Cambridge, England, 1977).

3. Cf. the remarks of G. Savino Pene Vidari, "Dote, famiglia e patrimonio fra dottrina e pratica in Piemonte," in *La famiglia e la vita quotidiana in Europa dal '400 al '600: Fonti e problemi* (Rome, 1986), pp. 109–21 at 121, where he points to the role of law and jurists, as well as litigants, in perpetuating suits.

That participation in civic politics for Florentines was fired by the requisites of family honor has become a cherished truism.[4] Family honor demanded not only wealth, social connections, and political participation but also some knowledge of and willingness to use law, keeping records and preserving legal documents, establishing familiarity with notaries and jurists.[5] Beyond its broad systemic features, law had discursive functions. Litigants and other "laymen" were participants in this discourse, not just its passive victims, if only because as an audience they needed to be persuaded to accept the practical effects of the law. After all, it is the litigants who, even today, more so in the past, bring the cases to the courts and choose to use legal mechanisms and to obey, break, or manipulate legal rules. It may well be that supremacy of law in some societies leads to high rates of litigiousness, but that supremacy also arises from a degree of acceptance and a willingness to use law.[6]

Just as honor was something one inherited (which, like material wealth, could then be squandered or increased by one's own actions), animosities and alliances were also inheritable. Inheritance itself became not only an economically pivotal moment in one's life but a socially identifying one as well. The *famiglia* or *casa* was a moral entity, made up of people and prop-

4. Cf. G. Brucker, *The Civic World of Early Renaissance Florence* (Princeton, N.J., 1977); N. Rubinstein, *The Government of Florence under the Medici (1434– 1494)*, 2d ed. (Oxford, 1997); M. Becker, *Florence in Transition*, 2 vols. (Baltimore, 1967–68); J. M. Najemy, *Corporatism and Consensus in Florentine Electoral Politics, 1280–1400* (Chapel Hill, N.C., 1982); D. Kent, *The Rise of the Medici: Faction in Florence, 1426–1434* (Oxford, 1978); L. Martines, *Power and Imagination: City-States in Renaissance Italy* (New York, 1979); and Martines, *The Social World of the Florentine Humanists, 1390–1460* (Princeton, N.J., 1963).

5. Cf. T. Kuehn, "Il diritto di famiglia e l'uso del diritto nelle famiglie fiorentine nel Rinascimento," in *Palazzo Strozzi: Metà millennio, 1489–1989* (Rome, 1991), pp. 108–25; Kuehn, "Antropologia giuridica dello Stato," in *Origini dello Stato*, ed. G. Chittolini, A. Molho, and P. Schiera (Milan, 1994), pp. 367–80; J. Kirshner, "Some Problems in the Interpretation of Legal Texts re the Italian City-States," *Archiv für Begriffsgeschichte* 19 (1975): 16–27; I. Baumgärtner, "Consilia: Quellen für Familie in Krise und Kontinuität," in *Die Familie als sozialer und historischer Verband: Untersuchungen zum Spätmittelalter und zur frühen Neuzeit*, ed. P.-J. Schuler (Sigmaringen, 1987), pp. 43–66; O. Cavallar, "Il tiranno, i *dubia* del giudice, e i *consilia* dei giuristi," *Archivio storico italiano* 155 (1997): 265–345; and essays by Cavallar, Kirshner, Kuehn, and Romano in *Legal Consulting in the Civil Law Tradition*, ed. M. Ascheri, I. Baumgärtner, and J. Kirshner (Berkeley, 1999).

6. Cf. R. C. van Caenegem, *Judges, Legislators and Professors: Chapters in European Legal History* (Cambridge, England, 1987), p. 163; O. Cavallar, "Lo 'stare fermo a bottega' del Guicciardini: giuristi consulenti, procuratori e notai del Rinascimento," in *Consilia im späten Mittelalter: Zum historischen Aussagewert einer Quellengattung*, ed. I. Baumgärtner (Sigmaringen, 1995), pp. 113–44.

erty (real and symbolic). The continuity of this entity was itself a moral imperative, captured in the term *ragion di famiglia*, evoked countless times in contemporary writings and elevated to the level of historical commonplace by the perceptive modern historians of cities like Florence.[7] This continuity was also an imperative of *publica utilitas*, captured primarily in statutes of Italian city-states seeking to preserve property in the male line.[8] The *Digest* of the Roman law dedicated fully one-quarter of its bulk to legal problems of inheritance, and with the addition of inheritance rules from the canon law, the feudal law, and myriad local statutes, it is no wonder that jurists expressed the belief that these were the most fundamental, important, and difficult areas of the law.[9] In the courts of cities like Florence—as in the courts of Satta's Nuoro—inheritance cases were a staple.

The collective demands of honor and the solidarity of families, however, should not blind us to evident moments of divisiveness or outright hostility among people who otherwise shared a common name, coat of arms, ancestry, even dwelling. Without going to the historically dubious step of postulating some Burckhardtian individualism to these historical actors, we can and must remain aware that each person figured as an agent in pursuit of culturally inscribed interests.[10] Inheritance especially was a moment

7. Among others, L. Pandimiglio, "Giovanni di Pagolo Morelli e la ragion di famiglia," in *Studi sul Medioevo cristiano offerti a R. Morghen*, 2 vols. (Rome, 1974), 2:553–608; F. W. Kent, *Household and Lineage in Renaissance Florence: The Family Life of the Capponi, Ginori, and Rucellai* (Princeton, N.J., 1977); C. Klapisch-Zuber, *Women, Family, and Ritual in Renaissance Italy*, trans. L. G. Cochrane (Chicago, 1985); D. Herlihy and C. Klapisch-Zuber, *Les Toscans et leurs familles: Une étude du catasto florentin de 1427* (Paris, 1978); A. Molho, *Marriage Alliance in Late Medieval Florence* (Cambridge, Mass., 1994); P. Cammarosano, "Aspetti delle strutture familiari nelle città dell'Italia comunale (secoli XII–XIV)," *Studi medievali* 16 (1975): 417–35; A. Tenenti, "Famille bourgeoise et idéologie au bas moyen âge," in *Famille et parenté dans l'Occident médiéval*, ed. G. Duby and J. Le Goff (Rome, 1977), pp. 431–40; Tenenti, "L'ideologia della famiglia fiorentina nel Quattro e Cinquecento," in *La famiglia e la vita quotidiana*, pp. 97–107; Kuehn, "'Nemo Mortalis Cognitus Vivit in Evo': Moral and Legal Conflicts in a Florentine Inheritance Case of 1442," in *The Moral World of the Law*, ed. P. Coss (Cambridge, England, 2000), pp. 113–33; J. Kirshner, "Baldus de Ubaldis on Disinheritance: Contexts, Controversies, *Consilia*," *Ius Commune: Zeitschrift für Europäische Rechtsgeschichte* 27 (2000): 119–214.

8. Guglielmo Durante, *Speculum iudiciale* (1479), De successionibus ab intestato, fol. 202va.

9. As Alberico da Rosciate's remarks on the law relating to substitutions, cited in A. Romano, ed., *Le sostituzioni ereditarie nell'inedita "Repetitio de substitutionibus" di Raniero Arsendi* (Catania, 1977), pp. 7–8.

10. F. W. Kent, "Individuals and Families as Patrons of Culture in Quattrocento Florence," in *Language and Images of Renaissance Italy*, ed. A. Brown (Oxford,

when siblings, for example, could come into evident conflict. The ubiquity of such conflicts was recognized and provided for with mechanisms such as arbitration—a less formal procedure deemed mandatory for the resolution of intrafamily disputes, notably involving inheritance.[11]

Inheritance cases thus furnish a primary, if not privileged, point of entry to questions of social identity. One such involved the estate of the wealthy Florentine merchant Paliano di Falco, who died in 1412. In his own actions, recoverable in good part from a surviving account book, in those of his son and daughters, and in those of jurists and notaries who became involved at various stages, we can see how the interests of family, honor, and property could find accommodation in the wider learned law and in local statutes and how the inherent ambiguity of the law allowed Florentines room to fashion a social identity.

INHERITANCE IN FLORENCE

As a *ius proprium* the statutes of Florence used the terms of the *ius commune*—civil and canon law as elaborated by academic jurists. *Ius commune* stood as supplement to *ius proprium*, filling its lacunae and acting as law where the statutes were silent.[12] Rules of custom or statute, for all that they were recognized sources of law, could clash with rules of *ius commune* or simply raise interpretive problems. The complexities of statute interpretation gave rise in the fourteenth century to a genre of learned treatises, such as those of Alberto Gandino (d. after 1307) or Alberico da Rosciate (d. 1360), and the elaboration of interpretive devices in juristic commentaries on the *Digest, Codex,* and *Liber extra*.[13] Academic jurists, ideologically wedded to the rules of *ius commune* as a *ratio scripta,* even as they conceded a *ratio* to statutes whose terms they could also comprehend as citi-

---

1995), pp. 171–92, advances the nice point that singling oneself out from among others of a lineage does not destroy all sense of lineage membership and necessarily thrust one into individualism.

11. Cf. T. Kuehn, *Law, Family, and Women: Toward a Legal Anthropology of Renaissance Italy* (Chicago, 1991), chap. 1; L. Martone, *Arbiter-Arbitrator: Forme di giustizia privata nell'età del diritto comune* (Naples, 1984).

12. F. Calasso, *Medioevo del diritto* (Milan, 1954); M. Bellomo, *Società e istituzioni in Italia dal Medioevo agli inizi dell'età moderna,* 3d ed. (Catania, 1982); P. Koschaker, *Europa und das römische Recht,* 4th ed. (Munich and Berlin, 1966).

13. C. Storti Storchi, "Prassi, dottrina ed esperienza legislativa nell' *Opus Statutorum* di Alberico da Rosciate," in *Confluence des droits savants et des pratiques juridiques* (Milan, 1979), pp. 435–89; M. Sbriccoli, *L'interpretazione dello statuto: Contributo allo studio della funzione dei giuristi nell'età comunale* (Milan, 1969).

zens and town dwellers, often restricted the operations of *ius proprium* and enlarged the effective range of *ius commune*.[14]

One statutory provision where such restriction commonly occurred was in regard to those statutes, found in almost all Italian cities, limiting the inheritance of daughters and other female relations from their fathers, grandfathers, brothers, and so forth to their dowry—thus contravening the rules of *ius commune* favoring equal division of patrimonies among all children without gender discrimination. These statutes enshrined a rationale of family and patrimonial preservation through agnation, to which women could not contribute a priori. The legacy of Roman law on this score was ambiguous, for it, too, at times privileged agnation, so learned jurists could find a professional basis for harboring sympathies with such statutes. On the other hand, they sought ways to reaffirm the practical import of equality in inheritance.[15] One place they could do so was where a statute, as in Florence, carried a qualifying clause that specified that the dowered woman was excluded from inheritance in favor of sons, brothers, paternal uncles, and so on, provided that these males were "born of a legitimate marriage."[16] Illegitimate males, like females, were deemed incapable of affecting agnatic and patrimonial preservation. Identity realized in terms of inheritance and agnation was a dubious quantity for women and bastards. Here moral prejudice against the *fragilitas sexus* of women, and against the *macula* or *defectus* of the bastard, emerged into legal view, so even formally legitimated males met arguments denying them the same privileges as those born legitimate.[17] Juristic interpretation of this statutory situation would come to play an important role in the disposition of Paliano Falchi's estate.

14. P. Grossi, *L'ordine giuridico medievale* (Bari, 1995).

15. Cf. Kuehn, *Law, Family, and Women*, chap. 10; L. Mayali, *Droit savant et coutumes: L'exclusion des filles dotées, XIIème–XVème siècles* (Frankfurt, 1987), esp. pp. 85–94; G. Savino Pene Vidari, "Dote, famiglia e patrimonio fra dottrina e pratica in Piemonte," in *La famiglia e la vita quotidiana*, pp. 109–21; F. Nicolai, *La formazione del diritto successorio negli statuti comunali del territorio lombardo-tosco* (Milan, 1940); J. Kirshner, "*Maritus Lucretur Dotem Uxoris Sue Premortue* in Fourteenth- and Fifteenth-Century Florence," *Zeitschrift der Savigny-Stiftung für Rechtsgeschichte (Kanonistische Abteilung)* 77 (1991): 111–55; and in general A. Romano, *Famiglia, successioni e patrimonio familiare nell'Italia medievale e moderna* (Turin, 1994).

16. ASF, Statuti del comune, 16, "Statuti del podestà dell'anno 1355," fols. 97v–98v; *Statuta populi et communis Florentiae, anno salutis mccccxv*, 3 vols. (Freiburg [Florence], 1778–83), 1:223–25; on which see Kuehn, *Law, Family, and Women*, chaps. 7 and 10.

17. Cf. Kuehn, *Law, Family, and Women*, chap. 7; and more fully Kuehn, *Illegitimacy in Renaissance Florence* (Ann Arbor, Mich., 2001).

INHERITANCE STRATEGIES OF PALIANO DI FALCO

The man whose inheritance set off a train of difficulties for his descendants was one of Florence's wealthiest at the end of the fourteenth century. Described variously as *tavoliere, campsor,* and *mercator et civis,* Paliano di Falco possessed wealth sufficient to place him as the twentieth most affluent citizen in the quarter of San Giovanni in 1403, one place ahead of the up-and-coming Giovanni di Bicci de' Medici.[18] From 1382 he was a business partner with two other prominent Florentines, Giovanni Portinari and Ardingo de' Ricci.[19] Operating from Perugia, Paliano struck up a relationship with a local widow, Marchnaia di Federigo. He never married her, perhaps because to do so while resident in Perugia would signal his willingness to take on Perugian citizenship.[20] They had three children, only one of whom, Bartolomeo, survived to adulthood.[21] As his mother's heir, Bartolomeo gained 60 florins ascribed to her in his father's accounts.[22] Inheritance from his natural father was a more difficult but also more lucrative matter.

Even as his Perugian concubine lay dying in 1390, Paliano contracted marriage with a Florentine woman, Margarita di Francesco Scodellai. The incentive to this match was both her Florentine ancestry and a handsome dowry of 1,000 florins, which consisted not of the usual cash and other liquid assets but of two farms and related holdings (indicating that his wife was a sole heir with no close male agnates).[23] This marriage was to remain barren, however. By her will of 1399, Margarita named Paliano her heir, and he realized from this estate a number of additional properties.[24] The

---

18. Cf. Martines, *Social World,* p. 356.

19. Bernardo di Giovanni Portinari's was the 10th highest assessed household head for San Giovanni in 1403, but Ardingo de' Ricci's was only 125th in the same quarter (ibid., pp. 356, 358).

20. Cf. J. Kirshner, "Mulier alibi nupta," in *Consilia im späten Mittelalter,* pp. 147–75.

21. The information on Paliano comes mainly from his *ricordi:* ASF, CS, ser. 2, 7. A son, Antonio, was born first on 12 October 1382, the same day Paliano opened his account book with the record of his business partnership (fols. 1r and 2v); but Antonio died 27 March 1383. A girl, Antonia, was born 18 September 1389 and died 17 August 1390, predeceasing her mother, who died 4 September. Bartolomeo was born 26 January 1388.

22. Ibid., fols. 4v–5r.

23. Ibid., fols. 9v–10r. Subsequently Paliano made *prestanza* payments for his mother-in-law (ibid., fols. 12v–13r) and gave her grain (fols. 20v–21r) and was involved in other matters (fols. 33v–34r).

24. Ibid., fols. 35r and 54r. These were mainly Ristori family holdings. They included three-fourths of a house in Campo Corbelini, where her mother had lived,

following year, as plague flared anew, Paliano also lost his brother, Nofri, and his nephew, Ghezo di Bartolomeo, and fell heir to them both. Three large *poderi* worth 1,000 florins were the result.[25] So the handsome inheritance Paliano was to leave was itself partly the result of several accumulated inheritances.

Earlier that same year Paliano had taken the precaution of drawing up his own will. He named as heir his only son, the bastard Bartolomeo, but he also made this identity conditional. In case he were to live to remarry, he provided that a sole daughter would get 1,500 florins as dowry (1,000 apiece to two or more girls) and that legitimate sons would become his heirs, while Bartolomeo got 1,000 florins (500 if he had two or more sons). He also ordered that Bartolomeo or any other son could not alienate or obligate any of the properties until he had reached age thirty and had children (of either sex) by a legitimate wife.[26]

Certainly here, as in other wills, there was a desire that the wishes of the testator could find practical expression in the law, although that did not in fact always happen.[27] Paliano's testament did not become the final word about his estate, but that was his doing in good part. Six years later he had it annulled and made another. In the interim, on 6 January 1401 he remarried; the bride was Giana di Currado di messer Gieri de' Pazzi, with a relatively modest dowry of 600 florins. This marriage was fertile, but not of sons. Paliano's transformation to legitimate father militated for changing his will as his first daughter, Niccolosa, born 13 May 1403, turned three.[28] Before his death in 1412, Paliano saw the births of two more daughters, Margarita and Caterina. The pregnancy of his wife in 1412 resulted, unfortunately for his hopes of a son, in the posthumous Gostanza. Paliano

---

half a *casa* in the countryside, a *podere*, a *casa* for a tenant, furnishings, and a pair of oxen—all coming to over 490 florins.

25. Ibid., fol. 56v.

26. Ibid., fols. 58v–60v. There is a discussion of this will from a different vantage point in Isabelle Chabot, "Per 'togliere dal pericolo prossimo l'onestà delle donzelle povere': Aspetti della beneficenza dotale in età moderna," in I. Chabot and M. Fornasari, *L'Economia della carità: Le doti del Monte di Pietà di Bologna (secoli XVI–XX)* (Bologna, 1997), pp. 22–23.

27. S. K. Cohn Jr., *Death and Property in Siena, 1205–1800: Strategies for the Afterlife* (Baltimore, 1988); Cohn, *The Cult of Remembrance: Six Renaissance Cities in Central Italy* (Baltimore, 1992); Cohn, "Le ultime volontà: Famiglia, donne e peste nera nell'Italia centrale," *Studi storici* 32 (1991): 859–75; but also my "Law, Death, and Heirs in the Renaissance: Repudiation of Inheritance in Florence," *Renaissance Quarterly* 45 (1991): 484–516.

28. Paliano recorded the cancellation of the first will; ASF, CS, ser. 2, 7, fol. 61r.

also took the step of formally legitimating Bartolomeo. Legitimation by rescript before a count palatine was an admission of sorts that Bartolomeo was not going to be *haeres universalis* in the second testament.

The second testament left Bartolomeo three *poderi,* including the obviously ancestral "podere di Paliano." Bartolomeo could not obligate or alienate these lands; they were to pass to his children. The legitimate daughters were designated *haeredes,* although Bartolomeo was substituted in the event they all died childless. Paliano chose his heirs by legitimacy over gender but also validated his son's attachment to his family and its ancestors. As we will see, Paliano also named *tutores* for his daughters.

BARTOLOMEO'S INHERITANCE

The events that transpired over the next decade following Paliano's death are vague. We can be certain only that Bartolomeo killed a man, Antonio di Baldo, and was condemned by the podestà of Florence for the crime. Bartolomeo fled into exile in his mother's native Perugia and was unable to return to Florence, where the relatives of his victim enjoyed legal impunity to exact their revenge. Paliano's widow remarried, to Berto Peruzzi, and so had to be excused from being *tutrice* for the girls. In the meantime, the two oldest daughters, Niccolosa and Margarita, married—the first to Niccolò di Bernardo Guadagni, the second to Priore di Mariotto Banchi, both men of some wealth who may well have been attracted to their brides not just by their nominal 1,000-florin dowries but by the fact that they were heirs to their father (and thus their dowries could be both augmented and consist of real properties, as had been the case with Paliano's first wife). Both these daughters succumbed to the plague, probably in 1423. Margarita left a daughter, Ginevra, who would become the first wife of Niccolò Serragli. Niccolosa had no children. She left her dowry by testament to her husband, who in turn soon died, leaving his father, Bernardo, as his heir. It was Bernardo Guadagni who moved the litigation of the 1420s.

Guadagni had lost a son and a daughter-in-law, but he also gained their properties. Recovering these assets was not only an economic step; it was a bid to reconstitute family fortunes. Guadagni was only modestly wealthy by the evidence of the 1427 catasto.[29] Almost immediately he moved to acquire Niccolosa's portion of Paliano's property by suit in the court of the podestà. Although the *tutores* of the young Caterina and Gostanza tried to

29. ASF, Catasto, 80, fols. 60r–61r, placing him 126th in the quarter of San Giovanni (Martines, *Social World,* p. 371).

delay the issue by not appearing in court, Guadagni was given a ruling that the case was properly initiated.[30] Guadagni then obtained the judgment that he was heir, through his son, to Niccolosa's portion of Paliano di Falco's estate. Bartolomeo had also been summoned to appear on the case but clearly was unable because of his exile. Through a *procurator* (the same Berto Peruzzi who married Paliano's widow), Bartolomeo stated the rule that "actor debet sequi forum rei" to transfer the case to Perugia.

Bernardo Guadagni need have felt no kinship to the illegitimate murderer who had inherited the three farms and a quantity of credits in the Florentine public debt (Monte comune). But Bartolomeo had on his side a certain moral weight—recognized and raised by his father, a *naturalis* (a legally and morally stronger position than other types of illegitimates), legitimated, left a handsome paternal legacy. He retained the services of several of Perugia's renowned jurists: Matteo Feliciani, Benedetto Barzi (who would in the 1450s write a *tractatus* on illegitimate succession), Francesco Mansueti, Giovanni da Montesperello (d. 1462), and two scions of famous jurists, Francesco di messer Baldo degli Ubaldi and his cousin Alessandro di messer Angelo.[31] They set out five legal questions relating to Bartolomeo's inheritance and proceeded to answer them. The questions themselves arose in the law, not in moral terms or the precise interests of the parties. They were (1) What could a *naturalis* inherit by the terms of the *ius commune* if there were no legitimate children? (2) Did legitimation remove the incapacity to inherit? (3) Did the failure to render subsequently an oath of loyalty to the empire void Bartolomeo's legitimation? (4) Was the petition lodged in Florence effective against him? And (5), because he had been resident in Perugia for more than ten years, was the summons issued for him to appear in Florence valid, or was the case to be moved to Perugia? These were questions about legal technicalities, the efficacy of legal mechanisms, and the use of law to postpone judgment or change venue. Only the first two questions raised the claims of illegitimate children, but all touched on Bartolomeo's status as heir to his father, as legitimated, as Florentine.

Questions of inheritance by bastards were not without difficulties, to be

30. This ruling was of some precedent, such that it was cited in a statute commentary by Alessandro Bencivenni: BNF, F.P., II.IV.435, fol. 3r; the same comment occurs in the other surviving commentary, that of Tommaso Salvetti: BNF, F.P., II.IV.434, fol. 16r. Since Bencivenni also died in 1423, this case came forward very quickly.

31. This first *consilium* is BNF, Landau Finlay, 98, fols. 155r–159v, and will hereafter be designated Consilium 1. Consilium 2 (fols. 160r–164v) and Consilium 3 (fols. 165r–166r) follow immediately in the same copyist's hand.

sure, but they could be dispatched. In the first place, *naturales* had inferior inheritance rights to those of *legitimi et naturales,* but they had some rights, unlike the *spurii,* whose conception in thoroughly illicit circumstances left them no inheritance rights.[32] At least *naturales* resulted from a sexual act "not reprehended nor approved, but tolerated" ("non improbato nec approbato tollerato tamen"). By *ius commune, naturales* could have two-twelfths of the patrimony, and the legacy to Bartolomeo totaling more than 2,000 florins came to around that. It was his legitimation that licensed a greater share. Illegitimacy was not a matter of natural law, said the jurists, but a product of written law, and written law provided means to remove the *defectus natalium.*[33] By means of legitimation through a count palatine, legitimacy was thus fixed in Bartolomeo's bones.[34] There was no question that Bartolomeo could receive a larger portion left him in his father's will.

As for the technicality of the oath that, interestingly, was supposed to be tendered to Ardingo de' Ricci, his father's business partner, the jurists rehearsed at great length arguments that failure to fulfill legal formalities should prevent an act's validity but decided the legitimation stood. Their argument rested on distinguishing what words or acts were integral to a legal ritual as opposed to simple after-the-fact actions.[35] The second *consilium,* by the same lawyers, minus Barzi, went straight to the missing oath and the powers of a count legitimating by rescript. Here was technical law at its fullest. The jurists dwelt on the exact words of the imperial privilege to the count to determine whether he had the power to legitimate.[36] The text of the legitimation was also inspected to affirm that it conferred the right to inherit. Then the lawyers were set to argue that the oath was not necessary.[37] It was at the end of this second *consilium* that the jurists returned to an issue of social identity. There it was pointed out that Bernardo Guadagni, along with others, had been named as *tutor testamentarius* by Paliano, but he had been excused from that office and, after Niccolosa took her quarter of the estate, arranged his son's marriage to her. This was a friend of the family who had exploited the situation and gained when the

32. Cf. Kuehn, "A Medieval Conflict of Laws: Inheritance by Illegitimates in *Ius Commune* and *Ius Proprium," Law and History Review* 15 (1997): 243–73.
33. Consilium 1, fol. 157r.
34. Ibid.: "unde semel legitimatione perfecta et ossibus ipsius Bartolomei legitimati infixa sunt iura legitimitatis unde perpetuo erit legitimus iudicandus. . . ."
35. Ibid., fol. 158v.
36. Consilium 2, fol. 161r–v.
37. Ibid., fol. 162v.

girl died. The dowry and marriage were suspect, said the jurists, but without elaboration.[38] Instead they raised the point that Niccolosa's will making her father-in-law her heir from her husband should not prejudice the substitution in Paliano's will in Bartolomeo's favor. Hence *iustitia* favored the son.[39]

Yet a third *consilium* was ultimately called for, with Dionigi Barigiani taking the lead (Feliciani missing this time). It went to the privilege of the count, the *persona agens*, in this legitimation. It also raised the issue of legitimation through a *procurator* representing father and son but resolved it with reference to authoritative jurists. Legitimation was greater than adoption, for here agnation was real, that is, natural.[40]

In sum, all this expensive legal talent had established Bartolomeo's legitimacy and inheritance, while also pointing to the substitutions in Paliano's will that shifted Niccolosa's share from her father-in-law, despite her testament in favor of her husband, to her sisters. In any case Bartolomeo held on to his farms and the Monte credits.

THE DAUGHTERS

These girls, one born posthumously, were subject to *tutela* as established in Paliano's will. Guardianship marked their legitimacy in family and society. Here was a legal institution heavily saturated with moralistic notions, recrafted under the influence of medieval canon law to allow mothers to serve as guardians and to erect numerous safeguards against guardians taking advantage of their vulnerable young wards.[41] The social and moral import of guardianship and the regularity of its incidence was such that Florence

38. Ibid., fol. 163v.

39. Ibid., fols. 163v–164r: "puto quod per testamentum dicte domine Niccolose preiudicare non potuit dicto Bartolomeo et non preiudicatur in iure substitutionis facte de dicto Bartolomeo qui capax est ut possit succedere vi dicte substitutionis quatenus sibi debetur in legitima debita dicte domine Niccolose computanda est dos sibi in testamento Paliani relicta quia et legata et dos data imputatur in legitima . . . et per premissa apparet et per alia tacta in alio consilio per me reddito concludo dictum Bartolomeum favere iustitiam."

40. Consilium 3, fol. 165r: "Nec legitimatio est agnatio dativa sed vera quia inheret naturali generationi et ideo legitimatio favorabilior est quam arrogatio, vel dicit ipse procurator non est hic proprie procurator sed supplicator. . . ." On these themes for Florence, see Kuehn, "L'adoption à Florence à la fin du moyen âge," *Médiévales* 35 (1998): 69–81; and in general Franck Roumy, *L'Adoption dans le droit savant du XIIe au XVIe siècle* (Paris, 1998).

41. Cf. G. Villata di Renzo, *La tutela: Indagini sulla scuola dei glossatori* (Milan, 1975).

established a civic magistracy with powers of appointment and oversight over the orphans (*pupilli*).[42] However, because guardianship also figured as a public burden (*munus publicum*), *tutores* could seek to be excused from the office.

Paliano had appropriately taken the precaution of naming ten guardians. The girls' mother, Giana, was excused in consequence of her remarriage to Berto di Bonifazio Peruzzi. This second marriage of a female of the Pazzi lineage to a prominent member of the equally prestigious Peruzzi did not render Giana a "cruel mother."[43] At least through her husband she remained involved in her daughters' lives. Berto's close ties with the Ricasoli may have been instrumental in arranging Caterina's marriage to Andrea di Bindaccio Ricasoli. Of the other nine *tutores*, three were dead by 1425, and Bernardo Guadagni and maestro Antonio di maestro Guccio da Scarperia had been excused.[44] In February 1425 the remaining *tutores* appeared before a notary. Vieri Guadagni, Bernardo's brother, then excused himself on the grounds that he was a member of the Ten on War and too involved in public affairs to deal with these girls' affairs. As the girls themselves had now reached legal adulthood (the youngest being now twelve), the *tutela* was legally transformed into a *cura adultarum* in the three remaining guardians—Corso di Zanobi Ricci, Antonio di ser Bartolomeo di ser Nello, and Guglielmo di Giunta. These three immediately presented an inventory of the properties and monies they managed on behalf of the two girls. The estate, in fact, had been liquidated into Monte shares in various packages acquired over the years, amounting to over 7,000 florins nominally, with another 260 turned up a month later after Corso de' Ricci had been appointed *procurator* for the other *curatores* to deal with the Monte.[45]

Clearly these young girls were good catches in the Florentine marriage

42. On this, see Kuehn, "Social Processes and Legal Processes in the Renaissance: A Florentine Inheritance Case from 1452," *Quaderni fiorentini per la storia del pensiero giuridico moderno* 23 (1995): 365–96, and the literature cited therein, esp. M. G. di Renzo Villata, "Note per la storia della tutela nell'Italia del Rinascimento," in *La famiglia e la vita quotidiana*, pp. 59–95.

43. This being the provocative formulation of C. Klapisch-Zuber, "La 'mère cruelle': Maternité, veuvage et dot dans la Florence des XIVᵉ–XVᵉ siècles," *Annales* 38 (1983): 1097–1109; trans. in Klapisch-Zuber, *Women, Family, and Ritual in Renaissance Italy*.

44. The three who died were Giana's brother Michele, Piero di Filippo, a *campsor* from Borgo San Lorenzo, and Bernardo di Buonaccorso di Berardo.

45. ASF, NA, 9040 (1422–29), fols. 176v–178v (16 February 1424/5) and 184v–185r (27 March 1425). Some of the amounts given were not for share values but for unpaid interest owed (*paghis retentis*).

market. By the fall the *curatores* had arranged the engagement of the barely nubile Gostanza to Benedetto di Marco Strozzi.[46] The groom acknowledged receipt of a 1,000-florin dowry three months later.[47] Benedetto Strozzi, however, seems to have run into difficulties. Less than a year after the marriage was contracted, on 3 August 1426, Gostanza, with her mother's husband as *mundualdus* and with her two remaining *curatores* (Antonio di ser Bartolomeo having died in the interim), presented an inventory containing her right to seek return of her dowry *constante matrimonio*, because her husband was going bankrupt.[48] The two guardians designated four notaries to act as *procuratores* to gain effective return of the dowry. The marriage did not end. The dowry was simply going to be managed by the *curatores* rather than the husband, whose financial difficulties might squander the dowry or burden it with debts. Strozzi's catasto declaration the next year listed his then sixteen-year-old wife while mentioning nothing about her dowry. Gostanza bore Strozzi a son in 1428.[49]

The *cura* over both girls continued. In July 1427 the *curatores* reported an addition to the inventory of 383 florins (as one-quarter of 1,534 florins in shares of the Monte of Pisa in their father's name). Caterina, by now married to Andrea Ricasoli, and her sister nominated Berto Peruzzi as *procurator* to cash out those shares.[50] The following May, Caterina, now over eighteen (statutory age of majority in Florence), with her husband as *mundualdus,* and Benedetto Strozzi acting for his wife, made a final receipt with Corso de' Ricci, acting for all his fellow guardians, regarding all aspects of the guardianship, except for some funds still owing from Bernardo Guadagni and from the other *curator,* Guglielmo di Giunta. Less than a month later, Priore di Mariotto Banchi, with the same exception noted, also released the guardians on behalf of his daughter as heir to the deceased Mar-

---

46. Ibid., fol. 206v (18 September 1425). One of the guarantors for return of the dowry was Gostanza's brother-in-law, husband of the dead Margarita, Priore di Mariotto Banchi.

47. Ibid., fol. 222v (10 December 1425). Benedetto's brother Carlo added his assent separately (ibid., fol. 239r [11 April 1426]).

48. Ibid., fols. 252r–v. On the *mundualdus,* see Kuehn, *Law, Family, and Women,* chap. 9. On retrieval of dowry from a bankrupt husband, see J. Kirshner, "Wives' Claims against Insolvent Husbands in Late Medieval Italy," in *Women of the Medieval World: Essays in Honor of John H. Mundy,* ed. J. Kirshner and S. F. Wemple (Oxford, 1985), pp. 256–303.

49. By the evidence of Tratte records computerized and shared with me in the form of a printout by the late David Herlihy. Strozzi's catasto declaration is in ASF, Catasto, 76, fol. 16r.

50. Ibid., fol. 302r (14 July 1427).

garita.[51] His simultaneous catasto declaration revealed that his Ginevra split two *poderi* in the Mugello, formerly belonging to Paliano di Falco, with her aunts Gostanza and Caterina. He also recorded the substance of the settlement with Corso de' Ricci on the *tutela*, namely one-third share of 350 florins, in addition to a third of 157 florins held by Bernardo Guadagni and of 11 florins held by Guglielmo di Giunta.[52]

The judgment of the wards, then, was that the testamentary guardianship had worked fairly well. Their property had been protected. They were married adults. There was still some unpleasantness, it seems, with their sister's father-in-law, where a portion of the estate was absorbed without a continuing interest on their part (for lack of offspring). More intriguing is the revelation in Banchi's catasto declaration that he and his brother Mariotto owed 1,200 florins to Camilla, Bartolomeo's daughter, of which they should receive over 980 from Bartolomeo. The reason for this transfer of funds is not apparent, but it is not hard to speculate that illegitimacy lay behind what may have been a subterfuge.[53] In some regard these women and the men around them did not lose sight of Bartolomeo or of the farms he had taken as his share of the estate, which were still subject to the substitution in favor of the legitimate half sisters should the exiled Bartolomeo die without male heirs. The daughter Camilla was no threat to that substitution, but sons were.

BARTOLOMEO'S HEIRS

Off in Perugia, Bartolomeo replicated the pattern of his father. Rather than marrying a Perugian girl, he struck a lasting concubinage with one, which produced sons who were, as he had been, *naturales tantum*. Around the same time his sisters were marrying and settling affairs with their remaining guardians, Bartolomeo transferred ownership to his natural sons of the farms he had inherited from his father.[54] From among his sisters, therefore, arose a challenge to his attempt to pass the farms to his sons. The case was

51. Ibid., fols. 349r–v (29 May 1428) and 353r–v (15 June 1428).
52. ASF, Catasto 64, fols. 423r–427r.
53. Ibid., fol. 426v: "Alla Chamilla figliuola di Bartolomeo di Paliano di Falcho de avere fi. 1200 e detto Piero e Mariotto anno avere da Bartolomeo suo padre fi. 980 s. 4 d. 1, siche resta avere la detta Chamilla fi. 219 s. 17."
54. The conjunction of these three jurists on this case was unlikely following di Castro's move to Padua sometime after 1424. All three were teaching in Florence in 1422–23. Cf. L. Martines, *Lawyers and Statecraft in Renaissance Florence* (Princeton, N.J., 1968), pp. 499–500.

brought to the attention of three prominent jurists in Florence, Antonio Roselli (1381–1466), who like Benedetto Barzi authored a treatise on illegitimacy but also fathered an illegitimate; Paolo di Castro (ca. 1360–1441), reviser of Florence's statutes; and Nello da San Gimignano (b. 1373). As with the first case, the issues here were in the realm of *ius commune*, not local statute. Could Bartolomeo alienate the farms to these sons, given that Paliano's will forbade their alienation except to his heirs? Second, did these boys prevent the substitution in favor of their father's half sisters?

Roselli took the lead defending Bartolomeo's actions and claims by citing a text of the *Digest* that gave validity to the *voluntas* of a testator who knew of *naturales* and so could not be said to die without sons, such that they excluded the substitutes who inherited if there were no sons.[55] As Paliano had favored Bartolomeo, a *naturalis*, one could regard the will as otherwise allowing *naturales*. The testator felt no shame in having *naturales* as his heirs, and so, despite the arguments of Bartolo da Sassoferrato, one should read *naturales* into the testament's terms.[56] Of course this conclusion still required that the language of the testament had not been (as it was in the first will) explicit that these children be born of a legitimate marriage. So Bartolomeo could indeed alienate the farms to his *naturales*, although such alienation was only possible because *naturales* were not subject to *patria potestas* and thus sufficiently separate from their father's *persona* to receive goods from him.

Roselli went on to defend the right of these *naturales* to alienate in turn to *extranei*. Here again he worked from a text of the *Digest* where a testator forbade his children to alienate so the goods remained in the *familia*. This was in fact a moral and legal imperative frequently found in wills and acts of alienation in Florence and elsewhere. The text in question, however, according to Roselli, placed the prohibition in the persons and not in rem. And as the prohibition in Paliano's will fell on Bartolomeo, not on the farms, the sons were not precluded from alienating them.[57] Paolo di Castro

---

55. BNF, Panciatichiano, 138, fols. 263v–265v, at 264r. This is a copy.

56. Ibid., fol. 264r–v: "Et ex hoc apparet quod non reputavit verecundiam sibi habere subcessores filios vel descendentes naturales, nec obviat predittos l. generaliter § fi. C. de insti. et substi. [C. 6.25.7(6),3] quia illa secundum Bar. debet intelligi et limitari dum dicit sine iusta sobole cum distintione dicti § siquis rogatus [D. 36.1.18(17),4], que dotrina reprehenditur per modernos qui est ad dictum tex. divinare, etiam michi non videtur vera sed tutor est solutio Dini quod si condicio liberorum apponitur a testatore tunc naturalis includitur secundum distintionem dicti § siquis rei rogatus."

57. Ibid., fol. 265r.

and Nello da San Gimignano concurred in these judgments, although the former added that, if the sons predeceased Bartolomeo, then the substitution did go into effect. The alienation was dependent on the timing of Bartolomeo's demise. If the substitutes died without children, their heirs still filled the substitution, according to Bartolo, but di Castro argued the opposite.[58] Here was another nice bit of legalism about the meaning of being an heir, but the effect of the argument was to draw a temporal boundary to the claims of the litigants. Those who bought the lands would thus only have to worry if Bartolomeo outlived his sons. They would not also have to worry about the female lines.

CONCLUSION

"In the Civil Code . . . the family was considered as distinct from property, but in real life the family that has nothing is an abstraction, a mere pompous way of talking, rather like an individual without property, whom the professional jurists refer to as a 'subject of law.'"[59] All the legal maneuvers and lawsuits revolving around the estate of Paliano di Falco were about giving economic and moral wherewithal to the family, but here only one of five children could propagate an agnatic line, and that with a cloud of illegitimacy over it. Law gave hope to plaintiffs not in possession to realize their pretended rights. It gave defendants weapons as well. It provided an institution to safeguard orphans—backed by a sense of obligation on the part of the guardians—and mechanisms to manipulate property. It gave bastards both legal disabilities and dubious identity but also the tenuous means of hope for agnation and inheritance.

Looked at in a discursive manner, legal language is not simply a transparent and plastic instrument of ideology, nor can it be reduced to a model for the circulation of commodities. Law functions as a "process of restricting conflict within the system to conflict over norms and words rather than interests or motives, conflict of an anodyne kind which will ideally take the form of disagreement over legal relevance and the legal meaning of terms of art."[60] Indeed, law would seem to be a fine and difficult art form. At various points, even as they asserted the sovereignty of legal discourse by citing its texts, jurists in the cases considered here referred to the artistic

58. Ibid., fol. 265v.
59. Satta, *Day of Judgment*, p. 41.
60. P. Goodrich, *Legal Discourse: Studies in Linguistics, Rhetoric and Legal Analysis* (New York, 1987), pp. 172–73.

character of legal reasoning in construing these texts. On the other hand, direct reference to immediate empirical interests (how much was at stake, even the name[s] of the parties) was left out—thus contributing to the sense of professional detachment. Legal language was an authoritative discourse with the past that arrived after the fact to reconstruct others' utterances (notably the will of Paliano) according to hermeneutic techniques that imputed legally relevant intentions to those who had already spoken.[61]

Where certain broad cultural notions of blood, honor, family, and ownership operated, there were texts and terms. But some of these were also familiar to people. They may not have shared with jurists the conclusions that legitimated sons inherited along with legitimate daughters or that the word "son" or "child" in a will included natural children, but they may have, especially if they stood to gain thereby. Even in their vendettas, as with Bartolomeo di Paliano's victim's relatives, and in the identity-defining legal maneuvers of Bernardo Guadagni (that, in consequence, also became identity-defining for Bartolomeo), Florentines found the law and its personnel useful.[62] They had to see some legal right to press their claims, to bring a matter to these Latinate, citation-making experts. They had to find a law that in some perceptible if imprecise way fed into the sense of personhood they sought to define or enhance by going to law.

In modern courts, the legal worldview "may be summarised in terms of procedures of individualisation and generalisation—both narrative and justificatory—which work to manipulate and transpose existent human beings and groups. . . . In broader terms, the legal use of language rewrites the individual, as it rewrites speech in terms of a notional and static unity of reasoned intentions." [63] In the Florentine cases what was operational was a notion of the person as relationally and notionally both subjective and objective. The *mens* or *voluntas testatoris* was not to be served on its own. It could not dominate and dispose of property freely, but it could govern inheritance and alienation through mechanisms like substitutions over a long period. The illegitimate son had to have arisen from a relationship such that he was able to inherit something, and even then not everything. His claim was strengthened by a reshaping or redefining of relations through legitimation. The girls were similarly objectified in their gender, but subject enough to consent to marriages and release their *tutores*. As

61. Cf. J. Kirshner, "*Consilia* as Authority in Late Medieval Italy: The Case of Florence," in *Legal Consulting in the Civil Law Tradition*, pp. 107–40.
62. Cf. Kuehn, *Law, Family, and Women*, chap. 2.
63. Goodrich, *Legal Discourse*, pp. 190–91.

6 Perceived Insults and Their Consequences

Acciaiuoli, Neroni, and Medici Relationships in the 1460s

Margery A. Ganz

In August and September 1466 the anti-Medicean movement that had been building since the death of Cosimo de' Medici two years earlier came to fruition. Luca Pitti, Niccolò Soderini, Manno Temperani, and especially Agnolo Acciaiuoli and Dietisalvi Neroni led a coup that attempted to depose the Medici from the leadership of Florence and to restore "a truly republican government" to the city. This event was the watershed in Medici rule because afterward life was never the same in Florence—neither for the Medici nor for the *ottimati*. The events of 1466 had revealed to the Medici the danger of alternate patronage networks, which, like the ones engineered by Agnolo and Dietisalvi, might compromise Medici control of Florentine government. Their growth could no longer be tolerated. Therefore, after the coup's failure and the attendant exile of Agnolo Acciaiuoli and Dietisalvi Neroni, both of whom had been important figures within the Medici inner circle as well as within the regime itself, most *ottimati* must have realized their choices had dwindled to becoming members of the Medici *amici*, and thus supporters of the Medici, or exile.

This chapter explores the public and private behavior of Agnolo Acciaiuoli and Dietisalvi Neroni, the two real leaders of 1466, as well as Medici behavior toward them during the years preceding the attempted coup. Because of the complicated network of personal bonds among members of the Florentine *reggimento*, good patron-client relationships were essential to the smooth functioning of politics, social life, and government. The relationships were reciprocal, trust being the essential glue that bound men together. Neither the patron nor the client could afford to forget that; if either did, then a high price might have to be paid. Thus, proper behavior was required on both sides of the patron-client relationship. As Ronald Weissman has pointed out, honor required that the client properly express his gratitude and demonstrate his loyalty to the patron; the patron, in turn, was expected to do favors and aid his clients in achieving their goals. A man with a wide network of friends and relatives was perceived as accruing honor and profit, while shame was attributed to those who failed to either demonstrate proper gratitude or produce the requested favors.[1] The Medici were the most powerful political patrons in fifteenth-century Florence because of the depth and breadth of their contacts, not only in Florence but throughout Italy and even Europe. Therefore, their clients could expect support and largesse beyond what any other Florentine patron could supply. When that support or favor was not forthcoming, clients felt betrayed, humiliated, and even insulted. These feelings on the part of Agnolo Acciaiuoli and Dietisalvi Neroni, patrons in their own right who understood the system, eventually contributed to their efforts to replace the Medici with a group of men who would function as the first citizens and thus patrons for the Florentine Republic.

This chapter examines the way the Medici could be perceived to have insulted their closest allies and friends during the last years of Cosimo's life and the first years of Piero's reign. By not supporting their clients, several Medici actions taken after 1458 humiliated both Acciaiuoli and Neroni. Apparently both Cosimo and Piero believed that they could afford such actions, but this was true only for Cosimo. Piero narrowly escaped having limitations placed on his political power by his family's former supporters. I will examine the steps—mostly political—taken by both sides during the crucial two years following the death of Cosimo. The private humiliations, which accumulated by 1464–66, led to more insults as each side imputed the worst motives to the actions or behavior of the other. In addition, this study addresses the question of whether Acciaiuoli and Neroni acted out of a sense of civic responsibility or for private gain. If the latter, their actions might be viewed as treasonous, but of course their motives may well have been mixed.

As early as 1466, many people wrote about this conspiracy. We find information about it in the Gaddi *Priorista*, the Parenti chronicle, Luca Landucci's *Diario*, Benedetto Dei's *Cronica*, Machiavelli's *Istorie fiorentine*, Fra Giovanni di Carlo's *Libri de temporibus suis*, and Alessandra Macinghi Strozzi's amazing letters. In this century Guido Pampaloni, Alfredo Municchi, and Nicolai Rubinstein have paid particular attention to this event.[2]

1. R. F. E. Weissman, *Ritual Brotherhood in Renaissance Florence* (New York, 1982), p. 26.
2. ASF, Tratte 132bis (Gaddi); Manoscritti, 119 (Dei). This is also available as Benedetto Dei, *La cronica dall'anno 1400 all'anno 1500*, ed. R. Barducci (Florence,

Unfortunately, the principal conspirators have not left *ricordi* to assist modern scholars in explicating the events of 1464–66. No volumes at all appear to have survived by Agnolo Acciaiuoli, and the two volumes of Dietisalvi Neroni's *ricordi*, which are really only account books, end before the death of Cosimo and are therefore almost useless for the purpose of this study. Instead, one must rely upon extant letters from the conspirators and their families and friends as well as other people's *ricordanze* for enlightenment. It is frustrating that of all the Florentine *ricordi* that survived from that period, not one from a leader of the conspiracy remains extant to help modern readers see more clearly the motivation behind the events of 1466. One cannot simply accept the winning side's assessment of the events and thus label Agnolo and Dietisalvi as well as the others as traitors. A more balanced view needs to be presented. The picture offered here, therefore, is pieced together from Agnolo and Dietisalvi's speeches in the *consulte*, from private letters and other correspondence with friends, family, and associates, from the *ricordi* of others, such as Parenti and Dei, from the reports sent back to Francesco Sforza and later to his successors by Milan's ambassador to Florence, as well as from public documents of the Florentine government and Medici papers.

Even before Cosimo de' Medici's death on 1 August 1464, the seeds of the 1466 conspiracy had been planted among its principal organizers. While Cosimo was alive, Agnolo Acciaiuoli, Dietisalvi Neroni, Luca Pitti, Niccolò Soderini, and Manno Temperani appear to have been content to work as members of the inner circle of Medici *amici*. This must have been due, in part, to their recognition of the fact that the Medici Bank provided Cosimo with the power to outstrip by far all other Florentines as a patron in the political and economic arena.[3] It was a realistic assessment of the way things actually were. All of them in one way or another needed Cosimo's

---

1985). BNF, Magl., XXV.272 (Parenti). Alessandra Macinghi-Strozzi, *Lettere di una gentildonna fiorentina del secolo XV ai figliuoli esuli*, ed. C. Guasti (Florence, 1877); Luca Landucci, *Diario Fiorentino dal 1450 al 1516*, ed. I. del Badia (Florence, 1883); Niccolò Machiavelli, *The History of Florence*, in Machiavelli, *The Chief Works and Others*, vol. 3, trans. and ed. A. Gilbert (Durham, N.C., 1965); Fra Giovanni di Carlo, "Libri de temporibus suis," in BAV, Vat. lat., 5878; G. Pampaloni, "Fermenti di riforme democratiche nelle consulte della Repubblica fiorentina," *Archivio storico italiano* 119 (1961): 11–62, 241–814; A. Municchi, *La fazione antimedicea detta "del Poggio"* (Florence, 1911); N. Rubinstein, *The Government of Florence under the Medici, 1434–1494*, 2d ed. (Oxford, 1997).

3. A. Molho, "Cosimo de' Medici, Pater Patriae or Padrino?" *Stanford Italian Review* 1 (1979): 30–33.

backing. Nonetheless, Agnolo and other prominent *ottimati* apparently viewed themselves as working *with* rather than strictly *for* Cosimo. Although Agnolo, Dietisalvi, and Luca had been willing to accept Cosimo's leadership because of his personal abilities, his links to other Italian and European states, and his following in Florence, they refused to defer to Piero in quite the same way. He was younger than they and not nearly the power his father had been. For thirty years they had ruled together with his father; now it was their turn to hold power in their own names, not simply as supporters of the Medici family but as patrons in their own right with their own network of clients. On the other side, Piero could not afford to lose any of his power or position. Thus, the battle lines were drawn.

This resentment of the continuing preeminence of the Medici was fostered among *ottimati* by Agnolo Acciaiuoli and Dietisalvi Neroni. Even before Cosimo's death, Agnolo wrote scathingly about the Medici to Francesco Sforza: he called Cosimo and Piero "cold men [*huomini freddi*], whom illness and old age have reduced to such cowardice that they avoid anything that might cause them worry or trouble."[4] The same day Agnolo made the point even more strongly in another letter by stating that Piero and Cosimo "were more cowardly than rabbits that were afraid of everyone."[5] These letters may have been the first open steps in Agnolo's attempt to convince Francesco Sforza that he, Agnolo, was a desirable ally and partner, who could replace the sick Medici. After all, Cosimo was an old man who was not in good health, and Piero suffered from gout and was often housebound. Clearly the Sforza needed a strong, talented partner who could continue what had become the traditional Milan-Florence alliance. Agnolo's letters were probably true in substance, but it is also essential to consider their tone. How could the outwardly close, friendly relationship between Agnolo and Cosimo have so deteriorated that Agnolo was willing to describe his patron in such terms to a Medici ally? One must ask whether

4. ASM, Sforzesco, Pot. est., Firenze, 271, fol. 133r: "Questo è vero: ma le nature de populi non sono apte ad intendere queste grandi cose dagli huomini freddi come è Cosimo e Piero, e quali e dal infirmità e dall'età sono tanto inviliti che fuggono ogni casa che habbi arrecare loro fatica o cura d'animo." On 23 April 1465, Agnolo wrote to Francesco Sforza once again about the ill health of Piero. The letter is in ASM, Sforzesco, Pot. est., Firenze, 272: "Dubito bene parlando con la S.V. come posso, che per la infirmità lui medesimo non invilisca in tale fatica e in tanta cura. . . ."

5. BAM, Ms. Z 247 sup., fol. 334r. Agnolo Acciaiuoli to Francesco Sforza, 12 July 1464: "Cosimo et Piero n'anno vogla: ma e sono più vili de' conigli: e per l'essere infermi e per non dispiacere a qualchuno."

Agnolo was concerned about the danger of putting on paper these heretical sentiments about his patron or if he was certain that his long-term relationship with Francesco Sforza would protect him and permit this severe evaluation of the Medici.[6] We must try to discover what had happened to separate Agnolo from Cosimo. It was essential for the continuing preeminence of the Sforza that they have a strong ally in Florence. Indeed, the Florence-Sforza alliance was one of the decisive factors in Italian diplomacy during the second half of the fifteenth century. But both sides needed to be strong. If the Medici had weakened, someone had to replace that family as the Sforza partner because above all the Sforza had to be concerned with their own self-interest. Could Agnolo, perhaps in association with Dietisalvi, supersede the Medici as Francesco's strong ally?

Dietisalvi's psychological estrangement from the Medici may have come even earlier than Agnolo's, although in public he supported Cosimo until the latter's death. Perhaps it began with Cosimo's projected addition to the Medici palace that would have reduced the light in Dietisalvi's home.[7] Although ultimately not completed, this planned infringement on Dietisalvi's physical space could well have been perceived as a diminishment of his political power. In an August 1463 letter Nicodemo da Pontremoli, one of Francesco Sforza's advisers, called Dietisalvi Neroni "Cosimo's greatest and most ambitious enemy."[8] The reasons for this statement remain unclear, but it is borne out by Dietisalvi's actions soon after Cosimo's death. Just seven days afterward, Dietisalvi clearly viewed the political situation in Flor-

6. Between 1451 and 1466 an extraordinary number of letters from Agnolo, and to a lesser extent from Dietisalvi, were written to Francesco Sforza; they exist in two collections, in Milan and Paris. The larger group is in Milan, where most are in the ASM, in the *Sforzesco, Potenze estere* section, while a smaller number are to be found in the Biblioteca Ambrosiana. The other collection is in the Bibliothèque Nationale in Paris. The letters cover a wide range of topics, including, but not limited to, daily happenings in Florence, the functioning of the Signoria and the *consulte*, Medici views on a variety of topics, Acciaiuoli or Neroni views on many issues and whether they differed from Cosimo's, accounts of visitors to Florence, Florentine governmental initiatives, family news, information on harvests from property in the *contado*, and many other topics that happend to have occurred to the writers. Often it was almost as if they were writing to friends and family away from Florence.

7. BAV, Vat. lat., 5878, fol. 96v. The citation to this manuscript is in R. Hatfield "Some Unknown Descriptions of the Medici Palace in 1459," *Art Bulletin* 52 (1970): 232–49. I would like to thank Susan McKillup for bringing this to my attention.

8. Paris, BN, Ms. Ital., 1589, fols. 196r (25 August 1463), 190r (17 August 1463): "Cosimo e li soy non hanno quì maiore né più ambitioso inimico che Dietisalvi." The letters are quoted in Rubinstein, *The Government*, p. 152 n. 3.

ence as changed. He lost no time in writing to Francesco Sforza, "While Cosimo was alive, decisions were left to him; now those who remain at the head of the regime are Piero and a number of citizens (i.e. Dietisalvi, Luca Pitti, and Agnolo Acciaiuoli) supporting him, who were brothers to Cosimo and who will now be fathers to Piero."[9] That letter demonstrates how Dietisalvi was positioning himself: it was now time for Dietisalvi to assume the paternal role, in effect to rule. He was to be the linchpin of the new Milan-Florence partnership. He was ready to set policy, and his bad advice to Piero about calling in debts right after Cosimo's death could be seen as an attempt to separate the Medici from their support among the masses.

One can see this changed perception of Medici rule in the surviving letters and other documents from the conspirators as compared with the literary prefaces previously dedicated to the Medici. In the late 1450s and early 1460s, Donato di Neri Acciaiuoli, Agnolo's younger cousin, provided an excellent portrait of the Medici as ideal patrons in his preface to the *Life of Hannibal and Scipio Africanus* when he wrote:

> Indeed, beyond a grateful soul, beyond these letters and concerns, I do not have anything which I can return to you for such benefits, the kindness which I received not only from you but also from Cosimo, your father, a very good and most wise man. For what has been his kindness towards me? What actions deserve such rewards? Is it love towards the study of letters, the practice of which is a virtue? He was a unique father of learned men. He was the patron; he was the everlasting promoter and helper. Moreover, you, Piero, are not only the legitimate heir of a very generous patrimony but you are also a most careful imitator of his admirable virtues, in the very esteemed tasks which public as well as private affairs bring to you.[10]

9. BAM, Ms. Z 247 sup., fol. 139r (8 August 1464): ". . . dove in vita di Chosimo si lasciava il pensiero a llui, hora questi che rimanghono nel governo dello stato che'è Piero chol favore di parecchi cittadini i quali erano fratelli ad Cosimo ora hanno ad essere padri ad Piero et tivonogli tucti di bonissima vogla ad volere seguitare nella amicitiia et conservatione dello stato."

10. BLF, Plut., LXVII, 20, fol. 1r: "Equidem praeter gratum animum et has litteras et vigilias meas, non habeo quod tibi reddam pro tantis beneficiis, quae non solum a te, sed etiam a Cosimo, patre tuo, optimo ac sapientissimo viro accepi. Quae enim illius erga me humanitas fuit? Quae merita? Qui amor erga studia litterarum exercitationes quae virtutum? Ille erat unus doctorum hominum pater. Ille patronus; ille perpetuus fautor atque adiutor. Tu autem, Petre, non solum amplissimi patrimonii legitimus heres, sed etiam admirabilium virtutum suarum diligentissimus imitator in maximis occupationibus, quas tibi cum publica tum privata negotis afferunt. . . ." This translation and a discussion of the prefaces can be found in M. Ganz, "Donato Acciaiuoli and the Medici: A Strategy for Survival in '400 Florence," *Rinascimento* 22 (1982): 49–54.

But even this protestation hardly compares to Donato's funeral oration for Cosimo, where the latter's death is described as "taking away from the citizens the humaneness, wisdom, excellence of that best father in whom all good qualities were found, which are sought by men."[11] When examining this oration or Donato's prefaces to his translations of Plutarch's *Lives of Alcibiades and Demetrius* or the previously cited preface to the *Life of Hannibal and Scipio Africanus* dedicated to both Cosimo and Piero, one must remember that he was not of Agnolo's generation, although they were first cousins; he was thirty years younger and had never perceived himself as Piero's, let alone Cosimo's equal. This was not the case for the men who had ruled with Cosimo for thirty years.

Although Donato and others of his generation always addressed their letters to Cosimo and Piero as "father," the letters of Agnolo, Dietisalvi, Luca, and even Niccolò Soderini do not include this deferential salutation. Every letter that I have been able to find from Agnolo or Dietisalvi to Piero as well as a significant numbers of letters to Cosimo address them not as "father" but as "brother."[12] In fact, several letters from Piero de' Medici to Agnolo as late as 1467 call the latter "father."[13]

Thus, from the standpoint of the leaders of the conspiracy, Piero di Cosimo de' Medici had not yet and never was to earn the right to be seen as a revered paternal figure the way Cosimo had been. Many younger Floren-

---

11. BLF, Plut. LXXXX, sup. cod. 37, fol. 86v: ". . . qui paucis ante mensibus vita fructus et auctoritatis et prudentiae suae ingens nobus desiderium reliquit. Erepta est enim nobis humanitas, sapientia, virtus illius optimi patris, in quo omnia bona reperiebantur, quae ab hominibus expeti solent." An analysis of the oration can be found in Ganz, "Donato Acciaiuoli and the Medici," pp. 49–50. The oration, as well as other pieces honoring Cosimo, is discussed by A. Brown in her important study, "The Humanist Portrait of Cosimo de' Medici, Pater Patriae" (1961), repr. in Brown, *The Medici in Florence: The Exercise and Language of Power* (Florence, 1992), pp. 3–52.

12. Almost all of the letters have the saluatation "Spectabilis vir et frater honorande." Examples of this phenomenon abound in the surviving letters of Agnolo Acciaiuoli. See, e.g., ASF, MAP, XVI, 126; XVII, 27; XVII, 110; CXXXVIII, 99; and LXVIII, 77. The last is dated 17 September 1466. Indeed, there are several surviving letters of Agnolo to Cosimo with the same salutation of "brother" (MAP, XI, 540; XII, 225 and 229). Dietisalvi's letters with similar salutations include the following: MAP, XVII, 109 and 428. Both Agnolo and Dietisalvi also addressed Cosimo's favorite son, Giovanni, in a similar manner while he was still alive: MAP, VII, 186, 785. Francesco Neroni, Dietisalvi's brother as well as coconspirator, also used the same vocabulary when writing to Piero: MAP, XVII, 531; XVII, 229; XVI, 73, 74, 449; XVII, 211, 229, 322.

13. MAP, LXXXIX, 109; XCVII, 251, 252; LXVIII, 77. Several of these letters begin with the following salutation: "Magnifice eques tanquam pater honorande."

tines, especially those seeking his assistance, had no trouble calling Piero "father," but the men of Cosimo's generation were unable to use that term in relation to Piero or to have the latter take power into his own hands at their expense.

Although I have been unable to find any specific incidents to fully explain Dietisalvi's enmity toward the Medici aside from the planned building, Agnolo's grievances had a basis in two private family incidents in the early 1460s. The first problem, which Agnolo blamed on Cosimo's interference, involved an adverse decision in the bishop of Cortona's court about his son Raffaello's marriage to Alessandra d' Ubertino de' Bardi. Although the two had married in 1456, by early 1463 Alessandra had fled the Acciaiuoli family home with the help of a cousin. In her court petition, she declared that her marriage to Raffaello was a fraud, since the latter had been dishonest toward her because he preferred boys to the proper conjugal relations with her. An additional claim was that Agnolo, her father-in-law, had been violent toward her.[14] Cosimo apparently intervened in the case on Alessandra's side: a divorce could have been achieved, but the Acciaiuoli would have lost Alessandra's dowry, the richest Florentine dowry paid up until that time—just over 8,500 florins.[15] Because of its size, repayment of the dowry was out of the question. Eventually, the marriage was patched up; the couple had three children, and Raffaello and his father were able to maintain control of that large sum of money. Moreover, the relationship not only endured but developed, so that much later Raffaello praised Alessandra highly for her care of his property and family while he was in exile.[16]

Nonetheless, Agnolo nursed his resentment of the interference of Cosimo, his putative ally and friend, in this private family matter.[17] But what

14. ASF, NA, 14198 (old M570), fols. 163r–164v; Machiavelli, *History of Florence,* in *The Chief Works,* 3:1351.

15. ASF, MC, 3735, fols. 25v, 27r, 122v; NA, 14198 (old M570), fols. 163r–164v; NA, 6144 (old D66), fol. 8v; BAV, Vat. lat., 5878, fols. 80v–81v. I would like to thank Anthony Molho for the original citations to Alessandra's dowry, as well as for the information that this was the largest dowry up until that time.

16. For more information on the tribulations of Alessandra due to the actions of her husband and father-in-law in 1466, see M. Ganz, "Paying the Price for Political Failure: Florentine Women in the Aftermath of 1466," *Rinascimento* 34 (1994): 237–57.

17. ASF, Dipl., Innocenti di Firenze, 17 September 1491; Catasto, 916, fol. 399r; Catasto, 1008, fols. 601r–602r; MAP, XCIV, 143, fols. 229–34; MAP, XCVIII, 463; CPGNR, 105, "Libro della luna restaurato," fols. 129r–131v; R. Hatfield, "A Source for Machiavelli's Account of the Regime of Piero de' Medici," in *Studies on Machiavelli,* ed. M. Gilmore (Florence, 1972), pp. 324–25; Machiavelli, *History of Florence,* in *Chief Works,* 3:1351.

he ignored at the time were the probable causes for Cosimo's intervention. Two possible reasons for that behavior have come to light: (1) Cosimo and others believed, according to Alison Brown, that Agnolo was a bad influence on Pierfrancesco de' Medici, Cosimo's nephew, who was married to Agnolo's daughter Laudomia;[18] and (2) Cosimo may have been influenced by the probable relationship between his wife, Contessina Bardi, and Alessandra, who I believe were cousins. Not supporting a major client could injure the patron-client relationship sufficiently to have severe consequences for both sides, but fighting with one's wife for nonsupport of her family could have been even more dangerous—especially when her family was the powerful Bardi clan.

The second disagreement concerned Agnolo's son Lorenzo, for whom Agnolo had sought the bishopric of Arezzo. At the last minute, Cosimo intervened on behalf of his own kinsman Filippo de' Medici and promised that Lorenzo could have the next vacant bishopric in Florentine territory. Unfortunately, the next vacancy was Pisa, probably the most important Tuscan post after Florence itself. While Cosimo would probably have preferred to make his cousin archbishop of Florence, that post was occupied by Francesco Neroni, Dietisalvi's brother, and so was outside Cosimo's reach at the time. Therefore, Cosimo reneged on his promise: he had Filippo appointed to Pisa, and Lorenzo was offered the now less desirable post of Arezzo.[19] So much for Medici promises to the Acciaiuoli; here, then, was a clear breach of the patron-client code. We can see why Agnolo must have felt betrayed by Cosimo, his supposed friend and patron. This may have also been a lesson to other *ottimati:* if such casual treatment could be accorded to Agnolo, a pillar of the regime, what might happen to them? Incidents like these—news of which must have circulated among Florence's political elite—suggest why Florentine *ottimati* were not necessarily surprised about the events that occurred after Cosimo's death.

Just six weeks after his demise, Alessandra Macinghi Strozzi wrote to her son Filippo that "new thoughts about governing the state were circu-

18. A. Brown, "Pierfrancesco de' Medici, 1430–1476: A Radical Alternative to Elder Medicean Supremacy," *Journal of the Warburg and Courtauld Institutes* 42 (1979): 81–103, especially 95; repr. in Brown, *Medici in Florence*, pp. 73–102. Brown argued that because of the way Cosimo and Piero had treated Pierfrancesco and his brother when their father's estate had been settled, Pierfrancesco might easily have looked to his father-in-law for guidance and help rather than to the uncle or cousin who he thought had cheated them. See also Hatfield, "A Source for Machiavelli's Account," pp. 324–25.

19. Vespasiano da Bisticci, *Vite di uomini illustri del secolo XV*, ed. P. D'Ancona and E. Aeschliman (Milan, 1951), pp. 494–95.

lating in Florence after the death of Cosimo."[20] For the surviving exiles of 1434 and their families, Cosimo de' Medici's death meant their possible recall. Although it would not occur for several more years, Alessandra's letter also expressed her hopes for the speedy return of her sons to Florence.[21] In a letter in December 1464 Alessandra wrote Filippo of what was occurring in Florentine politics, especially in the Signoria, and of the roles played by Agnolo, Dietisalvi, and Luca, all of whom were portrayed as friendly to the exiles,[22] men or sons of men who had been exiled at Cosimo's request after 1434.

The death of Cosimo liberated many among the Medici *amici* from their allegiance to the family: the glue that had kept Cosimo's careful coalition together for thirty years thinned with the accession of the less powerful Piero. Families that may have suffered either private insults or public disagreements with the Medici began to withdraw from their orbit. Nonetheless, Piero could ill afford to relinquish any appearance of authority. If he did, it could mean the beginning of the end for the Medici as the preeminent family in Florence. Whatever the reason for their discontent, Agnolo, Dietisalvi, and Luca, realizing that the institutional controls they had helped the Medici enact since 1434 had increased that family's power, began to turn against the government they had supported for thirty years. The reforms they advocated from late 1464 through early 1466 brought them greater exposure among Florentines of varied classes and persuasions. In the main, they acquired supporters from large numbers of citizens who were unhappy about the existing political system, who wanted a greater say in governing the state, and who sought to return Florence to its more traditional government.

Among the issues on which Agnolo and Dietisalvi took stances antithetical to Medici desires were the nonrenewal of the special powers, or *balìa*, of the Otto di guardia, closing the electoral *borse*, a subsidy for Milan, the extension of the life of the council of the Cento, and the public oath in May 1466. Although Piero de' Medici had wanted a renewal of the special pow-

---

20. Alessandra Macinghi Strozzi to Filippo Strozzi, 15 September 1464, in Strozzi, *Lettere*, p. 323: "Non è dubbio che gli animi d'alquanti cittadini per la morte seguìta non abbino fatto in tra loro nuovi pensieri del governo della terra; ma per ancora non si sente; chè la cosa è fresca, e Dietisalvi è stato ammalato."

21. Ibid., pp. 325–26: "La morte di Cosimo stimai lo sentissi più presto che da me, e però no lo scrissi. E di grado, estimo siate più tosto in migliore che piggiore: e per ora non è da scriverne a persona; quando sarà el tempo, vi si dirà."

22. Ibid., pp. 333–34. ". . . i'n'ho speranza che, scrivendo e chiedendolo cordialmente, riuscirà tutto. Faccia Iddio che debb'essere il meglio."

ers of the Otto, Agnolo and others disregarded his wishes and spoke out against the Medici position. At the *pratica* of 3 September 1465, Dietisalvi labeled Florentine government as corrupt and repressive.[23] Representing Medici interests, Tommaso Soderini, whose brother Niccolò was eventually exiled for his part in the events of 1466, labored hard and long to convince men with whom he had worked as Medici *amici* for many years of the advantages of prolonging the special powers of the Otto. Nonetheless, the concerted efforts of Agnolo, Dietisalvi, and others proved too strong for Tommaso, and the idea of extending the Otto's extraordinary powers was abandoned. The conspirators had won the first round in the constitutional reform battle.

Just a few days later the anti-Medicean faction turned its attention to widening the governing group and to the institution of the *accoppiatori*. In what may have seemed like a return to the politics of 1455, Manno Temperani led the attack here by stating that too much power was in the hands of too few individuals; ironically, Temperani himself was one of the *accoppiatori* in 1465, as were several of the other leaders of this faction.[24] Even though it might have meant a weakening of their own power, Dietisalvi, Agnolo, and Luca Pitti all agreed with Temperani's plan to close the *borse* and requalify those who had not been successful in the scrutinies of 1458 and 1463–64. The conspirators' position on this issue was certainly an indication of their loyalty to republican ideals as opposed to private gain. There was great feeling in the city in favor of the abolition of elections *a mano*, as well as for having more people participate in the *pratiche*. The Councils voted overwhelmingly to return to electing the Signoria by lot.[25] Several weeks later Agnolo wrote to his son Jacopo about what had happened. He told his son how the *accoppiatori*, to the great joy of the city, had restored to the electoral *borse* the names of the great majority of citizens who had been eligible for the *Tre Maggiori* since 1434.[26] The inclusion of

---

23. ASF, CP, 58, fols. 20v–22r; Rubinstein, *The Government*, pp. 159–64.

24. *Accoppiatori* in 1465 included Agnolo Acciaiuoli, Dietisalvi Neroni, Luca Pitti, and Manno Temperani as well as Tommaso Soderini; Rubinstein, *The Government*, p. 274.

25. ASF, CP, 58, fols. 28v–33v; Rubinstein, *The Government*, pp. 142–43. The Council of the People voted 175 vs. 19, while the Council of the Commune voted 146 vs. 6.

26. ASF, CS, ser. 3, 178, fol. 33r: "Noi seràmo le borse, e ritiràmo quasi tutti quelli che aveano vinto il partito dal 1434 in qua: e l'uno et l'altro è suto gravissimo a Piero. M'a tutta la ciptà è piaciuto; e in kalendi si trarrà e Priori secondo l'ordine antiquo. . . . La terra è tutta sollecita a volere che il governo torni al modo che l'ave-

men who had been excluded since 1458 meant that the Medici were certain to see among those chosen for the Signoria some who were not sympathetic to them and their attempts to restrict government, as well as those who were in favor of widening participation in the various major governmental posts. These proposals could have marked a return to Florence's more traditional pre-1434 government, which was the goal of Agnolo, Luca, and Dietisalvi. The selection of Niccolò Soderini as the first Standard Bearer of Justice from the new *borse* showed the conspirators how correct they were and confirmed to the Medici the danger of the conspirators' program.

But for Dietisalvi Neroni this victory was *for* Florence rather than against the Medici. He believed the restoration of free elections would benefit the city as well as its leading citizens. He wrote to Francesco Sforza that it would force Piero and Luca Pitti into working together for Florence.[27] His letter does not reflect personal joy at the downfall of Piero—rather happiness that the leading citizens would be forced to govern together as equals. His goal had been achieved. Needless to say, Piero saw the situation differently. Although Piero's own letter to Sforza has not survived, we do have Pontremoli's letter giving Piero's version of the events.[28] One wonders which story Francesco believed.

The breach between Piero and his former supporters—Agnolo and Dietisalvi—widened in the spring of 1466 with the death of Francesco Sforza. Dietisalvi and Agnolo had spent more than fifteen years serving as a private conduit between the Medici and Sforza families, but now a break in this pattern occurred.[29] In spite of their previous connection, Agnolo and Dietisalvi apparently turned against the Sforza heirs after Francesco's

---

vono ordinato e padri nostri; e delle cose qui della terra non t'ho da dire altro. . . ." Part of this letter appeared in Strozzi, *Lettere*, p. 484.

27. ASM, Sforzesco, Pot. est., Firenze 272, fol. 191r: "è stata cosa molto grata al populo, che pare loro havere riavuto la libertà. . . . Piero et Messer Lucha insieme con li altri principali cittadini si ristringhono insieme con molti altri cittadini, et saranno con più amore et fede l'uno con l'altro fussino mai; perchè hanno magiore bisognio l'uno dell'altro che per il passato. . . ." The letter was written on 23 September 1465.

28. Piero's version of the events went to Francesco Sforza in a letter written by Nicodemo da Pontremoli, the Milanese ambassador to Florence, on 14 September 1465. It can be found in Paris, BN, Ms. Ital., 1591, fol. 191r.

29. In the period between 1451 and 1466 there must have been about 750 letters that survive from Dietisalvi and Agnolo to Francesco Sforza or his chancellor as well as countless others from Milan's ambassador in Florence describing events in Florence and their interpretation by Agnolo and Dietisalvi. These letters can be found in three places in particular: the Bibliothèque Nationale in Paris, the Biblioteca Ambrosiana in Milan, and the Archivio di Stato in Milan. Indeed, a document

death on 8 March 1466. Perhaps one could more correctly say that they used Sforza's departure for their own advantage in Florence. Immediately following Francesco's death, Bianca Maria and Galeazzo Sforza requested some 60,000 florins from Florence to aid in the defense of the Milanese state.[30] After the immediate danger was past, Piero's opponents realized that to aid Milan was, in fact, to strengthen Piero's authority in Florence—something they did not want. Piero and his supporters were anxious to prove to Milan that the Medici could deliver on their promises; in contrast, Piero's opponents wanted to drive a wedge between Piero and Milan.[31] It was not that the anti-Medicean group wanted to attack Milan, which had been a strong ally of their city, but rather that they wanted to demonstrate their power and importance to the Sforza. It is ironic to consider that Agnolo and Dietisalvi had spent some fifteen years working with Francesco Sforza on behalf of Florence and/or the Medici and now refused to support the Sforza family. Agnolo and Dietisalvi as well as Niccolò Soderini led the group who opposed the loan to Milan. The opposition was successful in curtailing the loan and thus in lessening Piero's reputation.[32]

By early May 1466, things had become so bad that the Signoria called upon the leading citizens of the city to make peace with one another. The Signoria required all those who had been *veduti ai Tre Maggiori* to promise to forget all past injuries and to renounce all secret agreements and work together for Florence.[33] This decree was an extraordinary measure taken against both sides in the contest for control of Florentine government. Both the anti-Mediceans and the allies of Piero should have been humiliated by what was in effect a public rebuke by the Signoria in May. Yet, at the same time, the Signoria's action was also testimony to the conspirators' success in convincing the citizenry that their views were valid; there could be a return to the pre-1434 style of Florentine government.

The early May plea by the Signoria had not been enough. The next move by the conspirators and their supporters in the escalating fight for

---

exists which reveals large sums of money paid to Agnolo for his services to Milan (BAM, Ambrosiana Ms. Z 247 sup., fols. 355r–356v).

30. Municchi, *La fazione*, p. 43. The Parenti Chronicle (p. 40) says it was only 40,000 florins.

31. Municchi, *La fazione*, pp. 43–47.

32. Ibid., pp. 46–48, as well as 113–14 in the appendix. The appendix provides the document of instructions to Florence's ambassadors to Milan explaining the cut in funds. See also the Parenti Chronicle, pp. 39–40.

33. G. Pampaloni, "Nuovi tentativi di riforme alla Costituzione Fiorentina visti attraverso le consulte," *Archivio storico italiano* 120 (1960): 555.

control of Florentine government was the public oath on 27 May 1466. Although the name Medici was never mentioned, the oath of 27 May was clearly directed against that family's monopoly of important governmental positions; it did not contain the slightest hint of an organized attempt to oust Piero from his position as first citizen, let alone remove him from Florence. Simply put, 396 citizens swore to uphold the republican system of government with the Signoria being elected by lot, to prevent illegal pressure from being brought to bear on private citizens, and to protect such citizens' freedom to counsel and to decide public affairs.[34] The oath represented the most complete statement of the constitutionalist program that had yet been advanced. Luca Pitti was the first to swear to and sign the oath, Agnolo was second, Dietisalvi was fourth, and Niccolò Soderini was seventh.[35] All the great Florentine families were represented, and many of the signers had held prominent places in the Medicean regime. Numerous families had several signers: the Pitti had seven, the Acciaiuoli five, and the Dietisalvi or Neroni five. Some families were divided over whether or not to sign; even the Medici were represented by Pierfrancesco di Lorenzo, Piero's cousin, who was also Agnolo's son-in-law.[36] Several families who had lost their rights under the Medici also appeared as signers: two Strozzi and one Brancacci.[37] The large number of signatures from powerful families, plus the appearance of many of lesser status, demonstrated that this was not, as the Medici claimed, "the opposition of five or six men with private ambitions."[38]

The last step before the climactic events of August and September 1466 was the debate over the council of the Cento during late June and July. The *pratiche* debates over the continued existence of the Cento provide us with

34. G. Pampaloni, "Il giuramento pubblico in Palazzo Vecchio a Firenze e un patto giurato degli antimedicei (Maggio 1466)," *Bullettino senese di storia patria* 23 (1964): 233–34.

35. Ibid., p. 234.

36. Ibid., p. 236; A. Brown, "Pierfrancesco de' Medici, 1430–1476: A Radical Alternative to Elder Medicean Supremacy?" *Journal of the Warburg and Courtauld Institutes* 42 (1979): 91–92; repr. in Brown, *Medici in Florence*, pp. 86–87.

37. Pampaloni, "Giuramento," pp. 234–38.

38. ASM, Sforzesco, Pot. est., Firenze, 272: Agnolo della Stufa to Francesco Sforza on 8 November 1465 and Piero de' Medici to Francesco Sforza on 7 December 1465. Della Stufa wrote that those not loyal to Piero were "... pochissimi e non passano il numero di dua" and their motivation was "non so qual si sia o invidia o ambitione o paura per non esser cosi vixuti come lui. . . ." Meanwhile, Piero wrote to Francesco Sforza saying, "questi pochi che hanno voluto indebitamente caricare et mio padre et me. . . ."

an unbiased report of Dietisalvi and Agnolo's public stance immediately prior to the final confrontation. The following statements support the view of Agnolo and Dietisalvi as leaders of a pro-republican movement for Florence and not simply *ottimati* putting their own interests ahead of those of their city. In the *pratica*, Dietisalvi admitted that although abolishing the Cento might be against the interests of his own class, he was willing to do it; he said, "I like the council of the Cento, but if it causes trouble it should be abolished." [39] Agnolo argued even more strongly that "the Cento is all right for me, but not for the lower classes, and it can serve as an instrument for despotic government." [40] Niccolò Soderini also appeared as a backer of the lower classes. He criticized the Cento because of the disproportionate number of lesser guildsmen it contained. [41] Thus, at least in the *pratica* it is fair to say that Agnolo and Dietisalvi as well as Niccolò did represent the interests of the lower classes, or at least they presented themselves as disinterested in order to further their arguments. The debate over the Cento was so acrimonious that neither side really was truly successful. The debate so exacerbated the differences between the opposing camps that fear of an armed confrontation began to spread. On 1 August, in the *pratica*, Agnolo spoke of his apprehension for the city. He said that he feared the gulf between the two sides was so wide the city would be destroyed—it would, he suggested, be like returning the city to the hands of the duke of Athens, [42] which certainly would have been anathema to Florentines.

Both sides began—at this point and not before—to provide for men and arms in case they were needed. Piero called on his Sforza allies for assistance while his opponents searched for other sources of aid. There were some negotiations with Venice through Bartolomeo Colleoni, the Venetian Captain, with King Ferrante of Naples, through Agnolo's son Jacopo, who

---

39. ASF, CP, 58, fol. 177r. This is published in Pampaloni, "Nuovi tentativi," p. 571: "El Consiglio del Cento a me piace, ma havendo a fare scandolo sarei di parere che si levassi . . . né dico questo perche si levi o stia il Consiglio del Cento, ma per la pace et unione della città."

40. ASF, CP, 58, fol. 176v: "Noi siamo nel Consiglio del Cento che per me fa meno pe' populari et fa el bisogno di chi vuol tirannezare la città." Published in Pampaloni, "Nuovi tentativi," p. 570.

41. ASF, CP, 58, fol. 177v; Pampaloni, "Nuovi tentativi," p. 572.

42. Municchi, *La fazione*, p. 69; Pampaloni, "Nuovi tentativi," p. 575. In the *pratica* of 1 August 1466, Agnolo said, "Noi habbiamo divisa la terra et le divisione fanno i capi: i capi temono, el timore fa fare amici i quali a diritto a torto si bisognano aiutare. Verremo a questo modo a sospecto a noi medesmi et questo error condusse questa terra nelle mani del Duca d'Athene."

was established at Ferrante's court, and with some of the smaller cities of northern Italy that were not friendly with the Medici.[43] In the end, the anti-Medicean faction allied itself with Marquis Borso d' Este of Ferrara. It was this alliance that precipitated the crisis of 28 through 31 August. When news of the presence of Ferrarese forces in Tuscany reached the city on 27 August, Piero immediately requested that the Sforza troops waiting in the Romagna be mobilized and sent to Florence to counter moves made by his enemies.[44] On 28 August, the Signoria called on both Luca and Piero to disarm and keep the peace. Extremely interesting is the fact that it was Luca who was asked to disarm and not Agnolo or Dietisalvi. Though this is sometimes called the Pitti Conspiracy, Luca really played a secondary role to Agnolo and Dietisalvi. We know Luca did obey, but Piero's reaction is less certain. By 1 September, Luca had been to see Piero and made his own peace with the latter—he would "live or die with Piero."[45] From that point, Piero's opponents had lost the game, and the story was written only from the point of view of the victors. Luca's action was probably motivated by the 28 August drawing of a pro-Medicean Signoria to begin its term on 1 September 1466. Thus, during the *pratica* of 2 September, Luca called for a *parlamento* to remedy the upheaval in Florence. The fact that the *pratica* met in Piero's house on the Via Larga and not in the Palazzo Vecchio demonstrates that Piero had won all.

The Medici victory in September 1466 sent a strong message to both the vanquished and the victors. It moved Florence further away from the civic humanism of the early decades of the fifteenth century and closer to grand ducal form of government instituted in the sixteenth century: it prepared the way for both Lorenzo the Magnificent and later for Cosimo I. Having considered the various positions taken by Agnolo Acciaiuoli and Dietisalvi Neroni from 1464 through 1466, one must now evaluate that behavior in light of the results. From the Medici's public rhetoric the answer is sim-

43. Rubinstein, *The Government,* pp. 176–77, 183. ASF, MAP, LXXII, 236; ibid., LXXII, 233, as well as a missing letter referred to by Agnolo as being written on 29 August 1466. See also one of Jacopo's letters to Agnolo in MAP, LXVIII, 70.

44. We have evidence of the extent of Piero's military preparations from the letter of Nicodemo to Galeazzo Maria and Bianca Sforza on 1 September 1466; ASM, Sforzesco, Pot. est., Firenze, 272. Nicodemo's letter gives a figure of between three and four thousand troops that Piero was ready to send to strengthen the Sforza forces that were already in Tuscany on their way to his assistance.

45. ASM, Sforzesco, Pot. est., Firenze, 272, fols. 117r–119v. Piero de' Medici to Pigello Portinari on 13 September 1466: "Et adciò che tu intenda bene il tucto, t'aviso che M. Luca Pitti il dì inanzi al parlamento (1 September), veduto come le cose andavano, fu quì a me dicendomi essere disposto vivere et morire con meco. . . ."

ple—Agnolo and Dietisalvi, previously *amici,* were now traitors. They were men whose avarice and cupidity had led to an attempt to overthrow the state, which, happily, had been prevented by the populace's efforts to restore freedom.[46] Needless to say, this was not how Agnolo and Dietisalvi viewed the situation: in public at least they presented themselves as responsible citizens whose civic duty was to give Florence the best government possible. In every speech in the *pratiche* during the previous two years, this was how both Agnolo and Dietisalvi portrayed themselves. Nonetheless, at the same time they were ambitious men who were maneuvering to hold power in their own names while widening the governing group as a counterfoil to Medici power. Overall, of the surviving documentary evidence that could have been used in the September 1466 trials for treason, only the letters written to Francesco Sforza criticized Cosimo and Piero by name. Those four or five letters were almost certainly composed with the purpose of detaching Sforza from the Medici and substituting Dietisalvi and Agnolo as the new allies. Every public statement by Piero's opponents seems, as one would expect, to have had Florence's welfare at its heart, while the private, perceived insults that both men had suffered were never discussed, although it was clear that neither man had forgotten them. In the *pratiche,* Agnolo and Dietisalvi always spoke in favor of increasing the size of the power group—not restricting it. Obviously, none of the "conspirators" believed that he alone could rule—no one could replace Cosimo completely, not even his son. And that, of course, was the problem. They were unable to accept Piero as the father figure, the patron, while he was unwilling to see them as equal partners in governing Florence. Ultimately, their goal was always a return to the pre-1434 government, that government which Hans Baron characterized as having had such an impact on Florence's vision of itself.[47] Their public statements were a step-by-step attempt to dis-

---

46. The official version of the events can be found in several sources in the Florentine archives. ASF, Balìe, 30, fols. 5r–7r, is probably the fullest explication of the government's position. Nonetheless, one can also find mention of the government's view of the events in the Signoria's letter to the king of France, dated 23 September 1466 (ASF, Miss. I canc., 45, fols. 106v–107r): "Nonnulli, enim, cives nostri, inflati superbia atque avaritia et pessimis occecati libidinibus, dum sibi ad facinora et explendas cupiditates miseras adaperire tentant viam, etiam libertatem nostram in summum periculum adduxere. . . . Populus enim arma sumens, brevi, eorum perditissimum furorem penitus repressit, libertatem constituit, et, reducta concordia, rempublicam confirmavit stabilemque, etiam perpetuamque effecit."

47. H. Baron, *The Crisis of the Early Italian Renaissance: Civic Humanism and Republican Liberty in an Age of Classicism and Tyranny,* 2 vols. (Princeton, N.J., 1955); rev. ed. in 1 vol. (Princeton, N.J., 1966).

mantle the various controls the Medici had added to Florence's traditional government. Unfortunately, we have no way of knowing what was said in their homes or felt in their hearts. Even the surviving letters between Agnolo and his son Jacopo simply chronicle the events and relay instructions, but they do not display any personal animosity toward the Medici.[48] No letter complaining of Cosimo's interference in Acciaiuoli affairs has survived, if indeed one ever existed.

Nonetheless, the events of 1464–66 taught the Medici an important lesson: it was dangerous to appear to share power with anyone. Because *ottimati* like Agnolo and Dietisalvi had viewed themselves as having their own client networks and, therefore, as working *with and not just for* Cosimo, the latter's death was the signal to increase their own status in Florentine governmental circles. This was simply unacceptable for future Medici rule. Henceforth, political power was not to be a right but a gift bestowed on worthy followers by the Medici. After 1466, government was further tightened and restricted: the Medici were to be the sole patrons in the political arena; everyone else was to be a client. There were to be no more Dietisalvis or Agnolos or even Luca Pittis. It was to teach this lesson that Agnolo, Dietisalvi, and their families were exiled for twenty years and that Luca was deprived of any real power for the rest of his life.[49] From the Medici perspective, it was immaterial whether Agnolo and Dietisalvi were patriots or traitors or merely impatient and ambitious politicians. What was essential were the lessons these critical years had taught the Medici: in order to keep absolute control of political life in Florence, they had to ensure both the loyalty and the complete satisfaction of their clients, dependents, and supporters through a combination of rewards and threats. Therefore, although insults to clients were to be avoided, more important to the smooth functioning of the post-1466 patron-client system was the need for Medici clients to understand the limitations of their positions.

48. ASF, MAP, LXXII, 231, 233, 236; LXVIII, 70, 74; LXI; 78; CS, ser. 1, 136, fols. 28r, 29r, 30r, 31r, 32r, 33r–34r, 35r. Some of the letters had sections written with disappearing ink that had been treated or in code, but those sections could just as well have appeared in the main body of the letters.

49. ASF, Balìe, 30, fols. 18r–19r, 57v–58r: Dietisalvi and his family were to be exiled to Sicily while his brother Francesco was sent to Orvieto or Todi. Ibid., fol. 16v: Agnolo and his sons were exiled to Barletta for twenty years; Niccolò Soderini and his illegitimate son Geri were exiled to Provence under the guardianship of King Renato for twenty years. Benedetto Dei (ASF, Manoscritti, 119, fols. 23v–25r), also lists all those exiled and declared rebels. Luca Pitti and Giovannozzo Pitti and their families are conspicuously absent from these lists.

7   The War of the Eight Saints in Florentine Memory and Oblivion

David S. Peterson

I

Memory forgets, sometimes quite willingly. It is a process whereby individuals, groups, and entire societies conserve and record, but also filter, repress, and configure past experience to shape and accommodate their identities for presentation to self and others. The aims (or results) may range from explanation to concealment, self-congratulation to exculpation, self-justification and legitimation to the nurturing (construction, and elaboration) of grievances against others. Although memories may be preserved even fortuitously in texts and artifacts, their storage there can just as well be part of a deliberate and selective process. This is especially so when the objects concerned are carefully designed works of art, and the texts artfully composed narrative histories.

The memory of the Quattrocento Florentine Renaissance has long enjoyed an iconic status in narratives of Western civilization as a stage upon which its admirers have found enacted much of what they most prized in European culture and politics. Nor is this wholly accidental. The numerous vernacular memoirs (*ricordi*) of merchants like Giovanni Morelli, as well as the Latin histories of humanists like Leonardo Bruni and Poggio Bracciolini, reveal a society whose members were deeply self-conscious and historically minded. Much of the basis for accepting the notion of a Florentine Renaissance derives from the testimony of contemporaries like Matteo Palmieri

William Connell, Kenneth Gouwens, John Najemy, Kristin Ruggiero, and Brian Tierney kindly read this chapter and offered many valuable suggestions for its improvement, as did members of the European History Colloquium at Cornell University and the Medieval and Renaissance Studies Seminar at Washington and Lee University. Cornell and the Newberry Library in Chicago alike provided me with splendid facilities in which to write. The project of which this chapter is a part was supported by a generous Research Fellowship from the National Endowment for the Humanities.

and Giorgio Vasari that they were indeed having one, and on the determination of their fellows to furnish the necessary historical texts and artworks as proof. The Florentines' rediscovery of their ancient Roman ancestors carried in its train a recognition of themselves as an audience of modern posterity, making their Renaissance dialogue with the past an essential stimulus also to their own studied self-presentation to future generations.

Among the most notable examples of the Florentines' Renaissance are the works of art they commissioned for their churches and the texts composed by their humanist historians. Architects like Brunelleschi articulated a classicized Roman vocabulary of harmoniously balanced columns and rounded arches to solemnize the interior spaces of Florence's new cathedral and numerous other churches such as San Lorenzo and Santo Spirito that were rebuilt or remodeled in the late fourteenth and early fifteenth centuries. Painters like Masaccio and sculptors such as Donatello in turn adorned these churches with images and objects whose classical realism and naturalism give them heightened spiritual poignancy. Meanwhile, the city's humanist chancellors and historians from Coluccio Salutati onward recalled to Florentine citizens the genealogy of their descent from the Roman Republic, celebrated their republican institutions and their embrace of civic duty in the defense of their liberty, and lauded the ambition and unabashed entrepreneurial acquisitiveness that made possible their civic and charitable benefactions.

But although Florentine artists and humanists alike deployed classical motifs, the projects in which they engaged were in fact quite different. Artists employed pre-Christian art forms in the city's churches not to subvert religious space but to sacralize the city's urban fabric. The humanists, on the other hand, used classical rhetoric and historiographical models not only to connect the city's republican present to its Roman origins but also to secularize the vision of its history that informed contemporary political discourse. Underscoring the particularity of Florentine history did not, to be sure, require detaching it entirely from Christianity's universal eschatology. Even Machiavelli, after all, concluded *Il Principe* crying out for a new Italian redeemer. But Florentine humanists no longer recounted events to manifest the providence of God working directly through human agents. They highlighted instead the causal agency of human protagonists themselves and inscribed into their actions the civic and republican values that they aimed to recall to their contemporary and future readers. *Fortuna* was not *providentia Dei*.

The result has been that subsequent historians, taking their cues from Quattrocento and Cinquecento Florentine historians, long tended to portray the society as a whole in secular hues. But if we turn back from these textual sentinels to reconsider the city's churches not simply as works of art but as historical artifacts with a documentary significance of their own, and begin, as historians recently have done, to incorporate the archival study of religion and the church into Florentine social and political history, a paradox emerges: while Florentines were secularizing and de-Christianizing the discursive realm of their civic politics in the early Quattrocento, they were simultaneously sacralizing and re-Christianizing their built civic environment.[1] This is not to resurrect long discredited caricatures of the humanists as pagans, or to reposit a fundamental conflict (not even updated as "culture wars") between secularizing humanists and Christian reactionaries. Humanists from Petrarch onward were deeply Augustinian in their anthropology and attacked ecclesiastics not for their religion but for their lack of it. Nor is it necessary to pin religion and classicism on different elements of the social order. Leonardo Bruni wrote his classicizing republican panegyric and history of Florence to ingratiate himself with the same Florentine rulers who commissioned Ghiberti's *Gates of Paradise;* indeed, he helped select the biblical scenes to be represented.

Taken together, the written and material evidence furnished by Quattrocento Florentines points to a simultaneous rise of investment in a built Christian environment, concurrent with a surge of textual production that wrote secular values into the Florentine social and political world. The commemoration in Florentine churches of a Christian present contemporaneous with the textual recollection of a secular past that pointed directly to it suggests a fascinating instability of values. Societies, of course, need no more be consistent with themselves than are individuals. The Florentine case might simply be let stand as an example of mildly schizophrenic Renaissance self-fashioning. But because memory is the art also of selective (and collective) forgetting, and silences thus have histories of their own, it is worth excavating the documentary remains of those lying beneath Florence's ecclesiastical commemorations and historical recollections to see whether they do not converge at some point in the oblivion of a past that Florentines either chose to forget—or remembered very carefully.

1. G. Brucker's chapter "The Church and the Faith" was seminal in introducing the church as a factor in Florentine culture: Brucker, *Renaissance Florence*, 2d ed. (Berkeley and Los Angeles, 1983), pp. 172–212. See D. S. Peterson, "Out of the Margins: Religion and the Church in Renaissance Italy," *Renaissance Quarterly* 53 (2000): 835–79 (840). R. Goldthwaite summarizes the surge of fifteenth-century ecclesiastical building projects in *Wealth and the Demand for Art in Italy 1300–1600* (Baltimore, 1993), pp. 69–148.

II

In few societies have religion and politics been woven together so intimately —and conflictually—as they were in Renaissance Florence. As far back as the eleventh century, Florentine support under the Countess Matilda had been essential to the survival of the Gregorian reform movement, and from the formation of the Guelf entente in the 1260s down to the reigns of the Medici popes Leo X (1513–21) and Clement VII (1523–34) at the outbreak of the Reformation, no community in Europe was more vital to the economic and political fortunes (and misfortunes) of the papacy than its Tuscan neighbor, rival, and financier, Florence. Nor, in the two centuries from Dante's robust denunciation of the papacy in his *Commedia* down to Savonarola's project to fuse Christian and republican *renovatio* in a Florentine "New Jerusalem" that defied Pope Alexander VI (1492–1503), was any city so vigorous in condemning the papacy or so protean in generating new forms of religious thought and expression in artistic, political, and urban contexts.

The famous twenty-eighth maxim that Francesco Guicciardini (1483–1540) penned in the early sixteenth century appears to telescope the ambivalence many Florentines felt toward the church: "I don't know anyone who dislikes the ambition, the avarice and the sensuality of priests more than I do," wrote the papal governor of Modena and the Romagna. "Nevertheless, the position I have enjoyed with several popes has forced me to love their greatness for my own self-interest. Were it not for this consideration, I would have loved Martin Luther as much as I love myself." [2] In his ensuing maxim Guicciardini specified the cause of his dilemma, explaining that the Florentines had "the church as a neighbor, which is powerful and never dies." Essential to Guicciardini's schematization of his Florentine codependence with the church was the manner in which he identified clergy at all levels with the papacy, both with political power, and the necessity he therefore felt to partition his religious convictions from his political interests. Like Machiavelli (1469–1527), Guicciardini wondered whether it was possible "to control governments and states, if one wants to hold them as they are held today, according to the precepts of Christian law," and concluded that it was not. [3]

2. Francesco Guicciardini, "Ricordi, Seconda Serie," in Guicciardini, *Opere*, vol. 8, *Scritti politici e ricordi*, ed. R. Palmarocchi (Bari, 1933), p. 290; and in English in Guicciardini, *Dialogue on the Government of Florence*, trans. A. Brown (Cambridge, England, 1994), p. 171.

3. *Dialogo del reggimento di Firenze*, in Guicciardini, *Opere*, vol. 7, *Dialogo e discorsi del reggimento di Firenze*, ed. R. Palmarocchi (Bari, 1932), p. 162; trans.

There was much to justify these sentiments in the wake of Savonarola's late-fifteenth-century failure as an "unarmed prophet," when Renaissance popes had subverted the earlier efforts of conciliar reformers to curb their monarchical pretensions and had transformed themselves into ambitious Italian princes. But because Machiavelli's and Guicciardini's texts became the vehicles through which the preceding three centuries of Florentine history were synthesized and transmitted into the broader stream of European thought—and memory—historians in turn have read back out of the history of the Florentine republic the sixteenth-century identification of church with papacy, and the separation of religion from politics, that they wrote into it. Nor were these leanings without some foundation in earlier fifteenth-century humanist historiography. Leonardo Bruni (c. 1370–1444) and Poggio Bracciolini (1380–1459), upon whom they relied, embraced classical models that privileged political, military, and diplomatic narratives to focus their histories on Florence's development in its republican dimensions. In the process, they touched on local ecclesiastical or religious matters only so far as popes and prelates came on stage as players in Italian politics. The roles that religion and the local church played in shaping the Quattrocento Florentine cultural milieu that produced its foundational humanist historians were thus masked and obscured by the very selectivity and semiotics of the humanists' own narratives.

III

This is nowhere more evident than in their treatment of the cataclysmic War of the Eight Saints that Florence fought against Pope Gregory XI (1370–78) in 1375–78. Climaxing in the outbreak of the papal schism and the revolt of Florence's downtrodden Ciompi clothworkers, the war unfolded in two phases and encompassed two corresponding clusters of issues. It began as a Florentine effort to check the menacing expansion of the papal state in central Italy that the Avignon popes had set as a condition for their return to Rome and was fueled by the antipathy many Florentine citizens felt toward their Guelf fellows whose personal ties to the Papal Curia threatened to subvert the commune's sovereignty. Florence enjoyed a series of early successes, sponsoring uprisings throughout the papal state that were hailed by the republic's newly appointed chancellor Coluccio Salutati (1331–1406) as the triumph of Tuscan and Italian *libertas* over papal despotism. But as the war bogged down, the Florentines were confronted

---

Brown, p. 158. Machiavelli expressed a corresponding view (but without direct mention of Christianity) in his notorious fifteenth chapter of *The Prince*.

with rising military expenses that drove them to a momentous second step. Already under a papal interdict, the city's leaders determined in 1376 to finance the war by selling off local clerical property, and they proceeded to the most extensive liquidation of an ecclesiastical patrimony attempted anywhere in Europe before the Reformation. A war against the papacy was thus transformed into a referendum on the place of religion and the church within the Florentine community itself—again, one of the most literate and sophisticated in pre-Reformation Europe. The spoliation of the Florentine church, accompanied by efforts first to do without clerical ministrations, then, from 1377, to compel clergy to officiate and laity to attend services, turned the public sharply against the war. Flagellants took to the streets, the city's political leadership split bitterly, and Florence was forced to sue for peace. Gregory XI's timely death and the outbreak of the schism in the spring of 1378 enabled Florence to negotiate with the weak Roman pope Urban VI (1378–89). But there immediately ensued the revolt of the Ciompi. The war had a devastating impact on the Florentine church that shaped its politics and internal operations down to the mid–fifteenth century. And it impressed upon subsequent generations of Florentine rulers the vital importance of the legitimating power of the sacred in the city's economy of political interests, conditioning their policies not only toward papal Rome but, especially, toward the local Florentine church, even longer.

IV

Guicciardini omitted the war almost entirely from his youthful *Storie fiorentine,* beginning immediately afterward with the revolt of the Ciompi. But he blamed the uprising itself on the Otto di balìa, a special commission of eight magistrates who had been charged with the war's prosecution, for recklessly catering to Florence's lower classes.[4] He returned to the war twenty years later in his *Cose fiorentine,* written in the immediate aftermath of the Sack of Rome in 1527, on his return to a Florence in the last gasp of republican and messianic fervor. He prefaced his account with a speech by a confident Florentine councillor who favored the war "to preserve the dignity of our *patria* . . . [and] to maintain our liberty . . . undertaken not against the Church of God, nor against the vicars of Christ, but against evil pastors, against wicked governors."[5] To this he contrasted the

4. Guicciardini, *Storie fiorentine dal 1378 al 1509,* ed. R. Palmarocchi (Bari, 1931), pp. 1–2.

5. Guicciardini, *Le cose fiorentine,* ed. R. Ridolfi (Florence, 1945), p. 41: "per conservare la degnità della patria nostra . . . per mantenere la nostra libertà . . . si pigli

cautious Carlo Strozzi, who wondered how Guelf Florence could justify a war against the papacy, and predicted that the inevitable papal interdict would so traumatize the Florentines that "perhaps the greater part, on account of the damages and injuries of the war, will be disposed to return to the old faith." [6] But from these suggestive interpretive poles Guicciardini proceeded to narrate a tightly focused account of the political infighting between Florence's Ricci and Albizzi factions, and of the movements of armies and embassies, touching only minimally on the broader domestic impact of the interdict and the expropriation of church property. The veteran statesman's dry verdict was that "it is not enough to undertake wars with justice and generosity, if these are not accompanied by prudence as well." [7]

Machiavelli touched only glancingly on the war in his *Istorie fiorentine*. Nevertheless, he paused to offer an encomium to the Otto for having administered it "with such virtue and with such universal satisfaction that . . . they were called Saints even though they had little regard for censures, had despoiled the churches of their goods, and had compelled the clergy to celebrate the offices—so much more did those citizens then esteem their fatherland than their souls." [8] But though he lauded the Otto for their courage in placing devotion to the *patria* above fear of spiritual sanctions, Machiavelli nevertheless left open the possibility that their actions might indeed have been damnable. Recounting a meeting held just before the war of citizens concerned to end factional strife, Machiavelli inserted into the speech of their spokesman the lament that factionalism and the corruption of the city had arisen "because religion and fear of God have been eliminated in all." [9] While he reveled in the blow dealt the papacy by the Otto, Machiavelli echoed in his *Istorie* the view he had set forth in the *Discorsi*, that "as the observance of divine institutions is the cause of the greatness of republics, so the disregard of them produces their ruin." [10]

---

questa giusta, necessaria et sancta guerra non contro alla Chiesa di Dio, non contro a' vicarii di Christo, ma contro a' captivi pastori, contro agli scelerati governatori."

6. Ibid.: "et forse la maggiore parte, per e' danni et molestie della guerra, sin inclinerà a tornare alla anticha devotione."

7. Ibid., p. 62: "che non basta piglare le guerre con giustitia et con generosità, se anche non si piglano con prudentia."

8. Niccolò Machiavelli, *Istorie fiorentine*, bk. 3, chap. 2, in *Opere*, ed. A. Montevecchi, vol. 2 (Turin, 1971), p. 421; and Machiavelli, *Florentine Histories*, trans. L. F. Banfield and H. C. Mansfield Jr. (Princeton, N.J., 1988), p. 114.

9. Bk. 3, chap. 5; trans. Banfield and Mansfield, p. 110.

10. Machiavelli, *Discorsi sopra la Prima Deca di Tito Livio*, bk. 1, chap. 11, in Machiavelli, *Opere*, ed. E. Raimondi (Milan, 1976), pp. 154–55; Machiavelli, *The Prince and the Discourses*, trans. M. Lerner (New York, 1950), p. 148.

Writing a century before Machiavelli and only decades after the War of the Eight Saints itself, Leonardo Bruni, the founder of Florentine humanist historiography, was even more reticent. He could scarcely ignore the rising new Florentine cathedral and the numerous other ecclesiastical building projects that were visible throughout early Quattrocento Florence. Thus, in his famous "Panegyric" (*Laudatio*) of 1403–4, he commended the Florentines' piety and paused in his description of the city to offer lavish praise of their churches: "Indeed," he wrote, "in all of Florence nothing is more richly appointed, more ornate in style, more magnificent than these churches. As much attention has been given to decorating sacred buildings as to secular ones, so that not only the habitations of the living would be outstanding but the tombs of the dead as well." [11] At the same time, Bruni carefully circumscribed the churches' significance by inserting his description into a portion of the *Laudatio* devoted not to the city's history and institutions but to its architecture. Aiming to celebrate the republic, his parallel juxtapositions of buildings sacred and profane, of habitations for the living and the dead, effected an equality between the Florentine church and the republic, while separating the concerns of this world from those of the next.

Likewise, though Bruni celebrated the role of Florence's Parte Guelfa in championing the city's Roman republican ideals, he made only the briefest allusion to the Parte's origin as an alliance supporting the papacy. [12] While he could trace the many wars that Florentines had fought against tyrants in defense of their *libertas* back to the famous Guelf victory over the Ghibelline leader Manfred at Beneventum in 1266, he made no reference whatsoever to the great war that Florence had fought immediately prior to its recent victory over Milan's Giangaleazzo Visconti in 1402—the War of the Eight Saints. The omission was scarcely casual. Florence's victory over Milan in fact served Bruni, as it did many other Florentines, not only as an occasion for celebrating the triumph of Florentine republican ideals but also as a means of canceling the memory of an earlier war for Florentine *libertas*—that of the Eight Saints—that had gone terribly wrong.

Several decades later, when he turned to writing his *Historiarum florentini populi libri XII* (begun by 1415), Bruni could no longer completely

11. Leonardo Bruni, *Laudatio Florentinae Urbis*, in *From Petrarch to Leonardo Bruni: Studies in Humanistic and Political Literature*, ed. H. Baron (Chicago, 1968), p. 236, lines 13–17; trans. B. Kohl in *The Earthly Republic: Italian Humanists on Government and Society*, ed. B. Kohl and R. G. Witt (Philadelphia, 1978), pp. 139–40.

12. Ibid., p. 261, line 26.

ignore it. Rather, he focused on the first year of the conflict, which he could easily frame as a defensive war against papal aggression. Thereafter, throughout its second, domestic phase, Bruni kept his attention fixed squarely on the movements of armies and diplomats, turning to Florentine civic affairs only to note that the renewals of the Otto "provoked great jealousy among many."[13] Without ever mentioning Florence's assault on its local church and the political turmoil that ensued, he concluded his account by noting the outbreak of the schism, then partitioned the war from the city's internal life, and the Ciompi Revolt, with a chapter division.

v

The War of the Eight Saints had its ideological roots in a debate over ecclesiastical wealth and jurisdictions that had been intensifying throughout Europe for over a century. In sixteenth-century Italy, Machiavelli and Guicciardini took the temporal power of church and papacy for granted and distinguished both from true religion. But in the fourteenth century they were still conceivable as spiritual institutions, and it was the doctrine of papal *plenitudo potestatis*, upon which popes based their expanding claims not only to supreme authority within the church but also to myriad powers of intervention in temporal affairs, that occupied political theorists. It had inspired the growth of the radical Spiritual wing of the Franciscan order, and King Philip IV of France's challenge to clerical immunities from royal taxation and the courts, which elicited from Pope Boniface VIII the intemperate bull *Unam sanctam* (1302), strongly implying that all temporal rulers derived their authority from the pope and roundly designating all the faithful as his subjects. *Unam sanctam* became a rich target for critics that papal apologists like Giles of Rome actually widened by advancing fulsome claims for papal world *dominium* (lordship) that fused the issues of jurisdictions and property rights, thus effectively inviting opponents of papal authority to take aim at clerical wealth as well.

Among the sharpest antipapal reactions came from Italians. Dante articulated in his *Monarchia* (c. 1310) an ideal Aristotelian vision of a new Roman Empire, in which all political authority would be concentrated in a single temporal world ruler: restricting the church to a purely spiritual role

---

13. Leonardo Bruni, *Historiarum florentini populi libri XII*, ed. E. Santini and C. di Pierro, *Rerum italicarum scriptores*, 2d ed., vol. 19, pt. 3 (Città di Castello, 1914), bk. 8, p. 219: "magnam illis apud multos conflarat invidiam."

would secure humanity's common good by ending the destructive conflict between church and state. As he explained through Marco Lombardo at the center of his *Commedia*, all the evils of the world derived from misgovernment caused by a papacy which "striving to combine / two powers in one, fouls self and load and all."[14] In his *Defensor pacis* (1324), Marsilius of Padua added Roman corporation law to Dante's amalgam of Aristotelian and Franciscan arguments to propose reducing the church to purely spiritual powers and subjecting it to the supervision of a sovereign lay authority, the "faithful human legislator." Clergy would be subject to the penalties of the civil law and might, if necessary, be compelled by the state to perform services and to administer the sacraments.[15] The legislator would supervise appointments to ecclesiastical offices and any necessary inquisitions, and would oversee the administration of ecclesiastical property. Superfluous clerical property would be subject to taxation just like that of the laity.[16] Dante's *Commedia* became, of course, the cornerstone of Florentine literature, and an Italian translation (from the French) of the *Defensor pacis* circulated in Florence from 1363 onward, with numerous marginal arrows pointing to the passages on tithes and church property.[17]

Marsilius was soon joined at Ludwig of Bavaria's antipapal court by the brilliant English Franciscan heretic William of Ockham (c. 1285–c. 1347), who, followed by his Oxford countryman John Wycliff (d. 1384) later in the century, articulated political theories that also curtailed ecclesiastical jurisdictions and property rights, based not, however, on the church's presumed character as a spiritual institution but on its now evident forfeiture of that role. Wycliff wrote his *De civili dominio* (1378) with an eye on Florence's War of the Eight Saints, and the echo of his views in John Hus led to innumerable condemnations before (and after) the Czech's execution at the Council of Constance in 1415.[18]

14. Dante Alighieri, *Purgatorio*, canto 16, lines 128–29, in *Opere*, ed. F. Chiappelli (Milan, 1963), p. 626; and *The Divine Comedy*, vol. 2, *Purgatory*, trans. D. L. Sayers (Harmondsworth, 1955), p. 191.

15. Marsilius of Padua, *Defensor pacis*, trans. A. Gewirth (New York, 1956), Discourse 2, chap. 8, and chap. 17, p. 262.

16. Ibid., Discourse 2, chap. 17, esp. p. 264, on appointments; chap. 10 on inquisitions; chap. 21, pp. 296–97 on tithes; chap. 14, esp. p. 219, on administering church property; and chap. 17, par. 18, p. 266, on clerical taxation.

17. These marginalia are summarized in Marsilius, *Defensor pacis: Nella traduzione in volgare fiorentino del 1363*, ed. C. Pincin (Turin, 1966), pp. 547–48.

18. John Wycliff, *De civili dominio*, ed. I. Loserth, R. L. Poole, and F. D. Matthew II (London, 1900), bk. 2, chap. 9, p. 90, citing Gregory XI's interdiction of Florence in 1376 as a politically motivated abuse of papal spiritual authority.

VI

Florence's rulers had been given a powerful incentive to acquiesce in the expansion of papal controls over ecclesiastical wealth and appointments by Pope Martin IV's confirmation of the Florentine bankers' right to collect papal taxes in 1281, and papal actions touching the Florentine church could in any case easily be mediated privately by Florentines at the Papal Curia itself. Nevertheless, in (frequent) periods of domestic crisis, when Florence's patrician rulers sought to augment their power by admitting members of the lesser guilds and *novi cives* to a greater share of political offices, these new people (*gente nuova*) tended to pursue stricter constitutional protections of the commune's sovereignty, both against papal meddling from outside and against aristocrats' use of local ecclesiastical institutions to augment their power within Florentine politics. Under the "popular" governments of the Primo Popolo (1250–60) and of Giano della Bella (1293–97), and in response to interventions such as those of the papal legate Cardinal Latino Malabranca in 1279–80, and of Pope Boniface VIII in 1301–3, the Florentine councils passed a series of laws that prohibited the appointment of Florentine "magnates" to the bishoprics of Florence and Fiesole (which might be used as seigneurial power bases); required that ecclesiastics claiming fiscal and judicial immunities verify their clerical status; and denied that excommunications of communal officials could be cited to disqualify their decisions.[19] When, in the financial crisis of 1343–48 precipitated by the collapse of the Bardi and Acciaiuoli banking houses, Pope Clement VI (1342–52) used the inquisitor's office and an interdict to pressure Florentine bankers to treat ecclesiastical creditors preferentially, another broadly based government passed additional laws limiting clerical immunity from communal courts, restricting the inquisitor's power to investigate usury, and defying the interdict. At the same time, the Florentines also managed their fiscal crisis to a resolution by creating a funded public debt, the Monte, backed by papal juridical guarantees.[20]

Thereafter, the decades leading up to the War of the Eight Saints saw

19. R. Caggese, ed., *Statuti della repubblica fiorentina*, 2 vols. (Florence, 1910–21), vol. 1, *Statuto del Capitano del Popolo degli anni 1322–1325*, bk. 5, chaps. 78, 128, pp. 273–74, 320–23; and vol. 2, *Statuto del Podestà dell' anno 1325*, bk. 5, chaps. 61, 82–85, pp. 401, 412–15.

20. The legislation is published in A. Panella, "Politica ecclesiastica del comune fiorentino dopo la cacciata del Duca d'Atene," *Archivio storico italiano* 71 (1913): 271–370; and discussed by M. Becker, "Some Economic Implications of the Conflict between Church and State in Trecento Florence," *Medieval Studies* 21 (1959): 1–16.

broad Florentine-papal collaboration on matters of finance and appointments to benefices, as well as light Florentine taxation of the clergy.[21] But
distrust began to grow when Pope Innocent VI (1352–62) dispatched Cardinal Egidio de Albornoz from Avignon in 1353 to recover control of the
papal state in central Italy. Two factions emerged in Florence: the Albizzi
family and their followers identified the city's interests with those of the
papacy and the elite Parte Guelfa, while the Ricci and their supporters were
more willing to countenance closer relations with Milan as a counter to the
papacy's growing power on the peninsula and were more sympathetic to
the *gente nuova*'s mistrust of local ecclesiastical prerogatives.

VII

Gregory XI came to the pontificate in late 1370 in a moment of calm and was
personally congratulated by members of Florence's powerful philo-papal
Albizzi, Corsini, Strozzi, and Alberti families.[22] He was determined, however, to complete the papacy's consolidation of control over its central Italian
Patrimony, and to subdue its neighbors, in order to bring the Curia back to
Rome. Soon he was dispatching letters and embassies to neighboring Florence and other Tuscan cities with assurances that his assault on nearby Perugia portended no threat to their "Tuscan liberties," while he urged papal
loyalists like Lapo da Castiglionchio and other members of the Parte Guelfa
within the city to discourage any sharp Florentine response.[23] Florentine
councillors were deeply skeptical of the pope's motives. Gregory's increasingly indignant appeals for Florentine aid against Perugia, the Este of Ferrara, and Bernabò Visconti of Milan went unheeded or were minimally honored.[24] But his use of indirect political as well as formal diplomatic channels
to influence Florentine decision making facilitated erratic jumps of allegiance, such as Uguccione de' Ricci's spectacular defection to the Albizzi

21. My analysis draws heavily on G. Brucker, *Florentine Politics and Society,
1343–1378* (Princeton, N.J., 1962), chaps. 6–7; and R. C. Trexler, *The Spiritual
Power: Republican Florence under Interdict* (Leiden, 1974).

22. ASV, RV, 263, fols. 255r–256r, 257v (8, 13 February 1371).

23. Ibid., fols. 280r–v (8 June 1371), 76v–77r (7 July 1371), 80v–81r (11 July
1371), to Florence, Siena, and Lucca; ibid., fols. 272v–273r (2 May 1371), and RV,
269, fols. 346r–347r (22 November 1373) to Florentine Guelfs.

24. RV, 263, fols. 11v–12r (1 February 1371), demanding Florentine aid in the
papal state; and RV, 269, fols. 81v–82r (13 September 1373), that troops be dispatched against Bernabò. A commission of nine lawyers, including Lapo, Donato
Barbadori, and Donato de' Ricci, absolved Florence of any legal obligation to do so;
ASF, CP, 12, fol. 24v (10 May 1372).

side in 1373, and fueled a crescendo of factional strife that overtook the city in the next few years.

The pope also intervened aggressively in local ecclesiastical affairs and pressed the issue of "ecclesiastical liberties" with Florence. In 1371 he replaced Fra Andrea of the popular Ricci family with his own man, Fra Piero di Ser Lippo of Florence, to head the Florentine inquisition, in a move that could not but have been perceived in Florence as shoring up the political power of local Guelf families.[25] In 1373 Gregory deputed his own papal commissioners to reform the monasteries of the Florentine and Pisan dioceses, and he intervened aggressively in local ecclesiastical appointments.[26] When Antonio di Luca Abbati, a member of the minor Tuscan aristocracy and Gregory's *"serviens armorum atque familiaris,"* was summoned to appear before the communal courts, Gregory stridently protested this violation of ecclesiastical immunity.[27] Subsequently, the Florentines uncovered a scheme among members of the Albizzi and Corsini families to secure the appointment of a complicitous abbot to the strategically located monastery of Vallombrosa in the Apennines to facilitate the advance of papal troops toward the city. As the chronicler Stefani observed, "This affair was said to have a very long tail."[28]

Florence's councils responded to these provocations by passing new laws limiting the rights of churches to offer sanctuary to criminals and by refurbishing older measures that limited clerical judicial immunities and regulated access to ecclesiastical benefices.[29] The year 1375 revealed only further papal treachery to the Florentines. The city had been hit by a wave of plague and severe crop failures in late 1374, but appeals for permission to import grain from the papal lands around Bologna went unheeded. Rather, while Florence starved, Gregory ratcheted up his campaign in defense of ecclesiastical liberties by demanding now that the commune repeal its laws restricting the powers of inquisitors. For good measure, he fired some ex-

25. ASF, Dipl., S. Croce, 13 February 1373 and 15 March 1373, published in B. Bughetti, "Documenta quaedam spectantia ad sacram inquisitionem et ad schisma ordinis in provincia praesertim Tusciae circa finem saec. XIV," *Archivum Franciscanum Historicum* 9 (1916): 347–83 (350–51, 353–55).

26. ASV, RV, 265, fols. 81v–82r (5 November 1373).

27. RV, 268, fols. 274r–275r (28 June 1372).

28. Marchionne di Coppo Stefani, *Cronaca fiorentina*, ed. N. Rodolico, in *Rerum italicarum scriptores*, 2d ed., vol. 30, pt. 1 (Città di Castello, 1903), rub. 738, p. 285: "Dissesi avere questa cosa gran coda."

29. ASF, PR, 60, fols. 148v–149v (8 January 1373), limiting sanctuary; PR, 62, fols. 29v–30r (20 April 1373), against clergy fleeing communal jurisdiction; and PR, 61, fol. 183r–v (28 November 1373); PR, 62, fols. 76r–77v (27 June 1374).

communications on this issue over the Florentine bow at the rulers of neighboring Pistoia.[30] Then, in June, while papal envoys were in Florence seeking funds for the war against Bernabò Visconti, news arrived that the pope had secretly arranged a truce with the Milanese ruler. Papal troops led by the English mercenary John Hawkwood were now released from service and headed toward Florence, demanding a staggering 130,000 florins to spare the city from pillage. Later that month, a clerical plot was uncovered in Prato to yield the city to papal troops from Bologna.[31]

The clerics involved in the Prato plot were brutally executed, and Florence now organized for war. An executive priorate was drawn for the July–August term that contained an unusually large number of "new men" sympathetic to the antipapal leanings of the Ricci faction. Already the city had arranged a nonaggression pact with Hawkwood at a cost of 130,000 florins.[32] Now, without mentioning the clergy directly, the councils approved the priors' creation of a special commission of eight citizens, who in fact came to be known as the Otto dei preti, or Eight Saints, charged to levy a one-year, 130,000-florin forced loan (prestanza) on the clergy of Florence and Fiesole to pay off Hawkwood.[33] The old prohibition against Florentine magnates accepting the bishoprics of Florence or Fiesole was reinvoked, and a law was passed transferring jurisdiction over last testaments and usury cases from ecclesiastical courts to the commune's Monte offi-

30. ASV, RV, 271, fols. 15v–16r (9 March 1375), published in C. Eubel, ed., Bullarium Franciscanum, vol. 6 (Vatican City, 1902), doc. 1374, p. 549, to Florence; and ASV, RV, 271, fol. 16r (9 March 1375), to Florence.

31. A. Gherardi, "Di un trattato per far ribellare al comune di Firenze la terra di Prato nell'anno 1375," Archivio storico italiano, 3d ser., 10 (1869): 3–26.

32. ASF, Dipl., RAP, 21 June, 1375; and in A. Gherardi, "La guerra dei Fiorentini con papa Gregorio XI detta la guerra degli Otto Santi," Archivio storico italiano, 3d ser., 5 (1867): 35–131; 6 (1867): 208–51; 7 (1868): 211–48; 8 (1868): 260–96; published at 6 (1867): doc. 6, pp. 210–15.

33. ASF, PR, 63, fols. 69r–72v (7 July 1375), summarized in Gherardi, "La guerra," 6 (1867): doc. 12, pp. 217–18. They were Paolo di Matteo Malifici, Giovanni d'Angiolo Capponi, Antonio di Forese Sachetti, Antonio di Filippo Tolosini, Bardo di Guglielmo Altoviti, Recco di Guido Guaza, Salvi di Filippo Salvi, and Michele di Puccio albergatore. Gregory noted that the commission was referred to as the "Otto santi" in his condemnation of the city on 31 March 1376 (below, note 68), but the commune did not officially acknowledge that the tax fell on the clergy until August 1376: ASF, PR, 64, fols. 115v–117r (26 August 1376), fol. 115v. Stefani, Cronaca, rub. 753, pp. 293–94, recognized it immediately as a tax on the clergy, as did the author of the "Cronichetta d' incerto," in Cronichette antiche di varii scrittori del buon secolo della lingua toscana, ed. D. Manni (Florence, 1733), p. 203. The accounts are preserved in ASF, MC, 1742.

cials.[34] A month later, the councils approved the creation of another special commission, the Otto di balìa, empowered to make the military and diplomatic arrangements necessary to carry on a war against the pope.[35] By late summer they had worked out an alliance with Florence's and the papacy's traditional enemy: Milan.[36]

Both sides had already launched a war of propaganda. In May, Florence's ambitious young new chancellor Salutati addressed an "apology" to the pope, meant to be read out in Consistory, that actually detailed Florentine grievances running back to the arrival of Cardinal Albornoz in 1353. Protesting Florence's long-standing devotion to the church, Salutati ostentatiously (but menacingly) denied the rumor that Florence was preparing to sponsor an uprising in the Patrimony: the papacy's "most devoted sons" would never attempt "such a sacrilege."[37] Gregory responded with complaints of his own, notably of Florence's refusal to aid in the campaign against Bernabò Visconti and of its "tyrannical" violations of ecclesiastical liberties.[38] He invited Florence's citizens to put away their pride and return to the "old road" of humility, threatening that otherwise he would do everything in his power to defend the church, "against which not even the gates of Hell can prevail."[39]

VIII

But Florence's leaders, headed by members of the Ricci faction but including also many eminent Guelfs, were in no mood for the "old road." "Wake up!"

34. PR, 63, fols. 73r–75v (8 July 1375), pub. in A. Panella, "La guerra degli Otto Santi e le vicende della legge contro i vescovi," *Archivio storico italiano* 99 (1941): 36–49 (45–47).

35. PR, 83, fols. 81r–84r (14 August 1375), pub. in Gherardi, "La guerra," 6 (1867): doc. 24, pp. 222–31. The Otto are listed in Stefani, *Cronaca*, rub. 752, p. 293: Giovanni Dini *speziale*, Alessandro di Messer Riccardo de' Bardi, Giovanni Magalotti, Andrea di Messer Francesco Salviati, Tommaso di Marco degli Strozzi, Guccio di Dino Gucci, Marco di Federigo Soldi *vinattiere*, Tommaso di Mone *biadaiuolo*.

36. Gherardi, "La guerra," 6 (1867): docs. 18–22, pp. 220–22.

37. BAV, Fondo Capponi, 147, fols. 101–3 (19 May 1375), pub. in R. G. Witt, *Coluccio Salutati and His Public Letters* (Geneva, 1976), p. 97: "non putet vestra sanctitas nos sublimitatis apostolice devotissimos filios hoc sacrilegium actentasse."

38. ASV, RV, 271, fols. 22v–23r, 183r (13 April, 16 June 1375).

39. Ibid., fols. 46r–48r (8 August 1375), partially pub. in G. Mollat, ed., *Lettres secrètes et curiales du Pape Grégoire XI (1370–1378) intéressant les pays autres que la France*, 3 vols. (Paris, 1963), vol. 2, doc. 3412, pp. 137–38, fol. 46v: "adversus quam non possunt etiam porte inferni prevalere."

Salutati exhorted the Pisans. Moving to frame the anomalous Florentine war against the papacy in a broad historical context, he reminded them of how the ancient Greek republics had lost their liberty to the Macedonians by quarreling among themselves.[40] The dam burst on 11 November, when Città di Castello rose up against its papal governors. "Now indeed," crowed Salutati to Bernabò Visconti, "begins the ruin of the church!"[41] Like dominoes, Viterbo, Perugia, and dozens of other cities of the Patrimony rebelled as well. They were joined in the spring by Bologna, the crucial northern anchor of the papal state. Reports coming into Florence almost daily were read out "in the name of God and victory" to excited crowds summoned to the Piazza Signoria by the ringing of church bells. Troops of the Tuscan League entered the liberated cities to cries of "Long live Florence and liberty!" and red banners, "like those of Rome," emblazoned with the motto "*Libertas*," were distributed to Florence's new confederates.[42]

Euphoric letters now streamed out of the Florentine chancery exalting the Italians' re-embrace of their ancient liberty as they cast off the tyrannical yoke of servitude so long imposed on them by the barbarism, greed, and despotism of the papacy's Gallic prelates and governors. "Remember," Salutati urged the Orvietans, "that you are of Italian blood, the nature of which is to rule others, not to submit to them, and mutually and in turn you should rouse each other for liberty."[43] The war was not against the church, he assured Galeazzo Malatesta, but was "with barbarians, with foreigners who, born of the vilest parents and raised on filth," had been turned loose by the church to plunder *misera Italia*.[44] But as the war developed, Salutati was obliged (and not only by the protests of Florence's French and Angevin allies!)[45] to articulate a fuller and more complex vision of Italian

40. ASF, Miss. I canc., 15, fol. 16r–v (22 October 1375): "Exsurgiscimini!"

41. Ibid., fols. 22v–23v (11 November 1375), fol. 23v: "Iam enim cepit ecclesie ruina."

42. Stefani, *Cronaca*, rub. 753, p. 293; and "Diario d'anonimo fiorentino dall' anno 1358 al 1389," in *Cronache dei Secoli XIII e XIV*, ed. A. Gherardi (Florence, 1876), p. 304.

43. ASF, Miss. I canc., 15, fol. 41r–v (5 December 1375), fol. 41v: "Recognoscite, vos esse Italici sanguinis cuius est proprium imperare ceteris, non servire. Et vos ipsos vicissim ac mutuo, ad libertatis studia concitate."

44. Ibid., fol. 29r (7 December 1375): "non enim nobis cum ecclesia negocium est, sed cum barbaris, cum exteris gentibus, qui apud suos, vilissimis parentibus orti, turpissimeque nutriti, ut spolient . . . quasi ad predam, in miseram italiam per ecclesie presules destinantur."

45. BAV, Fondo Capponi, 147, fols. 15–17 (9 April 1376); and ASF, Miss. I canc., 17, fols. 27r–28v (15 May 1376), distinguishing Frenchmen from Limousins.

liberty, one that went beyond the *dictatores'* older, simple juxtapositions of liberty and despotism, and that enriched earlier Aristotelian and corporate views that proposed securing peace, "sufficiency of life," and the *bene comune* as the aims of legitimate government.[46] This was not a war simply for Florentine or Tuscan liberty but one fought to liberate all of northern Italy. Salutati had not only to address a variety of communities of differing traditions and political experience but also to enlist the support of foreign rulers. He was therefore inspired to elaborate a vision of liberty that went well beyond traditional communal ideals of self-rule and freedom from foreign domination in two new ways.

First, in soliciting the support of the Romans early in the war and, later, condemning their readmission of Gregory to the city, he articulated a new historical genealogy of Italian liberty. Reminding them of their "hereditary debt" (*debito hereditario*) as the "authors and fathers" of popular liberty,[47] he offered the Romans ever fuller lists of examples of their ancient forbears' resistance to tyrants (Tarquin) and foreigners (Hannibal), and linked their history to that of Florence and Italy.[48] By the end of the war, Salutati had developed a view of Roman liberty grounded in the rule of law. Its foundations had been laid under a dynamic republic, only to be extinguished subsequently by the Caesars themselves.[49]

At the same time, many of the cities in the Patrimony lacked such traditions and constituted in effect what Machiavelli would later describe as the problem of "new states." In the course of dispensing much practical advice to cities such as Città di Castello, Bologna, and Orvieto on how to choose rectors, avoid factional strife, and keep taxes low, Salutati was obliged to reflect on the roles and interests of nobles and *plebs*, merchants and artisans in civic affairs, and to develop a broad anthropology of liberty and its effect on human nature as the *"magistra virtutum"* that could be applied to Italian communities lacking clear republican traditions.[50] In phrases that

---

46. See the survey by N. Rubinstein, *"Florentina Libertas," Rinascimento,* ser. 2, 26 (1986): 3–26.

47. ASF, Miss. I canc., 15, fols. 40r–v (4 January 1375/76), fol. 40r: "vobis, tamquam publice libertatis auctoribus ac patribus."

48. Miss. I canc., 16, fols. 67r–v (4 February 1375/76).

49. BRF, Ricc., 786, fols. 139r–v (6 November 1377); and ASF, Miss. I canc., 17, fols. 117v–118r (2 August 1377). See D. De Rosa, *Coluccio Salutati: Il cancelliere e il pensatore politico* (Florence, 1980), pp. 87–134; and Witt, *Salutati and His Public Letters,* pp. 42–72.

50. To Bologna, ASF, Miss. I canc., 17, fol. 19v (16 May 1376), on taxation; fols. 41v–42r (1 July 1376), on the *plebs;* Miss. I canc., 15, fol. 81v (13 September

go well beyond older visions of the *ben comune* and that anticipate the republicanism of Bruni's *Laudatio,* Salutati praised liberty to the Bolognese as "[the] one thing alone [which], exalting cities, multiplies population immensely, enriches families, and adorns the status and majesty of the citizens with an air of ancient grandeur. . . . This is the teacher of virtues, since no one hesitates in his own republic which flourishes with liberty to demonstrate how much and what a virtuous man can do."[51] As the propagandist of Florence's strategy to guarantee its own security by republicanizing central Italy, Salutati developed an anthropology of liberty that made its Roman genealogy accessible to all Italians in an ideology that was, at the same time, new and distinctively Florentine.

IX

The war was immensely popular among the Florentines, even among some elements of the clergy. "Woe to those who are under you and don't rise up!" taunted the satirist Franco Sacchetti in a series of poems by turns sarcastic and enraged that he penned to Gregory XI, Pope *"Guastamondo."*[52] The Augustinian canon and humanist Luigi Marsili ventilated his own anticlerical sentiments from Paris to his friend, the *lanaiolo* Guido Del Palagio, and assured him that excommunications by the likes of Gregory XI's "shameless" (*sfacciati*) Limousin legates meant nothing to Christ: "Christ sent them [priests] to preach: but I see nothing in the Gospel that says he sent them to rule."[53] The Vallombrosan monk Giovanni dalle Celle likewise reassured Del Palagio that "no innocent person can be excommunicated. . . . You only have to beware not to vote that the pope should be taken or killed, and likewise for all other clergy and religious."[54]

1376), on the nobility; and BRF, Ricc., 786, fols. 17v–18r (14 March 1377), on merchants and artisans.

51. ASF, Miss. I canc., 17, fol. 50r–v (29 July 1376), trans. Witt, *Salutati and His Public Letters,* p. 55, here fol. 50r: "Hec quidem sola [libertas], civitates exaltans, populos mirabilibus multiplicat incrementis, res familiares amplificat, statumque et maiestatem civium decore mire venustatis exornat. . . . Hec est magistra virtutum quoniam nemo dubitat in sua republica que libertate floreat, quantum quidve virtuosum efficere possit, ostendere."

52. Franco Sacchetti, *Opere,* vol. 1, *Il libro delle rime,* ed. A. Chiari (Bari, 1936), no. 191, p. 208, line 66: "Guai a chi t'è sotto e non si leva!"

53. Luigi Marsili, *Lettere,* ed. O. Moroni (Naples, 1978), no. 4, p. 191: "Cristo gli mandò a predicare . . . ; ma nell' Evangelio non truovo che gli mandasse a signoreggiare."

54. F. Giambonini, ed., *Giovanni dalle Celle, Luigi Marsili: Lettere,* 2 vols. (Florence, 1991), 2:265–66: "niuno innocente può essere scomunicato. . . . Sola-

"Never," exulted Salutati in February, 1376, "has it been so easy to raise money from our citizens!"[55] The city's rulers were delighted with the war's progress. Even such "Archguelfs" as Lapo da Castiglionchio and Filippo Corsini now urged that the Otto "manfully pursue" what they had begun.[56] It took Gregory until the spring of 1376 to recover from the shock of his losses in the Patrimony. He then summoned dozens of Florence's leaders to appear before him at Avignon. The priors took the summons remarkably seriously and deputed the lawyers Donato Barbadori and Alessandro dell'Antella to present the Florentine case. Salutati now sent letters to Florence's Cardinal Piero Corsini and to the College of Cardinals responding to Gregory's charge that Florence had deliberately instigated the rebellions in the Patrimony. Reciting the long history of Florence's Guelf devotion to the papacy, he argued that "the damages the church has received . . . are to be blamed not on us, but on the excesses of its own officials."[57] The uprisings in the Patrimony were truly miracles, inspired by God's spirit, and would therefore be assessed by "divine judgment, not human counsel."[58]

X

Gregory, however, conceived the process not as a forum for debate but as a trial. The defense served up by Barbadori and dell'Antella was a breathtaking display of legal caviling that cannot have been meant to convince so much as to taunt, ridicule, and perhaps to generate sympathy for Florence among rulers north of the Alps. The lawyers began with a plea for postponement, then turned to twenty charges drawn up by the pope's advocate, Jacopo di Ceva, all of which they set out to refute. The charges were remarkably detailed, ranging from Florence's sponsorship of rebellion in the papal states to the formation of the commissions of the Otto di balìa and Otto dei preti, its execution of the Prato conspirators, passage of antiecclesiastical legislation, and unauthorized taxation of the clergy. But in each instance the lawyers argued provocatively that, lacking exact times, dates,

mente t'hai a guardare di non dare consiglio o di non mettere fava che 'l papa sia preso o morto, e così d'ogni cherico e religioso."

55. ASF, Miss. I canc., 15, fol. 46v (10 February 1375/76): "numquam tam facile fuit a nostris civibus pecuniam exigere."

56. ASF, CP, 14, fol. 14r (14 February 1375/76): "sollicitentur octo quod incepta viriliter prosequantur non obstantibus colloquiis pacis."

57. ASF, Miss. I canc., 16, fol. 68r (2 February 1375/76): "damna que in partibus italie recepit ecclesia non nobis sed officialium suorum excessibus imputaret."

58. Ibid.: "hoc totum divinum iudicium et non humanum consilium iudicabit." See also to the Cardinals, Miss. I canc., 17, fols. 1r–2v (8 March 1375/76).

and the names of all persons involved, the charges were "vague, obscure," and therefore legally inadmissible.[59] And they did more than simply quibble. Though they made no attempt to invoke Florence's traditional Guelf allegiance to the papacy, neither did they use this forum as an opportunity to champion the heroic vision of republican *libertas* that Salutati had elaborated in support of the war.

Instead, they framed the Florentine defense from beginning to end with the stunning assertion that Florence was, and always had been, "subject to the most holy Roman Empire," and that it therefore could not recognize the jurisdiction of the Papal Curia.[60] Florence indeed had renewed its privileges with Emperor Charles IV in 1369 and had been paying the emperor an annual *census* of 4,000 florins, a kind of ideological (and political) insurance policy that the lawyers now cashed in full.[61] Not only, they declared, were the Florentines innocent of Gregory's charge that they had violated the terms of their alliance with the church; the pope lacked competence to judge, both because he could not be plaintiff and judge alike in his own case and because the Florentine community and citizens "are laymen, and immediately subject to imperial authority."[62] Had they occupied the lands of Volterra, Pistoia, and other of their neighbors? On the contrary, argued the lawyers, Florentines served there as vicars of the emperor.[63]

Barbadori and dell'Antella did not, on the other hand, elaborate this new Florentine Ghibellinism into a bold vision of the prerogatives of the secular state along the lines set forth by Dante and Marsilius. Rather, they affected great respect for papal authority and the immunities of the church, while serving up denials of the papal accusations that were teasingly sophistic and mendacious. Responding to the charge that Florence had passed laws curtailing the freedom of the inquisitor and regulating access to eccle-

---

59. A notarized copy of the lawyers' deposition is preserved in ASF, Dipl., RAP, 31 March 1376, *quaderno* 1. Versions of the phrase "vagi et obscuri" (fol. 3r) are applied to all twenty charges.

60. Ibid., fol. 1v: "Ne videantur contepnere sanctitatem suam et huius sancte sedis protestationem premissam in principio medio et fine quod cum dicta civitas populus et comune et eius cives notorie sint subpositi et subiecti sanctissimo romanorum imperio ac serenissimo principi domino Karulo divina favente clementia romanorum imperatori non consentiunt nec consentire intendunt in dictum summum pontificem tamquam in iudicem competentem nisi si et in quantum de iure teneantur et debeant et iurisditionem eius."

61. Brucker, *Florentine Politics*, p. 238.

62. ASF, Dipl., RAP, 31 March 1376, *quaderno* 1, fol. 3r: "ipsa comunitas et cives sint layci et imperatorie maiestati immediate subiecti."

63. Ibid., fol. 5r, art. 10.

siastical benefices, they first disputed the laws' existence, then denied that they had been enforced, then pointed out that the *"clausula derogatoria"* attaching to them explicitly prohibited transgressions of ecclesiastical liberty.[64] Had clerics been tried and condemned in secular courts? Again they rejected the charge, adding, however, that these things had been done by Florence's podestà, a foreign official over whom they had absolutely no control.[65] Had the clergy been taxed and molested? Again, no: besides, the pope had failed to specify the sums and clerics involved; anyway, these were strictly voluntary loans.[66]

And so it went. Not surprisingly, Gregory flicked aside the Florentine defense as "frivolous and inane." (Nor would Charles IV have been amused, having only days earlier ordered the Florentines to desist from disturbing the Patrimony.)[67] In the interdict that he had ready for promulgation, Gregory compressed his condemnation of the Florentines into ten major (though quite detailed) counts, leaving himself ample space to elaborate on the economic penalties that, along with denial of access to the sacraments and the cult, were to be inflicted by the clergy and other Christians on these "impious sons of perdition" and their allies and abettors, the enemies of mother church and the Christian *"respublica."*[68] On hearing the papal sentence, which was at once a judgment, a polemic, and a curse, Barbadori collapsed to his knees, reciting the Psalms and calling upon Christ and the apostles as witnesses to Florence's innocence.

XI

In his history of Florence, Leonardo Bruni made Gregory's trial and condemnation of the Florentines the centerpiece of his account of the war, inserting lengthy speeches into the mouths of Barbadori and Gregory to set out the Florentine and papal positions. But what was a good Florentine republican, or even a Guelf, to make of Barbadori's and dell'Antella's defense, framed as it was within an imperial jurisprudence that not only ignored, understandably, Florence's Guelf traditions but also neglected to articulate the ideal of *libertas* that Salutati had made the centerpiece of the Florentine

64. Ibid., fol. 3v, arts. 3 and 4.
65. Ibid., fol. 4r, art. 5.
66. Ibid., fol. 5v, art. 12.
67. ASF, Dipl., RAP, 26 March 1376; pub. in Gherardi, "La guerra," 7, 2 (1868): doc. 188, p. 237.
68. ASV, RV, 290, fols. 5r–9r (31 March 1375); also transcribed in ASF, Dipl., RAP, 31 March, 1376, *quaderno* 2, and partially pub. in Mollat, ed., *Lettres secrètes et curiales du Pape Grégoire XI*, vol. 3: doc. 3929, pp. 32–34.

cause, and that offered instead a defense which, in the age after civil lawyers like Bartolus of Sassoferrato (1313/14–57), was anachronistically servile even by Ghibelline standards in its complete forfeiture of Florentine sovereignty?

Bruni rewrote the speech entirely, expunging every reference to Florence's submission to imperial authority, as well as virtually every charge leveled by the pope against the Florentines for their abuse of the church. This was no homage to the ancient historiographical tradition of rhetorical summation but a deliberate excision from the historical record undertaken to purify and sanctify Florentine public memory. In Gregory's speech, Bruni allowed the pope to express indignation only at Florence's provocation of the uprisings in the Patrimony. Then, drawing on the charges advanced against the church by Salutati in his letters, Bruni moved Barbadori to the offensive, blaming the war squarely on the tyranny and abuses of the papacy's Gallic legates: "If your governors, your holiness, or let us say legates, had bothered to establish a benevolent government, rather than a tyranny frightful to all men, neither would you have reason to accuse us at present, nor we to defend ourselves." [69]

But having recounted the legates' abuses at length, and following Salutati closely, Bruni then diverged from the course suggested by the chancellor's own letters. For rather than have Barbadori advance from traditional Aristotelian denunciations of the despotism of the papal legates to an articulation of Salutati's affirmative new vision of the ideal of *libertas*, as the chancellor himself had frequently done, Bruni next inserted into Barbadori's speech a history of Florence's Guelf loyalty to the papacy that went back not simply to the time of Manfred but, indeed, to that of Emperor Frederick I Barbarossa.[70] Why, if Bruni was using Barbadori as a mouthpiece for the Florentine position, did he not exploit this rhetorical opportunity to highlight one of Salutati's greatest achievements? In part, he was simply following the line of argument that Salutati himself had directed to audiences like the College of Cardinals, rather than that which he had developed to encourage Florence's allies. But Bruni was now writing a history meant to illustrate the theme of Florence's devotion to the cause of liberty that he had set forth in his *Laudatio*. It was one for which Salutati's many

---

69. Bruni, *Historiarum . . . Libri*, bk. 8, p. 211: "Si tui, beatissime pater, sive praefecti sive legati, quos ad gubernandas civitates Italiae misisti, gubernationem populorum amabilem ac non tyrannidem horrendam in cervices hominum fuissent meditati, nec tibi nunc accusandi causa foret, neque nobis excusandi."

70. Ibid., p. 213.

letters provided evidence in abundance. Surely Bruni had no intention of suppressing his mentor's achievement in order to appropriate it himself—though neither here, nor anywhere else in his history, did he ever mention his predecessor.[71]

Going through the chancellor's letters, Bruni will have found that Salutati's most frequent correspondent was Bernabò Visconti (1323–1385), the uncle of Florence's mortal enemy Giangaleazzo (1351–1402). And he will have discovered Salutati greeting him "not just as a friend, but as a brother," with whom he felt united "not just in a single will, but in a single body."[72] Bruni, of course, had written his *Laudatio* to celebrate the victory of Florentine *libertas* over Milanese despotism in the war of 1390–1402. Nowhere in his account of the War of the Eight Saints did he acknowledge Florence's crucial alliance with Milan. To have demonstrated that Guelf Florence had fought a war for *libertas* against a French pope was perhaps not terribly awkward. But to admit that the Florentines had actually justified that war, at the moment of truth, in Ghibelline terms, was impossible. To acknowledge, further, that his mentor and fellow Florentines had attained full historical awareness of their mission to champion the cause of *libertas*, not simply in a war fought against the papacy but as comrades-in-arms with Milan, was utterly unthinkable—indeed, not to be remembered. Barbadori's original speech to Gregory XI was consigned to the archives and erased altogether from Bruni's textual repository of Florentine civic memory.

Writing in the mid–fifteenth century, when Florentine relations with Milan were warming up as a result of the demise of the Visconti line of dukes (1447) and the rise of Francesco Sforza, Bruni's successor as chancellor and historian, Poggio Bracciolini, acknowledged in his account of the war that Florence indeed had allied with Bernabò Visconti. It had been a difficult but necessary choice forced on the Florentines by the need to defend their liberty against papal tyranny. And Poggio wholeheartedly framed the war as a Florentine struggle for liberty, praising the city's citizens in a manner that echoes Salutati and anticipates Machiavelli for "judging that the fear of religion is to be set aside when liberty is at stake, and that the censures of unfaithful men are not to be feared."[73] At the same

---

71. E. Cochrane noted the point in *Historians and Historiography in the Italian Renaissance* (Chicago, 1981), pp. 5–7.

72. ASF, Miss. I canc., 16, fol. 2v (25 July 1375): "facti sumus non amici sed fratres . . . in unius voluntatis confluentia, corpus unum."

73. Poggio Bracciolini, *Historia Florentina*, bk. 2, in *Opera Omnia*, ed. R. Fubini (1715; repr., Turin, 1966), 2:47: "Religionis timorem ponendum esse censebant, ubi is officeret libertati; neque censuras in perfidis hominibus verendas esse."

time he did so in a way that, like Bruni, entirely submerged Barbadori's original Ghibelline defense of the Florentine position. He may not even have known of it. And, again like Bruni, Poggio then narrated the subsequent course of the war as a purely military and diplomatic contest between Florence and Gregory. But there was also, in this second phase, a domestic history of the war that neither historian chose to touch upon.

XII

After some hand-wringing, Florence's leaders proclaimed on 11 May 1376 that as a sign of Christian devotion the city would observe Gregory's interdict. The laity would be denied all sacraments save baptism, confirmation, and penance; priests were to withdraw from public religious processions, and to withhold the consecrated host from the sight of Florentines.[74] The citizens' initial response was one of proud defiance: "But we see it in our hearts," declared an anonymous chronicler, "and God well knows that we are neither Saracens nor pagans; on the contrary, we are and will remain true Christians, elected by God, Amen."[75] Florentine spirits were buoyed by the auspicious rebellion of Bologna, which the city marked with a feast devoted to Saint Benedict, and further festivities were sponsored in honor of the Otto di guerra. Salutati spent the spring sending letters around to the rulers of Europe thanking them for their support and cautioning them of what Gregory's ambitions portended for their own kingdoms. Although Florentine merchants were subject to harassment everywhere, Gregory exempted many leading families from the penalties of the interdict (provided they refused to pay Florentine taxes), and in Italy only Naples and Florence's doughty little enemy Lucca, beyond the peninsula only Castile, officially enforced the interdict.[76]

But as the summer wore on, so did the war. Bologna, Perugia, and other recently liberated cities in the Patrimony began to totter. When the Romans admitted Gregory to their city in October, Salutati bitterly chided them: "What are you doing, my good men. . . . Still expecting the messiah

74. ASF, CP, 14, fols. 37v, 43r (12 April, 13 May 1376). Lapo da Castiglionchio's *consilium* for observing the interdict is in Florence, BLF, Aedilium 52, fols. 249r–251v, summarized by Trexler, *Spiritual Power*, pp. 119–21.

75. "Diario," p. 308: "Ma noi il veggiamo nel cuore, e Iddio il sa, che noi non siamo saracini nè pagani, anzi siamo e saremo veri cristiani eletti da Dio, ammè."

76. E.g., ASV, RV, 287, fol. 175r–v; RV, 289, fol. 18r–v (both 31 March 1376). Salutati's complaints to Castile and Naples are in ASF, Miss. I canc., 17, fols. 46r–47r, 56v (12 July, 15 August 1376); to Lucca, Miss. I canc., 15, fol. 77r (31 July 1376).

who will save Israel?"[77] In Florence, voices had been raised since the spring in the deliberations (*pratiche*) of Florence's priors and their advisers, urging the Otto dei preti to tax the clergy more heavily "so that they contribute just as do other citizens," and "so that laymen are not taxed on account of clerics."[78] In September a failed peace embassy produced rage and frustration in the councils. Salvestro de' Medici now advanced a radical proposal. "The bishops of Florence and Fiesole," he declared to the priors, "and all the prelates of the city of Florence, should be sent to the pope to get him to quit the war and make peace. And if not, all the goods of the clergy should be taken by the commune, and the war fought at their expense."[79]

On 25 September the councils brought this neo-Marsilian vision to life by creating yet a third commission of eight, the Otto livellariorum (or Otto dei livelli or livellari, the Eight of Rents), charged to survey the ecclesiastical patrimony and to expropriate clerical estates for sale to Florentine citizens. For the "defense of liberty and of the state," they promised that money could thus be raised "without inconvenience to anyone, and to the advantage of many."[80] But the public response was hostile. Within a few weeks, the councils were obliged to pass additional measures reassuring citizens that the expropriations would touch only "superfluous" ecclesiastical wealth and promising that the clergy would "infallibly" be inscribed "as creditors of the commune" for reimbursement of their lost revenues at an annual rate of 5 percent on the assessed monetary value of their property. But they also empowered the Otto to compel citizens to purchase the estates "willingly or unwillingly."[81]

---

77. Ibid., fol. 86r–v (12 October 1376), 86r: "Quid facietis, optimi viri . . . ? Expectabitisne semper messiam qui salvam faciat Israel?"

78. ASF, CP, 14, fols. 57v–58r (26 June 1376): "quod contribuant sicut alii cives"; and fol. 59r–v (2 July 1376): "quod laici pro clericis non graventur."

79. Ibid., fol. 86r (24 September 1376): "Quod episcopi florentinus et fesulanus et omnes prelati civitatis florentie mittantur ad papam et procurent eum removere a bello et deducere ad pacem. Quod si non fiat omnia clericorum bona veniant in comuni et fiat bellum eorum expensis."

80. PR, 64, fols. 137r–140v (25 September 1376), 137r: for the "defensione libertatis et status et hominum et populorum" of Florence, money would be raised "absque alicuius incommodo et cum multorum utilitatibus." The original Otto livellariorum were Matteo di Buonaccorso Alderotti, Niccolò di Buono Rinucci, Tommaso Soldani, Niccolò Giugni, Leonardo Beccanugi, Francesco di Ser Arrigo Rocchi, Bartolo di Michele *correggiaio*, and Bernardo di Luigi *calderaio*.

81. Ibid., fols. 153r–154v (18 October 1376). The appropriations would be carried out "sine gravi ecclesiarum periculo immo ut in pluribus cum ipsarum commodo" (fol. 153r); only estates would be appropriated "quorum frutus . . . transcendentur opportunitatem" (fol. 153v); citizens would be required to purchase

XIII

The Otto livellariorum proceeded to the most extensive liquidation of an ecclesiastical patrimony carried out anywhere in Europe before the Reformation. Hundreds of churches, monasteries, and hospitals suffered expropriations, and thousands of Florentines were forced to purchase ecclesiastical lands, many against their will. The hardest hit were the secular clergy and the older male religious orders. Fully 18,326 florins worth of episcopal estates, 87 percent of the bishopric's later 1427 catasto tax assessment, were sold to 585 purchasers, and virtually all of the cathedral chapter's property, 8,046 florins worth, was disbursed among 191 purchasers.[82] Though poorer parishes in the city went largely untouched, the city's dozen collegiate churches, such as San Lorenzo and Santa Maria Maggiore, were stripped nearly bare. In the countryside, poorer parishes in the Apennines were also spared, but all the large baptismal parishes (*pievi*) close to the city and south of the Arno were heavily imposed upon. Among religious, the ancient Florentine Badia lost over half its estates, and even deeper expropriations were made from dozens of other Benedictine, Camaldoli, and Vallombrosan monasteries. Mendicant houses and nunneries, on the other hand, suffered only token expropriations. Among hospitals, the city's flagship institution, Santa Maria Nuova, though more heavily endowed than the bishopric itself, escaped untouched. But from one-third to one-half of the estates of the Bigallo, the Misericordia, and San Paolo were taken, and even orphanages like San Gallo and La Scala suffered comparable expropriations.

Some Florentines exulted in the fleecing of the clergy. Jacopo Sacchetti urged the Otto livellariorum to squeeze them "down to the dregs," and the expropriations continued even after the death of Gregory XI in March 1378, beyond the election of Pope Urban VI in April, and down to the official

---

them "volentibus seu etiam invitis" (ibid.). Another measure, ibid., fols. 154v–157r (18 October 1376), specified that the clergy "intelligantur esse et sint creditores dicti comunis" (fol. 155r). In November the councils reiterated the Otto's power "to force and compel" (*cogere et compellere*) citizens to make the purchases and forbade the clergy to sell their property preemptively to sympathetic laymen; ibid., fols. 191r–192r (5 November 1376), fol. 191r.

82. Based on ASF, MC, 1558, a summary of purchases and restitutions as they stood in 1427. I have gauged the extent of appropriations by contrasting these figures with ASF, Catasto, 195, a survey of clerical property compiled by Florentine tax officials in 1438. Even allowing that the Otto surely assessed property values high for sale, and clergy declared them low for taxation, this permits a comparative assessment of the impact of the appropriations.

proclamation of peace in July 1378.[83] Nevertheless, more than Gregory XI's imposition of the interdict itself, it was the decision by the Florentine government—now clearly in the grip of its radical elements—to proceed with the spoliation of their local church that turned much of the Florentine populace against the war. It split the republic's leadership as well, alienating many of those Guelfs who had originally been willing to countenance the war only to check Gregory's territorial ambitions. Additional measures had to be passed compelling communal accountants to carry out their tasks and forcing citizens to accept assignment to the magistracy of the Otto livellariorum.[84]

This was scarcely the first time that a temporal power had gone to war with the papacy, and Florence had been interdicted over half a dozen times before.[85] But this interdict now gripped with exceptional force. Its impact cannot be credited simply to the financial and spiritual penalties inflicted on the Florentines, much less to the stature of the pope who imposed them. Temporal rulers since the time of Emperor Henry IV (1056–1106) in the investiture conflict and, more recently, King Philip IV the Fair of France (1285–1314) in his confrontations with Pope Boniface VIII (1294–1303) had found natural allies against the papacy among their own clergies, who resented the encroachments of centralizing papal administration on their own local prerogatives. The Florentine government's financial punishment of the Florentine clergy for the pope's offenses proved a colossal political blunder that forfeited the possibility of local clerical support. And turning a war against the papal state into an assault on local ecclesiastical institutions shifted public attention from Gregory XI's aims to the pretensions of Florence's own rulers. It required extending the state's coercive power not only over ecclesiastics but also over citizens. Florentines were now forced to comply with the profanation of a sacred ecclesiastical patrimony that they had endowed themselves, carried out in violation of what even the most cynical regarded as fundamental property rights. They had been assured that an interdict and denial of the cult by a manifestly evil pope and prelates meant nothing to Christ: but what if they were truly guilty of assaulting his shepherds?

83. CP, 15, fol. 34r (4 September 1377): "quod usque ad feces premantur clerici pro pecunia."
84. PR, 64, fols. 217r–218r (5 December 1376); PR, 65, fols. 162v–163v (16 September 1377); and CP, 15, fols. 22v, 40v, 48v, 92rv, 100v (July 1377–April 1378).
85. Trexler, *Spiritual Power*, pp. 20–29.

XIV

No sooner had the expropriations begun than the priors were forced to confront a surge of public penitential processions. The chronicler Marchionne di Coppo Stefani, who himself served in these months as a member of the Otto dei preti, observed that throughout the city and the *contado* "it seemed that a compunction overcame all the citizens, and every night, in almost every church, lauds were sung." [86] Every day there were processions of upwards of twenty thousand people, with relics and songs, "and all the people following behind." [87] Lay confraternities now formed groups of flagellants, recruiting members down to the age of ten, and in all five thousand. Wealthy young nobles were among their most enthusiastic recruits, and they took to dispensing alms, fasting, preaching by day, and sleeping out unsheltered by night. Stefani noted the paradox that "it seemed indeed that they wanted to defeat and humiliate the pope, and that they wanted to be obedient to the church." [88] The city's leaders directed the Dieci di libertà, a political police force, to investigate the meetings of the flagellants, while urging the Otto livellariorum to push on with the expropriations. [89] An atrocious massacre of civilians by Gregory's Breton mercenaries at the town of Cesena in early 1377 gave Chancellor Salutati a rich source of antipapal propaganda to broadcast to the rest of Europe, but it provoked only an increase of penitential processions in Florence itself. [90]

Gregory now had the upper hand in the war and was demanding over a million florins for a settlement. "He doesn't want to make peace," protested Salutati to Louis of Hungary, "he wants to sell it!" [91] That summer Bologna capitulated to papal forces, and that autumn Gregory raised the stakes further by condemning Florence's rulers for heresy. [92] They responded with a further act of defiance, accompanied by measures demanding complicity of all citizens. In October 1377, "in order that by attending masses and the clergy's other divine offices and orations, devotion and orthodoxy may

---

86. Stefani, *Cronaca,* rub. 757, p. 295: "parve che una compunzione venisse a tutti i cittadini, che quasi in ogni chiesa si cantava ogni sera le laude."

87. Ibid.: "con tutto lo popolo dietro."

88. Ibid., p. 296: "parea che volessero vincere e aumiliare il Papa, e che volieno essere ubbidienti alla Chiesa."

89. ASF, CP, 15, fol. 97r (25 October 1376).

90. "Diario," p. 331.

91. ASF, Miss. I canc., 17, fols. 99r–100v (23 March 1376/77), fol. 100r: "Heu, heu, pacem velle vendere, non veretur!"

92. ASV, RA, 203, fols. 30v–37v, 40r–44r (2 September, 13 November 1377).

grow," the councils passed a law requiring Florentines now to violate the interdict.[93] Not only would the priors attend mass daily in their private chapel: the podestà and Captain of the People were to compel clergy to officiate throughout the city, and laity to attend mass at least on Sundays and feast days.

But Bishop Ricasoli and other Florentine prelates had already fled the city.[94] Andrea Capponi, speaking for the government's Standard Bearer of Justice (Gonfaloniere di giustizia), denounced them as "rebels of the republic, and public enemies."[95] The mystical ascetic and church reformer Catherine of Siena, instead, who before the war had chided Florence's Bishop Ricasoli to "wake up from the sleep of negligence," now praised him for his "virile" resistance, while she condemned collaborative clerics for their "servile fear of men."[96] Gregory deputed her on a peace mission to Florence in the winter of 1377, believing, as he told her Dominican confessor and biographer Raymond of Capua, that "they would not molest her; she is a woman, and besides they hold her personally in high esteem."[97] At meetings of the Parte Guelfa, Catherine encouraged the politically divisive purges from public office (*ammonizione*) of accused Ghibelline sympathizers that the Parte was now promoting as a means of overturning the radical government and unblocking the path to peace. But according to Raymond, she was shocked by the political vendetta that in turn swept the city in the spring

---

93. ASF, PR, 65, fols. 176r–177r (20 October 1377), fol. 176r: "Ut ex frequentatione missarum et aliis divinis officiis et orationibus clericorum devotionis et orthodose fidei materia magis crescat." An accompanying measure guaranteed communal protection to all officials threatened with apostolic penalties and (menacingly) promised cooperative clerics security in their benefices; ibid., fols. 173r–176r (20 October 1377).

94. Salutati's demand (*requirimus et rogamus*) that he return is in BRF, Ricc., 786, fols. 119v–120r (10 October 1377).

95. ASF, CP, 15, fol. 47r (6 October 1377): "rebelles rei publice et hostes publicos omnium."

96. E. Dupré Theseider, ed., *Epistolario di Santa Caterina da Siena* (Rome, 1940), no. 37, p. 153, "che vi leviate suso dal sonno della negligentia"; and N. Tommaseo, ed., *Le lettere di S. Caterina da Siena*, 4 vols. (Florence, 1860), 3:329, no. 242: "essendo voi uomo virile . . . persevererete." Catherine's chastisement of complicitous priests is in Tommaseo, ed., *Le lettere*, 4:43, no. 284: "il timore servile delli uomini."

97. Raymond of Capua, "Legenda Maior," in *Acta sanctorum*, ed. D. Papebroch, April, tom. 3 (1675; repr., Brussels, 1968), rub. 421, p. 957: "ei, tum quia mulier est, tum etiam quia reverentiam habent ad eam, credo quod nihil mali facient"; trans. C. Kearns, *The Life of Catherine of Siena by Raymond of Capua* (Wilmington, Del., 1980), rub. 423, p. 383. ASV, Introitus et exitus, 347, fol. 40v (12 September 1376) records an 85-florin payment from the papal treasury to Catherine.

of 1378.[98] Stefani reported more dryly that "on that account she was regarded almost as a prophetess by those of the Parte, and by others as a hypocrite and evil woman." [99] That summer Catherine was among those obliged to flee the city by the July tumult of the Ciompi.

XV

Civic conflict, military reverses, and popular resentment of the war forced the government to sue for peace in March 1378. Gregory's sudden death on 27 March enabled the city to negotiate terms with the weak Roman pope Urban VI (el. 7 April), who, with the outbreak of the schism, was soon seeking Florentine support against his rival Clement VII (20 July 1378–1394) of Avignon. At the end of July, Florence agreed to pay Urban an indemnity of 250,000 florins (it had agreed to pay Gregory 800,000), to restore all church property confiscated since October 1375, and, after some hesitation, to repeal its laws touching the inquisition.[100] But the treaty was not formally signed in Rome until 28 August,[101] and Salutati spent September and October pleading with Florence's Roman ambassadors to secure an official bull of absolution to calm the religious crisis that had helped precipitate the Ciompi Revolt and upended the city's politics.[102]

The delay was caused by haggling over the first installment of Urban's indemnities. The broadly based guild regime (1378–82) that recovered control of Florence from the Ciompi promptly complied with the treaty by formally repealing the city's antiecclesiastical legislation in September. But the councils explicitly excepted all ordinances touching the Monte and thus preserved the republic's important fiscal claims against ecclesiastical courts in matters of contract and usury.[103] And Urban, though he counted heavily on the indemnities, never received much more than 30,000 florins. Only the Florentine populace's hatred of the "butcher of Cesena," Robert of Geneva, now Pope Clement VII, prevented the post-1382 Albizzi regime from accepting his offer to cancel them entirely, and from following Florence's

98. Raymond of Capua, rub. 423, p. 957.

99. Stefani, *Cronaca*, rub. 773, p. 306: "di che era costei quasi una profetessa tenuta da quelli della Parte e dagli altri ipocrita e mala femina."

100. The treaty is in ASF, Dipl., RAP, 28 July 1378. Hesitations were expressed in CP, 15, fol. 93r (27 March 1378).

101. As prescribed in BRF, Ricc., 786, fol. 101v (7 August 1378).

102. Ibid., fols. 104r–105r, 107r–v, 107v–108r (22, 25 September, 6, 11, 17 October 1378), pub. in G. Rigacci *Lini Coluci Pieri Salutati Epistolae*, 2 vols. in 1 (Florence, 1741), 2:199–209.

103. ASF, Balìe, 16, fol. 7r (1 September 1378).

Cardinal Piero Corsini into the lucrative Avignon camp.[104] But the Roman pope Gregory XII's (1406–15) revival of the claims was one of the reasons Florence withdrew allegiance from him on the eve of the Council of Pisa in 1408.[105] Among the first demands the city made of the newly elected Pisan pope Alexander V (1409–10) was the abrogation of the treaty, which he prudently granted.[106]

Restoring the clergy's confiscated property proved a longer and more complex process that for decades left ecclesiastics dependent on the (often inadequate) interest payments of their Monte shares and forced many lay-people to choose between restoring at a financial loss the property they had been compelled to purchase or retaining it against their religious con-sciences. Not until the civil disturbances had subsided in 1380 did the coun-cils, under pressure from ecclesiastics and "many officials and wise citizens, merchants, and artisans," pass into law a quintessentially Florentine scheme for making restitution.[107] Clergy would be issued 5 percent interest-bearing shares in the Monte for sums equal to the purchase price of the property they had lost.[108] Restitution itself would be made in accordance with draw-ings held twice annually. Citizens whose names were extracted would be repaid the price of the property they had purchased, which would then be restored to its original clerical owners. The clergy, in turn, were forbidden henceforth to deny laity who had not yet made restitution the last rites and ecclesiastical burial.[109]

Unfortunately, the government could afford to budget only 25,000 flo-rins annually for the restitutions.[110] The drawings did not get well under

---

104. Clement's offer is in ASV, RV, 293, fol. 158r–v (8 October 1381).

105. RV, 377, fols. 114v–115v (7 September 1407).

106. The city acknowledged a debt of 192,000 florins in ASF, LC, 4, fols. 103r–104v (9 July 1409). Alexander's bull is ASV, RV, 339, fols. 96r–101v (22 May 1409).

107. ASF, PR, 69, fols. 61v–69v (9 June 1380), fol. 61v: "actentis . . . consiliis multorum officiorum et sapientum civium mercatorum et artificorum"; and CP, 18, fol. 18v (4 October 1379), pressure from the abbot of Vallombrosa.

108. Such compensation had been promised in the original measures of Octo-ber 1376, but it had not been paid: PR, 67, fols. 144r–146r (27 June 1379).

109. PR, 69, fol. 64r. Clergy were free, of course, to buy back their estates from laymen directly and then await themselves drawing for repayment of the purchase price.

110. The councils passed additional measures allowing citizens to jump the lottery queue by forfeiting a 10 percent portion of the original purchase price, and encouraging them to turn over confiscated property to ecclesiastics by means of tax-free donations inter vivos, or in last testaments, and to hold the Monte shares them-selves: PR, 69, fols. 258r–259r (9 February 1380/81); PR, 72, fols. 76r–77v (10 June 1383).

way until 1383, and soon, from the late 1380s through the war against Milan to its climax in 1402, the government was frequently obliged to suspend the drawings, and later even the interest payments on the clergy's Monte shares, to free up funds to meet new war expenses "for the defense of Florentine liberty."[111] Only in the 1420s, with the reunification of the papacy under Martin V (1417–31), did the government press to complete the process, making possible in turn the compilation of Florence's new tax inventory of lay and clerical wealth, the catasto, begun in 1427.

The restitutions not only were protracted over half a century but also created in the meantime tremendous inequities among the clergy and friction with the laity. As late as 1420, a quarter of the episcopal estates remained in lay hands.[112] Though all of the city's smaller parishes had received their goods by 1407, most of the larger collegiate churches had to wait until 1427. Small institutions, whose possessions had been distributed among only a few purchasers, might receive all of them back within a few drawings—or be left waiting for decades. Among hospitals, the Misericordia and San Paolo had recovered all of their property by 1405 and 1408: the Bigallo waited until 1426, as did most monasteries, whose estates had been apportioned among numerous purchasers.[113] Nor were the restitutions always neat and straightforward: there was frequently an afterlife of litigation. Some properties had been improved by their lay owners, others allowed to deteriorate; some had been passed on whole in testaments, others sold or divided up among several new owners. There were myriad disputes over bookkeeping and interest payments. Hundreds came before the Monte officials; dozens were appealed to the councils and the priors themselves. The last case was not resolved until 1454.[114]

XVI

The war fundamentally transformed the financial relations between Florence, the papacy, and the Florentine clergy. Beforehand, Florence had needed

111. PR, 73, fols. 121v–122r (12 October 1384), fol. 121v: "pro defensione libertatis civitatis Florentie." Similar laws were passed in 1387–91, 1395, 1397, 1406, and 1409.

112. MC, 1558, fols. 8v–20r.

113. Ibid., fols. 80v–81r, 54v–57r, 88r, respectively.

114. E.g., PR, 72, fols. 229v–230v (17 February 1383/84), on the Cistercians at Settimo. Dozens of cases came before the priors in the decade 1415–25; SC Delib. spec., 16–19. Cases before the Monte officers are in MC, 1559 (the case of 1454 on fol. 154r–v), and MC, 1560. Thousands of deeds of restitution are contained in Dipl., RAP.

the papacy to serve as the judicial guarantor of the Monte. Now the relationship of dependence was reversed. Popes from Urban VI (1378–89) to Gregory XII (1406–15) relied on (meager) Florentine indemnity payments to keep their finances afloat, and after the schism Popes Martin V (1417–31) and Eugenius IV (1431–47) both sought to bolster papal finances by investing heavily in the Monte.[115] Through their Monte shares, the financial interests of the local Florentine clergy also became tied to those of the Florentine state. During the process of restitution, clergy depended on Monte interest for their livelihood. Afterward, though occasional calls in the *pratiche* for new expropriations of clerical property went unheeded,[116] offers of Monte shares were used to secure approval and prompt payment of further clerical taxes down to the mid–fifteenth century, while threats to withhold interest payments if cooperation was not forthcoming were made good against Pope Eugenius IV in 1446 and the Florentine clergy in 1452.[117] The detailed inventories of ecclesiastical wealth generated by the Monte officials and, from 1427, the catasto tax officials were used not only to carry out direct levies on the clergy but also to monitor the movement of benefactions from laity to ecclesiastical institutions, and even to appropriate the revenues of nonofficiating (absentee) clergy.[118] The Monte and the catasto thus became the basic bureaucratic instruments whereby Florence circumscribed, supervised, and manipulated the financial operations of the church within its expanding territorial state. The republic was still using Monte shares and interest as levers on the clergy when Pius II (1458–1464) assumed the pontificate.[119]

Further, the financial devastation wrought by the war did to church government in Florence what the schism did to the papacy: it precipitated a con-

---

115. J. Kirshner, "Papa Eugenio IV e il Monte Comune: Documenti su investimento e speculazione nel debito pubblico di Firenze," *Archivio storico italiano* 127 (1969): 339–82.

116. ASF, CP, 42, fol. 60v (18 August 1413); and CP, 50, fol. 119r (6 February 1434). Some properties were sold during the siege of 1529: PR, 208, fols. 58v–59r (20 December 1529); and MC, 1296.

117. On offering Monte shares as an inducement, see, e.g., PR, 123, fols. 94r–96r (27 May 1432), and Balìe, 26, fol. 62r–v (22 August 1444); on withholding interest, e.g., LC, 11, fols. 44r, 46r–v, 63r, 66r, 115v (16, 23 January, 17, 26 June 1445; 12 February 1445/46, threatening Eugenius IV); and PR, 143, fols. 3r–6r (24 March 1451/52, warning the Florentine clergy).

118. See D. S. Peterson, "State-Building, Church Reform, and the Politics of Legitimacy in Florence, 1375–1460," in *Florentine Tuscany: Structures and Practices of Power*, ed. W. J. Connell and A. Zorzi (Cambridge, England, 2000), pp. 122–43.

119. ASF, Miss. I canc., 42, fol. 121r–v (12 June 1459).

stitutional struggle that lasted beyond the schism to the mid–fifteenth century, in which the traditional principle of episcopal hierarchical authority was challenged by clerical experiments with corporate self-government. After decades of weak episcopal leadership, in the aftermath of the Council of Constance (1414–1418) that ended the schism, the secular clergy of the diocese took matters into their own hands by fusing conciliar and republican principles to form a self-governing corporation that challenged the hierarchical authority of Bishop Amerigo Corsini (1411–35; after 1419, archbishop) in order to defend themselves against Florentine and papal tax officials.[120] Only at midcentury was the reforming Dominican archbishop Antoninus (1446–59) able to intervene between Florence and the papacy to defend the clergy within the Florentine territory. Providing them with long-sought financial relief, he was able in turn to reimpose his own episcopal hierarchical authority over them.

XVII

Looking back, few Florentines doubted the justice of their city's war against Pope Gregory XI. In the view of the contemporary Stefani, the Otto di balìa "performed the greatest deeds that had ever been carried out down to that day."[121] Two decades later the pious, prosperous, but politically emarginated dyer Giovanni Morelli praised them in the *Ricordi* he wrote for his son as "the most famous, sagacious and valiant men ever seen in Florence."[122] Filippo Rinuccini, whose uncle Francesco had been forced to purchase estates from the monastery of Vallombrosa, likewise believed they had "conducted themselves valiantly" (*portoronsi valentmente*),[123] and his son Alamanno referred in his 1479 dialogue "On Liberty" to Florence's "greatest

120. See D. S. Peterson, "An Experiment in Diocesan Self-Government: The *Universitas Cleri* in Early Quattrocento Florence," in *Preti nel medioevo*, ed. G. De Sandre Gasparini, G. G. Merlo, and A. Rigon, Quaderni di Storia Religiosa, 4 (Verona, 1997), pp. 195–220; and Peterson, "Conciliarism, Republicanism, and Corporatism: The 1415–1420 Constitution of the Florentine Clergy," *Renaissance Quarterly* 42 (1989): 183–226.

121. Stefani, *Cronaca*, rub. 752, p. 293: "fecero pure i maggiori fatti che mai infino a quello dì si facessero."

122. Giovanni Morelli, *Ricordi*, ed. V. Branca (Florence, 1956), p. 317: "Questi furono i più famosi e i più segaci e valenti uomini che mai fussono veduti in Firenze per buona e vetturiosa prova."

123. Filippo di Cino Rinuccini, *Ricordi storici*, ed. G. Aiazzi (Florence, 1840), p. xxxiv; 3,850 florins worth of purchases are listed on pp. 44–46.

and most expensive war, the one against the terrible governors of the Papal States." [124]

But the humble Morelli also recalled another side of the war. "Our Lord God desired that his pastors be chastised," he explained, "but because that was not properly our task, since we are sinners ourselves as well, God chastised us in turn." [125] Even before the interdict was lifted, the Ciompi had risen in July 1378. The purges (*ammonizioni*) of suspected Ghibellines had opened up a power struggle among Florence's ruling orders between resurgent partisans of the Parte Guelfa and supporters of the Otto, while the government's assault on local ecclesiastical institutions had had the broad effect of destabilizing all public authority, lay as well as clerical, opening the way for the *popolo minuto* now to make a bid for political power. In July, half a dozen strategically located churches were used as centers of Ciompi operations: their leaders in fact styled themselves the "Eight Saints of the Balìa of the People of God." [126] Though their demands were more strictly political and economic than religious, Florence's traditional rulers viewed the Ciompi with horror and interpreted the uprising as a direct result of the war and, more specifically, of the city's assault on the local church. "For the sin committed against the holy church of God," noted the Florentine prior Alamanno Acciaiuoli in his chronicle of 1378, "having been led by evil Florentine citizens to make an assault [*impresa*] upon it, and to provoke so many cities and castles to rebel . . . and then, subsequently, for having sold the possessions and goods of ecclesiastics, carrying away so much money; and for the opprobrium, vituperation, and offenses that were inflicted daily on ecclesiastical persons, God promised to impose this punishment [*disciplina*] on this our city." [127] Chancellor Salutati explained to Prior Ubaldino

124. Alamanno Rinuccini, *De libertate*, ed. F. Adorno in *Atti e memorie dell'Accademia "La Colombaria"* 22 (1957): 267–303, trans. in R. N. Watkins, *Humanism and Liberty: Writings on Freedom from Fifteenth-Century Florence* (Columbia, S.C., 1978), pp. 208–9.

125. Morelli, *Ricordi*, p. 318: "Volle il nostro Signore Idio che i suoi pastori fussono gastigati; ma perché a noi non si appartenea, ché eziandio siamo pecatori, I' gastigò di poi noi." He pointed to the fates of the Otto di balìa, all of whom were eventually executed or banished, and whose descendants were still suspect to the early Quattrocento *reggimento*. Poggio, too, thought the point noteworthy: Bracciolini, bk. 2, p. 79.

126. Inquest of the Captain of the People of 17 December 1379, pub. in N. Rodolico, *La democrazia fiorentina nel suo tramonto (1378–1382)* (Rome, 1970), p. 442: "li Otto Santi de la Balìa del popolo de Dio."

127. Alamanno Acciaiuoli, "Cronaca (1378)," in *Il Tumulto dei Ciompi: Cronache e memorie*, ed. G. Scaramella, in *Rerum italicarum scriptores*, 2d ed., vol. 18,

Buonamici of the church of Santo Stefano that God had visited the schism on the papacy for its assault on Florentine *libertas* (and for the massacre at Cesena), the rebellion of the Ciompi on Florence for its liquidation of the clerical patrimony.[128]

XVIII

Salutati spoke for the members of the Guelf *reggimento* that returned to power in 1382 and found its political center in the Albizzi family. Thus, while they developed the use of institutions such as the Monte and the catasto to control the church in their expanding territory, they also articulated a variety of strategies aimed at pacifying society, and legitimizing their regime, not simply by reviving old papal Guelfism but by appropriating the legitimizing power of local religious life and ecclesiastical institutions. Embracing and shaping key (and acceptable) strains of public devotion, they made themselves stewards of a project to resacralize a city that had recently profaned itself.

The religious trauma of the war, followed by the outbreak of the schism, had stimulated a rise in the activities of *fraticelli* heretics and prophets; but it also generated a surge in confraternal foundations, new hospitals, ecclesiastical building projects, and lay benefactions to ecclesiastics. The regime turned first to coercion, and set boundaries, by passing a law in 1382 that condemned the *fraticelli* and required Florentine officials to carry out the orders of the inquisitor. Aimed at disciplining flagellants, prophets, and aristocrats of radical bents who had surfaced over the last few years, the measure also put an ideological brand on the upstart *popolo minuto* and distanced the regime from the Marsilian policies of the government of the Otto that had preceded it.[129] But executions in 1384 and 1389 provoked worrying public revulsion. More persistently, therefore, the government sought to shape and identify with, rather than repress, public expressions of religious sentiment. In the century down to 1450, sixty new confrater-

---

pt. 3 (Bologna, 1934), p. 18: "Per lo peccato commesso contro la santa Chiesa d'Iddio . . . essendosi per li mali cittadini di Firenze fatto la impresa contro a quella, di fare ribellarre tante cittade e castella . . . e poi suseguentemente di vendere le possessioni e beni eclesiastici, tanti danari quanti se ne trasseno, e li obro'brii e vituperii e le ingiurie che tutto dì si faceano nelle persone eclesiastiche; promise Iddio di dare questa disciplina a questa nostra città."

128. Coluccio Salutati, *Epistolario*, 4 vols., ed. F. Novati (Rome, 1893), 2:122–23 (3 October 1383).

129. ASF, PR, 71, fols. 175r–176r (13 December 1382).

nities were created in the city, the bulk of them penitential societies of *disciplinati*.[130] Though the government kept a wary eye on them,[131] confraternities provided an important release of social tension. The Albizzi regime actively encouraged the musical development of the *laudesi* and incorporated confraternities and *sacre rappresentazioni* into a ritual calendar of public religious holidays and dozens of new civic oblations to key religious institutions that it expanded dramatically over the next several decades.[132] When, in 1399, the great movement of Bianchi penitents reached the city gates, Florence's priors, unlike their counterparts in Milan and Venice, welcomed them into the city and organized additional processions throughout the surrounding countryside.[133]

The restitution of ecclesiastical property was accompanied by a surge of lay benefactions to ecclesiastical institutions that continued through the fifteenth century.[134] The completion of the cathedral, the decoration of Orsanmichele, and the rebuilding of such churches as Santa Trinita, San Lorenzo, and Santa Croce were but the most notable of numerous projects that conjoined art and power in a display of wealth and piety, carried out by *opere* that linked the city's priors, guildsmen (or, increasingly, leading parishioners), and ecclesiastics to rebuild, repair, or redecorate the city's churches and monasteries. The government's strategy of apportioning new ritual oblations to favored ecclesiastical institutions was replicated in the distribution of gabelle exemptions, fiscal subventions, and communal assistance in the judicial pursuit of testamental revenues to churches, monasteries, and especially hospitals. As Poggio's *De avaritia* attests, the aftermath of

130. J. Henderson, *Piety and Charity in Late Medieval Florence* (Oxford, 1994), pp. 38–46.

131. See, e.g., ASF, PR, 77, fol. 215r (2 December 1388), prohibiting public assemblies and parades by flagellants; and PR, 109, fols. 160v–162v (19 October 1419), pub. in L. Mehus, *Dell' origine, progresso, abusi e riforma delle confraternite laicali* (Florence, 1785), pp. 141–63, legislation aimed at curbing possible sedition from within confraternities by monitoring their membership.

132. R. F. E. Weissman, *Ritual Brotherhood in Renaissance Florence* (New York, 1982), chaps. 1–2; and B. Wilson, *Music and Merchants: The Laudesi Companies of Republican Florence* (New York, 1992). The new feast days and oblations are listed in *Statuta Populi et Communis Florentie . . . MCCCCXV*, 3 vols. (Freiburg [Florence], 1778–83), vol. 3, Tract. 3, pp. 287–370.

133. ASF, PR, 88, fols. 147v–149r (10 September 1399); and D. Bornstein, *The Bianchi of 1399: Popular Devotion in Late Medieval Italy* (Ithaca, N.Y., 1993), pp. 162–87.

134. S. K. Cohn Jr., *The Cult of Remembrance and the Black Death: Six Renaissance Cities in Central Italy* (Baltimore, 1992), esp. chap. 2; E. Conti, *La formazione della struttura agraria moderna nel contado fiorentino* (Rome, 1965).

the war saw the birth in Florence of modern charitable philanthropy. A comparable process unfolded in the sphere of Florentine sumptuary legislation. In the late fourteenth and early fifteenth centuries, the Florentine government superseded the episcopal court in the regulation of such life-cycle sacraments as baptisms, marriages, and funerals, as well as in enforcing laws regulating women's dress, gambling, and sexual conduct (including the supervision of nunneries).[135] Even hosting the Council of Pisa in 1409 was embraced as an opportunity not only to legitimize one of Florence's most recent territorial acquisitions but also to connect the sanctification of the republic to the broader effort to reunite a universal church whose own sanctity, and legitimacy, had been located by conciliar theorists in the community of the faithful. "Nothing," declared Antonio di Alessandro degli Alessandri to the priors, "would bring our republic greater merit before God, and fame among men."[136]

XIX

Bruni thus articulated his secularizing vision of Florentine republican history not only in the aftermath of the city's triumph over Milan in 1402, nor simply against a broad cultural backdrop of waning or merely persisting medieval religious sentiment. Florence in the early Quattrocento was a deeply penitential society, engaged in a process of civic resacralization in atonement for the profanation it had inflicted on its church during the War of the Eight Saints. The evidence of heightened Florentine religious sensibility abounds, as Bruni noted in his *Laudatio*, in the city's built environment. Bruni aimed not to contest but to complement this lavish display of Florentine piety. Though he has been lauded for his modern, critical approach to sources and documents, more lay behind his narrative selections (and omissions) than critical method, classical historiography, and rhetorical schematization.

Bruni would have been writing his account of the War of the Eight Saints in book 8 roughly in the years 1434–36. He had begun the *Historiarum florentini populi libri XII* upon his return to Florence in 1415 after a decade's service in the Papal Curia, and by the time he completed the first six books (to 1343) in 1429, his assumption of the chancellorate in 1427 had

135. On the sacraments, see the measures in the *Statuta*, vol. 2, bk. 4, pp. 366–90; on sexual regulations, M. Rocke, *Forbidden Friendships: Homosexuality and Male Culture in Renaissance Florence* (New York, 1996).

136. ASF, CP, 29, fol. 6r (7 February 1407/08): "nullus res . . . possit tractari a nostra republica maioris meriti apud deum, fame apud homines."

given them official status.[137] Hostilities with Milan had resumed under Giangaleazzo Visconti's son Filippo Maria (1392–1447) in 1423, and in 1436 Pier Candido Decembrio challenged republican Florence—and Bruni—by issuing his own imperial panegyric of Milan. In the biography of Dante that he wrote that year, Bruni disparaged the poet's Ghibelline *Monarchia* and, as we have seen, he omitted entirely from his history of the Eight Saints the Florentines' Ghibelline defense of their policies before Pope Gregory XI in 1376. At a time when many Florentines still wondered whether the destruction of papal power in central Italy had not in fact opened the door to Milanese aggression,[138] and when Florence had just joined Pope Eugenius IV in engaging the *condottiere* Francesco Sforza against Milan (1434), Bruni likewise deemed it inopportune to highlight the birth of Salutati's new historical vision of *libertas* in the war Florence had fought alongside Milan against the papacy. Rather, the triumph of Florentine republican *libertas* remained attached, in Bruni's historical narrative, to the Florentine victory over Milan in a manner that canceled the failures of its earlier conflict with the church.

Nor was this the moment to open up the domestic history of the war. In 1434 Pope Eugenius IV was forced to flee from Rome to Florence, where he found shelter for nearly a decade. But it was scarcely to appease this weak pope that Bruni suppressed from his account of the war every reference to the city's spoliation of its ecclesiastical patrimony. Rather, it was the religious sensibilities, anxieties, and memories of the Florentine public that he sought to assuage. Two years after Eugenius's arrival in the city—again in 1436—at great Florentine expense and with lavish ceremony, the pope consecrated the newly completed Florentine cathedral of Santa Maria del Fiore, which had been erected on the site of the old Santa Reparata, demolished in 1375. This was the capstone of that entire process of religious commemoration and civic resacralization that had been under way since the end of the War of the Eight Saints, one which the Albizzi regime had embraced and overseen, and which Florence's new Medici rulers aimed to inherit.[139] Two years later they underwrote the Council of Florence (1438–

137. In 1439 he formally presented these and the next three volumes (1343–89) to the Signoria: D. J. Wilcox, *The Development of Florentine Humanist Historiography in the Fifteenth Century* (Cambridge, Mass., 1969), pp. 2–5.

138. Domenico di Lionardo Buoninsegni, *Historia fiorentina* (Florence, 1581), p. 567.

139. See D. S. Peterson, "An Episcopal Election in Quattrocento Florence," in *Popes, Teachers, and Canon Law in the Middle Ages*, ed. J. R. Sweeney and S. Chodorow (Ithaca, N.Y., 1989), pp. 300–325.

39), again to connect the resanctified republic to a broader project to unify Christendom. Bruni chose not, in his history, to point back to the spoliation of its ecclesiastical patrimony that Florence had carried out during the war, and to the subsequent decades of restitution, that had necessitated this project. If the memories now being inscribed into the city's sacred urban fabric were to be piously conveyed to posterity, the legitimizing narrative of the Florentine republic would have to be detached from much of the history of its own church. The artistic commemoration of a Florentine *respublica christiana* entailed the construction of a purified, expurgated—and thus, secularized—narrative of the *respublica florentina*. The sacralization of Florentine space—and memory—required the textual secularization of Florentine history, and time.

The Florentine response to the War of the Eight Saints offers a remarkable study in the calculated disjunctures between historical events, historical writing, and public memory. Without the archival documents, it would be impossible to hear the silences in Bruni's and his successors' humanist texts. Those silences, in turn, echo the trauma of events willingly forgotten. Bruni was buried with a copy of his history: in his eulogy, Poggio praised it as a work "through which the fame and name of Florence will certainly come down to posterity and even into eternity," and an anonymous panegyric noted that Bruni "embellished a history in twelve books by which he kept alive the memory of many things done by Florence which were already being forgotten."[140] The reverse was also true. Bruni's authoritative history successfully reconfigured Florentine memory by attaching the theme of republican *libertas* to the war against Milan, while consigning the moment of Florentine Ghibellinism and sacrilege—and much of Florence's religious history since the Eight Saints—to oblivion.

XX

But the clergy remembered, and it fell to Archbishop Antoninus, who at midcentury supervised the last stage of the restitutions and reordered the clergy's finances and government, to recount the domestic history of the War of the Eight Saints and the city's assault on its church. In his universal *Cronica*, less widely circulated than his *Summa theologica*, and much less so than Bruni's history, Antoninus willingly acknowledged his debt to

---

140. Both quoted in Wilcox, *Development*, p. 8.

the humanist's work.[141] But Antoninus well knew the history of the Florentine church and was unwilling to accommodate the construction of a civic self-image that silently wrote it out of republican memory and into pious oblivion. Thus, where Bruni turned in his narrative to the movements of troops and diplomats, the archbishop instead brought the penitents and prophets back into the city's streets. He offered a full account of the Florentines' expropriation of clerical property, "so that all the while with the goods of the clergy they could fight against the church," explained in detail the restitution process, and noted that "nevertheless, many of [these goods] were lost, either through negligence, or in the oblivion and passage of time."[142] And, unlike Bruni and Poggio, Antoninus revived the views of Acciaiuoli and Salutati by connecting the war and the expropriations directly to the revolt of the Ciompi—and to God's chastising judgment on the city. The Florentines had spent "infinite" sums of money and had been interdicted and excommunicated while their enemies grew stronger. Then had come civic strife, the struggles between citizens and the *popolo minuto,* and finally the domination of the *"vilissima plebs,"* the Ciompi. Thus, reminded the strict archbishop, "the Florentines did not walk away unpunished."[143]

Antoninus's episcopal reforms enabled him to reassert ecclesiastical control of the sacred in Florentine life and gave him political capital that he spent defending the republic. Like their Albizzi predecessors, the Medici pursued a policy of cultivating religious legitimation that was a legacy of the "Eight Saints." But when they moved to consolidate their power in 1458 by pushing for the abolition of secret balloting in the city's councils, Antoninus threatened their partisans with excommunication.[144] They were obliged to abandon quiet subversion and to resort instead to an open coup (*parlamento*), at the same time choosing political power over the trappings of legitimacy. Thereafter, although Lorenzo de' Medici lavishly underwrote public religious festivals and married members of his family into families of the Papal Curia, the widening gap between private religious sensibility

141. Antoninus, *Cronica*, 3 vols. in 1 (Lyons, 1543), vol. 3, tit. 22, caps. 1–7, fols. 104r–106v, here, fol. 104ra.

142. Ibid., cap. 1, fol. 104rb: "ut cum bonis ecclesiarum diu contra ecclesiam possent dimicare," and, further on, "multa (bona) nichilominus sunt deperdita ex incuria vel oblivione et prolixitate tempis."

143. Ibid.: "Sed non transierunt impuniti florentini."

144. R. Morçay, *Saint Antonin, archevêque de Florence (1389–1459)* (Paris, 1914), pp. 243–69, 493–94.

and ostentatious public display became a staple of late-fifteenth-century Florentine discussion.

At the end of the fifteenth century, Savonarola, reaching deep into the city's civic memory, cited Antoninus as a precedent for his own efforts to revive Florence's republican and religious traditions.[145] But given the historiographical tradition they had inherited from Bruni, it was natural that neither Machiavelli nor Guicciardini should regard the prophet as other than an anomaly, or even notice his ties to the reforming Antoninus. In the wake of Savonarola's execution in 1498, with the Medici restored to Florence by their kinsmen Popes Leo X and Clement VII in the early sixteenth century, Machiavelli turned to ruminate on the possibility of exercising political power in a state without credible "divine institutions." Guicciardini, in turn, arranged his personal life and writings around that historical partition between politics and religion that he had inherited from his Quattrocento humanist predecessors. It has remained a staple of the European memory of the Renaissance virtually to this day.

145. D. Weinstein, *Savonarola and Florence: Prophecy and Patriotism in the Renaissance* (Princeton, N.J., 1970), p. 247.

8 Naming a Nun

Spiritual Exemplars and Corporate Identity in Florentine Convents, 1450–1530

Sharon T. Strocchia

In the winter of 1493 the nuns of the Benedictine convent of Sant'Agata gathered at the grate of their parlor to announce some good news. The sisters had decided to accept the five-year-old girl Lionarda di Giovanni Nelli as a nun in their community. Lionarda's entrance was supported by a fifty-florin dowry offered by her father and paid on the spot by his father-in-law. Henceforth, the nuns declared, little Lionarda would be known as Suora Eustochia.[1]

This episode, repeated countless times with minor variations in the monastic records of Renaissance Florence, offers a point of entry into a cluster of important questions raised by monastic naming practices. Taking a new name upon entry into the religious life often has been seen as a central act in the transition from a secular to a religious persona. The choice of a name held special significance in the fifteenth and sixteenth centuries, when names functioned in several meaningful ways: as markers of one's place in the social arena and guarantors of business transactions; as vehicles for invoking magical powers or celestial patronage; as signifiers of something essential about the person or thing named.[2]

My thanks to the Emory University Research Committee for generously funding archival research on which this project is based, and to Peter Lynch for helpful comments on an earlier draft.

1. ASF, CRSPL, Sant'Agata, 47, fol. 109r. Translations are my own. The Florentine year began on March 25; all dates in the text have been modernized.

2. Important works addressing the power and meanings of names in the late medieval and early modern period include L. Roper, *Oedipus and the Devil: Witchcraft, Sexuality and Religion in Early Modern Europe* (London, 1994); G. Ruggiero, *Binding Passions: Tales of Magic, Marriage, and Power at the End of the Renaissance* (New York, 1993); N. Z. Davis, *The Return of Martin Guerre* (Cambridge, Mass., 1993); J. Dupâquier, A. Bideau, and M.-E. Ducreux, eds., *Le Prénom: Mode et histoire* (Paris, 1984); and D. Herlihy, "Tuscan Names, 1200–1530," *Renaissance Quarterly* 41 (1988): 561–82.

Yet while we have become familiar with secular naming practices in Florence through the work of Christiane Klapisch-Zuber, the particulars of naming in religious communities remain unexplored.[3] The social and religious stakes invested in monastic naming practices were different but no less high than those obtaining among the elite families that placed their daughters in convents. Assuming a religious name detached a nun from her previous secular self and located her instead in a new network of filiation, one that combined devotional models with a communal identity. On a personal level, exchanging a given name for a religious one helped to make a nun "dead to the world" and gestured toward her integration into the community. That a change of name signaled a transformation of personal identity and status can be seen in reverse, in those rare instances when a nun left the convent to return to secular life. For instance, when the Medici nun Suora Girolama left Sant'Agata in 1509 after a decade inside the walls, she reclaimed the name of Maria Maddalena "by which she was known in the world."[4] On a more aggregate level, the pool of religious names selected by a convent indexed its choices of spiritual patrons and exemplary figures the nuns wished to emulate. That same pool also might provide an opportunity for an act of collective remembrance by "remaking" the name of a dead nun, slipping the fresh coloration of a new life over a fond memory. Viewed as a form of corporate representation, religious names mirrored the complex self-perceptions and distinctive history of each individual house and the nuns who inhabited it.

In this chapter I examine some of the patterns, practices, and meanings of naming nuns in late-fifteenth-century and early-sixteenth-century Florence. This period, from roughly 1450 to 1530, was characterized by the dramatic but uneven expansion in the population of female religious communities, as well as several profound political and religious upheavals. At the center of my analysis stand four established, affluent Benedictine houses, each of which played a significant role in Florentine parish and civic affairs over the course of the fifteenth century. These four houses—Sant'Ambrogio, Sant'Appollonia, Santa Felicita, and San Pier Maggiore—have left a rich legacy of documentary evidence that permits us to reconstruct naming practices in considerable detail. Less complete evidence from other houses,

3. C. Klapisch-Zuber, "The Name 'Remade': The Transmission of Given Names in Florence in the Fourteenth and Fifteenth Centuries," in Klapisch-Zuber, *Women, Family, and Ritual in Renaissance Italy*, trans. L. G. Cochrane (Chicago, 1985), pp. 283–309.

4. ASF, CRSPL, Sant'Agata, 49, fol. 193v.

such as the Benedictine convents of Sant'Agata and Le Murate, and material from other monastic orders provide important supplements and points of comparison.

In the first part of the chapter, I establish the basic chronology and prescriptive framework surrounding the adoption of a religious name. The following sections turn to a more detailed examination of exactly what names were chosen by religious women, focusing on three distinct patterns that emerge: first, the displacement of medieval saints' names in some convents by those of early Christian exemplars; second, the development of the cult of the angels; and, finally, the "remaking" of a dead nun by giving her name to a new novice. These trends in monastic naming practices signal both a new set of devotional models and an enhanced sense of corporate identity among religious women that were firmly in place by the demise of the last Florentine republic in 1530. I argue that the period from 1450 to 1530 saw a growth not only in female monastic personnel but also in female monastic self-consciousness that is reflected in naming practices. What was taking shape within these burgeoning religious houses was a new sense of community that was simultaneously religious, familial, and distinctively female.

THE CHRONOLOGY OF NAME CHANGES

The ritual transition from secular to religious status formed one of the central moments in the life experience of a nun. The liturgical rite of "consecrating virgins" assumed its definitive form in the 1295 pontifical of Guillaume Durand, with only minor modifications marking later pontificals such as the one ordered by Innocent VIII in 1485.[5] The *ordo* prescribed two main acts in the rite of consecration: blessing the nun's habit, with particular ritual emphasis on her veil; and placing a ring on the postulant's finger, which carried obvious parallels to secular nuptial rites. However, the declaration of a new name by which the newly made "bride of Christ" would be known did not figure into the official rite of consecration. Despite the symbolic importance of changing one's name as a way to mark a transformation in status, the assumption of a religious name was regulated by custom rather than prescription. There was no mandate for a name change in any of the three major rules—Benedictine, Augustinian, and Clarissan—

---

5. R. Metz, *La Consécration des vierges dans l'Église romaine: Étude d'histoire de la liturgie* (Paris, 1954), pp. 273–333.

governing the vast majority of Florentine convents.[6] Nor were name changes included as an integral part of profession rites in the Dominican constitutions that guided formal nunneries like San Jacopo di Ripoli, or tertiary communities like the Annalena.[7] Even in precept, then, name changes lacked the liturgical standing of either the ring or the veil, the crown or the tonsure.

Complicating our understanding of naming practices in the pre-Tridentine period is the fact that the process of becoming a nun involved several distinct phases, each of which might serve as the appropriate moment for a name change. In this sense, the profession of nuns as "brides of Christ" paralleled the disjointed episodes of secular marriage arrangements.[8] The first possible moment for the ritual transformation signaled by a name change was the acceptance of the postulant into the community and her subsequent investiture as a novice. At this ceremony, referred to as the "dressing" (*vestizione*), the postulant accepted the habit and veil of her community and officially entered the novitiate. It was at this point

6. For example, chapter 2 of the Rule of St. Clare specifies a number of particular details regarding the acceptance and eventual profession of novices, including their tonsuring and laying aside of secular dress, but makes no mention of a required name change; see "The Rule of St. Clare," in *Francis and Clare: The Complete Works*, trans. R. Armstrong and I. Brady (New York, 1982), pp. 209–25, at 211–13. It is worth noting that Dominican nunneries followed the Augustinian rule and the constitutions of the Dominican order, neither of which prescribe a change of name for religious women. P. D. Johnson, *Equal in Monastic Profession: Religious Women in Medieval France* (Chicago, 1991), p. 256, states that monastics in northern France first began to take new names upon entering the religious life only in the thirteenth century.

7. The rubric detailing the mode of profession at San Jacopo di Ripoli, dating from the late fourteenth century, reads as follows: "Ego Suora N. facio professione et promicto obedientiam deo et beate marie et beato domenico et tibi N. priorisse talis locis vice N. magistri ordinis fratrum predicatorum secundum regulam beati Agustini [*sic*] et institutiones sororum quarum cura predicto ordini est commisa. quod ero obediens tibi aliis que priorissis meis usque ad mortem." The prioress then blessed the prospective nun while giving her the new habit. The rubric also specified that no girl was allowed to take vows until she had reached the age of thirteen (ASF, CRSPL, San Jacopo di Ripoli, 25, fols. 24v–25r). The late-fifteenth-century constitutions of the tertiaries of San Vincenzo, called Annalena, do not specify changing one's name as part of their religious practices; "Constitutioni delle suore della penitentia a Santo Domenico del Terzo Ordine del Monastero di San Vincentio di Firenze vocato Annalena," Philadelphia, University of Pennsylvania Library, MS. Codex 104.

8. For a further exploration of these parallels, see K. J. P. Lowe, "Secular Brides and Convent Brides: Wedding Ceremonies in Italy during the Renaissance and Counter-Reformation," in *Marriage in Italy, 1300–1600*, ed. T. Dean and K. J. P. Lowe (Cambridge, England, 1998), pp. 41–65.

that the protagonist of our opening story, Lionarda Nelli, assumed her new identity, and it was this moment that became the defining event in name changes by 1500.

The liturgical aspects of the *vestizione* rite were relatively fluid and often minimal, as the following example demonstrates. In November 1457 a young serving girl named Daria, "inspired by God to renounce the world and live religiously," came with her employer, Monna Nanna Minerbetti, to the sacristy of San Pancrazio. There Daria sloughed off her worldly identity in favor of a new religious persona, henceforth to be known as Caterina. In the presence of the abbot Benedetto Toschi, two monks, and a priest, "with lit candles and holy water, reading the appropriate prayers as was usual for one who was taking the habit," Daria transformed herself into Caterina by means of small yet dramatic acts. As the account noted, "Caterina swore in the hands of the above named reverend abbot [the vows of] obedience, chastity and poverty; and then she placed her hands on a missal pledging to God to observe these promises." Since San Pancrazio housed Vallombrosan monks rather than nuns, it is not clear where Caterina eventually lived as a nun or, more likely because of her social class, as a serving sister (*conversa*).[9]

A second opportunity to alter one's name presented itself, however, when the novice formally professed and took the veil some years later, depending on her age, in a rite known as the "veiling" (*velazione*). Here the story of Maddalena di Orlando Gherardi offers a concise example of this ceremonial practice. In May 1456 Maddalena, who had been "dressed" as a novice by Archbishop Antoninus himself a short time earlier, formally asked the abbess and chapter of Sant'Appollonia to reduce the length of the one-year novitiate prescribed by the Benedictine rule. The nuns agreed, recited an unspecified prayer, and then bestowed on her the name of Suora Scholastica. It was in the guise of the newly made Suora Scholastica that this nun made her profession, promising stability of life, a change of habits, obedience, and service to God as laid out by the rule.[10]

---

9. ASF, AD, 296, unfoliated, dated 16 November 1457. The quoted passages read: "essendo la detta Catherina ispirata da Dio di volere rinuntiare al mondo e vivere religiosamente," she and her female patron resolved in the abbot's presence "con lumi accesi et acqua benedetta leggendo orationi convenienti come è usanza di fare a chi piglia quello abito, e detta Caterina giurò nelle mani di messer l'abate sopra nominato ubidienza, castità e povertà e così puose le mani in su il messale di così osservare a Dio. . . ." Since no dowry was mentioned, it is likely that Caterina became a serving sister rather than a choir nun.

10. ASF, CRSGF, 82, 1, fols. 345v–346r.

The profession of monastic vows was an act that carried legal as well as liturgical force. Notarial registers are dotted with instruments attesting to the profession of one or several nuns, mainly as a record of dowry agreements or as a quitclaim on inheritance. The notary Filippo Mazzei, who worked frequently for the Florentine bishopric, recorded the process by which the Bardi sisters Antonia and Camilla took their vows at Sant'Appollonia in 1435. After living for several years in the convent, these two girls, aged sixteen and fifteen, respectively, professed before the bishop, Amerigo Corsini, the abbess, Cecilia Donati, the assembled chapter of nuns, and eight other priests and friars. They agreed to live and die in observance of the rule and customs of the house; to be obedient to Abbess Cecilia and her successors; and to observe obedience, chastity, and poverty of their own free will. By this act the community officially accepted the girls; it did not, however, alter their names as part of the process.[11]

Relatively few Florentine nuns experienced the high drama of yet another rite, the group consecration known as the *sacra* (or *sagrazione*), held about every ten years, which effectively confirmed one's prior profession. These lavish rites became far more popular in Italy only in the late sixteenth and seventeenth centuries as part of post-Tridentine pomp and spirituality.[12] In addition to the occasions noted previously, nuns might spontaneously invent naming traditions that conferred a sense of distinctiveness on themselves and their community. For instance, when Suora Giana Bonsi was elected abbess of Le Murate in July 1534, she decided to change her religious name, which she had borne for fifty years, from Giana to Maria in honor of the convent's patron saint. Her four successors as abbess all imitated this practice, adopting the name of Maria on accession to the post.[13]

Documentary evidence thus points to considerable plasticity in monastic naming practices in Renaissance Florence. Yet these practices still have

---

11. ASF, NA, 13497, fols. 72v–73v, dated 9 February 1434/35.

12. C. A. Monson, *Disembodied Voices: Music and Culture in an Early Modern Italian Convent* (Berkeley and Los Angeles, 1995), pp. 21–22, 78–80. See also G. Zarri, "Ursula and Catherine: The Marriage of Virgins in the Sixteenth Century," in *Creative Women in Medieval and Early Modern Italy: A Religious and Artistic Renaissance,* ed. E. A. Matter and J. Coakley (Philadelphia, 1994), pp. 237–78. Nuns who were "consecrated" were to be at least twenty-five years old.

13. BNF, II.II.509, "Cronache del Monastero delle Murate di Firenze," by Suora Giustina Niccolini, dated 31 January 1597, fol. 94v. By taking the name of Maria, Murate abbesses also may have claimed a singular, elevated status, since the powerful name of the Virgin was not commonly used in the community; see the subsequent analysis of Murate names.

a history whose trajectory can be traced. In the period between the Black Death and the mid-Quattrocento, name changes were infrequent and erratic, especially in Benedictine communities, which enjoyed both decentralized governance and sometimes long-standing traditions of their own. Between 1350 and 1450, it was in fact more common for a nun to retain her secular name (very often a saint's name)[14] than it was to assume a new one. In this respect, naming practices before the mid–fifteenth century were not distinctly gendered: by and large, both monks and nuns kept their given names. After 1450, however, naming practices among male and female religious began to diverge dramatically, just as did their experiences in other realms, with monks retaining their given names and nuns adopting new ones with increased frequency. The retention of secular names among nuns prior to 1450 was particularly pronounced at the convent of San Pier Maggiore, which, as the oldest and wealthiest nunnery in Florence, vigorously maintained its own customs and stubbornly resisted change on numerous occasions. Here a systematic study reveals the irregular nature of renaming in that community. Of the eleven nuns who entered the house between 1375 and 1400, only two exchanged their secular names for religious ones. During the next half century, name changes became even less frequent; only one of seventeen nuns entering San Pier Maggiore between 1400 and 1450 assumed a new religious name.[15]

Although San Pier Maggiore was anomalous in its wealth and historic stature, it was not unique in the episodic nature of its naming practices in early Renaissance Florence. Evidence from other Benedictine houses confirms a similar penchant for retaining secular names among nuns before 1450. At Sant'Appollonia, often considered to be one of the city's more rigorous Benedictine convents, for example, name changes followed similar jagged lines, with only a handful of nuns changing their names. The sisters Piera and Margherita Portinari became known as Filippa and Benedetta when they entered Sant'Appollonia in January 1434. Yet, as mentioned earlier, the following year the Bardi sisters Antonia and Camilla kept their

---

14. Herlihy, "Tuscan Names," p. 574, states that in Florentine burial lists after 1349, "nine of the ten leading women's names refer to saints; in the Catasto of the city of Florence, seven out of ten do so."

15. These figures are derived from CRSPL, San Pier Maggiore, 50, 51, 52, 68, 69, 70, 72, 73; and from the Archivio Arcivescovile di Firenze. San Pier Maggiore, unnumbered volume, titled "Feste, ufizi, e mortori, 1351–1466." Don Gilberto Aranci, head archivist at the Arcivescovile, kindly informed me in July 2000 that this volume has not yet been reinventoried.

secular names upon taking their vows.[16] Similarly, Marietta Cambi became Suora Gabriella at the same house circa 1443; by contrast, Nanna Rustichi, the fourteenth child of the merchant diarist Antonio Rustichi, retained her given name after taking vows in 1456.[17]

The age of the postulant seems to have played an important role in several of these name changes and also may have entered into whatever negotiations took place about the specific name by which a nun would be known. While the passage of years did not necessarily guarantee a firmer sense of self, some evidence suggests that, during these decades when name changes were sporadic, older girls retained their secular names more frequently than their younger counterparts. In the preceding examples, for instance, the Portinari girls were seven and eight years old, respectively, when they shed their old names for new religious ones; by contrast, the Bardi sisters, who kept their secular names, were fifteen and sixteen years old at the time of profession. According to her father's diary, Nanna Rustichi, who also held on to her secular name, was twenty-two years old when she took vows, an exceptionally mature age for new Florentine nuns. Convent chapters may have been more hesitant to alter the identity of a novice who had already achieved adult status by contemporary standards.

How can we account for the episodic nature of name changes before the mid–fifteenth century? It would be far too simple to view these practices as a reflection of lax observance, especially since ritual and canonical prescriptions themselves were so vague about naming. A more forceful explanation lies in the understanding of enclosure that obtained in this period. Benedictine nuns in particular enjoyed a porous set of boundaries that allowed them to engage in neighborhood affairs as property owners, patrons, and members of kin groups. The two-way traffic in and out of the convent was often brisk, even when it did not involve serious infractions of convent discipline.

One figure who illustrates well the options open to nuns living within a permeable enclosure is Laudomina Rinuccini, a nun at San Pier Maggiore from 1394 to circa 1463. Suora Laudomina was surely one of the most energetic businesswomen to ever wear the veil; her career as an enterprising entrepreneur who actively swapped pieces of personal property as she

---

16. For the Portinari sisters, see ASF, CRSGF, 82, 10, fol. 49r; for the vows taken by the two Bardi sisters on 9 February 1434/35, see ASF, NA, 13497, fols. 72v–73v.

17. For Nanna Rustichi, who took vows on 9 May 1456, see CRSGF, 82, 10, fol. 81r; her birth on 2 May 1434 is recorded by her father in CS, ser. 2, 11, fol. 66v. For Marietta Cambi, see CRSGF, 82, 111, unfoliated, under the date 30 July 1443.

reached her prime in the second decade of the fifteenth century finds ample documentation in administrative and notarial records.[18] Besides possessing such worldly wiles, Laudomina and others of her cohort preferred the courteous form of address *monna* (madame) to that of *suora* (sister), thus further blurring the boundaries between secular and monastic worlds. For nuns like Laudomina Rinuccini, retaining one's given name signaled continuity rather than a disjuncture in their life experience.[19]

Before the mid–fifteenth century, entering the cloister did not necessarily mean abandoning all interest and involvement in extramural affairs, whether on a practical or a prescriptive level. Even before the Council of Trent mandated enclosure for all religious women, there were various gradations of how a life model of open reclusion was practiced. Although Benedictine nuns probably maneuvered within the interstices of ecclesiastical authority better than most religious women because of their loose, decentralized organization, even more tightly organized mendicant houses did not mandate a strict separation of spheres. For example, the constitutions governing the Dominican convent of San Jacopo di Ripoli in the late fourteenth century devoted an entire rubric to how nuns should comport themselves when they left the convent; however, these guidelines never challenged the nuns' ability to do so.[20] In this environment where *clausura* was still porous and Benedictine nuns trafficked heavily with the outside world, keeping one's secular name acted as a sustained, stable source of the self. It also measured the vitality of independent convent traditions that many nuns sought to protect.

Yet around the middle of the fifteenth century, this serendipitous naming regime gradually gave way to a highly regularized pattern of name changes. By 1500 it was the rule rather than the exception for nuns to exchange a secular for a religious name, even in the most elite, prestigious communities. Each of the four houses examined here experienced a slightly different pace and chronology, but the general trend nevertheless remained

18. Most of Laudomina's transactions are detailed in ASF, CRSPL, San Pier Maggiore, 52, 70, 72, and 73.

19. Latin documents of the period refer to nuns as "domina." Vernacular referents, however, were less consistent in their usage. In the late fourteenth and early fifteenth centuries, administrative records at San Pier Maggiore consistently refer to nuns as "monna." A similar practice prevailed at Santa Felicita, as was noted in 1622 by Suora Dianora Mazzinghi, a nun of that convent: "chiamavonsi le monache mone e non suore sino all'anno 1400 in circa" (ASF, CRSGF, 83, 239, p. 34).

20. ASF, CRSPL, San Jacopo di Ripoli, 25, fols. 33v–35v, rubric titled "Del entrare e del uscire de monasterii."

the same in all four houses. Regular name changes took effect at Sant'Appollonia by the 1460s; girls entering as novices were assigned a new name immediately upon their acceptance and from this point forward were referred to solely by their religious names in convent records. More regularized name changes took root at Santa Felicita and Sant'Ambrogio by the 1480s, but it was not until the 1490s that the stubborn aristocratic enclave of San Pier Maggiore succumbed to the practice. Even then, several young novices like Bianca Pazzi, who entered San Pier Maggiore in 1526, retained their secular names throughout their novitiates. Part of the resistance to this symbolic rupture no doubt stemmed from the convent's patrician clientele, whose influential families reckoned with powerful naming traditions of their own. In becoming Suora Laudomina in 1529, for instance, Bianca Pazzi had to turn her back on the rich heritage of a secular name derived from her grandmother Bianca, sister of Lorenzo the Magnificent.

In accounting for this change in naming practices around midcentury, we can point to the convergence of several different trends. What probably prompted more consistent name changes in some small part was the growing vogue for secular names drawn from antiquity, which became especially fashionable among the elite. Names like Camilla, the virgin warrior of Virgil's *Aeneid*, and Lucrezia, the violated Roman matron who killed herself rather than live with the shame, highlighted the tension between classicizing trends and religious ideals that was only partly diffused by the sexual integrity of these heroines. Thus at San Pier Maggiore, Camilla Pandolfini became Cecilia in 1493, while Camilla Particini assumed the name Felice in 1501.[21] Other traditionally popular Tuscan names were put aside as well. Unlike Ginevra Fioravanti, who professed at San Pier Maggiore in 1437 under her given name, her later namesakes in the house all changed theirs. Ginevra Strozzi was transformed into Elena (1518), Ginevra della Rena became Sibilla (1519), and Ginevra Taddei converted to Ippolita (1521).[22]

Yet the fashion for antique names cannot be the primary reason motivating these patterns, because even girls with saints' names surrendered them in favor of new ones. Once again San Pier Maggiore provides detailed evidence. Lisabetta Vernacci traded in her time-honored name for that of Giustina in 1495; Francesca Tornabuoni dropped that venerable patron to

---

21. CRSPL, San Pier Maggiore, 161, fol. 195r (Camilla Pandolfini); ibid., 76, fol. 8r (Camilla Particini).

22. Ibid., 31, fol. 10v (Ginevra Fioravanti); ibid., 131, fol. 47v (Ginevra Strozzi); ibid., 167, fols. 131v–132r (Ginevra della Rena); ibid., 167, fols. 195v–196r (Ginevra Taddei).

become Suora Clementia in 1503; and Maria Sapiti was renamed Caterina in 1508.[23] On occasion the pattern worked in the opposite direction. Some girls already bearing a saint's name altered it in favor of a more worldly one. Perhaps the most noteworthy example is that of Brigida Frescobaldi. Brigida entered the Observant Dominican house of San Jacopo di Ripoli, which fell under the stern supervision of the friars of San Marco, as Suora Fiammetta in 1523. It was as Suora Fiammetta Frescobaldi, bearing the name of one of Boccaccio's chivalric female protagonists, that this nun became a well-known writer and convent chronicler.[24] Clearly the issue turned less on the particulars of one's secular name than on the essential act of changing it.

What played a far more important role in this shift was the changing understanding of *clausura* that took shape throughout the Quattrocento.[25] Any assessment of this complex process must take into account the divergent, often competing perspectives of different Florentine constituencies, such as communal magistrates, ecclesiastical officials, nuns' kin and neighbors, and of course religious women themselves. As outsiders looking in, civic magistrates expressed their greatest concern with nuns' sexual behavior, establishing the Conservatori de' Monasteri in 1421 to guard the sexual purity of convents. Both Eugenius IV, resident in Florence in the 1430s, and Antoninus, archbishop from 1446 to 1459, pushed hard for a more rigorous separation between the convent and secular world. Even though stricter enclosure was neither a consistent goal nor a linear process in the fifteenth century, the personal force of Antoninus's intervention, coupled with a growing Observant movement, made the middle decades of the

---

23. Ibid., 161, fol. 247v (Lisabetta Vernacci); ibid., 80, fol. 8r (Francesca Tornabuoni); ibid., 165, fols. 57v–58r (Maria Sapiti).

24. G. Pierattini, "Suor Fiammetta Frescobaldi, cronista del monastero domenicano di Sant'Iacopo a Ripoli in Firenze (1523–1586)," *Memorie domenicane* 56 (1939): 101–6 and 233–39, at 236. One possible reason for the selection of "Fiammetta" as Brigida's religious name is that she had a younger sister bearing that name, to whom her dowry was transferred three years after her profession (p. 237). Should the secular Fiammetta die in childbirth, the religious Fiammetta could still carry on a familial naming tradition.

25. For an important preliminary sketch of the problem of enclosure in late medieval Italy, see K. Gill, "Open Monasteries for Women in Late Medieval and Early Modern Italy: Two Roman Examples," in *The Crannied Wall: Women, Religion, and the Arts in Early Modern Europe*, ed. C. A. Monson (Ann Arbor, Mich., 1992), pp. 15–47. E. Makowski, *Canon Law and Cloistered Women: Periculoso and Its Commentators, 1298–1545* (Washington D.C., 1997), discusses the legal framework of female monastic enclosure.

Quattrocento a turning point in conventual practices. Yet building higher walls and issuing entry permits were not the only means by which a greater degree of separation was achieved. Renaming nuns helped to symbolically demarcate a separate, distinct group of religious women whose lives were to be less entangled with external affairs.

Coercive oversight alone, however, cannot explain this development, especially since external supervision of convents by Florentine archbishops and monastic officials tapered off after 1460.[26] While Antoninus and others may have set this change in motion, ultimately new naming practices took root in the late fifteenth century because nuns themselves developed a stake in them. Naming offered nuns one of several strategies for fashioning the collective identity of the community. As the corporate, institutional influence of convents occupied a larger place in family strategies, neighborhood development, and civic affairs, naming allowed nuns to articulate their own set of values, models, and practices. In accepting the challenge of a *vita comune*, nuns used their new names to tell their own stories about themselves. Even tertiaries, whose attachments to communal life were historically thin, began to change their names more regularly by the end of the Quattrocento, perhaps as a way to distinguish themselves from secular, worldly women and to signal their dedication to an alternate life course.[27] Whether nun or tertiary, religious women began to find something valuable in taking a new name.

NAMING PATTERNS AND PRACTICES

In the second half of the fifteenth century, the population of Florentine convents experienced a rapid and dramatic expansion. Figures drawn from the 1427 catasto indicate that there were 553 female religious housed in convents within the city walls, and another 353 living in outlying institu-

26. G. Brucker, "Monasteries, Friaries, and Nunneries in Quattrocento Florence," in *Christianity and the Renaissance: Image and Religious Imagination in the Quattrocento*, ed. T. Verdon and J. Henderson (Syracuse, N.Y., 1990), pp. 41–62, at p. 56.

27. One example will have to stand in for many. On 13 March 1508/9, Suora Laurentia, known in the secular world as Smeralda di Goro di Benedetto Gori, took vows as a Franciscan tertiary at the convent of Sant'Onofrio di Fuligno. She knelt before the prioress Suora Appollonia Giunti, placed her hands in those of the prioress, and promised before God, the Virgin, and Saint Francis that she would observe the rule of the Third Order, live her entire life in obedience and chastity, and observe all aspects of the rule, including satisfaction of trangressions. CRSGF, 79, 387, insert 5, at that date.

tions, totaling 906 nuns. By 1500 the number of female religious had more than doubled to over 2,000. Convent populations swelled still more rapidly in the early decades of the sixteenth century; by 1515 the number of professed nuns in the city and its environs almost certainly exceeded 2,500.[28]

The full consequences of this demographic expansion for religious practices, monastic architecture, and lay patronage have yet to be examined and fall beyond the scope of the present study.[29] Here only the implications of such remarkable growth for monastic naming practices can be considered. It should be obvious nonetheless that the expansion of female monasticism forced an enlargement of the pool of religious names, especially if excessive and confusing duplication of names was to be avoided among the personnel of any given institution. The undesirable consequences of having several nuns bearing the same name are articulated explicitly by the merchant diarist Francesco di Tommaso Giovanni. Francesco noted in 1445 the terms by which he enrolled his nine-year-old daughter, Gostanza, in the Franciscan convent of Santa Maria in Monticelli, whose population was already on the rise by midcentury. Francesco explained that "because there were already two nuns [named] Gostanza the sisters gave her the name Suora Angelica, which they chose by lot."[30]

As the exchange of names became more regularized in the second half of the Quattrocento, the choice of a particular religious name became a highly conscious decision on the part of the community for several reasons. First, names provided a means of establishing spiritual patronage with a specific saint, who offered protection to his or her namesake. Second, a monastic name established a principal exemplar for a nun. We might think of a name as setting a novice on her spiritual itinerary, with the name and life of saint providing a kind of road map for a nun's behavior. During the course of her own life experience, a nun might find resources in the ready-made past supplied by her name saint. Such was certainly the case for the fifteenth-century holy woman Catherine of Bologna, whose writings articulate how she modeled herself explicitly after her name saint, striving for similar mystical experiences and imprinting similar interpretations on her visions.[31] Finally, the selection of names afforded a way to

28. These figures are given by Brucker, "Monasteries," p. 46.

29. I present a broader investigation of these issues in a forthcoming book provisionally titled "Nuns and Nunneries in Renaissance Florence."

30. ASF, CS, ser. 2., 16 bis, fol. 5r. "Perchè v'è 2 suore Gostanze poseno nome allei suora Angelica che così venne per sorte."

31. J. Wood, "Breaking the Silence: The Poor Clares and the Visual Arts in Fifteenth-Century Italy," *Renaissance Quarterly* 48 (1995): 262–86, at 272–76.

represent the identity of the community both to the nuns themselves and to the outside world. The mosaic of individual nuns' names—the individual "I" that contributed to a collective "we"—created a group portrait that made visible their lives together.

All the documentary evidence points to the fact that the ability and power to name rested with the community. Names were assigned to novices, not chosen by them. Convent records, whether kept by nuns or their male supervisors, consistently used one of two formulas to register name changes. They noted either that "we imposed on her" (*inponiamola*) a new name, which stressed the collective action of the group; or they rendered a more passive construction of a name "posted" to a new nun (*postila*). In either case, the nun's new name positioned her in a nexus of spiritual and social relationships. By virtue of her name, each nun stood in a different relationship to the group, but initially it was not a relationship of her own making. The willingness to be named by others also reinforced both the vow of obedience and the collective decision making that characterized convent life. It was thus through the shared agency on the part of the convent chapter that a new nun was fitted out with another self and a collective identity established.

For the community as a whole, naming was one area free from male clerical supervision. One of the great ironies of convent life was that, although women were stringently separated from men, they were still dependent on them for much of cult practice and administrative support. By contrast, naming was convent "business" in the purest sense of the term. It was not anchored to institutional systems governed by male clerics or laity but reflected the choices of religious women themselves. Naming was thus an important locus of control for the community. Even in houses like Monticelli, which apparently used a lottery system on occasion for selecting a name, the nuns themselves determined the prospective name pool. In turn, naming carried with it a kind of deferred agency for the individual nun, granting the future promise of the ability to position incoming nuns later in one's monastic career. Through the process of naming, a nun became a stakeholder in her community and in the complex of relationships that defined it.

The families of entering nuns may have expressed particular preferences that figured into a community's decision, but whatever negotiations took place about the choice of name have left no documentary traces in convent archives. In a few instances, it is possible to reconstruct how a nun's religious name may have paid homage to secular family members, although the evidence is extremely thin. For example, the choice of the religious name Francesca for the new nun Nera di Giovanni di Francesco della Luna, who entered San Pier Maggiore in 1454, probably deliberately honored her well-respected uncle, a man extremely active in civic affairs who in turn had "remade" her grandfather.[32] Yet reconstructing the households and natal kin of nuns within the limits of available evidence demonstrates few explicit connections between religious and given family names. Instead, as shall be described later, when a nun's name invoked her kin, that form of remembrance almost always harkened back to the religious name of another nun in the same convent, usually an aunt, whose good comportment had honored both family and community.

With these considerations in mind, let us turn now to the different strategies adopted by various communities as their populations swelled after 1450. Newly established institutions like Le Murate faced different problems in selecting names for incoming nuns than did venerable convents like San Pier Maggiore and Santa Felicita, in existence since the eleventh century, for two main reasons. First, new foundations often had to accommodate much larger numbers of entrants than did highly selective institutions that could afford low enrollments because of correspondingly high endowments.[33] Second, new communities also faced the challenging task of creating an entire pool of religious names *ex novo*, without either the guidance or the constraint of tradition. Implicit in this task was the opportunity to shape a fresh collective image of the convent unfettered by previous practices, and to broaden the spectrum of saintly life stories with which nuns could identify on both an intimate and a communal basis. By contrast, older houses not only had to find new names for their growing, albeit smaller ranks; they also had to decide how to distribute the time-honored, privileged names used in the past that carried the weight of personal histories and memories.

32. Among the many positions held by Francesco della Luna, Nera's uncle, from 1418 to 1446 were those of Standard Bearer of Justice, the city's highest political office (1418); supervisor of the civic foundling hospital, the Innocenti; adviser for the placement of the altar in the cathedral; and judge for the lantern designed to top the cathedral cupola; see D. F. Zervas, *The Parte Guelfa, Brunelleschi, and Donatello* (Locust Valley, N.Y., 1988), pp. 217–18. For Nera della Luna's experiences as a pupil and convent boarder at the Augustinian house of Lapo prior to taking vows at San Pier Maggiore, see my article "Learning the Virtues: Convent Schools and Female Culture in Renaissance Florence," in *Women's Education in Early Modern Europe: A History, 1500–1800*, ed. B. J. Whitehead (New York, 1999), pp. 3–46, at 12.

33. Brucker, "Monasteries," pp. 46–48.

THE RETURN TO EARLY CHRISTIAN EXEMPLARS

One of the most prominent trends in naming patterns in the second half of the Quattrocento was the emergence of patrons and role models drawn from the early Christian era. This trend was evident in a number of disparate communities such as the Dominican tertiary house of Annalena, which resisted attempts by both Antoninus and Savonarola to enclose it as a full-fledged nunnery.[34] Perhaps the clearest example of this pattern, however, can be found at the Benedictine house of Le Murate, which experienced the most rapid expansion of any convent in fifteenth-century Florence after its foundation in 1424.[35]

A single notarial document dated 18 April 1470, listing 137 nuns with 136 legible first names, offers an opportunity to conduct a small census of religious names at Le Murate, almost all of which had been given during the preceding thirty years.[36] The names of these Murate nuns articulate a communal vision that forged networks of spiritual clientage and created a gallery of exemplary female role models.

The most outstanding feature of this portrait gallery at the Murate was the return to early Christian exemplars. Slightly more than 62 percent of nuns' names (85 of 136) harkened back to the early centuries of Christianity. The single largest subset of names (60 of 136) reached deep into the early Christian past to recall some of the earliest saints, many virgin martyrs both famous and obscure, who offered models of sanctity for Murate nuns. Heading the list was Caterina, the most popular female Tuscan name in the 1427 catasto, with four namesakes, followed by Alessandra, who had

34. See ASF, NA, 10088, fol. 591v, for a roster of sixty-seven nuns dated 21 October 1494. A brief history of the house can be found in ASF, Manoscritti, 150, no. 3, fols. 53r–57v. For the nuns' mixed reception of Savonarola's interventions in convent affairs, see G. Zippel, "Le monache d'Annalena e il Savonarola," *Rivista d'Italia* 4 (1901): pp. 231–49.

35. Two recent articles offer a useful starting point for analyzing the Murate's extraordinary growth: K. J. P. Lowe, "Female Strategies for Success in a Male-Ordered World: The Benedictine Convent of Le Murate in Florence in the Fifteenth and Early Sixteen Centuries," *Studies in Church History* 27 (1990): 209–21; and F. W. Kent, "Lorenzo de' Medici, Madonna Scholastica Rondinelli e la politica di mecenatismo architettonico nel convento delle Murate a Firenze (1471–72)," in *Arte, committenza ed economia a Roma e nelle corti del Rinascimento (1420–1530)*, ed. A. Esch and C. L. Frommel (Turin, 1995), pp. 353–82.

36. The following discussion is based on ASF, NA, 7978, fol. 4r. My thanks to Gene Brucker for making his transcription of this document available to me, which I have subsequently amended slightly. One name is rendered illegible by a small hole in the document.

three representatives.[37] The virgin martyrs Barbara and Felicita each had two placeholders, as did Antonia and Giroloma, who stood in as feminized versions of male saints with popular followings in the fifteenth century.[38] Other than these few repeat names, however, there was remarkably little duplication. The Murate nuns preferred to individuate themselves by exercising considerable creativity even if it meant associating a new nun with a relatively obscure patron saint. Hence some less-known saints appear on the roster along with those of their more famous, popular peers. The Murate personnel included nuns named after such prominent female figures as Lucia, Agnesa, Dorotea, Gostanza, and Agata, as well as saints with only meager cult followings such as Anastasia, Eufrosina, Silvana, and Tecla. For nuns bearing the names of early Christian female saints, the paradigm of spiritual heroics was not penitence but martyrdom, even though that exalted act was available to fifteenth-century nuns only in a metaphorical sense. The strategy of using compound names to invoke the joint protection of two or more saints, which became a popular practice in both convent and secular life in the late sixteenth century, did not figure into the Murate roster of 1470, and instances of compound names were quite rare before the mid-Cinquecento in other houses as well.[39]

To understand the full significance of this cluster of early Christian saints' names, we must place it in relation to the second most popular subset, accounting for twenty-five names of Murate nuns. This grouping echoed the names of the apostles, prophets, and other biblical figures. The apostles Paul, Thomas, and Bartholomew each had two representatives bearing feminized versions of their names, along with a single stand-in for Andrew, Simon, and Phillip. The Murate nuns honored with one namesake

37. Herlihy, "Tuscan Names," p. 575.

38. For the complex fortunes of the cult of Saint Jerome, see E. F. Rice Jr., *Saint Jerome in the Renaissance* (Baltimore, 1985). Anthony was the most popular Tuscan male name found in the 1427 catasto, possibly because it enjoyed the double valence of the early Christian hermit Anthony and the thirteenth-century Franciscan preacher Anthony of Padua; Herlihy, "Tuscan Names," p. 578.

39. However, a contract from Le Murate dated 9 April 1467 lists a Suora Maria Salome Mariani in the house, along with a total of 152 nuns. Whether she was absent from witnessing the 1470 contract or had died by then is unclear. ASF, NA, 2308, fols. 69r–70r. My thanks to Bill Kent for this reference. Despite the fact that this document lists a greater number of names than the 1470 roster, it is less reliable for purposes of identifying nuns for two reasons: first, it gives first names and patronymics almost exclusively, with few surnames, making precise identification difficult; second, the patronymics given in the 1467 document differ in numerous instances from the 1470 roster, which corresponds more accurately to other contracts.

each the Old Testament figures Daniel, Zachary, Elias, Isaiah, and Jacob, whose teachings prefigured the Christian era. Four biblical women were represented in their own right: Susanna, the Babylonian wife whose beauty was paralleled only by her goodness; Elizabeth, mother of John the Baptist, figuring twice; Ann, mother of the Virgin; and Veronica, whose compassion for Christ on the road to Calvary earned her salvation. Variations on the Virgin's name (Maria, Marietta) appeared only twice; this name was simply too powerful to be used liberally in either the secular or the monastic world. Rounding out this biblical inventory were three namesakes related to the evangelists.

Taken together, these two subsets of early Christian saints and biblical figures represent the Murate nuns as a community that modeled itself after a more pristine, primitive Church. By selecting religious names from the deepest part of the Christian past, these nuns marked their allegiance to the quest for spiritual authenticity coming to the fore in the second half of the fifteenth century. The return to early Christian exemplars at the Murate was consonant with the broader Observant movement reshaping the Florentine religious landscape and registered the community's devotion to the ideals that won praise and patronage from contemporaries like Eugenius IV, Giovanni Benci, and later Lorenzo de' Medici.[40] Some of the inspiration for this cluster of religious names may have come from Archbishop Antoninus, who reportedly visited the convent often and personally professed fifty-eight Murate nuns during his thirteen-year tenure.[41] At the Murate, nuns' names became a sign, if not always the substance, of a particular brand of piety that celebrated the rigor, simplicity, and heroism of the early Church.

Yet these names also celebrated a different set of allegiances than those invoked by most Observant houses of men. Communities of Observant monks and friars belonging to the Franciscan, Dominican, and Carmelite orders frequently recalled the images and biographies of their founders, returning in their artistic commissions, for example, to various foundation myths that recalled the first principles of a particular monastic form.[42] Although the Murate nuns paid homage to their Benedictine roots in the form of two nuns named Scholastica, two called Benedicta, and two other major

---

40. See Kent, "Lorenzo de' Medici, Madonna Scholastica Rondinelli."

41. Antoninus's activities at the Murate are noted in BNF, II.II.509, fol. 44r.

42. C. Gilbert, "Some Special Images for Carmelites, circa 1330–1430," in *Christianity and the Renaissance: Image and Religious Imagination in the Quattrocento*, ed. T. Verdon and J. Henderson (Syracuse, N.Y., 1990), pp. 161–207.

Benedictine players, their names harkened back to a much deeper, more meaningful past.

The return to a biblically based Christianity represented by the 1470 roster of Murate nuns was registered as well by the rejection of medieval exemplars. In the Murate inventory of names, biblical and early Christian role models emphatically displaced medieval saints, ranging from the founders of major orders to local Tuscan figures. Despite the great age of Italian sainthood that had just transpired in the immediately preceding centuries, these saints were not the holy persons with whom Murate nuns chose to identify. Only ten nuns bore the names of late medieval saints, in comparison to the eighty-five celebrating early Christian role models. Franciscan ideals were honored by the presence of two nuns named Francesca, one Clare, a Lodovica, and a Gherardesca; the Dominicans were represented by a Domenica; the Bridgettines by one Bridget. The remaining names invoked a smattering of local Tuscan holy women such as Verdiana, Umiliata, and Fina, all of whom enjoyed local cults as patrons of nearby towns from which these particular nuns may have come.

The displacement of medieval saints as patrons and models in this Benedictine community is further corroborated by yet another group of names that outnumbered them. While ten nuns bore the names of medieval saints, sixteen nuns carried names of abstract virtues or prized qualities befitting religious women. The theological and cardinal virtues, along with other esteemed female attributes, made a respectable showing with one nun each named after such qualities as Prudenzia, Sapienza, Ubidienza, Pace, Benigna, Modesta, and so forth. Significantly, although all the virtues were linguistically gendered as female in the vernacular, two were socially gendered as male—Fortitude and Justice—and do not appear in the Murate roster or in any other listing of convent personnel encountered in my investigations.[43]

Stocking the Murate with the namesakes of early Christian figures, however, did not just identify the house with a particular form of piety. It also set it apart from other Benedictine convents, including its old, wealthy neighbor San Pier Maggiore, as well as Sant'Ambrogio, from whose parochial clutches it had been liberated by Eugenius IV.[44] These houses never

43. Rounding out the total of 136 names were ten angelic names discussed below, five popular Tuscan names such as Beatrice and Ginevra, three nuns named after gemstones that embodied praiseworthy properties (Diamante, Smeralda), and one miscellaneous name (Laudomina).

44. For the grant of parochial exemption, see BNF, II.II.509, fols. 13r–14v.

experienced the enormous expansion of the Murate, nor did they demonstrate a similar attachment to the heroics of early Christianity in their naming practices. In contrast to Le Murate, these two houses continued their allegiance to traditional, time-honored saints' names such as Catherine, Elizabeth, Margaret, Bridget, Constance, Cecilia, and Alexandra. Although several of these names had early Christian origins, they had been used in both the convent and the secular world for so long that they lacked a systematic reference and specificity of association. Only a handful of new names drawn from the early Christian period began to appear in these two communities circa 1470, with an occasional Domitilla being the most favored name.[45] The nuns at San Pier Maggiore and Sant'Ambrogio exhibited somewhat greater enthusiasm for naming new entrants after the various virtues, especially as their growth rate accelerated after 1500, with names like Concordia, Benigna, and Clemenzia making a minor showing. By and large, however, it was the tried-and-true saints of the medieval canon who won the naming battles at these two houses. Taken collectively, the pool of names used within a community spoke directly to its sense of identity and self-representation within a wider matrix.

THE CULT OF THE ANGELS

Where Le Murate shared greater common ground with other houses, including its older Benedictine neighbors, was in the new current of spirituality centering on the angelic. The cult of angels, especially in the guise of individual guardians, is best known as part of post-Tridentine spirituality, with its fifteenth-century antecedents lost in the scholarly shadows. An official liturgy of angels had existed since the time of Charlemagne, with Saint Michael occupying center stage in cult practice as the representative of the multitude of angelic beings.[46] Antoninus himself advocated devotion to angel guardians, who he thought were appointed to watch over every single person. Nonetheless, over the course of the Quattrocento the given name of Michael declined in popularity in Florence, surpassed by the model guardian angel Raphael.[47]

---

45. The first "Suora Domitilla" appeared at Santa Felicita in 1454 (ASF, CRSGF, 83, 113, fol. 5v); at Sant'Ambrogio in 1467 (CRSGF, 79, 455, fol. 36v); and at San Pier Maggiore in 1472 (CRSPL, San Pier Maggiore, 75, fol. 6r).

46. A. E. Sutton and L. Visser-Fuchs, "The Cult of Angels in Late Fifteenth-Century England: The Hours of the Guardian Angel Presented to Queen Elizabeth Woodville," in *Women and the Book: Assessing the Visual Evidence*, ed. L. Smith and J. H. M. Taylor (Toronto, 1997), pp. 230–65, at 231.

47. Herlihy, "Tuscan Names," pp. 578–79.

Angelic names seemed especially appropriate and meaningful for nuns seeking new sources of names. Angels formed themselves into corporations as did nuns; they acted as protectors of others' well-being, much as nuns did through their devotion to the *opus Dei;* and contemporaries perceived both angels and nuns to be important mediators between the human and divine, for which laypersons owed both groups gratitude and patronage.[48] Angelic names begin to appear sporadically in various houses as early as the 1440s, when Marietta Cambi became known as Suora Gabriella at Sant'Appollonia, and by the 1450s in other convents like Sant'Ambrogio, when Elena Bonvanni took the name Arcagnola in 1459.[49] However, the Murate nuns were in the vanguard with a more copious selection of angelic names, due in part to the pressing need for names there and in part because the convent owned a miracle-working image of Saint Michael from its earliest days. During the Spanish siege of Florence, a simulacrum of this much-venerated image appeared to a young girl over the roof of the church, fully armed and ready to defend the convent.[50] The cult of Michael may help to explain the early interest in angelic names at the Murate, where ten nuns bore the names of such beings in the 1470 roster.

By 1500 angelic names appear in all the convents under study to some degree, and their popularity only increased as Florence experienced continued crises in the early sixteenth century. So even the conservative bastion of San Pier Maggiore saw Lionarda Acciaiuoli accept the name Cherubina in 1517, while Maria Benvenuti was called Arcagnola at Sant'Appollonia in 1505. Seven of the nine founders of the Dominican convent of San Vincenzo in Prato adopted angelic names in 1504, by which time Prato and Florence were entwined in a complex regional monastic system.[51] The convent with the least numerous instances of angelic names was Santa Felicita, which is puzzling given the strong cult of the Archangel Raphael there. But clearly angelic names offered clever possibilities for nuns searching for solutions to sticky situations. These names enabled the blood sisters Gostanza and Loisia Strozzi to retain some semblance of their natal filiation when they

48. Sutton and Visser-Fuchs, "Cult of Angels," p. 230.
49. For the name change and dowry payments of Elena di Zanobi Bonvanni, see ASF, CRSGF, 79, 20, fols. 10r, 14r, 16v; and CRSGF, 79, 455, fol. 25v. Profession expenses on 4 May 1473 are recorded ibid., 79, 22, fol. 17r.
50. BNF, II.II.509, fol. 9r.
51. For Maria Benvenuti, see ASF, CRSGF, 82, 10, fol. 88r; for Lionarda Acciaiuoli, CRSPL, San Pier Maggiore, 166, fol. 162r. On the Pratese nuns, see S. Bardazzi and E. Castellani, *Il Monastero di S. Vincenzo in Prato* (Prato, 1982), p. 31. Four of the original nine nuns were from Florentine families.

professed at Sant'Appollonia in 1501 as Gabriella and Raffaella.[52] Still, angelic names provided only a secondary pool for both established and new foundations. Their appearance and popularity indexed a new current of spirituality gaining ground in the late fifteenth and early sixteenth centuries, but they never attained the stature of saints' names whatever their origin.

THE NUN "REMADE"

In more established houses like San Pier Maggiore, Santa Felicita, Sant'Ambrogio, and Sant'Appollonia, the problems raised by monastic expansion centered more on distributing the limited pool of privileged names that had acquired special resonance in each community than on creating new ones. The solution nuns developed was grounded in the fundamental principles of Florentine kinship: that is, they "remade" the name of a recently deceased nun in the person of a new novice. Remaking a nun was an act of remembrance of the most profound kind. As David Herlihy succinctly stated, "In some mysterious way, reused names undid death."[53] This naming practice both honored revered forebears and cast new nuns as placeholders in a system of filiation particular to that community. In this naming regime, it was less the case of a name being given to a person than a person being given to a name. Names bound nuns to the particular traditions of the house, with recycled names functioning as focal points for collective memory. At the same time, remaking a valued, deceased nun reinforced the notion of a convent as a fictive family, bound by the ties of names and the histories and memories those names represented. Significantly, this convent family reckoned filiation strictly through the female line, even though the names themselves might refer to male saints or archangels in their feminized form. Through the practice of remaking a dead nun, elite Benedictine houses began to celebrate a lineage of women that in turn symbolically strengthened female bonds. Moreover, it was a lineage that displaced secular family ties in favor of monastic ones. The case of Maria Minerbetti provides one telling example. As a secular girl Maria bore the name of her father's deceased first wife, who she "remade" in her honor. Once Maria entered Santa Felicita in 1506, she switched her filiation by remaking instead the dead abbess Piera de' Rossi, eventually rising to the post of abbess herself in 1571.[54]

52. ASF, CRSGF, 82, 10, fol. 88r.
53. Herlihy, "Tuscan Names," p. 571.
54. Anthony Molho, *Marriage Alliance in Late Medieval Florence* (Cambridge, Mass., 1994), p. 175; ASF, CRSGF, 83, 239, p. 39.

Surveying this naming practice over a long time span is essential in order to capture the transmission of religious names from one generation of nuns to another, particularly since some nuns lived exceptionally long lives.[55] At Sant'Appollonia, the first nun to be "remade" appeared in 1451, when Cosa Donati became Suora Cecilia. This young nun took the name of her kinswoman Cecilia Donati, abbess in the community from about 1429 to 1446. In turn, the privileged name of Cecilia was bestowed on the novice Marietta Orlandini shortly after the second Cecilia's death in 1498.[56] Similarly, Benedetta Portinari, one of the first nuns in the community to adopt a religious name in 1434, was remade a year after her death in 1460 by the novice Maria Bombeni; in turn, Benedetta Bombeni passed this name to the novice Alessandra Serristori in 1475, after which it was transferred to Albiera Gualterotti in 1485, five years after the previous Benedetta's death.[57] Similar chains of remembrance characterized the names Alessandra, Margherita, Brigida, Lena, Piera, Bartolommea, and Filippa, creating a set of interlocking personal memories that hopefully forged a stronger sense of both community and fictive kinship among nuns in this house.

The gap between old and new occupants of a prized name ranged from a few months to as many as five or even ten years, with the name of a dead abbess being recycled most quickly. For instance, Abbess Filippa Portinari, sister of the Benedetta noted earlier, died in May 1494. The next new novice to enter the convent in July 1494, Maddalena Corbinelli, was immediately assigned her name. A similarly short interval obtained between the death in February 1508 of Maria Barbadori, abbess of Sant'Ambrogio, and her remaking by her kinswoman Gostanza Barbadori at the same house two months later.[58] The practice of remaking a nun who spent a long tenure in the convent took such firm hold by the 1490s at Sant'Appollonia that a remaking provides a fairly reasonable indication of death in the absence of other evidence.

Not surprisingly, San Pier Maggiore, Sant'Ambrogio, and Santa Felicita all offer equally thick evidence of this practice. The favored names at Sant'Ambrogio were such old standbys as Maria, Maddalena, Margherita,

55. J. C. Brown, "Monache a Firenze all'inizio dell'età moderna: un analisi demografica," *Quaderni storici* 85 (1994): 117–52.

56. ASF, CRSGF, 82, 10, fols. 69r, 87v.

57. Ibid., fols. 84r, 86r, 86v.

58. ASF, CRSGF, 82, 9, fol. 30r (death of Filippa Portinari); CRSGF, 82, 10, fol. 87r (entry of Maddalena Corbinelli); CRSGF, 79, 27, fol. 230r (death of Maria Barbadori); CRSGF, 79, 60, fols. 102v–103r (entry of Gostanza Barbadori).

and Brigida, along with the early Christian martyr Domitilla. At San Pier Maggiore, several similar names enjoyed a privileged status, most notably Felice, Margherita, Maria, Brigida, Benedetta, and Laudomina. Here the circulation of the unusual name Laudomina will have to serve as one example among many. We have already met the first Laudomina in San Pier Maggiore in the person of Laudomina Rinuccini, the enterprising property owner who spent seventy years in the convent from her entry as a young girl in 1394 until her death after October 1463. This extraordinarily active nun was remade after her death in the person of "Laudomina" Gualterotti, who professed sometime between 1476 and 1485. Although this second Suora Laudomina did not distinguish herself as brilliantly as did her predecessor, nor spend so long a tenure in the house, the name was remade once again following her death after 1506. The community then pinned its hopes for a resurgent Laudomina on the novice Alessandra Antinori upon her entrance in 1510. Her monastic career was characterized by a number of property transactions, although not on the same scale as her illustrious predecessor. After thirteen years in San Pier Maggiore, this third Laudomina died of plague in 1523, and her name was then bestowed six years later on Bianca Pazzi, who had retained her given name throughout her novitiate.[59] In this way the singular figure of Laudomina Rinuccini was remembered and re-formed, with each new bearer adding her own talents and experiences to the fortunes of the name. It would seem that San Pier Maggiore needed the presence of this uncommon name as much as families needed the presence of a nun there who would look out for their varied interests.

Conversely, when a nun failed to comport herself well, her name dropped out of circulation. Piccarda Gianfigliazzi created an uproar at Sant'Appollonia after she transferred there from another house in the early 1450s because she was a malicious gossip, and the name was never remade in that convent, although it was reused several times at neighboring Sant'Ambro-

---

59. The imprecision in some dates results from a combination of missing account books and the severe water damage sustained by the *fondo* of San Pier Maggiore in the 1966 flood of the Arno River. Convent personnel for the years 1457 through the 1470s must be reconstructed from notarial records and other fragmentary sources. Suora Laudomina Gualterotti first appears on a notarial list dated 21 April 1485 as the ninth of eleven nuns ranked by order of profession date; ASF, NA, 10087, at that date. For the respective entries of Alessandra Antinori and Bianca Pazzi, see ASF, CRSPL, San Pier Maggiore, 165, fol. 59r; and ibid., 84, fol. 28v. The death of Alessandra Antinori is recorded ibid., 168, fol. 93v.

gio.[60] For "good" nuns like Laudomina and "bad" ones like Piccarda, the meaning of a nun remade was deeply embedded in the institution itself. Beneath the surface of this seeming traditionalism, then, with some Benedictine communities clinging to time-honored patrons, nuns were creating vital new traditions of their own.

Yet these naming practices also introduced another paradox characteristic of the complexities of Florentine convent life. As elite Benedictine convents restricted new membership to select families, many of whom had gained a foothold in the house through previous generations of nuns, new nuns sometimes ended up remaking their own kinswomen. At Sant'Ambrogio in 1502, for instance, Maddalena Zati took the name of her aunt Suora Lena in the same year in which she died. At Santa Felicita, Brigida Guicciardini, abbess from 1442 to 1480, was remade by her kinswoman Brigida, who professed in 1494.[61] It is difficult to tell from extant sources whether a convent purposely reserved an illustrious name with the knowledge that a close family member was likely to profess in the near future. Whatever the conscious strategies that lie hidden beyond our documentary reach, this practice had the unequivocal result of stamping family claims on the house so that, ironically, the boundaries separating the convent and the city became blurred once again. When the practices of remaking both a dead nun and a dead kinswoman overlapped or collided, nuns often responded with a clever solution. The elite, conservative, and honor-conscious nuns of San Pier Maggiore, for example, settled on a happy compromise in 1510 when they named the incoming nun Felice Buonafedi (or Buonafe) Suora Felicita. This variant of her own given name still successfully invoked the memory of her distinguished monastic ancestor, Suora Felice Buonafe, a longtime resident in the convent from 1385 until her death in 1438; yet at the same time it avoided direct duplication with another nun, Suora Felice Particini, who already had remade the name in 1501.[62]

The practice of remaking nuns' names belies a complex, emerging genealogical self-consciousness in the second half of the Quattrocento. As

60. The "scandal" surrounding Piccarda Gianfigliazzi is recorded in ASF, CRSGF, 82, 111, unfoliated, at 8 January 1451/2; and in ASF, NA, 13499, fols. 51v–52r, 53r–v.

61. ASF, CRSGF, 79, 26, fol. 110v (entry of Maddalena Zati); ibid., fol. 269v (death of Lena Zati); CRSGF, 83, 239, p. 36 (death of Brigida Guicciardini); CRSGF, 83, 115, fol. 28v (profession of Brigida Guicciardini).

62. ASF, CRSPL, San Pier Maggiore, 165, fols. 200v–201r, for the 1510 entry of Felice Buonafedi; ibid., 76, fol. 8r, for the entry of Camilla, later "Felice," Particini.

communities both expanded and turned in on themselves, they became more self-referential, more aware of their own history and traditions. A similar sense of a collective past that deserved to be known and celebrated surfaced in other forms of monastic record keeping, especially after 1500. For instance, in 1508 the abbess of San Pier Maggiore, Andrea Buondel-monti, ordered a retrospective inventory of all monastic goods and obliga-tions and inserted herself explicitly into the narrative of communal his-tory;[63] the Dominican house of San Jacopo di Ripoli began a comprehensive necrology in the same year; and the next generation of nuns started to chronicle the histories of their houses, reflecting the increased concern with memorialization in sixteenth-century Europe as a whole.

Despite these different strategies for choosing names, naming practices in these very diverse houses nevertheless shared a common underpinning. The narratives of naming allowed each community to define itself as it saw fit. There is no question that Le Murate and San Pier Maggiore stood at op-posite ends of the spectrum in terms of their size, wealth, heritage, social composition of personnel, devotional models, and spiritual reputation. Yet despite the fact that these houses inflected Benedictine ideals in different ways, they each engaged in fundamental acts of self-representation through their naming practices. The relationships they honored in their choice of names, whether spiritual or familial, formed the very foundation of their communities. Regardless of the pronounced differences between groups of religious women, naming practices furnish a crucial example of the ways that nuns created their own discrete identities and cultures.

63. ASF, CRSPL, San Pier Maggiore, 36, unnumbered front folio.

9 The Prophet as Physician of Souls
Savonarola's Manual for Confessors
Donald Weinstein

I

If by burning Fra Girolamo Savonarola and his two confederates the Florentine authorities thought they were lifting "the intolerable burden" of religious politics from the backs of a restive populace, they misfired.[1] Savonarolan millenarian ideology continued to be a factor, at times even a dominant force, for the four decades remaining in the life of the Republic.[2] Just as futile was the gesture of throwing the bones and ashes of the three friars into the Arno; even without relics to foster a martyr's cult, many believed that at least one saint had died in the flames of 23 May 1498.[3]

Another form of survival, even more broadly influential, was Savonarola's legacy of devotional and doctrinal writings, in the sixteenth and seventeenth centuries among the most widely read works of their kind.[4] Yet, although efforts are being made, we still do not have a comprehensive study

I wish to thank the trustees of the Bridwell Library, Perkins School of Theology, Southern Methodist University, for granting me a fellowship to use its superb collection of Savonarola materials. All of the early editions I cite in this essay are from the Bridwell collection. I am grateful to the Bridwell staff and its Endowed Librarian, Dr. Valerie R. Hotchkiss, for their hospitality and their help in my use of the collection. A translation of this article was published as "Il profeta come medico di anime: Il Manuale per Confessori del Savonarola," in *Memorie Domenicane*, n.s., 29 (1998): 21–38.

1. For the phrase, and for the thesis that Savonarola's career was "an aberrant moment" in Florentine history, see G. A. Brucker, "Savonarola and Florence: The Intolerable Burden" in *Studies in the Italian Renaissance: Essays in Memory of Arnolfo Ferruolo*, ed. G. P. Biasin et al. (Naples, 1985), repr. in Brucker, *Renaissance Florence: Society, Culture, and Religion* (Goldbach, Germany, 1994), pp. 333–47.

2. See now L. Polizzotto, *The Elect Nation: The Savonarolan Movement in Florence 1494–1545* (Oxford, 1994).

3. G. Schnitzer, *Savonarola*, Italian trans. E. Rutili, 2 vols. (Milan, 1931), vol. 2, chaps. 37–39; A. d'Addario, *Aspetti della Controriforma a Firenze* (Rome, 1972), pp. 255–56; Polizzotto, *Elect Nation*, pp. 441–43.

4. A. J. Schutte, *Printed Vernacular Religious Books 1465–1550: A Finding List* (Geneva, 1983); G. Zarri, "Note su diffusione e circolazione di testi devoti (1520–

of the friar's religious doctrine, a full appraisal of his influence on the Catholic and Protestant Reformations, or an adequate idea of his pastoral, as distinct from his more spectacular prophetic, career.[5] I should like to address myself particularly to the last of these questions, chiefly by examining one of Savonarola's least studied and, apparently, least regarded writings, the *Confessionale pro instructione confessorum,* which so far has not been given a place in the almost completed National Edition of his works.

It was not ever thus. Published about the time of Savonarola's death, the *Confessionale* was reprinted at least forty-two times in the next two centuries, no match for Saint Antoninus's three extraordinarily popular confession manuals, but successful enough to be described as *"fortunatissimo"* by a modern bibliographer.[6] Although its author was still under papal excommunication, the *Confessionale* even achieved something like official status, appearing in an approved edition in 1581 with a prefatory letter of Pope Gregory XIII.[7]

1550)," in *Libri, idee e sentimenti religiosi nel Cinquecento italiano* (Modena, 1987), pp. 131–54.

5. Still important is Schnitzer, *Savonarola,* vol. 2, chaps. 29–32. See also d'Addario, *Aspetti,* pp. 25–31; D. Weinstein, "Explaining God's Acts to His People: Savonarola's Spiritual Legacy to the Sixteenth Century," in *Humanity and Divinity in Renaissance and Reformation: Essays in Honor of Charles Trinkaus,* ed. J. W. O'Malley, T. M. Izbicki, and G. Christianson (Leiden, 1993), pp. 205–25. The recent outpouring of scholarship, much of it under the auspices of the Comitato Nazionale per le Celebrazioni del V Centenario della Morte di Girolamo Savonarola, is rich in new material and fresh insights, but with a few exceptions the friar's prophetic and political career continues to dominate research. See G. C. Garfagnini, ed., *Studi Savonaroliani Verso il V centenario* (Firenze, 1996); G. C. Garfagnini ed., *Savonarola e la politica* (Florence, 1997); G. C. Garfagnini ed., *Savonarola democrazia tirannide profezia* (Florence, 1998); G. C. Garfagnini and G. Picone, eds., *Verso Savonarola misticismo, profezia, empiti riformistici* (Florence, 1996–99). I address the issue of Savonarola's influence upon the Catholic and Protestant Reformations in my essay "A Man for All Seasons: Savonarola, the Renaissance, the Reformation and the Counter Reformation," forthcoming in the papers of the seminar "La figura de Jerónimo Savonarola OP y su influencia en España y Europa" (Valencia, 2000). While this article was in press (but after the appearance of its Italian edition), Gilberto Aranci published a study of the *Confessionale* valuable for its bibliographical references as well as for its analysis: "Il Savonarola tra pulpito e confessionale: *L'introductorium confessorum* nel progetto di riforma della chiesa e della città," *Vivens Homo* Anno X (1999): 265–94. He seeks to show connections as well as distinctions between Savonarola's *Confessionale* and his program of moral and ecclesiastical reform.

6. Girolamo Savonarola, *Operette spirituali,* 2 vols., ed. M. Ferrara (Rome, 1976), 2:267.

7. See the listing and description of twenty-eight editions in L. Giovannozzi, *Contributo alla bibliografia delle opere del Savonarola: Edizioni dei secc. XV e XVI*

Like other works of its kind, the manual is designed to prepare priests for hearing confessions by reviewing the catalog of sins, summarizing what has been said about them in papal decretals, conciliar decrees, and canon law, and instructing confessors in the techniques of interrogation, absolution, and the administering of penance. It is particularly intended for new and inexperienced confessors facing what Fra Girolamo calls "the uncrossable sea" of books, issues, canons, and the opinions they elicited from the Doctors. Of all priestly tasks the direction of consciences (*de regimine animarum*) is the most difficult, Savonarola says, and since his fellow priests have asked his help, he has put together this compendium of rescripts, problems (*questiones*), and natural, divine, and statute law, assembling them like a chain by which to lead a penitent from the beginning of confession to the end.[8] Given its nature, it is no surprise that the *Confessionale* neither rings with the apocalyptic fervor of Savonarola's sermons nor glows with the inspired spirituality of his *Triumph of the Cross* or his meditations on Psalms.[9] Beholden to previous models and to the pronouncements of authorities, most prominently Saint Thomas, Hostiensis, and Petrus of Palude, this is not the most original or exciting material in the friar's *Nachlass*, and its neglect by Savonarola scholars is understandable.

Understandable, but regrettable. The manual offers an unusual opportunity to view Fra Girolamo not as the lone prophet-reformer pitting himself against hierarchy and ceremonial religion (as he called it), not the visionary of a New Jerusalem in Florence, but in a less familiar, "insider's" role. Here Savonarola is a priest talking to priests about ecclesiastical authority and sacrament and advising them on casuistry, the art of applying doctrinal norms to the day-to-day sins of their charges. Whether we can recognize the Prophet in the Pastor, the visionary reformer in the casuist, is one of the questions I will address. Savonarola was nothing if not a *Bussprediger*, his constant pulpit cry, "poenitentiam agite!"; if his apocalyptic and

(Florence, 1953), pp. 24–33; and of an additional fifteen by Mario Ferrara in Girolamo Savonarola, *Operette spirituali*, 2 vols., ed. M. Ferrara (Rome, 1976), 2:267–68 n. 2.

8. Girolamo Savonarola, *Confessionale pro instructione confessorum* (Venice: Francesco Bindoni, 1524), fol. 2r–v. I cite this edition throughout as *Confessionale*. It has an introduction by Lucas Olchinensis to Antonio Contarini, Patriarch of Venice.

9. Girolamo Savonarola, *Triumphus Crucis testo latino e volgare*, ed. M. Ferrara (Rome, 1961); Savonarola, "Expositio in Psalmum Miserere Mei, Deus," and "Expositio in Psalmum in Te, Domine, Speravi," in Savonarola, *Operette spirituali*, 2:197–262 and nn. 339–419. For a brief discussion of these works, see Weinstein, "Explaining God's Acts," pp. 211–24.

pastoral selves connect anywhere it ought to be here, in his thinking about confession and the sacrament of penance.

The significance of this question goes beyond Savonarolan biography to some of the critical issues in the history of penance and confession at the turn of the sixteenth century. Thomas Tentler has nicely caught the balance between discipline and accommodation and between punishment and consolation in the thinking of the late medieval writers on confession and penance;[10] Steven Ozment, on the other hand, has emphasized "the burden of late medieval religion," citing the evidence of lay catechisms and vernacular manuals for confessors.[11] Because Savonarola was one of the most famous penitential preachers of his time, as well as the author of one of the most widely read works on confession, his views are relevant here. Was he, so severe in his judgment on the spiritual "tepidity" of the age,[12] also a rigorist in his instruction to confessors? Was the *Confessionale* another "intolerable burden" pressing down on the consciences of penitents?

A related question is the function of the *Confessionale* as an instrument of what has been called—not without dissent—social control.[13] Manuals routinely directed confessors to withhold absolution until the penitent made restitution of illegally or immorally acquired possessions or until they paid indemnities for antisocial acts.[14] John Bossy has even argued that while the primary concerns of the medieval penitential regime were the social sins, notably hatred and violence, sins that disrupted the Christian community, the growing individualization of society was accompanied by a shift toward an interiorized discipline for the individual conscience.[15] A

---

10. T. N. Tentler, *Sin and Confession on the Eve of the Reformation* (Princeton, N.J., 1977), p. 344 and passim. Another valuable study is P. Michaud-Quantin, *Sommes de casuistique et manuels de confession au moyen âge (XII–XVI siècles)* (Louvain, 1962). Neither author discusses Savonarola's *Confessionale*.

11. S. E. Ozment, *The Reformation in the Cities: The Appeal of Protestantism to Sixteenth-Century Germany and Switzerland* (New Haven, Conn., 1975), pp. 22–32.

12. On Savonarola and the concept of spiritual tepidity, see Weinstein, "Explaining God's Acts," pp. 217–18.

13. Tentler, *Sin and Confession*, p. 344 and passim. See the exchange between Tentler and L. Boyle in *The Pursuit of Holiness in Late Medieval and Renaissance Religion*, ed. C. Trinkaus and H. A. Oberman (Leiden, 1974), pp. 101–37.

14. A famous case, briefly described by Tentler, *Sin and Confession*, p. 367, was the refusal by a Dominican to hear the confession of Bartolomé Las Casas until he gave up his unfree Indians. Later, as bishop of Chiapas, Las Casas instructed priests to use the confessional to force the restitution of illegally acquired lands and Indians.

15. J. Bossy, "The Social History of Confession in the Age of the Reformation," *Transactions of the Royal Historical Society*, ser. 5, 25 (1975): 21–38. He expands

reading of the *Confessionale* may shed some further light on these controversial issues as well as on my initial question. Did Savonarola, ardent for
social harmony and political justice, attempt to enlist confessors in his campaign for moral and civic reform? Did he, in other words, regard confession
as a tool in building the New Jerusalem in Florence? Savonarola worked on
the *Confessionale* during the summit years of his ascendancy in Florence,
completing it just as his career and his life were coming to an end. Can we
make any connections? Did the *Confessionale*, like his prophetic sermons,[16]
reflect his Florentine experiences?

The *Confessionale* is a short, succinct treatise, some forty-four folios.
Savonarola refers to it as a "breve compendium" of the vast literature on
confession and penance and offers it as a mere outline of the principles and
procedure confessors should follow. In the first part he discusses the qualities of a good confessor and lists the types of ecclesiastical censure (major
and minor excommunication, interdict, etc.).[17] In the much longer second
part he outlines a routine for interrogating penitents, organizing it on a
well-established model in which the Decalogue serves as the fountain of all
spiritual and moral law.[18] *Caritas*, or love, encompasses all Ten Command-
ments, which are grouped into the familiar two tables. Love of God is the
subject of the first table: to the Lord, as to a prince, we owe fidelity, honor,
and service. Thus, failure to keep vows and pride (self-love) are as much
violations of the precept of fidelity as the lack of religious faith itself, while
vainglory, profanity, perjury, and blasphemy are some of the ways we violate the obligation to honor God. The most serious is *accidia*, or harboring
doubts of God's mercy, a sin against the Holy Spirit. The obligation of service to our God-Prince has both spiritual and ceremonial aspects. We err
spiritually by engaging in superstitious practices such as astrology and div-
ination or consorting with infidel Jews and Muslims. We violate our ceremonial obligations when we neglect divine worship on the Sabbath and
other holy days or fail in our sacramental duties. When *accidia* leads us to
neglect good works, it is a violation of the precept of service as well of honor.

---

his thesis of medieval communitarianism and its decline in Bossy, *Christianity in
the West 1300–1700* (Oxford, 1985).

16. On the connection between Savonarola's Florentine experience and his prophetic preaching, see D. Weinstein, *Savonarola and Florence: Prophecy and Patriotism in the Renaissance* (Princeton, N.J., 1970).

17. Savonarola, *Confessionale*, fols. 2v–14r.

18. Already in the thirteenth century, Raymond of Peñafort was dividing the
catalog of sins into two parts: those against God and those against one's neighbor.
See Michaud-Quantin, *Sommes de casuistique*, p. 36.

Savonarola's feudal-monarchical metaphor holds for the second table of the Law as well: our obligation to love God as our prince extends to loving his creatures, our neighbors, and guides us in our duties to society. Together the precepts of the second table form the basis of an extended Christian moral and social code. Thus, the command to honor our fathers and mothers is taken to include parents' treatment of their children (e.g., fairness in making wills) and governs relations between princes and subjects and masters and servants, as well as between social equals. Savonarola likes to remind his readers that we sin by speech and thought as well as deed, in heart and spirit as well as body.[19] Thus the Sixth Commandment includes social as well as physical murder—hatred and envy, spreading scandal and withholding fraternal correction; the Seventh covers other sexual sins besides adultery, namely, fornication, seductiveness in dress and behavior, and lust —in marriage as well as out; the Eighth Commandment, against theft, includes avarice (theft of the heart), simony, and usury.

Such a bare outline may give too negative and severe an impression. The *Confessionale* is more than a finding list for the vast library of sin, a road map through the dark forest of guilt. For all its terse brevity (which makes it, like other road maps, sometimes hard to follow), it is also an appeal for priestly understanding and a reminder of the complexity of human motivations. Savonarola was concerned that confessors show kindness rather than severity toward penitents. Before receiving penitents they should humble themselves and avoid self-righteousness; praying for divine guidance in directing consciences, they should rise in fear and trembling, not thinking so much about condemning sin as about the salvation of souls. Approaching the sinner and raising him from his knees, a confessor should be gentle (*dulcis*), affable, and compassionate, grave but not severe lest he terrify and confuse the penitent instead of encouraging him to show all his wounds. He should also be tolerant of poorly informed laymen; if a sinner is so ignorant as not to know how to make a decent genuflection, the sign of the cross, or other requisite gestures, he should be instructed and admonished, but gently.[20]

---

19. Of the seven deadly sins, Saint Thomas says that five are spiritual, two are carnal; *De modo confitendi et puritate conscientiae*, in Saint Thomas Aquinas, *Opera omnia* (Parma, 1852–73; photolithographic reproduction, New York, 1950), T. XVII, p. 308. Saint Antoninus speaks of sins of the heart and of action, citing Saint Thomas as his authority, also for holding that the latter are much graver, although he does not give a precise reference; Antoninus, *Medicina de lanima (Curam ille habe)* (Bologna, 1472), cap. xxvii.

20. Savonarola, *Confessionale*, fols. 2v–3r.

In the matter of contrition, or sorrow for one's sins, the all-important prerequisite to absolution, Savonarola was plainly no rigorist. Some, he observed, come to confession without a firm intention to give up their sins or, mistakenly believing themselves to be contrite, do not confess with sufficient diligence. But if a penitent exhibits attrition, or imperfect sorrow, his confession should be accepted as valid, for only by revelation is it possible to know whether anyone has true contrition. It is enough, then, that the priest has "sufficientes conjecturas." Better to give the penitent the benefit of the doubt, as Saint Thomas says, than to reject a less than perfect confession and raise innumerable scruples. Besides, Saint Thomas says an attrite person often becomes contrite in the course of making his confession.[21] If he confesses to an inherently mortal sin, the priest should try to find some reason to give him hope.[22] If the sinner is reluctant to recite his sins but is willing to answer when questioned about them, he should be helped to do so, encouraged to tell the circumstances and at least estimate the number of times he has transgressed, for as a physician of the body can only cure wounds that are shown to him, so disclosure is even more important for the physician of souls.[23] Even if a penitent shows no sign of contrition, the confessor should kindly exhort him to reconsider and to be as contrite as he is able.[24]

In urging confessors to speak softly and use the heavy rod of penance

---

21. Ibid., fols. 13r–14r. For Thomas on contrition, see *In quatuor libris Sententiarum* III-1, Quaest. XC, art. III and V, Dist. XVII, Quaest. II, art. I, *Opera omnia* (Parma, 1852–73; photolithographic reproduction), T. XXII. Astesanus de Ast said attrition may become contrition in the act of penitence, although it does not inevitably do so. *Summa de casibus conscientiae* (Venice: Johannes de Colonia & Johannes Manthen, 1478), bk. 5, chap. 9. On Saint Thomas's treatment of this issue, see Tentler, *Sin and Confession*, pp. 24–27, and for a discussion of contrition and attrition in general, ibid., chap. 5.

22. Savonarola, *Confessionale*, fol. 15r.

23. On the scriptural and patristic roots of the image of the physician of souls, see Tentler, *Sin and Confession*, p. 157 and n. 27. Alain de Lille used it in his late-twelfth-century *Liber Poenitentialis*; Michaud-Quantin, *Sommes de casuistique*, p. 17. It became a common trope in the literature of confession. Thus, Hostiensis writes that the physician is like a "medicus" of the body; in order to heal he must discreetly and astutely ask questions to extract what the patient himself does not know about his illness; Henricus de Segusio Cardinalis Hostiensis, *Summa* (Lyon, 1537; facsimile ed., 1962), bk. 5 (fol. 278r.) Some editions of the popular confessional manual of Saint Antonino, *Curam illius habe*, were entitled *Medicus de lanima*. See note 19 above for one.

24. "Si autem non apparent manifesta signa quam talis non sit contritus, eligat confessor in dubio benigniorem partem, inducens tamen eum per aliquam exhortationem quantum potest ad veram contritionem"; Savonarola, *Confessionale*, fol. 14r.

sparingly, Savonarola was in the mainstream of confessional thought. Since Gratian's endorsement of arbitrary penances in the twelfth century and Raymond of Peñafort's "capitulation to a milder regime" in the thirteenth, the penitential system had been on a course of moderation.[25] Within the tradition there was, to be sure, room for differences of interpretation and tone and degrees of rigorism.[26] Like Saint Antoninus before him, Savonarola was decidedly on the side of the moderates, and, like Antoninus, he warned against creating despair, stressed the priest's curative and consolatory functions, and granted him latitude in assigning penalties.[27]

Savonarola's emphasis upon discretion by confessors also reflects a long-standing tendency among some of the writers on the sacrament to adapt the penitential process to circumstances and persons.[28] Saint Antoninus cites the interrogatory formula of Petrus of Palude, the fourteenth-century Paris master: "Quis, quid, ubi, quibus, auxiliis, cur, quomodo, quando," and adds another from Raymond of Peñafort—"Quotiens?"[29]

Savonarola read and cited Petrus of Palude, although he does not invoke this formula literally; still, he too was concerned with motivations and psychological states. If a sin was not mortal in its nature, he declares, it may be

25. Tentler, *Sin and Confession*, p. 16.

26. Saint Antoninus, for example, while citing Saint Thomas and Raymond of Peñafort in support of his own discretionary approach to penance, noted that Thomas and Petrus of Palude strictly opposed absolution for certain types of recalcitrant sinners, while his own tendency was more liberal; see Antoninus, *Defecerunt*, chap. 32. On the diversity of medieval moralists in this regard, and the difficulty of assigning laxist or rigorist labels to particular authors, see Tentler, *Sin and Confession*, pp. 162–63.

27. Surprisingly, Savonarola cites Saint Antoninus only once in the *Confessionale*, on the subject of excommunication (fol. 2v).

28. Instead of applying a universal calculus of sins, confessors were instructed to concentrate on the moral and spiritual problems most relevant to penitents of diverse social status and occupation. In contrast to the former indifference of theorists to the circumstances of sin, the study of concrete situations became a regular exercise in the Paris Faculty of Theology by 1250. This was increasingly carried over to the manuals and summas, whose authors, citing the theologians as their authorities, instructed confessors to question penitents about the circumstances in which they had transgressed, take into account the psychological state of sinners at the time they sinned, and consider the intention as well as the consequences of the act, the thought as well as the deed. John of Freiburg's extremely popular *Summa for Confessors* helped consolidate the trend; Michaud-Quantin, *Sommes de casuistique*, pp. 45–46. Ozment thinks that interrogating penitents on the circumstances of sin contributed to the burden of penance (*Reformation in the Cities*, p. 26). If so, it was an unintended consequence of the scholastic teaching described earlier.

29. Antoninus, *Defecerunt*, chap. 25; Petrus de Palude, *In quatuor libros sententiarum et quodlibeta Duns Scoti* (Venice, 1583), Dist. 4, p. 16.

either mortal or venial depending on the sinner's intentions, and this is up to the confessor to determine. He should ask penitents *why* they had committed their sins ("quo fine hoc fecit") and probe for the accompanying circumstances. Intention ("de fine"), he writes, is the most important thing because "the end gives specificity to mortal acts. By this you will be able to recognize when sins are mortal, when venial." While the interrogation might lead in either direction, Savonarola clearly prefers to lighten rather than increase the gravity of the sin. In many cases the priest must refrain from judgment altogether. Especially as regards such interior sins as pride, human judgment is fallible, and confessors must leave much to God, the sole assessor of spirits. Only he has perfect knowledge of inner thoughts.

Evidence that the *Confessionale* reflects Savonarola's personal experience of confessors and penitents in Florence is mainly indirect and inferential. We may get some clues by considering how he distributed the space in his "brief compendium." Dipping into the "uncrossable sea" of penitential literature, he harvests only the matter he considers essential, treats most of it briefly, giving the main part of his attention to just five topics. Together these five topics take up almost half of the manual.[30] Leaving aside the opening section on excommunication and other ecclesiastical censures—mainly a recital of the canonical penalties for clerical misbehavior and for offenses against the Church—we are left with four dominant topics: marriage, lust, usury, and absolution. The first three were primarily, though not exclusively, concerns of the laity. Savonarola places them in the second table of the Law, which is to say he considered them to involve people in their social relations—to each other rather than to God or the Church.

Savonarola prefaces his discussion of marriage with the observation that whether or not a legitimate marriage exists between a man and a woman is determined in one way by a confessor ("in foro conscientiae") and in another by a judge in a court of law ("in foro contentioso"). For a confessor it is enough that two parties free to marry have agreed to do so, either now or in the future. If there has been "mutuum consensum," the marriage remains indissoluble unless a spouse commits fornication or decides, with the approval of the other and before consummation, to take religious orders. If consent was not mutual, there is no marriage even if carnal copulation has taken place. Nor does it affect the case if one of the parties enters the union

30. Excommunication, interdict, censure: 14 pp. (fols. 5r–12v). Marriage: 9 pp. (fols. 24v–29r). Lust (includes further discussion of marriage and women's ornamentation): 6 pp. (fols. 33r–35v). Usury (includes restitution): 5 pp. (fols. 37r–40r). Absolution and penance: 5 pp. (fols. 42r–44r).

with bad intentions, such as marrying for money or lust; so long as there was mutual consent, the marriage is valid. A confessor can determine the intentions of the parties and whether there was mutual consent by questioning them, but a judge must require that evidence be presented in court, either testimony as to what was said or some other kind of proof. Sometimes it happens that both the confessor and the judge rule correctly according to their respective criteria and come to opposite conclusions. If so, he says, (the confessor) may not retreat.[31]

Savonarola next takes up marital impediments. A contract of marriage involving a boy under fourteen or a girl under twelve is not valid, although it may be considered a betrothal—"unless," he says, "they are so close to that time that evil [*malitia*] makes up the deficiency in age."[32] By this opaque phrase the friar seems to mean that the minimum age requirement may be relaxed slightly if it seems that the betrothed couple is in danger of committing fornication. Confessors will find it difficult to judge on this point, he recognizes, and in such cases they should follow the safer course.[33] Nevertheless, the point is clear even if its application is not: canonical rules sometimes may be relaxed in order to accommodate human weakness.

An impediment to marriage that occupies the friar at greater length is consanguinity. He begins with the canonical principle: people in a direct line of descent from common ancestors may not marry; people related in a "transverse line" may marry if they are separated by more than four degrees of consanguinity. Thus, a man and woman may not marry if they are directly descended from a common parent, grandparent, great-grandparent, and so on ad infinitum, but they may do so if they descend from a common ancestor in collateral lines going back more than four generations or degrees. Parents must see that members of their households who are within the forbidden degrees of consanguinity or affinity do not engage in "carnalis copula interdicta," for sexual desire arises among people in daily contact with each other.[34]

To clarify the canonical impediments of consanguinity, Fra Girolamo takes pains to set up hypothetical kinship structures—transverse, to show

---

31. "a quibus recedere non potest"; *Confessionale*, fol. 25r. I take it that the intended subject here is the confessor, since the manual is addressed to confessors, not judges.

32. "nisi sunt ita prope illud tempus quod malitia suppleat etatem"; ibid.

33. "tenenda est in tali casu tutior pars"; ibid. The phrase is standard in the confession literature.

34. Ibid., fol. 26r.

when an imaginary Peter and Mary are allowed to marry; direct, to show when they may not. For direct lines the matter is simple: "no direct relatives may ever marry," however distantly they are related. If Adam were reborn, he would be allowed no wife but Eve, and if Eve were to reappear, she would be allowed no husband but Adam![35] For transverse lines the matter is more complex, but, he says, if confessors follow the infallible rule he lays out here, they will always be able to determine the exact degree of consanguinity.

Spiritual relationships such as those created by baptism and confirmation also entail impediments to marriage. Unions between godparents and their spiritual children as well as between people directly related to them are forbidden. Similarly, people related by the betrothal or marriage of their relatives—brothers- and sisters-in law, fathers- and mothers-in law, and so on—are also prohibited from marriage to the fourth degree. This holds even in cases where there have been sexual relations between them, for, the friar says—even though it is shameful to say it—it happens often nowadays that the brother of the prospective groom sleeps with the future bride, or has already done so, or that the groom sleeps with her sister or with her mother or with one of her other female relatives. If so, the betrothal is dissolved. Many, however, do nothing to stop such goings-on; worse, some do not care enough to take any notice.[36] Was sexual promiscuity as common among members of extended families and as casually accepted as Savonarola says, or was this rhetorical exaggeration? In the absence of other evidence, the latter explanation might seem more likely; still, while he mentions other lurid behaviors—such as husbands and wives plotting the deaths of their spouses in order to marry someone else—he does not claim, as he does in the case of sexual transgressions, that these are everyday occurrences.

Practically all confession manuals discuss sexual behavior between husbands and wives, and the *Confessionale* is no exception. Savonarola's views on the subject are fairly standard. He follows the canonical rule that payment of "the marriage debt" is obligatory, with each partner having the right to expect sexual intercourse from the other on request. Since the begetting of children is the main purpose of marriage, sexual intercourse between husband and wife is not only a duty but meritorious, and to refuse it is a mortal sin. If the partner requests sex on a holy day or when the

35. Ibid., fol. 26v.
36. Ibid., fol. 27r–v.

woman is menstruating or pregnant, the other spouse may remonstrate— "lightly"; but if the requesting partner insists, the spouse should comply. Sexual intercourse at such times is no sin if engaged in for "a reasonable cause" (presumably the desire to have a child), and if the reason is "the infirmity of concupiscence," it is still only a venial sin. So important is this obligation to a marriage that if a man conceals his impotence the contract may be invalidated, although not if the impotence is known and accepted beforehand. Temporary impotence caused by illness or by an evil spell (*ex maleficio*) for which there is a physical or spiritual remedy does not abrogate the marriage.[37]

Confessors should also interrogate married people about their sexual practices. Does the husband insert his penis exclusively in the one place nature intended (*vas debitum*), and does he release his semen only there? While not every alternative to vaginal intercourse is equally transgressive, sex in any form that prevents conception is a mortal sin. Savonarola allows that it is sometimes difficult to know when this is the case. Some say that conception is not impeded if, for example, the woman sits astride the male in intercourse. Nevertheless, the friar is sure such positions are illicit; variant modes of sexual joining stem from deadly concupiscence; penitents who are unwilling to abstain from them cannot be absolved. On the other hand, some infirm or pregnant spouses may truly be unable to perform in the required way; if so, they are not guilty of excessive lust. Less innocent are husbands and wives who, afraid to engage in coitus (presumably because of the possibility of conception), satisfy their lust by groping lasciviously (*inhoneste*); they turn their marriage into whoredom.[38]

Touching between spouses is not always damnable, but it is dangerous; better to ban it altogether. Betrothed persons need to be especially careful, for they do not yet have rights over each other's bodies and can easily slip from lascivious touching to worse corruption. Confessors need to judge such acts very carefully and warn against the dangers. Yet local practice varies, and the custom of the place determines what is sinful. In some places betrothed couples consummate their union even before they receive the Church's blessing; in other localities it is the custom to wait for the blessing, and not to do so is a mortal sin.[39]

37. Ibid., fols. 34v–35r. On the canonical requirement of paying the marital debt of sexual intercourse, see J. A. Brundage, *Law, Sex, and Christian Society in Medieval Europe* (Chicago, 1987), pp. 241–42 and passim.

38. Brundage, *Law, Sex, and Christian Society*, 241–42.

39. *Confessionale*, fol. 35r.

Luxuria, or lust, is the second of Savonarola's three main topics. Apart from lasciviousness among betrothed and married couples, he has much to say about youthful temptations of the flesh. Priests need to be very circumspect in their interrogation of sexual sins, especially with adolescents and particularly with boys, lest they put ideas into their heads or inadvertently teach them what they did not know. They should first ask youths whether they have heard bad language and what they felt when hearing it, then proceed cautiously from words and thoughts to inquire about acts; but of these it is not necessary to go into detail; the confessor need only know that such acts have taken place, how many times, and with what sort of persons—virgins, married people, relatives, whores, and so on and whether by force or consent, for to some extent these facts determine the gravity of the sin.[40]

While all voluntary sexual acts outside marriage are mortal sins, the degree of their gravity varies. Unnatural acts are worse than natural ones. The least of these is masturbation (*mollities*); more serious is sodomy, and graver still, bestiality. But the worst of these is incest, a breaking of the laws of consanguinity. Some kinds of illicit sex are sins against reason; in ascending order of gravity these are simple fornication with a woman; *stuprum*, or the deflowering of a virgin; adultery (double adultery when both partners are married); and sex with a person in religious orders, a form of sacrilege. All are compounded when accompanied by violence. By combining these categories, Savonarola comes up with the extreme of sexual sinning: the violent forcing of a close relation who is consecrated to God—a combination of rape, incest, and sacrilege![41]

Even acts that do not result in carnal copulation, such as touching and kissing, are mortal sins, according to the friar, if they are done for libidinous enjoyment, as gazing, listening, smelling, eating, and lascivious speech. Immodest dress, dancing, "and other things of this kind" are mortal sins if they aim at seduction, but only venial if they are motivated by a more moderate sensuality. Has someone by dress or speech intended to seduce a virgin or a youth? Have lustful thoughts merely passed through someone's mind, or were they entertained with pleasure; even worse, have these thoughts been accompanied by the wish that they could be made to come true? How hard has a penitent tried to expunge them? Obviously, the friar regards the mind of a sinner as a compelling field for investigation, where subterranean layers of sexuality await the tempered probe of a skillful confessor.

40. Ibid., fol. 33r–v
41. Ibid., fol. 33v.

Usury, the third of Savonarola's principal subjects, dominates the section on avarice. Usury, Savonarola writes, is the sin (*vitium*) of receiving or expecting to receive some gain in return for making a loan. This is a violation of the Savior's instruction, "Mutuum date, nihil inde sperantes" (Luke 6:35) and contrary to nature, since accepting something over and above the repayment of the loan itself would be to receive the same thing twice or to have sold something that does not exist.[42] The reasoning, and the definition, reiterate the classical arguments of Saint Thomas, Hostiensis, and other schoolmen,[43] but certain of Savonarola's qualifications reflect the more liberal position of Saint Antoninus.[44] A lender may, he says, accept recompense if it is not for the loan itself but "for *interesse* or some other reason," that is, if making the loan has cost the lender something, or if he has incurred a loss thereby ("ut ipsum damnum emergens ex tali mutuo recompensetur.") This, Savonarola argues, is not usury. He is less enthusiastic about charging borrowers for "damnum lucrum cessantis"—the profit the lender would have made had he invested the money in some other enterprise instead of making the loan. Some authorities, he acknowledges, hold that this is not usury, and he is "not displeased" to defer to their opinion. Still, he insists, the lender should not be allowed to charge the borrower an amount equal to the profit he thinks he passed up; not having actually opted for the alternative, he cannot know what his profit might have been. Such calculation of hypothetical profit ought to be left to experts. In any case, the friar warns, we should not talk or preach about this, "lest we open the floodgates of usury."[45]

If Savonarola sees the city as the place where lenders and investors skate on the thin ice of avarice, the countryside has its moral perils, too, although these reflect the invasion of urban capital. Where landlords furnish beasts of burden to their peasants (*rustici*) in return for an annual share of the yield in cash or in kind, or when a company (*societas*) contracts to provide sheep to herders either for a fixed sum or for a third or fourth share of the

---

42. *To receive the same thing twice:* i.e., the money or the value of the commodity loaned plus an unearned return on it; *to sell something which does not exist:* i.e., to receive payment for the use of the money or commodity loaned, since use is not an entity with an existence apart from the commodity or money loaned.

43. See J. T. Noonan Jr. *The Scholastic Analysis of Usury* (Cambridge, Mass., 1957), esp. chap. 3.

44. R. de Roover, *Saint Bernardino of Siena and Sant'Antonino of Florence: The Two Great Economic Thinkers of the Middle Ages* (Boston, 1967), pp. 27–33.

45. "ne aperiatur via voragini usurarum"; Savonarola, *Confessionale*, fol. 37v.

return, fraud or exploitation of one party by the other can find its way into the arrangements. Absentee owners who hire caretakers for their livestock might also be culpable by failing to pay them a wage equal to the value of their labor or refusing to share the risks of husbandry. But local variations make it hard to frame a general rule. Differences in soil and pasturage, climate, types of livestock, and custom shape practice, so many moral decisions must be left to the discrimination of the people on the ground. But, the friar insists, there should be equity between the parties, with neither exploiting the other.[46]

We arrive, like the penitents who were to be the ultimate beneficiaries of this handbook, out of the desert of sin into sight of the promised land of absolution. There is one more step to take: before receiving absolution, sinners who have caused a neighbor an injury must make restitution, and not only for material injuries but also for "spiritual" ones. Someone who leads another person away from a life in religion or from "a good life" must do whatever is possible to restore that person to his former state. In cases of theft and violence, restitution is incumbent upon all who participated, whether by giving orders or advice or in some other way abetting the injury, or by receiving some of the gain. Anyone who watched the crime without attempting to prevent it is also liable. Restitution should be swift, but some exceptions may be made. Savonarola notes that some authorities hold that a person who steals out of "extreme necessity" should be shown compassion, while a rich creditor who is not in any immediate need ought not demand repayment from a poor debtor but instead should charitably lessen the amount of the debt. The friar is in favor of these kinds of "equity" if they are carried out with prudence.[47] In the same spirit, gambling winnings must be restored if the loser's family would suffer as a consequence, or if the loser is a cleric living on his benefice (in which case restitution is decided by his ecclesiastical superiors). A winner who cheated or took advantage of someone who does not know how to play is also liable, as he is if the municipal laws require restitution. In other cases restitution is not necessary, but to give one's winnings to the poor is a good thing to do, just as it is good if finders of valuables give them to the poor when they cannot identify their owner.

As in questioning penitents, so in assigning penances Savonarola counsels discretion and moderation. Priests should be patient and understand-

46. Ibid.
47. Ibid., fol. 39r.

ing, adopting as their watchword, "Send no one away in despair." [48] If a sinner insists he is unable to perform a certain punishment, he should be urged, not commanded, to try it, and if he continues to refuse, to try just a part. Those who show "excellent" contrition need be prescribed only a mild penance, for contrition is far more important than any exterior satisfaction. By the same token, it is unwise to mete out a heavy penalty to a great sinner who is not sufficiently contrite, "lest the little flame [of contrition] be suffocated by heaping too much wood on it." Instead, the confessor should point out the magnitude of the sin and exhort the penitent to make his satisfaction directly to God. [49] Every penance should be an antidote for a particular sin: an act of humility for a proud man, the giving of alms for a miser, the assignment of work to a slothful one, and so on. [50] Above all, as physicians of souls, confessors should keep in mind that satisfactions are medicines to be prescribed for the spiritual health of sinners, not for their ruin.

II

Now that we have reached the end of Savonarola's chain of confession, I should like to return to the questions I raised at the outset. In some respects the pastoral and the prophetic Savonarola seem to occupy different moral universes. The nuanced approach of the *Confessionale*, its modest expectations about behavior, and its willingness to make concessions to human weaknesses contrast sharply with the unbending standards of the sermons. Absent is the stern moral censor, the jeremiads against irreligion, the harsh criticism of worldliness in laymen, priests, and prelates. Absent, too, is the visionary architect of the New Jerusalem. This is not only a kinder, gentler Savonarola than we are used to seeing—or, more to the point, than the crowds attending his sermons in San Lorenzo and Santa Maria del Fiore

48. Saint Antoninus, citing Hostiensis and Saint Thomas as his authority: "il confessore per niun modo debba lassare partire el penitente dase desperato"; in *Tractato volgare di frate Antonio Arcivescovo di Firenze intitolato Defecerunt, che insegna al confessore diche chasi & in che modo debbe domandare colui che egli confessa* (Florence, 1496).

49. "et hortandus est ut per seipsum deo melius satisfaciat"; Savonarola, *Confessionale*, fol. 42v.

50. Ibid. Saint Antoninus attributed this principle of antidotes or opposites to Raymond of Peñafort: *Defecerunt*, chap. 32. Saint Thomas said it with succinct alliteration: "Contraria contrariis curantur": Thomas, *In quatuor libris Sententiarum* IV, Dist. XVII, Quaest. II, art. I, *Opera omnia* (Parma, 1852–73; photolithographic reproduction), T. XXII.

were used to hearing—but also a counselor of moderate views and modest expectations.

If we can infer that in his own ministrations to sinners Savonarola employed the same soothing medicines he recommended to his younger colleagues, it would help explain why so many Florentines sought out the friar for spiritual counsel. Although it cut painfully into his time and energy for other tasks, it was a demand he found impossible to refuse, although he delegated the actual hearing of confessions to his two confederates.[51] At the same time, this "hands-on" experience gave him a familiarity with common spiritual and moral problems, a profitable supplement to his study of Saint Thomas, Hostiensis, and the other scholastic intentionalists. The *Confessionale's* special focus on the problems of marriage, sexual behavior, and usury further suggests that Savonarola was an attentive observer of life as it was lived by laymen and laywomen, that he knew at first hand which restraints chafed them most and which questions they most frequently brought before their confessors.[52]

Like some other authors of confessional manuals, Fra Girolamo had few illusions about the quality of lay piety. To some extent his pessimism seems to derive from experience. He reminds confessors that they may have to instruct penitents in the gestures and formulas required by the sacrament, even foreseeing the possibility that the sinner does not know how to kneel properly. His expectations for the clergy were not much higher. He leads confessors themselves step by step through the correct way to make the sign of the cross—right hand on brow reciting "In the name of the father,

51. After his imprisonment, one of the main things Savonarola's interrogators tried to find out was what he and his fellow friars talked about with the Florentines who came to San Marco to see them. Although the interrogators were chiefly interested in the political nature of these conversations, the responses reveal a great deal more. Savonarola told them he did not hear the confessions of visitors to San Marco, although he admitted questioning fra Domenico da Pescia and fra Silvestro Maruffi (his two fellow martyrs-to-be) about the confessions they heard. The surviving texts (considerably doctored by hostile scribes) of these interrogations are published in P. Villari, *La storia di Girolamo Savonarola e de' suoi tempi*, 2d ed., 2 vols. (Florence, 1926), vol. 2, documents XXVI–XXIX (appendices).

52. One of the best examples of Savonarola's observation of *borghese* behavior comes not from the tightly compressed *Confessionale* but from a sermon, although a sermon in a pastoral rather than a prophetic vein, the famous *Predica dell'arte del ben' morire*. Describing how people neglect to make spiritual preparations for death, the friar mimics the sickroom scene where well-meaning relatives cheerfully persuade a dying man that he is recovering instead of urging him to make his confession, See the two texts of the sermon in Girolamo Savonarola, *Prediche sopra Ruth e Michea*, 2 vols., ed. V. Romano (Rome, 1962), pp. 362–97, 446–74.

then over the navel saying *et filii*," and so on—and word for word he takes them through the recitation of the Confiteor in the vernacular ("Io mi confesso a Dio . . .")[53]—a pointed way of saying that some priests are as ignorant of the proper forms as the laity they professed to serve. Elsewhere he refers disapprovingly to the cursory manner in which priests conduct the sacrament, chiefly in their disinclination to probe more deeply into the circumstances and to determine the frequency of a sin—"a mistake which today many [priests] make." Without this information, he insists, the spiritual physician is unable to heal his patient, for he cannot know whether the wound needs mild or strong medicine.[54] Thus, Savonarola thought priests were forcing sins and sinners into objectified and superficial categories instead of treating each case as individual and, to some degree, psychological.

To be sure, Savonarola was not alone in advocating a comprehending moderation for confessors, nor did he claim to be an innovator. His purpose was to give young confessors easy access to the relevant body of canon law and to its main interpreters. Important here were authority, not originality, tradition, not innovation, and he leaned heavily on previous writers, especially those who taught confessors to look for intentions and mitigating circumstances. His advocacy of accepting imperfect contrition reflects the teaching of Saint Thomas.[55] His cautious approval of lenders charging interest in certain circumstances follows a fifteenth-century trend pioneered by Bernardino of Siena and Antoninus of Florence.[56] In other words, Savonarola allied himself with those late medieval authorities who worked to temper the discipline of confession with priestly compassion and tolerance, as well as with the "moderns" who adapted traditional morality to contemporary financial practice. Conversely, the popularity of his own manual for confessors furthered the cause of moderation and helped assure its continued influence in the pre-Reformation and Reformation eras.

With respect to Bossy's contention that there was at this time a shift from an emphasis on social sins to a concern for "interiorized individual

53. Savonarola, *Confessionale*, fol. 3r.
54. Ibid., fol. 14r.
55. Tentler, *Sin and Confession*, pp. 250–52. For Saint Thomas on contrition, see the passage cited in note 21; and ibid., III-I Quest. XC, art. III.
56. De Roover, *Saint Bernardino*, pp. 30–31. Noonan notes the influence of Laurentius de Ridolfis on Saint Bernardino. I think it accurate to say that Noonan regards the changing views on interest in the fifteenth century as more gradual than de Roover does. He also believes the controversy over *montes pietatis* in Italian cities was an important factor. Noonan, *Scholastic Analysis of Usury*, pp. 121–32.

discipline," I would argue that, at least on the evidence of Savonarola's *Confessionale*, change was incremental and inclusive rather than abrupt and exclusive. Newer concerns did not crowd out more traditional ones. Savonarola pressed confessors to try to sensitize consciences and heighten penitents' awareness of their personal spiritual responsibilities. His advice to them to first convince "great sinners" of the magnitude of their sins, then urge them to make their satisfaction directly to God, is a particularly striking example of his spiritual individualism.[57] But the *Confessionale* draws no hard-and-fast line between interior discipline and social responsibility. In Savonarola's catalog of sins, social injustice and violations of the peace and well-being of the community loom very large, while such sins of the heart as avarice and envy are especially damnable because of their social effects.

Nor do I find support in the *Confessionale* for Ozment's thesis that penance on the eve of the Reformation was a burden many found intolerable.[58] Instead, priestly humility, patience, tolerance in dealing with sinners, and a light hand with punishment—these are the dominant notes conveyed in this manual for confessors widely disseminated in the sixteenth century. These are not, as I noted earlier, what we hear in Savonarola's sermons, nor are they the virtues that come to mind when we consider the puritanical regime the friar and his colleagues were struggling to build in Florence. This striking contrast between Savonarola's preaching and penitential modes is not a little puzzling. To some extent of course—although an extent not easy to determine—the contrast between the preaching and the pastoral Savonarola is the result of the different purposes and different requirements of the two genres. In a sense preaching—certainly preaching of the apocalyptic, penitential, Savonarolan variety—and hearing confessions were complementary clerical functions, each with its appropriate rhetoric; it was the preacher's task to arouse feelings of guilt and fear among sinners and bring them to repentance; it was the confessor's responsibility to connect these awakened consciences, by means of the sacrament of penance, with the divine grace that offered them forgiveness of sin. But even if Savonarola the Confessor and Savonarola the Preacher were distinguish-

---

57. "Denunciandum tamen est ei quam magnum penitentiam meretur et hortandus est ut per seipsum deo melius satisfaciat"; Savonarola, *Confessionale*, fol. 42v.

58. See note 11 above. It would be a fair objection to point out that the *Confessionale* tells us what one well-known friar advises, not what confessors actually practiced; but this is an objection that applies to Ozment's evidence as well.

able only by their different rhetorical styles, this would be a distinction with a difference, for it would argue for a degree of moral flexibility and a complexity of personality that neither his devotees nor his critics have been willing to grant him.[59] Whether further study of Savonarola's thought and deeper insight can reconcile the Prophet with the Physician of Souls remains to be seen.

59. There have been observers, to be sure, who have regarded Savonarola as the consummately flexible opportunist. The classic judgment of this kind is Machiavelli's: "et così, secondo il mio iudicio, viene secondando e'tempi, et le sua bugie colorendo." Letter to Ricciardo Becchi, 9 March 1498, in Niccolò Machiavelli, *Lettere*, ed. F. Gaeta (Milan, 1961), p. 33. Hypocrisy is also a dominant note in Cordero's biography, in which the friar is depicted, somewhat inconsistently it seems to me, as both hysterically fanatical and coldly calculating; F. Cordero, *Savonarola Profeta delle meraviglie 1494–1495* (Bari, 1987), pp. 16–19 and passim. On the other side, Savonarolan devotees emphasize "the consistency and unbroken continuity of his character"; R. Ridolfi, *The Life of Girolamo Savonarola*, trans. C. Grayson (New York, 1959), p. 5.

10 Raging against Priests in Italian Renaissance Verse

Lauro Martines

To pick up the voice of anticlerical sentiment in the poetry of the Italian Renaissance is a recovery of lost conversation. In everyday life, the intensity of feeling against priests and friars was often muted, unless privacy or anonymity promised safety, such as around the statue of Pasquino in Rome during the early sixteenth century, when a cascade of anonymous poems raged against the turpitude of popes and cardinals.[1] At times fiercely humorous, the anticlerical theme is anything but funny for the history of Italy.

Becoming the motor of Italian political strife in the late eleventh century, galvanizing the Guelfs in the 1200s, and always thereafter to be in the thick of peninsular politics, popes and upper clergy inevitably drew the deadly venom of politics upon themselves.[2] Two early-fourteenth-century works, Dante's *De monarchia* and Marsilius of Padua's *Defensor pacis*, speaking out of a tormented political milieu, already simmer with fierce argument against the temporal power of the papacy. Henceforth in Italian literature, the fact that priests had a "vile" worldly side became a polemical claim; and this naturally was the side subject to diatribe or derision. Everyone could see the destructive irony of confronting the "carnality" of the clergy with their spiritual counterclaims.

The Avignonese papacy (1306–76), followed almost at once by the Great Schism (1378), fouled the image of the leading clergy in the fourteenth

---

1. See V. Marucci, A. Marzo, and A. Romano, eds., *Pasquinate Romane del Cinquecento,* 2 vols. (Rome, 1983).

2. G. Tabacco, "La storia politica e sociale: Dal tramonto dell'Impero alle prime formazioni di Stati regionali," in *Storia d'Italia,* vol. 2 *Dalla caduta dell'Impero romano al secolo XVIII,* 2 vols., ed. R. Romano and C. Vivanti (Turin, 1974), 1:113–223; G. Miccoli, "La storia religiosa," ibid., 1:480–530. See also P. A. Dykema and H. A. Oberman, eds., *Anticlericalism in Late Medieval and Early Modern Europe* (Leiden, 1998), esp. the essay by D. Weinstein, "Writing the Book on Italian Anticlericalism," pp. 309ff.

century; and the brutality of papal mercenaries in central Italy did not en-
dear their clerical bosses to a watchful people. In 1377, by order of Cardinal Robert of Geneva, mercenaries in Cesena slaughtered five thousand
men, women, and children. The city's moats and squares were piled with
bodies.[3] This episode was *not* typical, but it came at a time when for half a
century mercenary armies ravaged the countryside, plundered vast herds
of livestock, and blackmailed small cities.[4]

During the twelfth and thirteenth centuries, heresy attracted people
from all social classes; but this wide appeal was brought to an end in the fourteenth century, when the spiritual Franciscans still found some support
among poor artisans. And from this time on, the written record indicates
that anticlerical feeling was to be confined chiefly to the middle and upper
classes. In the fifteenth and sixteenth centuries, if Venice, Milan, Florence,
or other cities had artisans and workers who nursed acid resentments against
the clergy, little sustained evidence of this survives. Instead, where we do
find a stream of anticlerical sentiment is in tales (*novelle*), poetry, and diaries (*ricordanze*): that is, in the writings of educated men from the com-
fortable classes.[5]

Dante was not afraid to consign popes and prelates to hell or to the dark
labors of purgatory;[6] and up to about the time of his death (1321), feeling
against the clergy, if angrily voiced, was likely to be associated with heretical doctrine. But once heresy was suppressed, and popes held on stubbornly
in Avignon, criticism of the clergy, in orthodox circles, came forth more
loudly, particularly in attacks on the extremes of Minorite poverty or in
blasts against Franciscan hypocrisy and Dominican gluttony, as in the writings of the Florentine poet Antonio Pucci (d. 1388).[7] To denounce a poverty
that claimed to be apostolic in spirit could not fail to win the ready approval
of a pleasure-loving upper clergy and, in the cities, of an early "bourgeois"
society that was given to the pursuit of "profit and honor" (*utile ed honore*).[8] However, the Avignonese papacy's opulence and fostering of simony

---

3. M. Mallett, *Mercenaries and Their Masters: Warfare in Renaissance Italy*
(London, 1974), pp. 25–50.

4. See most recently W. Caferro, *Mercenary Companies and the Decline of
Siena* (Baltimore, 1998).

5. Thus Sercambi, Sermini, Masuccio, Gino Capponi, Francesco Accolti, Luigi
Pulci, Lorenzo Valla, and many Italian humanists.

6. Dante Alighieri, *Inferno*, III, 59; X, 120; XI, 8; XIX, 70, 82; XXXIII, 118; *Purgatorio*, XVIII, 118; XIX, 99; XXIV, 29.

7. In G. Corsi, ed., *Rimatori del Trecento* (Turin, 1969), pp. 815–17.

8. As set forth in Christian Bec, *Les marchands écrivains: Affaires et humanisme à Florence 1375–1434* (Paris and The Hague, 1967).

also generated bitterness, as in this anonymous *sonetto caudato*, in which Christ, with a sarcastic irony,

> consente il suo vicario sotto manti
> ricchi pompeggi nel ben senza novero,
> vendendo i benefici per contanti.
>   Adunque tutti quanti,
> cristian, fate concilio sopra a' preti,
> salvando sempre i divini secreti.[9]

(permits his richly robed vicar / to show off amidst endless wealth, / while selling church livings for cash. / Therefore, let all / Christians sit in council over priests, / always, however, reserving the mysteries of faith.)

The 1370s ended with a sharp rise in anger against the official church, a change connected with the presence of foreign governors in Italy, the spread of papal warfare, and the beginnings of the Great Schism. Invective against clerical corruption escalated: popes, simonists, and a greedy clergy came to be more often pilloried in verse. Attached to the court of the Visconti in Milan, the Aretine poet and nobleman Braccio Bracci, in the 1370s, produced three wrathful sonnets against the domineering ambitions, pomp, and cupidity of the papacy and deplored the scandalous spectacle of rival popes.[10] One of Saint Catherine of Siena's followers in Florence, the bankrupted Giannozzo Sacchetti (Franco's brother), then issued a passionate *canzone* against Pope Gregory XI, sharply condemning, as well, the simony and venality of all the upper clergy.[11] An unquiet spirit, Giannozzo died on the Florentine gallows in 1379, convicted of high treason, though the charge had nothing to do with his anticlerical stance. In the same years, Florence's antipapal War of the Eight Saints called forth anonymous poems against Pope Gregory and in defense of the republican commune.[12]

But protest against the divided church and its unworthy clerics was by no means restricted to Tuscany. An ironic *Lamento di Roma*, from the first half of 1376, is a plea for Gregory to abandon Avignon for Rome or be

9. Corsi, *Rimatori*, pp. 934–35, ll. 12–17; also, in comparison, see A. Classen, "Anticlericalism in Late Medieval German Verse," in Dykema and Oberman, *Anticlericalism*, pp. 91–114.

10. E. Sarteschi, ed., *Poesie minori del secolo XIV* (Bologna, 1867), pp. 43–45; also Corsi, *Rimatori*, pp. 413–15.

11. Giannozzo Sacchetti, *Rime edite e inedite*, ed. O. Sacchetti (Rome, 1948), pp. 94–96.

12. G. Volpi, ed., *Rime di trecentisti minori* (Florence, 1907), pp. 245–46; S. Morpurgo, ed., *Dieci sonetti storici fiorentini* (Florence, 1893), unpaginated, nos. 9 and 10.

stripped of his holy mantle and silver keys, to face the prospect of being declared a heretic by his college of cardinals.[13] About 1400, the Romagnol prince and poet Malatesta Malatesti produced a series of sonnets on the "leprous" state of the church:

> Dove solëa stare el tempio sancto
> e ivi orar la casta compagnia,
> hor c'è luxuria, vino e simonia,
> e chi più ne sa far, più se dà vanto.
> Non diede Christo a Pietro el ricco manto
> per usar tutto'l dì barattaria:
> hor non si può campar per altra via.[14]

(Where once the holy temple stood / and a chaste company prayed, / there now is lechery, wine and simony, / and those who best take to this brag the most. / Christ did not give Peter that rich mantle / so that he could spend his days as a swindler: / there seems to be no other way now [for priests] to live.)

In Bologna a few years later (ca. 1410), in the midst of the Great Schism, the jurist and local government official Nicolò Malpigli composed three blistering attacks on the papacy as corrupter of the entire Christian world:

> In ira al cielo, al mondo et a l'inferno
> Vegna toa pompa e perfida nequitia,
> Ingrata sinagoga, e toa militia
> Dispersa vada cum exilio eterno,
> Che cum color de spiritual governo
> Amorba el mondo, corrompe et avitia;
> Luxuria, gola, pompa et avaritia
> De ti se gode e studia in tuo quaderno.[15]

(May the wrath of heaven, earth and hell / overtake your pomp and treacherous wickedness, / ungrateful synagogue, and your army of priests / be scattered in eternal exile, / for under the color of spiritual rule / you infect, corrupt and deprave the world. / With you men enjoy lust, gluttony, pomp, and greed, / and learn these in your notebooks.)

13. A. Medin and L. Frati, eds., *Lamenti storici dei secoli XIV, XV e XVI*, 3 vols. (Bologna, 1887–90), 3:55–60.

14. Malatesta Malatesti, *Rime*, ed. D. Trolli (Parma, 1982), p. 160, ll. 1–7; see also pp. 154, 187–88, 190.

15. In L. Frati, ed., *Rimatori bolognesi del Quattrocento* (Bologna, 1908), p. 27, ll. 1–8.

Although Malpigli was briefly employed as a papal secretary, he made a blanket condemnation of the Curia and saw all clerics as evil:

> La bestia che più crudelmente agrappa
> Cum rostro sanguinoso e mortal branca
> Quella è che sotto la camicia bianca
> Tanti vitii nasconde e sotto cappa
>
> . . . .
>
>   Ma non è maraviglia,
> Chè 'l patre che vol dare il figlio a Cristo
> De tutti gli altri ognor li dà el più tristo.[16]

(The beast which clings most cruelly, / with bloody beak and deadly claw, / that's the one which under a white shirt / and cowl conceals so many vices / . . . / But no wonder, / for when a father chooses to give one of his sons to Christ / he always picks the worst of them.)

This astounding allegation about what fathers did with their worst sons (picked them for holy orders!) is a measure of the fury and pessimism in the anticlericalism of the early Quattrocento.

Although the Council of Pisa (1409) failed to unite the church,[17] the Council of Constance (1414–18), resulting in the election of Pope Martin V, largely healed the Schism. For a time, the anticlerical voice became less strident; but it was now permanently embedded in urban public opinion and in the literature of the age. Some degree of anticlericalism became a part of the conversation of many people, especially in well-informed male circles. Otherwise, while also bearing in mind the anticlerical influence of Boccaccio's *Decameron,* when we turn to the tales of Sercambi, Sermini, Lorenzo de' Medici, Masuccio, Morlini, Firenzuola, and others, how else can we account for the rich flow there of dramatic anecdote depicting the unbridled lechery, avarice, base ambitions, hypocrisy, and violence of a whole world of priests and friars? The conflict between their flesh and their spiritual vows obviously provided ideal narrative material, the backbone for good stories. Yet the ferocities and ill-concealed anger in such tales also disclose a profound resentment against the pretensions of the clergy. Down in the region of Naples, Morlini's early-sixteenth-century tale about the priest, Salvatore, aims to be screamingly funny; for his penis and bald head are suddenly attacked by two trained falcons one day, as he stands urinat-

---

16. Ibid., p. 29, ll. 1–4, 15–17.
17. L. Martines, *Lawyers and Statecraft in Renaissance Florence* (Princeton, N.J., 1968), pp. 288–96.

ing against a building, and he is then beset by a pack of hunting dogs. But the incident—replete with *Schadenfreude*—turns out to be condign punishment for his regular sexual intercourse (and symbolic incest) "cum commatre," that is, with the mother of a child of whom he was the godfather, having sponsored it at baptism.[18]

Since the great wealth of early Renaissance manuscripts reveals that Italian poetry circulated and was often anthologized, writers who took the trouble to compose anticlerical verse clearly desired to convey their views to a select public. This was surely so in the case of the celebrated law professor Francesco Accolti (1416–88), who at one point was a possible candidate for a place in the college of cardinals.[19] His *canzone*, "in detestazione e biasimo della Corte Romana e di tutti i preti," is a philippic.[20] Moving from the contrast provided by the purity of the early church, Accolti finds nothing but monstrous vice and corruption in the Holy See and ruling clergy of his day:

> Tenebrosa, crudel, avara e lorda
> gregge maligna, d'ogni vizio albergo,
>
> . . . .
>
> maladetta sie tu, po' che da tergo
> t'hai messa ogni virtù, al ben più sorda
> che l'angelica setta al ciel nimica.
> Ahi! meretrice e Sodoma impudica,
> nella qual Simon mago a Gezi regna,
>
> . . . .
>
> perché l'empia tua gola altro non grida
> che posseder tesoro, e tristo geme
> chi tra voi dignità sanz'oro aspetta.
> La santa Sposa, eletta
> a trionfar nel Ciel beata e bella,
> per ricchezze terrene in voi si strazia
>
> . . . .
>
> In sommo pregio è l'arte,
> per te, di chi, ruffianeggiando, tenta
> violar con ingiuria l'altrui letti;
> e per che me' la puzza in ciel si senta

18. Girolamo Morlini, *Novelle e favole*, ed. G. Villani (Rome, 1983), p. 16 (nov. 1).

19. F. Flamini, *La lirica toscana del rinascimento anteriore ai tempi del Magnifico* (Florence, 1977), pp. 270–75, 524.

20. In M. Messina, "Le rime di Francesco Accolti d'Arezzo," *Giornale storico della letteratura italiana* 132 (1955): 211–15.

di Ganimedi eletti
ogni camera tua bordel diventa.[21]

(Dark, cruel, miserly and filthy / malignant herd, hostel to every
vice / . . . be cursed, since you have put / behind you every virtue,
being more deaf to what is good / than even the [once] angelic sect
now enemy to heaven. / Ah, whore and indecent Sodom, / where
Simon Magus and Jezebel rule / . . . / why does your godless gullet
cry out / for gold alone? And sadly groan / those among you who
wait for office without money. / The Holy Spouse, chosen / to triumph blessedly and beautifully in heaven, / is torn apart in you by
[the scramble for] earthly riches. / . . . The highest worth for you
is in the art / of those who seek by pimping / to violate the beds of
others; / and so that heaven may better smell the stink / of your elect
bum lovers [*Ganimedi*], / all your bedrooms are turned into whorehouses.)

The poet then calls for the Roman Curia and top clergy to suffer the utmost
fear and pain, to be buried by the waves of the sea; but if this be not enough,
may fire rain down from heaven to destroy them, and may their poison be
punished there where Judas is ("veder poss'io punito il tuo veleno"). He
closes the *canzone* with a customary envoi, requesting that it go out only
to those who follow and honor virtue.

The hatred and venom in Accolti's poem was not unusual. He must have
known something that we, looking back, have trouble reconstructing, and
I shall come back to this suspicion later. At any rate, Accolti's passion is
found time and again in the anticlerical verse of the period. Two other Aretine writers show the same dislike of men in holy orders. The celebrated legal commentator and older contemporary Antonio Roselli (1381–1466), a
doctor of laws like Accolti, was first a professor at Florence and then, for
most of his career, at Padua.[22] Seeing the primitive church as poor and pure,
his *ternario* on avaricious priests and simonists attributes the origins of papal corruption to the false Donation of Constantine, because of which the
Holy See almost despises heaven:

per che da poi l'estituzion leggiadre
sempre son state strette da la soga
de' temporali e lor opere ladre.
Diventata è la nova sinagoga
madre di fornicar, Babilon magna,

---

21. Ibid., ll. 1–2, 4–8, 63–69, 103–8.
22. Martines, *Lawyers*, p. 500.

che fra' miseri avar ciechi s'afoga.
Puttaneggia costei, bramosa cagna. . . .[23]

(for ever since, they have been [happily] / tied by the rope / of their
properties, powers, and thieving deeds. / It [the church] has become
the new synagogue, / mother of fornication, great Babylon, / drowning
in wretched and blind misers. / This woman whores around, lusting
bitch. . . .)

Metaphors of female whoring abound, as so often in such verse. The poem
notes that later saints—Ambrose, Francis—failed in their efforts to re-
new the spiritual life of the clergy, "for nowadays almost every young and
happy / cleric hungers not for God and virtue / but for gold and silver":

ché quasi ciascun oggi lieto e fresco
cheric'ha non per Dio né per virtute,
ma per d'oro e d'argento aver gran desco. (vv. 49–51)

He imagines their like in hell, bent over in punishment like strung bows
("curvi come l'arco che si tira") because they had bought their spiritual dig-
nities and then, as prelates, chosen evil men over good ones for church benefices. Such men turn the Cross into a base worldly banner ("gonfalone")
and use "the keys and Cross" for theft and extortion. Decked out in their
great scarlet robes, they disdain the few good men in holy orders:

E quei che son devoti, onesti e miti,
voi isfrenati reputati stolti,
perché non seguon vostri bestial riti
di lussurie, rapine e varie pompe,

. . . .

Quanto gli esempli vostri mal corrompe
la sciocca plebe, poveri idioti. . . . (vv. 125–28, 130–31)

(And those who are devout, honest and gentle / you the unbridled consider stupid, / because they do not keep your brutish rites / of lecheries,
robberies and empty splendors / . . . / How your shows corrupt / the fool
populace, poor idiots. . . .)

The poem closes with a picture of one of the grand spectacles of the age,
witnessed by Roselli at Bologna, Florence, Padua, and elsewhere: the image
of prelates and papal ambassadors proudly entering a city in a grand caval-

23. A. Lanza, ed., *Lirici toscani del Quattrocento*, 2 vols. (Rome, 1973–75),
2:381–84, ll. 25–31. The corrupt papacy as whore is already in Dante, *Purgatorio*,
XXXII, 148.

cade, their horses richly caparisoned. Attended by servants, they ride under their great star-studded canopies and go in such dress and pomp that they make idols of themselves for the simpleminded folk who go out to gape at them. This was not the way of Jesus, the poet concludes:

> Non fé così quel benedetto agnello,
> che venne a tôr la colpa e 'l nostro danno,
> che, sedendo umil sopra d'uno asello,
> al popol venne suo divoto e pio
> pover vestito d'inconsutil vello,
> sì che ben si mostrò figliul di Dio. (vv. 143–48)

(He did not carry on this way, the blessed lamb / who came to take away our faults and injuries, / who, sitting on a mere donkey, / came to his people devoted and pious, / dressed poorly in a seamless pelt, / so that he truly showed himself the son of God.)

Roselli, the poet, cannot be linked to the heresy of the spiritual Franciscans, first anathemized by the Avignonese pope, John XXII, and long since destroyed. The fact is that the gaudy wealth of the papacy always met the disapproval of certain orthodox citizens, a note that would be loudly sounded in Florence by Savonarola and his great throng of followers.

If splendor worn on the backs of churchmen—a symbol of depravity— offered one approach to the anticlerical argument, a variety of individual vices provided other entries: notably, the ignorance of priests and their alleged predilection for base flattery, sodomy, adultery, usury, theft, and graft. All these Gambino d'Arezzo (ca. 1430–80) brings into his long poem on the people of Arezzo. Dealing with the city's fools ("Delle genti idiote d'Arezzo"), canto 7 of book 1 treats the wicked life of priests and their ignorance ("tratta de la diabolica vita dei Preti e di loro ignoranza"); and Gambino imagines them in hell, tormented by devils and in horrible pain.[24] Down to the sixteenth century, moreover, poets sometimes pitched into unnamed priests and friars in their occasional verse;[25] but these attacks were not necessarily turned into more sweeping indictments, to become generally anticlerical.

In the course of the fifteenth century, the power of the papal monarchy expanded dramatically. The pontificates of Sixtus IV (1471–84) and Alex-

---

24. Gambino d'Arezzo, *Versi,* ed. O. Gamurrini (Bologna, 1878), pp. 22–25.
25. E.g., Giovan Matteo di Meglio, *Rime,* ed. G. Brincat (Florence, 1977), pp. 61–63, rages against a vicious, thieving priest.

ander VI (1492–1503) were gateways to the deeper spread of simony and nepotism, in a démarche that continued far into the sixteenth century. Consequently, as Henry James would have said, the anticlericals "kept it up"—their verse continued to impugn men of the cloth, while always reserving the deadliest weapons for the ecclesiastical hierarchy. Trained in Roman and canon law, Accolti and Roselli had a keen sense of the church's historical development, however misplaced their accents. Anticlerical poets of a more popular or plebeian bent, having little or no Latin, were likely to produce more colorful compositions. The Florentine Francesco Scambrilla (fl. 1460s) penned four *sonetti caudati* against religious orders, specifically the Augustinians, Carmelites, Camaldolese, and Vallombrosans.[26] He accuses them of gluttony, lechery, and even hunting, of dressing too well and spending their days wooing women. Thus, the Augustinians walk around "fat and round" ("grassi e tondi"); the Camaldolese and others "go out at night, strewing their seed, / armed with sweet song and lovely sounds" ("vanno la notte spargendo lor seme, / armati con be' suoni e dolci canti").[27] The Vallombrosans of the *contado* go hunting; and the Carmelites, who often dressed in ermine,

> Con abito lattato
> pagoneggiando vanno fra le donne,
> onde e mariti mal contenti sonne.[28]

(In milk-white dress / they go out, showing off among the women, / whereupon, unhappy husbands!)

But more explosive are the sonnets of two other Tuscans, also from the late fifteenth century. One charges "the people of cloisters" with being depraved and lawless disseminators of "schism."[29] The other skewers an unnamed pope, probably Sixtus IV:[30]

> Ahi, babbilonio avaro e cismatico,
> imitator d'ogni cattivo stile,
> lupo rapace, crudo e 'n vista umile,
> leo febricoso, indomito e salvatico,
> a suponend' un puer se' sol pratico
> . . . .

26. In Lanza, *Lirici toscani*, 2:523–25.
27. Ibid., p. 524 (xliv), ll. 7–8.
28. Ibid., p. 524 (xliii), ll. 15–17.
29. Giovanni del Raggio, in Lanza, *Lirici toscani*, 2:638.
30. Bernardo de' Ricci, in ibid., 2:368, ll. 1–5, 7–9.

non vicar no, ma mostro di porcile,
da stare in sulle forche per istatico,
tu se' aversaro della Chiesa sacra. . . . (vv. 1–5, 7–9)

(Ah, miserly and schismatic Babylonian, / copier of every wicked style, /
predatory wolf, cruel yet humble to look at, / contagious and savage
lion, / you're only good for buggering boys / . . . / not vicar, no, but
porcine monster, / fit to be pinned to the gallows, / you're the enemy
of the holy church. . . .)

Miser, sodomite, schismatic, hypocrite, wild animal, rotter: all these
accusations had become nearly canonical. It would be wrong, however, to
suppose that literary anticlericalism was the terrain of "priest-haters" only
(*mangiapreti*); for men of remarkable piety were also bitterly critical of the
official church and clergy. The phenomenon of the "anticlerical cleric"—
Savonarola himself?—was a common feature of the topography of urban
Italy. In the early sixteenth century, two poets in holy orders, Teofilo Folengo and Francesco Berni, issued anticlerical satires that placed them in the
ranks of some of the toughest critics of the age.[31] But I choose, instead, to
highlight two laymen, the Florentines Feo Belcari (1410–84) and Bernardo
Pulci (1438–88). Writers of devotional verse and sacred drama, in addition
to being well known in Florence as pious men, they could also look upon
the clergy with terrible distaste and disapproval.

Belcari's melancholy sonnet on *Carità*, lamenting its absence in the
world, takes Lady Carità to Rome to encourage Peter's successor to live a
blessed life, but she can find no one there to "take me to the feet of the good
pastor" ("a' pie di questo bon pastore").[32] Another sonnet, an even stronger
attainder, reads like a final prophecy. He imagines the archangel Gabriel
preparing a fine new dress for the holy church:

Ma prima n'averà si gran fragello,
che molte terre belle e signorile
saranno fatte serve sozze e vile. . . .[33]

(But first shall there be such a great scourging, / that many lovely and
noble lands / will be rendered servile, filthy, and base. . . .)

The archangel Raphael will then purge us of our malady, but spiritual renewal will rest with the Germans:

---

31. Francesco Berni, *Rime*, ed. G. B. Squarotti (Turin, 1969), pp. 37, 55, 105,
174; Teofilo Folengo, *Baldus*, ed. E. Faccioli (Turin, 1989), bk. 8.
32. Belcari, in Lanza, *Lirici toscani*, 1:233–34.
33. Ibid., 1:240, ll. 5–7.

Gli Alamanni di questo avendo sete,
per la fede daranno a' ciechi el lume,
dando principio al viver virtüale. (vv. 12–14)

(Thirsting for this, the Germans / by their faith will bring the light to
the blind, / giving a start to the life of virtue.)

This was certainly not the sonnet of a *mangiapreti;* but its message constitutes a sharper rejection of the present state of the church in coming from
Belcari, who was renowned in Florence as a popular expert on theological
questions and much admired by the pious Lucrezia Tornabuoni, Lorenzo
de' Medici's mother.

After a trip in 1474 to the Rome of Pope Sixtus IV, the pious Bernardo
Pulci produced two sonnets denouncing the corruption of the Curia, a lascivious and greedy daughter ("figlia scelerata e ingorda"). He calls on Jesus
to save the church, metaphorized as a ship loaded with vice in dangerous seas:

ed a Piero, duttor della tua gregge,
che smarrito ha quaggiù la bianca chiave,
ricorda che per noi corresti a morte.[34]

(and remind Peter, the leader of your flock, / who has lost the white key
down here, / that you raced to your death for us.)

But the second sonnet is angrier still and takes its cue from a vision of historical Rome, once grand, noble, and divine but now the home of a hellish
smithy ("infernal fucina"):

Similmente i tua diletti figli,
degenerati e colmi d'ogni pecca,
hanno scurato la tua degna voce.
Misera, ha' tua nemici negli artigli,
ove il buon Cristo nella tua Giudecca
ogni dì mille volte è posto in croce.[35]

(So, too [Rome], have your beloved sons, / degenerate and loaded with
every sin, / obscured your worthy voice. / Wretch, you have your enemies in your claws, / there where the good Christ, in your ring of traitors, / is put on the Cross a thousand times a day.)

The Curia, in other words, with its hierarchy of clerics, so torments true
Christians that it puts Christ back on the Cross a thousand times a day. This

---

34. Ibid., 2:357–58, ll. 12–14.
35. Ibid., 2:358 (xcviii), ll. 9–14.

accusation was made by a man of unimpeachable piety. It did not issue, after all, from the pen of Bernardo's brother Luigi, the famous author of the *Morgante*, whose satires on religious belief provoked anger and hostility, not least from Marsilio Ficino, himself a priest.[36]

Moving on from the death of the Pulci brothers (1480s) to the next decade, we come at once on the Savonarolan crusade for spiritual renewal; and the early sixteenth century then sees a shower of violent anticlerical verse in Rome. Savonarola's plea for a purified clergy turned him, ironically, into one of the most famous of all anticlerical clerics, despite the fact that his great Florentine enemies, the city's intransigent oligarchs, looked upon his citizen followers as credulous, priest-infested fools. When fused with political crisis, however, the Savonarolan campaign of reform was a natural response to the swelling might of the papal monarchy, which had entered one of its most energetic periods in the middle of the fifteenth century. Later, although Luther, Calvin, and the Northern Reformation were the obvious outcome of so great an accretion of priestly authority, no such schism was possible south of the Alps, because the ruling part of the Italian upper classes, ensconced in their domineering cities, were too closely linked to the wealthy sector of the clergy, to the papal court and to the whole structure of church lands, benefices, religious houses, clerical appointment, the pursuit of careers for sons, and convents for girls removed from the expensive marriage market. In short, however explosive, anticlericalism in Italy led either to tiny (clandestine) Protestant communities, such as at Lucca, and then to exile, *or* to a stifled rage, as in Guicciardini's famous outburst, declaring that but for his career in papal service, he would have loved Martin Luther quite as much as he, the *fiorentino*, loved himself.[37]

In scanning the social history of anticlericalism in Renaissance Italy, we discover that the main voice of criticism belonged, on the whole, to well-placed, educated men. In a series of trenchant considerations (*Ricordi*), drafted for his sons in 1420, the aging Gino Capponi, an influential Florentine statesman, proffered this chilling advice: "Non v'impacciate con preti, che sono la schiuma del mondo" (Don't get involved with priests: they're the scum of the earth).[38]

Why such anger and contempt? In the course of his long career at the

36. Luigi Pulci, *Opere minori*, ed. P. Orvieto (Milan, 1986), pp. 193–201.

37. Guicciardini, *Opere*, ed. V. de Caprariis (Milan and Naples, 1953), p. 103 (*Ricordi*, n. 28).

38. G. Folena, "Ricordi politici e familiari di Gino di Neri Capponi," in *Miscellanea di studi offerta a Armando Balduino e Bianca Bianchi* (Padua, 1962), pp. 29–39 (n. xiii).

summit of politics in Florence, Capponi had often dealt with important clerics and papal legates, including friars in the service of the commune. As a distinguished parishioner, he also had necessary relations with local clergymen. We can only infer, therefore, that he had seen more than enough to disgust him. In this respect, he shared the views of Guicciardini's father, who prevented the youth in 1503 from taking up an ecclesiastical career because it struck him, a rich and eminent politician, that the official church was too disorderly and corrupt.[39] The young and ambitious Guicciardini, believing a cardinal's hat to be within his reach, had longed to succeed his uncle Rinieri—a known homosexual—as bishop of Cortona. Rinieri had the right to treat this dignity as private property: he could bequeath it.

Again and again, as in Bracci, Sacchetti, Malatesta, Malpigli, Accolti, Roselli, Belcari, Pulci, and others, we come on well-connected men who railed against different aspects of the church's institutional hierarchy: against the practice of simony, ruthless ambition, the lack of vocations, mendicant hypocrisy, ignorance, the incidence of sodomy and adultery, the temporal authority of priests, or even just their sheer malice. Belcari sat in Florentine magistracies at the head of state, notably the Lord Priors and the Dodici Buonuomini; so he was not just an obscure citizen, innocent and unworldly. Roselli, Malpigli, and Accolti, trained at Bologna in civil and canon law, had studied at the feet of clerics, could claim them as university colleagues, and were surely, as legal experts, retained now and then by religious houses, as Guicciardini would be. Their relations with men in holy orders were thus unusually close, and at the outset not necessarily tainted with animosity. Like the top men in government, they had all been in positions to observe the push of ambition, the buying of office, and the spin of grievous misconduct among ecclesiastics. They witnessed a detailed history that largely vanished from the historical stage, until it is fetched forth from archives,[40] or—with prudence—from the anticlerical literature.

The papal bureaucracy grew from a corps of several hundred clerics in the late fourteenth century up to a total of about two thousand in the pontificate of Leo X (1513–21). From the time of Pius II (1458–64), moreover, to meet rising political expenses, popes began to organize, as formerly at

---

39. Guicciardini, *Opere*, p. 7 (*Ricordanze*).

40. As in the books by B. M. Hallman *Italian Cardinals: Reform and the Church as Property, 1492–1563* (Berkeley and Los Angeles, 1985); and R. Bizzocchi, *Chiesa e potere nella Toscana del Quattrocento* (Bologna, 1987).

Avignon, the systematic sale of expensive curial offices, thereby encouraging bankers to operate as brokers for profit-seeking clerics.[41] In the later fifteenth century, Florence and other states were driven increasingly to voice insistent complaints against the invading competence of papal courts in their lands.[42] The highest councils of state, even in Venice, were occasionally penetrated by papal spies;[43] and when the pope himself was the enemy, how could this fail to be deeply distressing? No wonder the Roman Curia and its small army of clerics, living under their own code of laws, provoked anger and hatred as they claimed, on the one hand, a sovereign spiritual authority, while also, on the other, fighting for every inch of their worldly jurisdictions, in a sphere in which material penalties and brutalities were common: that is, the confiscation of property, reprisals suffered abroad, prison, and even torture. Excommunication for failure to abide by the rulings of church courts constituted a spiritual penalty, but the consequences were also temporal, such as in loss of the right to draw up a last will and testament.[44]

I offer some concluding observations. First, the poems cited often pivot on accusations that seem to be commonplaces; and the metaphor of prostituting the church had biblical roots, to be sure. But neither topoi nor roots explain the anger or diminish the attendant energy; and despite the repetition of charges in the poems, it is important to bring such verse to the attention of historians. The fact that the extremes of anticlericalism came in flurries points to the impact of changing conditions in the wide world of the church, not to individual eccentricity or to an immobile fund of biblical metaphor.

Since the church was conventionally metaphorized as mother, spouse, or even daughter—and these had their true correlatives in the surrounding world of family life—the image of the prostitute and pander occurred naturally to poets when ecclesiastical corruption and simony were the issue. In the eyes of the Italian Renaissance male,[45] just as there could be nothing more noble among women than a virgin daughter or a chaste wife

41. Bizzocchi, *Chiesa*, pp. 164, 169.

42. Martines, *Lawyers*, pp. 270–86.

43. Domenico Malipiero, "Annali veneti dall'anno 1457 al 1500," *Archivio storico italiano* 7 (1843): 661–62, 668–70.

44. As in Sixtus IV's excommunication of Lorenzo de' Medici and Florence's Lord Priors of March–April and May–June 1478.

45. L. Martines, *Strong Words: Writing and Social Strain in the Italian Renaissance* (Baltimore and London, 2001), pp. 199–231.

and mother, so the corrupt church, when imagined as a woman, had to be seen as a whore and her bosses as pimps.

The invective, as we have seen, was leveled primarily at the wild and flagrant immorality of popes and upper clergy. Was this because informed contemporaries were satisfied with the authority of the church in *temporal* affairs? Not in the least. The trick was to expose the evils of the clergy in the realm of the spirit. This done, all their other claims collapsed as well.

Anonymity was the best cover for anticlericalism in poetry: the poet could then be forthright about expressing the intensity of his feelings. But if a poem was scandalously critical of clerics and carried the author's name, then it was put out mainly to friends, unless there was open war between the papacy and the city of the offending poet.

Anticlerical verse was written by men, not by women. Down to about the 1530s, women's verse was overwhelmingly religious, and the rare exceptions underline this claim. Among the propertied classes and even at the princely courts, generally speaking, women were not at all brought up like their men: they were more closeted and got a more narrow religious education.

The ranks of lawyers, humanists, men in government, and educated merchants were the ones most likely to generate anticlerical views, not only because such men were more familiar with their clerical compeers but also because they were more likely to have a superior grasp of Christian doctrine.

The Great Schism (1378–1415), the outbreak of the Italian Wars (1494–95), and the unashamed power politics of High Renaissance popes and cardinals produced the prime moments of anticlerical sentiment. But after 1494, fury with religious leaders mingled with a profound political malaise, making for a most explosive mixture.[46]

Can it be claimed that the severest critics of the official church, such as Accolti and Roselli, had been foiled or frustrated when aspiring to ecclesiastical careers, and that their venom, therefore, issued from a taste for revenge? Such a claim depends upon reducing politics and the historical condition of the church to quirky points of individual psychology, leading to monocausal poverty. Bracci, Malpigli, Pulci, and the many others had not aspired to church place. It may well be, however, that the political corruption of the dominant oligarchies in Florence and Bologna, for example, had got so out of hand in the fifteenth century that the demand for something higher and finer in the church was also an oblique quest for principle, for

46. Ibid., pp. 249–63.

some kind of justice in the surrounding world.[47] If the top men in the church were no better than despicable rotters, what could citizens expect from the cruel world of urban politics?

Literary anticlericalism seems to have been Tuscan preeminently. Was this simply because the production of verse in Tuscany vastly exceeded the like from other parts of Italy? Possibly so, although Venice, which must have nourished some degree of anticlerical feeling, reveals nothing of the sort in its poetry. I leave it to Venice experts to throw light on this point. Where, as in Perugia and parts of the Romagna, nearly all the upper-class families looked to the church for the military, political, and ecclesiastical careers of their sons, there the expression of contempt for priests was bound to be more private, more covert, or compensatory and colluding. I have yet to come on any poetry from Perugia, later than 1350, that is strongly directed against the clerical order. Yet we know that Bologna and Rome were major venues for such expression. When Pope Julius II expelled the ruling Bentivoglio family from Bologna in 1506, a spasm of anticlerical anger passed through the city, and there was a sudden outpouring of verse against the pope. The attorney (*notaio*) Ercole Ugolotti was hanged when he confessed to having written and posted an anonymous twenty-five-line poem, calling for an uprising against the new government of "pitiless priests."[48]

47. L. Martines, "Corruption and Injustice as Themes in Quattrocento Poetry," in *La Toscane et les Toscans autour de la Renaissance: Cadres de vie, société, croyances. Mélanges offerts à Charles-M. de La Roncière,* ed. Jean-André Cancellieri (Aix-en-Provence, 1999), pp. 377–86.

48. Giovanni Gozzadini, *Memorie per la vita di Giovanni II Bentivoglio* (Bologna, 1839), pp. 214–17.

11 Liturgy for Nonliturgists

A Glimpse at San Lorenzo

William M. Bowsky

This is a suggestive essay written by a historian of medieval Italy who himself only recently turned to liturgical sources in an effort to widen his investigation of the secular Church of San Lorenzo in Florence in the thirteenth and fourteenth centuries. One of Florence's oldest churches, San Lorenzo was dedicated by Saint Ambrose during the closing years of the fourth century and lay claim to being the city's first cathedral. The parish of San Lorenzo was the city's largest, and its parishioners an extremely varied lot. Among them were Guelf and Ghibelline nobles, great merchants, tradesmen, small shopkeepers, and workers and laborers of all sorts. The parish was home to large numbers of the town's most recent immigrants and to many of its poorest inhabitants. Alongside all these was a host of religious of nearly every hue and stripe.

In only a slightly later period, so brilliantly studied by Gene Brucker, the parish of San Lorenzo would become the centrum of Medici power and the basilica itself the object of their lavish support. Not surprisingly, then, the Church of San Lorenzo has not lacked for scholarly attention. Most, however, has focused upon the Renaissance church, thanks in great part to the immense architectural changes wrought by Brunelleschi in the fifteenth century and to Michelangelo's sculptural and architectural contributions in the sixteenth century.[1] By contrast, medieval San Lorenzo has received little scholarly attention, almost none of which has dealt with what actually

The University of California, Davis, and a grant from the American Philosophical Society facilitated this study. Friends and colleagues and the personnel of the Biblioteca Medicea Laurenziana aided me. I especially appreciate the kindness of Professors Andrew Hughes and Richard W. Pfaff, outstanding liturgists who patiently helped to introduce me to the mysteries of their craft. Errors, however, are completely my own. In the traditional phrase of scholars of an earlier era, I seek the understanding of the Benevolent Reader, for whose aid a supplementary bibliography has been included at the end of the notes. All manuscripts cited are housed in the Biblioteca Medicea Laurenziana. Archivio San Lorenzo manuscripts are cited as ASL. References to notes also refer to the pages on which they appear.

1. For our purposes see esp. R. Gaston, "Liturgy and Patronage in San Lorenzo, Florence, 1350–1650," in *Patronage, Art and Society in Renaissance Italy*, ed. F. W.

went on within the church and the nature and activities of the clerics who directed its daily activities.[2]

The present study began as a search for evidence concerning spirituality, a topic much discussed, if variously defined, in recent decades. We need think only of the work of André Vauchez or of the seventeen-volume *Dictionnaire de spiritualité*.[3] In this quest I turned to liturgy.

Despite some forays into liturgy by such a brilliant and eclectic a scholar as Ernst H. Kantorowicz, whose *Laudes Regiae* is known to every graduate

---

Kent and P. Simons (Oxford, 1987), pp. 111–33. See also P. Roselli and O. Superchi, *L'edificazione della Basilica di San Lorenzo: Una vicenda d'importanza urbanistica* (Florence, 1980); H. Burns, "San Lorenzo in Florence before the Building of the New Sacristy: An Early Plan," *Mitteilungen des kunsthistorischen Institutes in Florenz* 23 (1979): 144–54; C. Elam, "The Site and Building History of Michelangelo's New Sacristy," *Mitteilungen des kunsthistorischen Institutes in Florenz* 23 (1979): 155–86; I. Hyman, *Fifteenth Century Florentine Studies: The Palazzo Medici and a Ledger for the Church of San Lorenzo* (New York, 1977); V. Herzner, "Zur Baugeschichte von San Lorenzo in Florenz," *Zeitschrift für Kunstgeschichte* 37 (1974): 89–115; H. Saalman, "San Lorenzo: The 1434 Chapel Project," *Burlington Magazine* 120 (1978): 361–64; Saalman, "The New Sacristy of San Lorenzo before Michelangelo," *Art Bulletin* 67 (1985): 199–228; J. Ruda, "A 1434 Building Programme for San Lorenzo in Florence," *Burlington Magazine* 120 (1978): 358–61; J. Clearfield, "The Tomb of Cosimo de'Medici in San Lorenzo," *Rutgers Art Review* 2 (1981): 13–30; S. E. Reiss, "A Medieval Source for Michelangelo's Medici Madonna," *Zeitschrift für Kunstgeschichte* 3 (1987): 394–400; Reiss, "The Ginori Corridor of San Lorenzo and the Building History of the New Sacristy," *Journal of the Society of Architectural History* 52 (1993): 339–343; U. Baldini and B. Nardini, eds., *San Lorenzo: La basilica, le sagrestie, le cappelle, la biblioteca* (Florence, 1984); W. E. Wallace, *Michelangelo at San Lorenzo: The Genius as Entrepeneur* (Cambridge, England, 1994).

2. For the medieval church of San Lorenzo, in addition to the works cited below, see, e.g., A. Benvenuti, "San Lorenzo: La cattedrale negata," in *Le radici cristiane di Firenze*, ed. Benvenuti, F. Cardini, and E. Giannarelli (Florence, 1994), pp. 117–33. Embarrassing though it is to note, my own works are almost the only modern studies to treat the actual workings of the medieval church of San Lorenzo. See esp. W. M. Bowsky, *Piety and Property in Medieval Florence: A House in San Lorenzo,* Quaderni di "Studi Senesi," 69 (Milan, 1990), now in Bowsky, *La Chiesa di San Lorenzo a Firenze* (Florence, 1999), pp. 1–90; Bowsky, "Chiostro con vista: I canonici di San Lorenzo a Firenze," *Ricerche storiche* 25 (1995), in Bowsky, *La Chiesa,* pp. 157–96; and Bowsky, "The Confraternity of Priests and San Lorenzo of Florence: A Church, a Parish, and a Clerical Brotherhood," *Ricerche storiche* 27 (1997), in Bowsky, *La Chiesa,* pp. 197–245; and Bowsky, "'Populus Sancti Laurentii': Care of Souls, a Parish, and a Priest" (cited at note 39 below).

3. *Dictionnaire de spiritualité ascetique et mystique, doctrine et histoire,* ed. M. Viller et al., 17 vols. (Paris, 1937–95). See, e.g., A. Vauchez, *The Spirituality of the Medieval West* (Kalamazoo, Mich., 1993), trans. from the 1975 French edition; Vauchez, "Un colloque sur la notion de spiritualité," *Studi medievali,* ser. 3, 23 (1982): 447–49; Vauchez, *The Laity in the Middle Ages,* ed. D. E. Bornstein, (Notre Dame, Ind., 1993); Vauchez, *La sainteté en occident aux derniers siècles du moyen*

student of medieval history,[4] liturgy is a field that has been relatively little utilized by traditional historians. Liturgy had been a terra incognita to this institutional historian who, after decades devoted to the study of Siena, only later in life turned to her archrival, Florence, and to ecclesiastical history. In liturgy,[5] I hoped to find not only feasts of saints especially revered at San Lorenzo,[6] but also stories and homilies apparently particularly emphasized in what were or might have been its liturgical books, and to compare those manuscripts with liturgical documents related to other churches, or at least Tuscan churches.[7]

I attempted to ascertain what liturgical manuscripts belonged to the chapter of medieval San Lorenzo, then to discover their scriptoria, when they

---

âge (Paris, 1981). Cf. B. Calati, R. Grégoire, and A. Blasucci, *La spiritualità del medioevo*, Storia della spiritualità, 4 (Rome, 1988); *Chiesa e riforma nella spiritualità del sec. XI*, Convegni del Centro di studi sulla spiritualità medievale, 6 (Todi, 1968); J. Leclerq, F. Vandenbrocke, and L. Bouyer, *The Spirituality of the Middle Ages* (London, 1968), trans. from 1961 French edition. A projected twenty-five-volume series, "World Spirituality: An Encyclopedic History of the Religious Quest," already includes *Christian Spirituality: Origins to the Twelfth Century*, ed. B. McGinn, J. Meyendorf, and J. Leclerq (New York, 1985); and *Christian Spirituality: High Middle Ages and Reformation*, ed. J. Raitt, B. McGinn, and J. Meyendorf (New York, 1987).

4. Ernst H. Kantorowicz, *Laudes Regiae: A Study in Liturgical Acclamations and Mediaeval Ruler Worship* (Berkeley and Los Angeles, 1946). I offer this example only because it is so well known. This is not the place for even a select bibliography of historical works that utilize liturgy.

5. See the interesting working definition of liturgy adopted by the art historian Robert Gaston in his "Liturgy and Patronage," p. 115 n. 12: "In this study, liturgy is defined as any ritualized act of Christian worship performed publicly or privately by an individual cleric or layman, or by groups of clergy or laymen; such acts may take place in any context, including churches, private homes, and *palazzi*, civic buildings, confraternity halls, or public streets and squares." For a convenient definition of liturgical texts, see P. Salmon, *Les manuscrits liturgiques latins de la bibliothèque vaticane*, 5 vols. Studi e Testi 251, 253, 260, 267, 270 (Vatican City, 1968–72): vol. 1, *Psautiers, antiphonaires, hymnaires, collectaires, bréviaires*; vol. 2, *Sacramentaires, épistoliers, évangéliaires, graduels, missels*; vol. 3, *Ordines Romani, pontificaux, rituels, cérémoniaux*; vol. 4, *Les livres de lectures de l'office. Les livres de l'office du chapitre. Les livres d'heures*; vol. 5, *Liste complémentaire*. See the "Tables générales," at 1:vi–vii.

6. See the brief but valuable treatment of fourteenth-century liturgy of San Lorenzo and its festal calendar in R. Gaston, "Liturgy and Patronage in San Lorenzo," pp. 117–19. In the context of the present essay I shall not treat liturgical information that can be derived from such documents as the extant constitutions of the Church of San Lorenzo, as that involves a different sort of investigation and analysis than that necessary for what traditionally are considered liturgical texts.

7. I shall discuss elsewhere documents related especially to other Tuscan and particularly Florentine churches, prominent among them the cathedral.

came to the Ambrosian basilica if not written, illuminated, and bound there, and how long they might have remained in use.[8] Quickly I discovered that many apparently reasonable goals are naive, given the nature, quantity, and location of archival documentation and the present state of scholarship.

While secular churches as well as regular foundations had their liturgical books, one may be surprised at the small number contained in the late medieval sacristy of even so important and ancient an ecclesiastical institution as San Lorenzo.[9] Of course not all manuscripts may have been kept in the sacristy, and medieval inventories sometimes omit service books. And at any time individual clerics possessed their personal copies of some books and manuscripts.

Initial exploration suggests that others who do not specialize in liturgy may appreciate some indications of the possibilities and pitfalls for the nonspecialist in this fascinating but technical and underutilized field of study.[10] While my evidence derives from documents in the Biblioteca Medicea Laurenziana, the famed Laurentian Library in Florence, it is especially some more general observations that I wish to emphasize here.

One of the first problems that one confronts may perhaps seem surprising. That is the need to ascertain the nature of manuscripts that one is examining. Even when working only with published liturgical documents, one quickly perceives the importance of a phrase in Robert Reynolds's definition of a Divine Office lectionary: "The lections or readings themselves could be

---

8. A. Hughes, *Late Medieval Liturgical Offices: Sources and Chants* (Toronto, 1996), p. 53, in his "recommendations for the cataloguing of liturgical books," urges that "the words *provenance* and *origin* should be eliminated," and replaced by more precise terminology.

9. F. Baldasseroni and P. D'Ancona, "La Biblioteca della Basilica fiorentina di San Lorenzo nei secoli XIV e XV," *Rivista delle biblioteche e degli archivi* 16, nos. 10–12 (1905): 175–201, at 182: a 1393 copy of a 1387 inventory (Inv. A), twenty listings, with thirty-three manuscripts.

10. R. W. Pfaff, *Medieval Latin Liturgy: A Select Bibliography* (Toronto, 1982), remains the first work to consult. J. W. Harper, *The Forms and Orders of Western Liturgy from the Tenth to the Eighteenth Century* (Oxford, 1991), is an excellent introduction to medieval liturgy, and I thank Katherine Gill of the University of Connecticut for first bringing it to my attention. See also C. Vogel, *Medieval Liturgy: An Introduction to the Sources* (Washington, D.C., 1986). H. L. Spencer, *English Preaching in the Late Middle Ages* (Oxford, 1993), chap. 2, "Setting the Scene," contains a useful summary of liturgical matters. Difficult but absolutely essential for medieval liturgy is A. Hughes's splendid *Medieval Manuscripts for Mass and Office: A Guide to Their Organization and Terminology* (Toronto, 1982); see, e.g., pp. 3–13, for the liturgical year. C. Jones, G. Wainwright, E. Yarnold, P. Bradshaw, eds.,*The Study of Liturgy*, rev. ed. (London, 1992), is less useful than its comprehensive title would suggest.

gathered into separate sections within the lectionaries according to the temporale (a liturgical cycle arranged according to feasts of the ecclesiastical year) or sanctorale (a liturgical cycle arranged according to the feasts of the saints), or they might be mingled."[11] I would emphasize that intermingling, and the inclusion of elements of one type of liturgical work within the body of another, seems to be the rule, not the exception.

We must bear in mind Aime George Martimort's observation that distinctions between office books of biblical readings, patristic readings, and hagiography frequently are honored in the breach. Various types of readings often appear side by side even in a description of the same celebration. In a single lectionary, sacramentary, or missal, saints' feasts can "alternate with the solemnities, Sundays and weekdays of the liturgical year."[12] Guy Philippart's effort to distinguish various types of lectionaries and legendaries only highlights the problem of such intermingling.[13] Even Henri Barré, who insists on sharp distinctions between homiliaries, lectionaries, and legendaries, notes that "the distinction of genres cannot always be respected rigorously," and that there are, for example, "homiliary-legendaries."[14]

My own search began with the five-volume catalog of manuscripts housed in the Laurentian Library. Compiled by Angelo Maria Bandini, its head librarian from 1757 to 1803, and printed in folio volumes with double columns, it is buttressed by a three-volume supplement.[15] Excellent for its

11. R. E. Reynolds, "Lectionary," in *Dictionary of the Middle Ages*, ed. J. R. Strayer, 13 vols. (New York, 1982–89), 7:534, especially on Mass and Divine Office lectionaries. Cf. his "Divine Office," ibid., 4:221–31. For Office lectionaries, see esp. Salmon, *Les manuscrits liturgiques latins*, 4:vi–xi. S. J. P. Van Dijk, ed., *Latin Liturgical Manuscripts and Printed Books: Guide to an Exhibition Held during 1952* (Oxford, 1952), too frequently overlooked, contains useful brief definitions of liturgical terms.

12. A. G. Martimort, *Les lectures liturgiques et leurs livres*, Typologie des sources du moyen âge occidental, 64 (Turnhout, 1992), pp. 69–70.

13. G. Philippart, *Les légendiers latins et autres manuscrits hagiographiques*, Typologie des sources du moyen âge occidental, 24–25 (Turnhout, 1977), p. 24.

14. H. Barré, "Homéliaires: Caractères généraux," and "Homéliares latins," in *Dictionnaire de spiritualité*, vol. 7, pt. 1 (1969), cols. 597–600, 600–606, at 598. On Barré's definition of homiliary, see Salmon, *Les manuscrits liturgiques latins*, 4:vii.

15. A. M. Bandini, *Catalogus codicum latinorum Bibliothecae Mediceae Laurentianae*, 5 vols. (Florence, 1774–78). (This is abbreviated below as Bandini.) See also Bandini, *Bibliotheca Leopoldina Laurentiana: Seu catalogus manuscriptorum, qui iussu Petri Leopoldi . . . Imperatoris in Laurentianam translati sunt . . . A. M. Bandinus, recensuit, illustravit, edidit*, 3 vols. (Florence, 1791–93). See, too, Bandini, *Dei princìpi e progressi della Real Biblioteca Mediceo Laurenziana (Ms. laur. Acquisti e Doni 142)*, ed. R. Pintaudi, M. Tesi, and A. R. Fantoni (Florence, 1990), pp. xi–xiii for discussion of the Bandini volumes themselves.

time and genre, Bandini's probably is typical of such eighteenth-century catalogs of manuscript collections. Mutatis mutandis, similar observations and similar cautions can and should be applied to other eighteenth-century catalogs that include descriptions of unpublished liturgical manuscripts.

In Bandini I focused on the Plutei manuscripts, a collection that includes ecclesiastical and liturgical manuscripts of every variety, from the earliest Christian writings through Wycliff, among them bibles, psalters, breviaries, kalendars [16] and missals, saints' lives or *vitae*, martyrologies, sermons, homiliaries, and lectionaries.[17] I sought every manuscript that might have belonged to the Church of San Lorenzo.

For most manuscripts there is no indication of either their scriptoria or where they were used. *Pluteo* 17.1, a well-illustrated fifteenth-century breviary given to the city of Todi by Pope Leo X (1513–21), is a relative exception, most probably preserved because of its illustrations.

As with so many such works, the copies of catalogs that are housed with the collections that they describe often contain invaluable marginalia or even added notes, sometimes signed. Father Martino Bertagna, OFM, pasted a slip of paper into a Laurenziana copy of Bandini. He wrote that *Pluteo* 20.6, a short collection of saints' lives used in the Florentine cathedral, had to date "from the first half of the trecento because it contains a vita of San Lucchese [of Poggibonsi] (whose last miracle was in 1321) and a compendium of the life of Santa Fina taken from a more ample redaction of the beginning of the fourteenth century."[18]

While we may be grateful for such modern notes and marginalia, Father Bertagna's addition also highlights a limitation as to what the nonliturgist can accomplish. Although one may make a start by utilizing the Bollandists' *Bibliotheca hagiographica latina*,[19] detailed knowledge of the contents and dating of variant versions of saints' lives is the provenance of a specialist. This stricture applies to other comparisons and variants in any type of

16. For kalendars, see especially Hughes, *Medieval Manuscripts for Mass and Office*, p. 447 (index) s.v.; and Salmon, *Les manuscrits liturgiques latins*, 4:xii.

17. The Plutei manuscripts are not discussed as a collection in Bandini, *Dei principi*.

18. The Biblioteca Laurenziana possesses three sets of Bandini, which I arbitrarily call a, b, and c: (a) Vols. 1–11, Sala di Consultazione (vols. 1–5, Latin manuscripts; vols. 6–8, Greek manuscripts; vols. 9–11, the 1791–93 Supplement); (b) a set without a call number in the Ufficio Manoscritti; and (c) an incomplete set. The Bertagna note is in Bandini (a), 1, cols. 616–17. Bertagna includes a reference to his own 1969 article on San Lucchese.

19. *Bibliotheca hagiographica latina antiquae et mediae aetatis (BHL)*, vols. 1–2 (Brussels, 1898–1901), *Supplementum* (1911), *Novum Supplementum* (1986).

liturgical or indeed religious manuscript. A complete study, for example, requires specialized knowledge of the variant versions of lessons, homilies, legends, and so forth concerning every saint who appears in a particular manuscript, a quest made more difficult because the overwhelming majority of such manuscripts remain unpublished.[20] Andrew Hughes estimates that "10,000 manuscripts of the late office liturgy are extant," and as for "saints' feastdates . . . each country, each diocese, each church may have its own correct date."[21]

In very few cases Bandini states that a manuscript had belonged to a particular church. In rare instances the manuscript itself vouchsafes him this information, as with *Pluteo* 20.6. Bandini rightly dates this to the fourteenth century, apparently, as with most manuscripts, on the basis of its calligraphy. By very occasionally noting changes in hand, however, Bandini can lull one into thinking that he accounts for all of them, which is far from the case. And while his dating may have taken manuscript illustration into account, this is problematic.

Dating manuscripts was not Bandini's greatest strength. Ordinarily he tended to date manuscripts as older or earlier than they actually are, an error that has misled scholars who relied upon his catalogs rather than the manuscripts themselves. We should certainly forgive our eighteenth-century savant, however, for even the best known and most useful modern study of medieval Italian manuscript illuminations can misdate.[22]

---

20. Despite its misprints and omissions, an invaluable research tool that includes lists of religious feasts and of principal saints is A. Cappelli, *Cronologia, cronografia e calendario perpetuo* (Milan). The medievalist may use any edition. Now essential, and for far more than its lists of kalendars, feast names and dates, is Hughes, *Late Medieval Liturgical Offices: Sources and Chants*. Despite its own shortcomings, *Bibliotheca Sanctorum*, 14 vols. (Rome, 1961–70, 1987 [Prima Appendice]), is a fine modern hagiographic reference work. More difficult to obtain, at least in the United States, is a complete set of J.-L. Baudot and L. Chaussin, eds., *Vies des saints et des bienheureux selon l'ordre du calendrier avec l'histoire des fêtes, par les rr. pp. Bénédictins de Paris* 13 vols. (Paris, 1935–59). D. Cambiaso, *L'anno ecclesiastico e le feste de santi in Genova nel loro svolgimento storico*, Atti della Società ligure di storia patria, 17–18 (Genoa, 1917–18), remains useful. *Analecta Bollandiana* (1882–), 114 volumes by 1996, contains numerous articles concerning saints and their vitae as well as studies of variant versions. Individual volumes possess indices of saints mentioned as well as of works reviewed in them. Not to be overlooked is the classic Bollandist series, *Acta Sanctorum* (1643 ff.), which appeared in various editions.

21. Hughes, *Late Medieval Liturgical Offices: Sources and Chants*, pp. 2, 51.

22. E. B. Garrison, *Studies in the History of Mediaeval Italian Painting*, 4 vols. (Florence, 1953–62), tends to date initials and other illuminations, and hence the manuscripts themselves, as later or more modern than they are. For this, see especially K. Berg, *Studies in Tuscan Twelfth-Century Illumination* (Oslo, 1968).

Dating of course is essential. With liturgy this demands a knowledge of hagiography. When did the feasts of individual saints first appear in Italian and in Tuscan manuscripts? When did they become common, or universal? What saints did a church or order especially venerate, and why? How much space did they receive in manuscripts created or used in that institution? Were their octaves included, when they were not included elsewhere? Their translations?[23] What significance, if any, lies in a feast's appearance in a sanctorale out of its apparent chronological order? Might a church be celebrating not the death of an apostle, martyr, confessor, or virgin but the translation of relics, even to its own sanctuary? Knowledge of a saint's canonization aids in the dating of the portion of a manuscript in which he or she appears.

Dating manuscripts means dating their parts as well. Here one is aided not only by calligraphy but also by the art historian's study of manuscript illumination, initials in particular, and the materials used. Despite enormous strides made in this century, this complex and specialized field is not an exact science. Even experts can disagree by as much as a century. Long-lived artists and illustrators make dating estimates especially hazardous. Nor is it always easy to have the necessary sets of scholarly art historical volumes at one's side while working in many archives. And even should one go to the expense of obtaining color photocopies of selected initial letters, there is too much that they cannot reveal. Nonetheless, the nonspecialist can obtain insights by studying initial letters, the differences in their size, filigree, elaboration, and decoration, and artistic content. The very colors of the initials of saints may suggest relative importance.

Before dating parts of a manuscript, one must ascertain those divisions. Splendid eighteenth-century leather bindings frequently combine disparate manuscripts and wrongly separate others. Catchwords at the foot of a folio verso that also begin the next recto can help. A catchword followed by a different word may reveal the loss of an entire fascicle. Such gifts to the scholar are infrequent. We must search out the threads in the middle of each fascicle, often a difficult process in a tightly bound volume, and determine the nature of every fascicle, from a cover to each separate quire. Folios from which a sheet was cut off and the remainder skillfully glued to another folio, particularly toward the end of a manuscript, lie hidden to confuse us. They certainly have misled me on more than one occasion.

23. For translations of relics, see M. Heinzelmann, *Translationsberichte und andere Quellen des Reliquienkultes* (Turnhout, 1979); and P. Geary, *Furta Sacra*, 2d ed. (Princeton, N.J., 1990), passim.

Closely allied to foliation is calligraphy. It is not even impossible to mistake a change in pens for a different hand. Writers' ages and when and where they trained can lead to apparent variations that may not, in fact, mean that folios or quires were written at different times. It only is a rule of thumb that writers still unfamiliar with a script tended to write with letters clearly detached, while those more familiar with it tended to run their letters together.

Let me sound a warning given me by an outstanding liturgist. Differences among manuscripts that might suggest differing outlooks or emphases, or spiritualities if you will, are not to be sought merely in a manuscript's treatment of the particular saints in whom one is interested. They may occur in the treatments of any other of the numerous saints in a given manuscript. Similarly, we must remember that certain Sundays and feasts of the temporal calendar can displace, move, or change the content of some feasts in *sanctorale* celebrated on the same day, as too can feasts of the temporal calendar likewise affect Sunday lessons.

Mention of Sundays suggests yet another caveat. Some liturgical documents reckon Sundays after Trinity and not after Pentecost—the Roman style. I mistakenly thought that one could have an indication of the scriptorium of a manuscript according to its division of the liturgical year, before a kind liturgist disabused me of this notion.[24]

Similarly, I had hoped that by seeking out variations in liturgy, even in choice of pericopes or assigned scriptural readings,[25] one might ascertain whether a manuscript, or part of it, had been created by one or another religious order or in a secular church, regardless of where it came to be utilized. Thus in referring to England, H. Leith Spencer explains that

> variations in the liturgy might be caused . . . by who was reciting it: secular or religious. The religious Orders . . . might well follow a rite of their own. . . . The Benedictines generally followed the practice of the diocese. . . . The Augustinian canons, too. . . . The Dominicans used the pericopes appointed in Sarum. The Franciscans . . . did not, but agreed with the Roman rite of the papal court.[26]

This, too, however, is far from ironclad, and local variations alone seem well nigh innumerable. In passing I should add that in medieval Europe "the pa-

24. See, e.g., Spencer, *English Preaching*, p. 24.
25. For pericopes, see below note 29.
26. Spencer, *English Preaching*, p. 23.

pal rite of the Roman court" is not to be equated with "the Roman rite," itself an elusive quarry.[27]

Moreover, even when we know that a manuscript was used in a church such as San Lorenzo, ordinarily we must remain ignorant not merely of its scriptorium but also of when it reached that church and when it may have been superseded by other liturgical documents. I have come across more than one manuscript most of whose fascicles apparently were written elsewhere, but that at some time came to San Lorenzo. And, we may ask legitimately, how long did a twelfth-century or a thirteenth-century homiliary, for example, remain in use in the Ambrosian basilica? The mere existence of a later homiliary does not tell us when, or even that, an earlier one was abandoned.

A peril of another sort derives from the very detail and completeness of manuscript catalogs such as those of Bandini. For this apparent completeness can mislead as well as aid the liturgical researcher. Thus, for most manuscripts Bandini creates his own sections, paragraphing the contents of a manuscript with his own Roman numeration.[28] These descriptions contain surprisingly few errors. Yet as even his large folio volumes are insufficient for detailed discussions of contents, Bandini tends to omit saints or feasts contained within a portion of a manuscript devoted to another topic or to the life of another saint. When he believes that the contents of a section (or paragraph) replicates passages in manuscripts that he already has described, he frequently refers to "pages," that is, columns, of earlier parts of his catalog, and to his own section numbers. Unfortunately, examination of the manuscripts themselves occasionally reveals that cited passages only

27. See the basic study by S. J. P. Van Dijk and J. H. Walker, *The Origins of the Modern Roman Liturgy: The Liturgy of the Papal Court and the Franciscan Order in the Thirteenth Century* (Westminster, Md., and London, 1960). Cf. Van Dijk, *Sources of the Modern Roman Liturgy: The Ordinals by Haymo of Faversham and Related Documents (1243–1307)*, 2 vols., Studia et documenta franciscana, 1–2 (Leiden, 1963). M. A. R. Tuker, *The Liturgy in Rome*, 2d ed. (London, 1925), a far less sophisticated work, while essentially modern in focus, is a convenient introduction with numerous references to some medieval practices and parallel Latin and English texts. For "Roman Use," see Hughes, *Late Medieval Liturgical Offices: Sources and Chants*, pp. 52–53.

28. His failure to offer this fulsome treatment to *Pluteo* 20.5, an Office lectionary used in the Church of San Lorenzo, describing it only in about a half column (vol. 1, col. 615: "Festivitates sanctorum incerti auctoris"), led me to examine this manuscript in some detail, which I shall elaborate in a forthcoming publication. For now, see A. R. Fantoni, "La Biblioteca Capitolare di San Lorenzo," in *San Lorenzo: I documenti e i tesori nascosti* (Florence, 1993), pp. 21–33 (27).

resemble one another, and that in fact they contain important variations, omissions, or additions.

While some scholarly approaches are open to all, others remain available only to specialists. Among these last are the study of differences between monastic and secular church documents that may suggest breaks and changes within a manuscript. This includes the order of psalms, versicles, and responses for different hours and offices, and of the pericopes, or biblical passages especially from the Gospels, Epistles, and Acts, included within such documents as homiliaries, lectionaries, breviaries, and missals. Here, too, however, the nonliturgist may make at least a good beginning, starting with the aid of a scholarly work now a century and a half old.[29]

On the simplest level, we may note, for example, that a first written unnumbered folio recto in *Pluteo* 20.5 contains lections numbered nine through twelve and ends in midsentence.[30] The main portion of matins in the Divine Office consists of nocturns, containing psalms, antiphons, canticles, and lessons. These differed both geographically and among religious entities. Offices in most secular churches, with the exception of some in the hands of regular canons, consisted of nine lessons for major feasts, otherwise three, with some singlets. The monastic office comprised twelve lessons, three nocturns of four lessons each. This suggests that the unnumbered folio was taken from a monastic sanctorale, in this case probably a lectionary with lessons from the Gospel of Matthew. The remainder of this manuscript is an office lectionary, probably a hagiographic cycle, or sanctorale, for the entire liturgical year intended for use at matins by the chap-

29. For pericopes see E. Ranke, *Das Pericopensystem aus den ältesten Urkunden der Römischen Liturgie dargelegt und erläutert* (Berlin, 1847), particularly for changing and competing pericopes in various early lectionaries (*comites*), including for important liturgical events such as the dedication of a church and for feasts of the temporal calendar of the liturgical year, as well as for the sanctorale. Section III (pp. 264–399) contains the pericopes (readings) for the entire liturgical year. The Appendix Monumentorum (pp. I–XCII) contains the pericopes of various lectionaries. Ranke also is useful for citations of seventeenth- and eighteenth-century editions of early lectionaries, homiliaries, and kalendars. For comparative assigned biblical readings, especially from the sixth century through the Carolingian era, various medieval rites, and the sixteenth-century Roman rite, see also F. Cabrol et al., eds., *Dictionnaire d'archéologie chrétienne et de liturgie*, 15 vols. (Paris, 1907–53), vol. 5, pt. 1 (1922), cols. 246–344: "Épitres"; and cols. 852–923: "Évangiles"; cf. vol. 8, pt. 2 (1929), cols. 2270–2306: "Lectionnaire." The index in the *editio princeps* of the Roman missal, R. Lippe, ed., *Missale Romanum Mediolani, 1474*, 2 vols., Henry Bradshaw Society, 17, 33 (London, 1899–1907), includes incipits of texts used for some gospel citations. The publications of the Henry Bradshaw Society are essential for liturgical studies.

30. The verso is blank.

ter of the Church of San Lorenzo.[31] And while its liturgical year properly ends with the Common of the Saints interspersed with the feasts of several saints,[32] we should not be surprised that there follow folios in several different hands, including the original one, that contain yet other saints' feasts, translations and alternative readings.

Another area reserved to the specialist is the study of musical liturgical manuscripts, which remains the domain of the musicologist. Different churches have different types of musical notations and lettering, and the nonspecialist treads here at her or his extreme peril.[33]

In my quest for clues regarding spiritual life that liturgical manuscripts might offer for that of the Church of San Lorenzo in Florence, in addition to studying the Bandini manuscripts I sought others that the collegiate chapter might have possessed. The 1393 inventory described by Baldasseroni and D'Ancona[34] can be supplemented with an imperfect but essential twentieth-century inventory of manuscripts still in the chapter archive. It, however, lists no missals, breviaries, or psalters earlier than the end of the fourteenth century.[35] Such a gap makes it all the more difficult to establish a norm for that church's liturgical celebrations.[36]

Might litanies, liturgical supplications and responses, suggest something about the relative importance of different saints to the San Lorenzo clergy?

31. Bandini, vol. 1, col. 615. For reasons that I have yet to ascertain, this is one of the relatively few Plutei manuscripts that Bandini does not describe in detail, and discusses in but half a column. Its analysis will form a portion of my study of the liturgy of San Lorenzo. Other manuscripts utilized by the Church of San Lorenzo include *Pluteo* 27.1, "Vitae sanctorum patrum," Bandini, I, cols. 779–84 (779–80), a complex document that requires detailed and accurate analysis. For now, see Fantoni, "La Biblioteca Capitolare," pp. 26–27.

32. *Pluteo* 20.5, fols. 115v–129r.

33. See especially Hughes, *Late Medieval Liturgical Offices: Tools for Electronic Research* (Toronto, 1994); and Hughes, *Late Medieval Liturgical Offices: Sources and Chants.*

34. Baldasseroni and D'Ancona, "La Biblioteca."

35. Two indices of documents still extant in the Chapter archive, housed in the reading room of the Laurentian Library and prepared by Stefano Caroti, are "Archivio del Capitolo di San Lorenzo. Inventario," a–i and 1–23. Volume 23 includes the missals, breviaries, and psalters. It just is possible that further detailed analysis may suggest that *Pluteo* 16.8 belonged to San Lorenzo. Bandini described this (I, cols. 171–87) as "MARTYROLOGIUM BEDAE, Seu potius Missale et Sacramentarium ad usum Ecclesiae cuiusdam Florentinae praevio Kalendario" (col. 171), and dated it as "Saec. XII. ineuntis. . . ." (col. 187). Bandini rightly recognized fourteenth-century additions in the kalendar, and a thirteenth-century hand elsewhere. Berg, *Studies in Tuscan Illumination* does not refer to *Pluteo* 16.8.

36. Cf. Harper, *The Forms and Orders*, chap. 12, "Establishing the Order of a Latin Liturgical Celebration," pp. 191–200.

Litanies of saints appear in most types of liturgical books, especially in long and elaborate ones, those that included the Vigil of Easter or Holy Saturday, and the Offices of the Dead, and of the Dying.[37] Within the sections in a litany of saints, their order of appearance might suggest relative importance, although Saint Lawrence, the patron saint of San Lorenzo, is important everywhere. A *ii* (two) after a name, meaning that it is to be repeated, also might suggest relative importance. Do unexpected or local saints appear in a litany? It is unfortunate, though, that no publication lists the order in which saints appear in litanies. Rather, one must seek out and compare individual litanies.

One source definitely used in the Church of San Lorenzo that contained such litanies was the gradual, of which two housed in the chapter archive seem to date from about 1352–60.[38] If, as I suspect, these manuscripts were not made for San Lorenzo, we cannot even be certain when they came to that church, no less how long they were utilized. These graduals, moreover, are very richly decorated. Were others, less well illustrated, not carefully kept but rather consumed? The same warning applies to other liturgical manuscripts. Breviaries and missals faced their own special risks engendered by frequent usage and handling.

While the scholar concerned with liturgy certainly will not overlook homiliaries,[39] other religious works should prove worthy of examination even

37. See M. Coens, "Anciennes litanies des saints," *Analecta Bollandiana* 54 (1936): 5–37; 55 (1937): 49–69; 59 (1941): 272–98; 62 (1944): 126–68, a collection of largely Carolingian litanies; and see 54 (1936): 6–7 for references to published litanies. For a lengthy and detailed litany in *Pluteo* 17.3, which he calls an eleventh-century psalter, see Bandini, I, cols. 324–37, at 326–33, with a reference to other published litanies.

38. ASL, Corale E, fols. 267r–270v; and Corale F, fol. lvii r–v. These manuscripts are discussed briefly by M. Assirelli in *San Lorenzo. I documenti . . .* , pp. 139–40. Cf. A. Morandini, "Note su alcuni corali conservati nel Archivio del Capitolo di San Lorenzo in Firenze," in *Miscellanea di studi in memoria di Anna Saitta Revignas*, Biblioteca di Bibliografia Italiana, 86 (Florence, 1978), pp. 289–95 (294). Harper, *Forms and Orders*, p. 100, defines the gradual as "The choral chant sung after the first reading at Mass. . . . A book containing all the choral chants for the Proper of the Mass."

39. The Church of San Lorenzo certainly made use of *Pluteo* 17.39, which Bandini describes (I, col. 401) as "Homiliarium Diversorum Patrum. Continens Homilias, quae leguntur a Dominica Resurrectionis usque ad Dominicam XXVI. post Pentecosten, et in Festis propriis Sanctorum, et in Communi eorundem." Bandini dates this as "Saec. XI," while recognizing that it includes in another hand a copy of a sermon in praise of San Lorenzo attributed to Saint Ambrose and copied from a work held by the Church of San Lorenzo fuori le Mura in Rome (I, col. 413). Berg, *Studies in Tuscan Illumination*, no. 25, p. 239, states that the "Provenance" of *Pluteo* 17.39 is unknown, describing it as "Tuscan, third-to-fourth quarter, twelfth

if they were not utilized directly in public service. In the case of San Lorenzo, I quickly came upon a theological manuscript that was not to be overlooked. *Pluteo* 18.15, a discussion of the biblical text of Job by Pope Gregory the Great, is dated by Bandini as eleventh century,[40] and by Knut Berg as the second quarter of the twelfth century.[41] It turns out to be one of the few manuscripts listed in the 1393 sacristy inventory, where it is described as "un libro grande di morali di Sancto Gregorio."[42] Provided with beautifully illustrated initial letters, it was at the very least begun by one Stantius for the Ambrosian basilica, from which it was ordered never to be removed, and indeed it never was.[43] This reminds us that such manuscripts might remain in use for centuries in the same ecclesiastical institution. Yet here, too, the specialist is called for, in this case an expert in the history of theology, who might shed light on any of the manuscript's peculiarities, and their meaning for the church that it served.

In the present state of research it is far too early to assess fully the liturgical life of San Lorenzo, especially in a comparative sense. Some of the very few short, recent studies are too confident in their assertions, and even a bit slipshod. It also remains true that liturgists and other specialists must examine medieval liturgical manuscripts to uncover the precise nature of their content, scriptoria, and intended destinations, and their relation to the entire corpus of such sources. I hope, however, to have suggested how an institutional-social historian can attempt to utilize even specialized manuscripts and contribute modestly to such studies, and to have shown that this is a worthwhile way in which to investigate a variety of important themes and issues in medieval religious history—among them the study of a Florentine church.

---

century." For the sermon falsely attributed to Saint Ambrose and its utilization by the Church of San Lorenzo in Florence, see W. M. Bowsky, "'Populus Sancti Laurentii': Care of Souls, a Parish, and a Priest," revised version in *Miscellanea Domenico Maffei*, ed. Antonio Garcia y Garcia and Peter Weimar, 4 vols. (Goldbach, Germany, 1995), 4:147–91 (174–75); now in Bowsky, *La Chiesa*, pp. 91–156; originally published in *Le radici cristiane di Firenze*, pp. 135–81.

40. Bandini, I, col. 468, describes it as "DIVI GREGORII EXPOSITIO IN IOB. . . . B. Gregorii Papae-Expositionis Moralia In Librum Iob Libri XXXV."

41. Berg, *Studies in Tuscan Illumination*, no. 28, p. 240. Fantoni, "La Biblioteca Capitolare," p. 24 n. 37, accepts Berg.

42. Baldasseroni and D'Ancona, "La Biblioteca," p. 182.

43. *Pluteo* 18.15, fol. 1r, written across the bottom of both columns in the same hand as the rest of the folio is "Stantius noster devotus pro redemptione animae suae incepit hunc librum ad honorem dei & Sancti Laurentii ut numquam ab ecclesia eius alienetur." (Cf. Bandini, I, col. 468.) The manuscript is clearly written in several hands, all apparently from the same period.

BIBLIOGRAPHY OF USEFUL WORKS NOT PREVIOUSLY CITED

Dix mille saints. Turnhout, Belgium, 1991. Updated translation of *The Book of Saints,* 8th ed., 1988, by Benedictines of Ramsgate Abbey, with an added liturgical calendar.

Dubois, Jacques, and Jean-Loup Lemaitre. *Sources et méthodes de l'hagiographie médiévale.* Paris, 1993.

Grégoire, Réginald. *Homéliaires médiévaux: Analyse des manuscrits.* Spoleto, 1980.

———. *Les homéliaires du moyen âge: Inventaire et analyse des manuscrits.* Rerum Ecclesiasticarum Documenta. Series major. Fontes 6. Rome, 1966.

Jungmann, Josef A. *Mass of the Roman Rite.* 2 vols. New York, 1950–55.

———. *Pastoral Liturgy.* New York, 1962.

Kaftal, George. *The Iconography of the Saints.* 4 vols. Florence, 1952–65.

Kellner, Karl Adam Heinrich. *Heortology: A History of the Christian Festivals from Their Origin to the Present Day.* London, 1908. Translated from second German edition.

Palazzo, Eric. *Le moyen âge: Des origines au XIIIe siècle.* Histoire de livres liturgiques. Paris, 1993.

Philippart, Guy, ed. *Hagiographies: Histoire internationale de la littérature hagiographique latine et vernaculaire en Occident des origines à 1550.* Vol. 1. Corpus Christianorum, Hagiographies, 1. Turnhout, 1994. To be followed by three volumes of texts, indices, etc.

Reynolds, Roger E. *Law and Liturgy in the Latin Church, 5th–12th Centuries.* Variorum Reprints. Brookfield, Vt., 1994.

Salmon, Pierre. *The Breviary through the Centuries.* Trans. Sister David Mary. Collegeville, Minn., 1962.

———. *L'Office divin au moyen âge: Histoire de la formation du bréviaire du IXe au XVIe siècle.* Paris, 1967.

Tolhurst, John B. L. *Introduction to the English Monastic Breviaries.* London, 1942. Vol. 6, no. 80 of Tolhurst, ed., *The Monastic Breviary of Hyde Abbey.* 6 vols. London, 1932–42. Henry Bradshaw Society, 69–71, 76, 78, 80.

Weiser, Francis X. *Handbook of Christian Feasts and Customs.* New York, 1952.

12 The Florentine Criminal Underworld

The Underside of the Renaissance

John K. Brackett

All the artistic glories of the society of the High Italian Renaissance could not mask the fact that the sixteenth century was a troubled time for Italy and for Florence. The creation of Michelangelo's frescoes in the Sistine Chapel in Rome, particularly the *Last Judgment,* is one example of the creativity and the anxiety that were equally present in Italian society. In Florence, Michelangelo erected his giant sculpture *David* ("Il Gigante") in the piazza Signoria. Benvenuto Cellini's sculpture *Perseus Holding the Head of Medusa* was also put up in Florence in the Loggia next to the signorial palace. Other creations of the artists included the construction of the Uffizi offices designed by Vasari and the elaboration of the Pitti palace into a trend-setting royal residence. And there were many other wonders too numerous to list. But from 1494 until about 1550, Italy was also a battleground for the competing armies of the French king Francis I and Charles V, the Holy Roman Emperor, with most of the peninsula ultimately losing its political independence to the empire. Florence survived these times only marginally better than did some of her sister states, such as Naples and Milan, in that the Florentines, thanks to the maneuvering of Cosimo I de' Medici, escaped direct Spanish rule.[1] Though learning to adopt Spanish black in their dress, the Florentines remained at least formally independent under the ennobled Medici family, a satellite of the Spanish Habsburgs, while the Milanese and the Neapolitans labored under the tutelage of Spanish viceroys. Subsequently, and very quickly, what had been a merchant elite undertook to

---

1. F. Diaz, *Il Granducato di Toscana* (Torino, 1976). The complete story regarding Cosimo's successful endeavors to maintain some independence for Florence is told here. See also G. Spini, *Cosimo I e l'indipendenza del principato mediceo,* rev. ed. (Florence, 1980).

transform itself in the aristocratic image of its conquerors.[2] This social and political restructuring of the elite required a redefinition of its relationship with those at the bottom of the social hierarchy, the working poor and the indigent, who were usually called, simply, "the poor."[3]

In this chapter I wish to explore the style of life of the urban poor and demonstrate how Florentine men of the new aristocracy perceived a supposedly spreading criminality as a threat to decent society. The new elite was composed of merchants and landowners, clerics, artists, and intellectuals; the last of these groups received substantially more training in the humanist vein than the others, although humanist ideas became prevalent in all of the constituent parts of the controlling class in the sixteenth century. A humanism strongly influenced by Aristotle's *Politics* and *Ethics* resulted at Florence in the general acceptance of an imaginary cityscape—of an aristocratic vision of the way Florence should have been—that can be compared with the results of research I have conducted in criminal records in the Florentine State Archive. I have organized these findings so as to provide for the period of the early Grand Duchy, between 1537 and 1609, both a rough social profile of Florentine lawbreakers and a "topography" of crime in the city. The chapter follows Judith Walkowitz and Peter Burke in rejecting the conceptual opposition "representation/reality" that informs most historical work. As my findings show, representation and reality resist separation and, in human affairs, inevitably merge with one another.[4]

Using a variety of sources that I can only wish were available for Renaissance Florence (newspapers especially), Walkowitz, in her book on the Jack the Ripper murders in late-Victorian London, *City of Dreadful Delight*, traces the origin and development of the imagined life of the poor of

---

2. R. B. Litchfield *Emergence of a Bureaucracy: The Florentine Patricians, 1530–1790* (Princeton, N.J., 1986).

3. P. Burke, "Perceiving a Counterculture," in his *The Historical Anthropology of Early Modern Italy* (Cambridge, England, 1987), pp. 63–75, doubts that this topos can ever be completely linked with reality, and I have not done that here. But it cannot be definitively refuted given that to do so would require discounting much documentation. To define poverty is not easy, but J. Henderson, *Piety and Charity in Late Medieval Florence* (Chicago, 1994), gives us a useful definition in three parts: endemic, epidemic, and episodic poverty. The category of endemic poverty included the elderly and the chronically sick; epidemic poverty was composed of those who were plunged below the level of subsistence by severe dearth or outbreaks of epidemic disease; the third category (episodic) was associated with those at the more vulnerable periods of the life cycle, for instance, widows and orphaned children.

4. J. Walkowitz, *City of Dreadful Delight: Narratives of Sexual Danger in Late-Victorian London* (Chicago, 1992). I would like to acknowledge a conceptual debt owed to this book; and also to Burke, "Perceiving a Counterculture."

nineteenth-century London, as it was conceived and discussed by educated middle-class men. Many of these men, employed in government bureaucracies, were not all that different in their education, work, and expectations from the patrician/aristocrats of grand ducal Florence. Of particular interest is their perception of the city as divided between an approved-of upper realm that prospered, while simultaneously it was undermined by the immoral habits of the poor inhabitants of a dark underworld (which nonetheless had its imagined pleasures associated with sin and crime). I hope to demonstrate that Florentine men of the same social class shared much the same vision of the poor in their city, albeit at a much earlier date. For example, no less a figure than Leonardo da Vinci wrote in a letter that, in his conception, the ideal city would be divided into upper and lower realms, inhabited by the rich and the poor, respectively.[5] The area reserved for the poor was infested by disease. In Florence this meant the coexistence of the poor with the plague and syphilis (the plague of prostitutes). Scipione Ammirato, court philosopher to Ferdinando I, was disturbed in 1591 by the sight of beggars on all the street corners and in front of the churches of his beautiful city. He identified the cause of their condition to be their own laziness.[6]

The link between certain kinds of poor people and a dissolute lifestyle was not new in the sixteenth century but can be found, according to Michel Mollat, as early as the beginning of the fourteenth century.[7] Then, the concern was derived from two sources. The first was a group of social outcasts who lived literally on the edges of society in the forests; many of these individuals, having cut all ties to society, were professionally engaged in crime, at war with normal society. The second was new to the Middle Ages: the problem of urban poverty, endemic and episodic, as the cities began to recover economic activity and expand in population. This last problem would become more severe throughout the late Middle Ages and the Renaissance.[8] In Florence, the Ciompi Revolt of 1378, an explosion of discontent by unorganized clothworkers, brought to a head the tension between the poor and oligarchs. The result was the political consolidation of the oligarchy and a growing rift between them and the poor of all types.[9] In their work on Flor-

5. Henderson, *Piety and Charity*, p. 410.
6. E. Cochrane, *Florence in the Forgotten Centuries, 1527–1800* (Chicago, 1973), p. 112.
7. M. Mollat, *The Poor in the Middle Ages: An Essay in Social History*, trans. A. Goldhammer (New Haven, Conn., 1978), "Introduction," pp. i–viii.
8. Ibid.
9. R. F. E. Weissman, *Ritual Brotherhood in Renaissance Florence* (New York, 1982).

entine confraternities, from the Middle Ages to the end of the sixteenth century, both John Henderson and Ronald Weissman point to the periodic suppression of these religious and charitable organizations by the Medici, paranoid that their meetings were actually devoted to political conspiracy rather than religious devotions.[10] In the grand ducal period the Medici moved from suppression to co-optation to reorganization according to occupation, under the auspices of the state. Without state supervision the poor could not be trusted to administer charity to themselves and their neighbors. This suspicion combined with an earlier belief from the Middle Ages, that vagabonds were organized into a highly structured countersociety to feed the sense among the elite that the practices of the poor constituted an organized and deliberate threat to the existence of normal society.

The notion of an organized society of beggars constituting a medieval criminal underworld is as well known as it is controversial. Bronislaw Geremek, in his essay "Lo scoperto di un altro mondo," is the most prominent proponent of the view that such a countersociety did exist in fact.[11] Peter Burke, in his essay "Perceiving a Counterculture," states that it is difficult to connect this literary topos to social reality.[12] On the other hand, it cannot be rejected completely, since that would mean ignoring a great quantity of evidence supporting Geremek. But more about this further ahead. The point is that social stability was far from being a given for intellectuals of the Renaissance influenced by humanism. Especially important was the formative role that the family played in the creation of society in the first place; family was the bedrock of the social order. But, as we know from Leon Battista Alberti's *Della famiglia,* the existence of the family could not itself be taken for granted but had to be carefully and thoughtfully nurtured to survive and prosper. Several factors were key: attention to the proper upbringing of children; good marriages with carefully selected families; and wealth. The lives of the poor, especially the wandering poor, seemed to display none of these necessary qualities. Their world must have been the mirror image of the world of the elite. These two worlds coexisted in Florence in the minds of the patriciate.

As Walkowitz notes, the experience of the city as a whole, as opposed to a relatively confined localism, is a defining aspect of male bourgeois subjec-

---

10. Ibid., pp. 172, 173, and passim; Henderson, *Piety and Charity,* pp. 37, 412, 419, 420–21.

11. B. Geremek, *La stirpe di Caino: L'immagine dei vagabondi e dei poveri nelle letterature europee dal XV al XVII secolo* (Milan, 1988), pp. 55–127.

12. Burke, *Historical Anthropology.*

tivity. It establishes a right to the city, not available to those less advantaged, which speaks of possession and distance. Although Walkowitz wrote about nineteenth-century London, her observations are equally pertinent to Renaissance Florence, a conclusion I hope to demonstrate through an examination of some Florentine histories and one Regolamento discussed later.

The important humanist histories of the Renaissance were preceded by other forms of writing: these were medieval chronicles and diaries, which were peculiarly Florentine. The chronicles recorded in chronological fashion events of interest that had occurred in the city. Some of these, like Dino Compagni's, were extremely accurate and served as sources for Dante and humanist historians; the writers were from Florence's elite or from a slightly lower level of society. All the chronicles were to some extent expressions of Florentine civic pride or apologies for one political faction or the other. Vittore Branca, a historian of Italian literature, notes that the merchant-writers of family diaries discussed themes dominated rhetorically by the myth of *libertas*, that is, Justice, Peace, and Civic Unity in the commune.[13] The idea of *bene comune* was the civic principle justifying charity in the medieval period.[14] These writers, reflecting their merchant training and experience, measured and characterized time, persons, and things. They attempted to foresee and control the future as far as possible, a predominant aspect of the mentality necessary to the conduct of business. For them, the family was the basic unit of society: the state could not exist without it; society itself therefore could not exist.

Even though there is a difference in style and conceptualization of history, chronicler and diarist share common concerns with the humanist historian, of which Leonardo Bruni is the best exemplar. Bruni's *Laudatio Urbis Florentiae*, written in 1403–4, based on a panegyric of Athens written by Aristides, a little-known second-century Greek orator, transformed simple patriotism, as love of one's home, into an ideology. To Bruni, Florence was the modern Athens. In his studies of Aristotle's *Politics* he worked out the tenets of what Hans Baron has identified as "civic humanism": the superiority of the active to the contemplative life, of wealth over poverty, of matrimony to celibacy, of political to the monastic vocation. Bruni put these views into practice: he gave up his clerical benefice and got married, he accumulated wealth, and he held high and important political offices.

13. D. J. Wilcox, *The Development of Florentine Humanist Historiography in the Fifteenth Century* (Cambridge, Mass., 1969); V. Branca, ed., *Mercanti scrittori: Ricordi nella Firenze tra Medioevo e Rinascimento* (Milan, 1986).

14. Henderson, *Piety and Charity*, pp. 411–12.

These writers, and others like them, wrote and acted as though Florence belonged to men of their ilk. They were active citizens in a republic because they had a stake in the welfare of the state; the res publica really was their "public thing." This view held in the sixteenth century and beyond, even as the shape of the polity altered radically.

Sixteenth-century history writers of interest include Machiavelli and the equally great Francesco Guicciardini, along with lesser lights such as Benedetto Varchi, Scipione Ammirato, Luca Landucci, and Giuliano de' Ricci. All were of the elite class except Landucci, who was the owner of an apothecary and had no humanist education. It is the *Cronaca* of Giuliano de' Ricci that best serves my purposes. Although he aspired to produce an important history of his city, Ricci did not share the intellectual ability of his maternal grandfather, Niccolò Machiavelli; nor did he have access to the documents and people who could have served him as sources; thus, he was not able to compose the high-level history of Florence that Niccolò produced. Born in 1543, Giuliano demonstrated a lively intelligence that seemed to suit him for study. He took up philosophy, astronomy, astrology, and music. His intellect was better formed, then, than those of other writers of his social level—Landucci, who had no intellectual training, or the principal author of the anonymous chronicle published by Carlo Morbio, who was a cleric and wrote primarily on religious matters—but by 1573 Giuliano was forced by family circumstances to give up his intellectual ambitions and take over his father's business. Thus, his *Cronaca* duplicates the immediacy of life in Florence as seen from a shop in the heart of the city that is captured by Landucci, but Ricci is better able to conceptualize and generalize his impressions. For example, when he discusses the rapid deaths from illness of three Florentines on 7 October 1569, he attributes these deaths to the peculiar location and climate of Florence, where the air penetrates the body easily, and the quality of that air is humid, caused by the Arno and trapped by the surrounding mountains. These sorts of deaths occur rarely elsewhere but frequently in Florence. Giuliano proceeds to recommend that, to protect their health, Florentines discharge their various commissions and duties during times of the day when the weather is best, before sundown, well after sunrise.[15] Ricci is referring to the health effects of the humoral theory of Hippocrates and Empedocles, summarized by Galen and common knowledge in Renaissance medicine.

15. Giuliano de' Ricci, *Cronaca, 1532–1606*, ed. G. Sapori (Milan and Naples, 1972), pp. 18–19.

Like other members of his class and generation who experienced the popular revolution of 1527–30, or who carried about with them the legacy of that period or other similar rebellions against the oligarchy, Ricci despised the poorest of Florentines—calling them the "popolaccio."[16] His book is filled with their misdeeds, along with his assessment of the more or less competent attempts of police officials and criminal courts to apprehend and punish wrongdoers. Giuliano was, for example, initially supportive of Lorenzo Corboli, who between 1560 and 1587 was secretary of the Eight on Public Safety (Otto di guardia), the chief criminal magistracy of the city. Corboli was for years a fine director of the court and its police until he succumbed to greed and became involved with a corrupt lawyer in a scheme to provide false evidence of innocence for a price to suspects who appeared before his own court.[17] On the whole, Giuliano had a favorable impression of the reign of the first Medici Grand Duke, Cosimo; an unfavorable view on his successor, Francesco; and a positive assessment of the third Grand Duke, Ferdinando. The honesty and effectiveness of officials in maintaining public order in the city reflected the interest of the princes in establishing and maintaining good government.[18]

Referring to book 4 of Aristotle's *Politics*, Giuliano affirms that the causes of the fall of states are often to be found in small things.[19] He states:

> Having learned from my reading of histories, from that which Aristotle wrote in his Fourth Book, and from experience that most times the causes of the changes of States, and particularly of Republics, have had weak beginnings, and the origin of these changes has been something frivolous and light, for this reason I do not hold it inconvenient to recount minutely what during the previous year has happened in the city of Genoa.[20]

16. According to G. Sapori, ibid., p. xxi.

17. Ibid., pp. 478–98.

18. J. K. Brackett, *Criminal Justice and Crime in Late Renaissance Florence, 1537–1609* (Cambridge, England, 1992), "Conclusion," pp. 139–43.

19. In book 4 of the *Politics*, Aristotle developed his catalog of regimes.

20. Ricci, *Cronaca*, p. 59: "Addì 4 di agosto 1473. Havendo io dalla lettione delle historie, da quello che scrive Aristotile nel ¼ della politica et dalla esperientia, conosciuto manifestamente che il più delle volte le cagioni delle mutationi delli Stati, et particolarmente delle Republiche hanno hauto deboli principii, et l'origine di esse mutationi è stata cosa frivola et leggieri, per tanto non ho per inconveniente il raccontare minutamente quello che da uno anno in qua è seguìto nella città di Genova. . . ." Ricci goes on to discuss in detail the problems of Genoa, which the Florentine followed with great interest, given the intervention of the great powers in Italy. The issues were related to the factional conflict between the Adorno and Fregoso clans and to laws passed by the Genoese government that extinguished certain fam-

It is for this reason, namely, the potential inherent in even small events, that Ricci includes the criminal notices that appear throughout his book. For example, he chooses to write extensively on 30 December 1573 about a German counterfeiter because this activity was a "thing of moment."[21] On another occasion he notes the executions of two thieves, some highwaymen (*latrocinii*), and purse snatchers. Also mentioned are wounds received by the gentleman Claudio Caetani.[22] It is important to mention that Giuliano was not the only history writer to include mention of assaults, murders, robberies, executions, and so forth in his work. Luca Landucci does the same for his diary of the period 1450–1516, for example. But it is Giuliano who is able to conceptualize a link to an important theme in Aristotle's *Politics*, a central text to educated Florentines writing on the life of their city, from Bruni to Machiavelli and Guicciardini. I mentioned earlier the importance attached to the observation of small things, which could have great consequences in the life of states, but there was another lesson to be learned from the Philosopher. Although Guicciardini and Machiavelli both ignored crime in their histories of Florence and of Italy, Guicciardini shared the Aristotelian citation with Ricci because it supported their common view on the superior didactic value of experience over pure intellection. Experience, gained as the result of observation of the smallest details, demonstrated the uniqueness of human events and was thus a better guide to foreseeing and controlling the future, as far as that was possible. Giuliano believed that his observations on crime and the reasons for their commission were important as a key indication of the status and well-being of his city.

For Ricci, the cityscape of sixteenth-century Florence included more than the construction of the Uffizi or the pristinization of the Ponte Vecchio as a home for goldsmiths and jewelers, more than the elaboration of the Pitti palace and the building of lesser palaces. The city also had its dark side as a home for alien "Others," predators on decent people, careless of the consequences of their actions. Ricci records the murder of Giulio di Giovanbattista Giovanni, occurring in the night of 29 August 1586, while he was returning home. Four persons were responsible, but only one was caught and hanged as an assassin (*sicario*). This had been a murder for hire.[23] Giuliano wrote in February 1586 that "one finds always and at every time men

---

ily names, forcing families admitted to the governing class to amalgamate against their will.

21. Ibid., p. 71.
22. Ibid., p. 76.
23. Ibid., pp. 497–98.

who for the smallest price put themselves at every risk and danger." One group of men, stealing stones from a construction site at Boboli, caused a poor workman to be buried alive. Others "for little money went wounding and killing this one or that one."[24] These people did not stay confined in their neighborhoods but circulated through the city's arteries committing murders for hire, thefts from persons and from shops, and assaults in the various piazzas and streets of the city. In February 1584 he wrote that many violent arguments, disorders, fights, and murders continually occurred in Florence. The new head of the police was diligent in tracking down the malefactors, executing one and wounding another after finding them in the countryside.[25]

The tumults caused by these killers for hire were joined by the violent intimidations of Florentine citizens that were carried out by the bravos of nobles from other states who resided in the city under the protection of the Grand Dukes. Ricci lamented the consequences for the life of the city when especially violent crimes went unsolved or unpunished. On 22 December 1574 he wrote, "Niccolaio di . . . Carducci was wounded and died without it being known by whom or for what reason: a common thing in this city, in which at present there occur many and frequent homicides, woundings, and insults, and never is the criminal found or punished."[26] The peace and order of the city (state) depended on the Grand Dukes and their functionaries finding and punishing those who committed crimes against persons and property; that is, leaders must fulfill their proper governing role to execute justice. After all, as Giovanni Della Casa, sixteenth-century writer on manners and morals, concluded in his *Trattato degli uffici communi tra gli amici superiori e inferiori,* the poor were given to a certain *riottosità.*[27] Another duty of political leaders toward the poor was dispensing aid to those who deserved it and banishing or otherwise punishing those miscreants who did not, who, in effect, stole aid from the legitimate poor.

In the seventeenth century, other concerned elite citizens allied with the Medici Grand Dukes to voice their concern about the numbers, habits, and

24. Ibid., p. 459.
25. Ibid., pp. 421–22.
26. Ibid, p. 137: "Addì 22 [di dicembre 1574] fu ferito et morto Niccolaio di . . . Carducci senza sapersi da chi né per che conto: cosa solita in questa città, nella quale al presente occorre assai et spessi homicidii ferite et insulti, né mai si truova o è gastigato il delinquente."
27. P. Pissavino, "I poveri nel pensiero politico italiano tra Cinque e Seicento," in *La città e i poveri: Milano e le terre lombarde dal Rinascimento all'età Spagnuola,* ed. D. Zerdin (Milano, 1995), pp. 151–89.

appearance of the poor. By way of providing context, from the late fifteenth century into the sixteenth century and seventeenth, to about 1650, Florence and Tuscany witnessed a series of economic problems, famine, intermixed with a severe episode of the plague in 1527 and 1633, and an economic depression in 1619–22. During this period the poor-relief system also experienced disarray and reorganization. In 1540, amid a serious famine, Cosimo I appointed Francesco Cavalcanti and Francesco Inghirami as commissioners and providers of the begging poor, with broad powers to order, provide, and manage benefits, accommodation, and subvention of these poor.[28] These men were both members of the Compagnia di Santa Maria della Misericordia, the city's chief agency battling the plague of 1527–28. They were to administer the rationing of food supplies in the 1540 famine. Both Cosimo I and Francesco I considered providing for the needs of the poorest citizens to be an indispensable justification for their rule,[29] but this ad hoc approach was insufficient. The traditional system of relief supplied by confraternities and hospitals was supplemented in 1542 by centralization of the state's hospitals, through a reorganization of the old and wealthy confraternity of Santa Maria del Bigallo.[30] The hope was that greater efficiency in expenditures would be the result, but this reform also proved unsuccessful, as Medici dukes were never able to sufficiently grasp control of the many hospitals in the territory outside of Florence itself to produce either this efficiency or hoped-for cash surpluses.

By 1621, the consequences of failed reform had matured. Highly visible poverty convinced Florentines that at last they must attempt what was for them a new solution to the problem of large numbers of homeless and occupation-less persons from the countryside. They turned to the construction of a workhouse to enclose the poor away from decent society, but more about this later. Along with the resident poor, the wandering poor thronged the city streets and church entrances from the early sixteenth century into the seventeenth. The visibility of these desperate poor was considered by the city's elite to be a stain upon the Florentine honor (and Florentine honor was special to men with views as diverse as Leonardo

28. N. Terpstra, "Competing Visions of the State and Social Welfare: The Medici Dukes, the Bigallo Magistrates, and Local Hospitals in Sixteenth-Century Tuscany," *Renaissance Quarterly* 54 (2001): 1319–55.

29. Ibid., p. 8.

30. N. Terpstra, "Confraternities and Public Charity Modes of Civic Welfare in Early Modern Italy," in *Confraternities and Catholic Reform in Italy, France, and Spain*, ed. J.P. Donnelly and M.W. Maher (Kirksville, Mo., 1999), pp. 97–121.

Bruni and Savonarola), and thus had to be removed.[31] In addition, the sixteenth century was a time when writers like Erasmus of Rotterdam and Giovanni della Casa were elucidating standards of proper dress and behavior for the aristocracy. As Norbert Elias wrote in *The Civilizing Process*, his pioneering analysis of manners and behavior in Europe, these standards defined a self-image bound up in the new term, *civilité*, which was in the process of emerging from 1530 and after.[32] Erasmus wrote that bodily carriage, gestures, dress, and facial expressions constituted outward behavior that expressed the inner or whole person. Excellent persons sometime needed proper instruction to avoid behavior improper for their status. While a peasant may wipe his nose on his cap or coat, a sausage maker on his elbow or arm, a decent person should use a cloth, preferably while turning away.[33] Being demonstrated above all were self-control, discipline, and composure in thought and action—quite a change from medieval standards for the aristocracy, according to which emotionalism and lack of self-restraint governed behavior. Elias attributes the new values to the victory of court society and the political demands of the centralized state.

In Florence, the Medici certainly did emphasize restraint and proper behavior for members of the new aristocracy, discouraging if not outright prohibiting them from dueling, for example.[34] Cosimo I was ambivalent about dueling. His was a new ruling house only a generation removed from its mercantile past, and chivalry and the code of honor were an essential

---

31. D. Lombardi, *Povertà maschile, povertà femminile: L'ospedale dei mendicanti nella Firenze dei Medici* (Bologna, 1988), pp. 9–10.

32. N. Elias, *The Civilizing Process: The History of Manners and State Formation and Civilization*, trans. E. Jephcott (Oxford, 1978), pp. 42–3.

33. Ibid., p. 44.

34. D. Weinstein, "Fighting or Flyting? Verbal Dueling in Mid–Sixteenth Century Italy," in *Crime and Disorder in Renaissance Italy*, ed. T. Dean and K. J. P. Lowe (Cambridge, England, 1994), pp. 204–20. Weinstein writes that the Italians created the duel, reworking medieval forms to do so. Italian masters taught fencing to Europe's gentlemen and developed the perfect weapon for it, the rapier. Even though an act of violence, the duel was elevated above the street brawl as an affair of gentlemen over honor, a concern, in the minds of aristocrats, worlds removed from the preoccupations of the poor. The duel was a means of resolving a private, moral dispute. These were not affairs of wild passion (those could be left to commoners) but were structured by rules and rituals. There is not much evidence to show that a great number of duels really took place. Weinstein's article, in fact, deals with verbal dueling where an actual physical encounter certainly did not take place. See also F. R. Bryson, *The Sixteenth-Century Italian Duel: A Study in Renaissance Social History* (Chicago, 1938); and now D. Weinstein, *The Captain's Concubine: Love, Honor, and Violence in Renaissance Tuscany* (Baltimore, 2000).

part of the princely image. But Cosimo was also in the process of shaping a "service nobility" so that some restraint among them was called for.[35] Florentines remained, of course, very concerned about honor, and this meant recourse to violence, even though it might not be permitted in duels. The records of the Eight on Public Safety are replete with examples of violent, informal confrontations between patrician/nobles in the streets and squares of the city.[36] While the transformation to self-restraint was far from complete in the sixteenth century, that period did mark a watershed in aristocratic self-concept and in behavior: sixteenth-century Florence was a far better behaved society without the factionalism of the medieval period. Moral concerns, the underlying principle of self-restraint, played a key role in this change.

Michel Mollat wrote that, by the sixteenth century, poverty had become associated with sin, a totally new development.[37] Appearance and behavior now marked both groups, rich and poor, and associated morality and immorality, respectively, as an inner quality identifiable by outward dress and behavior. It does not take much imagination to understand with what horror the poor—many physically deformed by disease or hunger, dirty and dressed in tattered clothing—must have been perceived by the Florentine elite of this age, and why the latter wanted these contaminating indigents out of sight. Nor do we have to strain to understand how the new nobility could downplay its violence by clothing it somewhat in ritual forms and basing it on the idea of the defense of honor. The poor did not and could not possess honor; uncontrolled violence was associated with the undisciplined, immoral poor, who were, as Aristotle wrote, rebellious in spirit.

Focusing on how elite Florentines conceptualized the problem of the poor, what was retained from the medieval period, and what was new in the late Renaissance? Social crisis and transformation are two issues that were new, as was the growing association of poverty with sin and wealth with morality. A new method of dealing with the poor was also being created in many places in Europe, where institutions of enclosure were being developed to treat the poor. For Florence, Daniela Lombardi has already more than competently illuminated the development of a workhouse (Pia casa dei mendicanti).[38] Suffice it to say that the Florentines, much later than residents of many other cities in Italy and France, established this institution,

35. Weinstein, "Fighting or Flyting?" p. 218.
36. Brackett, *Criminal Justice and Crime*, p. 102.
37. Mollat, *The Poor in the Middle Ages*, p. 297.
38. Lombardi, *Povertà maschile*.

which quickly came to enclose only women. Workhouses seem to have grown out of the medieval idea of specialization in hospitals, that is, targeting certain groups of the poor for treatment and therapy in one place.[39] In Italy, new hospitals had been proposed and constructed as early as 1400 in Milan;[40] the Visconti had been the first to order enclosure of the poor in already existing hospitals in 1396. These institutions brought honor to the cities funding them, really a continuation of the medieval Christian requirement that legitimate rulers tended to the needs of the poor, but doing so in the late Renaissance meant subjecting them to a regime of reform. Focusing on Florence, according to an undated and anonymous Regolamento included in the files of the Pratica Segreta (1531–43), a hospital was first proposed to serve four types of poor persons: the crippled, the blind, orphans, and, controversially, the unemployed.[41] Florentine residents would receive shelter, food, and spiritual assistance aimed at helping them reform, while nonnatives would receive alms and be sent on their way. This proposal was rejected by Cosimo I as too costly; it should also be noted that, in this period of time, no further proposals for dealing with the poor included provision for the able-bodied unemployed. Nicholas Terpstra believes that Cavalcanti and Inghirami were likely authors of this document; both men were among the first five appointees to the reformed Bigallo.[42]

From the documents establishing the Pia casa dei mendicanti years later, we learn that Florentines continued to be disturbed by the numbers ands ragged appearance of the poor. Many came to the city during plague, famine, or dearth seeking assistance unavailable in their villages in the countryside. At times like these, Henderson's categories of endemic, episodic, and epidemic poverty converged to create a real crisis. Records indicate that the city housed about one thousand persons in temporary shelters, yet officials complained that their streets remained just as clogged by this unsavory, begging mass as before. Since not all these persons were proper subjects for enclosure, aid was extended only to women and young girls, leaving the men and boys to shift for themselves.[43] Any male not obviously crippled was deemed able to support himself.

Discrimination had been present in medieval poor relief, in Europe generally and in Florence specifically, as we learn from Michel Mollat and John

39. Mollat, *The Poor in the Middle Ages*, p. 285.
40. Ibid.
41. ASF, Pratica Segreta, 184 (F).
42. Terpstra, "Competing Visions," pp. 1327–28.
43. Lombardi, *Povertà maschile*, p. 89.

Henderson.[44] Those who could work, that is, able-bodied men, should work or be made to work; it was a sin to aid them, since such assistance amounted to theft of alms from the legitimate poor, at the same time that the alms-giver was defrauded. Such men were parasites on the body of society.

While many able-bodied male poor were left on their own, continuing to be deemed the illegitimate poor as they had been in the Middle Ages, women were another matter. Humanists like Leon Battista Alberti had established as a feature of the culture of Renaissance Italy that the proper place for women was in the home, under the authority of a man—father, husband, or uncle. The motive was to achieve male control of female sexuality; women on their own would entice men into the commission of extramarital sex, leading themselves and ultimately their society to corruption. Prostitutes, for example, as the most blatant example of such women, were controlled by the Officials of Decency (Onestà), instituted at the beginning of the fif-teenth century for their control. As the legend of Saint Nicholas demon-strated, even noble but poor women could face the danger of falling into prostitution because of their poverty, without some intervention of society.

The female homeless now posed the same kind of threat; all women posed an actual or latent sexual threat to men. To help blunt it in the sev-enteenth century, educated and well-to-do Florentine men, like Francesco Rondinelli, also extended temporary shelter in houses that they owned to women and girls whom they found wandering the streets near nightfall. Providing shelter to young girls and lone women was not new but contin-ued from the medieval period as a targeted form of poor relief, extended primarily by hospitals established for that purpose. This was a civic service performed to prevent these women and girls from resorting to prostitution to support themselves, bringing further dishonor on the city. The work-house came to focus exclusively on the enclosure and reform of women and girls as a hoped-for permanent solution. In the medieval period, in convents such as those of the Convertite,[45] a regime of prayer had constituted the program. But in the late Renaissance the regime of the Pia casa dei mendi-canti added work as a new element along with prayer and sermonizing.

---

44. Mollat, *The Poor in the Middle Ages*, p. 134; Henderson, *Piety and Charity*, p. 242. For both writers, discrimination is evident in positions taken by the church from about the beginning of the fourteenth century. The issue, of course, was who deserved assistance and who did not. The poor lived in "humility," both in the spiri-tual sense and in the sense of experiencing the contempt of society.

45. S. Cohen, *The Evolution of Women's Asylums since 1500: From Refuges for Ex-Prostitutes to Shelters for Battered Women* (New York, 1992).

Sexual danger, represented by the presence in the city of numbers of un-controlled women and girls, was an important element in the conceptual-ization of the legitimate resident or wandering poor that was conjoined to the presumed criminal propensities and corruptive influences of poor but able-bodied men who chose not to work. Here, two problem groups from the Middle Ages came together: the wandering poor, continually viewed as a threat to social order, and not without reason; and the urban working poor, who appear at the beginning of the fourteenth century.[46] By the be-ginning of the sixteenth century, at least in Florence, dearth, political un-rest, disease, and economic difficulty brought these groups together within the city gates but not for the first time. The late medieval period had also witnessed the same phenomenon.

New in the late Renaissance were the social and political context, the changing self-image of the patriciate/aristocracy, and the depths of the po-litical crises affecting the state, beginning with the death of Lorenzo de' Medici in 1492. In 1494, the invasion of Italy by Charles V set off a series of changes in the regime, first leading to the exile of the Medici from Flor-ence and the initiation (1494–98) of the Savonarolan period. During the post-Savonarolan period (1498–1512), other opponents of the Medici ruled. The period 1512 to 1527 saw the Medici restored; then, between 1527 and 1530, the last republic came and went. From 1530 on, the Medici were re-stored and ennobled as supporters of the Spanish Habsburgs. Finally, in 1537, radical change in the very configuration of the polity and society is confirmed as Duchy becomes Grand Duchy. Within the context of this po-litical instability, the threat that the poor could pose to the social and politi-cal order, their *riotossità*, was of great concern. It had been demonstrated by the Ciompi Revolt of 1378; suspicion of it evidenced in the periodic sup-pressions of the confraternities into the sixteenth century. The humanists expressed disdain in writing about the poor. For Donato Giannotti, for ex-ample, the *plebe* had no value to the city other than the physical labor that they performed.[47] According to the humanists, then, the poor had to be iden-tified and controlled through some regime of discipline, preferably work, their only legitimate function in society. Without discipline, even a society that appeared prosperous and well ordered on the surface could suddenly collapse because its moral foundations had been eroded from below.

This fear was pervasive among elite Florentines, and from Pissavino we

46. Mollat, *The Poor in the Middle Ages*, pp. 165–71.
47. Pissavino, "I poveri," pp. 164–65.

learn why. Giovan Francesco Lottini, an experienced Florentine public official writing during the Counter Reform period, paraphrased Aristotle's *Politics:* "One thing is certain, that if one ever has fear of the poor, while one might value their labors, and as long as they are able to purchase bread, even though being followers of low thoughts, and being always occupied by their small incomes, [it is because] they do not know, nor do they have the time to think of big things." [48] Lottini found in Aristotle examples that contradicted the usual citations locating rebelliousness in the poor: it was the great and ambitious whose actions disturbed the tranquillity of the state. Similar sentiments are also found in *Republica fiorentina*, composed during the last Republic (1527–30) by the Florentine humanist Donato Giannotti.[49] The poor, as opposed to the rich and the *mediocri*, have no place in the governance of the city, but the city only benefits from their physical labor. Consequently, the poor were of concern when they were not able to work or provide for their subsistence; then they were subject to manipulation by the ambitious in their schemes against the state.

Two views of the danger to the state posed by the poor coexisted: either the innate rebelliousness of the poor was a danger, or their gullibility could, when their subsistence was threatened, make them unwitting pawns of some politically ambitious but unscrupulous faction in its schemes against the state. On the other hand, Francesco Guicciardini, serving the Medici at the time of the transition from republic to principate, wrote in his *Ricordi* that the poor were "an insane animal, full of a thousand errors, of thousands of confusions, without taste, without refinement [*diletto*], without stability." [50] The intensity of these opinions only grew as it became clear that the poor could not be completely hidden away, or perhaps even finally controlled. Lottini credited the fiscal policies of Medicean absolutism—falling upon those people who could not find work, or those who found work but were still unable to make ends meet—with pushing them to revolt against authority. Writing well toward the end of the sixteenth century, Scipione Ammirato, another Florentine humanist and servant of the Medici, used words similar to those of Guicciardini in describing the poor as a *"canaglia"* (group of persons given to evil deeds) and as "vile plebs," who were a threat to the good order of the state. They remained a fearful alien presence in the midst of the city, a constant threat to society, as an unorganized mass, which, unrestrained, gave birth to a well-organized criminal underworld.

48. Ibid., p. 164.
49. Ibid. Donato Giannotti, *Republica fiorentina*, ed. G. Silvano (Geneva, 1990).
50. Pissavino, "I poveri," p. 165.

Thus were joined two images. The first was composed of the stereotypical picture of the world of medieval rogues, believed to be structured in a highly organized underworld described in police and literary documents for the elite. This criminal underworld became connected to the world of the poor in the city, which actually was becoming more completely segregated from the society of decent persons, socially, spiritually, and physically. Leonardo da Vinci had conceived the division of the ideal city, cordoned off into a healthy upper city for the elite and an unhealthy lower city for the poor. Earlier I have discussed the social and spiritual separation inherent in the idea of *civilité*. Sixteenth-century Florence was also a city in the process of increasing the actual physical separation of rich from poor. Samuel Cohn Jr. has written that, in the aftermath of the Ciompi Revolt, the residences of the poor were increasingly located on the outskirts of the central city.[51] Similarly, in the heart of the city, certain groups of the poor were segregated from the rest of society. These included some of the most suspect poor: women denounced as prostitutes to the *Onestà*, who were forced to live in specific streets of the central city that had acquired an unsavory reputation.[52] Also at the heart of the town were found the *Convertite* for the reform of prostitutes; the convents that accepted unmarried women, enclosing them to keep them from prostitution; and the prison of the Stinche and various other city jails. What we see is a city divided conceptually into high and low, moral and immoral, but not so in spatial terms. (Leonardo's was, after all, an ideal city.) Physically, the city was divided into outer and inner, center and periphery, but the center was itself also segregated into islands of honor and dishonor, where the dishonorable were to be enclosed away from view, walled away from the rest of society while they underwent reform. The problem, then, was how to make the poor invisible actually in the physical sense and, when in view, docile in their behavior, tamed as far as possible by work and religion.

Thus far I have discussed both perception and practice; now I would like to give, in outline form, some idea of the problem of crime in Florence through the presentation of a social profile of violators and a topography of violations.[53] Modern attempts to understand crime often focus on the connection between age, sex, marital status, occupation, and socioeconomic

51. S. K. Cohn Jr., *The Laboring Classes in Renaissance Florence* (New York, 1980).

52. J. K. Brackett, "The Florentine *Onestà* and the Control of Prostitution, 1403–1680," *Sixteenth Century Journal* 24 (1993): 273–300.

53. Brackett, *Criminal Justice and Crime*. Most, if not all, of these conclusions come from my book. The book's penultimate chapter briefly summarizes my con-

position, and the incidence of specific crime. My information permits only partial answers to some of these questions.[54]

The sex of those convicted of crimes was overwhelmingly male. Women did commit some violations, but they were few in number. Incidents in which women assaulted each other can be found, but there are also examples in which they were involved in assaults on policemen or court messengers who had been sent to arrest their close male relatives for nonpayment of debts. At such times they were not averse to swinging a frying pan while a husband, brother, or father escaped out the back door. Women were also convicted of giving aid and comfort to banished relatives; they were naturally convicted of sexual violations such as adultery—men were not, however—and fornication. Women were exclusively implicated in cases of infanticide. Role expectations were different for women: it was not expected, nor was it desirable, that women engage in aggressive acts for any reason; to do so was to threaten male identity.

It is difficult to formulate conclusions about the marital status of women or men, since this information is of more interest to modern researchers than it was to Florentine officials. Unmarried men or men temporarily separated from their wives may have been more prone to commit misdeeds. Certainly, soldiers and noble exiles were a source of problems, as well, unrestrained by the obligations of family and work. But married men were also involved in thefts and assaults.

The records often list occupations. My research reveals ninety-four categories of occupations and titles—noble, clerical, and bureaucratic— demonstrating that violators spanned the Florentine social spectrum. But prosecutions did not occur on an equal basis: the Eight seems to have been reluctant to move against other aristocrats without the sanction of the Grand Dukes. The court did, however, prosecute some patricians; others, especially those close to the circle of the Medici, could be subject to extra-judicial punishment by the chief of police (bargello) acting on orders from the Grand Dukes. Of course, the lurid misdeeds of the royal family, real and imagined, were not punished by any court on earth. On the whole, it was the poor—not just the marginal poor—who were most often hauled before city tribunals by the police.

Evidence from the records of the Eight on Public Safety permits the construction of a topography for seven types of Florentine criminality. For

clusions about crimes in Florence as the result of my research on the city's criminal justice system.

54. Ibid., pp. 133–38.

murder and other forms of violent death, and also for assault, theft, sexual crimes, property damage, gambling, and the sale of stolen goods, it is possible to ascertain typical locations and circumstances.

Among family members, murder and unintended death occurred most commonly in the home, where these acts were often the result of accumulated tensions. Murders that arose from quarrels among friends and acquaintances most often occurred in or near public places—taverns, places of work, and in streets and city squares. Assaults happened in the same areas. These places were the centers and the limits of the social networks of the Florentine world of the poor.

Thefts occurred in markets, churches and monasteries, homes, and hotel rooms and from businesses. Interestingly, in the city, these acts were seldom accompanied by violence of any sort. Sexual crimes sometimes occurred in the home of the aggressor but much more often in that of the victim, and occasionally in churches (a favorite trysting place of gay men). Property damage was a form of insult, a public gesture, visited on homes and businesses by the enemies of their owners. These actions took the form of throwing rocks against doors or windows, accompanied by shouts; of breaking down doors; of placing sets of animal horns and excrement over a doorway. Gambling occurred everywhere in Florence, in public and in private. Casinos catered to the well-to-do, while the homes of prostitutes often sated the gaming spirit of the poor. However, the average man seems to have preferred to gamble at work, after working hours, or in public near the city gates, which were unguarded at night, or along the banks of the Arno, also at night. Taverns were another location, but a less than desirable one, since they were susceptible to unexpected visits from the police. Stolen property could be disposed of locally in the shop of a less than scrupulous merchant or in the establishments of secondhand-clothes dealers or pawnbrokers, who were not always careful to check the pedigree of items offered to them for resale.

There were some professional criminals in Florence, who associated loosely together. Most notorious was a coterie of professional assassins. As we have seen, Giuliano de' Ricci wrote that the sixteenth-century city was the home of many killers for hire. A second element was composed of registered, professional prostitutes, whom we must be careful to distinguish from the wealthy courtesans who catered to the nobles of court society. The homes of registered prostitutes were often the sites of brawls among the women's regular *amici* that were motivated by jealousy. Gambling was a major pastime in these residences, and the disposal of stolen property given as gifts or in payment for sexual services also occurred. Florence also hosted professional gamblers who operated casinos. This was a continuation of the practice in the medieval period, when the gambling of professional *barattieri* was protected by law, and games of chance were regulated and taxed by the commune, much like prostitution, rather than prohibited outright.[55] Professional thieves were also present; most were constantly on the move, passing through Florence as they pursued their trade.

This brief topography demonstrates that, despite the presence of only a few professional criminals in Florence, there was no underworld, located in one or several places, and little in the way of elaborate structure or organization to their activities. Violence, even murder, could occur anywhere but was most disturbing to people like Ricci when committed at night by unknown persons. Professional thieves did tend to live briefly in hotels or even hospitals for the wandering poor because of the transient nature of their trade. But these types did not commit most thefts. Stolen goods could be disposed of with the aid of sellers of used cloths or in the shops of a variety of merchants who were not too concerned about the origins of goods that persons might bring to them for quick sale. Prostitution and gambling were often linked and located in specific locales within the city, in state-run whorehouses, the homes of prostitutes, and taverns. But the poor were also found gambling in places of work after working hours. For historians to define this situation as constituting an "underworld," however, is to go too far in accepting the structured mental landscape of the Florentine elite.

This mental landscape was composed of a grid structured by the interweaving of several ideas and images. The social and political ideas of humanists, influenced by Aristotle's *Politics*, about the place in society and the nature of the poor were very important to this merchant elite. But there were different understandings about the role of the regime in roiling the instability of the poor. Humanists went with the ancients in blaming unrest on a poorly run regime; less educated types reversed this understanding, blaming political instability on the undisciplined poor. An emerging concept of *civilité* is clearly discernible among the Florentine aristocracy. Honor and morality were completely ascribed to the elite, identifiable not only by their dress but also by their restrained and refined behavior. Conversely, the poor looked and behaved the part, building on the spiritual contempt directed at them beginning in the fourteenth century. In addition, a kind of class consciousness of the city's history (the memory of the

---

55. On the public regulation of gambling in Florence in the Middle Ages, see the essays reprinted in L. Zdekauer, *Il gioco d'azzardo nel medioevo italiano*, ed. G. Ortalli (Florence, 1993), esp. pp. 17–92. On prostitution in the fifteenth century see M. S. Mazzi, *Prostitute e lenoni nella Firenze del Quattrocento* (Milan, 1991).

Ciompi and similar revolts), experience in the streets and churches of the city, and class interest also played their part in creating this grid, not only organizing reality but also actually creating it. For example, women appearing in public seemed both endangered and a source of sexual danger to men in the streets, as Walkowitz argued was true for nineteenth-century London. Women were not and should not be autonomous; thus they were the bearers of meaning pertinent to their gender, not its creators. Further, the symbolism associated with the prostitute identified her as the incarnation of female sexual danger, thrown up from the very dregs of society. In the sixteenth century, they were to be enclosed or segregated and marked by particular dress, a yellow scarf or veil. Of course, many men liked to flutter around this danger, like moths around a candle. But the sixteenth century also witnessed the negative association between whorehouses and syphilis, which made prostitution and its environs seem even more sinful, since acquisition of the disease was undeniable, visible proof of sinful behavior. Poor men and women (potential or actual prostitutes) were to be banished from the city's better streets and neighborhoods, from its public squares, from its churches, monasteries, and convents—poor women and girls in workhouses, prostitutes hidden in habitations located in the worst streets of the city's various neighborhoods, the men expelled through the city gates. It remains only to explain the actualization of this mental image.

Daniela Lombardi argues that the *classe dirigente*, many of whose members were entrepreneurs in the cloth industry, absorbed the image of the rogue, a medieval literary topos resident in the collective unconscious, and applied it to the poor because they feared that their pool of specialized labor might withdraw itself completely from their industry. The combination of withholding aid while prohibiting begging, and castigating the unemployed as lazy good-for-nothings who lived immoral lives, endangering their city in the process, amounted to a self-serving strategy to discipline in other ways those whom they could not discipline in the marketplace.[56] The idea of a collective unconscious as repository for a literary topos is really impossible of historical proof. We need a more satisfactory solution.

Peter Burke writes that to reject outright the idea of an organized world of beggars means also to reject too much evidence attesting to the existence of organized begging. But Burke cannot completely accept the idea as reality, either. He rejects even the attempt to squeeze the idea into categories of "fact" or "fiction." Instead, he outlines a process of "culturally stereotyped

56. Lombardi, *Povertà maschile*, pp. 129–33.

perceptions" at work on the general level, a process of simplifying a complex reality into a story occurs that can then be assimilated to the interests of the listener or reader. So, information on different kinds of beggars is simplified into the image of the rogue, and fairly informal organization of some categories of beggars is also simplified into a formal hierarchy. To understand the point of this stereotyping, historians must look at who is doing it and why. I agree that this is a simple process that works for human beings broadly and on many levels. Applied to the situation in late Renaissance Florence, one can see how stereotyping worked for groups of the elite mentioned at the outset of this chapter by identifying their interests. Businessmen were concerned to control the labor force and keep costs down. Seeing themselves as having become rich through their own efforts, it was easy then to see the unemployed as being too lazy to work. Next, they turn on its head the humanist formulation that political disorder contributed to unrest among the poor and instead assign blame for social and political disorder to the lack of discipline of the poor. Oligarchs then assimilate the undisciplined and undisciplinable poor to the familiar image of the rogue, whose activities were argued to be part of a dangerous underworld, whose values were the reverse of those of decent society. Intellectuals, on the other hand, were concerned with the misbehavior of the poor, which their bookish sources convinced them to read as evidence of a disordered polity. They developed such a negative semantics of poverty because the impatient and rebellious poor *were* politically dangerous. Rejecting a failed status quo, the poor were willing to experiment with new things (*novità*), since any change might improve their situation. Their restive presence contributed to the fear of revolution, a fear that would have been all the more palpable given the newness of the Medicean Grand Duchy, and the recent history of foiled attempts at restoring the republic. So, then, even though the poor were not to blame for disorder, it was imperative that they be controlled, since, having neither interest in government and politics nor training in the arts necessary to exercise such participation—hence the employment of such descriptors as *"plebe"* and *"canaglia"*—they were ready prey to be manipulated by a dissatisfied clique of the elite looking for an opportunity to overturn the regime.

The different perspectives of the Florentine elite ultimately converged into an image of the undeserving poor, mainly unemployed men, and women without men. It was they who posed a moral danger (women in the sexual sense), who emerged from and spread a disordered and immoral life cycle, creating and perpetuating an underworld of persons averse to work, who begged, stole, and committed other types of crime, eroding the foundations of society as they warred against decency.

13   Lay Male Identity in the Institutions of a Tuscan Provincial Town

James R. Banker

I

The formation of identity in the fifteenth century in the Tuscan town of Borgo San Sepolcro may be viewed as a process by which an individual was placed, or chose a place, in several among a wide panoply of institutions existing within and without the town.[1] An individual did not conceive of himself as fashioning a self from the disparate parts of his society. From this town of four or five thousand people and from the vast majority of Italians in the fifteenth century, there are no documents of self-fashioning such as *ricordanze*, or instructions on how to divide one's consciousness as a means of focusing on aspects of appearance or behavior for their reconstruction. However, two novel programs for individual reformulation appeared in the course of the fifteenth century. The first was a more intensive religious program required by lay confraternities. This model of comportment and character may appear to twentieth-century eyes as traditional and thereby easily accessible to fifteenth-century men, but instead it was a radical departure from prevailing modes of behavior. The second program of self-

---

1. In its original conception, this essay was intended to examine institutions available for women, but limitations of space made such a discussion impossible. Though the choices may have been less numerous and public, women in Quattrocento towns of northern and central Italy possessed the opportunity to construct a large number of varied identities. It should also be stated that male and female identities associated with religious professions have not been discussed here. My purpose of demonstrating the wide number of life choices available in small towns in Quattrocento Italy is analogous to the purpose discussed by N. Davis for French peasants in her *The Return of Martin Guerre* (Cambridge, Mass., 1983). The excellent study by C. Gardner von Teuffel on the continuity of images and symbols of the town of Borgo San Sepolcro in the late Middle Ages and Renaissance appeared too late for inclusion in the conception of my study; see "Niccolò di Segna, Sassetta, Piero della Francesco and Perugino: Cult and Continuity at Sansepolcro," *Städel Jahrbuch* 17 (1999): 163–208.

scrutiny was found in texts from classical antiquity and Italian commentaries on this tradition.

But is it possible to know Renaissance selves beyond general categories or specific activities? I believe so if we forgo methodologies that purport to examine intentions or the consciousness of the individual. One might wish to delineate Renaissance personality in the modern sense, that is, to portray the individual as articulating an identity to itself and others through autonomously constructed reflections and acts. Modern ideas of individuality tend to emphasize a person's autonomy and ignore the vast number of institutions that are accepted without conscious choice. The lack of evidence to describe Renaissance personality with modern assumptions in this provincial town precludes the employment of this strategy.[2]

I propose here a method that is apt for delineating the Italian Renaissance form of identity. An individual participated in a number of institutions, some that he chose and others that presented themselves as a given or a necessity. This method focuses on the variety of institutions that groups of individuals chose or in which they were placed. But the context that surrounded an individual was made up of more than institutions. It consisted of the constellation of traditions and communities in which an individual moved. Individuals relied upon complex systems of social relationships to establish their professional career, religious and social life, and economic well-being and thereby to construct their identities. An analysis of this context will provide the basis for understanding social selves.[3]

II

In the biographies written by the Renaissance humanists, the individual was defined by the events and communities in which she or he participated with a summary appended of the permanent character traits.[4] For example, when Leonardo Bruni wrote his biography of Dante, he recounted the poet's ancestors, his public education in conversations with other men, his mil-

2. The phrasing and this definition are taken from T. C. Price Zimmermann, in his "Paolo Giovio and the Rhetoric of Individuality," in *The Rhetorics of Life-Writing in Early Modern Europe: Forms of Biography from Cassandra Fedele to Louis XIV*, ed. T. F. Mayer and D. R. Woolf (Ann Arbor, Mich., 1995), p. 39. And see pp. 60–61 n. 53 as well as for his definition of classical character.

3. See the comments of S. Chojnacki, "Social Identity in Renaissance Venice: The Second *Serrata,*" *Renaissance Studies* 8 (1994): 342–43, and his use of the term "social self."

4. Zimmerman, "Paolo Giovio," pp. 39–40.

itary service together with an account of the battle of Campaldino, his involvement in "cultural and civic affairs," his wife and children, his political offices and resultant banishment, and his property; finally, he included a discussion of poetry as means of defining Dante's literary achievements.[5] Bruni constructed a biography out of the social and political worlds within which Dante moved. One gains no knowledge of the contents of *The Divine Comedy* or of any private activities or thoughts. Dante is a public man defined more by his participation in the social, intellectual, family, and political communities than by his poetry. Bruni recognized the poetical traditions within which Dante wrote and some problems of genre, but Dante's life attained significance in social intercourse.

The basic assumption underlying my approach is that the individual participated in his society's symbolic systems, communities, and institutions, affirming and, at times, rejecting adhesion to them, and in this process the individual constructed a public or historical persona that might be best termed a "social self." This conception of self as deriving from one's context has analogues in some forms of postmodernism, but it rejects other parts of that movement that emphasize a restless, changing self, on the one hand, and rejects its opposite, that individuals are simple replicators of social or cultural institutions.

Any discussion of identity in Tuscany in the Renaissance must begin with three fundamental elements: the core of selfhood was an identification with one's city, with religion, in most cases Christianity, and with family.[6]

Numerous historians of medieval and early Renaissance city-states have discussed *campanilismo* as a term to express the intense devotion of urban men and women to the city of their origins. Often Dante is quoted from the *Purgatorio* when he placed in the mouth of a woman of the noble Tolo-

---

5. I have used A. F. Nagel's translation of *La Vita di Dante* in *The Humanism of Leonardo Bruni: Selected Texts*, ed. G. Griffiths, J. Hankins, and D. Thompson (Binghamton, N.Y., 1987), pp. 85–95. It is clear that Bruni's organization of the biography around communities derived from ideas commensurate with those of Aristotle in *The Politics*, which Bruni translated into Latin.

6. "Family" in Quattrocento Borgo San Sepolcro will not be discussed here in part because of reasons of space and in part because of the many excellent discussions of the Renaissance family; but see especially F. W. Kent, *Household and Lineage in Renaissance Florence: The Family Life of the Capponi, Ginori and Rucellai* (Princeton, N.J., 1977); and the several books of D. Herlihy and C. Klapisch-Zuber, especially their *Tuscans and Their Families: A Study of the Florentine Catasto of 1427* (New Haven, Conn., 1985); and Klapisch-Zuber's *Women, Family and Ritual in Renaissance Italy* (Chicago, 1985). Identities forged through economic activity are also not addressed in this essay.

mei family the words "Siena made me," thereby indicating that the place and the social relationships of Siena had formed her.[7] While noting this fundamental importance of identification with one's birthplace, I shall go about indicating the definition of this corporate sense through an examination of the myths and symbols of the town of Borgo San Sepolcro.

A defining event in the history of Borgo San Sepolcro accounts for its origin, the town's name, and a substantial part of its corporate self-conception. According to the earliest narrations of the history of the town, two pilgrims, Arcano and Egidio, passed through the Tiber valley on their return from Jerusalem, carrying with them pieces of the Holy Sepulcher. They received a vision while resting by a fountain and subsequently built an oratory on the site. Though the date of these, perhaps legendary, events is unknown, the earliest account of the history of Borgo San Sepolcro, which was written by an unnamed Camaldolensian monk in the early 1440s, fixed the founding date in 937.[8] Rural families constructed houses around the oratory and its sacred objects, thereby creating Borgo San Sepolcro. Again according to the anonymous chronicler, pieces of the church of the Holy Sepulcher were brought from Jerusalem in 1012 to the oratory, and then a monastery of Benedictines was constructed in 1027.[9] In the course of the twelfth century, the reforming Camaldolensians took control of the monastery, and from the abbey church the Camaldolensian abbot ruled the townspeople as their secular and spiritual leader. His abbey was at the center of the town, and the townspeople viewed it as a location of its spiritual authority.

In 1301 the abbot sold his temporal rights over the town to the citizens, but the religious origin of the town remained as the center of the originating myth celebrated by subsequent writers.[10] Though there had been conflicts between citizens and abbots prior to 1301, in Borgo San Sepolcro the two pilgrims and the early reliquaries of the Holy Sepulcher came to be powerful symbols of the town's corporate conception. The image of Christ emerging triumphant from the tomb is evident in an early altarpiece that

7. See, e.g., D. Waley, *The Italian City-Republics,* 3d ed. (New York and London, 1988), p. xiv, and the discussion that follows. Dante is quoted from *Purgatorio,* canto V, 134.

8. BLF, Plut., LXVI, cod. 25, fol. 1r–v. Subsequent authors, however, did not all accept this date, though they placed the date in the tenth century; see L. Coleschi with F. Polcri, *La storia di San Sepolcro,* rev. ed. (Borgo San Sepolcro, 1966), p. 128.

9. BLF, Plut., LXVI, cod. 25, fols. 2v, 4r–v.

10. For the act of 1301, see G. Degli Azzi, "Inventario degli archivi di San Sepolcro," in *Archivi della Storia d'Italia,* ser. 2, 4 (1914): 171–74.

rested on the high altar of the abbey from at least the 1360s. The two pilgrim saints, Arcano and Egidio, were not depicted on the altarpiece, nor does one often find their names given to the sons of the town in the fourteenth century. But by the time of Piero della Francesca's altarpiece for the Misericordia confraternity, commissioned in 1445, the two pilgrims had reemerged in the minds of the men and women of Borgo San Sepolcro and flanked the major saints in that painter's polyptych. And of course the image of Christ emerging from the sepulcher painted by Piero, now in the Museo Civico of Borgo San Sepolcro, remains where he painted it, in the chambers of the then principal lawmaking council of the town in the Quattrocento. That this was a recurring image that the town's political authorities exploited is evident from later practices. In January 1468 the town executives gave authority for painting the arms of the town above the central portal of their residence. This central door looked toward the abbey and inward into the legislative council room and Piero della Francesca's *Resurrection*. The insignia of the city, as stated here, is the "sepulcher of Jesus Christ."[11] In the statutes of 1571, the standard (*gonfalone*) of the city presented a painted image of the "sepulcher with a triumphant Christ," with the arms of the city and the Medici on a white and black field.[12]

Therefore, in the representations in the earliest extant paintings and writings, the origins of the town are not specifically political but religious. Other towns and cities would celebrate their earlier conflicts with resisting bishops or nobles or define themselves through celebrations of their liberation from or domination of other towns. But, in fact, here the most important conflict was between the abbot of Borgo San Sepolcro and the nearby bishop of Città di Castello over spiritual authority in the town. This conflict dragged throughout the fourteenth and fifteenth centuries, absorbing the energies and conceptions of the people of Borgo San Sepolcro. The communal government eventually took up the cause and, after a half century of appealing to papal authorities and the Medici in Florence, Pope Leo X rewarded Borgo San Sepolcro with a bishop. This secured Borgo San Sepolcro and its religious authority against threats of absorption into the authority of the bishop of Città di Castello. These images of origin and conflict served religious and political purposes. They served the secular government's needs to integrate the townspeople into a corporate group as well as serving the local church's purpose of stirring devotion. In the first account of the most important reliquaries of the town, written in 1418, the sacred objects are in

11. BSS, AC, ser. 2, reg. 7, fol. 13v.
12. Degli Azzi, "Inventario degli archivi di San Sepolcro," p. 180.

strongboxes in the possession of the local government. The most valued objects of the town are those related to the sacred objects of the Crucifixion and Resurrection of Christ: a piece of the wood of the cross; some of the stone of the Holy Sepulcher, "in whose name was built this town [*terra*]"; the cloth that held the body of Christ; "blood from the images of Christ"; and the container in which the sacred images were brought to the town from Jerusalem by Arcano and Egidio.[13]

The foundation of the town was linked to one of the fundamental mysteries of the Christian religion. The sacred objects of the Holy Sepulcher and the Resurrection were the symbols of the town. The enduring conflict in the period of the Renaissance was with the bishop of Città di Castello and therefore largely religious in nature. These were the enduring symbols and representation of corporate identity of the people of Borgo San Sepolcro in the Renaissance. Other than the short account of the history of Borgo San Sepolcro by the anonymous Camaldolensian monk, there are no chronicles of the town written in the Renaissance. This lack of narratives is striking in Borgo San Sepolcro. Historians from other towns will use political events to achieve an idea of change over time, a sense of a political organism that evolves in accord with a sense of corporate self and deepens itself after challenges from external forces. At best in the history of the Camaldolensian monk and in the first lay historical work of Bercordati, around 1600, the writers copy documents verbatim to prove the claims of the abbot of Borgo San Sepolcro's rights of spiritual jurisdiction over the bishop of Città di Castello.

In the High Middle Ages and Renaissance the people in Borgo San Sepolcro enjoyed few years of independence. In the first seventy years of the fourteenth century, the townspeople had moments of self-rule, but in turn they were subject to Arezzo, their dreaded enemies in Città di Castello, and finally papal authority. In 1371 Pope Urban V sold rule over the town to the Malatesta from Rimini for 18,000 florins. This family exercised authority in Borgo San Sepolcro for sixty years. And it was to Malatesta rule that later writers would look to as a period of prosperity and beneficent rule, rather than to any precise moment of self-rule.[14] Thus the people of Borgo

13. BSS, AC, ser. 18, reg. 1, fol. Iv–IIr, in the hand of Francesco dei Largi. There followed five other reliquaries, but, other than the milk of Mary, the reliquaries were fragments from lesser saints. See also A. Goracci, *Breve istoria dell'origine e fondazione della città del Borgo di San Sepolcro* (San Sepolcro, 1636), p. 152, repr. in *Collezione di cronisti italiani*, vol. 7.

14. E.g., see F. Bercordati, "Cronaca di San Sepolcro," par. 239 in a display case in BSS, AC.

San Sepolcro did not recall the animating and integrative experience of casting off a foreign foe and constructing a popularly based government as an integral part of their history.[15]

In 1430 the papacy reestablished its claim over Borgo San Sepolcro only to lose it to a series of military lords; this decade witnessed continuous conflict and finally the victory of the papacy and Florence over an army of Milan and its allies, including Borgo San Sepolcro, at Anghiari in 1440. Pope Eugenius IV promptly lent rights over Borgo San Sepolcro to Florence for 20,000 florins. The defeat at Anghiari led to the integration of Borgo San Sepolcro into the Florentine dominion (see map), and it began a long process in which the townspeople were drawn slowly into the Tuscan economy and culture.

Despite the nearly continuous foreign rule, the townsmen did exercise internal autonomy. This was true prior to and after the Florentine victory. When Florence gained authority over the town, it agreed to maintain the statutes that had been rewritten in 1430 under the papacy.[16] Moreover, as has been recently argued, Florence, at least in theory, privileged local law in its dominion, even when local law contradicted Florentine statutes, although I should add that specific Florentine laws and practices often fundamentally changed local practices.[17] The men of Borgo San Sepolcro, however, tied identity to political participation just as if they were completely independent from external rule. They may have accepted one half of Leonardo Bruni's definition of liberty as the free access to political office while ignoring the other definition as freedom from external rule.[18]

Numerous offices existed from which their occupants could derive local authority and honor. The men of the town sought to occupy the offices just as if the town were completely autonomous. Within rule by a foreign state

15. Goracci, *Breve istoria*, pp. 202–4; P. Farulli, *Annali e memorie dell'antica e nobile città di San Sepolcro* (Foligno, 1713), p. 33; and Bercordati, "Cronaca," par. 253, discuss a rebellion in 1417 or 1420 that could have established the basis for a historiography of resistance.

16. Goracci, *Breve istoria*, p. 211. See BSS, AC, ser. 32, reg. 182, fol. 7v, "Specchio" of Francesco dei Largi, where he writes that he had copied the 1430 statutes as reformed by the papal governor Bishop Didaco.

17. J. Black, "Constitutional Ambitions, Legal Realities and the Florentine State," in *Florentine Tuscany: Structures and Practices of Power*, ed. W. J. Connell and A. Zorzi (Cambridge, England, 2000), pp. 48–64.

18. The libraries of men of San Sepolcro in fact demonstrate a special interest in the writings and translations of Bruni; see, e.g., the library of the doctor of law Jacopo di Jacopo degli Anastagi, J. Banker, "A Legal and Humanistic Library in Borgo San Sepolcro in the Middle of the Fifteenth Century," *Rinascimento*, ser. 2, 33 (1993): 163–91, esp. 186–91.

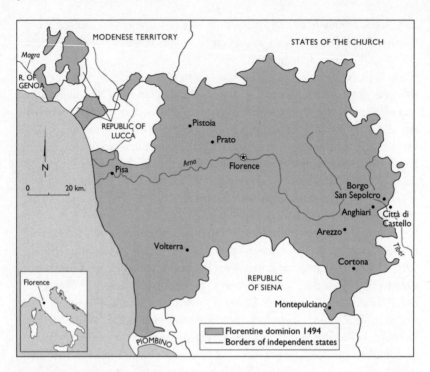

Borgo San Sepolcro and the Florentine Dominion, ca. 1494.

and alien political groups, towns like Borgo San Sepolcro constructed a vigorous public culture. A regular round of selection to political office and decision making was commensurate with foreign rule. Documents sufficiently plentiful to evaluate the nature of Florence's dominion over Borgo San Sepolcro after 1441 show that Florentine priors and councils made decisions on defense, foreign relations, fiscal policy, and the parameters of politics, but that the men of Borgo San Sepolcro nevertheless possessed and regularly made profound decisions on the life of the town.[19]

Florence exercised its authority in Borgo San Sepolcro through a captain, who was Florentine and selected in Florence every six months. The captain brought with him his retinue, or *familia*, which consisted of a judge, three notaries, three knights, and several personal servants, in addition to twenty-five provisionaries, twelve custodians, two trumpeters, and the five castellans of the town gates, totaling between fifty and sixty men.

19. See, e.g., the chancellery records of Francesco dei Largi from 1441 to 1447; BSS, AC, ser. 2, reg. 2.

Many of these men were Florentine, or at least Tuscan, and were paid by the town of Borgo San Sepolcro a total of 3,600 lire a year.[20] Florence commanded the town to pay this sum through its traditional taxes (*gabelle*) on goods coming through its gates, grinding of grain, contracts, wood, wine, and a variety of other sales taxes. For compensating its own officials and financing its own initiatives, the town had to apply the *dazio*, an extraordinary and unpopular tax on real property. Though the *dazio* could be applied more than once a year, the monies from this property assessment seldom if ever yielded more than the 3,600 lire a year paid to their Florentine rulers. The income from the *dazio* paid for the salaries of the town doctor, grammar school teacher, chancellor, and servants, for gifts to churches and other ecclesiastical bodies, for maintenance and construction of communal property, for grain in years of famine, and finally for the cloth *palio* (150 to 210 lire) sent to Florence yearly as a symbol of the subjection of Borgo San Sepolcro to Florentine authority.[21]

To make corporate choices within the general arc of Florentine protection and guidance, the people selected a large number of officials by lot for short terms of office. The chief executives of the town were four conservators, one of whom was the Standard Bearer of Justice (after 1469), each serving for two months. They administered the local government and proposed legislation to a council of the Twelve Good Men, who served three months, and to a council of sixty men, who served four months. At times the conservators would debate issues among themselves and on other occasions with one or both of the councils. These three magistracies would yearly require 252 men to fill their posts. The council of 60 was drawn from a larger council called the Council of the People, consisting of 300 men, who were organized into twenty groups of fifteen men, each led by a *capolista*. There were, in addition, a larger number of other offices also selected by lot, most for a year, and many with prohibitions against holding more than one office or holding offices consecutively, totaling another approximately 70 men.[22] Given a town of between 4,000 and 5,000 people in the fifteenth century and a low percentage of adults, perhaps 800 to 1,000 adult

20. BSS, AC, ser. 2, reg. 2, unfoliated at this point, to the day, 18 July 1441 and 7 November 1442. From these and subsequent documents, it is not clear if the castellans and custodians of the gate and their servants were paid from the 3,600 lire or from some other source by the people of Borgo San Sepolcro.
21. See, e.g., the expenses of 1461; BSS, AC, ser. 2, reg. 5, fols. 29r–30r.
22. This description is drawn from an examination of the earliest *Tratte* records of the town, 1477–81; see BSS, AC, ser. 3, reg. 1. Some terms of offices were differ-

males, a relatively high percentage—perhaps a quarter of the townsmen—would yearly participate in civic offices.

Within this wide political participation, it is clear that an elite composed of several families monopolized the highest offices and repeatedly were selected as the conservators and the Twelve Good Men. The Pichi, Graziani, Rigi, Dotti, Roberti, and Carsidoni families predominated.[23] With the exception of the Rigi family, these houses had also monopolized offices from at least the late fourteenth century, as can be seen from their numbers as *capoliste* in the council of 300 in 1391.[24] The predominance of these socially and economically powerful families within local politics attests to the fact that these offices were valued. A vibrant public culture of frequent debate yielded honor and status to the holders of public office. The town had attempted to express and to focus honor on the conservators in 1460 when Niccolò Acciaiuoli was captain by gaining for them continued habitation and meals within the Communal Palace and with one of them being symbolic head of the town as Standard Bearer of Justice. The Florentine governors refused to grant this obvious imitation of Florentine practices in that year but in 1467 did grant these honors to their subject town.[25]

This vibrant representative culture, however, existed within a watchful Florentine supervision. The meetings of the conservators and the communal councils were convened by the command of the Florentine captain or his representative, his judge. One or the other usually sat in the executive and legislative meetings. The men of Borgo San Sepolcro made frequent and expensive embassies to Florence seeking to mitigate the force and costs of Florentine rule. Though legislative changes were frequent, prior permission was often sought from Florence to post revisions.[26]

The dual political machinery of internal republican government and external Florentine control yielded an ambivalent political identity. Whereas prior to 1441, much of the culture of Borgo San Sepolcro was shared with the Marches to the east and Umbria and Rome to the south, after 1441 Borgo San Sepolcro was slowly drawn more into a Tuscan orbit. Florence sent over one hundred representatives there yearly and required many

---

ent earlier in the century, especially the conservators who served for three months; see BSS, AC, ser. 2, reg. 2, no foliation at this point, to the day, 15 October 1443.

23. This conclusion is derived from an analysis of the names listed in the *Tratte* from 26 December 1476 to 22 July 1481; BSS, AC, ser. 3, reg. 1, fols. 1r–52r.

24. BSS, AC, ser. 2, reg, 1, fols. 7r–12r, 1 January 1391. The council at this point was called the "New Council of the Commune."

25. BSS, AC, ser. 2, reg. 6, fols. 62v–63r.

26. See the experiences of the 1440s in BSS, AC, ser. 2, reg. 2.

of the men of the small town in the Upper Tiber Valley to commute to Florence as ambassadors and to seek loans and serve in Florentine wars. Preexisting economic links intensified after 1441. The pride of Borgo San Sepolcro in its history and culture had to be newly conceptualized within Florentine attempts to funnel the town's trade through Florence, appoint Florentines and Tuscans to its churches, and limit its choices within the general will of Florence.

This yielded a split attitude on at least political arrangements between the two towns. On the one hand, Borgo San Sepolcro adhered to Florentine symbolic practices by sending the yearly *palio* "in recognition especially of the humanity and benevolence which the people of Florence have toward the people of Borgo San Sepolcro" and by having its conservators take office only after kneeling before the captain and vowing to rule faithfully and according to the statutes that had been approved in Florence. The people of Borgo San Sepolcro, moreover, paid Florentine agents, operated within laws sent from Florence that optimized the opportunities of Florentine merchants and drew their economic activity within a Tuscan economy, and accepted Florentine foreign policies as their own. For this, Borgo San Sepolcro and its people gained the protection of the Florentine state. Given the frequent conflicts and sieges of the town in the 1430s, the relative peace after 1441 and the economic opportunities within the Florentine economy stimulated the society and culture of Borgo San Sepolcro.

On the other hand, the men of Borgo San Sepolcro continually attempted to limit and test the controls of the center city over them. The town exploited its strategic position at the head of the Tiber Valley and in the southeast corner of the Florentine state that bordered on both the Marches and Umbria. When Borgo San Sepolcro rebuilt its walls in the late 1440s, it sought to have Florence pay for the new construction because its strength enhanced the security of all the Florentine state. Throughout the second half of the fifteenth century, the political leaders sought to reduce their payments to Florentine officials, claiming an inability to pay given the town's poor economic conditions. While the public records do not recount any expressed resentment against the Florentine rule, there is a continuous debate on how to loosen the yoke.[27] There existed a pride in participation in the Florentine state but also a stubborn adherence to a prior and powerful local identification.

But there were other means of achieving or supplementing identity be-

27. See, e.g., the discussion of 21 May 1441 on how many florins should be expended on the *palio* that the town sent to Florence yearly; BSS, AC, ser. 2, reg. 2, unfoliated at this point, to the day.

yond political office in the town of Borgo San Sepolcro. It is clear that as in modern societies a male could choose from a variety of institutions from which he could derive honor and a sense that he was participating in the construction of the well-being of his town and Christendom. Though a fifteenth-century man would not articulate it in this way, he was provided numerous possibilities for individuating his self through his acceptance of the ideas and institutions of the Christian church. I shall here assume the existence of the ecclesiastical structure and its clerical leadership and instead concentrate on religious institutions that an individual chose to join, specifically lay confraternities.[28]

Confraternities were self-governing voluntary associations of laymen and laywomen with the purpose of gaining merit with God through charitable acts and/or a more intense devotion than that required by the Church. In the fifteenth century a man in Borgo San Sepolcro had a rich panoply of confraternities from which he could choose.

The most prestigious confraternity, the Fraternity of Saint Bartholomew (Fraternità di San Bartolommeo), had from the thirteenth century supervised burial in the town, aided the poor at death and through weekly distribution of food to them, and received donations from its thousands of members as well as the remnants of candles after every burial. The communal government had made the administrative heads of the fraternity legal representatives of the poor already in the thirteenth century. By the fifteenth century, membership was inconsequential; of sole importance was selection as one of four priors who governed the fraternity's vast agricultural estates and urban property. They also supervised the non-confraternal hospitals, distributed clothing and food to the poor, as well as selling large amounts of grain in a weekly market for profit. The priors were administrators with a large number of obligations for supervising the poor, orphans, testamentary bequests, and other social functions today associated with state institutions. In fact, from 1436, the priors were selected by lot in a process identical to that in which political officials were designated. In addition, the priors were given several privileges in the terms of their offices, including exemption from guard duty or any other communal office, or war service.[29]

The names of those who held this position in the fifteenth century and beyond are the same as those who held the position of conservator. Thus

---

28. N. Terpstra, *Lay Confraternities and Civic Religion in Renaissance Bologna* (Cambridge, England, 1995), pp. 77–82.

29. See Largi, "Specchio," fols. 5v–13r, esp. fol. 5v.

only elite males could attain this position of prior and take the opportunity of gaining political honor and serving the poor as part of one's Christian stewardship. An individual would not seek to be selected as prior if he wanted to discover novel ways of expressing his Christian faith or indeed even attend mass or other services. By the fifteenth century the priors were the Fraternity, and they administered property and agricultural goods for the well-being of the community.[30]

Nonelite men of Borgo San Sepolcro could join the confraternity of Santa Maria della Notte if they wished to aid the poor and the community through administrative service.[31] Founded in about 1300, this confraternity was composed of laymen who traversed the streets of the town singing praises of Mary and her Son. In the following two hundred years this *laudese* confraternity gained a large landed patrimony, especially of agricultural properties, from testators of the town and from income from these properties. The number of members was severely limited, probably to the apostolic twelve, with nearly all occupying one of the many offices of the confraternity continuously and each heading the confraternity as one of the two priors within a two- or three-year period. The commune honored the heads of the confraternity of Santa Maria della Notte with privileges and immunities equal to those of the elite who served as priors of the Fraternity of Saint Bartholomew. The landed property of this confraternity was approximately the same as the two most wealthy entities of the town. In an *estimo* of landed property in the mid–fifteenth century, the Camaldolensian abbot, the Fraternity of Saint Bartholomew, and the confraternity of Santa Maria della Notte each possessed approximately one hundred pieces of land.[32]

Given the wealth, responsibilities, privileges, and distinction conferred on the confraternity and its priors, it is striking that its members, who were also officers, derived from modest origins. Few of them had family names, none appear at the top of the lists of the legislative Council of the People, and the membership remained agrarian and artisanal. The twelve or so members administered their vast agricultural lands. By the fifteenth century this confraternity had evolved an elaborate exchange system between town and country that made the confraternity indispensable. The confra-

---

30. For the foregoing, see J. Banker, *Death in the Community* (Athens, Ga., 1988), pp. 75–109.

31. For the following discussion, see Banker, *Death in the Community*, pp. 110–44.

32. BSS, AC, ser. 32, reg. 173; and Banker, *Death in the Community*, p. 102, table 3.9.

ternal leaders hired agricultural workers, including members who, according to an eighteenth-century historian, exited the town at dawn singing praises to the Virgin and Christ as they processed to the confraternal lands to trim the grapevines, prepare the soil, and perform a variety of other agricultural tasks. From their rural holdings they brought grain, beans, and other agricultural goods into the town. Then, from the town administrative center and large oratory on the central piazza, which today serves as the seat of the town government, the members sold grain and dispensed a wide range of charity. Finally, a finely articulated system of restoring fertility to the soil of the confraternal lands was achieved by hiring laborers to move night soil from stables and town homes to the countryside.[33]

Members administered large landed estates and accounts as well as a large corps of laborers and as often performed the manual labor on the land. This economic entity was at the same time a religious charitable institution; members gained honor by profitably managing the estates and distributing charity to the poor. During the Renaissance the elite never succeeded in wresting control of the confraternity from its artisans and agricultural workers, perhaps because of the manual labor associated with membership.

Yet again, a citizen of Borgo San Sepolcro of the fifteenth century had other vastly different choices with which to construct a religious persona. If he wanted to demonstrate his devotion to the Virgin and God solely through song without the administrative and agricultural labor of Santa Maria della Notte, he could join the *laudese* confraternity of Santa Maria della Badia that congregated near the high altar of the abbey. Here artisans in particular had the opportunity for periodic worship.[34]

A more critical choice that would require a decidedly different form of life than those of the heretofore-discussed confraternal members and those who simply complied with the church's standards of a Christian life was that of joining a flagellant confraternity. In the Renaissance a man in Borgo San Sepolcro could choose to join one of five discipline brotherhoods that required corporate and at times public flagellation; in the confraternities of Santa Maria della Misericordia, Santa Caterina, Sant'Antonio, Santa Maddalena, and Santa Croce, an individual underwent self-scrutiny and confraternal scrutiny. Here the member's social as well as some private behavior was regarded as problematic. The flagellants' behavior was to be held to

---

33. See the expenses in ASF, CRSPL, 3362, *filza* 27.

34. E. Battisti, *Piero della Francesca*, 2 vols. (Milan, 1971), 2:231, document CXXII.

a higher standard in a variety of forums with the purpose of constructing a sacred community.

Incoming members had to undergo scrutiny of their behavior to assure existing members that the newcomers would not taint the purity of the brotherhood. They also had to confess their sins just prior to entering the confraternity so they would be in a sacred condition, and members had to confess again prior to taking one of the many offices. The statutes of the confraternity required monthly confessions, which constituted much more self-examination than the annual confession to the member's parish priest required by ecclesiastical law. The confraternities forbade a number of vices and several that were more prominent or divisive in urban settings. For example, if an incoming member had been usurious or had cheated another, he had to go to the abbot to receive a penalty and make the proper restitution to the injured parties prior to reapplying for membership. Other prohibited urban acts included drinking in taverns on the days of confraternal services, frequenting houses of prostitution, practicing sodomy, and playing games of chance with money at stake.[35]

A more intensive devotional life was also required of these flagellants. First, brothers were obligated to meet every Sunday in their oratories and on the festivals of the Virgin Mary, Christ, and a variety of saints. Attendance was also obligatory at funeral processions of members and on other occasions when prayers were offered for the soul of each member. Prayers, particularly "Our Fathers" and "Hail Marys," and appeals to the divine were to be repeated at waking, eating, retiring to bed, on Friday in honor of Christ's passion, and on other specific moments of the day and week. Most important, these discipline confraternities required members to flagellate themselves as identification with the flagellation of Christ and as a means of purification of their bodies.

These prohibitions and new requirements were largely behavioral, and the statutes did not demand changes in interior states. Most often the discussions of the requirements of membership point to behaviors rather than psychological states. This is consistent with our introductory remarks on the necessity of understanding Quattrocento individuals through their social behaviors.

The confraternities and especially the flagellant brotherhoods sought a more intensive devotional life modeled on monastic and especially mendicant forms of what they called the "honest life." For laymen, this was a rad-

35. Banker, *Death in the Community*, pp. 153–58.

ical departure and required focusing on one's individual behavior. This novel mode of uniting the lay and mendicant approach to life was so appealing that a high percentage of individuals joined confraternities. The confraternal members took a more aggressive attitude, a more active devotional life either in flagellation or in working for the poor in their larger community. This could have driven the confraternal members to more individualistic spirituality, but in Borgo San Sepolcro the new devotion emphasized reciprocity. Members prayed for one another in life and at death and sought to secure the well-being of the poor and less fortunate through a large number of charities and administration of hospitals.[36]

The revival of knowledge of classical culture provided a second program for life that was newly available for the men of Borgo San Sepolcro in the Quattrocento. Though not contradictory to the confraternal program, humanism presented a variety of other choices. Given the large number of studies of humanism and the limited evidence for Borgo San Sepolcro, the humanistic program there will be presented through an examination of one of its several Quattrocento libraries. No one from the town attained a great reputation as a humanist in the fifteenth century, but interest in the humanistic program is evident in several large libraries with numerous humanistic treatises and commentaries.

The libraries at the beginning of the fifteenth century were professional and composed primarily of books collected from the lectures of a university education. Lawyers collected texts on civil and canon law, doctors kept books on medicine, and grammar school teachers had texts of grammar and rhetoric.[37] By midcentury libraries reveal broader interests that are best described as providing instructions on behavior and examples of living a socially responsible public life. Rhetorical and ethical texts, histories, letters, and orations from specific historical occasions supplemented books concentrating on one's profession.

The best example is that of the library of Maestro Michelangelo Palamidessi, whose books were inventoried in 1466 soon after his death.[38] Michelangelo was a merchant and also collected humanistic texts. His books reveal an interest in the humanistic program of Francesco Petrarca and the

36. See the statutes of the confraternity of Santa Croce in ibid., Appendix III, pp. 210–34.
37. E.g., see the inventory of the books of the doctor of law Battista di Matteo di Cecchi Orlandi of San Sepolcro, ASF, NA, 7009, fol. 129r, 9 December 1422.
38. For the following see the inventory of Michelangelo Palamidessi's books in ASF, NA, 7053, acts of Mario di Matteo Fedeli, no. 9, 24 April 1466, fols. 13r–14v, with another copy beginning on fol. 21v.

next generation of humanists in Florence, especially Leonardo Bruni. He concentrated his attention on Bruni's translations of Greek texts: Aristotle's *Ethics* and *Politics* and the Pseudo-Aristotelian *Oeconomica*, among others. He also collected classical rhetorical and ethical texts, especially those of Cicero: *De officiis, De amicitia,* and a collection of orations that Michelangelo himself had copied. A third group included works of contemporary Italian humanists: Poggio Bracciolini's *De varietate fortunae, Epistulae,* and *Orationes;* Filelfo's *Orationes;* and an oration by Matteo Palmieri. Michelangelo's humanistic texts demonstrate his interest in, and probably commitment to, values and techniques that were essential for his participation in the town's public life and that were different from those advocated in the confraternities.

But within this varied Christian society there were fissures and groups that were set apart from the community, especially rural workers and Jews. The agricultural laborers in the district of Borgo San Sepolcro became highly vocal in the last three decades of the fifteenth century. Concentration of wealth and landownership in the hands of the urban elite appears to have been common throughout most of Tuscany in the Quattrocento and as well as in Borgo San Sepolcro.[39] At three points in the last third of the fifteenth century, 1470, 1484, and 1494, the rural workers organized to seek a redress of their conditions. Two aspects of these moments of rural unrest are of paramount interest. The first is the fact that the rural workers sustained their opposition to urban exploitation for a quarter of a century. Second, the rural workers accepted the overall political framework within which they operated and looked beyond their local government to Florence for redress of their economic misfortunes. Their opposition focused on specific criticisms of the urban elite and their Florentine overlords.

Both this local elite and the agricultural workers frequently claimed to be suffering economic problems after the 1450s. On 3 July 1470 approximately two hundred "laborers and contadini" congregated and elected the merchant Urbano di Marcolino dei Pichi as their syndic to represent their view to the political officials of Florence. They enumerated the problems of

39. Herlihy and Klapisch-Zuber, *Tuscans and Their Families;* and D. Herlihy, "The Distribution of Wealth in a Renaissance Community: Florence," in *The Medieval City,* ed. P. Abrams and E. A. Wrigley (London, 1977), pp. 131–57. See also the general discussion of D. Hay and J. Law, *Italy in the Age of the Renaissance, 1380–1530* (London, 1989), pp. 51–64. For the late fifteenth century and sixteenth century, see the excellent study by G. Benadusi of the coalescing elite of Poppi and their ownership of rural property, *A Provincial Elite in Early Modern Tuscany* (Baltimore, 1996), pp. 138–62.

production in the countryside and ascribed as the source of their problems the intrusive control of the local government and heavy tax burdens. The agricultural laborers appealed directly to Florence, and the Florentine Signoria sent two arbiters, who proposed a traditional Florentine solution: the election of a new magistracy to oversee town-rural relations.[40]

That magistracy, known as the Office of the Regulators and Accountants (Offitio dei regolatori e ragionieri), failed to end the problems and criticisms by the agricultural workers of Borgo San Sepolcro. In 1484 they again gathered and asserted that they were the "maiorem partem dictorum laboratorum et comitatinorum" and again elected syndics, on this occasion ten of their own men, to represent them in an embassy to Florentine officials. The syndics were empowered to narrate and explain their necessities and to point out that heavy taxes had been applied contrary to Florentine law. The syndics were to argue for repeal of the recent laws because they were antithetical to the form of the ancient statutes.[41] It is not clear if and how Florence responded to this appeal.

The opposition and criticisms of the policies of the local and Florentine elites continued and in 1494 flared into rebellious actions.[42] On 1 April an unknown number of agricultural workers entered the communal piazza in front of the residence of the communal government, apparently brought there by the passage that day of the application of "gabelle de monete bianche" by the communal magistrates. From among the armed country laborers, Luca d'Andrea di Piccone shouted to the magistrates, "Why have you sold the *dazio* and posted the expenses that we told you not to apply?" The Standard Bearer of Justice replied, "The chancellor explained to you why." This dismissive response enraged the agricultural workers, who then "violently" sent the conservators out of their residence. The rioters then ascended to the balcony of the conservator's residence, threw communal documents into the piazza, and proceeded to burn what we may assume were tax assessments. Moreover, they held the central piazza for fifteen days with the conservators as virtual prisoners in the captain's palace. Only when the Florentines sent a new commissioner to replace the captain was the siege lifted and the conservators reconfirmed in their office.[43]

---

40. ASF, NA, 16730, fols. 92r–93v, 3 July 1470. Title in the margin: "Sindicatus laboratorum terre Burgi."

41. ASF, NA, 19260, fol. 6r–v, 15 February 1484.

42. In an act of 1485 the *contadini* and laborers sought through four representatives greater activity of the Regolatori in their interests; see ASF, NA, 19261, fol. 40v. Again this attests to the continuity of the agricultural laborers' organization.

43. ASF, NA, 7154, fol. 394r, 1 April 1494.

The criticisms by the agricultural laborers of the taxes of Borgo San Sepolcro apparently were not addressed by either the local or the Florentine government. The notary who inserted the foregoing account in his protocol had little sympathy for the laborers and therefore did not mention their specific criticisms and possible reforms, though the occasion of the rebellion suggests that the gabelle of "white money" finally stimulated the rural workers to violent action after a quarter century of seeking redress through their representatives. The extant public Florentine documents treat the problem as one of public order and the result of a pusillanimous Florentine captain.

The initial corporate acts of the working rural class in 1470 and 1484 suggest an identification of the men of this group with the town and with a Tuscan lordship under Florence. Their appointment of representatives to the magistrates of Borgo San Sepolcro and embassies to Florence demonstrates their assertion of a role, and a corporate expression of a will to participate, in both the local government and the Florentine state. Though obviously an important part of the social and economic body of Borgo San Sepolcro, the agricultural workers and their families did not in the Quattrocento have political representation, though at some later point one of the four conservators had to be a rural inhabitant.

In Renaissance formulations the agricultural workers were conceived as part of the Christian commonwealth. The other marginal group in Borgo San Sepolcro was composed of a small number of Jews. They chose to be a separate religious community and on that basis were excluded from the political and many aspects of the social community. In the Quattrocento there were probably never more than two or three families of Jews in Borgo San Sepolcro. Not surprisingly, their community tended to be broader than the walls of Borgo San Sepolcro and to extend to the families of Jews from Umbria to Emilia. The nature of Jewish identity is only suggested in the extant documentation, but their economic and marriage networks indicate this broad community.[44]

Through most of the fifteenth century the central occupation of the Jews of Borgo San Sepolcro was to administer banks there owned by Jews in Città di Castello, Florence, and Bologna. These banks were sold this privilege not by the local government but by the political overlords of Borgo San Sepolcro: the Malatesta, the papacy, and the Florentines. The banks gave loans with pawns (*a pegno*) but as well loaned money through written documents

---

44. Of many examples of marriages and banks, see ASF, NA, 7037, fol. 81r–v; ASF, NA, 7040, fols. 35r, 114r–v, 116r–v.

(*a carta*) in small sums of two or three lire for consumption or much larger to the merchants and local government of Borgo San Sepolcro.[45]

The small community of Jews maintained their separate identity through their service of providing usurious loans that were regarded as reprehensible by Christian theologians, though Christians often made the same types of loans and paid usurious rates when necessary. The local government enforced the repayment of the loans *a carta* to Jews, though on at least two occasions the authorities of the town applied pressure to the bankers to lighten the burden of loans and on another arrested a Jewish banker for some inexplicable reason.[46] These appear to be exceptions; extant documents report only occasional hostility toward Jews by individuals, despite the vitriolic preaching of the Observant Franciscans in Borgo San Sepolcro against the Jews and subsequent anti-Jewish legislation.[47] Christians served as witnesses for contracts between Jews, and Jewish contractors were often present in the homes of Christians.

From the point of view of the Christians, Jews were defined negatively as those outside the Christian community and practicing a condemned behavior. Though the extant documentation on Jews in Borgo San Sepolcro is limited, it is clear that the Jews affirmed and sought to maintain their separate heritage. When they had children, they brought in a Jewish master to teach them and provided books in Hebrew.[48] As their children approached adulthood, the parents sought spouses from Jewish communities throughout central Italy.

Defined negatively by the larger Christian community, the Jewish families nevertheless maintained a positive identity. There is no indication that any Jew in Borgo San Sepolcro converted to Christianity, and the Jewish bank there maintained a vigorous life even after the town instituted a communal pawn bank (Monte della pietà), the purpose of which was to eliminate Jewish pawn bankers. Despite the small number of Jews in Borgo San

45. For one among hundreds of loans, see ASF, NA,19287, fol. 15v.

46. F. Corazzini di Bulciano, *Appunti storici e filologici su la Valle Tiberina superiore* (San Sepolcro, 1874), Letters XXI and XXII, pp. 18–19. And see ASF, NA, 7036, unfoliated, 14 November 1455, for the pressure applied by the abbot of San Sepolcro on the Jewish banker David Abrami. For the arrest of Salomone di Bonaventura, see BSS, AC, ser. 2, reg. 2, unfoliated, to the day, 19 January 1442; Salomone was released on the request of Florentine officials.

47. See the anti-Jewish legislation following the preaching of the Franciscan Observant Fra Jacopo delle Marche; BSS, AC, ser. 2, reg. 2, unfoliated, to the day, 8, 12, 29 October 1445.

48. E.g., see the purchase of a Hebrew Bible on 23 August 1446, ASF, NA, 19315, unfoliated, to the day.

Sepolcro, they sustained a viable community within the larger Christian society.

Part of the purpose of this essay has been to demonstrate the large number of choices that were available to men in the construction of their lives as a means of understanding the nature of identity in provincial Renaissance Italy. It may be argued that most men passively accepted the family's religion, occupational traditions, and town loyalty. That may be a powerful argument from an abstract point of view, especially for those with modern conceptions of freedom. But within these traditions and institutions, men and women of the Renaissance possessed a wide variety of choices whose combinations conferred specific identities.

Maestro Michelangelo Palamidessi was introduced earlier as the collector of humanistic texts, but he also can be viewed as an individual who made a series of uncommon choices, thereby forging his unique social identity. First, he went to an unknown university where, not content with simply gaining the title of "maestro" and the privilege of teaching, he obtained a doctor's degree in the liberal arts. He was the only layman in Quattrocento Borgo San Sepolcro who earned this distinction. Despite his preparation, he apparently never taught in the communal grammar school or gained employment based on his degree. Instead, he combined several part-time activities, a professional amateur as a merchant, ambassador, public man, and intellectual. He was instrumental in bringing the Observant Franciscans to Borgo San Sepolcro by supervising the construction of their residence and place of worship. He frequently served the communal government as an ambassador, especially in pleading his town's needs to their Florentine overlords and in seeking the independence of the abbot of Borgo San Sepolcro from the bishop of Città di Castello. Michelangelo also exercised his liberty in choosing books for his library. Doubtless the town councillors chose him as a frequent ambassador because of his oratorical skill, for which the numerous rhetorical texts in his library had prepared him. But he went beyond humanistic texts and purely professional formation in choosing books for his library. These books show an interest in cosmology and astrology, as well as in scholastic and Aristotelian logical texts, especially the *Posterior Analytics* upon which Michelangelo's friend Niccolò Tignosi had lectured at the university in Florence. As in his life choices, so in his books Michelangelo does not fit into the usual social categories of his and our day.[49]

The aforementioned lack of self-conscious articulations of these choices

---

49. I intend to treat Michelangelo more fully in a future study. For the library, see note 38 above.

in Borgo San Sepolcro limits our discussion to the social selves, even with Michelangelo. Some men with the benefit of family wealth served in public offices almost continuously, content to derive honor and exercise influence within the town. Others left the town for an education, for a military career, or for mercantile activities as a preparation for a return in which honor would be derived from possession of wider Italian contacts and knowledge. Some men combined an artisan activity with religious devotion, and others were omnipresent and omniactive, exercising several occupations, joining several confraternities, serving in public offices, witnessing nearly daily notarial contracts, and dying with honors after having lifted their families from agrarian or artisan origins to the elite of the town. Finally, we not should forget those others whose identities were obliterated in their own day due to an early death from plague or those who were denigrated because they failed to maintain the wealth and position of their forefathers.

14 Insiders and Outsiders

The Changing Boundaries of Exile

Alison Brown

I

There is no exile without a homeland from which to be expelled. The effectiveness of exile as a political punishment depended on strong affective bonds between the exile and the city of his birth that made leaving it a penalty—as well as a guarantee of loyalty.[1] For exile was a double-edged weapon, as Savonarola realized: "If you send away your citizens and exile them, they will go to princes and will reveal the secrets of your state, which could damage you quite a lot."[2] It was also economically dangerous, for in exiling wealthy citizens, the city lost their "great riches" and the "universal benefit" such wealth would bring to the city if they returned.[3] Randolph Starn has argued that exile lost its bite in the course of the fifteenth cen-

---

1. On the distinction between exile and banishment, see page 340. Recent work on exile includes R. Starn, *Contrary Commonwealth: The Theme of Exile in Medieval and Renaissance Italy* (Berkeley and Los Angeles, 1982); G. Ulysse, "De la séparation et de l'exile: Les Lettres d'Alessandra Macinghi Strozzi," in *L'exil et l'exclusion dans la culture italienne* (Aix-en-Provence, 1991), pp. 89–112; S. F. Baxendale, "The Alberti Family In and Out of Florence, 1401–1428," *Renaissance Quarterly* 44 (1991): 720–56; and M. Ganz, "Paying the Price for Political Failure: Florentine Women in the Aftermath of 1466," *Rinascimento*, ser. 2, 34 (1994): 237–57. There are in addition two recent general books on exile in Italy, J. Heers, *L'esilio, la vita politica e la societa' nel medioevo* (Naples, 1997); and C. Shaw, *The Politics of Exile in Renaissance Italy* (Cambridge, England, 2000, reviewed by A. Brown in *English Historical Review* 115 [November 2000]). See also D. Cavalca, *Il bando nella prassi e nella dottrina giuridica medievale* (Milan, 1978); and, as a basis for my work on this topic, as for so many others, G. Brucker, ed., *The Society of Renaissance Florence* (New York, 1971), pp. 21, 38, 49, 63, 116, 130, 136. I thank Catherine Harbor for her help preparing the graphs and appendix to this chapter.

2. Girolamo Savonarola, *Prediche sopra i Psalmi*, vol. 1, ed. V. Romano (Rome, 1969), no. 1 (6 January 1495), p. 13: "se tu mandi via de' tua cittadini agli confini, andranno a' principi e reveleranno i secreti del tuo stato, che ti potrebbe nuocere assai."

3. Ibid., p. 14: "i tuoi che sono in luoghi lontani con grande richezze . . . torneranno e saranno le loro richezze beneficio universale a tutta questa città."

tury as a weapon against political dissidents. This was partly for the practical reasons highlighted by Savonarola. It was also, he argues, the result of more profound changes in the external relationship between Renaissance states and in their internal organization that intensified "pressures for ideological conformity."[4] My purpose here will be to reexamine the practice of exile in the fifteenth century to see if there was a change and, if so, what it may tell us about wider changes in the period. Despite the difficulty of probing the feelings of exiles and of distinguishing their situation from that of other Florentine emigrants, a study of changing political and financial strategies may help to explain how the threat of exile retained its power to hurt—although its power, I shall argue, was now exerted more through internalized fear and behavioral controls than through the external frontiers of the city's medieval walls.

Exile from an Italian city-state meant much more than simply losing one's political and financial privileges as a citizen—the *onori e utili* that made office-holding so sought after. It meant crossing the frontier between death and salvation both as a Christian and as a citizen. To be exiled was to lose the double protection of the city's encircling walls, which—as numerous paintings illustrate—were themselves held in the warm embrace of its patron saint, safe from the clutches of the devil hovering above and the wild beasts outside. Cities, as we know from Gino Capponi, were for men, and the countryside for animals, and to a much greater extent than in less urbanized countries, city dwellers in Italy believed they could not be fully human outside their city. So to lose one's city was to lose not just the perks of city life but life itself—to become, in Remigio Girolami's evocative words, no more than "a painted image or a form of stone."[5] It is for these reasons that we can talk of exile as the crossing of a moral as well as a political frontier, one symbolized by the city walls and by the names used to distinguish insiders (*intrinseci*) from outsiders (*estrinseci* or *fuorusciti*). Just as in the

4. Starn, *Contrary Commonwealth*, chap. 4, "Facts and Rules of Inclusion," at p. 87.

5. "Unde destructa civitate remanet civis lapideus aut depictus," *De bono comuni*, ed. M. C. de Mattei, *La "Teologia politica e comunale" di Remigio de' Girolami* (Bologna, 1977), p. 18; cit. A. Brown, "City and Citizen: Changing Perceptions in the Fifteenth and Sixteenth Centuries," in *City-States in Antiquity and Medieval Italy*, ed. A. Molho, K. Raaflaub, and J. Emlen (Ann Arbor, Mich., 1991), p. 94; repr. in Brown, *The Medici in Florence: The Exercise and Language of Power* (Florence, 1992), p. 283. For Capponi, F. W. Kent, *Household and Lineage in Renaissance Florence: The Family Life of the Capponi, Ginori and Rucellai* (Princeton, N.J., 1977), p. 60.

wider map of Universal Judgment the walls of the Heavenly City segregated the saved from the damned in two distinct zones,[6] so the walls of temporal cities segregated good people from bad: good citizens not only from exiles, who were allowed to return only when "reformed, civil, full of good,"[7] but also from criminals who crossed the walls to be executed in the liminal space outside.[8]

Exile was an effective weapon because it operated within this intimate and integrated system of values, but by the fifteenth century both the spiritual and the political maps of Italy had changed. The maps of Universal Judgment removed the strict boundary between saved and damned by admitting an intermediate purgatorial zone and then were replaced altogether by a more internalized map of guilt and salvation. At the same time, the political map of Italy altered old boundaries by expanding many of the small city-states into larger territorial states, whose rulers, joined by political and marriage alliances, no longer guaranteed safe havens for partisan exiles.[9] This new map of Italy certainly helped to reduce the numbers of exiles

6. S. Y. Edgerton, *Pictures and Punishment: Art and Criminal Prosecution during the Florentine Renaissance* (Ithaca, N.Y., 1985), pp. 22–33; C. Frugoni, *A Distant City: Images of Urban Experience in the Medieval World* (Princeton, N.J., 1990), pp. 135–38.

7. Shakespeare, *Two Gentlemen of Verona*, 5.4.154–156: "Forgive them what they have committed here, / And let them be recall'd from their exile. / They are reformed, civil, full of good," quoted by A. B. Giamatti, *Exile and Change in Renaissance Literature* (New Haven, Conn., 1984), p. 148. Cf. Francesco Guicciardini, who thought those who rejected citizen honors had "lo animo male disposto e come pernizioso si vorrebbe separarlo ed esterminarlo dalla patria"; *Dialogo del Reggimento di Firenze*, ed. R. Palmarocchi (Bari, 1932), p. 120; trans. A. Brown, in Guicciardini, *Dialogue on the Government of Florence* (Cambridge, England, 1994), p. 116. On exile and otherness, M. R. Menocai, *Shards of Love: Exile and the Origins of the Lyric* (Durham, N.C., 1994).

8. A. Zorzi, "Le esecuzioni delle condanne a morte a Firenze nel Tardo Medioevo tra repressione penale e cerimoniale pubblico," in *Simbolo e realtà della vita urbana nel tardo medioevo*, ed. M. Miglio and G. Lombardi (Rome, 1993), pp. 27–32 (though, as Zorzi reminds us, not all criminals were hanged outside the walls: some exemplary hangings were conducted "nel cuore della vita publica," including at the podestà's palace); Edgerton, *Pictures and Punishment*, p. 141. On the walls as boundaries, R. C. Trexler, "*Correre la Terra*: Collective Insults in the Late Middle Ages," repr. in Trexler, *Dependence in Context in Renaissance Florence* (Binghamton, N.Y., 1994), pp. 113–70.

9. On purgatory, J. Le Goff, *The Birth of Purgatory* (Chicago, 1984); and on personalized salvation, Edgerton, *Pictures and Punishment*, esp. pp. 172–83; on political boundaries, R. Starn, *Contrary Commonwealth*, esp. chap. 4, pp. 86–120. The new resident ambassadors also undermined the safety of places of exile in spying and reporting on their compatriots there; ibid., pp. 93–94.

compared with the mass expulsions of Guelfs and Ghibellines in the thirteenth and fourteenth centuries. And the expansion of the Florentine state
also changed the terms and places of exile. Although the same terminology
continued to be used, inherited from both German and Roman law, the
frontiers were no longer the same. The German *bannum* meant expulsion
from the empire and loss of the right to legal protection as a result of rebellion (the equivalent of the Roman *interdictio aqua et igni*), a punishment that continued to be imposed, although "the empire" no longer meant
the German empire but Florence's own territory or dominion, and the practice of levying bounty was—as we shall see—increasingly condemned as
inhuman and immoral.[10] Roman *relegatio* meant either exclusion *from* certain places (from Florence, or so many miles from the city or its territory)
or temporary relegation *to* a certain place (to a town or to an island, *ad insulam*) becoming permanent deportation with loss of civil, but not human,
rights and confiscation of property if the terms of exile were broken, whereas
confinatio meant confinement *inside* a certain place (inside the walls of Florence or in its prison, the Stinche).[11] Here change can be seen in the sentences imposed on exiles, which no longer defined *relegatio* and *confinatio*
in terms of the city and its walls but in terms of its wider dominion, replacing the Roman relegation *ad insulam* with the concept of exile outside the
frontiers of "Italy" itself. So whereas in 1466 two of the Pitti conspirators
were confined to the island of Sicily, "beyond the lighthouse," in 1482 three
of the surviving Pazzi conspirators exchanged imprisonment in Volterra for
relegation, or exclusion, not from Florentine territory or to an island but
from "the whole of Italy." At the same time imprisonment inside the city
walls was redefined to mean confinement inside Florence's new territory,
in Pisa or in Livorno, or inside the new high-security prison in Volterra, il
Maschio, which replaced the old prison of the Stinche in Florence. This was

10. See the comment of Francesco Guicciardini in his *Dialogo del Reggimento
di Firenze*, ed. Palmarocchi, p. 167, trans. Brown, p. 163, cited in note 78 below. The
increased bounty of 4,000 florins on Piero de' Medici's head in September 1495 was
imposed by the Otto di guardia within the Florentine "empire," OGBR 102, fol. 81r;
see Alison Brown, "The Language of Empire," in *Florentine Tuscany: Structures
and Practices of Power*, ed. W. J. Connell and A. Zorzi (Cambridge, England, 2000),
pp. 32–47, esp. pp. 41–42. On legal objections to the transference of these powers
to Florentine magistrates in 1478, O. Cavallar, "Il tiranno, i *dubia* del giudice, ed i
consilia dei giuristi," *Archivio storico italiano* 155 (1997): 265–345, esp. pp. 284–90
(whom I would like to thank very warmly for letting me read and cite this article
before publication).

11. See especially Cavalca, *Il bando* (esp. pp. 55 and 95, citing Bartolus on the
bando); Starn, *Contrary Commonwealth*, esp. pp. 17–29.

where the Pazzi prisoners were sent, whereas moral deviants such as adulterers and homosexuals, who needed to be isolated from the healthy community, were punished with imprisonment inside a new purgatorial zone on the malarial frontiers of the state around Livorno.[12]

Perhaps the most striking boundary change, however, is the least commented on: the changing boundaries of trade. The new interest in cartography was fired by voyages of exploration to Africa and the New World. The translation of Ptolemy's *Geographia* in Florence around 1400, the acquisition of Pisa and her trading posts in 1406, and the creation of her galley fleet in the 1420s transformed Florence into a maritime power.[13] What impact did this have on people's perception of inside and outside? Some exiles were now exiled to Pisa and Livorno, with the proviso that they could "sail in every part of the world on Florentine galleys sent by the commune of Florence."[14] When exiles like the Alberti, the Strozzi, the Pazzi, and the Medici had houses and trading posts throughout Italy and Europe, exile surely lost much of its power to hurt.[15] Far more effective than exile as pun-

12. ASF, OGBR, 61, fol. 29v (13 April 1482): "extra totam Italiam" (cf. note 27 below). The crimes of breaking open tombs in front of Santa Maria Novella during Easter 1483, adultery, and two cases of sodomy merited exile in Livorno for periods of ten, five, three, and two years; ibid., 64, fols. 36r, 40r–v (28 March and 3 April 1483). There are examples of exile to Pisa and/or Livorno in OGBR, 67, fol. 2r (1 March 1484); and OGBR, 224 (on 224, see note 24 below), fols. 94v–95v, 96v, 104v–107r, 110v–111r, 113r–114r (1458/59–1462). These exiles also helped to colonize this frontier territory, as we can see from a proposal in 1460 for a law, "per quam exules, exceptis certis criminibus, in agro pisano reduceretur ob inopiam agrestium hominum," ASF, CP, 56, fol. 76r–v (8 March 1460); thus in October 1496, one citizen hoped that Livorno would not be lost, because "tornerà una terra castellana e sarà peggio di Siena, perché quella ha qualche porto" (CP, 62, fol. 205v). On the state of Pisa, see M. Mallett, "Florence and Pisa in the Fifteenth Century," in *Florentine Studies: Politics and Society in Renaissance Florence*, ed. N. Rubinstein (London, 1968), esp. pp. 407–9; and ASF, Misc. rep., XI, 266 (proposals to reform Pisa in 1490).

13. S. Y. Edgerton, *The Renaissance Rediscovery of Linear Perspective* (New York, 1975), esp. pp. 97–99; K. Lippencott, "The Art of Cartography in Fifteenth-Century Florence," in *Lorenzo the Magnificent: Culture and Politics,* ed. M. Mallett and N. Mann (London, 1996), pp. 131–49 (with relevant bibliography); M. Mallett, *The Florentine Galleys in the Fifteenth Century* (Oxford, 1967), esp. chaps. 1 and 2, pp. 3–39; B. Dini, "L'economia fiorentina dal 1450 al 1538," in *La Toscana al tempo di Lorenzo il Magnifico,* 3 vols., ed. R. Fubini (Pisa, 1996), 3:805.

14. ASF, OGBR, 224, fol. 107r (16 April 1461): twenty years' exile to Livorno and twelve years' exile to Pisa and Livorno, "salvo che possono navichare in ogni parte del mondo sopra legni di fiorentini mandati per lo comune di Firenze."

15. As G. Ulysse argues, commenting on the voluntary departure of three Strozzi cousins to trade in Spain and Bruges, as well as in Naples and Rome ("De la séparation et de l'exil," p. 99). On the Salviati's trade in Bruges and Madeira, see

ishment for such people, Francesco Guicciardini argued in the 1520s, would be ostracism from merchants' communities abroad, "because the sight of people visiting and conversing with members of the trading community is taken as a sign that they have quite a lot of friends and allies in the city; and on the contrary, to see them abandoned and shunned by everyone suggests things are going badly for them." [16]

No one has attempted to assess fully the effect on exile of Florence's new trading empire, nor answer the pertinent question raised by Richard Goldthwaite in 1987 about "the problem of the exiled merchant" and why businesses were unaffected by it: "When Cosimo de' Medici himself went into exile late in 1433 . . . he simply opened up shop elsewhere (at Venice) and continued to do business as usual." [17] Part of the answer, as he suggests, must be the solidarity of the business community that made it relatively impervious to government controls. Thus in 1363 only 21 out of 121 Florentine bankers suffered reprisals after obeying the extraordinary papal mandate to desert their own government, while in 1414 the exiled Alberti were able to survive Pope John XXIII's attempt to bankrupt them by paying the loan of 80,000 florins he asked for in only four days, half the time allowed. [18]

This is only part of the explanation, however, and it does not address the question of change and the growing powers of fifteenth-century governments. Their unwillingness to confiscate merchant wealth was not simply a result of impotence in the face of international capitalism but also was due to other considerations, such as the strength of family bonds, the fear of losing the hens that laid the golden eggs—and perhaps also the sheer difficulty of the operation. [19] Savonarola, as we have seen, was well aware of the

---

Dini, "L'economia fiorentina," pp. 801, 811. On the Pisan exiles in Sicily, see G. Petralia, *Banchieri e famiglie mercantili nel Mediterraneo aragonese: L'emigrazione dei Pisani in Sicilia nel Quattrocento* (Pisa, 1989). On the economic effects of exile, especially on the women left behind, see Baxendale, "The Alberti Family In and Out of Florence"; Ganz, "Paying the Price for Political Failure."

16. Guicciardini, *Dialogo del Reggimento*, p. 168; trans. Brown, p. 164.

17. R. A. Goldthwaite, "The Medici Bank and the World of Florentine Capitalism," *Past and Present* 114 (1987): 23.

18. According to S. Raveggi in *Ghibellini, Guelfi e Popolo grasso: I detentori del potere politico a Firenze nella seconda metà del Dugento*, ed. S. Raveggi, M. Tarassi, D. Medici, and P. Parenti (Florence, 1978), pp. 58–61, the merchants had to leave Florence and hand over lists of all their partners, otherwise all their goods would be sequestered by the pope. On the Alberti, Baxendale, "Exile in Pratice," p. 737; the money was moved from London to Rome via Venice.

19. That is, the difficulty of separating the exile's account from those of his partners' (demonstrated, e.g., by the accounts of the "Sindaci super rebus Pieri de Medici" in ASF, CS, ser. 1, 10, no. 11, fols. 186r–89v, concerning the division of a

danger of losing the exiles' wealth, as were the citizens who in 1431 debated whether or not to exile citizens for tax debts. "It is not good to force citizens into exile," one citizen said, "they should be kept here and made to pay what they can by degrees"—"taxing them month by month without reducing their original debt," as another put it.[20] The revenue drawn from taxing the property of exiles in their absence was considerable, as Baxendale has shown in the case of the Alberti, and since debt disqualified citizens from political office, it was mutually beneficial for government and exiles not to break their umbilical cord.[21] For this reason the property of exiles was sequestered as surety for taxes and good behavior, but it was confiscated only if the exiles broke the conditions of their exile and became outlawed as rebels.[22] Cosimo was thus able to "empty the great treasure of [Florence] into the bosom of St. Mark" by transferring at least 15,000 ducats from Florence to his bank in Venice and some 10,000 florins' worth of Monte credits to Rome, as well as by depositing another 10,000 ducats from his manager's house in two Florentine monasteries.[23]

II

If there was change, it was not immediately evident. The policy of not being unduly harsh toward exiles was at first continued by the Medici regime

battiloro company, 6 May 1495) and also the problem created by returning exiles illustrated by Cavallar, "Il tiranno" (note 10 above), esp. pp. 331–32, citing Guicciardini's *Storie fiorentine*, ed. R. Palmarocchi (Bari, 1931), p. 101, on the "sommo timore" of those who had acquired rebels' goods on their return in 1494.

20. E. Conti, *L'imposta diretta a Firenze nel Quattrocento (1427–1494)* (Rome, 1984), pp. 166–67 (3, 5 July 1431): "Ponere cives in exilio . . . non est bonum. Potius retineantur cives et paulatim exigatur ab illis quod possibile est, tassando de mense in mense, sine diminutione principalis debiti."

21. Baxandale, "Exile in Practice," pp. 734–38.

22. On the Tower Officers and the Officers of the Goods of Rebels, see *Statuta Populi et Communis Florentiae*, 3 vols. (Freiburg [Florence], 1778), 2:7–13; G. Guidi, *Il governo della città-repubblica di Firenze del primo Quattrocento*, 3 vols. (Florence, 1981), 2:286–87. Starn demonstrates a decline in the sequestration of rebel property from 525 in 1365–76 to 239 in 1431–1509; *Contrary Commonwealth*, p. 113.

23. "e del tuo gran tesoro ti vota sempre, et empie a Marco il seno," cited by A. Molho, *Florentine Public Finances in the Early Renaissance, 1400–1433* (Cambridge, Mass., 1971), p. 190; cf. Dale Kent, *The Rise of the Medici: Faction in Florence 1326–1434* (Oxford, 1978), p. 296. On Cosimo's fortune in being exiled to Venice, where he was honored and favored by the government, see Giovanni Cavalcanti, *Istorie fiorentine*, ed. G. di Pino (Milan, 1944), bk. ix, chap. 37, p. 292; cited by R. Trexler, *Public Life in Renaissance Florence* (New York, 1980), p. 422.

after 1434. For although the number of exiles in 1434 was 118, vastly more than the 8 Medici and 3 others exiled in 1433, their terms of exile were initially not very long, nor were their places of exile inhospitable, many being sent to locations where they could well have conducted business.[24] Moreover, even the toughest sentences were accompanied by placebos and modified in time. The sentences against the Pitti conspirators in 1466 were softened by the return of 29 earlier exiles, and after representations to the government that Dietisalvi and Francesco Neroni "shouldn't be punished for their failings," the brothers were allowed to exchange exile in Sicily "beyond the lighthouse" for a choice of places nearer home.[25] The hardest of hearts could be guaranteed to be moved by the demands of "mercy and pity" in the course of time, even in the case of the Pazzi. First those who fell sick in the harsh prison at Volterra were allowed to be given medication by the Medici's doctor, George of Cyprus; then, following the opinion of "the most noble and wisest citizens," "the frailest and least capable of doing harm" were allowed out to live one hundred miles from Florence; later, "for the public good and moved by just and laudable reasons to be merciful," three more left to live outside Italy; and finally Lorenzo de' Medici's nephew was repeatedly allowed to stay with his mother, "wherever she is, even in Florence."[26] The success of "caressing" the 1466 rebels—in winning them over to the regime—made Piero Guicciardini, a severe critic of

---

24. See Tables I and II, "Exiles by Year" and "Places of Exile." ASF, OGBR, 224 (beautifully written on vellum on or after 1458, copied in ASF, Manoscritti, 441) lists sentences of exiles, as well as when they reported in their place of exile. Cf. Dale Kent, *Rise of the Medici*, Appendix II, pp. 355–57, listing 109 exiles in 1434; and N. Rubinstein, *The Government of Florence under the Medici (1434–94)*, 2d ed. (Oxford, 1997), pp. 2–4, 123–26. Although some *popolani* were relegated to the category of magnates in 1434, they became a juridical rather than a social class; Kent, *Rise of the Medici*, pp. 346–47.

25. See the lists in M. Phillips, *The Memoir of Marco Parenti* (Princeton, N.J., 1987), pp. 203–6; and ASF, Balìe, 30, fols. 57v–58r (30 October 1466), allowing Dietisalvi to replace Sicily with Novara or Alessandria, and Francesco with Foligno, Orvieto, or Todi. Similarly, Alessandro Tornabuoni's exile in Sicily was modified after a year to exile two hundred miles from Florence; OGBR, 68, fol. 124r (October 1484); ibid., 72, fol. 17r (November 1485). On Tornabuoni's exile, see Luca Landucci, *Diario fiorentino dal 1450 al 1516*, ed. I. del Badia (Florence, 1883; repr., 1985), p. 48.

26. ASF, OGBR, 55, fols. 10v–11r; ibid., 56, fols. 46r, 77v; ibid., 57, fol. 81r–v ("communem nobiliorum sapientiorumque suorum civium sententiam . . . qui debiliores sunt et minus nocere possunt"); ibid., 61, fol. 29v ("pro bono publico & ad faciendam misericordiam . . . iustis & laudabilibus causis moti"); ibid., 68, fol. 1v, in March, August, and October 1480; February 1481; April 1482; July 1484, renewed in November and every year until November 1488. Cf. Landucci, *Diario*, p. 40.

the 1478 sentences, expect that even the 1434 exiles would eventually be won over by similar blandishments.[27]

It would be wrong, however, to deduce from this that exile had lost its bite under Medici hegemony in the fifteenth century, since quite the reverse was true. What is striking about a comparison of numbers of exiles from 1433 to 1494 (figure 14.1) is not only the large number who were exiled in 1434 but also the fact that the second highest peak is in 1458—a relatively understated moment of crisis, precipitated by disagreement within the regime about the need for reform—when forty men were exiled, one more than in 1466. Perhaps, compared with the 1434 exiles, the measures against Girolamo Machiavelli and his supporters seemed mild, but both the numbers of new exiles and the novelty of their punishment suggest that the political threat was more serious than chroniclers at the time, or later historians, have acknowledged.[28] And although the sentences of 1466 were mitigated by the recall of earlier exiles, the numbers of people they exiled were again high, six more than in 1478, when the punishment was generally reckoned to have been particularly harsh, both in terms of the number of innocent Pazzi who were exiled and also for the barbarism of the initial retribution, when more than eighty people were hanged from the windows of the Bargello without a proper legal process or being allowed to take the last rites.[29]

Another novel feature of the fifteenth century was the new "scatter" policy of sending exiles to many different places, as figure 14.2 demonstrates. It seems that more important than where they went was the fact that they were scattered far and wide, especially in 1434, when the Albizzi exiles were sent to forty-two different cities, including Rhodes, Ragusa, Avignon,

27. Rubinstein, *Government*, p. 365: "carezzati" (Appendix XI: Piero Guicciardini on the scrutiny of 1484).

28. See Rubinstein, *Government*, p. 124, commenting on the mildness as well as the "sense of mistrust" shown by the regime in extending the 1434 sentences, though perhaps understating the political threat.

29. Jacopo Guicciardini was very critical of Lorenzo's vendetta against the Pazzi, according to Francesco Guicciardini, *Memorie di familia*, in Guicciardini, *Scritti autobiografici e rari*, ed. R. Palmarocchi (Bari, 1936), p. 42. Cf. his *Storie fiorentine*, p. 78, and *Dialogo*, p. 32; trans. Brown, p. 31 (although as Osvaldo Cavallar reminds us, Francesco's professional opinion was rather different; Cavallar, *Francesco Guicciardini giurista* [Milan, 1991], p. 111); and A. Brown, "Lorenzo and Guicciardini," in *Lorenzo the Magnificent*, ed. Mallett and Mann, pp. 286, 289. According to Edgerton (*Pictures and Punishment*, pp. 104–5, 108, 145 n. 30), Lorenzo de' Medici was personally responsible for the epitaphs placed below the *pitture infamanti* of eight traitors.

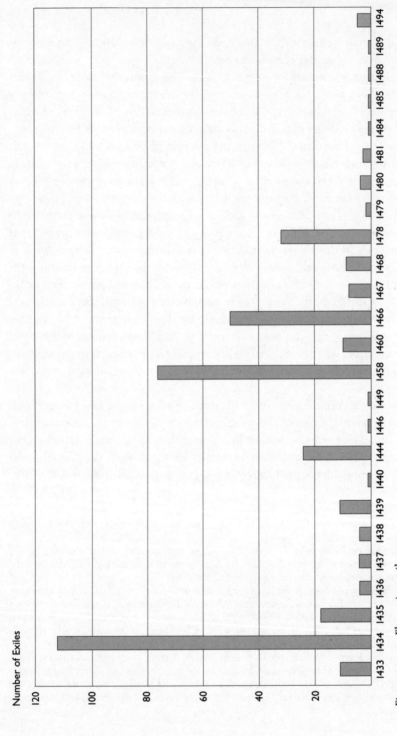

Number of Exiles

Figure 14.1. Florentine exiles, 1433–94.

and Barcelona outside Italy. This policy was doubtless intended to prevent the formation of cells of opposition such as later developed in Ferrara, Venice, Rome, and Naples. According to Giovanbattista Busini, a sixteenth-century exile, Cosimo and his party initiated it, although we do not know whether social discrimination also formed part of this policy, as it did in the sixteenth century, when Busini complained that the Papal States were chosen for those of "the lowest condition," like himself.[30]

Moreover, though heavily reduced in numbers, exiles were subject to increasing controls. It is in 1444 that we can begin to see the emergence of what Nicolai Rubinstein has defined as a new strategy of eliminating exiles as a political class.[31] The Balìa of that year took the first steps in this new strategy by renewing the decrees of 1434 for another ten years, the Balìa of 1453–54 extending them for another ten years until 1464, and the 1458 Balìa for another ten until 1474—and then for an extra twenty-five years.[32]

Ammonizione, or loss of office, was also part of this strategy. Described by Gene Brucker as "a brilliant new technique" when it was introduced by the Guelf Party in about 1359, it had fallen into disrepute with the decline of the party and the factionalism that it represented.[33] So although the exiles of 1433 and 1434 had been automatically deprived of offices, with their

30. According to G. B. Busini (*Lettere . . . a Benedetto Varchi*, ed. G. Milanesi [Florence, 1860], p. 190), the policy of dispersing exiles "qua e là . . . fece Cosimo e la sua parte." Busini was sent to Benevento, whereas "infiniti nobili ebbero il campo largo"; on his exile in 1530, see C. Pincin in *Dizionario biographico degli Italiani*, vol. 15 (Rome, 1972), pp. 534–37. The later cells are discussed below, p. 360.

31. Rubinstein, *Government*, p. 125: "to eliminate . . . any danger that might accrue from a return of the exiles to political life: in many cases, the new sentences amounted to banishment, or at least disqualification, for life."

32. ASF, Balìe, 26, fols. 24v, 28v–29r, 41r–42r, 58v (29–30 May, 22 June, 6 August 1444); Balìe, 27, fol. 217v (14 March 1454); Balìe, 29, fol. 10r; and OGBR, 224, fol. 85v (11 August and 13 November 1458, to one hundred miles beyond Florentine territory); Rubinstein, *Government*, pp. 20–21, 124–27. In 1444, twelve leading citizens (and one wife) were sent from the Stinche to exile outside the Florentine state after they had paid their fines and debts to the commune (Balìe, 26, fol. 26r–v, 29 May 1444). These terms did not apply to those exiled within the Florentine state after 1434, whose condemnations "cancellentur facta certa declaratione" (marginal note, ibid., fol. 58v).

33. G. Brucker, *Florentine Politics and Society, 1343–1378* (Princeton, N.J., 1962), pp. 170–71, describing it as "a more humane method of proscription. . . . Those marked for exclusion were not financially penalized, nor did they suffer the humiliation of being branded in the courts as a criminal." See also pp. 370–71, on its reform in 1378; and, in 1382, see Guidi, *Il governo*, 1:212; 2:114–17. On the attempt to revive it in 1430 by Mariotto Baldovinetti, exiled in 1434, see D. Kent, *Rise of the Medici*, p. 251.

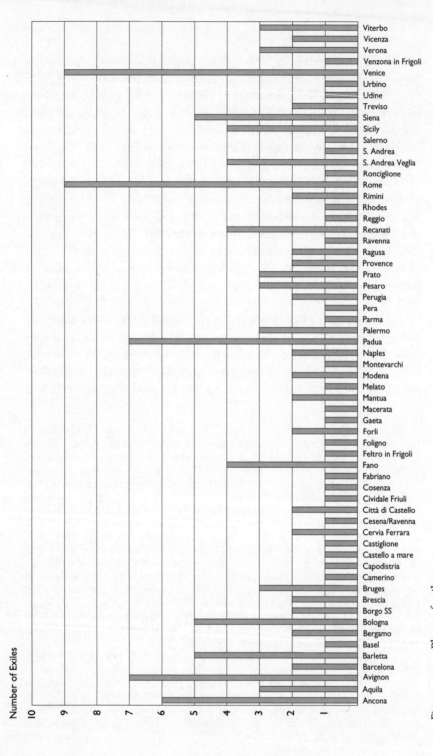

Figure 14.2. Places of exile, 1433–94.

sons, as a condition of their exile (the Medici, as well as six exiles in 1434 also being proscribed as magnates or supermagnates), the only people to be punished solely by loss of political office in 1434 were the Signoria (and their sons) of September–October 1433 who called the *parlamento* that exiled the Medici, together with four other citizens.[34] In 1444 this political blacklist was extended to include the scrutineers of 1433 and their sons and brothers; ten years later the Balìa of 1452–54 (like that of 1444 not related to a major political crisis or rebellion) added to these groups all those deprived of office between 1434 and 1444;[35] and in 1458—after the Otto di guardia had been given special powers in matters of exile and loss of offices—they and their male descendants were deprived of offices for twenty years and then, with all the members of eleven listed families, for life.[36]

Moreover, in 1466 it was decreed that the name tickets of the disenfranchised exiles were to be taken out of the bags and destroyed *before* they were drawn instead of afterward—not only saving time and preventing boredom, as it was claimed, but also depriving them of the publicity that it was thought they no longer merited.[37] Thereafter loss of office either for a long period (twenty or twenty-five years) or for life became established as one of three ingredients (with exile and monetary fines and/or confiscation of goods) in a punitive cocktail dispensed in varying doses and measures to political opponents of the regime.

It is the third ingredient in this cocktail that is particularly interesting. Economic sanctions were seemingly less important than political ones, and it was surprising to Goldthwaite that so little use was made of them. Initially the Medici regime continued the statutory policy of confiscating Monte credits and the possessions of exiles only when the exiles were denounced as rebels, otherwise sequestering them as surety for the payment of taxes and good behavior.[38] And although in 1434 as in 1433, additional sureties

34. ASF, Balìe, 24, fols. 10v–11r; Balìe, 25, fols. 55r, 61r, 64v, 65v, 68r. The loss of office was for life.

35. OGBR, 224, fol. 78r (2 June 1444); and ASF, Balìe, 27, fol. 217r (13–14 March 1454).

36. OGBR, 224, fol. 85v (13 November 1458); Rubinstein, *Government*, pp. 124–25. On the *balìa* given to the Otto in and after 1453 and its importance, ibid., pp. 125–26 and 126 note 3.

37. ASF, Balìe, 30, fol. 85r–v (24 December 1466): "e non meritano essere pure ricordati nella città nostra se non come capitali nimici di quella." The Palace Officials and friars were authorized to open and hunt through all the election bags to read the name tickets, destroying those of *confinati* or *ammoniti* before refolding and replacing the rest diligently in the bags.

38. D. Kent, *Rise of the Medici*, p. 296; Ganz, "Paying the Price," p. 242. As it was expressed in ASF, Balìe, 30, fol. 75v (11 December 1466), Monte credits and

were demanded from rich bankers, the size of these sureties was in fact much smaller in 1434 than in 1433.[39] Only Rinaldo degli Albizzi was listed as having lost his Monte credits to the Otto di guardia after being declared a rebel on 25 February 1435, and we know of some fourteen exiles or their heirs who lost their property to the Monte officers for nonpayment of taxes in 1438–39.[40]

Nevertheless, here, too, there was change. For not only were fines levied on exiles and opponents of the regime, but increasingly nonrebels were threatened with the confiscation of their goods, mobile as well as immobile. The first evidence I have found of these changes is in 1458, a year already noted for its high number of exiles. The arrest of Girolamo Machiavelli and his brother Piero on 3 August was followed by sentences punishing them with exile for twenty-five years, loss of office for life (and for their male descendants), confiscation of goods—despite not being rebels—and a fine of 800 *fiorini larghi*. It was a condition of this and subsequent fines of the same sort that the threatened confiscation would not take place if half the fine was paid within ten days, a gambit that eventually, if not initially, proved successful in procuring cash rapidly. For although in 1458 seven such fines drew in only about 1,000 florins, in 1466 ten larger fines succeeded in procuring 8,625 florins in cash for the treasury.[41] Since both Girolamo and his brother were condemned as rebels the following year, their property was

---

possessions of the exiles "remaneant obligata communi Florentino pro solutione onerum & pro observantia confinium ipsorum. . . . Et quod vendi alienari seu obligari alicui alteri nequeant quoquo modo etc. Salvis iuribus quorumcumque qui essent creditores confinatorum predictorum. . . ."

39. Cosimo's surety was 20,000 *fiorini d'oro*, Averardo's and Lorenzo's 10,000, Giuliano di Averardo's 5,000, and Orlando's 3,000 (on 29 September, when they were declared magnates, Monte credits belonging to their banking companies were exempted from this restriction), whereas ten sureties of 1,000 and two of 500 *fiorini d'oro* were demanded from members of seven families in 1434, including the Strozzi, Peruzzi, and Bardi; ASF, Balìe, 24, fols. 11r, 23v (11, 29 September 1433), ed. A. Fabroni, *Magni Cosmi Medicei Vita*, 2 vols. (Pisa, 1789), 2:92–93; and Balìe, 25, fols. 58r, 65r (6, 17 November 1434); cf. D. Kent, *Rise of the Medici*, p. 296. The freeze on assets (on Monte credits and *bona immobilia*) is stated in Balìe, 24, fol. 11r, ed. Fabroni, *Magni Cosmi . . . Vita*, p. 92; Balìe, 25, fols. 63r–v, 65v–66r; 30, fol. 17v (11 September 1466); cf. OGBR, 224, fol. 13r.

40. According to the one listed volume of confiscated *beni* I have identified in the Monte Comune *fondo* (pt. II, no. 1289). Rinaldo's credits are listed in OGBR, 224, fol. 72r. They could not be spent or alienated by the Otto "se non per occisione et persecutione di Rebelli."

41. ASF, OGBR, 224, fols. 80r, 81r, 82r, 83r–v, 84r, 134r–135r, 137r–138r, 139r, 140r.

in the end forfeited, as was that of a new listing of families condemned in 1460, updated to include their sons and male descendants.[42]

By 1466 the idea of confiscating the goods of nonrebels encouraged new developments that suggested the boundary between rebels and nonrebels was growing less clear. The Balìa appointed by the *parlamento* on 2 September 1466 condemned the principal opponents of the Medici—Angelo Acciaiuoli and his son Neri, the Neroni brothers Dietisalvi, Francesco, and Angelo, and Niccolò Soderini and his son Geri—to twenty years' exile in southern Italy, Sicily, and Provence; and it sequestered their Monte credits and possessions as surety for the payment of taxes. Despite the fact that none of these people was as yet condemned as a rebel (Angelo and his sons were condemned only in January–February 1467), grain belonging the Acciaiuoli and the Neroni was confiscated and given to the Office of the Abundantia in September, and in its last month of office the Balìa appointed Five Officers of the Rebels to arbitrate claims on the sequestered (and later confiscated) possessions, which it claimed the Tower Officers and the Otto di guardia were too busy to deal with.[43] The success of these economic sanctions can be seen in Angelo Acciaiuoli's bitter letters of despair at having "lost my goods at home and my credits in Milan and what the king [of Naples] gave me four years ago."[44]

In 1478 and 1494, following the Pazzi Conspiracy and the exile of the Medici, the same situation recurred in that possessions were seized before

---

42. Ibid., fols. 97v, 99v (29 November and 8 December 1459); and 104r (12 July 1460), listing members of fifteen families.

43. ASF, Balìe, 30, fols. 15v–18r, 75v–77r, 93r–v (11 September 1466 and 11, 29 December 1466, the last a modification); OGBR, 224, fols. 13v (11 September 1466), 125v (29 January, 3 February 1467); Ganz, "Paying the Price," p. 242 n. 14). Cf. Phillips, *Memoir*, pp. 202–3. There was in fact nothing new in this, since Officials of the Rebels had similarly been appointed in 1434 (replacing the Quinque Officiales Rerum Condemnatorum) to deal with claims on the estates of the exiles and to prevent the sale of Monte credits; in 1468 the Tower Officers were once again in charge of the "rerum et bonarum rebellum et confinatorum et exbannitorum"; see their *quadernus* beginning 4 April 1468, ASF, CPGNR, 132. On these offices, see note 22 above.

44. ASF, CS, ser. 1, 136, fol. 41 (to Piero Dietisalvi in Naples, 24 July 1470): "'gni persona sa che io ho perduto la roba della patria, et quella di che ero creditore ad Milano; et quello che il Signor Re mi havea data et sono iiii anni. Questa è una prova vera della povertà mia." On the confiscation of his grain, see his letter to Piero de' Medici, 17 September 1466, ed. A. Fabroni, *Laurentii Medicis Vita*, 2 vols. (Pisa, 1784), 2:36; trans. in J. Ross, *Lives of the Early Medici as Told in Their Correspondence* (London, 1910), p. 105: "Io l'aiutai che non li [Cosimo] fusse tolta la roba, ora e' tolgono a me & grani & certe miserie di masserizie."

the exiles had been legally condemned as rebels. Perhaps it was self-evident in May 1478, five days after Giuliano de' Medici had been murdered in the cathedral, that "because of what has happened, many have become rebels of the commune and that decisions have to be made about how best to profit from the residue of their possessions after their creditors have been paid." Nevertheless, to sequester the goods of the Pazzi on the day following the murder—even before the appointment of Five Officers of the Rebels on 1–2 May 1478—and then to confiscate and sell their possessions before they were legally condemned as rebels was surely jumping the gun.[45] All of their clothes, cloths, and furnishings were auctioned by the Five under the roof of the Mint on 1 June, "filling it from end to end, for they were very rich." Yet it was not until 4 August, two months later, that the podestà legally condemned the conspirators as rebels (with the confiscation of their goods) on the grounds that because they were rebels "at the time of their death . . . the goods of each and every one of them had been and are confiscated and seized for the communal fisc."[46] Eighteen months later, toward the end of the debilitating war that followed the conspiracy, six "Officials, Procurators and Syndics for the Affairs of the Pazzi" were appointed to settle the Pazzi's accounts, beginning work in May 1480.[47]

45. See F. Sacramoro to the dukes of Milan, 27 April 1478, cited in Lorenzo de' Medici, *Lettere*, vol. 3, ed. N. Rubinstein (Florence, 1977), p. 9 n. 2 (where their debts are estimated at 40,000–50,000 ducats); and ASF, PR, 169, fols. 16v–17r (1–2 May 1478), appointing "5 cittadini fiorentini" with the authority "quella e quanta hanno havuto gli uficiali de ribelii suti nell'anno 1434"; on 16 September 1478 the authority granted in May was said to apply to the "casi de ribelli e confinati da dì venticinque d'aprile insino allora" (ibid., 70r). The Officers of the Rebels were renewed on 25 April 1479 (PR, 170, fols. 17r–18r), with authority "solo a quegli che sono stati giudicati o pronunciati ribegli o de' quali la memoria è suta dannata o confinati o che furono privati di vita a dì xxvi d'aprile proscimo passato . . . ed non circha altri ribegli o confinati," for whom the Tower Officers remained responsible (cf. note 47 below). I am very grateful to Bill Kent for verifying this for me, as well as the records of the Otto cited in the following note. ASF, CPGNR, 77, lists some 427 claims by Pazzi and Salviati creditors made to the Officers of the Rebels in 1478.

46. Landucci, *Diario*, p. 22; ASF, Atti del Podestà, 5160, ed. A. Perosa in Angelo Poliziano, *Della congiura dei Pazzi* (Padua, 1958), p. 80. Whereas the Atti del Podestà incorporate sentences of the Otto against the rebels dated 28 April, 7 and 10 May 1478 (ed. Perosa, pp. 83–90), the records of the Otto itself contain no such sentences until 1 July (ASF, OGBR, 48, fol. 27v).

47. ASF, PR, 170, 100v–102r, 24 December 1479, appointing six citizens as syndics of the affairs of the Pazzi who had been confined and sentenced "da dì 26 aprile"; they were to enjoy the same authority hitherto accorded to the syndics "di falliti cessanti"; cf. Balìe, 38, "Liber sive Quaternus Officialium Procuratorum et Sindicorum super rebus et negotiis Pactiorum," 1480–82. Three officials were to be creditors of the Pazzi; the other three, representing the commune, had repeat-

The zeal of these auditors is demonstrated both by their records and by the complaints later made against them by the Pazzi. They met on average seven to eight times per month over two years, writing to Bruges, Valencia, Ragusa, and Pisa in pursuit of Pazzi wealth and drawing up lists of creditors, debtors, and their debts, especially from the salt farm in France that the king of France retracted after the conspiracy. Their sales ranged from the *domus magna* of Guglielmo Pazzi in Borgo degli Albizi, sold to Carlo Borromeo for a price to be brokered, to a pair of Niccolò Pazzi's used sheets, which the banker Filippo da Gagliano bought for eight florins.[48] When the Pazzi returned from exile in 1494, they complained bitterly of the great injustice done to them by the auditors in falsely denouncing their debtors as creditors, taking their possessions, and selling credits at less than half their proper value.[49] And, as we now know from Osvaldo Cavallar's important discussion of the legal implications of these confiscations, it was claimed on behalf of the Pazzi that since neither Lorenzo de' Medici nor the Otto di guardia enjoyed legitimate authority in Florence, the confiscations were also illegal.[50]

This situation was repeated in 1494. Despite the fact that no official

---

edly refused to serve until in May they were given a salary, fol. 2r–v. Their office was distinct from that of the Office of the Rebels (see note 45 above), and when it ended (they were renewed once), they were to be replaced by the Tower Officers. On their business interests, see M. Spallanzani, "Le aziende Pazzi al tempo della congiura del 1478," in *Studi di storia economica nel Medioevo e nel Rinascimento in memoria di Federico Melis* (Pisa, 1987), pp. 305–20.

48. The house was sold on 10 October 1480 for a price to be agreed by Antonio di Taddeo and Giovanni Portinari, ASF, Balìe, 38, fol. 26v. Renato Pazzi's palace was sold to Ercole d'Este for 4,000 florins on 3 January 1480; C. Elam, "Lorenzo's Architectural and Urban Policies," in *Lorenzo il Magnifico e il suo mondo*, ed. G. C. Garfagnini (Florence, 1994), p. 361; Pisa, Salviati Archive, MS. IV, 1, fol. 27 left (29 February 1480): f.8 1s.9d. for "dua paia di lemzuola usate . . . auto da gl' uficiali di rebelli e quali mi dettono per chomto di Niccholo di messer Piero de Pazzi." On their first meeting, on 29 May, they cited eighty debtors to appear, some of whom (fourteen) they imprisoned until they paid up and others (twenty-four) they inscribed in the *Specchio* (ASF, Balìe, 38, fols. 5v–6r, 12v–13r, 39r). They cited some seventeen creditors (fol. 54r), and estimated the final sum owed by Francesco Capponi for the French salt farm as 21,500 florins (fols. 79r–83v).

49. ASF, PR, 195, fols. 53v–54v (25–26 January 1495): "et ingiustamente furono chiariti loro creditori e' quali non erano o non di tanta quantità ma più presto erano debitori, et per cagione non vere et crediti non veri a decti tali così chiariti furono consegnati de' loro beni, etiamdio mobili molti ne rapirono et con tituli fraudulenti ne occhuporono et alchuni etiamdio de loro beni per meno che la metà del giusto prezo conperorono et in effecto molti loro beni et ragioni et donati et finiti furono."

50. Cavallar, "Il tiranno."

charge of rebellion was brought against Piero de' Medici and his brothers until 20 November, nor against the others, a *bando* was issued on the day following Piero's flight from the city on 9 November confiscating all his possessions, as well as those of his family and his intimates.[51] Between then and the end of the year, nearly one hundred former exiles were recalled.[52] Moreover, despite the fact that the government was forced to revoke the charge of rebellion (with its corollary, confiscation of goods) on 25 November as one of the terms of Florence's treaty with Charles VIII of France,[53] the work of reclaiming debts owed by the Medici bank nevertheless continued steadily: six auditors were appointed on 14 December "for the affairs and the possessions of Piero de' Medici and the heirs of Lorenzo de' Medici & Co.," and in January another six auditors were appointed to review all government accounts since 1478.[54] The Medici auditors, like the Pazzi ones, were intended to deal with private claims on the Medici company and also to recover money owed to the commune, combining the authority of "syndics of bankrupts" and "syndics of rebels."[55] And they, too, were equally

51. ASF, SC Delib. ord., 96, fol. 87r–v (10 November 1994): "quod omnes res & masseritie Pieri Laurentii de Medicis & Juliani eius fratris carnalis et eorum vel alterius eorum familie. Ac etiam Antonii Bernardi Miniatis Dini et ser Ioannis ser Bartolomei de Pratoveteri & ser Simonis Grazini de Staggia & ser Laurentii ser Antonii de Doane & ser Pieri & Ioannis Baptiste & Bernardi ser Francisci de Bibbiena & eorum vel alicuius eorum familie"; fol. 96r–v, ed. G. L. Moncallero, *Il Cardinale Bernardo Dovizi da Bibbiena. Umanista & diplomatico (1470–1520)* (Florence, 1953), pp. 140–41: Piero de' Medici is declared a rebel "propter inobbedientiam et indignationem" with a price of 2,000 florins on his head (and prices of 1,000 and 500 florins, respectively, on the heads of his secretaries Piero and Bernardo Dovizi).

52. See the Appendix. These are the names listed in ASF, SC Delib. ord., 96, of those recalled and who paid the tax demanded by the government on their return.

53. Edited by G. Capponi, in *Archivio storico italiano*, vol. 1, Appendix III (1842), p. 372, sections 17–18: "quod . . . non imponent aliam poenam dicto Petro de Medicis . . . quam poenam relegationis . . . in qua poena nullo modo venit confiscatio bonorum"; confirmed on 2 December; ASF, SC Delib. ord., 96, fol. 102r–v.

54. ASF, PR, 185, fols. 19v–21v (28 December 1494) and 26r–v (13 January 1495). The decision to use Medici silver held by the commune to pay their debts to the king of France, and to appoint two custodians to receive Medici property from those still possessing any was doubtless an attempt to regularize the situation, SC Delib. ord., 96, fols. 107v, 111r (4 and 10 December), 114v (14 December). On the work of the government auditors, anticipating the five appointed in 1527, cf. Alison Brown, "The Revolution of 1494 in Florence and Its Aftermath: A Reassessment," in *Culture in Crisis: Italy in the 1490s*, ed. J. Everson and D. Zancani (Oxford, 2000), pp. 22–23.

55. ASF, PR, 185, fol. 20r: "provedere et ordinare le cose de privati et maxime quelle di più importanza et dove il comune etiam ha qualche interesse" with "tanta auctorita quale et quanta et come hanno havuto insino a qui qualunche sindachi di

hardworking. We know that they met two or three times per week over the next year, even in the dangerous period during the king of France's return from Naples, when they were officially disbanded.[56] The calling in of accounts, the permission granted to the auditors in June 1495 to store "goods and furniture in the church and houses of San Lorenzo," and the steady sale of Medici houses over at least three years all tell their own story.[57]

So, too, do the letters of Piero de' Medici's former secretary, Bernardo Dovizi, from Pisa in 1496. Despite being in a rebel city and free to negotiate with the emperor Maximilian on behalf of his patrons, he was very upset to find that Maximilian, although well-disposed to the Medici, was not only living in their house but also wanted to be given their cattle, "since he had been told they belonged to Florence." After reassuring his patrons that the emperor had "changed nothing" in their house—unlike the king of France, who had knocked the Medici palace in Florence about "to make a thousand little stairways and exits so he could go secretly to visit Madonna Caterina in San Lorenzo"—he nevertheless expressed how upset he was that their "goods and possessions had gone badly" and confessed to other untoward fears about the situation.[58]

falliti cessanti et fugitivi sopra i beni et ragione d'alchuno qualunche fallito et cessante et tale et tanta quale et quanta hanno hauto qualunche uficiali de ribelli. . . ." ASF, CS, ser. 1, 4, is a notebook recording their work: "Deliberazioni degli officiali sopra i fatti e negotii di Piero de' Medici," with accounts of Piero de' Medici and Co. di Pisa, inventories of clothes, etc., now edited by O. Merisalo, *Le Collezioni Medicee nel 1495: Deliberazioni degli Ufficiali dei Ribelli* (Florence, 1999).

56. From 12 May to 20 June 1495, ASF, SC Delib. ord., 97, fols. 51v, 68v.

57. See, e.g., ASF, MAP, 81, no. 74; MAP, 82, nos. 119,446–62; and MAP, 83, no. 55. For debts listed in the Monte Comune books, see A. Brown, "Lorenzo, the Monte and the Seventeen Reformers," in *Lorenzo de' Medici: Studi*, ed. G. C. Garfagnini (Florence, 1992), p. 132 n. 80, revised in Brown, *The Medici in Florence* (Florence, 1992), p. 178. For permission to store, see ASF, SC Delib. ord., 97, fol. 64v. For sales of possessions, see SC Delib. ord., 97–100 passim. On the 11,000 florins and 600 *libbre* of worked silver recovered from the Medici, leaving a deficit of over 62,500 florins in 1500, see A. Brown, "Lorenzo and Public Opinion in Florence," in *Lorenzo il Magnifico e il suo Mondo*, ed. G. C. Garfagnini (Florence, 1994), pp. 81–82; and Brown, "The Revolution of 1494," pp. 22–23.

58. Bernardo Dovizi in Pisa to Piero and Cardinal Giovanni de' Medici, [7–10] November and 12–13 November 1496, ASF, Signori, Dieci, Otto. Legazioni e commissarie. Missive. Responsive, 66, fols. 178–80, 196r–v, 200r: "Il re dei Romani alloggiò in Casa vostra . . . et in casa non innovò nulla come il Re di Francia, che la bucò tucta et li fece mille scalette et usciolini da fraccurra di per andare secretamente a visitare Madama Chaterina da San Lorenzo"; "Io sono assai di mala voglia perché oltre al trovare le robe et beni de' mia patroni essere andati qua non bene, mi vanno per la mente assai dubbi poco a proposito nostro"; "S.Maestà mostrò grande

It appears from this evidence that the Pazzi and the Medici auditors were more successful than we have thought. Does their work suggest that the distinction between confiscation and sequestration was being eroded? Outwardly, at least, the old forms were observed. The Medici auditors had to wait until Piero broke his confines in September 1495 and was again condemned as a rebel before gaining control of his possessions deposited in San Marco, and at the end of their term of office in December, their work was taken over by the five Officials of the Rebels and Syndics of the heirs of Lorenzo de' Medici, who were responsible for initiating the repayment of Medici debts.[59] Yet the fact that there was confusion between the work of the Medici and the communal auditors suggests it was difficult in practice to distinguish the Medici's private from their public debts,[60] and this in turn may have blurred the distinction between confiscating their goods as rebels and confiscating them as tyrants. Interestingly, when contrasting Florence's policy toward exiles with Genoa's in the 1520s, Guicciardini in his *Dialogo* suggested that Florence's policy of confiscating the goods of rebels acted as a powerful deterrent. For "if one did as they do in Genoa, where citizens rebelling against the state are deprived of their homeland but not their goods, there would be far more who would attempt to overthrow and conspire against the state than hold back through fear of becoming poor."[61]

Although the Medici were a special case because of their status outside Florence as cardinals and then popes in Rome, Guicciardini's comparison of Florence and Genoa suggests that the government's fiscal policy was increasingly stringent. Now that its long arm pursued debts as vigorously abroad as at home, it could raise the specter of poverty as a powerful sanction. At the same time, the crime of rebellion was itself becoming more fearful. Even to think or plot the death of a Medici was already in 1481 con-

---

admiratione et dixe non haver inteso che fussino [el bestiame] vostre ma che li era stato decto da' Pisani proprii che questo bestiame era de' Fiorentini et che però lo voleva. . . ."

59. ASF, PR, 186, fols. 120r–121v (10 October 1495), referring to the Otto di guardia's decree of 25 September increasing the bounty imposed on Piero's head in 1494 to 4,000 florins (OGBR 102, fols. 80v–84v); SC Delib. ord., 97, fol. 105r (26 September), on his books; PR, 186, fols. 148r–150r (6 December 1495), electing five Ufficiali de' Ribelli and establishing an order for repayments; and on handing over books to them, ibid., fol. 150v (6 December), and SC Delib. ord., 97, fol. 129r–v (31 December).

60. On 1 October 1495, the auditors of the communal accounts were told not to get involved in the "bona illorum de Medici" until 7 [October?—September is written], and the Medici auditors vice versa, ASF, SC Delib. ord., 97, fol. 106v.

61. Guicciardini, *Dialogo*, p. 168: "cittadini rebelli"; trans. Brown, p. 164.

sidered lese majesty, for which all the goods and possessions of the conspirators were confiscated—"money, clothes, household goods, books, writings,
arms and every other single thing." [62] And by the time the Medici became
dukes in the mid–sixteenth century, the punishment for this "atrocious
and wicked crime of *lesa Maestà*" was enough to frighten any person of
property, "of whatsoever sex or condition"—women, that is, as well as
men: confiscation of their "goods, property, accounts and investments of
every sort . . . even possessions subject to any kind of restitution whatsoever, trusts or transfers either by last wills or by gifts or subsequent contracts to descendants . . . whether held by personal and allodial law or by
emphyteutic and feudal law . . . as well as shares of paternal, grandpaternal
or maternal or grandmaternal possessions." Also following the precedent
established by the fifteenth-century Medici, all the descendants of this
"corrupted root," legitimate or illegitimate, were deprived of every type of
office and bequests in wills, and they were perpetually exiled from Florence
and from the Florentine state from the age of twelve.[63]

So although the Medici's strategy against dissent has been discussed
mainly in the political context of office-holding and exile, we can see that it
achieved its effect by threatening family power and inheritance, disqualify-
ing the whole male descent from office, and depriving a family, with ever-
extending tentacles, of its matrilineal as well as its patrilineal possessions.
The desire to procreate was closely linked in Florence to the expectation
of acquiring wealth and political status, and of being able enjoy the fruits
of one's success and pass them on to one's family—whereas to be deprived of

62. ASF, OGBR, 58, fols. 66r, 67v (5, 7 June): "bona omnia & singula mobilia &
immobilia solemniter incorporaverunt," listed in the *bando* as "alcuna cosa o beni
come sono danari, panni, masseritie, libri, scripture, armadure o altra qualunque
cosa o beni. . . ." On this charge, see Brown, "Lorenzo, the Monte and the Seventeen Reformers," pp. 152–53 n. 6; *Consorterie politiche e mutamenti istituzionali
in età Laurenziana*, ed. M. A. Timpanaro, R. M. Tolu, and P. Viti (Florence, 1992),
pp. 163–64; and Cavallar, "Il tiranno," p. 300 n. 104, who provides a full discussion
of the crime of lese majesty, particularly in relation to the Pazzi rebels.

63. *Legge dell'illustrissimo et excellentissimo Signore il Signore Duca di Fio-
renza hoggi Gran Duca di Toscana*, 11 March 1548, *pubblicata* 5 March 1565 (Florence, 1627; London, B.L. 1570/898 [14]), pp. 4, 10, and 13. The law also gave arbitrary power to the judge of confiscations to declare when the delinquents began to
"cogitare di commetter sì atroce delitto" to prevent evasion of the law (p. 12);
and it decreed that dowries were to be converted into Monte credits or *beni immobili, paghe* or revenues from which could be paid during the wives' lifetimes. Illegitimate children were already penalized in the fifteenth century, e.g., Alessandro
Barbadoro in 1458 (ASF, OGBR, 224, fol. 82r) and Giulio di Francesco (later Cardinal) Soderini in 1466 (though Giulio's sentence was rapidly revoked, Balìe, 30,
fols. 96v–97r).

them was considered slavery.[64] The Florentine Republic had long separated exiles from their families by encouraging wives and young children to remain in the city to protect their property—and the taxes they provided. And thanks to the recent work of Susannah Baxendale and Margery Ganz, we now know the extent to which women bore the brunt of exile in economic and social terms. So perhaps Guicciardini was right in thinking that it was loss of possessions that frightened early-sixteenth-century citizens more than loss of *patria*.

III

Fear of loss is all-embracing, and it is difficult to untangle the strands that contribute to it. Loss of possessions was closely bound up with love of one's family, since to lose one was also to destroy the other, as the Medici well realized. When Savonarola spoke in 1498 of having been threatened with exile, he told his Florentine audience: "It is you who are afraid of exile, you who have wives and children—I don't care, let him do it."[65] Yet the loss of family and friends was as frightening for fathers away on business as it was for exiles. We can see this from letters of the period, such as the correspondence between Lorenzo's secretary Niccolò Michelozzi, emissary in Naples in 1492, and his banker Filippo da Gagliano, a voluntary exile in Bologna, Ferrara, and then Venice in 1495. First it was Gagliano who comforted Michelozzi when his wife was sick and his daughter nearly died, news that he relayed only "now that [the baby] seems safe and better."[66] Then it was Filippo's turn to hear about the children's illnesses from Niccolò, whom he urged to "write as often as you can, since I have no other comfort."[67]

---

64. Machiavelli, *Discorsi sopra la prima deca di Tito Livio*, ed. S. Bertelli (Milan, 1973), bk. II, chap. 2, p. 284.

65. *Prediche sopra l'Esodo*, ed. P. G. Ricci (Rome, 1956), p. 327: "Abbiate paura voi de' confini, che avete moglie e figliuoli. . . . Io non me ne curo, faccia lui. . . ."

66. Filippo da Gagliano to Niccolò Michelozzi in Naples, Florence, BNF, Fondo Ginori Conti, 29,69, no. 3421564, 21–24 May 1492: ". . . la vostra figliuola magiore à auto ancora lei male, cominciò la rosolia e dopo quella auto febre . . . il male non n'e' ssuto picchiolo e anche di natura che in parte secondo dicie Il maestro," concluding the letter three days later, "La vostra binba da lunedì di qua à avuto un gran male, in modo che a dirvi il vero, ora che apare sia migliorata e al sichuro, abiamo dubitato assai di lei, pure come dicho è a buon termine." A week later another younger baby, Filippo's goddaughter, was sick; also they feared from "roxolia" (German measles), ibid., no. 3421567.

67. "Piaciemi ch'el fanciullo vostro sia presso a ghuarito e ch gli altri stieno bene, baciateli per parte mia," "è molto magiore il contento ò a vedere vostre lettere e di leggierle . . . però seghuitate di scrivermi quanto spesso potete non mi sendo rimasto altro conforto," Bologna, 14 September, and Ferrara, 30 September 1495, ibid.

If it is difficult to distinguish between the fears of exiles and those of merchants abroad, it is equally difficult to distinguish between the excitement that both experienced abroad. At the beginning of the fifteenth century, Gregorio Dati described this excitement when he said that in Florence, "whoever is not a merchant and hasn't investigated the world and seen foreign nations and returned with possessions to his native home is considered nothing."[68] Filippo da Gagliano, too, was excited by foreign travel, as we can see from his letter to Niccolò Michelozzi from Venice. How bored he would be, he wrote, without the pastime of seeing life in the maritime city, where "every hour something happens that, as I've said, I'm delighted to have seen—like this morning, when I saw five galleys entering the harbor and coming as far as the customs to unload . . . and as well five or six ships returning from Crete and from other places in the Levant laden with merchandise, it seemed to me quite magnificent!"[69] Filippo's own brother Giuliano had worked in Lyons as a banker for twenty years, and when Filippo wanted Giuliano back in Florence to help him defend himself against charges of peculation, Giuliano refused to come, partly for tactical reasons, partly "for fear of the journey"—and partly, too, no doubt, because Lyons was by then his home.[70] There was a large Florentine community in Lyons, as in Rome, and although Filippo was apprehensive of finding himself as much a foreigner there as in Ferrara, and of not "knowing how to comport myself," his brother as a long-term resident clearly did not share these fears.[71]

Despite this, exiles did experience special fears when abroad, especially

68. *L' "Istoria di Firenze" di Gregorio Dati dal 1380 al 1405*, ed. L. Pratesi (Norcia, 1904), p. 60: "chi non è mercatante e che non abbia cerco il mondo e veduto l'estranie nazioni delle genti e tornato alla patria con avere, non è reputato da niente."

69. 19 November 1495: "E se non fussi quello passatenpo di vedere queste cose di qua mi darebbe piu noia assai, ma ogni ora achade qualcoxa che come vi dissi ultimamente ò carissimo (?) avere visto, come è suto questa mattina, che ho veduto entrare in porto e venire fino alla doghana a scharichare a un tratto 5 ghalee . . . e oltre 5 o vero 6 navi che tornano di Candia e da altri luoghi di Levante chariche di [ ] merchantantie, che m'è parso una gran magnificenza."

70. 30 September 1495, ibid.: "Conoscho ancora Io sarebbe neciessario ci fussi Giuliano per molti conti. . . . In effetto io gli ò scritto tante volte che vengha, che sa quello a fare e di qua non ò modo a schriverli altrimenti o l'andare io da là," and again referring to Giuliano, "il quale non era partito per dubio del camino." Giuliano left for Lyons on 27 May 1475; Pisa, Archivio Salviati, MS. IV,1, fol. 163r.

71. Ibid.: "e tanto mi sarei forestiero là quanto qui, e . . . il disagio il quale non so come mi conportessi." On the Florentine community in Lyons, see M. Vigne, *La Banque à Lyon du XVe au XVIIIe siècle* (Lyons and Paris, 1903), p. 87; B. Dini, "L'economia fiorentina," pp. 805, 809, referring to twenty-nine Florentines at the

in the centers where they tended to congregate. After the 1466 exiles broke their confines, they created cells of opposition throughout Italy—one going to "the king of Naples, another to the duke of Modena, another to the Signoria of the Venetians, each moving and rising up against his native city, one to Siena, another to the duke of Savoy, one to the Romagna, another to Piombino, trying by might and main to return to their native city."[72] In these cities, and in Rome, Ferrara, and Bologna, it was as dangerous to be seen with exiles as to be one.[73] In Naples in 1481, for example, the Florentine ambassador's secretary, ser Francesco di ser Barone, was careful to explain that he was obeying an order when he visited the dying Francesco Neroni, whom he found with two other exiles, Raffaello Acciaiuoli and Simone Neroni.[74] Six years later, Cosimo de' Pazzi was ostracized in Rome by Piero de' Medici and his companions because Lorenzo had ordered his son not to go around with anyone "who might give people something to talk about."[75] Bernardo Dovizi was worried by his position in Pisa in 1496, remembering how he had been urged by the duke of Milan to come in disguise and on leaving to be very careful "not to be seen by the Florentines."[76] And Machiavelli was also fearful about visiting his friend Fran-

---

meeting of their nation in Lyons in 1488; and M. Cassandro, "I forestieri a Lione nel '400 e '500: la nazione fiorentina," in *Dentro la città: Stranieri e realtà urbane nell' Europa dei secoli XII–XVI*, ed. G. Rossetti (Naples, 1989), pp. 151–62; in Rome, see A. Esposito, "I 'forenses' a Roma nell' età del Rinascimento: Aspetti e problemi di una presenza 'atipica,'" ibid., pp. 163–75, esp. pp. 169–70; M. Bullard, "*Mercatores Florentini Romanam Curiam Sequentes* in the Early Sixteenth Century," *Journal of Medieval and Renaissance Studies* 6 (1976): 51–61.

72. Benedetto Dei, *La cronica*, ed. R. Barducci (Florence, 1984), p. 70: "movendo e sollevando ciaschuno per chontro alla patria sua. . . . operando ciaschuno sua industria e ssuo ingegnio pe' ritornare alla città loro."

73. E.g., ASF, Balìe, 25, fol. 127v (31 December 1434): that no Florentine territorial can write or communicate with a rebel or exile except with permission of the Otto di guardia. There are regular payments to "spie secrete," "exploratores," or "notificatores secreti" in the *stanziamenti* of the Otto.

74. Ser Francesco di Ser Barone to Niccolò Michelozzi, 13 July 1481, BNF, Fondo Ginori Conti, 29,101a: "Et se agl' Otto ne fusse dato notitia alchuna di tal mia gita *ut fit*, ve ne voglo havere scripto per mia cautela et difesa peroche feci quanto mi fu comandato da chi per allhora comandare ne potea" [i.e., Piero Nasi, the ambassador].

75. Jacopo Salviati to Ser Francesco di Ser Barone, 18 November 1487, ASF, MAP, 61, 24, cited by A. Brown, "Between Curial Rome and Convivial Florence," in Brown, *Medici in Florence*, p. 254.

76. Letter of [7–10] November cited in note 58 above: "Ricordòmi con che parole et efficacia V. di Milano mi commandò che io venisse sconosciuto et al partire da là si guardassi bene non fussi visto . . . da Fiorentini, che denota practica con Firenze."

cesco Vettori in Rome in 1513 because if he came, he "would be forced to visit and talk to" the Soderini, which he feared might land him in prison on his return to Florence.[77]

So there are many threads that contribute to the web of fear surrounding exile—social and familial, as well as economic. To draw them together to describe the experience of exile at the end of our period is not easy. Some of the fears were not unique to exiles, and others—like the fear of prison—must always have been present, even if unexpressed. But if we are discussing exile in terms of changing boundaries, then clearly something had changed by the end of our period. The boundaries of the city, the territory, and the known world had expanded, making the city walls no longer an effective moral or political marker between good and bad. Nor were the old norms of accepted behavior considered valid. Despite the fact that the government in 1495 defended the right to kill a rebel according to not only statutory but also divine law, Guicciardini argued some thirty years later that to treat a rebel as nonhuman and place a price on his head was both ineffective and morally wrong, since if it was wrong to take pains to ensure that someone was murdered, it was equally wrong to encourage men by paying them to do it.[78] Guicciardini, as we saw, also believed that ostracism from merchants' communities abroad would be far more effective punishment than exile, since the sight of exiles being shunned would damage them far more. And by rejecting the exiles' appeal to return to Florence in 1537 on the grounds that the state is founded on power, not legitimacy, he removed the last prop of the old normative system.[79] He pro-

---

77. Niccolò Machiavelli to Francesco Vettori, 10 December 1513, in Machiavelli, *Lettere*, ed. F. Gaeta (Milan, 1961), pp. 304–5.

78. ASF, PR, 186, fol. 120r: "secondo e' nostri statuti . . . etiam dalle sacre leggi è permessa"; Guicciardini, *Dialogo del Reggimento di Firenze*, p. 167, trans. Brown, p. 163, that bounty "è una persecuzione morta che rarissime volte fa effetto; e pure chi allegassi la conscienzia, se è contro a conscienzia el curare con diligenzie particulari e strette che siano amazzati, è anche illecito el darne occasione ed invitare gli uomini con le taglie." On Piero de' Medici's bounty, cf. notes 10 and 59 above.

79. See Francesco Guicciardini, "Risposta per parte del Duca alle querele de' Fuorusciti," in his *Opere inedite*, vol. 9, ed. G. Canestrini (Florence, 1866), esp. pp. 355–56; discussed by D. Marrara, "Il problema della tirannide nel pensiero di Francesco Guicciardini e di Francesco Vettori," *Rivista storica del diritto* 39 (1966) 99–154; and Cavallar, "Il tiranno." On the "paura inespressa" in an anonymous pro-Medicean dialogue on these exiles, see P. Simoncelli, "Repubblicani fiorentini in esilio. Nuove testimonianze (1538–1542)," in *Renaissance Studies in Honor of Craig Hugh Smyth*, 2 vols., ed. A. Morrogh, F. Superbi Gioffredi, P. Morselli, and E. Borsook (Florence, 1985), vol. 1, p. 221.

vides a useful guide to the changes I have been examining. For by replacing the old external boundaries on which it had relied—the frontier controls of the city walls—with new internalized norms of behavior based on fear and self-awareness, he helps to show how exile adapted itself to the new boundaries, economic and political as well as moral, of early modern Europe.[80]

80. Norbert Elias, *The Court Society* (1933), trans. E. Jephcott (New York, 1983); cf. R. Chartier, *Cultural History: Between Practices and Representations*, trans. L. G. Cochrane (Ithaca, N.Y., 1988), chap. 3: "Social Figuration and Habitus: Reading Elias," pp. 71–94. On similar changes in the laws prosecuting homosexuals, see M. Rocke, *Forbidden Friendships: Homosexuality and Male Culture in Renaissance Florence* (New York, 1996), pp. 227–335, esp. p. 233.

Appendix: *A List of Florentine Exiles, 1433–1494*

The following table is based on ASF Otto di guardia repub. 224 (see note 23; cf. also D. Kent, *Rise of the Medici*, Appendix II, listing the 1434 exiles) to 1468. It is supplemented with names from Balìa 24 (1433), Balìe 24–30 (1434–66), and with some exiles recorded in the incomplete Otto di guardia volumes, 1478–96, as well as those recalled in November and December 1494 in SS. Deliberazioni ordinaria autorità 96. Sons, brothers, and descendants (ss bb dd) are listed when named in these records; otherwise they are understood to be included, according to the relevant decrees (see p. 349). If the place of exile is known, it is given in preference to the generic decree. This list does not attempt to be comprehensive. It does not include all the artisans and laborers without surnames listed in Otto di guardia repub. 224 unless they recur and are clearly involved in a political exile, nor does it include all the exiles listed in other volumes of the Otto di guardia. It is intended to serve as an initial checklist and a basis for future research.

ABBREVIATIONS

Names

bb	brothers
cc	cousins *(cugini)*
dd	descendants in the male line
m	messer
nn	nephews or grandsons *(nipotes)*
ss	sons

Place of exile

mc	miles outside the contado
mF	miles outside Florence
mFt	miles outside Florentine territory
m[city]	miles outside city named

Ammonizione

off	loss of offices for specified time
per	loss of offices for life

Length of sentence The length of exile is indicated only when different from the period of *ammonizione*.

Fine in florins, unless specified as lire (£)

C	fine and confiscation of all goods
pd	half fine paid within ten days, which canceled the remaining half and the threatened confiscation of goods
mcs	Monte credits
S	amount sequestered as surety
SS	Monte credits and *bona immobilia* sequestered as surety

Rebel Denounced as rebel = R (in year, if known), leading to confiscation of goods

ex	executed
mag	magnate
supmag	supermagnate

Other If preceded by an asterisk, the additional information pertains to the item that is followed by an asterisk in the same row; otherwise it is general.

acc	*accoppiatore* or scrutineer in 1433
GG	gonfalonier of justice in September 1433 responsible for Medici exile
prior	member of Signoria in September 1433 responsible for Medici exile
rev	revoked by the 36 votes of the Signoria and Colleges

Florentine exiles, 1433–1494

Last Name	First Name	Father's Name	Year of Sentence	Year Sentence Revoked	Place of Exile	Ammonizione	Length of Sentence	Fine	Rebel	Other
Acciaiuoli	Angelo m	Jacopo	1434*		Cosenza		10 yrs			*February
Acciaiuoli	Angelo m	Jacopo	1466		Barletta	off	20 yrs	1,000 + grain	1467	in Corato
Acciaiuoli	Jacopo	Angelo	1466		Barletta	off	20 yrs	*beni* C	1467	in Corato
Acciaiuoli	Neri	Angelo	1466	1484	Barletta	off	20 yrs		1467	+ ssdd 1467
Acciaiuoli	Raffaello	Angelo	1466		3mF	off	20 yrs		1467	
Albizzi	Ormanno	Rinaldo	1434		Gaeta		10 yrs	2,000 S	1435, 1458	+ ssdd 1460, R
Albizzi	Rinaldo m	Maso m	1434		Naples or Trani*			4,000 + SS	1435, 1458	*100mF
Albizzi	Tobbia ss [family]	Rinaldo		1494						
Aldighieri				1494						
Aldobrandini	Jacopo	Lorenzo		1494						
Aldobrandini	Luigi	Giovanni	1434		outside F	per	3 yrs			acc, 1444 loss off 20 yrs
Alessandri	Alessandro	Jacopo		1494						+ dd 1494
Alessandri	Niccolò	Jacopo		1494						+ dd 1494
Allegri	Domenico ssdd	Antonio	1458	1484		off				Domenico prior; rev
Altoviti	Angelo	Ruberto	1466		5mF	off		2,000 C pd		
Altoviti	Antonio	Vieri	1434		Vicenza		5 yrs	300 S		
Altoviti	Giangualberto	Ubaldo	1480						1480	
Altoviti	Ruberto	Giovanni	1466		5mF	off	20 yrs	2,000 C		
Altoviti	Sandro	Vieri	1434		outside F		3 yrs			
Amari	Bartolomeo	Filippo	1435		Stinche*					*50mF 1445
Amoraccia, dell'										see Franceschi
Anselmi	Bernardo	Anselmo	1437		10mc					
Anselmi	Filippo	(Filippo?)	1437							38mF 1 yr

Surname	Name	Father	Year		Place		Term	Sum	Years	Notes
Anselmi	Niccolò	Anselmo	1437		10mc					
Antella, dell'	Antonio	Lionardo	1434						1435, 1458	
Antella, dell'	Luigi	Ruberto		1494					1435, 1458	
Antella, dell'	Ruberto	Lionardo	1434							
Ardinghelli	Bartolomeo	Jacopo	1444		Ancona	off	10 yrs			acc
Ardinghelli	[family]		1458		100mFt	per	20 yrs			
Ardinghelli	Francesco	Piero	1458		Bologna		25 yrs			
Ardinghelli	Luigi	Piero	1458		Bologna					
Ardinghelli	Niccolò	Piero	1458	1466	Pera					
Ardinghelli	Piero	Jacopo	1444	1466						acc + ss
Arnoldi	Andrea	Neri	1434		Mantua		3 yrs	5,000 S pd		+ ssdd 1458
Arnoldi	Francesco	Giovanni	1435		Venice		3 yrs			
Arnolfi	Doffo ssdd	Giovanni	1458			off	25 yrs			
Arnolfi	Giovanni	Doffo	1458	1466						
Arrighi	Bartolomeo	Filippo	1435		Stinche*			"denari" 1435		*outside Ft 1444
Arrighi	Giovanni	Piero	1434						1435	
Arrigucci	Michele	Alessandro	1434		Palermo		10 yrs		1435, 1458	
Attavanti	Domenico	Bartolo	1458	1494						+ ssdd 1494
Attavanti	Domenico m	Lionardo	1494							cleric
Azzi, d'	Daniello	Nofri	1458	1466		per		2,000		+ ssdd
Baldesi	Andrea	Segnino	1434		Stinche*		5 yrs	200 S	ex	*outside Ft 1444
Baldovinetti	Amorotto	Guido	1481							
Baldovinetti	Bartolomeo	Mariotto	1458		Venice	per	25 yrs			
Baldovinetti	[family]		1458		100mFt	per				
Baldovinetti	Guido	Soletto	1434		Reggio	per	3 yrs	500 S		+ ssdd 1458
Baldovinetti	Mariotto	Niccolò m	1434		Salerno	per	10 yrs	1,000 S		prior
Baldovinetti	Mariotto ssdd	Niccolò m	1458		100mF					
Baldovinetti	Soletto	Guido	1458		Venice					
Baldovinetti	Uberto	Guido	1458		Mantua	per	25 yrs			

(continued)

Florentine exiles, 1433–1494 (continued)

Last Name	First Name	Father's Name	Year of Sentence	Year Sentence Revoked	Place of Exile	Ammo-nizione	Length of Sentence	Fine	Rebel	Other
Balducci	Alessandro	Giovanni		1494						+ ssdd 1494
Balducci	Alessandro magister	Baldo		1494						+ ssdd 1494
Balducci	Antonio	Giovanni	1481						ex	
Balducci	Francesco	Giovanni		1494					R	+ ssdd 1494
Banchelli	Vincenzio	Lucha ser	1468					beni C		
Bandini	Piero	Giovanni		1494	Bruges					
Barbadori	Alessandro	Antonio	1458	1494	outside Ft	per	25 yrs	400 C pd		
Barbadori	Alessandro	Giandonato		1494						
Barbadori	Antonio	Giovanni	1458	1494	Bologna*	per	25 yrs	400 C pd		*outside Ft
Barbadori	Cosimo	Niccolò	1434		Verona or Venice		5 yrs		ex	
Barbadori	Cosimo ss	Niccolò	1458			off				
Barbadori	Donato	Lodovico m		1494						
Barbadori	Giandonato	Antonio	1458		outside Ft	per	25 yrs	400 C pd		
Barbadori	Lodovico	Donato		1494						
Barbadori	Niccolò	Donato m	1434	1494	Verona	per	10 yrs	600 + 300 S	1458	
Barbadori	Piero	Niccolò	1444		Stinche*					*outside Ft 1444
Bardi	Andrea	Simone	1458		Pesaro					
Bardi	Bardo	Francesco	1434		Padua		5 yrs	1,000 S	mag	+ ssdd 1458
Bardi	Bernardo	Cipriano	1434		Macerata		5 yrs	500 S	supmag	+ bbssdd 1458
Bardi	Bindello	Simone	1458		Pesaro				1460	
Bardi	[family]		1434							1458: 100mFt, 25 yrs
Bardi	Francesco	Bernardo		1494						
Bardi	Jacopo	Simone	1458		Ronciglione*				1460	*Castello di R.
Bardi	Lionardo	Ridolfo	1434		Perugia		10 yrs	1,000 S		+ ssdd 1458

Surname	Name	Father	Date	Date 2	Place	Status	Term	Amount	Reg.	Notes
Bardi	Matteo	Bernardo	1434		Barletta		10 yrs	500 S	mag	+ ssdd 1458
Bardi	Simone	Jacopo	1434		Urbino		5 yrs			d. 1437; + ssdd 1458
Baroncelli	Giovanbattista	Francesco		1466						
Baroncelli	Jacopo	Piero	1444			off	20 yrs			acc + ssbb
Baroncelli	Jacopo ss	Piero		1466						
Baroncelli	Niccolò	Bartolomeo		1494						
Baroncelli	Pagolo	Piero	1439						R	
Baroncelli	Piero	Giovanni		1494						
Baronci	Michele	Galeotto	1434		Rhodes		10 yrs			
Bartoli	Giovanni	Jacopo	1479		Stinche		5 yrs			
Bartoli	Giovanni	Piero	1434		Ragusa		10 yrs		1435, 1458	
Bartolini	Niccolò	Bartolino	1466			off	20 yrs	2,000 C		+ ssdd
Bartolini	Niccolò	Bartolomeo	1458		20mF	off	1 yr			from porta a Faenza
Bartolini	Niccolò ssdd	Bartolomeo		1466						
Bate	Antonio	Giovanni	1435						1435, 1458	
Bate	Giuliano	Guardi	1435						1435, 1458	
Beccanugi	Simone	Piero m	1466	1494		off	20 yrs			+ ssdd
Belfredelli	Bartolomeo	Zanobi	1458		Rome				1460	+ ssdd
Belfredelli	Bernardo	Salvestro	1434		Treviso		5 yrs	300 S	1435, 1458	100mF + ssdd 1458
Belfredelli	Bertoldo	Zanobi	1460						1460	
Belfredelli	[family]		1458		100mFt	per	25 yrs			
Belfredelli	Zanobi	Adoardo	1434		Vicenza	per	4 yrs	1,000 S	ex	+ ssdd
Belfredelli	Zanobi ss	Adoardo	1458			off				+ exile
Benini	Giovanni	Tommaso	1458		outside F	per	1 yr			
Benini	Piero	Tommaso	1458		outside F	per	1 yr			
Benizi	Alessandro	Piero		1494						
Benizi	Antonio	Piero	1458		Siena*	per	25 yrs	2,000 C		*outside Ft + ssdd
Benizi	Carlo	Piero	1458		Avignon	per	25 yrs	2,000 C	1460	

(continued)

Florentine exiles, 1433–1494 (continued)

Last Name	First Name	Father's Name	Year of Sentence	Year Sentence Revoked	Place of Exile	Ammonizione	Length of Sentence	Fine	Rebel	Other
Benizi	Filippo	Piero	1458		Recanati*	per	25 yrs	2,000 C		*outside Ft
Benizi	Giovanni	Matteo	1458	1466	Recanati*	per	10 yrs			*outside Ft + ssdd
Benizi	Jacopo	Adoardo	1436		Avignon					
Benizi	Jacopo	Piero	1436	1494	Avignon		3 yrs	2,000 S	1460	
Benizi	Matteo	Matteo	1434							
Benizi	Matteo	Piero	1434		Foligno		3 yrs	1,000 S		
Benizi	Niccolò	Doffo	1434	1466	outside F		3 yrs			
Bernardini	Giuliano	Bartolomeo	1434							
Besso, del	Girolamo	Francesco	1434	1466						
Bettini			1434	1494						
Biffoli	Giovanni	Simone	1434		Città di Castello		6 yrs	£1,000 S		1445 to Bologna
Biffoli	Niccolò	Agnolo	1434	1494	Forlì					
Biffoli	Niccolò ser	Simone	1434	1494	Forlì		10 yrs			
Biffoli	Smeraldo	Simone m	1434	1494						
Bindelli-Bardi	[family]		1434		outside F		5 yrs			
Bischeri	Bernaba	Bartolo	1434		Palermo		10 yrs			
Bonciani	Guido	Carlo	1466			off	20 yrs	2,000 C pd		
Bordoni	Niccolò	Pagolo	1434	1494	Stinche*		1 yr			*outside Ft 1444 + ssdd 1494
Bordoni	Pagolo	Niccolò	1466	1494						
Borghini	Giovanni	Tommaso	1458	1466	outside F	per	1 yr			+ ssdd
Borghini	Piero	Tommaso	1458	1466	outside F	per	1 yr			+ ssdd
Bracciolini	Giovanfrancesco m	Poggio m	1466	1494						
Bracciolini	Jacopo	Poggio m	1466			off	20 yrs	2,000 C	1478	
Brancacci	Branca	Luigi ser	1434	1494						
Brancacci	Branca ser	Bonfigliuolo	1434		Stinche*		5 yrs			*outside Ft 1444
Brancacci	[family]		1458		100mFt		25 yrs			
Brancacci	Felice	Michele	1435		Capodistria	per	10 yrs	800 S	1435, 1458	

Brancacci	Luigi ser	Branca ser	1458		Rome				1460	
Brancacci	Silvestro	Guasparre	1434	1494					1435, 1458	+ssdd 1458
Brancacci	Simone	Guasparre	1434						1435, 1458	+ssdd 1458
Brighaio	Filippo	Salvestro	1439			per				
Brunelleschi	Piero	Simone	1449							+14 others
Bucelli	Bartolomeo	Francesco	1460						1460	
Bucelli	Filippo	Francesco	1460						1460	
Bucelli	Francesco	Giovanni	1434		Ravenna		10 yrs		1435, 1458	
Bucelli	Simone	Piero	1494							
Bulletta, del	Lorenzo	Giovanni	1434		Udine			1,000 S		1m outside Impruneta
Buondelmonte	Pierantonio	Ghino	1479		8mF		5 yrs			
Busini	Francesco	Antonio	1468		Stinche	per				
Busini	Giovanni	Tommaso	1466	1494		off				
Caccia, del	Marco	Salvadore	1466			off	5 yrs			
Caccia, del	Salvatore	Marco	1468		Siena*	per*	5 yrs			*3–20mF
Caccini	Francesco	Domenico	1458		outside F	per*	1 yr			*+ssdd
Caccini	Francesco ss	Domenico		1494						
Caccini	Matteo	Domenico	1458	1466	outside F	per*	1 yr			*+ssdd
Cambi	Neri	Stefano	1489	1494		off				
Campigli	Piero	Giovanni	1435		Rome		10 yrs			
Canigiani	Bernardo	Francesco	1444			off	20 yrs			acc
Canigiani	Bernardo ss	Francesco		1466						
Canigiani	Giorgio	Francesco	1444			off	20 yrs			
Canigiani	Giorgio ss	Francesco		1466						
Casa, della	Antonio	Agnolo	1494							+dd 1494
Casa, della	Antonio	Ghezzo	1435		Avignon		10 yrs			
Casa, della	Antonio ss	Ghezzo		1494						
Casa, della	Bernardo	Filippo	1434		Avignon	off	10 yrs	1,000 SS	1435, 1458	+dd 1494
Casa, della	Filippo	Ghezzo		1494						

(continued)

Florentine exiles, 1433–1494 (continued)

Last Name	First Name	Father's Name	Year of Sentence	Year Sentence Revoked	Place of Exile	Ammo-nizione	Length of Sentence	Fine	Rebel	Other
Casa, della	Filippo	Tedaldo		1494						+ dd 1494
Casa, della	Francesco	Agnolo		1494						+ dd 1494
Casa, della	Francesco	Tedaldo		1494						+ dd 1494
Casa, della	Giovanni	Agnolo		1494						+ dd 1494
Casa, della	Giovanni	Tedaldo		1494						+ dd 1494
Castellani	[family]		1458		100mF	per	25 yrs			
Castellani	Francesco	Filippo	1434					SS		
Castellani	Francesco m	Matteo m	1444	1466		off	20 yrs		mag	acc + ss
Castellani	Jacopo	Vanni m	1434		Recanati*		3 yrs	1,000 SS		*100mFt + ssdd 1458
Castellani	Otto	Michele m	1434		100mF			1,000 SS		+ ssdd 1458
Castellani	Paolo	Giovanni	1434		outside F		3 yrs			+ ssdd 1458
Castellani	Piero	Vanni m	1434		Recanati*		3 yrs	1,000 SS		*300mF + ssdd 1458
Castellani	Richo	Giovanni	1434		outside F		3 yrs			+ ssdd 1458
Cavalcanti	Rosso	Rosso	1439		in F		1 yr			
Cavallereschi	Piero	Cavalcante	1434						mag	
Chiaro, del	Domenico	Piero		1494						+ nn
Cigliani	Alberto fra	Niccolò		1494						
Corsi	Bardo	Bartolo	1478			off				
Corsi	Bartolo	Bernardo	1478		5–25mF		10 yrs			
Corsi	Bernardo	Bartolo	1478		5–25mF		10 yrs			
Corsi	Corso	Lapo	1435			off				
Corsi	Corso ssdd	Lapo	1458		100mF	per	25 yrs			prior
Corsi	Lorenzo	Bartolo	1478			per				
Corsi	Simone	Lapo	1434			off	5 yrs			
Corsi	Tommaso	Lapo	1434			off	5 yrs			

									R	
Davanzati	Francesco	Luigi	1460							
Davizi	Gherardo	Giovanni	1466			off	20 yrs	2,000 C pd	1460	1468: 3–16mE, 8 yrs
Doffi	Bernardo	Lodovico ser	1434		20mF		3 yrs			
Donati	Geri	Melchiore		1494						
Doni	Alessandro ssdd	Gherardo	1458	1466		off	25 yrs			1437: +10mE, +1yr; *legnaiuolo*
Fagnoni	Bartolomeo	Francesco	1434		outside F		3 yrs			
Falconi	Ridolfo	Clemente		1494						
Farineo	Piero	Fallo	1434		100mF				1435	
Fibindacci	Bindaccio	Granello	1434		in F		3 yrs	SS	mag	
Fibindacci	Bindaccio ss	Granello		1466						
Fibindacci	Carlo	Granello	1434					SS	mag	
Forese, del	Lorenzo	Stefano ser	1434		Viterbo		3 yrs	100 S		
Fortini	Bartolomeo	Benedetto ser	1444	1466		off				acc
Fortini	Benedetto	Paolo ser	1444	1466						
Franceschi	Francesco	Oddo	1460						1460	
Franceschi	Oddo	Francesco	1434		Camerino		5 yrs	1,000 S	1460	al. dell'Amoraccia
Franzesi	Albizzo	Giovanni		1494						
Franzesi	Antonio	Napoleone		1494						
Frescobaldi	Battista	Bardo	1481						ex	
Frescobaldi	Stoldo	Lionardo	1434	1466						
Fronte	Antonio	Fronte	1466		3mF	off	20 yrs			
Gaballino	Giovanni	Tommaso		1494						
Gacci	Bernardo	Benedetto		1494						
Gaetani	Benedetto	Francesco m		1494						
Gerini	Piero	Attaviano	1468		in F	off	1 yr			
Gherardini	Jacopone	Bartolomeo	1458	1466	outside F	per*	1 yr			*+ ssdd
Giacomini	Piero ser	Tommaso	1466		3mF	off	20 yrs	3,000 C		
Gianfigliazi	Baldassare	Francesco	1434		Brescia		10 yrs	1,000 S	1434, 1458	
Gianfigliazi	Francesco	Rinaldo m	1435		Feltro in Frigoli	per		1,000 S	1435	*see Gianfigliazi, Mea (wife)*

(continued)

Florentine exiles, 1433–1494 (continued)

Last Name	First Name	Father's Name	Year of Sentence	Year Sentence Revoked	Place of Exile	Ammonizione	Length of Sentence	Fine	Rebel	Other
Gianfigliazi	Giannozzo	Giovanni	1435		Fabriano				1435, 1458	
Gianfigliazi	Giovanni	Rinaldo m	1434		Verona		5 yrs	1,000 S	1434, 1458	
Gianfigliazi	Jacopo	Rinaldo m	1434		Brescia		10 yrs	2,000 S	1435, 1458	
Gianfigliazi	Mea	Antonio Santi	1439		Stinche*		2 yrs	200		*and 1440; outside Ft 1444
Gianfigliazi	Niccolò m	Antonio	1438		Venice		3 yrs		1458	
Gianfigliazi	Rinaldo	Baldassare	1434						1460, mag	+ Baldassare's sddd
Gianni	Astorre	Niccolò	1444			off	20 yrs			acc
Giannuzi	Santi	Cristofano	1435						1435, 1458	
Ginori	Domenico	Giuliano	1458	1466	outside F	per*	1 yr			*+ sddd
Ginori	Margherita	Benvenuto								see Neroni, Margherita
Girolami	Tommaso	Zanobi	1466		outside Palazzo	per		50 pd		
Gondi	Carlo	Salvestro	1466			off	20 yrs	5,000 C pd		
Gondi	Mariotto	Salvestro	1466			off		5,000 C pd		
Grassi	Ridolfo	Clemente		1494						
Guadagni	Antonio	Bernardo	1435		Barcelona			500 S	1435, ex	
Guadagni	Antonio ss	Bernardo	1458			off				+ exile
Guadagni	Bernardo	Vieri	1434		100mF	per				GG; 1444 off 20 yrs as acc
Guadagni	Bernardo sddd [family]	Vieri	1458		100mFt	per	25 yrs			
Guadagni	Filippo	Bernardo	1435		Barcelona	per	25 yrs	500 S	1435, 1458	+ sddd 1458
Guadagni	Francesco	Vieri	1435		Stinche*		10 yrs	500 S	1435, 1458	*1444: 80mFt + sddd 1458
Guadagni	Giovanni fra	Filippo		1494						

Surname	Name				Place					Notes
Guadagni	Manno	Vieri	1434		Stinche		2 yrs	*beni*		+ sddd 1458
Guadagni	Migliore	Vieri	1435			off	10 yrs		1435	1440 to the Marche
Guadagni	Vieri	Migliore	1458		Parma					
Guasconi	Biagio	Jacopo	1434	1494	Ancona*		3 yrs	1,000 S		*outside F; + sddd 1458; 1458: 100mFt, 25 yrs + per
Guasconi	[family]		1434			off				
Guasconi	Giovachino	Biagio	1458	1494	Bruges					
Guasconi	Giovanni	Tinoro	1458	1494	Fano					
Guasconi	Girolamo	Tinoro	1458	1494	Fano					
Guasconi	Jacopo	Bernardo	1434	1494	Padua		3 yrs	400 S		+ sddd 1458
Guasconi	Marino m	Tinoro	1458	1494	Ancona					
Guasconi	Niccolò	Zanobi m		1466						
Guasconi	Tinoro	Niccolò m	1434	1494	Cesena or Ravenna		5 yrs	1,000 S		+ sddd 1458
Lamberteschi	Andrea	Domenico	1460						1460	
Lamberteschi	Antonio ss	Domenico	1460						1460	
Lamberteschi	Antonio ss	Domenico		1494						
Lamberteschi	Bernardo	Lamberto m*		1494						*di Alterio; + dd in 1494
Lamberteschi	Domenico	Antonio		1494						
Lamberteschi	Domenico	Bernardo	1434		Cividale Friuli or Verona		5 yrs	1,000 + 3,000 S	1434, 1458	
Lamberteschi	Domenico	Jacopo		1494						
Lamberteschi	Enea	Jacopo		1494						
Lamberteschi	Goccio ser	Goccio ser	1434	1494	Cervia Ferrara		1 yr		1436	
Lamberteschi	Goccio ser ssdd	Goccio ser	1436	1494	Cervia Ferrara		1 yr		1436	*chiavaiuolo*
Lamberteschi	Jacopo	Domenico	1460						1460	
Lamberteschi	Jacopo ss	Domenico		1494						

(continued)

Florentine exiles, 1433–1494 *(continued)*

Last Name	First Name	Father's Name	Year of Sentence	Year Sentence Revoked	Place of Exile	Ammo- nizione	Length of Sentence	Fine	Rebel	Other
Lamberteschi	Lamberto	Bernardo	1439	1494					1439	+ dd (di Alterio) 1494
Lamberteschi	Lamberto dd	Alterio		1494						
Lamberteschi	Piero	Domenico	1460						1460	
Lamberteschi	Scipio	Jacopo		1494						
Lamberteschi	Sebastiano	Jacopo		1494						
Lamberti, de'	Massaio fra	Guido	1434		Stinche* outside Ft	per				*outside Ft 1445
Lapaccini	Salvestro	Lorenzo	1468							
Larioni	Lorenzo	Giovanni		1494						+ ssdd 1494
Lotti	Bernardo	Pagolo	1466			off	20 yrs			
Luna, della	Francesco	Francesco	1444			off	20 yrs			
Luna, della	Francesco ss	Francesco		1466						
Luti	Jacopo	Giovanni	1434			per				prior
Luti	Jacopo ssdd	Giovanni	1458		100mF	per	25 yrs			
Machiavelli	Agnolo	Piero		1494						+ dd 1494
Machiavelli	Girolamo	Agnolo m	1458		Avignon*	per	25 yrs	800 C pd	1459	*300mF and 20m from Naples
Machigni	Piero	Agnolo m	1458		Viterbo* outside F in Ft	per	25 yrs	800 C	1459	*100mF
Macigni	Giovanni	Carlo	1466				10 yrs			
Mancini	Andrea ssdd	Taddeo	1458	1484		off				Andrea prior; rev acc
Mancini	Taddeo	Duccio	1444	1466		off	20 yrs			
Mangioni	Cipriano	Lippozzo	1440		Stinche*	per			1460	*1444: outside Ft 5 yrs + 500 S
Manovelli	Terrino	Niccolò	1434		Perugia		4 yrs			
Manovelli	Terrino ssdd	Niccolò	1458	1484		off				rev
Marchi	Piero	Marco m	1434			per				prior
Marchi	Piero ssdd	Marco m	1458		100mF	per	25 yrs			

Marsili	Luigi	Sala	1466		outside F*	per	10 yrs			*outside Palazzo forever
Marsuppini	Jacopo	Carlo m	1468		in F*	off	5 yrs	300		*1 yr
Martini	Baldassare	Piero*		1494						*di Puliciano
Martini	Giovanni ss	Luca		1466						
Martini	Lorenzo	Doffo ser	1434		Siena*	off	2 yrs		1458	*outside Ft
Martini	Luca ssdd	Martino	1466			off				Luca prior; *pianellaio*
Masi	Tommaso ser	Giovanni		1494						
Masini	Piero	Niccolò	1439		Castiglione*					*della Pescaia
Medici	Averardo	Francesco	1433		Naples		5 yrs	10,000 SS	mag	+ 5 yrs
Medici	Bernardo	Salvestro	1433		Rimini		3 yrs		mag	
Medici	Cosimo	Giovanni	1433		Padua		5 yrs	20,000 SS	mag	+ 5 yrs
Medici	[family]		1433						mag	
Medici	Giovanni	Pierfrancesco		1494	1mF	per				
Medici	Giuliano	Averardo	1433		Rome		2 yrs	5,000 SS	mag	+ 1 yr
Medici	Gregorio	Salvestro	1433		Rimini		3 yrs		mag	
Medici	Lorenzo	Giovanni	1433		Venice		2 yrs	10,000 SS		+ 1 yr
Medici	Lorenzo	Pierfrancesco		1494	1mF	per				
Medici	Nanni	Andrea	1433		Fano		3 yrs		mag	
Medici	Orlando	Guccio	1433		Ancona		3 yrs	3,000 SS	mag	+ 2 yrs
Medici	Piero	Lorenzo		1494	100mFt				R	
Michi	Lorenzo	Francesco		1466						
Montecastelli	Francesco	Filippo	1434			off				
Morelli	Francesco	Giovanni	1467			off				
Nannucci	Silvestro	Jacopo		1494	Stinche	per	25 yrs			rev June 1494
Nardi	Bartolomeo	Andrea	1467					*beni C*	1467	
Nardi	Bernardo	Andrea	1467					*beni C*	1467	
Nardi	Salvestro	Andrea	1467							
Neri	Neri	Viviano ser	1444			off	20 yrs			acc + ss
Neroni	Alessandro	Antonio	1466		Prato					+ ssdd

(continued)

Florentine exiles, 1433–1494 (continued)

Last Name	First Name	Father's Name	Year of Sentence	Year Sentence Revoked	Place of Exile	Ammonizione	Length of Sentence	Fine	Rebel	Other
Neroni	Angelo	Nerone	1466		Sicily*	off	20 yrs	grain + 2,000 C pd	1468	*in Palermo
Neroni	Angelo ss	Nerone	1466	1494	3–20mF in Ft	off		2,000 C pd		
Neroni	Antonio	Nerone	1466		S. Andrea*	off	20 yrs	1,000 + 3,000 S		*in Ciercino; 3–20mF
Neroni	Antonio ss	Nerone	1466	1494						
Neroni	Bartolomeo	Nigi	1466	1493	S. Andrea a Veglia*					*3mF; rev 1493
Neroni	Carlo m	Antonio		1494						
Neroni	Dietisalvi m	Nerone	1466	1494	Sicily*	off	20 yrs	grain	1467	*in Novara/Alessandria see Neroni, Margherita (wife)
Neroni	Dietisalvi ss	Nerone	1466	1494	3–20mF					*3–20mF + ssdd
Neroni	Filippo	Nerone	1466	1494	Prato*	off	20 yrs	2,000 C pd + 3,000 S		
Neroni	Francesco	Nerone	1466	1494	Sicily*	off	20 yrs		1467	*Foligno/Orvieto/Todi
Neroni	Francesco Maria	Antonio	1466	1493	3–20mF					rev 1493
Neroni	Girolamo	Antonio	1466	1493	3–20mF					rev 1493
Neroni	Lorenzo	Dietisalvi	1466		Modena	off	20 yrs		1466	3–20mF + ssdd
Neroni	Lottieri	Nigi	1466		S. Andrea a Veglia*		20 yrs	2,000 S		*3mF; 1475 in Siena (Ft) 8 mos
Neroni	Margherita	née Ginori	1467		Bologna*		10 yrs			*10mFt + dd 1494
Neroni	Nerone	Nigi	1466	1494	Siena					
Neroni	Niccolò	Nigi	1466		S. Andrea a Veglia*		20 yrs			*3mF (in Casa di Nigi)
Neroni	Nigi	Nerone	1466		Palermo	off	20 yrs	2,000 C pd		+ ssdd

Surname	Name	Father	Date	Rev.	Place		Term	Amount	Year	Notes
Neroni	Nigi ssdd	Nerone	1466	1494	3mF in Ft		20 yrs			*3mF; rev 1493
Neroni	Piero	Nigi	1466	1493	S. Andrea a Veglia*					
Neroni	Simone	Dietisalvi	1466		Modena*	off	20 yrs		1466	*3–20mF
Neroni	Zanobi	Dietisalvi	1466		3–20mF	off	20 yrs		1466	
Niccolini	Giovanni	Mariotto		1494						
Noceto	Antonio	Giovanni	1488		outside F in Ft		10 yrs	10,000 S		
Pace, del	Antonio	Jacopo	1494							
Paganucci	Tommaso	Alberto	1494							
Panciatichi	Piero	Giovanni	1434					1,000		
Panzano, da	Matteo	Matteo	1434		Borgo San Sepolcro		5 yrs			
Panzano, da	Matteo ss	Matteo	1466					500 S		
Pazzi	Alessandro	Cosimo	1478		5–20mF	per				*80mFt
Pazzi	Andrea	Giovanni	1478	1494	20mTerra Leonis*	per				*Volterra; outside Italy 1482 + ssdd 1494
Pazzi	Andrea	Piero m	1478	1494	Stinche*	per				
Pazzi	Andrea ss	Piero m	1478		5–20mF	per				
Pazzi	Antonio	Cosimo	1478		5–20mF	per				
Pazzi	Antonio	Piero m	1478		Melato*	per				*his bishopric
Pazzi	Bartolomeo	Andrea	1478		outside Ft	per				
Pazzi	Carlo	Renato	1478	1494	outside Ft	per				
Pazzi	Federigo	Giovanni	1480	1494	outside Ft	per				
Pazzi	Francesco	Antonio	1478						1478	
Pazzi	Galeazzo	Giovanni	1480	1494	outside Ft	per				
Pazzi	Galeotto	Piero m	1478	1494	Stinche*	per				*Volterra; 100mF, 5 yrs; + ssdd 1494
Pazzi	Giovanni	Antonio	1478	1494	Stinche*	per				*Volterra; outside Italy 1482

(continued)

Florentine exiles, 1433–1494 (continued)

Last Name	First Name	Father's Name	Year of Sentence	Year Sentence Revoked	Place of Exile	Ammonizione	Length of Sentence	Fine	Rebel	Other
Pazzi	Giovanni ss	Antonio	1478	1494	5–20mF	per				*Volterra; 100mF, 5 yrs; + ssdd 1494
Pazzi	Giovanni	Piero m	1478	1494	Stinche*	per				*
Pazzi	Giovanni	Renato	1478	1494	outside Ft	per				
Pazzi	Guglielmo	Antonio	1478	1494	5–20mF	per				+ ssdd 1494
Pazzi	Guglielmo	Cosimo	1478	1494	5–20mF	per			1479	
Pazzi	Jacopo	Andrea m	1478						ex	
Pazzi	Lionardo	Piero m	1478	1494						+ ssdd 1494
Pazzi	Niccolò	Piero m	1478	1494	Stinche*	per			1485	*Volterra; outside Italy 1482; + ssdd 1494
Pazzi	Piero	Cosimo	1478		5–20mF	per				
Pazzi	Piero	Renato	1478	1494	outside Ft	per				
Pazzi	Raffaello	Giovanni	1480	1494	outside Ft					
Pazzi	Renato	Piero m	1478		5–20mF	per			1478	
Pazzi	Renato ss	Piero m	1478		5–20mF	per				
Pecora	Benedetto ser	Lorenzo ser	1434		10mF		1 yr	£200 S		1435: 4 yrs in Prato prison
Pepi	Ottaviano	Chirico	1434		Bergamo		3 yrs	1,000 S		
Peruzzi	Amideo	Amideo	1435						1435, 1458	+ ssdd
Peruzzi	Antonio m	Ridolfo	1438		Rome		3 yrs			+ ssdd 1458
Peruzzi	Bartolomeo	Averano	1434		outside F		5 yrs			+ ssdd 1458
Peruzzi	Benedetto	Giovanni	1439		Stinche*		5 yrs	200 S		*outside Ft 1444
Peruzzi	Bernardo	Bindaccio	1434		Venice*		5 yrs	1,000 S		*100mF; + ssdd 1458
Peruzzi	[family]		1434			per				1458: 100mF, 25 yrs

Family	Name	Patronymic	Year	Year	Place	Status	Term	Amount	Dates	Notes
Peruzzi	Filippo	Francesco	1458		50mFt	per			1460	
Peruzzi	Filippo	Ridolfo	1458	1494						
Peruzzi	Francesco	Ridolfo	1458	1494						
Peruzzi	Giovanni	Bindaccio	1434		Venice*		5 yrs	1,000 S		*100mF + ssdd
Peruzzi	Giovanni	Lorenzo	1439		Stinche*		5 yrs			*outside Ft 1444
Peruzzi	Lorenzo	Bindaccio	1434		Venice*		5 yrs	1,000 S		100mF + ssdd
Peruzzi	Luigi	Ridolfo	1434		Ancona*		5 yrs	1,000 S		*100mF
Peruzzi	Mariano	Giovanni	1434		Stinche*		5 yrs	300 S		*outside Ft 1444; + ssdd 1458
Peruzzi	Piero	Donato	1444	1466		off				
Peruzzi	Ridolfo	Bonifazio	1434	1494	Aquila*		10 yrs	10,000 S		1458 to Avignon w/ssdd; + ssdd 1494
Peruzzi	Ridolfo	Luigi		1494						
Peruzzi	Ridolfo ssdd	—		1494						
Peruzzi	Stefano	Amideo	1439						1439, 1458	+ ssdd 1458
Peruzzi	Vincenzio	Antonio m	1458		50mFt	per				
Petrucci	Antonio	Domenico		1494						
Petrucci	Antonio	Tano		1494						
Pezaio	Piero	Lorenzo	1444			off	20 yrs			acc
Pianellaio	Luca ssdd	Martino	1458		100mFt	per	25 yrs			
Pieruzi	Filippo ser	Ugolino ser	1444		12mF		20 yrs			
Pitti	Girolamo	Silvestro		1494						
Pucci	Giovanni	Antonio	1433		Aquila		10 yrs			
Pucci	Puccio	Antonio	1433		Aquila		10 yrs			
Raffacani	Antonio	Lionardo	1434		Città di Castello		3 yrs	500 S	1435, 1458	acc; 1444 off 20 yrs
Redditi	Tommaso	Francesco	1466			off	20 yrs			
Renzi	Andrea			1494						
Ricasoli	Bindaccio	Granello		1494						see Fibindacci
Riccialbani	Francesco	Vieri	1466	1494			20 yrs			
Riccoldi	Paolo ser	Riccoldi	1434	1494	Rome	off	10 yrs		1435, 1458	

(continued)

Florentine exiles, 1433–1494 (continued)

Last Name	First Name	Father's Name	Year of Sentence	Year Sentence Revoked	Place of Exile	Ammo- nizione	Length of Sentence	Fine	Rebel	Other
Ridolfi	Bartolomeo	Jacopo	1444			off	20 yrs			acc
Ristori	Bono	Jacopo	1458	1466	outside F	per*	1 yr			*+ ssdd
Rondinelli	Andrea	Rinaldo	1444			off	20 yrs			acc
Rondinelli	Andrea	Vieri	1434		Ragusa		10 yrs	2,000 S		+ ssdd 1458
Rondinelli	[family]		1458		100mFt	per	25 yrs			
Rondinelli	Luigi	Andrea	1458		Rome				1460	
Rondinelli	Vieri	Andrea	1458		Rome				1460	
Rossi	Lodovico	Giovanni	1434		Viterbo		10 yrs	£50(?)	1435, 1458	
Rossi	Paolo	Onofrio		1494						
Rucellai	Cosimo	Bernardo	1494	1494	Prato	per				
Salviati	Francesco	Bernardo	1478						1478	
Salviati	Jacopo	Bernardo	1478						1478	
Salviati	Jacopo	Jacopo	1478						1435	
Salviati	Jacopo	Simone	1434		Fano*		10 yrs	1,000 S	1435, 1458	*100mF
Santi	Cristofano	Giannozzo	1434		Borgo San Sepolcro*				1435	*100mF
Scambrilla	Manetto	Tuccio	1434		outside F		3 yrs			
Scambrilla	Piero	Manetto	1434		Montevarchi		10 yrs			
Scelto, dello	Giovanni	Matteo	1434		Treviso*		10 yrs	500 S	1435, 1458	prior; *outside F
Scelto, dello	Giovanni ssdd	Matteo	1458		100mF	per	25 yrs	£50(?)		
Serragli	[family]*		1444	1466		off	20 yrs			*exc. Giorgio di Piero + bbss
Serragli	Piero	Pagolo	1435			off	10 yrs			
Soderini	Francesco	Tommaso m	1438		Stinche*		3 yrs			*Venice 1444
Soderini	Geri	Niccolò m	1466	1494	Provence*	off		500	1467	*jurisd. King René
Soderini	Giulio	Francesco	1466	1466	10mF					
Soderini	Lorenzo	Tommaso m	1468		Siena*		10 yrs	3,000 S		*3–20mF

Surname	Name	Father			Place		Term	Amount		Notes
Soderini	Niccolò m	Lorenzo	1466	1494	Provence*	off	20 yrs		1467	*jurisd. King René at 18 yrs
Soderini	Niccolò ss	Lorenzo	1466		100mF	off	20 yrs			
Soldani	Goro	Bernardo		1494						
Solosmei	Matteo	Nuccio	1434			off	10 yrs	SS		
Solosmei	Nuccio	Benintendi	1434			off	10 yrs	SS		
Sozi	Tonino	Sinibaldo ser		1494		off				
Spini	Bartolomeo + ssdd	Bartolomeo	1458		100mF	per	25 yrs			prior
Stechuto, dello	Mariotto + ssdd	Giovanni	1458	1484		off				prior
Strozzi	Alessandro	Giovanfrancesco		1494						
Strozzi	Bardo	Lorenzo		1494						
Strozzi	Carlo	Giovanfrancesco		1494						
Strozzi	[family]	Matteo	1458		100mFt	per	25 yrs			
Strozzi	Filippo	Palla m	1458	1466	Rome			beni C		
Strozzi	Giovanfrancesco	Niccolò	1467						1467	
Strozzi	Giuliano*		1468		Stinche	per	2 yrs			*al. Cientella; + 200mF 10 yrs
Strozzi	Lionardo	Stagio	1467		60mF		25 yrs			
Strozzi	Lorenzo	Matteo	1458	1466	Bruges					
Strozzi	Lorenzo	Palla m	1434		Padua		3 yrs			+ ssdd 1458
Strozzi	Matteo	Matteo	1458		Castello a mare					
Strozzi	Matteo	Simone	1434		Pesaro		5 yrs			
Strozzi	Niccolò	Palla m		1494	Padua					+ ssdd 1458
Strozzi	Nofri	Palla m	1434		Padua		5 yrs	2,000 S		+ ssdd 1458
Strozzi	Palla	Giovanfrancesco		1494			5 yrs			
Strozzi	Palla m	Nofri	1434		Padua*		5 yrs	10,000 S		*+ 5 yrs; + ssdd 1458
Strozzi	Palla m ssdd	Nofri		1494						
Strozzi	Roberto	Giovanfrancesco		1494						
Strozzi	Smeraldo	Smeraldo	1434		Barletta		5 yrs	1,000 S		+ ssdd 1458
Stufa, dalla	Lorenzo	Giovanni	1458	1466	outside F	per*	1 yr			*+ ssdd
Temperani	Giovanni	Manno m	1467		5mF			3,000 S		

(continued)

Florentine exiles, 1433–1494 (continued)

Last Name	First Name	Father's Name	Year of Sentence	Year Sentence Revoked	Place of Exile	Ammo-nizione	Length of Sentence	Fine	Rebel	Other
Tobbiano, di	Antonio	Nanni		1494						+ dd 1494
Tobbiano, di	Vieri	Nanni		1494						
Tornabuoni	Alessandro	Filippo	1484	1494	Sicily*	per				1485: *200mFt
Tornaquinci	Andrea	Piero		1494						
Tornaquinci	Giuliano	Piero		1494						
Tornaquinci	Pero	Chirico	1439		Basel		5 yrs			
Tosinghi	Francesco	Pierfrancesco		1494						
Valori	Giovanni	Niccolò	1460	1494					1460	al. Botticello
Velluti	Donato	Piero	1434		Stinche*	per	10 yrs	500 S	1460	1444: *50m from Feltro in Frigoli
Velluti	Luigi	Donato	1446		Bologna		3 yrs			
Verrazano	Banco	Fruosino	1468	1473	Stinche*	off	5 yrs			*6 mos; for 5 yrs within 20mF
Vespucci	Giovanni	Simone	1444		Stinche*		3 yrs	1,000 S		*outside Ft 1445
Vespucci	Marco	Piero m	1478		5–25mF	per				
Vespucci	Parigi	Francesco	1439		Stinche		8 mos			
Vespucci	Piero m	Giuliano	1478		Stinche	per				
Vespucci	Simone	Giovanni	1485	1494		off				
Viviani	Agnolo	Pagolo		1494						
Viviani	Nicola	Viviano	1444	1466						
—	Alessandro	Andrea	1437		3mF*					*from the walls
—	Antonio fra	Guido								see de' Lamberti, Massaio
—	Antonio ser	Niccolò	1434		Venice		10 yrs		ex	
—	Antonio ss	Niccolò	1458			off				

—	Bernardo	Filippo*	1434	Avignon	off	10 yrs		1435	*di Ghezo
—	Bernardo ss	Giovanni	1458			10 yrs		1435, 1458	fabbro
—	Bindo	Ciuccio	1434	Bergamo		10 yrs			
—	Cristofano	Agnolo	1434	outside F		3 yrs		R ex 1435	*fabbro; d'Aronta in Mugello
—	Davizino	Fammeo*	1434	100mF					
—	Francesco	Tommaso m*	1458	100mF	per	25 yrs		1458	*di Guccio; + ssdd son of Francesco above
—	Giovanbattista	Francesco	1458	outside F					orafo
—	Giovanni	Guarente	1466				2,500		Lana Guild
—	Giovanni	Pagolo ser	1466		off	20 yrs			
—	Giovanni	Stefano	1466						acc coltriciaio
—	Lorenzo	Benino	1444		off	20 yrs			
—	Michele	Giorgio	1478	10–20mF		10 yrs			
—	Michele	Giovanni	1435	Venzona in Frigoli				R 1436, ex	di ser Matteo
—	Nanni	Stefano	1438	Stinche		2 mos			
—	Neri	Viviano ser	1444		off				
—	Paolo ser ss	Lando ser	1444		off				acc
—	Piero	Chiaro	1434	Padua		10 yrs			armaiuolo
—	Piero	Fammeo*	1434					ex 1435	*fabbro; d'Aronta in Mugello + ssdd
—	Piero	Tommaso	1466	3mF in Ft	off	20 yrs	3,000 C pd		
—	Piero ser	Benedetto	1458					1458	
—	Pietro	Sano	1466	10mF		10 yrs			
—	Stefano	Salvi	1434	Ancona		5 yrs	1,000 S	1435	calzolaio; al. della Cora
—	Tommaso	Antonio	1434 (1494)						
—	Zanobi	Lorenzo	1434	outside F		3 yrs			chiavaiuolo

15 The Identity of the Expatriate

Florentines in Venice in the Late Fourteenth and Early Fifteenth Centuries

Paula Clarke

In recent decades, the work of the *Annales* school and, in particular, that of Fernand Braudel has drawn attention to the importance and the permanence in history of broad social movements such as immigration. This, together with increased stress on economic and social history and on the history of the lower classes, has led to a growing interest in immigration as a fundamental but neglected phenomenon in the history of medieval and early modern Europe. This interest has extended to Italy and resulted in important studies elucidating problems such as the incidence of immigration, its origins, and its economic or artistic consequences.[1] Nevertheless, as regards medieval and Renaissance Italy, the subject is still in its infancy. Even questions fundamental to modern immigration studies, such as the experience of the immigrant or the process of assimilation into his new environment, have barely been broached. What follows is intended as an effort to promote discussion of such subjects through an analysis of assimilation within one immigrant group—Florentines in Venice during the late fourteenth and fifteenth centuries. Moreover, as far as possible within the limitations of the evidence at our disposal, it will attempt to approach the more elusive but intriguing problem of how the immigrant's personal identity or self-perception changed as he passed from membership in one political entity to integration into another.

In such a study, the concepts and conclusions elaborated by historians of modern phenomena of immigration can offer a framework for discussion.

---

1. E.g., *Strutture familiari, epidemie e migrazioni nell'Italia medievale*, ed. C. Romba, G. Piccinni, and G. Pinto (Naples, 1984); *Forestieri e stranieri nelle città basso-medievali* (Florence, 1988); *I Toscani in Friuli*, ed. A. Malcangi (Florence, 1992); R. Starn, *Contrary Commonwealth: The Theme of Exile in Medieval and Renaissance Italy* (Berkeley and Los Angeles, 1982); L. Mola, *La comunità dei Lucchesi a Venezia: Immigrazione e industria della seta nel tardo medioevo* (Venice, 1994).

Classic analyses of modern immigration, such as those carried out by sociologists in the United States, suggest that the immigrant goes through a number of phases of assimilation which occur gradually and at differing rates.[2] First he adapts fairly quickly to the external aspects of the new world in which he finds himself, adopting the local language or dialect and local customs and manners. However, such "cultural" assimilation can occur without the immigrant's truly becoming part of the new society in which he finds himself. The latter requires the formation of basic personal bonds, such as friendship and marriage with members of local society, along with entry into social groups through which the immigrant can create such attachments and become accepted into a new social world. According to some authorities, once this stage of "structural" assimilation occurs, the immigrant is on his way toward full assimilation, including that of identification with his new world rather than his old.[3] However, this general model has been contested by others, who point out that immigrants do not experience these phases at the same rate or in the same manner. In particular, the question of identity has proved controversial and complex, as some research has indicated that, even after "structural assimilation" has occurred, the descendants of immigrants may still, for generations, identify at some level with the place of their family's origin, and may even draw people of other origins into their own ethnic world through structural bonds such as marriage.[4]

To explain the strength and long-term survival of national identity, as well as the differing rates of assimilation among immigrant groups, scholars have suggested various factors which influence immigrants' reactions to their new world. Obviously, the presence of a sufficiently large immigrant group to supply its members with their most intimate relationships and support networks is one of the major factors retarding structural assimilation and helping to preserve a sense of identity with one's place of origin. It has, further, been generally accepted that the concentration of an immigrant group within a particular area of residence has a similar effect of slowing the newcomer's assimilation into the new society in which he finds himself. Related to the question of residence is that of work, for residence in the same area often depends on the type and location of employment, while work associations among immigrants can clearly reinforce their sense

2. Cf. in particular the fundamental work of M. M. Gordon, *Assimilation in American Life: The Role of Race, Religion and National Origin* (New York, 1964), esp. chap. 3.

3. This is the view of Gordon, ibid., pp. 80–81.

4. Cf., e.g., K. N. Conzen, "Immigrants, Immigrant Neighborhoods and Ethnic Identity: Historical Issues," *Journal of American History* 66 (1979): 612.

of cohesion. However, as has also been noted, with or without physical proximity, this same cohesion and the survival of one's original identity can be achieved by involvement in national or ethnic institutions which both maintain immigrants' traditions and encourage intimate relations among them. Similarly, close personal relations among immigrants, even without institutional support, can militate against assimilation, as can continuing contacts with the home country and those resident there. Finally, the immigrant's traditional identity can be maintained to some degree merely by a process of "socialization" within the family, whereby national or ethnic customs and a sense of family origins are transmitted to subsequent generations.

The limited number of studies devoted to immigration in later medieval Italy suggests that modern findings are to a large degree applicable to earlier times. In particular, a recent study regarding Lucchese immigration to Venice in the fourteenth and fifteenth centuries indicates that a strong sense of national identity was maintained within this group not only because of the relative coherence created by massive immigration and by continuing contacts with the home country but also by common economic activities which formed an employment environment essentially national in character and a concentration of residence which reinforced the primacy of the national group.[5] This identification with the place of origin was further strengthened by the creation of "national" institutions which promoted frequent and intimate relations among the immigrants. Yet, even while this study reaffirms the importance of residence, work patterns, and national institutions in maintaining immigrants' identity and cohesion, it raises other questions regarding our subject. In particular, it suggests that Lucchese immigrants experienced a personal conflict or "tension" between their desire for assimilation and their continuing sense of national identity. This, however, contrasts with the conclusions of modern immigration studies, which tend to see the immigrant group as a springboard toward further assimilation and hypothesize a situation of anxiety and conflict only for marginal figures who abandon their national group without gaining complete acceptance into their new environment. Indeed, even this conclusion has been questioned by other researchers, who suggest instead that marginal individuals may find their lives enhanced by the wider horizons and additional possibilities opened up by connections with multiple national groups.[6]

Other studies on exile and immigration in medieval Italy suggest that

5. Cf. Mola, *La comunità dei Lucchesi,* esp. chaps. 2 and 3.
6. Cf. the discussion in Gordon, *Assimilation,* pp. 56–57.

there may well be a special factor in the Lucchese experience—exile. This phenomenon is rarely taken into consideration in modern immigration studies because of its marginal nature in recent times, but it was very common in medieval Italy; indeed, it formed one of the major reasons for immigration itself. Exile may well have affected assimilation in that people forced to leave their homeland undoubtedly felt a greater nostalgia for the country they had left behind.[7] They may therefore have felt less desire for integration into local society and have maintained a more lively and long-lasting sense of identity with their native land. Whether this factor helps to explain the differing behavior of immigrants in our period is one of the questions which will be treated here.

As a related issue, some studies involving late medieval immigration in Italy stress the importance of the immigrant's desire for acceptance into his new society as one of the primary factors affecting the speed and degree of assimilation.[8] Whereas, again, this has not been given much attention in modern immigration studies, where the immigrant's desire for assimilation is assumed, it is relevant in late medieval Italy, where, as I have been suggesting, there may be a wider variety of reasons for immigrants' transferring abroad. Not only could exile make a difference; so did the tendency of merchants to move, sometimes permanently, to another center for business purposes, becoming effectively immigrants, with citizenship and structural ties in their new home. However, the fact that they viewed their new place of residence in primarily instrumental terms and maintained close connections with their place of origin meant that their attitudes might be very different from those of an immigrant who had left everything behind and was intent on building a new life abroad.[9]

Finally, this in turn raises yet another issue which applies more to the late medieval period than to modern times—that is, the question of what effect differences in socioeconomic status had on rates and degrees of assimilation. While modern immigrants to the United States have usually been relatively humble people, in late medieval Italy even people of notable status and wealth might find themselves permanent expatriates, whether for political or commercial reasons. With a tradition of influence and pres-

7. Cf. Starn, *Contrary Commonwealth*, esp. chap. 5.
8. In particular, P. Braunstein, "Appunti per la storia di una minoranza: La popolazione tedesca di Venezia nel medioevo," in *Strutture familiari*, pp. 514–15.
9. Cf. the comments of P. Corrao regarding the Genoese in Sicily in "La popolazione fluttuante a Palermo fra '300 e '400: Mercanti, marinai, salariati," in *Strutture familiari*, pp. 440–41.

tige in their native land and, possibly, with property and family there, such individuals might well have been more reluctant to forget their old world and more inclined to retain a sense of belonging to it.

After this survey of the influences affecting assimilation and "national" identity, we can now turn to an analysis of the behavior of our chosen immigrant population—that is, Florentines resident in Venice in the late fourteenth and early fifteenth centuries. This group is particularly useful for our purposes because it offers a variety of expatriates whose motives for being in Venice differ, as does the length of their stay there. On the one hand, we have what we might call ordinary immigrants—those who left their homeland because of personal problems such as bankruptcy or because they sought better opportunities abroad or merely because their commercial activities led them to take up permanent residence abroad. Some of these were still newcomers to Venice at the end of the fourteenth century, whereas other families had been in the Veneto-Friuli area as early as the late thirteenth century. In addition, however, the Florentine population in Venice contained a relatively large number of exiles, whether of new or recent date. What we might call the "old exiles" consisted often of Ghibelline and/or magnate families who had been forced to abandon Florence as early as the late thirteenth century, and some of whom, after various peregrinations, had fixed their residence in Venice. The more recent exiles, relatively numerous, were a product of the particular circumstances which occurred in both Florence and Venice toward the end of the fourteenth century. On the one hand, in Florence, when the broadly based regime instituted after the Ciompi Revolt of 1378 was overthrown in 1382, a considerable number of its supporters were exiled or felt compelled to abandon the city. At about the same time, in Venice, the year 1381 saw the termination, with Florentine support, of the War of Chioggia with Genoa—a war which had exacted a huge effort from Venice and had left considerable financial problems in its train;[10] hence the efforts of the Venetian government to infuse new life into the city's economy by attracting immigrants with skills and/or capital to invest in manufacture and trade. The incentives offered such immigrants, together, undoubtedly, with the economic potential of Venice and the possibility of living under a republican regime famed for its just government, must have influenced many Florentine exiles to choose Venice as their per-

10. Cf. R. Mueller, "Gli effetti della guerra di Chioggia (1378–81) sulla vita economica e sociale di Venezia," *Ateneo veneto*, n.s., 19 (1981): 27–41, mentioning also the special privileges granted Florentines in return for their city's contribution to the termination of the war.

manent place of residence, particularly if they had already had contacts of one sort or another with it.[11] Thus, the last decades of the fourteenth century witnessed an unusually high Florentine immigration into Venice, adding an important group of "new exiles" to the expatriates already there. This variety of immigrants provides us with an excellent opportunity to test the various factors mentioned earlier to determine how and to what degree they really influenced assimilation and identity.

We can begin this examination with the problem of the effects of exile, first analyzing the behavior of the new exiles and then comparing it with that of new immigrants before turning to the long-term residents. These new exiles ranged from families prominent in the upper echelons of the 1378–81 regime, such as the Alberti, Gucci, Velluti, Benini, and Dini; to leading figures of the lesser guilds, including the Da Carlone and Casini; to more obscure individuals, such as Ser Cione di Paolo di Cione, a *pizzicagnolo* turned notary, who shared in the punishments meted out by the victors of 1382.[12] Among such figures, only recently departed from their homeland and undoubtedly profoundly resentful of the political circumstances which had forced them to leave, we would expect to find a high degree of cohesion, a strong sense of Florentine identity, and, initially at least, a very limited degree of assimilation. What we do find is, first of all, as modern studies in immigration would lead us to expect, a considerable degree of rapid superficial assimilation, presumably undertaken with the pragmatic motive of making life abroad, even if unwelcome, as convenient as possible. This first phase of assimilation was not, however, so much cultural, in the sense, for example, that these Florentine exiles did not abandon their Tuscan speech for the Venetian dialect.[13] Rather, it was institutional in form. In particular, most of those who could aspire to Venetian

11. Of the exile families mentioned below, the Gucci were present in Venice by the mid–fourteenth century: R. Mueller, "Mercanti e imprenditori fiorentini a Venezia nel tardo medioevo," *Società e storia* 55 (1992): 47, 53; Piero Benini was active in the eastern Mediterranean: *I libri commemoriali della repubblica di Venezia, Regesti,* II (Venice, 1878), Libro VI, doc. 5, 9 May 1357.

12. On internal political events in 1382, see G. Brucker, *The Civic World of Early Renaissance Florence* (Princeton, N.J., 1977), pp. 60–101. The published source providing the fullest information on these political punishments is M. Stefani, *Cronaca fiorentina,* ed. N. Rodolico, in *Rerum italicarum scriptores,* 2d ed., vol. 30, pt. 1 (Città di Castello, 1903–55), pp. 393–408. For the origins of Ser Cione di Paolo di Cione, see ASF, Mercanzia, 1177, fol. 185r, 22 March 1379.

13. Cf., e.g., the will of Antonio di Berto, probably a Benintendi, written by Benedetto di Bartolomeo Gucci: ASVe, Notarile, Test., 108, n. 181, 9 September 1405. This will was written in Tuscan, despite the many years which Gucci had spent in Venice.

citizenship rapidly acquired it, availing themselves of the special regulations in effect or even seeking special treatment on the basis of what they could offer Venice in its period of need.[14] Citizenship was desirable from the point of view of legal treatment, property-owning, and business activities, and it involved certain obligations to Venice, such as the payment of taxes. However, it did not imply any major assimilation into Venetian society or a fundamental shift in identity away from the *patria*.

In fact, apart from citizenship and its obligations, the world of these exiles remained, initially, essentially Florentine; as modern sociologists would say, structural assimilation was slow in coming. Even if some work relations were quickly established with Venetian institutions,[15] the principal personal relationships of our exiles, such as friendships or marriage, were generally with other Florentines, normally exiles themselves, or recent immigrants to Venice.[16] No less revealing are the spiritual associations these exiles formed, for religion represented an extremely important facet of life, and connections in this sphere expressed very deep personal commitments. It is therefore significant that several exiles chose spiritual advisers from among the Florentine religious present in Venice. For Francesco Gucci, it was the fervent Giovanni Dominici, who provided spiritual guidance in business matters as in personal life, while Piero Benini turned to the Florentine theologian who was then the head of the Venetian province of the Servites, itself an order founded by a Florentine.[17]

However, while our new exiles maintained Florentine contacts, they by no means formed a single community, despite their common experience and interests. Often, it is assumed that expatriates compose just such an all-embracing community, which reinforces national identity by re-creating a

14. On the privilege accorded Alessandro and Francesco Gucci to set up a shop producing woollen cloth in Venice and for their citizenship, see Mueller, "Gli effetti," p. 38; and Mueller, "Mercanti e imprenditori," p. 54. Piero Benini acquired citizenship within Venice "de gratia" in 1388. Giovanni Dini's son Piero acquired it in 1396, and Bernardo Velluti and Cione di Paolo in 1391 on the basis of special regulations introduced that year: ASVe, Senato, Privilegi, 1, fols. 82v, 97r, 131r.

15. E.g., Bernardo Velluti rapidly became sufficiently prominent in the Venetian wool guild to be selected as one of its representatives in an initiative to construct fulling mills: ASVe, CI, Notai, 224, fols. 11right and ff.

16. E.g., Piero Dini established close relations with a bankrupt Florentine banker, Matteo di Miniato di Nuccio: cf. ASVe, CI, Notai 92, 30 June 1395; and Notarile, Test., 824, 1 November 1424; ASF, NA, 15191, fols. 275r ff. Antonio di Berto's will (note 16 above) shows that he married Caterina d'Alessandro di Benedetto Gucci.

17. Cf. Francesco di Benedetto Gucci's will of 12 November 1392, ASVe, Notarile, Test., 574, n. 567; and that of Piero Benini, ibid., 1072, fol. 37r, 5 December 1392.

miniature home country abroad. On the contrary, as modern sociologists point out, even immigrants tend to associate not with all immigrants of the same origin but, rather, with those of backgrounds and socioeconomic status similar to their own.[18] This trend may, in the case of our Florentines, have been reinforced by a lack of "national" institutions bringing together immigrants of all classes. While a Florentine consulate certainly existed at Venice, with considerable theoretical powers in commercial matters, it most probably affected principally Florentine merchants. Nor is it clear that a permanent Florentine confraternity existed prior to 1435.[19] Moreover, the relative dispersion of Florentine émigrés in Venice and the wide variety of their professional activities must have militated against close contacts among them.[20] In fact, our exiles seem to have formed rather separate social worlds which, once we take into consideration the common contemporary phenomenon of patronage, recognized the social distinctions of the time. Moreover, it is evident that relationships already formed in Florence helped to determine immediate social contexts abroad. Thus, for example, a group of prominent new exiles was formed by the Alberti, Benini, Gucci, and Dini, who had been accustomed in Florence to collaborating not only in politics but also in commerce. It was natural that these relations should continue in exile, with business associations formed among them and close commercial cooperation maintained.[21] This cooperation extended to personal matters, with, for example, both the Dini and the Benini marrying into branches of the increasingly persecuted Alberti clan.[22] These families also established relations with other Florentines, generally of similar sta-

18. Cf. Gordon, *Assimilation*, pp. 51–52, on the concept of "ethclass"—i.e., a group not only of the same ethnic origin but also of the same class that forms an immigrant's immediate world.

19. These questions will be dealt with more fully in a forthcoming work on Florentines in Venice and Venetian-Florentine commercial relations.

20. While S. R. Ell, "Citizenship and Immigration in Venice, 1305 to 1500" (Ph.D. diss., University of Chicago, 1976), p. 63, is undoubtedly correct about exceptional concentrations of Florentines in certain parishes, his information was, as he recognized, incomplete. I shall deal with the question of the residence of and trades practiced by Florentines in a forthcoming study.

21. On the commercial contacts of one branch of the Dini with Piero Benini: ASF, Mercanzia, 1183, fols. 74r–75v, 89v–92r. For cooperation between the Dini and Alberti, see the will of Luigi Dini, who evidently had worked for the Alberti in England (ASF, NA, 10466, fols. 39r–v, 24 August 1399), and the catasto declaration of Giannozzo and Tommaso Alberti in 1427 (ASF, Catasto, 77, fol. 122r). In Venice, the Benini and Gucci formed a partnership with activities in Puglia: ASVe, Notarile, Test., 1072, fols. 55v–56r, 20 March 1397.

22. For Piero Dini's marriage to Antonia d'Alberto Alberti, Magdalena di Piero Dini's marriage to Tommaso di Giannozzo Alberti, and Margherita di Piero Benini's

tus, already resident in Venice.[23] However, they do not seem to have had close relations with more humble exiles, even with the leaders of the lesser guilds, such as the Casini or Da Carlone families. Although the Da Carlone arrived in Venice at about the same time as the other exile families, and established themselves as rapidly as Venetian citizens, they initially chose marriage partners from more obscure Florentine families still resident in Florence or from families from the Florentine territory which had immigrated to Venice.[24] Thus, the social distinctions which existed in Florence were maintained abroad, creating a number of relatively separate social spheres even within a wider, alien world.

Despite this initial Florentine orientation of their social worlds, there are relatively early signs among our exiles of a degree of assimilation, perhaps aided by this relative lack of cohesion among exile groups. An intermediate, if ambiguous stage was created by the contacts the exiles established with other immigrants, especially those of Tuscan origin. Presumably, particularly for poorer, less distinguished families, acceptance came more easily and earlier from other foreigners than from Venetians. Moreover, Tuscans in particular shared various elements of culture, not least language, which must have marked them out from the Venetian population and given them a sense of common origins and traditions. Above all, it was the Lucchese with whom Florentines most frequently established close bonds, undoubtedly because of common interests in the textile industries as well as a common Guelf heritage. The relatively humble Da Carlone family, for example, formed multiple marriage relations with Lucchese families.[25] For the upper-class Benini, cooperation with the Lucchese probably arose through their contacts with the Servites in Venice, whose church had become the center of Lucchese "national" worship and of the Lucchese confraternity.[26]

---

marriage to Lorenzo di Benedetto Alberti, see L. Passerini, *Gli Alberti di Firenze: Genealogia, storia e documenti*, 2 vols. (Florence, 1869), 1:194, tables III and IV.

23. See note 16 above.

24. For the citizenship of the sons of Benedetto da Carlone, see ASVe, Senato, Privilegi, 1, fol. 121r, 2 September 1396 (*de intus*); and fol. 139r, 25 February 1401 (*de extra*). For the marriage of Niccolò di Benedetto da Carlone to Fioretta di Bartolo Dardi, see ASF, NA, 10466, fol. 37v, 25 April 1398. Caterina di Sandro da Carlone married Guccio di Piero da Scarperia, who had immigrated to Venice: e.g., ibid., 10657, 7 October 1404.

25. Isabetta di Benedetto da Carlone married Matteo Lotti da Lucca: cf. ASVe, Notarile, Test., 858, n. 94, 23 June 1405. By 1427, Nanni da Carlone was married to Camilla di Francesco Tedaldini: ibid., 554, n. 282, 16 August 1427. On both of these Lucchese, see Mola, *La comunità dei Lucchesi*, as indicated in index.

26. Cf. ibid., pp. 87–105.

Presumably, it was at least in part through the Servites that the Benini established their connection with the Sandei family, with whom they had formed a commercial company by the end of 1408.[27] Beyond the Lucchese, the Sienese and even Pisans were among the first non-Florentine families resident in Venice with whom the exiles established relations; the Dini in particular distinguished themselves by the creation of a truly inter-Tuscan partnership with Niccolo Tegliacci da Siena and the Pisan, Gaspare da Calci, called Gaspare de Lavaiano.[28] In addition, the Bolognese, with whom Florentines often had close relations because of Bologna's key position on the route between Florence and Venice and its importance as a center of exile activity, also supplied occasional personal ties, including a marriage with the Da Carlone.[29]

Beyond such connections with non-Florentine immigrant groups, there are other indications of gradual assimilation among the new exiles. In particular, the entry of members of exile families into Venetian monastic communities and confraternities represents ties with local institutions which are fundamental for structural assimilation, while it also created deeper spiritual bonds with the city.[30] In fact, paralleling, or even preceding, such structural assimilation are signs that a change of identity was beginning to occur—that is, that the exiles were beginning to feel themselves at least a little Venetian. This development can, to a degree, be charted. Initially, as we would expect, the exiles' vision was directed primarily homeward,

27. Cf. ASVe, CI, Notai 192, fol. 107v, 8 December 1408. For the Sandei family and Niccolò d'Arrigo, the Benini's partner, see Mola, *La comunità dei Lucchesi,* as indicated in index. However, he makes no mention of this company.

28. There are many indications of this partnership, from 21 July 1405: ASVe, CI, Notai, 92. Tegliacci had close relations with Florence, of which his son became a citizen in 1447: ASF, PP, 17, fols. 50r–58v. I am grateful to Brenda Preyer for this and other information regarding Tegliacci. De Lavaiano was among the wealthiest Pisans in the catasto of 1427–28: B. Casini, "Patrimonio ed attivita del fondacho del taglio di Simone di Lotto da Sancasciano e fratelli," in *Studi in onore di A. Fanfani,* 6 vols. (Milan, 1962), 2:258.

29. Before 17 October 1414, Isabetta da Carlone had married Bettino Pellacani, of a wealthy Bolognese family that had immigrated to Venice: cf. ASVe, Notarile, Test., 1234, fol. 89.

30. A son of Piero Dini entered the monastery of Santo Spirito at Venice, together with two sons of his friend, Matteo di Miniato di Nuccio: ASF, NA, 15191, fols. 275r ff., 17 October 1425; ASVe, Notarile, Test., 824, 1 November 1424. Niccolò di Nanni da Carlone and Bartolomeo Gucci entered the confraternity of San Cristoforo: ASVe, Scuole piccole, 406, fols. 29r, 59r. Bernardo Velluti's nephew Nofri was a member of the Scuola grande of San Giovanni Evangelista: e.g., ASVe, Scuola grande di San Giovanni Evangelista, 72, fol. 39r, 7 March 1428.

toward family, possessions, and obligations left behind. Contacts were maintained through communication with relatives, business activities, and, where possible, return visits.[31] Even the regulations of exile required on occasion contacts with Florence,[32] while, for almost two decades, various of our exiles were involved in plots against the Florentine regime, clearly expressing a refusal to accept permanent exclusion from their native city.[33] For some Florentines, particularly the Alberti, this refusal to accept the fact of exile was apparently permanent. They evidently did not seek Venetian citizenship, presumably in part because their international commercial network made it less important for business affairs but also, perhaps, because they were sufficiently distinguished to feel that their history was irrevocably involved with Florence's, while they were sufficiently powerful to expect that even the increasingly severe punishments inflicted on them might eventually be annulled—as, of course, finally occurred in 1428. However, if the Alberti represent the highest echelons of exiles, for whom assimilation was a low priority, their aloofness from Venice was not typical of the exiles as a whole. For the latter, continued residence in the city, a deeper integration into its business world, and, perhaps most important, the failure of the repeated plots against the post-1382 Florentine regime led to a growing acceptance of the finality of their separation from Florence and an increasing sense of identification with their new home.

This process can be traced most clearly in the Benini family. Already, in 1397, even before the disastrous plot of 1400 which saw his brother imprisoned and tortured, Antonio Benini expressed in his will a desire for his patrimony and that of his late father to be invested in property in Venetian territory.[34] Much later, in 1409, the brother who had been involved in the plot, Michele, expressed his shift in perspective, as well as his loyalty and gratitude to the Venetian government, by providing that in certain circumstances his patrimony was to devolve to the Venetian Signoria itself.[35] Even

31. Cf. Piero Benini's will of 5 December 1392, ASVe, Notarile, Test., 1072, fols. 37r–38v.

32. Exiles were frequently required to give regular proof of their residence in the places assigned them, or guarantees that they would observe the punishments inflicted on them. Cf. the promise of Bernardo Velluti's sons in this sense: ASVe, CI, Notai, 223, fol. 62left, 23 June 1386.

33. For a plot in 1383 involving Bernardo Velluti, see Brucker, *Civic World*, p. 69. For another plot of 1397 involving Cristoforo di Niccolò da Carlone, see G. Morelli, *Ricordi*, ed. V. Branca (Florence, 1956), pp. 372–77. For that of 1400, cf. in particular the confessions of the participants published by Passerini, *Gli Alberti*, 2:266ff.

34. ASVe, Notarile, Test., 1072, fols. 55v–56r, 20 March 1397.

35. ASVe, Notarile, Test., 1234, n. 461, 20 April 1409.

before then, another member of the same family had expressed his pride in his acceptance into Venetian society by canceling the designation "de Florentia" in a legal act, to replace it with the titles of citizen and inhabitant of Venice.[36] While this instance by no means represents a denial of his Florentine origins, it does indicate a shift in identification and suggests that his more immediate loyalties were beginning to lie with his city of adoption.

However, the degree of assimilation and identification with Venice evident among our new exiles remained limited. The social world of even the younger generation of almost all of these families remained predominantly Florentine, while contacts were maintained with Florence not only through relatives but also through business activities and matriculation in Florentine guilds.[37] In addition, representatives of various of these families eventually returned to their original home, even if the reasons for this return are not always clear.[38] Significantly, the family that achieved the greatest degree of assimilation and most successfully established itself as Venetian was one from the lower guilds—the Da Carlone. Only they, for example, from an early stage, repeatedly contracted marriage as well as business connections not only with the non-Florentine immigrant groups mentioned earlier but also with local families.[39] Moreover, whereas other exile families generally continued in Venice the trade which they had pursued in Florence, the Da Carlone abandoned cloth manufacturing, with which they had been associated in Florence, to take up a profession which was perhaps more lucrative, as well as more appropriate to the Venetian world—that is, retail commerce in spices.[40] They were remarkably successful in building a

36. ASVe, CI, Notai, 192, fol. 51r, 21 February 1407.

37. Francesco di Piero Dini matriculated in the family's traditional guild of doctors and druggists sometime before 1410, when he could not have been more than sixteen: ASF, Arte dei medici, speziali e merciai, 7, fol. 64r.

38. The remaining members of the Benini family seem to have returned to Florence by 1427: cf. ASF, Catasto, 68, fol. 251. The absence of any business interests in this tax declaration suggests that a business failure may have caused them to leave Venice. The fact that Francesco Dini filed such a return in 1457–58 (ibid., 804, fols. 214, 219) when his family had not originally done so, together with his matriculation in a Florentine guild, suggests that he also returned. Of the Velluti, Bernardo seems to have died in Venice (cf. his will of 12 August 1405, ASVe, Notarile, Test., 575, n. 762), and his nephew Nofri, at least, remained in Venice, acquiring citizenship on 29 December 1419: ASVe, Senato, Privilegi, 1, fol. 187v.

39. E.g., Nanni di Benedetto was, by 4 November 1411, married to Ursa di Giovanni da Pellestrina: ASVe, CI, Notai 36 (Giovanni Campio).

40. Stefani (*Cronaca*, pp. 355, 400) called Benedetto da Carlone *pianellaio* and *carditore*, while Niccolò da Carlone, a dyer, was one of the first consuls of the guild of dyers and other crafts instituted in 1378. Cf. N. Rodolico, *I Ciompi: Una pagina di storia del proletariato operario*, 3d ed. (Florence, 1980), pp. 240–45. In Venice,

new life in Venice, founding a major spice shop which became a supplier to the Venetian Signoria, and eventually marrying into noble Venetian families.[41] This success, in a new world defined by a new profession and, increasingly, by new social contacts, undoubtedly explains their permanent commitment to Venice and their gradual turning away from their Florentine ties, even if they by no means lost contact with other Florentine expatriates.[42] That this degree of assimilation was the result of a choice on this family's part, as well as of their humble origins and their discouragement with Florentine politics, is indicated by the fact that this pattern is not repeated by other exile families of the lower guilds.[43]

When we turn to the "ordinary immigrants" of the same period to see whether they display the same pattern of a continuing strong attachment to their native land, modified by a small degree of assimilation, we find that, rather than a single pattern, a whole gamut of responses emerges. Starting with the question of socioeconomic level, it is significant that we cannot offer examples of Florentines of high status and wealth who voluntarily immigrated to Venice in this period. Local patriotism was such that those who could, remained rooted at home, even if they went abroad for long periods for commercial purposes. The upper rank of our first-generation immigrants is, therefore, composed of relatively well-to-do merchants who are socially, however, not of the first rank. We can begin by considering their case before turning to the attitudes of more humble immigrants.

Perhaps the best example we can offer of merchants permanently resident in Venice is Zanobi di Taddeo Gaddi, a member of a rather modest family which had initially achieved renown as painters and sufficient capital to en-

---

Niccolò's son Cristoforo continued his father's trade as a partner of a Lucchese dyer, Zonta Bonifazio, who also had a company with the Florentine *setaiuolo*, Geri Niccolosi: ASVe, GP, SG, 10, fol. 105; Mola, *La comunità dei Lucchesi*, as indicated in index. Although Mola claims Niccolosi as Lucchese, he was, in fact, Florentine. By 1403 the sons of Benedetto da Carlone had become druggists: ASVe, Notarile, Test., 1072, fol. 105r, 23 June 1403.

41. As purveyors to the Signoria: ASVe, Rason vecchie, busta 25, Notatorio, 2, fol. 94, 19 March 1462. For a marriage into the Pasqualigo family: ASVe, GP, SG, 105, fol. 59r.

42. The fact that Niccolò da Carlone sought out another Florentine to underwrite insurance (ASVe, GP, SG, 74, fol. 32r–v, 8 February 1437) indicates continuing contacts with Florentine immigrants. However, so far, no indications of business activities of the Da Carlone in Florence have come to light, while their wills suggest that they no longer possessed property or had close ties there.

43. The Casini, for example, seem to have maintained structural ties solely with families of Florentine origin.

ter the commercial world. While the reason for Zanobi's transfer to Venice remains, as usual, unclear, he became an expert in commercial affairs in that center, acting as an agent for major Florentine companies, such as that of Francesco Datini, as well as engaging in commerce in his own right.[44] It was undoubtedly because his commercial success was built on his knowledge of the Venetian market and his expertise in it that he ended up remaining all his life in Venice, where he sought the advantages of citizenship in 1384. However, as has been suggested,[45] Zanobi's citizenship was undoubtedly of the superficial, pragmatic variety which has been noted among Italian merchants elsewhere. At heart, Zanobi remained a thorough Florentine. Much of his business was conducted with or for Florentines; he married into a family of Florentine exiles of the 1380s which had emigrated to Venice, consorted principally with Florentines, must frequently have visited Florence, where he was on occasion selected for official posts, matriculated in a Florentine guild, and, when requested, acted as a representative of the Florentine government.[46] Moreover, he seems never to have called himself a Venetian citizen, defining himself always instead as a Florentine. This commitment to Florence is particularly evident in his will, drawn up in Venice by a Florentine notary in 1400.[47] Surrounded by Florentine merchants resident in the city, Zanobi disposed of his considerable possessions, which were primarily in Florence and its territory, principally to Florentines, many of whom were living in Florence itself. His sense of obligation or gratitude to the city which had furnished him his livelihood for so many years was expressed in the provision of 200 florins [*sic*] for pious causes in Venice or its territory and small bequests to Venetian monasteries, in one of which he wanted to be buried. Yet he also anticipated the possibility of his dying in Florence, and his sense of deeper commitment to the city of his birth was expressed nicely in his designation of the larger sum of 300 flo-

---

44. On Zanobi, see Mueller, "Mercanti e imprenditori," pp. 44–47.

45. R. Mueller, "Stranieri e culture straniere a Venezia: Aspetti economici e sociali," in *Componenti storico-artistici e culturali a Venezia nei secoli XIII e XIV*, ed. M. Muraro (Venice, 1981), p. 76.

46. Zanobi married Caterina di Messer Donato del Ricco Aldegheri, whose father had been executed in the political reaction of early 1382 and whose family had subsequently emigrated to Venice: cf. Zanobi's will of 27 June 1400 in ASF, NA, 6178; Stefani, *Cronaca*, pp. 392–93. Zanobi was selected as a representative of his guild of doctors and druggists on 12 February 1399: ASF, Mercanzia, 232, fols. 37v–38v. For his famous role in Florence's guarantee for Venice's observance of the Peace of Turin, cf., e.g., ASF, PR, 71, fols. 48v–49v, 82v–83r, 23 May and 21 July 1382.

47. Cited in the preceding note.

rins for pious causes in the Florentine territory. It was, moreover, only Florentines whom he entrusted with the execution of his last wishes, whether in Venice or Florence, and to a Florentine that he wanted his wealth consigned for investment until his sons came of age.[48]

Zanobi Gaddi demonstrates that the Florentine merchant permanently abroad could be more firmly oriented toward his homeland than even the exile. However, the sentiments of such merchants, who not only retained the possibility of returning home but probably never abandoned the intention of doing so, are not typical of the more humble Florentine immigrant of the time. Among these latter figures the norm is relatively rapid assimilation, in which the passage from the first to the second generation is often decisive. This is understandable given that the younger generation, often born and raised in Venice, tended to be well inserted into local society, through marriage, personal associations, habits, and even language, although the degree of Florentine identity passed on through socialization within the family is often difficult to ascertain. As an example of this we can take the obscure Zanobi di Andrea, who, at the time of making his will in 1421, still felt sufficiently attached to his old life in Florence to specify not only the parish but even the street in which he had lived there.[49] However, his son Donato, married into a Venetian family of druggists and an apothecary himself, seems to have felt little connection with his father's homeland. Donato's will of 1464 shows him well integrated into Venetian society, closely connected with Venetian nobles (some of considerable standing), and a member of a major Venetian confraternity. There would be nothing to suggest even a memory of the family's Florentine origins if the language of the will, written by Donato himself, did not contain hints of a Tuscan origin.[50]

Although this is the typical pattern for poor Florentine immigrants, there are indications that personal choice could create much more rapid as-

48. I.e., to Antonio di Ser Bartolomeo di Ser Nello di Ghetto di Sinibaldo da Montecuccoli, one of the sons of a notary who had worked for many years for Zanobi's guild of doctors and druggists and whose sons matriculated in the same guild. Although they concentrated their business activities in Bologna, they also had interests in Venice, where Antonio, having accepted Zanobi's request, was living in 1404: ASF, NA, 10657, 30 January 1404. The relations will be treated in a separate article, with the publication of Gaddi's will.

49. ASVe, Notarile, Test., 586, n. 168.

50. Donato's will, in ASVe, Notarile, Test., 1238, n. 197, does use Venetian expressions, such as "muier" for "moglie," and does show the Venetian tendency to drop consonants and replace the "c" with a "z." Yet it is by no means written in a full-fledged Venetian dialect.

similation, and even a decisive change in identity. To illustrate this I shall first cite the case of another poor immigrant whose loquacity has left us an unusual insight into his personal attitudes. This individual, called Jacopo di Cristoforo, or Papi for short, arrived in Venice before the end of the fourteenth century, evidently as a relatively young member of a destitute family.[51] Needing to find work to support himself and his family, he established a business relationship with Antonio Velluti, for whom he sold used clothes in the Venetian markets. This work, although carried on within a Florentine association, nevertheless brought Papi constantly into contact with Venetians, with whom he gradually established friendships. Indeed, he seems consciously to have sought out in particular Venetian nobles with whom to establish instrumental connections, undoubtedly with the intention of acquiring protectors or influential contacts within the world in which he now lived. Thus, Papi created a social world which was Venetian as well as Florentine—a fact clearly demonstrated at the celebration of his marriage in 1410, to which, as he deliberately tells us, both Venetians and Florentines were invited.

This sense of belonging to two worlds—of Florence and of Venice—accompanied Papi throughout his life without creating any evident personal conflict. On the one hand, he maintained business contacts with Florence and even purchased property there, as though initially planning to return.[52] In Venice, his principal religious connections were also with Florentines, as he became close to the Umiliati of the monastery of San Cristoforo, among whom both the prior and the *proposto* were, during Papi's maturity, Florentine. However, at the same time he gradually established closer relations with Venice, of which he became a citizen in 1413,[53] subsequently acquiring property there. That this sense of belonging to his adopted city was compatible with a continuing Florentine identity is illustrated by the attitudes Papi expressed in his will of 1435. On the one hand, as he there informs us, he had just helped to found the Florentine national confraternity of San Giovanni Battista, thereby expressing an ongoing sense of his Florentine identity. On the other hand, he had meanwhile made a decision to remain permanently in Venice, and this, as we shall see, had important ef-

51. All information regarding Papi, unless otherwise indicated, comes from his will of 15 November 1435: ASVe, CI, Miscellanea, Notai diversi, 25, n. 1787. It is possible that his father left Florence for political reasons, but he cannot be identified as one of those condemned for political motives.

52. Cf. also Papi's catasto declaration of 1427: ASF, Catasto, 79, fol. 490r–v. For his trade with Florence: ASF, NA, 13278, fol. 295v, 21 June 1410.

53. ASVe, Senato, Privilegi, 1, fol. 172r, 10 October 1413.

fects on his personal identity. Papi's reasons for consciously choosing Venice as his residence were related to his own experience and, above all, to his rational and practical assessment of the economic opportunities offered by the city. Papi attributed his own, if modest, success to the wealth which circulated in Venice and to the openness which Venetians displayed in their willingness to do business with foreigners like himself. Undoubtedly affected by a sense of gratitude to the city and its inhabitants for the possibility they had given him to make a good life for himself and his family, Papi came to the conclusion that Venice was the best possible city to live in. Hence his own decision to commit himself permanently to it and his advice to his sons, expressed in the same will, not to seek better conditions elsewhere. That such a commitment had an effect on Papi's personal identity is clear from the change of tone evident in his will. At the point in which he expressed this preference for Venice, Papi stopped referring to the city and its inhabitants as something different from, and alien to, himself. Rather, he expressed devotion to the government to which he was consciously attaching his fortunes and referred to it for the first time as "our" Signoria. Thus, in Papi's case, we can locate a moment in which an identity as a member of the Venetian city-state was consciously assumed, as well as see the personal motives behind such a development. We can also ascertain that, even if Papi made a conscious choice between Florence and Venice, this did not destroy his Florentine identity but, rather, placed it in a new dimension, as another, perhaps subsidiary, level of consciousness, but one which could exist harmoniously with his newfound Venetian-ness.

If Papi's story demonstrates how an immigrant could consciously create a new identity for himself, other examples exist to show that such a conscious shift in identity could be yet more radical, with a first-generation immigrant renouncing his allegiance to his native land, apparently completely. Here we can cite another humble used-clothes dealer called Giovanni di Jacopo, who died around 1403. By that date, Giovanni was married to a non-Florentine wife and had a daughter also married to a non-Florentine.[54] Nor, in his will of that year, did Giovanni mention any attachments either to Florence or to Florentines in Venice. Indeed, he did not even define himself as a Florentine, and the only way in which we know that he was Florentine in origin is that his wife specified this in her own legal acts.[55] Evidently, Giovanni's ties to Florence had long been broken, and, having created his

54. Cf. his will of 31 May 1403, ASVe, Notarile, Test., 108, n. 97.
55. Cf. ASVe, CI, Notai, 242 (Zaccaria Ziera), 18 June 1403, and her will of 13 April 1400: ASVe, Notarile, Test., 108, n. 244.

own niche within Venetian society, he had ceased even to think of himself as Florentine. His assimilation into Venetian society must have been deliberate, given his apparent decision to marry a non-Florentine and his evident failure to maintain contacts with other Florentines in the city. Presumably, there was little in his Florentine existence that he wished to remember, while he could no longer have possessed property, close family, or other obligations to bind him to his native city. Nevertheless, while, to Giovanni, his desired assimilation must have seemed complete, to his wife, herself presumably Venetian, his Florentine origin was not forgotten but remained a defining element of his identity—a factor which made him at some level a permanent alien. Here, then, while on the one hand we have an example of deliberate total assimilation within the first generation, on the other hand, we can see how collective memory—on the part of the host population—made such rapid assimilation an illusion on the part of the immigrant's own sense of himself and the way he was perceived by those around him.

Several conclusions may be drawn from these examples of differing identities on the part of Florentines resident in Venice. First, their appreciation for the economic opportunities which Venice offered and the importance of these for their residence in and attachment to the city are obvious. Equally evident, however, is the difference between poorer immigrants who owed all their success and their livelihood to the city to which they had gone, as opposed to those of independent means, who may have experienced success in Venice but did not see it as determining who and what they were. For, perhaps, the poorest stratum, represented by such figures as Giovanni di Jacopo, the Florentine connection evidently offered little of value and could therefore be rejected in favor of a thorough assimilation into a more welcoming world. For Papi, the decision to choose Venice rather than Florence came rather late but was taken with a sense that he had been able to create his life because of and through Venice. His gratitude and admiration for the city was a major contribution to his conscious formation of a new identity, even if this did not cancel his sense of origin, which itself had contributed during his early life in Venice to his survival and his success. For him, as suggested by one current in modern immigration studies, belonging to two different nationalities probably represented a widening of his acquaintances and opportunities, including precisely the possibility of choosing the city-state which could offer him more. On the other hand, for those who saw Venice as a place to which they went merely for employment, the question of identity hardly arose because they had been formed by another environment and felt themselves permanently attached to it. In this group belongs initially the exile, whose attitude to his new place of residence is understandably instrumental at the start. However, if he comes to accept the permanence of his stay and feels gratitude for acceptance into a new and productive world, his attitudes, too, appear to change. An increasing sense of distance from his homeland is accompanied by a growing identification with his adopted city and a gradual assimilation into it. This last can occur more quickly or more slowly, depending on the desire of the immigrant as well as, to a degree, on his socioeconomic level. Thus, our findings so far suggest that personal choice may be a major determinant of national identity, accompanying or even preceding, rather than following, structural assimilation. In addition, despite its initial importance, exile may not, over the long term, prove as significant as other factors in influencing expatriates' identity.

On the basis of these suggestions, we can now turn to a consideration of the remaining categories of our expatriates—that is, the "old exiles" and "old immigrants." Significantly, all our examples of such long-term residents come from the upper ranks of Florentine society, for, although we can follow immigrant families of humble status for a couple of generations, they subsequently, as indicated earlier, tend to disappear into the context of local society. On the other hand, families of higher standing remain distinguished by their names, at least, and we can begin by asking whether the social, economic, and even political distinction suggested by these names results in their retaining a Florentine identity beyond the period evident in families of lower status.

There are indications that it was possible even for families of prominence to transfer their interests outside their native city and remain abroad for a sufficient period that in their homeland they were eventually looked on as foreigners. A Florentine example of this phenomenon is offered by the branch of the Guidotti family which moved to Bologna during the fourteenth century and, by the end of this century, no longer having a presence or property in Florence, was known within Florence itself as Bolognese.[56] There are, in Venice, similar examples of Florentine families whose origins had become so obscured with time that there is no overt indication of any remaining identification on their part with Florence. Such, for example, are

---

56. Cf. a procuration of 8 March 1385 in Giovanni di Filippo Guidotti da Bologna: ASF, NA, 14896. Also, a summons by the Mercanzia, which treated Piero di Filippo and brothers as foreigners having no residence in the city: ASF, Mercanzia, 1229, fol. 16r, 16 November 1402.

the Amidei and Bombeni clans, both of whom had been active in Friuli from the early fourteenth century, probably before their transfer to Venice.[57] By our period, both these families had abandoned all reference to themselves as Florentine, while they had become well assimilated into Venetian society through marriages and through membership in prestigious Venetian religious institutions,[58] as well as insertion into the manufacturing and commercial world of their adopted city.

However, there are, equally, indications that, connected as these old, distinguished families were to the traditions and the history of their native land, the memory, at least, of their origins lived on, both among themselves and in their native and adopted cities. Even the Guidotti were prepared, when it proved useful, to appeal to the Florentine Signoria for aid, justifying this request precisely on the basis of their Florentine origins; and the Signoria was prepared to assist them, for the same reason.[59] Similarly, the Amidei in Venice maintained relations with others of their clan who, while in Friuli, still retained their self-definition as Florentines.[60] They must therefore have continued to view themselves as part of a wider clan of Florentine origin connected by travel and communication despite its being spread over such distances. Similarly, the Bombeni did have business relations and, possibly, marriage connections with Florentines resident in Venice.[61] Consequently, they, too, probably retained within the family a memory of their origins which was reinforced through both personal and business contacts.

57. Cf. A. Battistella, *I Toscani in Friuli e un episodio della Guerra degli Otto Santi* (Bologna, 1898), pp. 141, 145–48, 150–52; A. Falce, "Colonie mercantili toscane in Venezia-Giulia ai tempi di Dante (secoli XIII–XIV)," *Rivista storica degli archivi toscani* 4 (1932): 81, 82, 165–67, 188, 199, 263–64, 276.

58. A Niccolò and a Battista Amidei and five Bombeni were members of the confraternity of San Cristoforo: ASVe, Scuole piccole e suffragi, 406. In 1398–99, Niccolò Amidei was *guardiano grande* of the Scuola grande of Santa Maria della Carita: ASVe, CI, Notai, 92, 26 April 1398 and 10 March 1399. Bombeni married into the Trevisan and Grasso families: ASVe, GP, SG, 5, fol. 80r–v; ASVe, Notarile, Test., 1234, n. 547, 29 October 1418.

59. And, undoubtedly, because the Guidotti's contacts made them politically useful. Cf. the letter of the Florentine Signoria to Duke Leopold of Austria in favor of Bartolomeo Guidotti: ASF, Miss. I canc., 25, fol. 71v, 6 April 1402.

60. Lapo Amidei de Florentia living in Friuli creates as procurator Niccolo Amidei of San Polo in Venice: ASVe, CI, Notai, 92, 30 June 1390.

61. E.g., Jacopo Bombeni and his son Lodovico had business involvements with Donato di Filippo Nati: ASVe, GP, SG, 65, fol. 53v. A daughter of Bartolomeo Bombeni mentions as a brother-in-law Cino da Firenze: ASVe, Notarile, Test., 1233, 20 July 1411.

Other examples of long-term Florentine residents in Venice confirm this sense of the importance of family tradition and historical memory in maintaining the original national identity of prominent families. To illustrate this, I shall, for the sake of brevity, confine myself to two interrelated families of long residence in Venice, the Ubriachi and the Figiovanni. The former, the Ghibelline branch of the Ubriachi clan, represents the exiles of the late thirteenth century and was present in Venice shortly thereafter, while the Figiovanni must have arrived there toward the middle of the fourteenth century.[62] Although relations between these families remained very close, they represent two rather different patterns of assimilation and identity. On the one hand, the descendants of Ugolino Ubriachi, despite their initial status as exiles, adopted the policy of seeking integration into Venetian society. Thus, they established business relations with Venetians, entered Venetian religious associations, and married into prominent Venetian noble families which could provide them with contacts and status within their new social world.[63] The result of this, by the end of the fourteenth century, was that they had ceased to designate themselves as Florentines and begun to identify with the Venetian world.[64]

Nevertheless, these Ubriachi's consciousness of their Florentine origins must have survived.[65] Continued contacts with the branch of the family still in Florence and with Florentines in Venice, particularly the Figiovanni, must have served as a constant reminder of their associations with their native city.[66] Moreover, like many prominent Florentine families, they may

62. On the Ubriachi, see in particular BNF, Manoscritti Passerini, 158bis; and R. Trexler, "The Magi Enter Florence: The Ubriachi of Florence and Venice," *Studies in Medieval and Renaissance History*, n.s., 1 (1978): 129–213. Information regarding the Figiovanni comes, unless otherwise indicated, from the will of Giovannino di Jacopo di Giovanni Figiovanni of 1418 (no day or month): ASVe, Notarile, Test., 486.

63. Ugolino's grandson Maso married into the Contarini clan. His son Giovanni chose his wives from the Bragadin and the De Vidore families. The principal business associates of Giovanni and his brother Antonio were Francesco Cavazza "a ferro" and the mercer, Jacopo Testa. Giovanni, at least, was a member of the Scuola grande of San Giovanni Evangelista. Cf., e.g., Giovanni's will of 11 August 1396, ASVe, Notarile, Test., 571, n. 198, cit. also by Trexler, "The Ubriachi," p. 162.

64. As Trexler points out, ("The Ubriachi," p. 133), in his will of 1416, Giovanni di Maso emphasized his citizenship in and loyalty to Venice.

65. Pace Trexler ("The Ubriachi," p. 161), who states that the great-grandchildren of Ugolino were "Venetian to the core."

66. On the contacts between Giovannino Figiovanni and the Ubriachi, see the wills of both, cited above. Giovanni Ubriachi also established relations with the Benini: ASVe, CI, Notai, 92, 26 August 1394, and Ubriachi's will of June 1416, pub-

well have kept record books (*ricordi*) which preserved, through family traditions, the memory of their important historical role in Tuscany.[67] Further, toward the end of the fourteenth century, their connections with Florence were expressed and reinforced by the arrival in Venice of a member of
the Florentine branch of the clan, Baldassare di Simone Ubriachi. A banker
and merchant whose trade in ivory carvings has made him famous, Baldassare was evidently forced by financial difficulties to leave Florence soon after 1390.[68] Presumably, his choice of Venice as his future residence was motivated in part by the presence of the other branch of his clan, with whom
he established close personal and business relations.[69] The effects for the
Ubriachi already resident in Venice were notable. On the one hand, in the
will which Giovanni di Tommaso drew up in 1396, along with his Venetian
relatives, friends, and business partners, who figured prominently among
the executors and beneficiaries of his bequests, a strong Florentine component was represented both by his Figiovanni cousin and, in particular, by

lished in Trexler, "The Ubriachi," p. 212. See ibid., p. 137, for Baldassare's contacts
with Maso di Manfredo Ubriachi resident in Venice.

67. The detailed genealogical information on the Ubriachi supplied by Figiovanni in his will (see below and Trexler, "The Ubriachi," p. 133 and genealogical
table) must have come from some sort of documentation, which was most probably
in the Ubriachi's possession.

68. Trexler suggests that his financial problems were created by his sons-in-law
seeking the dowries due them: "The Ubriachi," pp. 142ff., 159–60. It is more likely,
however, that Baldassare's sons-in-law sued for the dowries after his finances were
in a critical state rather than before. In fact, Baldassare's problems had begun earlier. On 27 August 1392, Messer Guccio de' Nobili prepared to renounce his banking partnership with Baldassare, refusing to be held responsible any longer for him:
ASF, NA, 14757, fols. 2–3r. By 27 September 1392, Baldassare was attempting to
recover old claims by sequestrating money deposited by Florentines in Venice: ASF,
Mercanzia, 11310, fols. 57v–58r. He was probably by then living in Venice.

69. Trexler ("The Ubriachi," pp. 164–65, 174, 180–81) asserts that Giovanni
and Antonio Ubriachi and Giovannino Figiovanni not only ran Baldassare's affairs
in Venice but also worked with or for him in Paris and possibly elsewhere. While
these three were certainly his procurators in Venice, there is no evidence that their
role went further than that, at least not before Baldassare's death. Whereas Trexler
declares that Giovanni Ubriachi was working with Baldassare in Paris in 1401–2, he
was almost certainly in Venice for part of that period (He was created a procurator
there on 28 May 1401 and 8 February 1402, while he created procurators himself
on 19 May 1402: ASVe, CI, Notai, 92). The business affairs with his brother that
Giovanni discusses in his will of 1416 are evidently those of the old company they
had with Cavazza, and no mention is made of any commercial claims against Baldassare. When Giovanni and Antonio traveled to Paris and elsewhere, it may well
have been for their company rather than for Baldassarre's interests. On Figiovanni,
see below.

Baldassare Ubriachi, who was not only named an executor but also considered as an alternative to Giovanni's own partners as an investor of the patrimony which Giovanni would leave to his young children. In the case of his brother Antonio, who married one of Baldassare's daughters and became one of his father-in-law's heirs, the bond with Florence was further strengthened. In fact, Antonio's widow returned to Florence with at least one of her children, while one of her and Antonio's sons subsequently married there. Thereby, although the principal headquarters of this branch of the Ubriachi remained Venice, the family's ties with the city of their origin were reestablished, even in such areas as possessions and tax payments.[70]

If this example of the Ubriachi indicates the strength of family associations in maintaining national identity, the case of Giovanni and Antonio's Figiovanni cousin demonstrates how personal perceptions and self-image could create the same result at an even more intense level. Unlike the descendants of Ugolino Ubriachi, the Figiovanni had not become truly assimilated into Venetian society. Indeed, the very close links they maintained with the Ubriachi in Venice militated against the creation of wider social contacts. Their quasi dependence on the Ubriachi was apparently increased by the fact that the Figiovanni seem to have been less successful in the economic field. The last of the family resident in Venice, Giovannino di Jacopo di Giovanni, while involved to a degree in the business matters of his Ubriachi relatives and in some trading on his own, was primarily a broker in the Rialto market.[71] He was, moreover, alone, unmarried, and without children.[72] It was perhaps because of this relative lack of success and lack of integration into Venetian society that Giovannino tended to see himself in terms of the past, as a reflection of his more successful Ubriachi relatives, and therefore to identity principally with the Florentine tradition from which both sprang. The results are very evident in his will of 1418, where, exceptionally, he provides genealogies not so much of his own family as, significantly, in much greater detail, of the branch of the Ubriachi which had emigrated to Venice and with which he himself was related. As though trying to illuminate himself and his own ancestors with the reflected glory of the more prestigious and successful Ubriachi, he highlighted every con-

70. Cf. the catasto reports of Ginevra di Baldassare Ubriachi and her children: ASF, Catasto, 64, fols. 310v–311r, 372v; ibid., 72, fol. 320v; Trexler, "The Ubriachi," pp. 190–91.

71. He is called such in the will of a woman living in his house: ASVe, Notarile, Test., 554, n. 291, 12 July 1399. Again, Trexler perhaps exaggerates the role that Giovannino played in Baldassare Ubriachi's business.

72. This is evident from his will of 1418.

nection between the two families, including his own position as patron of a confraternity connected with an Ubriachi foundation of the early fourteenth century.[73] Moreover, Giovannino's sense of who he was is indicated by the fact that his own social world not only remained principally Florentine but was determined in large part by his Ubriachi relatives. In his will, he particularly mentioned his best friend, Domenico di Masino, a banker who was living in Giovannino's house at the time, and who was a nephew of Baldassare Ubriachi's master ivory carver.[74] Moreover, Giovannino had opened his house to a widowed daughter of Baldassare and also to the widow of another Florentine merchant, Dante di Salvesto Nati, thereby creating a kind of Florentine oasis in his parish of Santa Marina.[75] Figiovanni's world thus remained primarily Florentine because his own sense of who he was, of his worth and dignity, remained closely attached to Florentine tradition and to a Florentine social world, maintained over generations within a foreign environment.

Thus, these examples of the Ubriachi and Figiovanni families demonstrate not only how important contacts with the motherland were to maintain a sense of connection with it on the part of its expatriates, and how ties with immigrants of the same origin reinforced an identification with the *patria*. They also suggest how identity could be affected by more elusive factors such as a desire to maintain one's sense of dignity and value. In both cases, the fact that these families belonged to the old Florentine patriciate was an important factor in contributing to a pride in their origins which implied a commitment to their Florentine history and a continuing connection with Florence itself. Therefore, once again, the status of the expa-

73. Trexler claims that this will proves that the Hospital of San Giovanni Battista on Murano must have been founded by the Figiovanni rather than by Corsolino di Giovanni Ubriachi: "The Ubriachi," pp. 133, 163. However, Giovannino in fact says that the founder of the hospital was Corsolino di Giovanni, and therefore he must have been patron of the confraternity later associated with this hospital. In fact, he tells us that his father was buried in Corsolino's tomb in the Frari, and therefore it is possible that the Figiovanni had a close connection with the hospital, but through the confraternity.

74. Cf. the will of "magister Johanes Jacobi de Florentia," who is undoubtedly this ivory carver, and who includes his nephews Manetto and Domenico di Masino among his executors: ASVe, Notarile, Test., 670, n. 25, 15 November 1404. While Trexler points out the importance of not confusing this person with Figiovanni, he seems to do this himself, calling the ivory carver "maestro Giovanni di Jacopo Giovanni" ("The Ubriachi," pp. 163, 192), when, in fact, he must have been "maestro Giovanni di Jacopo di Manetto": cf. Mueller, "Mercanti," pp. 49–50.

75. Cf. ASVe, GP, SG, 12, fol. 99r–v, [August 1404]; ASVe, Notarile, Test., 1231, n. 372, 7 May 1416.

triate influenced his identity, in the direction of reinforcing the sense of belonging to, because created by, one's original city-state.

In the end, then, this brief survey of assimilation and identity among Florentine expatriates suggests many implications regarding the applicability to late medieval Italy of conclusions reached in modern immigration studies. On the one hand, the importance of certain factors in influencing rates of assimilation and changes in identity is confirmed. For example, that the maintenance of personal contacts, friendship, marriage, and religious associations among immigrants of the same origin retards structural assimilation seems as true in our period as in recent centuries. Moreover, the phenomenon of "ethclass" seems a more relevant concept than that of a community embracing all the immigrants from any one location. On the other hand, this study suggests that, in our period, more attention must be given to the motive with which expatriates went abroad, as residence abroad resulting from political exile or commerce could, as we have seen, retard assimilation of every sort. In addition, our results suggest that the socioeconomic status of expatriates does make a difference in the degree to which they wish to, or can, sever ties with their native city. Various examples given here suggest, moreover, that assimilation at the level of identity might, *pace* such scholars as Gordon, actually occur before structural assimilation, and that the latter may well be a result as much as a cause of a shift in identity. Connected with this and, perhaps, the most interesting conclusion which we can draw, is the degree to which human perceptions and human will can influence a sense of identity and the rate of assimilation. If the case of Giovannino Figiovanni indicates how a desire for self-respect and belonging can make one into a traditionalist committed to a vision directed toward the past, the example of Papi suggests the capacity of human beings to choose not only where they want to live but also what they want to be. In both cases, these personal desires or perceptions can overcome what would be the natural effect of time, in that they can preserve an earlier identity essentially intact for generations or create a new identity in only one. In the end, then, it is perhaps precisely this capacity of the human being to choose his own destiny and create his own identity which emerges as the most novel and striking of the factors explaining the variety of responses to immigration which has been charted here.

16 Clement VII and the Crisis of the Sack of Rome

Paul Flemer

For full on seven months, from May to December 1527, the Roman pontiff was the prisoner of imperial soldiers in Castel Sant'Angelo. From the ramparts of the fortress, which even today afford one of the best views of the city, Clement VII daily gazed down on scenes of carnage and destruction. Beginning with the entry of the duke of Bourbon's undernourished and unpaid troops into Rome on the morning of 6 May, the Holy City, which had undergone a splendid *renovatio* during the preceding eighty years, was steadily reduced to a suffering mass of half-ruined palaces and churches, its streets and alleys littered with unburied and decaying corpses.[1] An anonymous Spanish observer recorded the horrifying and humiliating scene stretched out before the pontiff:

> In Rome, the capital of Christendom, no bells ring, no church is open, Mass is not said, neither Sundays nor feast days are celebrated. The rich shops of the merchants are turned to stables; the most splendid palaces are plundered; many houses are burnt to the ground; in others the doors and windows are broken and carried away, the streets are changed into dunghills. The stench of dead bodies is terrible; men and beasts have a

An earlier version of this chapter was presented at the annual conference of the Renaissance Society of America in Los Angeles, 1999.

1. There are many accounts of the Sack, all of which include, to some degree, reports on the havoc wreaked by Bourbon's army in the city. An invaluable collection of contemporary accounts is C. Milanesi, *Il sacco di Roma nel MDXXVII: Narrazioni dei contemporanei* (Florence, 1867). This volume includes Luigi Guicciardini's account (pp. 3–244), now translated into English: L. Guicciardini, *The Sack of Rome*, ed. and trans. J. H. MacGregor (New York, 1993). See, too, K. Gouwens, *Remembering the Renaissance: Humanist Narratives of the Sack of Rome* (Leiden, 1998). J. Hook, *The Sack of Rome, 1527* (London, 1972), remains useful. On Renaissance Rome generally, see C. L. Stinger *The Renaissance in Rome* (Bloomington, Ind., 1985); and P. Partner *Renaissance Rome, 1500–1559: A Portrait of a Society* (Berkeley and Los Angeles, 1976). In this chapter, I have relied heavily on the work of André Chastel, who, alone among more recent scholars, has made Clement's response to the Sack a central focus of his study; Chastel, *The Sack of Rome, 1527*, trans. B. Archer (Princeton, N.J., 1983).

common grave, and in the churches I have seen corpses that dogs have chewed. . . . I know of nothing else that compares with this except the destruction of Jerusalem.[2]

Penned barely a month after Bourbon's troops entered Rome, this account not only provides a fairly accurate report on the condition of the city but also hints at the moral and religious indignation felt by many contemporaries.[3] More shocking to observers than the wanton destruction of property by the soldiers was the widespread abuse of religious, nuns as well as monks, and the desecration of holy objects and relics:

> All the monasteries and churches of the friars as well as of the holiest nuns are pillaged; many friars are murdered, even priests at the altar; many old nuns are beaten; young nuns are violated and robbed and taken prisoner; all the vestments and chalices have been taken; the church plate has been carried off; all the tabernacles where the corpus Domini was are gone, and the consecrated hosts thrown now on the ground, now in the flames, now trampled under foot, now roasted, . . . now broken into a hundred pieces; all the relics despoiled of the silver vessels which held them, and the relics discarded.[4]

These acts, according to André Chastel, transformed the assault on Rome and gave it the character of "vast profanation" that called into question the very legitimacy of papal Rome.[5]

Of course, the challenge to the legitimacy and authority of papal Rome

2. Quoted in L. von Pastor *Storia dei papi dalla fine del medio evo,* ed. A. Mercati (Rome, 1956), vol. 4, pt. 2, p. 278. The translation is mine.

3. Pastor quotes from a wide range of diplomatic letters as well as from chronicles, diaries, and historical narratives. On this point, see the letters of Francesco Gonzaga, Matteo Casella, Cardinal Giovanni Salviati, and Giovanni Battista Sanga, from 7 May to 27 June 1527, included in Pastor, *Storia dei papi,* vol. 4, pt. 2, Appendix, pp. 723–27 nn. 114–17. In October 1528, when Francesco Gonzaga returned to Rome, he "marveled" at the ruined state of the city; ibid., p. 730 n. 120. The entries in Sanuto are useful here: Marino Sanuto, *I Diarii,* 58 vols. (Venice, 1879–1903), XLV, col. 164 and passim.

4. "Tutti li monasteri e chiese tanto di frati quanto di monache santissime saccheggiati; ammazzati molti frati, preti allo altare; bastonate molte monache vecchie; violate et rubate molte monache giovane et fatte prisione; tolti tutti li paramenti, calici; levati li argenti delle chiese; tolti tutti li tabernaculi dove era il corpus Domini, e gettata l' ostia sacrata ora in terra ora in foco, ora in messa sotto li piedi, ora in la padella a rostirla, ora romperla in cento pezzi; tutte le reliquie spogliate delli argenti che erono attorno, e gettato le reliquie dove li e parso"; "Copia d' una del Cardinale di Como a uno suo segretario, data a Civitavecchi alli 24 Maggio 1527," in Milanesi, *Il sacco,* pp. 484–85. The German contingent of *Landsknecht*s was not the only group among the imperial force involved in these acts, although they did boast of them; see Pastor, *Storia dei papi,* vol. 4, pt. 2, pp. 262–65.

5. Chastel, *Sack of Rome,* chap. 3, pp. 96ff., and p. 186.

was more explicit when important curial figures were the targets of the soldiers' insults. On more than one occasion the occupying troops paraded leading religious figures into Campo dei Fiori to be insulted. In addition, the soldiery paraded outside Castel Sant'Angelo enacting a mock deposition of Clement and the elevation of Luther to the leadership of the Church.[6]

The sacking of the Holy City, with Clement powerless to affect the course of events swirling around him, is an enduring image of his pontificate. Indeed, his contemporaries perceived the Sack to be the defining moment in Clement's life. Writing in the immediate aftermath, Francesco Vettori observed Clement's reputation had been transformed "from a great and renowned Cardinal into a little and despised Pope."[7] Francesco Guicciardini, one of Clement's closest advisers prior to the Sack, and a man who knew Clement as well as he knew himself, concluded the experience of the Sack robbed Clement's life of all its happiness.[8] Luigi Guicciardini, Francesco's brother, thought the shock of the Sack would compel Clement to curse his very existence: "Wherefore, then, hast thou brought me forth out of the womb? Oh, that I had died, and no eye had seen me!"[9]

These remarks may reveal as much about the anxieties of their authors as they do about Clement's reaction to the Sack. Certainly Francesco Guicciardini was deeply disturbed by the Sack, for which he imagined himself almost solely responsible. The writings he composed in the months after the Sack, the *Consolatoria*, the *Oratio accusatoria*, and the *Defensoria*, as well as certain *ricordi*, were deeply reflective and display traces of a neo-Stoic "philosophy," which he adopted as a defense against the vicissitudes of the times.[10] This "philosophy" became a central element in his later writing. It forms an undercurrent of the *Storia d' Italia*, and it is clearly present in his representation of Clement as a kind of "exemplar," demonstrating the fleeting happiness of life and *fortuna's* inconstancy.[11]

---

6. Ibid., p. 107. Also, *Letters and Papers, Foreign and Domestic of the Reign of Henry VIII*, 21 vols., ed. J. S. Brewer (London, 1872), 4:2 n. 3473, pp. 1571–72.

7. "Sommario della Storia d' Italia dal 1511 al 1527," in *Francesco Vettori, Scritti Storici e Politici*, ed. E. Niccolini (Bari, 1972), p. 207. It is likely that Vettori's opinion of Clement's took shape over the preceding years and then received definitive expression after the Sack.

8. Francesco Guicciardini, *Storia d' Italia*, 3 vols., ed. S. Seidel Menchi (Turin, 1971), 3:2069 (bk. 20, chap. 7).

9. Luigi Guicciardini, *The Sack of Rome*, p. 116. McGregor identifies the quotation from Job 10:18.

10. R. Ridolfi, *The Life of Francesco Guicciardini*, trans. C. Grayson (New York, 1968), pp. 184–87.

11. Guicciardini, *Storia d' Italia*, 3:2069–70.

Although there is plenty of evidence to suggest that Clement experienced a similar personal crisis following the Sack—the most obvious external sign of this was his growth of a beard as a sign of mourning over his and Rome's misfortune[12]—the depths of this crisis, and its specific contours, have not been charted. Despite the magnitude of events associated with Clement's pontificate, or perhaps because of them, Clement has not been the subject of a modern biography but instead is treated primarily as a character in another story. Thus, Pastor, in his *Storia dei Papi,* set his treatment of Clement against the background of the failure of the Renaissance papacy to address the problem of reform in the Church. He concluded that after the Sack of Rome, Clement comported himself like a Medici prince (as if it was completely clear what this meant) rather than as the shepherd of Christ's church.[13] Peter Partner substantially echoed Pastor's judgment in his study of Renaissance Rome, asserting that for two decades, during the reigns of Leo X and Clement VII, the papacy was sacrificed to the interests of the Medici dynasty.[14] While this is the perspective of papal historians, Florentine scholars, not surprisingly, express exactly the opposite view. For example, J. N. Stephens, in his detailed work *The Fall of the Florentine Republic, 1512–1530,* argues that the Florentine economy supported Clement's papal policy to its own ruin.[15] However, this emphasis on either a Florentine or a Roman perspective has severed interests and concerns that were inextricably combined in Clement's character.

12. Chastel, *Sack of Rome,* pp. 185–89. Possibly the beard was grown not only in outward imitation of Julius II but also in the spirit of a deeper emulation of a pontiff's character that was so alien to his own. On Julius II's beard, see L. Partridge and R. Starn, *A Renaissance Likeness: Raphael's Portrait of Julius II* (Berkeley and Los Angeles, 1982), pp. 43–46, 100–101.

13. Pastor, *Storia dei papi,* vol. 4, pt. 1, pp. 327–28: "Il papa mediceo si professa apertamente un genuino politico della realta: dal punto di vista meramente umano si spiega che in un tempo , in cui quasi esclusivamente il potere materiale dava autorita, ... ma l'ufficio di vicario di Cristo avrebbe tuttavia richiesto una concezione e un atteggiamento piu elevato e cristiano."

14. Partner, *Renaissance Rome,* p. 27: "The fact remains that the election of a pope of the former Florentine ruling dynasty in 1513 gave a new stamp to the whole nature of papal policies and to the nature also of Roman curialist society. Papal policy was geared for twenty years (with the exception of the brief pontificate of Adrian VI from 1521 to 1523) to the needs of the Tuscan dynasty."

15. J. N. Stephens, *The Fall of the Florentine Republic, 1512–1530* (Oxford, 1983), pp. 181ff. The tension between Florence and Rome has formed the context for two important studies: R. Devonshire-Jones, *Francesco Vettori, Florentine Citizen and Medici Servant* (London, 1972); and M. M. Bullard *Filippo Strozzi and the Medici: Favor and Finance in Sixteenth-Century Florence and Rome* (Cambridge, England, 1980).

An appreciation of the combination of Florentine and Roman interests is essential to a proper understanding of Clement's behavior during the last years of his pontificate. This combination of interests was the product of the concerted policy pursued by his uncle, Lorenzo the Magnificent, immediately following the failed Pazzi Conspiracy of April 1478. Lorenzo, shocked by the complicity of Pope Sixtus IV in the conspiracy, which claimed the life of his brother Giuliano, Clement's father, and nearly cost him his own, looked to secure Medici fortunes by establishing a family presence in the Roman hierarchy.[16] The result was a "Romanization" of Medici dynastic ambitions that culminated in the second and third decades of the sixteenth century with the election to the papacy of his son, Giovanni (Leo X), and then his nephew Giulio (Clement VII).[17] By 1527, Clement was the last direct heir of the Laurentian legacy, and the Sack of Rome and its aftermath threatened to obliterate it. Clement's appreciation of this threat and his attempt to salvage his uncle's legacy gave a distinctive shape to the activities of the last years of his papacy. In several important aspects, Clement's diplomacy after the Sack of Rome shows a profound awareness of the Laurentian legacy and of the memory and myth of the Laurentian "golden age," which had come to occupy such a large place in the consciousness of Florentine intellectual circles after 1494.[18]

With his own life in danger, and all that he worked for seemingly in ruins around him, it might have been natural for Clement to look back over the whole course of his life, as the remark of Luigi Guicciardini quoted earlier suggested, in order to understand how he had arrived at that crisis of May 1527. But if such a reaction is perhaps the common psychological response to a life-threatening crisis, more specific reasons prompted Clement

16. The Pazzi Conspiracy resulted in the closure of the Rome branch of the Medici bank for almost two years. When this reopened, Lorenzo realized that the bank by itself did not guarantee the Medici sufficient influence with the cardinals and pope. See M. M. Bullard, "In Pursuit of Honore et Utile," in Bullard, Lorenzo il Magnifico: Image, and Anxiety, Politics and Finance (Florence, 1994), pp. 133–53. Bullard believes that Lorenzo's efforts profited even more from the establishment of a parentado with Pope Innocent VIII through the betrothal of his daughter Maddalena to the pope's son Franceschetto Cibò (pp. 136ff.).

17. The high point was reached with the election of Leo X to the papacy in 1513, the appointment of Giulio (Clement VII) to the cardinalate, and the nomination of Leo's nephews, Lorenzo and Giuliano, as Roman citizens. Thus, contemporaries worried that the Medici might turn the papal office into a hereditary possession, and it was believed that both Lorenzo and Giuliano would be given states created for them from the lands of the Church.

18. F. Gilbert, Machiavelli and Guicciardini: Politics and Culture in Sixteenth-Century Florence (1965; New York, 1984), chaps. 3 and 6.

to look backward in time. The Sack of Rome, which began on 6 May 1527, occurred ten days after the anniversary of the murder of his father, Giuliano, by the Pazzi conspirators and three weeks prior to Clement's forty-ninth birthday.

It is difficult to imagine that the coincidence of dates would have escaped Clement's attention. Beginning when he was three years old and continuing at least until he was thirteen, his father's assassination was annually commemorated in Florence on the last Wednesday in April.[19] These childhood memories were later supplemented by more mature reflection. In 1519, as a cardinal at the age of forty-one, Clement assumed an active part in the commemoration of his father and Lorenzo the Magnificent when he negotiated the commission for the funerary chapel in the New Sacristy in the Church of San Lorenzo, where three generations of the Medici dynasty were to be honored.[20] Contemporaneously he commissioned Machiavelli to write a history of Florence. In the summer of 1525, Clement received from Machiavelli the first part of his *Florentine Histories*, the last book of which opens with the Pazzi Conspiracy and the murder of his father, and concludes with a eulogy of Lorenzo.[21] Less than a year later, in February 1526, his cousin Giovanni delle Bande Nere, who had been appointed by Clement to lead papal troops in northern Italy, and who, according to Paolo Giovio, was the living embodiment of Clement's father, was killed.[22]

While these activities and events suggest the memory of his father and uncle were deeply embedded in Clement's consciousness, the spectacle and visual panorama of the Sack could have triggered further reflection on his

19. Lorenzo de' Medici commemorated his brother's murder with gifts of property to the *opera* of San Giovanni and to the Calimala guild on 6 May and 7 November 1482. The day chosen for the celebration of the office was the first Wednesday after the feast of Saint Mark, 25 April. See R. C. Trexler, "Lorenzo de' Medici and Savonarola, Martyrs for Florence," *Renaissance Quarterly* 31 (1978): 297. On the importance of funerary rites for the definition of personal and family identity in Renaissance Florence, see S. T. Strocchia, "Death Rites and the Ritual Family in Renaissance Florence," in *Life and Death in Fifteenth-Century Florence*, ed. M. Tetel, R. G. Witt, and R. Goffen (Durham, N.C., 1989), pp. 120–45.

20. J. Cox-Rearick, *Dynasty and Destiny in Medici Art: Pontormo, Leo X and the Two Cosimos* (Princeton, N.J., 1984), p. 42; S. E. Reiss, "Cardinal Giulio de' Medici as Patron of Art, 1513–1523" (Ph.D. diss., Princeton University, 1992), chap. 10.

21. Niccolò Machiavelli, *Florentine Histories*, trans. L. F. Banfield and H. C. Mansfield Jr. (Princeton, N.J., 1988), bk. 8, pp. 317–63. According to Machiavelli's modern biographer, Clement VII was pleased with Machiavelli's work and hoped to have him continue his history into the sixteenth century: R. Ridolfi *The Life of Niccolò Machiavelli*, trans. C. Grayson (Chicago, 1963), pp. 242–43.

22. Paolo Giovio, *Gli elogi: Vite brevemente scritte d' huomini illustri di guerra antichi et moderna* (Venice, 1557), bk. 3, fol. 127v.

condition and the fate of his forefathers. The source of some of Clement's first memories of his father's assassination was in all likelihood the medal commissioned by Lorenzo the Magnificent from Bertoldo di Giovanni to commemorate the Pazzi conspiracy.[23] The medal, which Lorenzo probably intended to distribute to family and supporters,[24] showed portraits of the two brothers, Lorenzo on the obverse and Giuliano on the reverse (figure 16.1), superimposed over a narrative depiction of the assault in the choir area of the cathedral. On the side dedicated to Giuliano, the narrative depicts three scenes: within the choir area the mass is being conducted, the priest, attended by deacons, stands before the altar, and behind them is a group of churchgoers. In the left foreground, outside the choir screen, the attack on Giuliano begins: Giuliano, standing, at this point, is stabbed in the back and side by two figures; then, in the right foreground, Giuliano is shown fallen beneath four figures with knives raised over their heads. Inscribed beneath the choir screen rail in eulogy to Giuliano are the words "LVCTVS PVBLICVS" (public mourning).

As noted, this medal in all probability was the source of some of Clement's first memories of his father's death. Bertoldo's composition, with its circular feel (conveyed by the rendering of the choir structure as well as the shape of the medal), its "bird's-eye perspective,"[25] and the head of each of the Medici raised above the struggle depicted below, strangely prefigured the scenes laid out before Clement, who, as a captive in Castel Sant'Angelo, looked down on the violence that ruled in the streets of Rome. However, if Clement did not consciously recollect Bertoldo's composition, certainly the inscription honoring Giuliano with the words "luctus publicus" summed up Clement's most visceral response to the Sack as expressed in a letter to Charles V in October 1528:

> We should rejoice after such a shipwreck that, though stripped of everything, we have reached safe harbor: but our distress over the devastation of Italy, visible to anyone, particularly the misery of this city, and even our own personal misfortunes, has been exacerbated by the way Rome looks. Our only hope is to be able to heal the many wounds of Italy and

23. Bertoldo di Giovanni, was a "servant and familiar . . . artist and advisor of Lorenzo 'il Magnifico.'" J. D. Draper, *Bertoldo di Giovanni: Sculptor of the Medici Household* (Columbia, Mo., 1992). Bertoldo cast his medal on the Pazzi Conspiracy in the same year, 1478. The minting of coins and medallions to commemorate significant events was a widespread practice. Employed first by the princes of Italy, it flourished in Florence in the last quarter of the fifteenth century under Lorenzo's patronage.

24. Ibid., p. 87.

25. Ibid., p. 92.

Figure 16.1. Bertoldo di Giovanni. Medal. Recto inscribed: LAVRENTIVS MEDICES. SALVS PVBLICA. Verso inscribed: IVLIANVS MEDICES. LVCTVS PVBLICVS. The Metropolitan Museum of Art, bequest of Anne D. Thomson, 1923 (23.280.44).

Christendom by the means you offer us, and to revive this city by our presence and that of the Curia, for we have before our eyes, my beloved son, nothing but a dismembered corpse, and nothing can alleviate our despair, nothing can restore this unhappy city or Church but the hope of peace and tranquillity, which depend solely on you.[26]

Even if Bertoldo's medal did not directly inspire Clement to interpret his dilemma in the light of the crisis experienced by his forefathers, the religious symbolism that quickly attached itself to the account of his father's murder would have resonated with the desecration of the Holy City. In written accounts of the Pazzi Conspiracy, the attack on Giuliano and Lorenzo was elevated to a form of sacrilege; Giuliano, especially, became identified with the Holy Eucharist, since according to the testimony of the conspirators, the Elevation of the Host was to be the signal for their attack.[27] This

26. Letter of 24 October 1528 written to Charles V on Clement's return to Rome after his exile in Orvieto, where he had gone following his escape from Castel Sant'Angelo in December 1527. Quoted in Chastel, *The Sack of Rome, 1527*, p. 180. There are clear echoes of Lorenzo's correspondence with the king of Naples following the Pazzi Conspiracy.

27. See J. McManamon, "Continuity and Change in the Ideals of Humanism: The Evidence from Florentine Funeral Oratory," in *Life and Death in Fifteenth-Century Florence*, p. 77. The precise moment chosen for the attack is somewhat uncertain, although it seems to have been during the priest's preparation for Communion. Poliziano states that it followed the priest's taking of the wine: see Angelo Poliziano, "The Pazzi Conspiracy," trans. E. B. Welles, in *The Earthly Republic: Ital-*

identification of Giuliano with the sacred Eucharist persisted even after Clement's own death.[28] By virtue of the sacrilege committed by the imperial army and the insults directed at his own official authority, Clement's suffering in the summer of 1527 could easily revive the memory of his father's demise.

During the long summer of 1527, on more than one occasion, Clement would have reflected on his captivity only to stir memories from his past. His liberation in December 1527 and his subsequent return to Rome after nearly a year in exile would inspire Clement to confront the dual crisis— Florentine and Roman—which the Sack and its aftermath created.

The art historian André Chastel has demonstrated the extent to which the last years of Clement's pontificate were dominated by his attempts to "repair" the effects of the Sack.[29] Chastel's investigation focused on a series of artistic projects commissioned by Clement in the years after 1528. These projects—coins and medals Clement commissioned from Benvenuto Cellini, the placement of two statues of Saints Peter and Paul on the Ponte Sant'Angelo, and a fresco in the Church of Trinità dei Monti—while employing symbols traditionally associated with the papacy, and modeled closely on some of the projects sponsored by his predecessors Julius II and Leo X, nevertheless presented a uniquely Clementine story. Although Chastel was not primarily interested in this personal story, he identified the specifically Clementine component in these projects by the prominence accorded to Castel Sant'Angelo and its patron, Saint Michael the Archangel, to whose protection Clement "twice owed his life."[30]

According to Chastel, these elements formed a Saint Michael "cycle" within the various commissions that otherwise had as their primary theme the defense of Roman primacy.[31] For example, one of the medals Clement commissioned from Cellini to commemorate the anniversary of his escape depicts Saint Michael liberating Saint Peter from prison. Cellini's composition, reminiscent of Raphael's fresco in the Stanza d'Eliodoro, with its large

---

ian *Humanists on Government and Society*, ed. B. G. Kohl and R. G. Witt (Philadelphia, 1981), p. 312 n. 34. On the Pazzi Conspiracy generally, see the narrative of Harold Acton, *The Pazzi Conspiracy: The Plot against the Medici*, (London, 1979).

28. An account of the Pazzi Conspiracy accompanied the portrait of Giuliano in the 1557 collection of Giovio, *Gli elogi*, pp. 146ff. In the poem by Pietro Angelo Bargeo, Giuliano was called "the honor of his country, a pure, innocent figure . . . whose innocent blood stained the holy altars"; fol. 152r.

29. Chastel, *The Sack of Rome*, chap. 6.

30. Ibid., p. 191.

31. Ibid., pp. 184–98, 219.

grille as a backdrop to the angel leading Saint Peter from prison, shows that Clement clearly "identified his own escape from Castel Sant'Angelo" with Saint Peter's "miraculous liberation" from Herodianum.[32]

At Castel Sant'Angelo itself the Clementine experience was to be narrated also. Late in 1528, Clement had plans prepared for a huge project that involved restoring the angel, which had been destroyed in 1497, to its place atop the fortress and to destroy two chapels that stood at the entrance to the bridge (from the city side), from which imperial soldiers had directed fire against the fortress during the siege. In their place, Clement planned to raise two statues, of Saints Peter and Paul, the twin martyrs of the city, and patrons of the papacy.[33]

Only the bridge portion of this project was completed, but Chastel maintains that the whole project has its counterpart in a fresco painted for a chapel in the Church of Trinità dei Monti entitled *Apparition of the Archangel Michael above Hadrian's Mausoleum*.[34] The angel's appearance, according to popular belief, was in response to Pope Gregory the Great's prayer that the plague then ravaging the city would come to end. In homage to divine mercy symbolized by the angel's appearance, Pope Gregory decided to commemorate the event with an annual procession held in honor of the Archangel on 7 May. The scene in the fresco depicts this procession, and Clement VII, identifiable from the Medici crest on the hood of the pontifical cape, fills the role of the historical pope.[35]

As already noted, Chastel did not pursue the subject of Clement's personal crisis; he was more interested in the projects as they related to the contemporary images of Rome and the papal office.[36] Thus, for Chastel, the significance of the "intervention" of Saint Michael in the narrative of the Sack was that it presented the Roman "theory" of the papacy and the city: the archangel's aid and protection were a sign of divine protection and approval for the Apostolic See.

However, if Castel Sant'Angelo served as a "divine" refuge for Clement, it bears remembering that this aid was necessitated by the failure of the pope's earthly protectors. The pope's temporal agents, the commanders of the Holy League, had twice failed him. First, they had failed to prevent

32. Ibid., p. 190.
33. Ibid., pp. 191ff. and 279 n. 44. According to Chastel, the Castel Sant'Angelo was at the center of an "entire composition" (p. 193).
34. Ibid., p. 194ff.
35. Ibid., p. 198.
36. Ibid., p. 179.

Bourbon's army from reaching Rome; later, they failed to liberate Clement from the siege and occupation. Seen in this context, the archangel stood as a loyal, dutiful, and obedient servant of the pope (and Rome) and served to remind others of their obligations to the pope.

The assault by Bourbon's army and his incarceration would have naturally raised the issue of the loyalty of the League's captains in Clement's mind that summer, 1527. But the matter would have become more painful owing to the fact that he would have celebrated the feast of Saints Peter and Paul (29 June) in captivity. The feast celebrated the twin patrons of the Holy City, whose martyrdom in the city established the primacy of the Roman See in the Latin Church.[37] An important aspect of this feast was the renewal of fealty to the pope by the papal vassals.[38] The Sack, however, interrupted the normal course of this celebration. In that fateful summer of 1527, instead of sitting in state in the Vatican palace, receiving oaths of loyalty from papal vassals, instead of receiving foreign envoys bearing expressions of respect from their masters (from kings and emperors, and even cities), Clement found himself negotiating for his life and liberty. He found himself melting down the papal plate and the papal tiaras (with the significant exception of that belonging to Julius II) to turn into coins to meet the ransom demands of a sacrilegious soldiery; he found himself pathetically reduced to hiding jewels in the lining of his garments to preserve some little collateral in the vain hope of raising an army to come to his rescue. If this was not bad enough, his feeling of betrayal and abandonment would have increased with the news of Florence's rebellion (16 May) and the loss of territories belonging to the church in Romagna and Emilia, where the Venetians and the duke of Ferrara moved in.

Of all the persons whom Clement could have blamed for his humiliation,

---

37. On the feast day of Peter and Paul, see the article "Paolo, apostolo," *Bibliotheca sanctorum*, section 6, Feste liturgiche, p. 201. See also J. P. Kirsch, "Le feste degli apostoli Pietro e Paolo nel Martirologio Geronimiano," *Rivista di archaeologia cristiana* 2 (1925): 54–83; M. Maccarrone, "La concezione di Roma citta di Pietro e Paolo da Damaso a Leone I," in *Romana ecclesia, cathedra Petri*, ed. Piero Zerbi, Raffaello Volpini, and Alessandro Galuzzi (Rome, 1991), pp. 175–206.

38. I have been unable to discover the exact moment that this occurred. The origins of the practice may go back to the widespread granting of the *patrocinium* (protection) of Saint Peter granted to monastic houses in the late eleventh century, and quickly extended to vassals in the Patrimony of Saint Peter. The earliest such grant of *patrocinium* occurred in 863, when Count Gerald of Roussillon commended two monasteries to Saint Peter. The most famous was that to Cluny in 910. Several such grants to princes date from the late eleventh century; I. S. Robinson, *The Papacy, 1073–1198: Continuity and Innovation* (Cambridge, England, 1990), chaps. 6, 8.

he chose the Duke of Ferrara, Alfonso d' Este. Above all others, Alfonso became the object of Clement's wrath, the target of a campaign designed to deprive him of his whole state. Because of Clement's enmity for Alfonso, we must look beyond Rome, to Modena, to further explore Clement's response to the crisis initiated by the Sack.

The city and territory of Modena became a part of the papal state as a result of Julius II's campaigns against Duke Alfonso in 1510. Despite a brief period between 1510 and 1514 when it was under imperial administration, the church ruled Modena until 6 June 1527. On that day, exactly one month after the duke of Bourbon's soldiers entered Rome, and on the very day that Rome finally capitulated to the imperial army, Duke Alfonso's troops entered Modena and reclaimed it as a part of the Estense dominion. For this action, Clement reckoned Alfonso his bitterest enemy, and Modena became permanently associated in the pope's mind with the assault on Rome.

Clement initiated his punitive campaign against Alfonso early in 1528 while he was being courted by his erstwhile allies of the Holy League, Venice and France, as well as by Charles V. In the aftermath of the Sack, with armies still in the field, both sides hoped to bind Clement to their cause.[39] Clement, for his part, looked to turn their need to his advantage by demanding the restoration of occupied lands as the price of his allegiance.[40] Clement eventually decided that Charles offered him the best chance to avenge himself against Duke Alfonso. Negotiations between the pope and the emperor led to the Treaty of Barcelona, signed 29 June 1529, in which Charles promised to support Clement's claim to Modena, albeit without any prejudice to imperial claims.[41] Clement hoped for a quick offensive against Alfonso, but Charles delayed, alleging that his campaign against Florence, also undertaken on Clement's behalf, was absorbing all his resources.[42] Perhaps, however, Charles came to realize what Machiavelli accused the French of failing to appreciate: that his own position in Lombardy would be weakened by the reestablishment of papal authority in neighboring Emilia.[43]

---

39. Pastor, *Storia dei papi,* vol. 4, pt. 2, pp. 316ff.

40. Ibid., p. 316.

41. Ibid., p. 317.

42. Ibid., p. 320; Hook, *Sack of Rome,* p. 282.

43. At the end of chapter 3 of *Il Principe,* Machiavelli condemned the French for failing to understand that no power could control Italy so long as the church (papacy) was strong. Had Charles and his advisers learned this lesson? Charles explained his lack of activity in the case of Modena by claiming that his troops were overextended. Several of his advisers at the time cautioned Charles against further military action because his Spanish troops were meeting with increasingly hostile crowds throughout the peninsula.

Despite Charles's hesitation, Clement hoped to spur him into action when the two men met in Bologna to negotiate a settlement for the peace of Italy and to prepare for the imperial coronation. With this plan in mind, Clement refused to allow Duke Alfonso to come to Bologna or to be represented in any of the peace negotiations. At the same time, he presented Charles with a formal declaration of charges against the duke, a *proposito*, which repeated his demand that Modena be returned to the church and Alfonso's state devolve to Rome.[44]

The series of charges brought against Alfonso reads like a laundry list of accusations, ranging from economic issues, such as the illegal manufacture of salt, to political issues, such as the duke's violation of his oath of obedience to the pope.[45] Despite casting a wide net, Clement's brief failed to persuade Charles to act unilaterally against Alfonso. Rather, Charles encouraged face-to-face negotiations between Clement and Alfonso. As dependent on Charles's support as he was, Clement could not reasonably resist him on this point, although he did manage to postpone any negotiations with the duke until after the imperial coronation. When negotiations began in March 1530, Clement and Alfonso adhered to their separate claims to Modena, so little progress was made toward their reconciliation. Finally, under pressure from Charles, who was anxious to leave Italy and turn his attention to the problems besetting his German territories, Clement and Alfonso consented to allow Charles to act as an arbiter in their dispute. They agreed to suspend their hostilities for six months, to place the disputed territories into imperial custody, and to cooperate in the holding of an inquest. Based on the testimony gathered at the inquest, Charles would propose a resolution to their dispute.

It was in connection with the inquest and the months following it that Clement's campaign against Alfonso showed most clearly the effects of the

44. "Proposito nuntiorum papae super causa Ferrariens," in H. Sudendorf, *Registrum oder merkwürdige Urkunden für die deutsche Geschichte*, 3 vols. (Berlin, 1851–54), 3:187–95.

45. Ibid. The list of offenses included the accusation that he had illegally manufactured salt; that he had occupied lands belonging to the state of the Church; that he had aided the pope's enemies, which resulted in the destruction Rome and the imprisonment of the pope; that he had failed to aid or send aid to the pope, his lord, when he was captive; that he had profited from his lord's suffering by expanding his state at his lord's expense; and that he had oppressed his subjects and sheltered lawbreakers. Thus, the duke not only had done irreparable injury to the pope and Rome but also had shown himself personally unworthy as a vassal and as a lord. Clement argued the law required that the duke should forfeit his whole state to the Church for these actions.

Sack of Rome. The inquest was convened in Modena in September 1530 and lasted six weeks. The imperial governor, Don Pedro Zapata Cardenas, who had temporary custody of the city, presided over the hearing for Charles; the pope and the duke were represented by their own legal counsel.[46] Two hundred witnesses appeared before the court, one hundred for each side. By the time the proceedings had concluded, the notaries had recorded nearly six thousand pages of testimony.[47] This material was packed up and transported over the Alps to the imperial court, where its sheer mass so overwhelmed the resources of the imperial councillors that Charles was forced to postpone a decision in the case.[48]

During this period, as the imperial councillors were examining the testimony collected at the inquest, Clement ordered his consistorial advocates to prepare an *allegatio* for Charles presenting its side of the dispute.[49] Al-

46. Although the papal side was represented by a team of six individuals, three of whom were notaries, the printed sources identify only one representative on the papal side: the vice-legate and governor of Bologna, Umberto Gambara. Francesco Guicciardini was not present during the entirety of the inquest, but he did appear to give testimony. It is possible that the two principal legal representatives on Clement's behalf were Niccolò Aragonia, auditor of cases (*causarum auditor*), and Giovanni Francesco Burla, *aulae concistorialis advocatus*, since these two men were witnesses to the *laude* that Charles V delivered on the case. See Sanuto, *Diarii*, LIV, col. 437; and ASV, Politicorum, 51, fol. 51r. The duke was represented by Filippo Rodi, *consultore*, Jacopo Alvarotti, ducal *consigliere*.

47. This is the number given by Tomaso dei Bianchi called Lancellotti, in his *Cronaca modenese* (Parma, 1862–64), vol. 3. These numbers seem to be accurate, although they might be smaller than actually appeared. The *allegatio* in ASV, Archivum Arcis, Armadi AA, Arm I–XVIII, n. 4842 (see note 51 below) refers to witnesses by number, and these numbers exceed one hundred. According to contemporaries, the men who appeared for the pope were primarily "nobili bolognesi," while "nobili Ferraresi" appeared on behalf of the duke.

48. A. Frizzi, *Memorie per la storia di Ferrara*, vol. 4, 2d ed. (Ferrara, 1847–48; reprint, Bologna, 1970), p. 312. Frizzi claims Charles asked for an additional six months within which to render his decision. During this period, the duke's ambassador (*orator*) Matteo Casella was resident at the court, having accompanied Charles soon after he left Bologna. Frizzi, following Muratori's *Antichità estense*, vol. 2 (Modena, 1740; repr., 1984), p. 358, states that the court was in Flanders when the testimony arrived. However, this may be incorrect. In fact, the court was at Augsburg until November 1530; then it went to Speyer, and then to Cologne. See T. Ascari, "Casella, Matteo," in *Dizionario biografico degli italiani*, vol. 17 (Rome, 1978), pp. 314–16. For the activity of the imperial court at Augsburg, see G. G. Krodel, "Law, Order and the Almighty Taler: The Empire in Action at the 1530 Diet of Augsburg," *Sixteenth Century Journal* 12 (1982): 75–106.

49. An *allegatio* was one of the three types of legal *consilia* prepared by medieval and early modern lawyers. It was "the true legal brief of defense written by the lawyer and was the most partisan of *consilia*"; P. R. Pazzaglini and C. A. Hawks,

though the *allegatio* itself is undated, internal evidence suggests that it was produced after the inquest had been conducted in Modena.[50] Individuals who had testified at the inquest are cited throughout the document. Additionally, references to individuals who appeared before the imperial court at Augsburg, where Charles arrived on 15 June 1530 and remained until November 1530, are common.[51]

In its basic structure the *allegatio* resembled the *proposito* presented to Charles a year earlier in Bologna. The accusations against the duke were repeated, but whereas in the *proposito* they formed a relatively brief statement, in the *allegatio* they were separated into nineteen *causae*, each carefully elaborated according to the *mos italicus*. Each *causa* opened with a sentence stating the specific charge and the sentence desired, namely, the forfeiture of the duke's state to the pope. This statement was followed by a citation from the *ius commune*, frequently a law from the Digest or Code, but because the duke held Ferrara as a fief from the pope, feudal law precepts also were cited. These citations, which established the legal basis for the specific charge (the *causa*), often were accompanied by references drawn

---

Consilia: A Bibliography of Holdings in the Library of Congress and Certain Other Collections in the United States (Washington, D.C., 1990), p. xiv.

50. If I am correct in supposing that those who witnessed this document were those who testified at the inquest in Modena, the document (consulted in ASV, AA. Arm. I–XVIII, n. 4842) would appear to be a later redaction of the *allegatio* prepared by Giovanni Francesco Burla and Niccolò Aragonia in April 1530, immediately after Clement had agreed to let Charles act as arbiter in the case. Two manuscripts of this *allegatio* exist in the Biblioteca Apostolica Vaticana: "Directum civitatum Mutinae et Regii dominium ad Romanam Ecclesiam pertinere," in BAV, Chigi, IV.120, fols., 26r–75v; and BAV, Barb. latino, 2372, pp. 122–86. Cf. "Burla, Giovanni Francesco," in *Dizionario biografico degli italiani*, vol. 15 (Rome, 1972), p. 431; and the letters of May 1530 preserved in ASV, Arm. 40, vol. 31, fols. 123r and 143r. There is no reason to think that Burla and Aragonia were not also the primary authors of this document as well. Both were listed as witnesses to the decision Charles delivered in Cologne on 21 December 1530 (see note 48 above). Like the "Pro divo Carolo . . . apologetici libri duo," to which this was partly a response, the document was probably prepared by a team of curial advocates, who nevertheless represented the sovereign's (i.e., Clement's) official stance. On the composition of the "Pro divi Caroli," see J. M. Headley, *The Emperor and His Chancellor: A Study of the Imperial Chancellery under Gattinara* (Cambridge, England, 1983), chap. 5. Headley attributes the authorship of this document to Gattinara and the Latin secretary Alfonso de Valdes, a follower of Erasmus.

51. ASV, Archivum Arcis, Armadi I–XVIII, n. 4842 causa 3, fol. 13r: "sunt praeterea sex testes, fere omnes de familia olim Ill.mi Ducis Borbonii augusti examinati"; causa 3, fol. 17r: ". . . ex iis qui examinati Mutinae fuerunt"; and causa 3, fol. 17r: ". . . etiam eos qui in Augusta civitate fuerunt examinati."

from the corpus of important legists: older authorities like Andrea d' Isernia (d. 1316), Bartolus (d. 1357), and Baldus (d. 1400) and more recent experts like Johannes Crottus (d. 1500), Jason de Mayno (d. 1519), and Philippus Decius (d. 1536/37). Next, the names of witnesses who had testified that the alleged act actually had occurred were recorded. However, because the testimony of witnesses merely established the fact of the events narrated, not the legal ramifications of the action, and because the witnesses themselves could become the source of controversy, the citation of specific laws and/or legal opinions frequently multiplied.

Of the nineteen *causae*, three dealt explicitly with the Sack of Rome, while one treated the loss of Modena. Judging from this small number of specific references, it would not seem that the Sack exerted a particularly powerful influence on the pontiff at the time that the *allegatio* was crafted. From one perspective this was true: the Sack made up only one aspect of the overall case being made against the duke. The whole case presented against Alfonso argued that he was a traitor and a tyrant, unfit to serve any lord as a vassal or rule any state as a prince. To make this case, the *consilium* could not concentrate solely on the Sack and the loss of Modena because a pattern of felonious behavior needed to be established to counter the duke's argument that his actions in 1527 were committed in self-defense.[52] Therefore, twelve *causae* allege violations of the terms of the investiture of the Duchy of Ferrara that the duke accepted in 1522 from Clement's predecessor, Adrian VI. The violation of the investiture provisions illustrated the duke's infidelity, his disregard for the faith and duty that a vassal owed his lord.[53] Among the charges that illustrated Alfonso's infidelity were the manufacture of salt in the Val di Comacchio; the sheltering of outlaws and rebels; placing himself under the protection of another lord; plundering (*spolatio*) several cities under papal government; conspiring with the Bentivoglio of Bologna against papal rule; and producing images in contempt of the Apostolic See.[54] Despite the range these charges covered, they were not wholly

---

52. The right to act in self-defense was undeniable and was often alleged in cases involving treason. On the right to self-defense and its place in legal procedure, see K. Pennington, *The Prince and the Law, 1200–1600* (Berkeley and Los Angeles, 1993); and as justification for assault on one's lord, see S. H. Cuttler, *The Law of Treason and Treason Trials in Later Medieval France* (Cambridge, England, 1981), p. 5 and passim. The formal shape this resistance was to take was *diffidatio*— the formal withdrawal of loyalty before recourse to war.

53. Cuttler, *Law of Treason*, p. 5. In feudal law, treason was synonymous with infidelity.

54. ASV, Archivum Arcis, Armadi I–XVIII, n. 4842 causae 6–10, respectively.

unrelated to the Sack, for they occurred within the broader context of the Italian Wars and so were linked more or less explicitly to the Sack, too.

Yet, if Clement hoped to impress Charles with the sheer number of the duke's transgressions, he could not allow him to forget the unique outrage of the Sack or the duke's central role. The third *causa* was crucial for this purpose. This *causa* accused the duke of having given aid and transit to the enemies of the pope. More specifically, it recounted the support Alfonso gave to the duke of Bourbon and his army in the early months of 1527. The *causa* alleged Alfonso gave transit, aid, and hospitality to Bourbon, and that he had furnished him with supplies (*auxilium*) and instruction in the use of arms. Alfonso furnished this aid even though he knew that Bourbon was intent upon the pope's complete destruction. By these acts Alfonso showed himself to be Bourbon's "friend" and Clement's "enemy." Yet, as treacherous as these acts were, worst of all was the subsequent calamity that befell Rome, Clement, and the Apostolic See. No punishment, the *causa* argued, could avenge that offense.[55]

Alfonso had tried to counter the charge against him by alleging that his cooperation with Bourbon was necessary for his own welfare and that he did not intend any harm should come to Clement. He claimed he could not oppose Bourbon without exposing himself to harm. The papal lawyers dismissed this defense, reminding Charles that it was widely known at the time that the duke's army was already underpaid and ill-provisioned, threatened daily by desertions of both officers and men. However, for the sake of argument the papal case allowed that Bourbon's army may have appeared to Alfonso stronger than it was. Even if it had, the argument continued, Alfonso should have resisted Bourbon. Here was the crux of the argument and Clement's own dilemma. The papal brief argued that history, modern and ancient, provided examples where a smaller force had resisted a larger one: the recent victory of Charles's forces at the battle of Pavia (1525) demonstrated what a handful of loyal and determined soldiers could achieve against a stronger enemy; so, too, did the exploits of the Roman consul Decimus Brutus, who in 43 B.C. defended the same city of Modena (Mutina) against the superior troops commanded by Mark Antony. Nothing more specific than this was said about Decimus Brutus, except to state that Charles and his circle had shown that they were familiar with him. This latter remark seems to imply that there was more to the story of Decimus Brutus than was being told here, but what was it?

---

55. Ibid., causa 3, fol. 18r.

The simple lesson proposed by Decimus Brutus was that in the same place and under the same conditions, he, unlike Alfonso, did not surrender to a more powerful enemy. By this act he showed himself superior in virtue: he carried out his duty, he resisted, and he snatched victory from what had seemed to be certain defeat. Presented against this background, Alfonso's collaboration with Bourbon, whether in self-defense or not, was condemned.

Decimus Brutus's presence in the *allegatio* marks a rare intrusion of humanist culture into this otherwise highly specialized legal text. His appearance is more intriguing because he was not one of the figures from antiquity which humanist writers commonly presented as an "exemplar" of moral and political action.[56] The fact that he was familiar to Charles and his court suggests one explanation for his presence; however, given the hostility of some of Charles' closest advisers for the humanist culture of the Roman Curia, his inclusion was not without a certain risk. Thus, Decimus Brutus's place in the text seems to derive from the significance he held for Clement as much as the impact he might have on Charles and his advisers.

There are two principal sources for the life of Decimus Brutus: a small number of letters written between him and Cicero in 44–43 B.C. familiar to Renaissance readers in Cicero's letters *Ad familiares,* and a more substantial body of narrative material contained in Cicero's *Orations against Mark Antony,* better known as the *Philippics.*[57] These orations comprise Cicero's last great defense of Rome, this time against the tyranny of Cae-

---

56. T. Hampton, *Writing from History: The Rhetoric of Exemplarity in Renaissance Literature* (Ithaca, N.Y., 1990), p. 25, observes that "the smallest semantic unit of the exemplar, his name, contains within it the entire history of the hero's deeds, the whole string of great moments which made the name a marked sign in the first place. . . . The task of the Renaissance reader who is well schooled in ancient history and poetry is to unpack those great deeds from the mere appearance of the name, recognizing them as models by which to measure his own action in the world." What pertains to the reader of the name applies as well to the narrator or writer of the name. In other words, the choice of a historical figure from antiquity to serve as an exemplar reveals an association with the self of the author just as it seeks to establish a relationship with the reader. The writer who selects an exemplar has already come to know the figure, has already "read" and "unpacked" his deeds, and has made them a part of his identity. Thus, the appearance of Decimus Brutus in the causa sheds light on Clement's outlook and permits us to probe more deeply into his psychological response to the Sack. Also, see the articles on exemplarity in the *Journal of the History of Ideas* 59 (1998), especially F. Cornilliat, "Exemplarities: A Response to Timothy Hampton and Karlheinz Stierle," pp. 613–24.

57. Cicero suggested the name in a letter to Marcus Brutus because these orations resembled those delivered by Demosthenes against Philip of Macedon.

sar's supporters, above all against Mark Antony. Poggio Bracciolini had edited these speeches in 1425 and again in 1428.[58] As a result of Poggio's work, and his correspondence with Niccolò Niccoli in Florence, these speeches were probably known to Cosimo de' Medici at this time.[59] Before the end of the century, the *Philippics* could be found along with the rest of the Ciceronian corpus in the "public library" of San Marco in Florence.[60] During the sixteenth century, the *Philippics* were among the most popular of Cicero's works. They were "glossed and commented" on by ten different scholars and appeared in thirty-six separate editions.[61] In addition, Erasmus included references from them in his *Adages*, occasionally even alluding to them by title.[62]

More closely related to our case was the reference Erasmus made to them throughout his *Ciceronianus* (1528) before giving a synopsis of their theme near the end of the dialogue as he reviewed the dispute that took place between the Flemish/French scholar Christophe Longueil and the Roman literary establishment in 1519. Longueil, one of the leading "northern" scholars of the day, had won renown for the elegance of his Latin compositions among such leading figures of the Roman Academy as Pietro Bembo and Jacopo Sadoleto, who endeavored to have him made an honorary Roman citizen. This honor attracted the enmity of other members of Rome's cultural circle, who summoned Longuiel to demonstrate his skills before a panel of Roman judges convened at the Capitol. Longueil composed two speeches modeled on Cicero's *Philippics*, which he did not deliver but which were quickly put into print. Erasmus's "praise" of Longueil conveyed a double attack against Rome: Longueil's trial demonstrated how petty and frivolous intellectual pursuits had become in Rome, and how far removed from Christian subjects, while Longueil's speeches, absolutely

58. Cf. Poggio Bracciolini in P. W. G. Gordan, ed. and trans., *Two Renaissance Book Hunters: The Letters of Poggius Bracciolini to Nicolaus de Niccolis* (New York, 1974), letters XXXV and XXXIX, pp. 93–94, 98–99.

59. Ibid. The *Philippics* were in that part of the collection of the Library of San Marco of which the Medici were patrons. The actual date of their appearance is uncertain, but it was at least as early as the beginning of the sixteenth century; B. L. Ullman and P. A. Stadter, *The Public Library of Renaissance Florence* (Padua, 1972), passim.

60. Ullman and Stadter, *The Public Library*, p. 226. This edition had belonged to Niccolò Niccoli.

61. J. O. Ward, "Renaissance Commentators on Ciceronian Rhetoric," in *Renaissance Eloquence: Studies in the Theory and Practice of Renaissance Rhetoric*, ed. J. J. Murphy (Berkeley and Los Angeles, 1983), pp. 152ff.

62. Desiderius Erasmus, *Adages*, II, ii, 1 and III, iii, 100, in *Collected Works of Erasmus*, vol. 34 (Toronto, 1992), pp. 37, 75.

faithful to Cicero's orations yet composed when no danger threatened Rome, could not be equaled even by Italian authors in 1528: "Yet in treating this topic, this exceptional young man performed with such ability, with such nimbleness of mind, that I know of no one even today, even among the Italians—may I be forgiven for saying so—whom I consider able to perform a similar feat." [63] Erasmus's attack on Roman learning was doubly sharp because it both struck at the intellectual caliber and orientation of the Curia, as he perceived it, and mercilessly reminded them of the recent occupation of Rome by Bourbon's troops. Not even the Sack, Erasmus believed, could properly inspire the Roman Curia. [64]

Cicero first mentions Decimus Brutus at the beginning of the Third Oration that he delivered to the Senate on 20 December 44 B.C. However, with respect to the presentation of his case to Charles V, the Fifth Oration was most likely Clement's source. Slightly more than halfway through this oration, delivered before the Roman Senate on 1 January 43 B.C., Cicero turned his thoughts to the men whom the Senate should most honor for their service to the state. Because it was customary, he said, that discussion begin with consuls-elect, he would adhere to that practice and begin with Decimus Brutus. He would not speak on Decimus Brutus's past accomplishments, which had been generally approved by the Senate, but without any official proclamation. Instead, he would concentrate on Decimus Brutus's recent services to the state at this time of crisis and suggest an appropriate expression of gratitude to be made by the Senate. Cicero first commended Decimus Brutus for organizing an army for the defense of the province of Gaul. Although he took this step on his own authority, before he had received a command from the Senate, this action deserved their praise because it had tied Antony down to a long siege in Emilia and saved Rome from certain assault. As a result, Cicero maintained, no honor was too great to bestow upon Decimus. "This gratitude then is due to Decimus Brutus, who, without waiting for your authority, but by his own decision and judgment, refused to accept that man as a consul, but kept him out of Gaul, as

63. Erasmus, *Ciceronianus*, in *Collected Works of Erasmus*, vol. 28 (Toronto, 1986), p. 434.

64. Of course, what Erasmus wished was to see the religious reform of the Curia. He criticized Longueil for having wasted his talents praising Rome. He would have preferred that he had "employed his oratorical skills on a few speeches intended to inspire that city and those of its inhabitants in particular who profess good letters with reverence for Christ and a love of holy living"; ibid., p. 434.

being an enemy, and chose rather to be besieged himself than to see this city (Rome) besieged." [65]

That the fifth Philippic served as the inspiration for the insertion of Decimus Brutus into the argument of the third *causa* of the *consilium* is suggested by several elements. First, the few lines devoted to Decimus Brutus in the third *causa* echo the basic narrative content of Cicero's speech. Second, few other passages in the *Philippics* treat Decimus Brutus so thoroughly, and, with the exception of the Third Oration, nowhere else in the *Philippics* does Cicero speak so directly and at such length about him. [66] Finally, the actual circumstances under which Cicero delivered the fifth Philippic parallel the presentation of the *allegatio* to Charles. When Cicero delivered the fifth Philippic, he wanted to persuade the Senate to persevere in its opposition to Antony. Two weeks earlier, on 20 December (the date of the Third Oration), the Senate had for all intents and purposes declared Antony an enemy of the state. But now, as a result of lobbying by Antony's friends, the Senate was leaning toward a more moderate course. [67] This situation paralleled the course of Clement's efforts against Duke Alfonso. In the Treaty of Barcelona, Charles had (in the pope's mind, at least) condemned Alfonso. Now, however, Charles was granting Alfonso a new hearing that might absolve him of any wrongdoing. Just as Cicero urged the Senate to maintain the hard line it had adopted toward Antony, Clement was determined to prevent any show of leniency from Charles toward Alfonso.

Looking more closely at Cicero's narration of Decimus Brutus's actions reveals the basic outline of this relationship. Whenever Cicero referred to the defense of Modena, he emphasized that Decimus acted on his own initiative, on his own authority, independent of the orders of the Senate. In effect, he knew the proper course of action to take before the Roman people did. When Cicero made this point during his commendation of Decimus Brutus before the Senate, he stressed that a moral verdict was implied in this action. Decimus's defense of Modena condemned Antony as a criminal and an enemy of the state; conversely, his action legitimated the Roman state, the Roman people, the Roman Senate. Decimus did not waver or question; he turned himself into Rome's defender and reaffirmed her legitimacy. By presenting Decimus Brutus as an exemplar to condemn Duke Alfonso's

---

65. *Philippic* V. xiii, in Loeb Classical Library, trans. W. C. A. Ker (London, 1926), p. 295; and D. R. Shackleton Bailey, *Philippics* (Chapel Hill, N.C., 1986).

66. Forming a pair with the Fifth Oration; see note 70.

67. Ker, "Introduction to Philippic V," ibid., pp. 253–55.

betrayal, Clement simultaneously affirmed his own legitimacy. On the one hand, Clement wanted Charles and his councillors to reaffirm it by condemning Alfonso; on the other, faithful to his *impresa*, "Candor illaesus" (unblemished whiteness), he affirmed it for himself through the invocation of the figure of Decimus Brutus.[68]

Yet, for all the ways in which Decimus Brutus could help Clement restore his lost dignity, the fact remained that the two stories had different conclusions: Decimus Brutus's actions had spared the Rome of his day from the outrage of an armed assault, and while he had been hailed as a savior of his country, the same could not be said of Clement. Clement fully realized this fact. His most basic response to the Sack had been to assume a posture of mourning, clearly symbolized by the beard he grew during his incarceration and which he retained until his death.[69] Yet, on this subject, too, Decimus Brutus helps to establish a link to Clement's past experiences.

As already mentioned, the invocation of Decimus Brutus was not without risk for the papal case. Although the imperial side had already referred to Decimus in the service of its own cause, and the mention of him in the papal *consilium* could be seen merely as a reaffirmation of that figuration of the ancient Roman, the event that preceded Decimus Brutus's defense of Modena was the assassination of Julius Caesar. Decimus Brutus had been one of the conspirators who plotted against Caesar; in fact, he had persuaded Caesar to go to the Senate when it looked like he might remain at home that day. After the assassination, Decimus Brutus, like his coconspirators, left Rome. He traveled to Modena to take possession of the government of the province of Cisalpine Gaul, a post that, ironically, he had received largely through the efforts of his former patron Julius Caesar. In Rome, meanwhile, besides Mark Antony's enmity, there remained a certain number of men in the Senate who had been loyal to Caesar and remained hostile to Decimus Brutus. Their hostility was sharpened by Decimus Brutus's betrayal of their common patron. Cicero needed to silence the complaints raised against Decimus Brutus by this faction in the Senate. Cicero's solution to this delicate situation was imaginative, if not entirely convincing. Invoking the gods themselves, he argued that divine favor had taken a

68. The impresa *Candor illaesus* (whiteness undamaged, innocence unharmed) was fashioned for him by Domenico Buoninsegni, when Clement was still a cardinal. It was directed against those rivals who had plotted against his life. Clement wanted Brutus's verdict applied to himself: his legitimacy was indisputable, irresistible, undeniable. Hence Clement's personal appeals to Charles throughout, from Bologna to the mission of Fabio Mignanelli (on which see below).

69. On Clement's beard as a symbol of mourning, see note 12 above.

hand in guaranteeing the survival of the city, for how else could one explain that one of Caesar's own favorites (Decimus Brutus) had taken a hand in preserving Rome's liberty, first by murdering Caesar, then by defending the state from his supporters. It is not clear how Charles, as Caesar's "heir," would have responded to this aspect of Decimus's story. However, such praise of Decimus Brutus as one of Caesar's assassins might not have offended Charles as much as it might appear at first glance because, through the teaching of Erasmus, Charles would have been familiar with Caesar as a man who met his violent end as a consequence of his unbridled ambition.[70]

Still the conspiracy to assassinate Caesar and the onset of political crisis would have struck a deeper chord in Clement. To a considerable degree Clement's whole life had been shaped by the consequences of one conspiracy after another. The *impresa* mentioned earlier was developed to present a facade of invincibility in the face of widespread plotting against his life by Cardinal Colonna and his faction prior to his election as pontiff.[71] This enmity between Clement and Colonna had lingered just beneath the surface until November 1526, when Colonna invaded Rome and forced Clement to seek refuge in Castel Sant'Angelo.

Similarly, Clement had been the target of conspirators in Florence as well. In May 1522, five months after Leo X's death, the anti-Medicean elements in the city contemplated a coup that would return the city to popular rule. As a youth of eighteen in 1494, he was forced into exile with rest of the Medici in the wake of the French invasion. The grand tour of the continent that he undertook with his cousin Cardinal Giovanni was interrupted when they were arrested and temporarily imprisoned by the king of Hungary in 1499.

Clement was not always the target of conspiracy; he was a conspirator, too. For example, he participated in the machinations to return the Medici to power in Florence in 1512. As a cardinal he conspired against Duke Alfonso and he would do so again as pope. Yet, despite the frequency with which conspiracy intruded into his existence, all these episodes must have receded before the memory of the Pazzi Conspiracy of 1478 discussed earlier.

In the end, Charles did not render the verdict Clement desired. The settlement he worked out left the duke in possession of Modena as a fief of the empire rather than the church. However, to placate Clement, Alfonso was

70. Erasmus developed this view of Caesar in his treatise *On the Education of a Christian Prince*, prepared specifically for Charles V.
71. Chastel, *The Sack of Rome, 1527*, p. 149.

commanded to pay 100,000 ducats in damages. The settlement would be sealed by the duke's payment of the monies in Rome before the feast of Saints Peter and Paul. Although Clement's treasury was short of funds, he refused to accept payment from the duke's representatives. Clement was indignant that Charles had not recognized the church's claim to Modena, which was just as good as its claim to Ferrara, or so Clement argued. But this disappointment was made worse by the fact that the duke did not have to appear in person with the payment. Clement, ever sensitive to his appearance, called upon Giovio to mark the occasion on which he turned down monetary compensation for the sake of his dignity.[72] Clement tried to dislodge Alfonso by launching a surprise assault against Ferrara, but the duke discovered the plot that subsequently dissolved into nothing.[73] Despite this failure, Clement never did reconcile with Alfonso. The two men died within a month of one another, and it was left to their successors to settle their dispute.[74]

One of the last commissions sponsored by Clement in Florence was in the Salone of Lorenzo the Magnificent's villa at Poggio a Caiano.[75] The decorative scheme for this room was begun in 1520–21, but work had been interrupted by Leo X's death. Clement had been involved in planning the earlier work for the room, and, with the Medici return to Florence after 1530, he wanted to resume the project. (Finished frescoes from the earlier period included the *Triumph of Cicero* by Franciabigio and the *Tribute to Caesar* by Andrea del Sarto.)[76] Under Clement's guidance mythological subjects were to complete the decorative program. Among the cartoons prepared for the room was a representation of *Hercules Crushing Antaeus*.[77] This would have been a fitting homage to Lorenzo, who had closely identified himself

72. Paolo Giovio, *La vita di Alfonso da Este duca di Ferrara* (Florence, 1553), p. 122. For Giovio, T. C. Price-Zimmermann, *Paolo Giovio: The Historian and the Crisis of Sixteenth-Century Italy* (Princeton, N.J., 1995), is essential.

73. R. Ridolfi, *Life of Francesco Guicciardini*, trans. C. Grayson (New York, 1968), pp. 218–19.

74. Which Paul III and Ercole II did in 1535, without, however, any reference to the dispute of their predecessors. See ASV, Politicorum, n. 51, fols. 47r–49v: "Capitula concordie que proponebantur inter S.S. nostrum Paul III et Ducem Ferrarie a. 1535."

75. I have relied on J. Cox-Rearick, *Dynasty and Destiny in Medici Art*, chap. 4, for the details of the decorative plans for the Salone. Although Cox-Rearick sees a close relationship existing between Rome and Florence during the years of Leo's pontificate, she devotes little attention to Clement VII.

76. Ibid., p. 90.

77. Ibid., p. 91.

with Hercules,[78] but not unlike Clement's struggle against Duke Alfonso "nothing [came] of this campaign."[79]

The impact of the Sack of Rome on the collective mentality of the age was such as to challenge the very identity of individuals. It was characteristic of the humanist culture of the Renaissance to encourage the refashioning of identity by making the past—including its events, symbols, and texts—available for use in the present. Clement turned to the past in his moment of crisis. The fact that the past failed him only testifies to those broader political and cultural changes that were then gathering force in Europe.[80]

78. Ibid., p. 146.

79. Ibid., p. 91. According to Cox-Rearick, the decorations for the Salone were not completed until 1578–82.

80. F. Gilbert, surveying the impact of the whole period 1492–1530 on Guicciardini's historical consciousness, remarked: "But the political catastrophe which showed the futility of all human calculations also dealt a death blow to such pragmatic uses of the past . . . although Guicciardini did not share the humanist view that history exemplifies general rules or guides man's behavior, he returned to the humanist concept of the moral value of history: history appeals to man to become conscious of his own intrinsic value." See Gilbert, *Machiavelli and Guicciardini*, p. 300.

Contributors

JAMES R. BANKER, Professor of History at North Carolina State University, has written on problems of medieval and Renaissance religion, especially in his *Death in the Community: Confraternities and Memorialization in a Late Medieval Commune*, and on the relationship of Renaissance art and society, especially in his studies of Piero della Francesca.

WILLIAM M. BOWSKY, Emeritus Professor of History at the University of California, Davis, is the author of numerous books, including *Henry VII in Italy; Finance of the Commune of Siena; A Medieval Commune: Siena under the Nine, 1287–1355;* and *La chiesa di San Lorenzo a Firenze nel Medioevo.*

JOHN K. BRACKETT, Associate Professor of History, University of Cincinnati, is the author of *Criminal Justice and Crime in Late Renaissance Florence, 1537–1609.*

ALISON BROWN is Emeritus Professor of Italian Renaissance History at Royal Holloway College, University of London. Her recent publications include an edition of all of Bartolomeo Scala's humanist treatises and political writings; a revised edition of her Cambridge Seminar Studies book, *The Renaissance;* and several articles on Savonarola and the period before and after the 1494 revolution in Florence.

PAULA CLARKE, Associate Professor of History, McGill University, is the author of *The Soderini and the Medici: Power and Patronage in Fifteenth-Century Florence.*

WILLIAM J. CONNELL, Associate Professor of History, holds the Joseph M. and Geraldine C. La Motta Chair in Italian Studies, Seton Hall University, and is a member of the Institute for Advanced Study, Princeton. He is the author of *La città dei crucci: Fazioni e clientele in uno stato repubblicano del '400* and editor (with Andrea Zorzi) of *Florentine Tuscany: Structures and Practices of Power.*

PAUL FLEMER is a Lecturer at St. Mary's College, Moraga, California. His research focuses on the Papal State in the sixteenth century, including studies of Francesco Guicciardini and papal administration under Clement VII.

MARGERY A. GANZ, Professor of History, Spelman College, is the author of numerous studies of elites in fifteenth-century Florence.

DALE KENT, Professor of History at the University of California, Riverside, is the author of *The Rise of the Medici: Faction in Florence 1426–1434; Neighbours and Neighbourhood in Renaissance Florence: The District of the Red Lion in the Fifteenth Century* (with F. W. Kent); and *Cosimo de' Medici and the Florentine Renaissance: The Patron's Oeuvre.*

F. W. KENT, Professor of History, Monash University, and Director of Monash University in Prato, is the author of *Household and Lineage in Renaissance Florence: The Family Life of the Capponi, Ginori, and Rucellai; Neighbours and Neighbourhood in Renaissance Florence: The District of the Red Lion in the Fifteenth Century* (with Dale Kent); and *Bartolommeo Cederni and His Friends: Letters to an Obscure Florentine* (with Gino Corti). He is also the editor (with Patricia Simons) of *Patronage, Art, and Society in Renaissance Italy* and general editor designate of the correspondence of Lorenzo de' Medici.

JULIUS KIRSHNER, Professor of History, University of Chicago, is the author of numerous studies of the legal and social history of the Italian Renaissance, including *A Grammar of Signs: Bartolo da Sassoferrato's "Tract on Insignia and Coats of Arms"* (with Osvaldo Cavallar and Susan Degenring). He is the editor of *Origins of the State in Italy, 1300–1600* and *Legal Consulting in the Civil Law Tradition* (with Mario Ascheri and Ingrid Baumgärtner).

THOMAS KUEHN is Professor of History at Clemson University. He is the author of *Emancipation in Late Medieval Florence; Law, Family and Women: Toward a Legal Anthropology of Renaissance Italy;* and *Illegitimacy in Renaissance Florence* and editor (with Silvana Seidel Menchi and Anne Jacobson Schutte) of *Tempi e spazi di vita femminile tra Medioevo ed età moderna.*

LAURO MARTINES, former Professor of History at the University of California, Los Angeles, resides in London. His many works include *The Social World of the Florentine Humanists, 1390–1460; Lawyers and Statecraft in Renaissance Florence; Power and Imagination: City-States in Renaissance Italy;* and *Strong Words: Writing and Social Strain in the Italian Renaissance.*

JOHN M. NAJEMY, Professor of History, Cornell University, is the author of *Corporatism and Consensus in Florentine Electoral Politics, 1280–1400* and *Between Friends: Discourses of Power and Desire in the Machiavelli-Vettori Letters of 1513–1515.*

DAVID S. PETERSON teaches history at Washington and Lee University. He is the author of many studies of the Florentine church in the fourteenth and fifteenth centuries.

SHARON T. STROCCHIA, Associate Professor of History, Emory University, is the author of *Death and Ritual in Renaissance Florence.*

DONALD WEINSTEIN, Professor Emeritus, Department of History, University of Arizona, is the author of *Ambassador from Venice: Pietro Pasqualigo in Lisbon; Savonarola: Prophecy and Patriotism in the Italian Renaissance; Saints and Society: The Two Worlds of Western Christendom 1100–1700* (with Rudolph M. Bell); and most recently *The Captain's Concubine: Love, Honor, and Violence in Renaissance Tuscany.*

Index

Compositor:	G&S Typesetters, Inc.
Text:	10/13 Aldus
Display:	Aldus
Printer and binder:	Edwards Brothers, Inc.